THE
BUSINESS LAW
$URVIVAL
GUIDE

AN ANTICIPATORY THINKING APPROACH

101
BUSINESS LAW TIME BOMBS
AND
THE WINNING $TRATEGIES TO DEFU$E THEM

HOW TO EFFECTIVELY MANAGE
THE
LEGAL RISKS OF COMMERCIAL TRANSACTIONS

BY
MARTIN E. SEGAL

NEW & UPDATED
CONTRACTS & SALES EDITION

NEW AGE PUBLISHING CO.
P.O. BOX 01-1549
MIAMI, FL 33101
newagepub2003@yahoo.com

SPECIAL THANKS for assistance in cover design to:
Designapolis, Inc., Coral Gables, Florida

DISCLAIMER

This is not a book of self-help legal advice. They are available in the Business section of bookstores or online. Rather, this book provides the reader with a practical and effective method of identifying, analyzing and eliminating many of the most common legal risks of commercial transactions in the planning and negotiating stages, before binding final decisions have been made, so that one's ultimate business decisions are programmed for success.

Although the suggested strategies to avoid specific business law time bombs should be helpful, the information and opinions in this book are not guaranteed to produce favorable results and may not be suitable for every reader. The information contained herein is believed to be accurate as of the date written, and has been approved by sources believed to be reliable, but laws, rules of usage, professional standards and interpretations frequently change, and may vary from state to state, especially in Louisiana where the legal system is based upon French civil law.

Although the author is a licensed attorney, this book should not be construed as a solicitation of legal business. The reader is strongly urged, in every instance, to consult an independent qualified legal professional in their jurisdiction to verify the soundness of any intended courses of action before making any final business decisions.

Any personal opinions expressed or experiences shared are solely those of the author.

ABOUT THE AUTHOR

MARTIN E. SEGAL, also known as Doctor Law (Dr-Law), has had a career as a transactional lawyer, commercial litigator, business entrepreneur and risk management consultant. In meeting these challenges, he developed his anticipatory thinking approach to preventive law to assist in analyzing, evaluating and structuring business transactions.

He brought this experience to his current career as a lecturer in Business Law at the University of Miami, Coral Gables, Florida, where he is a multiple winner of the School of Business Administration's prestigious Excellence in Teaching award. He is also faculty advisor for Project Sunshine, a campus volunteer organization to bring smiles to the faces of children with life-threatening illnesses.

His courses cover a wide spectrum, combining the technical aspects of business law with the practical problems of everyday commerce, resulting in a unique perspective that identifies and defuses the potential legal time bombs that permeate the business marketplace.

Books he has previously written: *Florida Real Estate Tax Certificates, A Financial Bonanza (Business Finance); The Guru Is You, How to Play and Win the Game of Life (Self-Empowerment); Peeling The Sweet Onion, Unlayering the Veils of Identity and Existence (Personal Growth); Blame It On The Buddhists, and other Stories (Popular Fiction).*

His most recent commercial publication, bridging the gap between the worlds of business commerce and academia is *Preventative Law For Business Professionals.*

He also writes the popular *Ask Doctor Law* column appearing bi-weekly in the Business Monday section of the Miami Herald.

His philanthropy includes annual gift grants from The Segal Family Foundation; scholarships for deserving minority high school seniors provided by the Martin E. Segal Scholarship Fund, and an annual scholarship for a deserving UM minority legal studies undergraduate through the Martin E. Segal Business Law Department Donor Scholarship.

TABLE OF CONTENTS

SUBJECT	**PAGE**

INTRODUCTION

"The world is a place of business."
Henry David Thoreau

"The best laid schemes o' mice and men . . ."
Robert Burns

This book is not just about the law; its subject is real life. Our shared business life. We are all in business in one form or another every single day. After all, what is business of any kind but a sequence of one or more commercial transactions that usually involve contractual agreements and sales of goods or services. We are all students of business in one form or another, and we all need to understand how to manage our commercial transactions.

And we share a common predicament, through the millions of large and small transactions we engage in everyday in the marketplace, and the seemingly endless number of disputes that occur. Our age, prior experience, and station in life do not matter.

Look at your daily newspaper. On every page there are stories of transactions that seemingly have blown up in the faces of the participants. What started as simple buyer-seller, borrower-lender, and consumer business transactions became differences of opinion that grew into full-blown lawsuits. And the wheels of litigation just keep turning.

So the book is also of interest and benefit to business managers, executives, entrepreneurs and lawyers. Their daily business lives require dealing with the same disputes as students, just from a different perspective.

Beyond the unique factual patterns of these business disputes, their ultimate cause is usually the same, whether the parties are students trying to learn the intricacies of commerce, Mom and Pop in the business world or Fortune 1,000 Companies. In each case, one of the parties made a binding business decision without being fully aware of its possible adverse legal consequences.

Once the agreement is made, the contract signed, the merchandise shipped or the required payment made – the legal rights of the parties have already been seriously compromised.

Business law time bombs are everywhere, hidden to most parties until they explode. And most of them can be traced back to how most contract and sales transactions are created.

In my experiences as lawyer, businessperson, teacher of business law, risk management consultant, and plain old consumer - I was constantly reminded that most people are unaware they are surrounded by a complex web of legal rights and duties.

When we blindly enter into business transactions praying for the best, but fearing the worst - if a dispute arises we will meet the dreaded four L's that will surely sink our venture - Liability, Lawsuits, Lawyers and Losses.

Agreements that suddenly can't be enforced, business plans gone awry, and unforeseen problems that ruined that appeared to be golden opportunities brought me to ask, "What if we could locate in advance the time bombs that potentially sabotage most commercial transactions and either avoid or minimize them?"

This led to my *anticipatory thinking approach,* the foundation of the *preventive law method,* my appellation as Dr-Law, and the best way to fail-safe commercial business transactions.

By putting up red warning flags as a transaction is being planned, negotiated and structured, the parties could maximize their chances for success and avoid most disputes. This could be done on a project-by-project basis of new matters or in periodic legal audits of existing business. In either event, the bottom-line financial impact would be significant.

When I discuss how to manage the legal factor with young students they often remark, "I didn't know something like that problem could happen, but now that I do, it won't happen to me."

When I conduct business seminars about the legal implications of everyday commerce, the participants usually say, "I experienced that problem and it was a very expensive lesson. Now that I'm aware of it, I won't make that mistake again."

When clients consult me who want to be extricated from self imposed legal problems, they truly seem surprised at suggestions that they could probably have avoided the situation in the first place by advance legal planning.

Different people sharing a common predicament - every business transaction is a potential minefield of liability, and we need a good map to get us through it.

If we attempt our business journey without knowing what are the best roads to take, where are the hidden obstacles, and what is the optimum way to get from our starting point to our destination - we are in a no-win situation.

We are then forced to treat irreversible symptoms, rather than preventing the problem from occurring and finding its cure. In business terms, all that remains is how much we will have to pay for the mistake.

This guidebook can be used in a variety of ways, none of which is mutually exclusive:

- In the classroom - as a lecture text, teaching supplement or discussion workbook to encourage group participation, to highlight how business decisions are made, and to assist in avoiding their potential perils and pitfalls through preventive legal risk management.

- In private enterprise - as a handy and useful AAA desk reference guide for business managers or anyone planning a transaction in the business marketplace, to gain:

    1) *AWARENESS* of the existence of potential problems.
    2) *AVOIDANCE* of them if possible.
    3) *ASSESSMENT* of damage if no detour was possible, and use of effective strategies to lessen their adverse impact.

- In corporate boardrooms and governmental settings – to verify existing contracts, analyze pending transactions, and brainstorm future ventures.

- As a template for managing the legal factor, and highlighting the legal implications of executive decision making through individual initiatives and group discussions.

- In consumer transactions - as a trouble-shooting reference.

- In the home – as a business desk reference and source guide.

Keep a reference copy for yourself, have one in your business office, carry it in your car, place one in your residence, and distribute it to your staff, employees, and executives. Provide copies for family and friends.

As your commercial business transactions unfold you can become a skilled planner as you identify and defuse the legal areas where you are vulnerable.

Dr - Law is here to help you. The office is open 24 hours a day, and we make house calls. Visit our Website at www.dr-law.com. Contact us by email at askdoctorlaw@yahoo.com.

Enjoy the book, and prosper!

NOTES

THE BUSINESS LAW SURVIVAL GUIDE

PREFACE

" Tell them what you are going to tell them,
then tell them ,then tell them what you have just told them. "
Trial Lawyer's Credo

This 2nd edition of the book is separated into the major business law areas of contracts and sales impacting most commercial transactions. It is organized in the same practical sequence that business decisions need to be made in the marketplace, whether you are student or teacher, business employee, manager, executive or entrepreneur.

We proceed, step by step, through the most common commercial transactions, highlighting at least 101 business law rules that create the time bombs that may blow up into a typical dispute, and the alternatives to minimize or avoid these problems.

Some of these legal time bombs are obvious, like the requirements that certain types of contracts must be in writing, rather than verbal, to be legally enforceable. They stand out like bright red flags waving their warnings at us.

Others are subtle, hidden below the surface, yet potentially lethal like icebergs. Gifts and contract price adjustments, which may be legally cancelled notwithstanding the promise of one of the parties to the contrary, fall in this category.

One party's business law time bomb is another party's business opportunity. Ignore the problem or be unaware of it and you blow up financially. Avoid the problem or defuse it and you have a successful result.

There is a common thread woven throughout the world of business law disputes. One of the contracting parties wants to enforce it because he believes he made a good business deal. The other party does not want to be legally bound because he believes he made a bad business deal. The respective motivations of the litigants are as basic as that. They each will argue the rules of law or exceptions to those rules that support their positions and are consistent with the outcome they desire. They will interpret the facts of their dispute in a way most favorable to their legal position.

Each unit of the book explores these points of view in detail, as well as presenting through text material and case examples typical business law problems encountered in everyday commercial transactions and practical strategies to avoid them.

The scales of justice diagram is used throughout as a visual metaphor, to remind us that navigating successfully through life in general and business in particular is a daily balancing act. We walk the tightrope, trying to maintain an acceptable balance, constantly adjusting our position as problems arise.

The numbered chapters begin with a discussion of the Anticipatory Thinking Approach, which is the foundation of the Preventive Law Method, providing the opportunity for skillful planning of one's commercial transactions.

We then examine and gain a realistic understanding of our legal system, answering important questions along the way including:

- Why do we have laws?
- What are the sources of laws?
- To sue or not to sue?
- How to hire a lawyer?
- What legal remedies are available?
- Where to file suit?
- How to sue?

For some readers this material is a reminder of known or forgotten concepts. For others it is new ground to be explored. For all however, it is an explanation of how to legally protect oneself in our complex world of everyday commerce.

We then examine, chapter by succeeding chapter, the perils, pitfalls and planning skills involved in:

- Creating a contract
- Legal enforcement of the contract
- Legal excuses for non-performance
- Special rules for sales of goods
- Special rules for products liability
- Special rules for e-commerce and cyberlaw

The book concludes with two thought-provoking chapters. Business Ethics examines examples of the good, the bad, and the ugly in the impact of company actions on the social framework in which they were made, and suggests that the following of certain ethical guidelines in today's fast-paced business environment may still make it possible to be both successful and socially conscious in executive decision making. Trends in the Law notes and briefly discusses some of the main legal "hot spots" in the ever-changing contemporary business law landscape.

The case study method of learning-analysis-problem solving is used throughout with numerous examples and actual court cases. Some of the cases involve well-known persons or companies. Others involve famous disputes. While others involve parties like you and I who become involved in a business law drama. Similar cases are being heard and decided everyday in our courts.

The actual reasoning of the presiding judges is used throughout, their direct quotations giving a voice to how cases are actually decided, so as to present a more realistic and useful presentation.

I.   WHAT?   THE BUSINESS LAW RULES

Each chapter contains a summary of the basic governing rules of business law. These are the legal right and duties of which the public is usually unaware. Not complying with them creates the potential problems that result in most business disputes. These basic business law rules are explained and then illustrated with hypothetical examples of typical situations.

II.   WHERE?   LOCATING THE TIME BOMBS

Each chapter also highlights the business law time bombs that often trap the unsuspecting parties and sabotage their commercial transactions. They are also identified, explained and then illustrated with hypothetical examples of typical situations, and how they might have been avoided by anticipatory planning.

III.   HOW?   DEFUSING THE TIME BOMBS

The time bombs are illustrated, defused and replayed in a real-life setting by actual court cases in each chapter, involving real-life situations and often presented in business disputes between well-known companies and famous personalities.

The reader is presented alternate ways the transaction could have been structured by the losing party to avoid the original explosive situation and achieve the desired result. This is Monday morning quarterbacking at its best, learning from the costly mistakes of others and using them for a better outcome.

IV.   CHAPTER EXERCISES

At the end of each chapter the reader/student/user is offered Discussion Exercises, Case Exercises and Case Research Cybercises to enhance the problem solving process of learning, analyzing, evaluating, understanding and utilizing the material. An area for reader's Notes ends each chapter.

V.   CHAPTER CASE UPDATES

At the end of the book there is a concluding section of chapter-by-chapter case updates of recent cases and legal developments that will help to keep the chapter material in its proper context for understanding, learning, discussion and practical application.

VI.   OVERVIEW

There are hundreds of potential business law time bombs, hypothetical examples and illustrative actual court cases presented in the chapter text material to assist the reader in navigating the commercial minefields of modern business. They may also be used by the reader as a risk management Quick-Find, to locate a particular problem and analyze it to assist in creating a transaction to avoid it, or minimize its impact in an existing problem area. In this manner, one can tell at a glance if a proposed business plan or transaction will work smoothly, or if there may be trouble ahead that requires restructuring with one or more of the replay strategies.

If used properly as a guidebook to effectively manage the legal risks of most commercial transactions, *THE BUSINESS LAW SURVIVAL GUIDE* can provide an effective prescription for business success.

1.

THE PREVENTIVE LAW METHOD:
THE POWER OF ANTICIPATORY THINKING

"An Ounce of Prevention is Worth a Pound of Cure"
The Farmer's Almanac

The anticipatory thinking approach is the foundation of preventive law. It is also the basis of practical problem solving in business. It enables us to evaluate the plus and minus factors involved in all types of commercial transactions, past, present or future, and then act skillfully to preserve, protect and plan.

We also use this approach all the time in our everyday lives. We ask ourselves, "What do I need to succeed?" If we can't accomplish our goal directly, perhaps we can do an end run to reach the finish line.

We are confronted with a potential problem - an apparently impassable situation – and we diagnose it and devise a strategy to solve it.

In fact, anticipating and preventing are two sides of the same coin. Webster's dictionary says:

> *Anticipate - to forestall*
> *Prevent – to keep from happening*

Simply stated, they both mean, "look before you leap."

It sounds deceptively simple. But in order to legally anticipate we must know WHAT types of problems create liability time bombs that could sabotage our plans. And then we must know WHERE to locate them. And when we do find them we must know HOW to defuse them.

Everyone involved in a business transaction hopes it will be completed smoothly and profitably. But there always are potential perils and pitfalls that may jeopardize its success.

And a large part of our problem is the fact that we are poor contract shoppers when it comes to the due diligence needed to protect us. We would never buy a car without inspecting it and taking it for a test drive. But most of us enter into binding agreements every day without a clue as to our legal rights and duties.

Using anticipatory thinking to prevent legal problems will often allow us to successfully complete our commercial transactions - sometimes we can move in a straight line toward our goal and at other times we must zig-zag to skillfully dodge its hazards.

There are legal implications in every important business decision. Properly managing the legal factor bears a direct relationship to maximizing revenues by minimizing expenses, thus achieving greater net profits. And the converse is also true. Mismanagement usually occurs because the affected party is unaware or negligent in complying with the legal rules governing their transaction.

The more potential time bombs that can be exposed before the transaction is finalized, the greater chances we have for structuring it in a way that will avoid potential disputes and provide the best opportunity for a positive result.

The extent to which we make use of the Anticipatory Thinking Approach to prevent legal problems is our barometer of business success or failure.

In the initial structuring of any transaction we should routinely ask the following questions, which will highlight where in our path might lie potential business law time bombs:

1) What is my objective? What do I want to accomplish? What is the desired result? How do I propose to structure this transaction? (This is our own initial view of the deal, based upon whatever is our current level of experience and expertise.)

2) What could go wrong? What result do I want to avoid? What are the potential legal time bombs in my path? (This requires us to view the proposed transaction it its worst possible light. We exercise the power of negative thinking to identify our potential business law problems. But this critical step requires knowledge of the many rules that may create these obstacles, so this is where we must use this guidebook to identify the areas where we need to restructure our transaction.)

3) What are my alternative choices in changing the transaction? Will it have to be fully or partially revised? Will I be able to completely avoid the potential time bomb? Can I minimize its impact? What are the risks, rewards and offsets involved in being able to finalize my business deal?

   Often the creation of needed detours around the business roadblocks that impede us require quite a bit of give and take. We need to determine which aspects of our transaction are deal breakers, and thus non-negotiable, and which ones can be used as bargaining chips to still allow us to reach our desired destination.

4) What does my new transaction look like? Will my new map of the liability landscape realistically enable me to get from the points of inception to conclusion with minimal or no legal hazards? Does this new concept actually work?

We may be able to enter into a similar transaction with a small amount at risk to test it, or use contract conditions to prevent loss.

5) But the best way to verify that our new plan of action is viable in our state is with the assistance of a legal professional. Although you may choose to proceed to complete your transaction without a lawyer, it is not recommended.

6) Can I be insulated from liability even if an unseen business law time bomb explodes? How can my potential business risks be further reduced? The legal form of organization used to conduct business is every bit as important as the nature of the business itself. There are simple ways to do business so that our personal liability is limited just to the amount we have chosen to invest in the particular enterprise, rather than putting our total assets in jeopardy.

By training ourselves to ask these questions during the planning and negotiating phases of our commercial transactions, before binding business decisions have been made, we can completely avoid many business law time bombs, lessen the impact of many others and in so doing, greatly increases our chances for success.

The contrary is also true. If there is a lack of anticipatory planning, the results can be financially disastrous, as happened in *City of Everett v. Mitchell, 631 P.2d 366 (Wash. 1981)*. An estate hired an auctioneer to sell some of the deceased's items. Included was a used safe that had an inside locked compartment which, for some reason, neither the executor nor the auctioneer opened before the sale. Mitchell bought the safe for $50, hired a locksmith to open the inside compartment, and finding it contained over $32,000 in cash, the locksmith called the city police who impounded the contents, pending a court determination of ownership. Mitchell won the case and kept the money.

"The Mitchell's were aware of the rule of the auction that all sales were final. Furthermore, the auctioneer made no statement reserving rights to any contents of the safe to the Estate. Under these circumstances, we hold reasonable persons would conclude that the auctioneer manifested an objective intent to sell the safe and it s contents and the parties mutually assented to enter into that sale of the safe and the contents of the locked compartment."

In *Dempsey v. Norwegian Cruise Line, 972 F.2d 998 (9th Cir. 1992)*, plaintiff's passenger ticket reduced the standard 3-year limitation period for filing personal injury lawsuits to one year, as allowed under the Federal Maritime Act. The ticket stated in bold letters, "Passengers are advised to read the terms and conditions of the Passenger Ticket Contract set forth below."

Plaintiff sued for an alleged injury on that cruise more than one year later, but within three years of the voyage. Summary judgment was entered for the defendant based upon the failure to sue within the one-year limitation period, and the appellate court affirmed.

"Congress has provided that vessels may contract for a one year limitations period ... Passengers like Dempsey who purchase tickets containing this limitation 'benefit in the form of reduced fares reflecting the savings that the cruise line enjoys.' Moreover, when a passenger is involved in an accident, it is reasonable to expect the passenger to consult his or her ticket or an attorney to determine his or her rights. The passenger can fully protect his or her rights by filing suit within one year of the injury."

In *Scott-Pontzer v. Liberty Mutual Insurance Co., 710 N.E.2d 1116 (Ohio 1999)*, plaintiff's husband, Pontzer, was killed when a drunk driver collided with his vehicle. That driver's insurance only had minimum limits of liability. Prior to the accident, Pontzer was employed by Superior Dairy, which had a policy of commercial auto liability insurance written by defendant, containing a provision for underinsured motorist coverage as well as umbrella/excess liability coverage.

Plaintiff sued on behalf of her husband's estate, claiming coverage under the defendant's policy. It moved for summary judgment, claiming that under the policy, Pontzer was not a named insured because the policy was issued to a corporation, not an individual, and he was not operating a 'covered' vehicle because the accident occurred when he was off-duty. The trial court granted defendant's motion.

The appellate court determined that, "the policies in question were 'ambiguous as to the insureds' under the underinsured motorist coverages," and that Pontzer, "as an employee of Superior Dairy, was an insured under the policies issued by (defendant)." But the court then affirmed because the insurance coverage "is available only to those employees injured while acting within the scope of their employment," and this excluded Pontzer.

The Ohio Supreme Court reversed the appellate court, and ruled for the plaintiff. It first agreed that Pontzer was "an insured for purposes of underinsured motorist coverage" due to the ambiguous wording of the policy. "Courts universally hold that policies of insurance, which are in language selected by the insurer and which are reasonably open to different interpretations, will be construed most favorably to the insured."

It then disagreed with the appellate court and ruled for the plaintiff, due to discrepant wording in the defendant's umbrella/excess and underinsured motorist policies:

"The Liberty Fire policy contains no language requiring that employees must be acting within the scope of their employment in order to receive underinsured motorist coverage. Thus, we find that appellant is entitled to underinsured motorist benefits under the Liberty fire policy."

There were two dissenting opinions that suggested the decision was incorrect, and that the specific language requirement of the majority was unnecessary.

"Despite the named insured ('you') being superior Dairy, the majority finds coverage for an off-duty employee driving his wife's car by saying that because UIM coverage protects persons and not vehicles, and because corporations cannot drive cars or sustain injuries, UIM coverage cannot protect a corporate entity. But, of course, a corporate entity has insurable interests for which countless policies are issued every day."

"This concept of Superior Dairy having corporate insurable interests defeats the majority's reasoning for extending coverage to the off-duty employee as an 'insured.' Though business entities like Superior Dairy operate through their employees, this employee was not acting for Superior Dairy at the time of the accident. So, there is no basis for saying he qualifies as an insured by virtue of his Superior Dairy employment."

The fallout from the majority opinion in Ohio has been tremendous. Most insurance policies did not have specific exclusionary language that limited recovery in these UIM claims only to that plaintiff's injured, "within the scope of their employment." Therefore, the case created a liability loophole through which many claimants have successfully sued for underinsured or uninsured motorist coverages.

A liability fund of almost $1 billion was set up by Ohio insurers to pay these so-called *Scott-Pontzer* claims, and they are still being decided in favor of plaintiffs. Now, in Ohio and other states that have witnessed the Ohio experience, liability policies are closely monitored to make sure they extend coverage, "only to officers, owners or employees acting in the course and scope of employment."

DISCUSSION EXERCISES

1. Discuss at least three examples of situations in your personal life where you used anticipatory thinking to provide a positive alternative to a problem that appeared to have no workable solution. Then discuss some examples of your failure to do so.

2. Discuss at least three examples of potential business problems you were able to identify in advance and avoid, solve or re-structure for a successful outcome. Then discuss some examples of your failure to do so.

3. Discuss some of the advantages of using the preventive law approach in planning and evaluating commercial transactions.

4. Discuss some of the disadvantages of the preventive law approach.

5. Discuss and rank the top five obstacles to successful implementing of anticipatory thinking in your everyday life?

CASE EXERCISES

FAILURE TO RENEW A LICENSE ALMOST COSTS $34,000

The case of *Wilson v. Kealakekua Ranch, Ltd., 551 P.2d 525 (Hawaii 1976)*, is a graphic example of a lack of anticipatory thinking that was almost disastrous.

Wilson was an architect who performed agreed architectural services totaling almost $34,000 for the defendant, and then sued for breach of contract when his bill was unpaid.

He had originally been licensed as required under Hawaii law, but neglected to pay his $15 annual renewal fee, causing his certificate of registration to expire until reinstated. He also failed to pay the $30 reinstatement fee. The services in question in this case were rendered during this period of license expiration.

ANALYSIS

The trial court ruled that Wilson had violated a regulatory law and his contract was void. It cited the law that stated, "any person who practices architecture without having first registered in accordance with this chapter and without having a valid unexpired certificate of registration shall be fined not more than $500 . . ."

Fortunately for him, the appellate court reversed, holding that since he was originally licensed, the failure to renew only violated a revenue-raising law and did not invalidate his contract. It noted that, "while the provisions of the statute requiring initial registration are clearly designed to protect the public from unfit and incompetent practitioners of architecture, we think that the provision requiring renewal, with which Wilson failed to comply, is purely for the purpose of raising revenues."

"Additional punishment (beyond the $500 fine), especially a disproportionate forfeiture (of up to $34,000) is not justified and could not have been intended by the legislature."

DEFUSE REPLAY

If the Hawaii law had stated, "and failure to comply with these provisions shall be deemed a violation of a regulatory law and invalidate any contracts made during a period of license suspension or expiration," Wilson would have lost his $34,000. A very expensive lesson, indeed.

Wilson could have insulated himself from this type of problem by including in his agreement to perform architectural services a provision that stated, "sums due hereunder for the rendition of valuable services rendered shall not be deducted or denied due to any inadvertent or negligent failure of Architect to comply with local license renewal laws."

(See the later chapter on illegality for a discussion of the legal distinctions between regulatory and revenue-raising laws as they relate to enforcement of contracts)

CONCLUSION

Wilson almost blew himself up financially due to his failure to comply with the licensing law. Since all states always notify a licensee when renewal is due, he could easily have avoided the problem by prompt compliance. He could also have avoided it by prompt reinstatement. He did nothing, and was very fortunate.

A. Do you agree with the court's final decision?
B. Is the $500 fine for late renewal sufficient to teach Wilson a lesson?
C. What would have been the result if he were not originally licensed?

ONE WORD IN A CONTRACT OFFER LOSES A CASE

In *Osprey L.L.C. v. Kelly-Moore Paint Co., 984 P.2d 194 (Okla. 1999)*, the defendant Kelly entered into a 15-year commercial lease with the plaintiff. It had a six-month renewal clause that stated:

"NOTICES. All notices required to be given hereunder by Lessee or Lessor *shall* be given in writing and *may* be delivered either personally or by depositing the same in United States mail, first class postage prepaid, registered or certified mail, return receipt requested."

On the last day, Kelly faxed its renewal notice during the day and also sent a copy of that notice by Federal Express, which arrived the following day.

Plaintiff rejected the fax notice, claiming it was late because it didn't comply with the terms of the lease, and sued to remove Kelly from the premises. Kelly claimed its fax renewal was effective.

The case was the first time an Oklahoma court had been called upon to decide whether a faxed delivery of a written notice to renew a commercial lease is the same as "personal delivery".

ANALYSIS

The trial court ruled in favor of Kelly, and the Court of Appeals reversed, determining that "the plain language of the lease required it be renewed by delivering notice either personally or by mail, and that Kelly-Moore had done neither."

The Oklahoma Supreme Court vacated the decision of its appellate court and affirmed the trial court, stating, "because the lease provision concerned uses the permissive "may" rather than the mandatory "shall" and refers to personal delivery or registered or certified mail, but does not require these methods of delivery, to the exclusion of other modes of transmission which serve the same purpose . . . a substituted method of notice which performs the same function and serves the same purpose as an authorized method of notice is not defective."

DEFUSE REPLAY

The landlord who offers lease renewal is "master of his offer" and can word it in any fashion to limit acceptance to its specific terms and to the time, method or manner of acceptance.

Landlords also customarily draft the lease agreements they offer to prospective tenants, especially in commercial leases. Here, Osprey chose to use the word "may" when referring to the method of renewal notice, rather than the word "shall", and suffered the adverse legal consequences.

If Osprey had done a better job of anticipatory thinking when they drafted their lease form, they would have prevented the legal problem they encountered.

CONCLUSION

There is a trend that is emerging in various court decisions in cases such as this that is related to the numerous electronic and technological methods of legal communication that now exist.

Formerly, almost all decisions required strict adherence to the contract terms that specifically refer to a method of delivering notice of lease renewals or exercise of option contracts.

Now, a shift has occurred whereby a majority of courts have moved from the "strict compliance rule" to a more liberal "alternative method rule", which allows a substituted method if it is furnished in the same time frame. The practical philosophy here is "no damage, no foul."

      A. Do you agree with the court's final decision?
      B. Did the punishment suffered by Osprey fit his offense?
      C. What are advantages/disadvantages of the strict v. liberal compliance rules?

This chapter concludes with two cases involving banks that may well be the most costly, yet easily preventable, examples of how the lack of an anticipatory thinking approach to preventive law can lead to financially disastrous results.

FAILURE TO "AFFIX" AN ENDORSEMENT TO A PROMISSORY NOTE COSTS THE BUYER BANK $19MILLION

In *Adams, et al v. Madison Realty & Development, Inc., et al, 853 F.2d 163 (3rd Cir. 1988)*, Empire, a federal savings bank in Deland, Florida, purchased thirty-five promissory notes for $19.5 million in the secondary market from Consolidated Mortgage Co. and Putnam Funding Co. as part of a bulk investment of negotiable instruments.

These notes were the debt instruments of separate investors in real estate partnerships that had been offered for sale to the public by Madison Partnerships. Approximately 18 months later, a massive fraud by Madison was discovered and the investors sued to have their notes legally canceled.

Empire was the holder and owner by endorsement of these notes, whereby the endorsements on separate sheets of paper had not been stapled or otherwise attached to the notes ("affixed") as required by law, but rather had just been loosely inserted within each note. They claimed that since they had not participated in the fraud, they were still protected by the Negotiable Instrument Laws that insulate a holder in due course from any transactional problems of the party from whom they purchased the notes.

ANALYSIS

The trial court ruled in favor of Empire. It acknowledged that the separate, unattached sheets of paper carrying the endorsements did not comply with the Uniform Commercial Code, which reads, "An indorsement must be written by or on behalf of the holder and on the instrument or on a paper so firmly affixed thereto as to become a part thereof."

But the trial court still ruled for the indorsee, saying that even if the indorsee had been exposed to some risks, "that is no reason to absolve the notemakers, who are in no way injured by the use of an unattached indorsement, of their obligations." The failure to properly attach the indorsements was excused as being "hypertechnical".

The appellate court reversed, vacating the lower court judgment. While admitting the affixation requirement was technical, the court also agreed with the argument that "the privileged status of holder in due course is also a technical creation bestowed only after strict compliance with the statutory prerequisites."

The appellate court was not sympathetic to the bank's self-imposed predicament, and took a position of insisting upon strict adherence to the governing law of the UCC:

"Financial institutions, noted for insisting on their customers' compliance with numerous ritualistic formalities, are not sympathetic petitioners in urging relaxation of an elementary business practice."

DEFUSE REPLAY

How could Empire have avoided this very costly problem?

The critical wording of the UCC provision required the endorsements to be "firmly affixed" to the promissory notes. "A purported indorsement on a mortgage or other separate paper pinned or clipped to an instrument is not sufficient for negotiation . . . the loose indorsement sheets accompanying Empire's notes would have been valid allonges had they been stapled or glued to the notes themselves."

By being "loosely inserted" with each note, the separate indorsements resulted in Empire not being a legal "holder" and therefore not entitled to the protective legal provisions of the UCC that allow a holder-assignee to take free of any transactional defenses that may be legally enforceable against their seller-assignor.

CONCLUSION

The law of negotiable instruments is highly technical in its requirements, because it affords special protection to the parties who purchase and seek to enforce their notes, drafts, and other types of commercial paper.

At first analysis, this clerical error of not physically attaching the indorsements to their corresponding promissory notes seems harmless. There was no question that Empire had bought them and was in possession of all the original documents.

But the technical nature of the law itself is exactly why Empire was duty bound to be meticulous is strict compliance.   Compare the cost of thirty-five missing staples with the amount Empire had at risk. A $19 million mistake!

      A. Do you agree with the court's final decision?
      B. How could Empire avoid such problems in the future?
      C. Where would you draw the line between technical and hypertechnical compliance with the law?

FAILURE TO RETURN BAD CHECKS ON TIME COSTS BANK $25MILLION

In *ChicagoTitle Insurance Company v. California Canadian Bank, 1 Cal. App. 4th 798 (Cal. App.. 1991),* a mortgage broker and its client used a title company to act as escrow agent in closing various real estate transactions.

They wrote checks totaling $17M payable to the title company, drawn on their account at the California Bank's San Mateo, Ca. branch. The title company deposited these checks for collection at its account at Bank of San Francisco, who sent the checks for payment to California Bank. The next day, California Bank sent the checks to its San Mateo, Ca. branch for payment, where they were dishonored due to insufficient funds.

Unfortunately, the mortgage broker and its client were engaged in a massive check fraud operation, where they had diverted the $17M to their own use before their fraud was discovered, with the title company paying funds out of its escrow account that were supposedly backed by these "good" checks.

The title company sued the bank, claiming it violated the usual banking procedures and statutory laws that established a "midnight deadline" rule to the effect that a bank that receives for collection a check of its account holder presented for payment at another bank must return dishonored items no later than midnight of the next business day, or be "accountable" for any losses.

The obvious purpose of the "midnight deadline" rule is to provide prompt notice of dishonor to check payees so they can protect themselves. The title company claimed it suffered the loss because of the bank's delay in returning the bad checks to their Bank of San Francisco.

ANALYSIS

The trial court determined that the "midnight deadline" rule requires. "a bank which performs bookkeeping at a computer center to *return* checks to the Clearing House by midnight of the day following receipt . . . ," and entered judgment against California Bank, for $25 million which included accrued interest.

It also noted the bank's own internal policy and trade practice, "to return checks by delivering them to a clearinghouse or the bank on which drawn prior to the 'midnight deadline'."

The bank argued unsuccessfully that "it could somehow suspend the running of the midnight deadline by sending the checks to its own computer center, thereby getting them out of the bank branch proper before the deadline expired."

On appeal, the trial court's decision was affirmed. "Since the bank did not return the checks in question before the applicable midnight deadline, it is 'accountable' or strictly liable for the amount of the checks under (the California law)."

DEFUSE REPLAY

The "midnight deadline" rule is one of the basic principles of banking law. It requires banks that receive collection items to approve or dishonor them within the required one business day time limit, or suffer the financial consequences.

That rule is absolute, no matter how complex the internal routing structure is of the bank in question.

The testimony at the trial showed the internal practices of the bank were extremely sloppy. It admitted its returns of in-county checks were routinely late, "and that its own policy and procedure manual made no distinction between in-county and out-of-county checks." That manual stated:

"An office, regardless of its location . . . must return (dishonored checks) the same day."

CONCLUSION

The effect of this case was far-reaching on the California Bank in particular, and other banks across the country in general.

When the trial court decision was rendered, the bank realized this problem could repeat itself unless they drastically improved their internal procedures. They did this while their appeal was pending. It was too late to save then from this loss, but there would be no repeats in the future. It was like locking the barn door after all the cattle had escaped.

When the appellate decision was widely reported, the entire banking industry took note.

It reviewed, evaluated and restructured its compliance procedures where necessary. The dramatic financial loss of California Bank served as an industry wake up call.

    A. Do you agree with the court's final decision?
    B. Is the "midnight deadline" rule too strict?
    C. How could California Bank avoid such problems in the future?

CASE RESEARCH CYBERCISES

The following cases also relate to the material in this chapter and illustrate the types of disputes that may occur. For each one do the following written assignment:

1. Locate the case using the Internet (Lexis-Nexis, West or any other research cite which provides case transcripts).
2. Briefly summarize what it was about – the nature of the dispute involved.
3. Who won at the trial court level? Who won at the appellate level?
4. Who won if there was a third level of Supreme Court review?
5. What were the legal rules of law and the reasoning used to reach the final decision?
6. Do you agree or disagree with the decision, and explain why?
7. What business law time bomb(s) were involved?
8. Could the time bomb(s) have been avoided by structuring the transaction differently? Discuss.
9. Could the adverse effects of the time bomb(s) have been defused by a different reaction or response by the affected party? Discuss.
10. Replay the facts of the case to achieve a different successful result.

1. *FDIC v. Hughes Development Co., 684 F.Supp. 616 (Dist. Minn. 1988) (loan cancellation allowed four years after the fact).*
2. *Oclander v. First National Bank of Louisville, 700 S.W.2d 804 (Ky. App. 1985) (charges from credit card left in estranged spouse's possession were allowed).*
3. *Pinner v. Schmidt, 805 F.2d 1258 (5ᵗʰ Cir. 1986) (erroneous credit report).*

NOTES

THE BUSINESS LAW SURVIVAL GUIDE

2.

THE PURPOSE OF LAWS:
WHY DO WE HAVE THEM?

"We are a government of laws, and not of men."
John Adams

"Laws are generally found to be nets of such a texture, as the little creep through, the great break through, and the middle-sized are alone entangled in."
William Shenstone

A. LAWS PROVIDE OUR FRAMEWORK OF SOCIETY

Laws are the rules of conduct that govern our everyday lives. They tell us what we can and cannot do. They set the permissible boundaries of our individual, corporate and governmental behavior.

Every day there are literally hundreds of them we obey and hundreds that we disobey, some with full knowledge of their existence, many others in ignorance until after the fact. The threat of enforcement of laws and the consequence of violating them is one of the threads that hold the fabric of our society together.

Many laws act as a deterrent to criminal behavior. "If you can't do the time, don't do the crime," says the jailhouse adage.

Equally as many laws deter personal or corporate civil misconduct. If one's private actions or non-actions violate certain laws, their behavior may be adapted accordingly due to our judicial system. If a large company is inclined to abuse its powers of size, influence and financial strength, it may refrain due in large part to the possibility of lawsuits that protect and compensate the affected parties with large damage awards.

The contracts and sales laws of the commercial marketplace are the heart of transactional business:

- The parties make an agreement to buy or sell goods or services

- One party believes it made a bad business deal and seeks a way to legally be excused from having to perform

- The other party believes it made a good business deal and seeks to legally enforce the agreement

- This dispute is ultimately resolved based upon the governing rules of law

If the game is baseball or basketball, soccer or squash, we can't be skilled players unless we know the rules of the game.

The same applies to the game of business. Knowledge of the laws help us to plan proposed transactions, evaluate their advantages and disadvantages, consider alternate courses of action, negotiate terms and avoid disputes. If disputes do occur, the laws assist in predicting their probable outcome and provide a basis to negotiate compromises. In totality, they provide the framework of acceptable conduct in both personal and business interactions.

B. LAWS HELP TO PREDICT THE OUTCOME OF DISPUTES

Since life in our busy world invariably leads to disputes of one kind or another, some being simple misunderstandings and others having more far-reaching legal implications – it would be very helpful to be able to predict their probable outcome.

We are not talking about something so imprecise as intuition or psychic skills. Our laws, whether they be legislative statutes, judicial court decisions or executive orders, are created as a result of disputes of one kind or another that have ripened into lawsuits, or raised sufficient public attention to be the subject of laws passed by our political bodies to help protect our perceived health, safety and general welfare.

The past is the best predictor of the future. When a new dispute arises, judges look to prior cases or legislative enactments, or administrative orders or other sources of law to guide them. We can do the same thing in evaluating a current dispute and making our best management decisions.

For some disputes, the available authorities are so clear and pervasive that an answer can be stated with reasonable assurance. For others, the law on the subject may be confused or inconsistent. For some disputes, the situations are so novel and unique that no governing laws exist. This sliding scale of predictability leads us into another aspect of laws – their ability to change to meet necessary challenges.

In *American Heart Association, et al v. County of Greenville, 489 S.E.2d 921 (Sup. Ct. S.C. 1997),* the dispute involved conflicting claims of ownership to the will of the infamous "Shoeless Joe Jackson", a member of the Chicago "Black" Sox baseball team accused of throwing the 1919 World Series. The original will contained a rare example of his original signature, worth approximately $100,000 to autograph collectors.

That will was in possession of his wife until she died in 1959, until it was filed with the defendant as required by law, as a part of the probate of her estate. Her will devised it to the plaintiff charities. They and the defendant brought a declaratory judgment action to determine legal ownership of the will document.

The trial court granted summary judgment declaring the defendant owner of the original will, and the decision was affirmed on appeal.

Plaintiffs asserted, "a will is a person's personal property since individuals may during their lifetime own, possess, use, enjoy, and dispose of their will any way they see fit and upon death, the will becomes part of one's estate, passing directly to the personal representative."

The courts disagreed. "The trial court ruled that the Jackson will is a public record and must remain in the care, custody and control of the Probate Court . . . original wills, which are required by state law to be filed with the Probate court, constitute 'public records.' . . . the probate code neither intends nor provides that the deliverer of a will, even if a devisee under it, gain ownership in the actual document."

C. LAWS CHANGE TO MEET CHANGING SOCIAL CONDITIONS

"If our existing case law is inadequate to accommodate the business transactions made in today's business world, and if, as the Court's opinion concedes, our law is not in accord with that in a majority of jurisdictions, it simply does not do to continue to decide 1980 controversies based on what in 1912 was thought to be the better law to follow." *Hoffman v. S V Company, Inc., 628 P.2d 218 (Idaho 1981).*

Contrary to the layperson's view of the law, it is flexible and in a constant state of flux, on a delayed basis, as it tries to respond to the ever changing needs of society. The process of change is slow, but sure. Once a certain critical mass of events are reached, combined with media attention and public outcry, the wheels of change begin to turn and eventually a landmark case or legislative enactment occurs that completes the process.

We have seen this happen in landmark cases such as *Brown v. Board of Education of Topeka, 347 U.S. 483 (1954)* (school integration), *Bakke v. Regents of the University of California, 483 U.S. 265 (1978)*(reverse discrimination), *Roe v. Wade, 410 U.S. 113 (1973)*(abortion rights), and *Miranda v. Arizona, 384 U.S. 436 (1966)* (right to criminal counsel).

We have seen it happen in laws passed to abolish slavery, grant women the right to vote, prohibit child labor and unsafe working conditions, end discrimination and job harassment, establish a minimum wage, grant social security, provide social assistance such as medicare and medicaid, assist the consumer, protect the environment, and so on.

We have also seen the pendulum swing back and forth. Alcohol sale and consumption was prohibited by the Volstead Act and 18th constitutional amendment on moral and religious grounds.

It was then repealed by the 21st amendment when the growth of organized crime and the public's thirst combined to end that experiment in legislating morality. "Right to Life" v. "Pro-Choice" signals the uncertain legal future of abortion. Muhammad Ali was a "draft-dodger" in the eyes of the law when he refused to serve in the Vietnam War, and then was later considered a hero for his courage in opposing it.

Our immigration laws, at the turn of the century that resulted in populating many of the major industrial areas of the country with a work force were ostensibly passed in the spirit of freedom and liberty. But some had originally been passed as exclusionary protection against certain "undesirables." These laws are still in a state of flux depending upon where local pressures exist.

We have seen our laws change recently in the evolution of lawsuits for money damages by cigarette smokers against tobacco companies.

For many years these lawsuits were routinely dismissed at the trial court level. The U.S. Supreme Court routinely affirmed the lower court rulings on appeal by a unanimous 9-0 vote. Gradually similar cases were heard where the tobacco companies prevailed, but the votes began to change as some Justices wrote dissenting opinions.

Then a lifelong smoker who began smoking as a teenager before mandatory health warnings, and continued until her diagnosis of terminal lung cancer brought a lawsuit. She claimed her permanent injuries were caused by a combination of the defendant's deceptive advertising, fraudulent concealment of health risks, and their industry wide conspiracy to "hook" smokers and maintain their nicotine addiction.

That landmark 1992 case, styled *Cipollone v. Liggett Group, Inc., 505 U.S. 504 (1992)*, was heard by the U.S. Supreme Court after it slowly traveled the trial court – appellate court route, with majority opinions in favor of the defendant and dissenting opinions in favor of the plaintiff until the Court ruled for the first time that the Federal Cigarette Labeling Act did not bar such lawsuits against tobacco companies.

Following *Cipollone*, more and more lawsuits were heard by trial courts around the country, and eventually juries began to enter large damage awards against the defendants in both individual actions and the much larger class actions filed on behalf of smokers within a particular state or nationwide. The law in this area had come full cycle from no recovery to full recovery, with most plaintiffs' verdicts carrying hefty awards of punitive damages, as mentioned in the chapter on Remedies.

But the law in this area continued to evolve, as States successfully sued the tobacco companies and recovered hundreds of millions of dollars in settlements for the large sums they were forced to pay to medicare and medicaid patients suffering from related smoking ailments.

Success in these typical cigarette smoker cases then led to class action litigation on behalf of flight attendants for damages caused by direct and secondhand smoke. Now, another type of tobacco lawsuit is being filed on behalf of users of smokeless tobacco products, based upon the same arguments that proved successful in the tobacco smoking cases - concealing smoking dangers, failing to warn consumers of true risks and manipulating nicotine levels to make the products more addictive.

Once the tobacco company litigation began to emerge as a viable plaintiff's source of recovery, similar lawsuits were filed as test cases against alcohol manufacturers and sellers for a variety of alcohol related personal injuries, as well as the same type of Medicare and Medicaid reimbursements requested in the tobacco cases.

The results were different however, with few if any recoveries allowed. While similarities between alcohol and tobacco exist in that neither activities are prohibited by law, there are far less instances in the alcohol cases of corporate misconduct such as misleading advertising, hidden data on harmful effects to health and safety, and enhancements of addictive contents of the products.

Another area of litigation that followed the tobacco cases was lawsuits against manufacturers and distributors of inexpensive small handguns known as "Saturday Night Specials", on the theory that there was a link of negligence liability between the proliferation of their availability and the resulting violence in their usage that resulted in damage to the public.

The gun companies made the same arguments about lawful sale, but ingenious counter-arguments were made by plaintiffs that the defendants were "negligent" in their failure to properly safeguard the guns against intended or accidental usage by minors, and allowing such cheap, easily concealable weapons to be available.

Such arguments did not lead to any successful court cases, but created enough congressional pressure to result in many of the largest gun manufacturers voluntarily agreeing to create and provide gun-locking devices, so that handguns legally in one's home for protection could not be protected against accidental or unauthorized use by juveniles and intruders.

A new trend in the gun cases may now be emerging due to the recent unreported West Palm Beach, Florida court case of *Grunow v. Valor Corp.*

In it for the first time in U.S. judicial history a jury found a major handgun distributor contributorily negligent for 5% of the damages suffered when a 13-year-old boy took one of their small guns manufactured without a safety mechanism from a family friend to his high school and shot and killed one of his teachers. The widow brought a wrongful death action that named the gun distributor as one of the defendants.

The jury verdict in *Grunow* was subsequently overturned, but additional test cases will no doubt be filed to test the judicial limits of recovery in the gun cases.

Our society has always been preoccupied with physical appearance, with the inevitable court disputes. In the late 1800's, the "full figure" was considered attractive and healthful. We have now come full circle, from "big is beautiful" to "thin is in." But more people than ever suffer from overweight and its related ailments, burdening individual and governmental pocketbooks. We are a fast-food, sugarholic society.

This is now reflected in obesity lawsuits being filed against deep-pocket fast food chains like McDonalds and Burger King. None have survived early dismissal but, like the gun cases, a litigation trend may emerge.

Another drastic change has occurred in how lawyers may attract new legal business. Every state has statutory provisions that disallow improper solicitation. Advertising of any kind by lawyers was strictly prohibited. Terms like "ambulance chasing" have crept into our vocabulary to signify unlawful conduct by lawyers or their agents, who sought to sign up new clients, literally while they were being treated for their personal injuries. There were also common law protective doctrines to prevent abusive attorney-client practices.

Then the tables turned, when lawyers were allowed to advertise by virtue of the landmark case of *Bates v. State Bar of Arizona, 433 U.S. 350 (1977)*. In the years that have elapsed since that decision, lawyer advertising is now the norm rather than the exception. Lawyers and law firms, large and small, have now remade themselves as service industries to meet increased competition and make fees affordable. Larger firms, innovations such as isolated tasks done by lower-paid assistants, standardized forms, office automation and increased use of technology have all become a part of this revolution.

In *Saladini v. Righellis, 687 N.E.2d 1224 (Mass. 1997),* the Massachusetts Supreme Court recognized this new trend, and struck down the old common law rules of champerty (selling an interest in a lawsuit) and barratry (bringing frivolous lawsuits), leaving it up to judges in individual cases to determine the fairness of contractual payment arrangements made to finance litigation.

Sometimes events occur that cause a legislative or judicial response and new laws result such as the death of the Lindbergh baby in the 1930's.

It resulted in federal kidnapping laws. The explosion of a Union Carbide chemical plant in Bhopal, the Three Mile Island Nuclear disaster, and the Exxon Valdez oil spill led to stronger rules to protect the environment. The Justice Clarence Thomas judicial confirmation hearings raised the national sensitivity to workplace sexual harassment. The accounting scandals at Enron and World Com will lead to greater corporate accountability. Our society often cannot know where legal protection is needed until situations arise which make such needs evident.

C. LAWS TRY TO ACHIEVE A BALANCE OF FAIRNESS

Contrary to popular belief, in addition to our hundreds of general laws that govern our personal and business relationships, there are just as many exceptions to these rules designed to prevent one party from taking unfair advantage of the other. Visualize the scales of justice. They also appear as the governing image in courtrooms throughout the land. Their motto is, "we who labor here seek only truth." It is usually achieved by the presentation of conflicting points of view. Our legal system tries to achieve this balance.

In *Flagiello v. Pennsylvania Hospital, 208 A.2d 193 (Pa. 1965)*, the plaintiff was injured in a fall that broke her ankle, while a patient at the defendant's non-profit hospital for an unrelated ailment.

She claimed the defendant was negligent and sued for money damages. The defendant claimed that the legal rule of charitable immunity established in prior cases insulated it from liability. After the trial court granted judgment based on this general rule of law, the Supreme Court reversed, citing the following fundamental rule of legal fairness:

> "From the earliest days of organized society it became apparent
> to man that society could never become a success unless the
> collectivity of mankind guaranteed to every member of society
> a remedy for a palpable wrong inflicted on him by another
> member of that society."

Our legal system is based upon a system of checks and balances. The plaintiff and defendant have a dispute. They both determine their legal rights by consulting a lawyer, who researches the sources of law and evaluates their respective positions. Let us assume they both believe they are right, are unable to mutually settle their differences and the dispute becomes a lawsuit. Both sides are bound by the same sets of rules for when to sue, where to sue and how to sue.

Even the conduct of a lawsuit resembles a pendulum as the parties alternate in their trial presentations. Plaintiff files complaint, defendant answers, both sides discover all surrounding facts and circumstances. If either party objects to anything, the other presents their counter arguments. Plaintiff presents its case, and then defendant does the same. They may cross-examine each other.

They argue their cases to the jury, first plaintiff and then defendant. Point – counterpoint.

Both sides request a decision in their favor. But it is an adversarial process and there can only be one winner. When the trial court decision is rendered, the loser has the right to appeal. Again, point – counterpoint. Ultimately a point of finality is reached. In the process both sides have been allowed a full presentation of their conflicting positions.

Our governmental structure is also based upon checks and balances. The framers of our Constitution implemented the scales of justice concept by devising the structure of our government. The executive branch cannot usually do anything without the advice and consent of Congress. Congress cannot usually legislate unless both the House and Senate concur. The lower court decisions are subject to review by higher courts until one final decision is made.

We have two judicial systems operating simultaneously to cover the wide spectrum of human and business relationships – Criminal Law and Civil Law.

A. Criminal Laws are offenses against society, and are enforced by the governmental authority. Sanctions may be warnings, license suspensions, fines, probation, imprisonment and loss of life.

The more serious the offense, the more severe the penalty. The Criminal law system acts as a deterrent to criminal conduct, assuming we know the rules and don't break them, and also keeps the peace by enforcing with appropriate judicial action those laws that are broken.

Notice these 10 significant characteristics of the Criminal Law system:
- Cases are heard in separate criminal courts
- The State or other governing authority is the complainant
- The party who violated the law is the defendant
- If there is an injured party, they may be a witness, but not one of the main parties to the proceeding.
- The defendant is not required to testify due to our constitutional privilege against self-incrimination
- Jury decisions are called verdicts, and must be unanimous decisions of guilty or not guilty. Otherwise there is a 'hung jury' and the case will either be retried or the defendant will be acquitted
- Criminal juries are usually 9 to 12 persons
- The State may not appeal a verdict in favor of the defendant
- The State must prove its case 'beyond and to the exclusion of every reasonable doubt'
- If the State wins its case, the guilty defendant may face imprisonment.

B. Civil Laws are the rules of conduct that relate to all areas other than criminal matters, and they govern commercial business transactions. The usual legal remedy in a civil action is money damages. They may include many different kinds of monetary recovery, including actual losses (compensatory), projected losses (consequential), special aspects of personal injury cases (pain and suffering, mental anguish and loss of consortium), and monetary punishment of a defendant to deter egregious conduct (punitive).

There are also non-monetary remedies available in appropriate cases. The most common are specific performance (defendant is required to honor his contract to sell you his unique one-of-a-kind painting), injunctive relief (defendant is legally restrained from a specific unlawful act, such as stalking a former spouse), child custody and adoption.

Notice these 10 significant differences of the Civil Law System:
- The disputes are between private parties
- The complaining party, called the plaintiff, sues the defendant
- Plaintiff may file a civil lawsuit without an attorney
- Defendant can be interrogated and must testify at trial
- Defendant must provide full discovery of material information, including pertinent documents, experts reports and lists of witnesses
- Cases may be decided by the judge alone or be heard by a jury. Either party may request a jury trial. The jury's decision is called a 'judgment', and need not be unanimous.
- Most civil juries consist of 6 persons.
- In most cases, the losing party has the right to appeal the adverse decision
- Plaintiff's burden of proof is much less than in a criminal case. It must prove its case 'by the greater weight of the evidence'
- The winning plaintiff usually recovers money damages from the defendant and can collect them, if not voluntarily paid, by having the court seize the defendant's assets and sell them at public sale

One of the most graphic examples of the differences between the criminal and civil law systems was the O.J. Simpson legal drama that took place in 1999. In *State of California v. Simpson,* he was acquitted by a jury of murdering his former wife Nicole and her friend, Ron Goldman. In *Goldman v. Simpson,* he was ruled responsible by jury for the wrongful death of Ron Goldman and liable for money damages, under the same facts.

The identical facts of each case produced different results due to the basic differences between the two legal systems under which they were presented.

D. LAWS SOLVE PROBLEMS IN DIFFERENT WAYS

Strict constructionists are judge's who exercise judicial restraint, and won't change laws on their own, even if they think they are bad laws. They take a narrow view of their role in the legal system. They refuse to function as legislators.

Judicial activists do not wait for what they consider bad laws to be repealed or good laws passed, and sometimes attempt to meet the current needs of the culture with their court decisions. Their decisions may even rewrite statutory laws that they feel no longer serve the needs of society.

In *Flood v. Kuhn, 407 U.S. 258 (1971)*, the major league baseball player, Curt Flood, challenged professional baseball's reserve clause which considered players to be the property of their ball clubs and allowed them to be traded from one club to another without their consent. He claimed this violated federal antitrust laws in that it restricted fair competition, and sought a ruling overturning the long-established antitrust exemption for baseball. He demanded to be made a free agent to make his own bargain with any other team of his choice.

The high court ruled against him, as it had in other cases brought over the years. Justice Blackmun said, " In view of all this, it seems appropriate now to say that with its reserve system enjoying exemption from federal antitrust laws, baseball is, in a very distinct sense, an exception and an anomaly...
And what the Court said (in 1922), and what it said (in 1953), we say again here in 1972: the remedy, if any is indicated, is for congressional, and not judicial, action."

Interestingly, as a result of this case and the refusal of the Court to allow free agency, the baseball player's labor union ultimately won this right in its collective bargaining agreement, resulting in the huge salaries baseball players receive today. This, in turn, has led to more labor turmoil and another assault on baseball's antitrust exemption as the baseball owners claim they cannot operate profitably, threaten contraction of certain small market teams, and seek to implement a salary cap on the players.

In *Kreimer v. Bureau of Police, 765 F.Supp. 181 (N.J. Dist. 1991)*, a homeless person was ejected and barred from a local public library because of its policy of nuisance exclusion based upon "annoyance of other persons" or "offensive personal hygiene". The policy also stated that patrons who are not actively "using library materials shall be asked to leave the building."

In holding this library policy unconstitutional, Judge Sarokin took a judicial stance of social consciousness in saying, "Society has survived not banning books which it finds offensive from its libraries; it will survive not banning persons whom it likewise finds offensive from its libraries. The greatness of our country lies in tolerating speech with which we do not agree; the same toleration must extend to people, particularly where the cause of revulsion may be of our own making.

If we wish to shield our eyes and noses from the homeless, we should revoke their condition, not their library cards."

In *Bush v. Gore, 531 U.S. 98 (2000),* the 2000 presidential election brought into play both strict construction of the Federal Constitution by the 5 majority Justices and the attempt to mold a fairness remedy to a unique problem by the 4 dissenting Justices.

The presidential election held November 7, 2000 resulted in an unprecedented constitutional crisis. Mr. Gore won the popular vote.

But under our laws, presidents are elected by a majority of the electoral votes apportioned to each state. The winner of the election hinged on the Florida vote. Mr. Bush had an original victory margin of 1,784 votes, which was later reduced by machine and manual recounts to a winning of 537 votes which was certified by Florida's secretary of state as required by law.

Mr. Gore contested the results and demanded a full manual recount, based upon various allegations of error and impropriety. At Mr. Bush's request, the U.S. Supreme Court agreed to consider the situation. The Florida Supreme Court twice invoked its equitable powers to create a remedy to meet this unique problem, and sided with Mr. Gore by requiring the counting of various previously identified votes, a manual recount of other undervotes, and "such other orders as were necessary to add any legal votes to the total statewide certifications."

The U.S. Supreme Court reversed the Florida Supreme Court by a 5-4 vote, and Mr. Bush was officially declared President. The majority ruled that any recount would be unconstitutional because it violated the equal protection clause of the Federal Constitution's 14th Amendment. Their ruling stated, " . . . there was no recount procedure in place (under the Florida ruling) that comported with minimal standards required under the Fourteenth Amendment . . . for the recount could not be conducted in compliance (with the 14th amendment) without substantial additional work." This represents an example of the "strict construction" aspect of the judicial restraint approach.

The dissenters argued that, "this was not an occasion which required federal judicial intervention in a state election." They were also concerned that the majority's "concern about the December 12 deadline was misplaced, and (the majority's conclusion that) a constitutionally adequate recount was impractical was a prophecy which the Court's own judgment would not allow to be tested."

Rather than being concerned with what was technically incorrect, inconvenient or impractical, the dissenters focused on the fact that, "under the very special circumstances of the case at hand, basic principles of fairness might have counseled adoption of a uniform and specific standard to guide the manual recount ordered by the Florida Supreme Court."

The dissenters, as well as the Florida Supreme Court, followed a judicial activism approach to try and solve the unique problem facing them.

DISCUSSION EXERCISES

1. Discuss any other situations where laws may provide a societal framework.
2. Discuss any other situations where laws may help predict the outcome of disputes.
3. Discuss any other situations where laws were created to meet changing social conditions.
4. Discuss any other situations where laws try to balance fairness.
5. Discuss how laws may impact the business marketplace to:

   - Encourage existing business activity
   - Restrict existing business activity
   - Create new business opportunities

CASE EXERCISES

JOHN LENNON'S LONG AND WINDING ROAD TO STAY IN THE U.S.

Lennon v. INS, 527 F.2d 187 (1975) tells this story. In 1968 police officers from Scotland Yard made a warantless search of John Lennon's London apartment, found one-half ounce of hashish, and placed him under arrest. He claimed he was unaware of its presence, but pleaded guilty to possession of cannabis resin and was fined 150 pounds.

In 1971, John and his wife Yoko arrived in the U.S. to seek custody of his daughter by a former marriage to a U.S. citizen. Since his conviction rendered him excludable under the U.S. Immigration Act ("any alien who has been convicted of . . . any law or regulation relating to the illicit possession of . . . marijuana"), he and his wife were issued temporary visas. Under the law, when the visa expired they were required to leave the U.S. or face deportation.

When the visa expired, the INS notified the Lennons that they had to leave the country. They applied for and received 3rd preference immigrant visas which are given to "qualified immigrants who . . . because of their exceptional ability in the sciences or the arts will substantially benefit prospectively the national economy, cultural interests, or welfare of the United States." This status was a pre-requisite to petitioning for permanent residency.

Deportation hearings were held by INS and 10 days after approval of their immigrant status, the Lennons applied for permanent residence.

Yoko Ono's petition was granted because she had previously gained permanent residence status in 1964 while married to her first husband, but John Lennon's was denied and he was ordered deported.

ANALYSIS

The order of the Immigration Judge was based upon the belief that Lennon's 1968 conviction made him excludable under the Immigration Act, and was upheld by the Board of Immigration Appeals.

The Board conceded that the Immigration Act "does not exclude aliens convicted of possession under laws which make knowledge immaterial to the offense."
However they concluded that, "a person who was entirely unaware that he possessed any illicit substance would not have been convicted under the British Dangerous Drugs Act."

Lennon argued that he was not excludable because, "he had not been convicted of violating a law forbidding *illicit* possession." He urged that, under British law, guilty knowledge was not an element of the offense, and therefore his possession could not have been illicit.

That Act states, "A person shall not be in possession of a drug unless . . . authorized."

The U.S. Court of Appeals ruled in favor of Lennon, agreeing with his contention that the British law made guilty knowledge irrelevant. They said:

"Under British law, a person found with tablets which he reasonably believed were aspirin would be convicted if the tablets proved to be heroin. And a man given a sealed package filled with heroin would, if he had any opportunity to open the parcel, suffer the same fate – even if he firmly believed the package contained perfume."

The Court also noted that the purpose of the Immigration Act's exclusionary clause was to bar undesirable aliens. "There is also, we note, some indication that Congress, in enacting (the Law) was far more concerned with the trafficker of drugs than with the possessor."

There was a dissenting opinion that suggested the Immigration Act's exclusionary language was very clear in that it would, "exclude any alien who has been convicted of a violation of any law or regulation relating to the illicit possession of narcotic drugs or marijuana."

"Since the statute applies to any alien, it makes no difference whether he be John Lennon, John Doe or Johann Sebastian Bach."

"The undisputed fact, however is that Lennon did plead guilty to the possession of cannabis resin, and while this may have been convenient or expedient because of his wife's pregnancy and his disinclination to have her testify in court, it is elementary that we cannot go behind the plea."

DEFUSE REPLAY

The majority decision brought into its reasoning many factors outside the limited issue of comparing the wording of the British and U.S. laws that seemed to justify their ruling as being the right and proper thing to do.

They noted after reviewing INS records of over 1,800 deportable aliens against whom no proceedings had been instituted that, "Many aliens granted such status had criminal records far more serious than Lennon's. Some were convicted of murder or rape, and one was described in his file as "an admitted heroin addict" who was reputedly on of the "largest suppliers of marijuana and narcotics in the area."

They also took note of Lennon's argument that he was being singled out for deportation because the INS "instituted deportation proceedings because they feared he might participate in demonstrations that would be highly embarrassing to the then-existing administration."

The dissenting opinion refused to consider any such matters they deemed extraneous to the real issue at hand, being Lennon was an alien convicted by his own guilty plea of possessing a banned substance. The argument that the U.S. law required criminal intent and the British law did not was disregarded.

"It is the unusual case where contraband such as this is surreptitiously planted in one's reticule or blue jeans pocket. Yet by disregarding convictions under the British Statute or any other foreign counterpart, the majority would admit to the United States those who knowingly possessed any illicit drugs."

CONCLUSION

This Case is a fine example of the different points of view involved in judicial activism (majority opinion) and judicial restraint (dissenting opinion).

The majority goes outside the narrow confines of the legal issue before it to recommend changes in the immigration laws, their interpretation, and in effect attempts to rewrite certain provisions.

The minority takes a more rigid view of strict construction, to maintain the separation between the functions of the judicial and legislative branches of government and refuse to bend or modify the existing law.

The majority also considered social justice and how our immigration laws should be viewed under current times:

"We have come a long way from the days when fear and prejudice toward alien races were the guiding forces behind our immigration laws . . . Deportation is not, of course, a penal sanction. But in severity it surpasses all but the most Draconian criminal penalties. We therefore cannot deem wholly irrelevant the long unbroken tradition of the criminal law that harsh sanctions should not be imposed where moral culpability is lacking."

"The excludable aliens statute is but an exception, albeit necessary, to the traditional tolerance of a nation founded and built by immigrants. If, in our two hundred years of independence, we have in some measure realized our ideals, it is in large part because we have always found a place for those committed to the spirit of liberty and willing to help implement it. Lennon's four-year battle to remain in our country is testimony to his faith in this American dream."

> A. Do you agree with the court's final decision?
> B. How do you think a current court would rule on this dispute after the terrorist attacks of 9/11/02?
> C. What changes in our Immigration Laws, if any, do you think are currently necessary?
> D. Discuss what part, if any, you believe Lennon's substantial financial resources played in permitting him to maintain the four-year legal proceedings and to ultimately prevail.

"MODERN VULGARISM" UNDERCUTS SEX HARASSMENT LAWS

In *Breda v. Wolf Camera, 222 F.3d 890 (11ᵗʰ Cir. 2002)*, plaintiff was hired as a full-time sales associate in Defendant's camera and film store in Savannah, Georgia. She alleged that she was subjected to sexual harassment throughout her employment, resigned approximately 14 months later, and filed suit under Title VII of the Civil Rights Act, claiming her employer knew or should have known of the harassment and failed, as required by law, to take remedial action.

The defendant had a clear and established policy regarding suspected harassment that stated, "Anyone who believes that he or she is being subjected to harassment or who has witnessed such harassment must immediately notify his or her manager."

Plaintiff followed this procedure and complained on at least four or five occasions to her store manager of the conduct of a fellow employee. The manager insisted her complaints did not constitute sexual harassment, but were "only general animosity between co-workers."

The trial court granted summary judgment to the employer, which was reversed on appeal (222 F.3d 886) and remanded back to the trial court, "to allow the district court to resolve factual disputes regarding the timing, extent, and nature of Appellant's complaints."

The behavior complained of by Plaintiff included allegations that her co-workers used sexual epithets and obscenities, waited for her outside the restroom and berated her for taking so long, told her that she made sales because male customers wanted to have sex with her, and used the store's telephoto lenses to ogle her.

ANALYSIS

The trial court, after the remand, ruled again in favor of the employer and dismissed plaintiff's complaint, basing its ruling in part on the view that the conduct complained of was not sufficiently severe to violate her civil rights.

"The modern notion of acceptable behavior – as corroded by instant-gratification driven cultural influences (e.g. lewd music, videos and computer games, perversity-programming broadcast standards, White House internal affairs and perjurious coverups of same, etc.) has been coarsening over time. . ."

"Today, a victim may have to accept a certain amount of boorish behavior or workplace vulgarity as normal rather than a civil violation in today's "Slouch Toward Gomorrah" society."

In finding the alleged behavior not legally actionable, the court said:

"The conduct is juvenile, offensive, and at times even mean-spirited, but merely inserting every last rude or sexualized comment/gesture/joke into a lengthy list accumulated over the years of employment does not a Title VII claim make."

DEFUSE REPLAY

Title VII liability for hostile work environment sexual harassment requires a plaintiff to establish:

(1) she is a member of a protected group,
(2) she received unwelcome sexual harassment,
(3) the harassment was because of her sex, and
(4) the harassment was *sufficiently severe* to alter her employment conditions

The trial courts own words highlight the opposing points of view:

"Sensitive judges might find a case laden with sexually crude jokes and behavior sufficient to send the case to a jury, if not support a jury's 'hostile environment' determination."

In contrast, judges desensitized by contemporaneous, 'Vulgarians-at-the-Gate' cultural standards might find the same facts insufficiently severe, then grant the defendant summary judgment."

CONCLUSION

This case demonstrates a number of our concepts about the purpose of laws.

First, it is a fine example of how changing social conditions will influence not only changes in the law, but how existing laws are interpreted by courts hearing disputes. Had this case been decided at the time of passage of Title VII in the 1960's or even through the 1980's - when the terms "obscenity" and "pornography" had a workable legal framework that defined and limited one's actions – the plaintiff would probably have been a clear winner.

However, any lines of acceptable behavior that previously existed have certainly been blurred by the times in which we now live.

Second, the trial judge interestingly labels himself as being "desensitized" by current standards of our culture, and rules for the employer. His approach is a form of reverse judicial activism, because while he considers all external factors, his ruling is against the party seeking relief.

A ruling for the plaintiff would therefore be made by a "sensitive" court that limited its analysis just to the specific acts, rather than the surrounding social arena. Such a decision would fall within judicial restraint, because it is limited in focus to the specific acts, rather than the times in which they occur.

A. Do you agree with the court's final decision?
B. What arguments would you make in support of judicial restraint? What arguments would you make in support of judicial activism?
C. How should judges interpret pre-existing laws that were created in different social times?

CASE RESEARCH CYBERCISES

The following cases also relate to the material in this chapter and illustrate the types of disputes that may occur. For each one do the following written assignment:

1. Locate the case using the internet (Lexis-Nexis, West or any other research cite which provides case transcripts)
2. Briefly summarize what it was about — the nature of the dispute involved
3. Who won at the trial court level? Who won at the appellate level?
4. Who won if there was a third level of Supreme Court review?
5. What were the legal rules of law and the reasoning used to reach the final decision?
6. Do you agree or disagree with the decision, and explain why?
7. What business law time bomb(s) were involved?
8. Could the time bomb(s) have been avoided entirely by structuring the transaction differently? Discuss.
9. Could the adverse effects of the time bomb(s) have been defused by a different reaction or response by the affected party? Discuss.
10. Replay the facts of the case to achieve a different successful result.

1. *Rochin v. California, 342 U.S. 165 (1952) (forced stomach pumping yields controlled substance).*
2. *Price Waterhouse v. Hopkins, 490 U.S. 228 (1989) (employment sex stereotyping).*
3. *United Steelworkers v. Weber, 443 U.S. 193 (1979) (affirmative action racial preferences).*

NOTES

THE SOURCES OF LAWS:
WHAT ARE THEY?

*"The chess board is the world,
the pieces are the phenomena of the universe,
the rules of the game are what we call the laws of Nature."*
Thomas Henry Huxley

If we are to learn to use the Anticipatory Thinking Approach to Preventive Law, it is essential to identify the particular rules of law that may govern our business transaction.

We cannot realistically plan anything until we know the legal constraints that we are operating under. Once we plug the factual aspects of our proposed transaction into the legal rules that apply to it, we will have a much better picture of our prospects for success.

Perhaps we will receive confirmation that allows us to proceed exactly as planned. Maybe we need a substantial reworking of our ideas to circumvent a potentially explosive legal time bomb or two, and proceed down a different road. At worst, we may be forced to abandon the proposed transaction entirely, but even if this occurs, we know we have located a potentially fatal problem and avoided its financially deadly consequences. Our finances remain intact and we have preserved our financial ability to find another deal on another day.

We are presumed to know the laws that pertain to our transaction. We may not raise 'ignorance of the law' as a legal defense in the event of a dispute. And we know to a certainty that it is impossible to be aware of those laws relevant to our proposed deal unless they are researched properly. All the more reason to learn how to find them and become familiar with those that apply to our intended course of conduct *before* it is finalized, so that we may weigh all the possible alternatives and choose wisely.

Knowledge is power, and in the marketplace of commercial transactions advance knowledge usually results in wise decisions. In our legal system, the laws that govern our everyday lives are found in these sources:

- COURT CASES. When a factual dispute between the parties becomes a lawsuit, brought in the appropriate Federal, State or Municipal court jurisdiction, and is concluded with a final judgment in favor of either plaintiff or defendant, we have legal precedent created by the judicial branch of government. Notice the root word, "precede", meaning that which comes before. This ruling may be used as persuasive authority in a future dispute involving similar facts.

This source of law began in this country as the English common law, and then has evolved on a case-by-case basis.

The public usually becomes aware of cases when an appellate court decision is published by the court, becomes a matter of public record, and is then a part of the information superhighway available through services such as Westlaw, Lexis-Nexis and the main Internet search engines. Trial court decisions and results of arbitration proceedings are not automatically reported, although they may be the subjects of news stories when they involve disputes of interest.

- STATUTES. These are formal laws adopted by the legislative branches of government in their formal law-making sessions. These laws are usually enacted by the U.S. Congress on the Federal level, the State legislatures, and may also include laws of local governments, called ordinances, covering a variety of areas including, building codes, zoning regulations and traffic laws.

  Sometimes laws on a given subject are codified by recognized authorities such as the "Restatement of Contracts", which seeks to review and analyze various conflicting laws on the subject from various states, and present one recommended legal view. Though not binding on the parties as governing law, it nevertheless is often cited as persuasive authority on the subject.

  The "Uniform Commercial Code", which applies to sales of goods, is a body of statutory law that has been adopted in whole or part by all states. It governs these transactions, unless the parties provide otherwise, and overrides local laws or common law rules that may be conflicting. It is binding on the parties as a primary source of law.

  All state laws also include "statutes of limitations", which are laws that specify time limits for filing lawsuits. No matter how strong the plaintiff's case, the defendant may raise its untimely filing as a defense, and the matter will be legally dismissed.

  There are different time periods for each type of legal action. For example, in malpractice cases, parties usually have one year to sue from their first reasonable opportunity to discover the alleged negligent act. In contracts and sales cases, the limitation periods range from three to seven years from the date of breach, depending upon the state in which the contract or transaction was finalized.

- **ADMINISTRATIVE REGULATIONS.** As society has become more complex and government has expanded, a large group of regulatory agencies have been created on all levels of government to enact and oversee the enforcement of certain types of laws that seek to protect the public. These agencies include the Internal Revenue Service (taxes), Securities Exchange Commission (investments), Food and Drug Administration (consumables), Environmental Protection Agency (pollution), and many others.

- **CONSTITUTIONS.** They establish the structure of our Federal and State governments. There is one U.S. Constitution, the supreme law of the land, and 50 different State Constitutions. The Federal and State Constitutions are similar in their creation of the basic three branches of government:

  - Judicial (Courts) to enforce the laws
  - Legislative (Congress/Legislatures) to enact the laws
  - Executive (President/Governors) to interpret the laws

  While similar in format to the U.S. Constitution, State constitutions may differ significantly and court disputes sometimes involve these conflicts.

- **BILL OF RIGHTS.** They guarantee to each citizen certain fundamental rights and privileges such as freedom of religion, freedom of speech and freedom of the press. They are constitutional amendments that have been approved over the years for the benefit of the public. They are a form of governmental commandments, the "thou shalt not" duties having been replaced with a form of "thou shalt" have certain guaranteed rights.

These sources of law have an enforcement priority in the event of a dispute. The U.S. Constitution takes precedence over all other laws. Federal Laws govern over State laws. State laws prevail over local laws. Statutes have a higher priority than administrative regulations.

Contracting parties may also negotiate specific clauses in their agreements that designate (1) where disputes must be decided (forum selection), (2) the rules of law to be applied (choice of law), and (3) whether or not lawsuits or arbitration will be the means of dispute resolution (choice of remedy).

Before any domestic transaction is finalized, the parties must be aware of and analyze the federal and state laws that may be involved, as well as the laws of foreign countries if the proposed transaction is international. This strategic advance planning could be critical to the successful outcome of a dispute.

*Ex: Triton, Inc., a New York Corp. discusses the sale of $1,000,000 worth of computer parts to Vailtronic Co., a Colorado Corp. (All buyers of goods prefer full seller warranties in the event of any product defects, and all sellers of goods prefer to sell without warranties.)

In its negotiations, the buyer is firm in requiring any disputes to be heard in Colorado rather than New York. The seller huffs and puffs, but finally gives in on this if the law of Japan will apply to the transaction. The buyer assumes that Japanese and U.S. law are similar, since both countries are very active in the sale of goods. (Japan has no warranty laws!)

The contract is finalized, the goods are shipped, one-half of the agreed price is paid upon shipment, and the buyer refuses to pay the balance when it discovers the goods are defective after they arrive.

Seller sues buyer in Colorado (forum selection) and wins the case, because that court must use the Japanese law agreed upon by the parties (choice of law).

Where can we find these sources of law, so that they can be reviewed in detail, and analyzed, hopefully prior to completing the agreement, so that we may know the particular rules of law that may pertain to our particular transaction?

- A lawyer's initial consultation – explain your problem or proposed transaction and learn the basic legal rules that govern. This is traditionally done by contacting an attorney, making an appointment, and discussing your matter in the law office.

  Newer innovations also exist such as being able to speak directly to an attorney in your state over the telephone for a fixed fee per inquiry ("ask an attorney" service of lawexpress.com), and having a lawyer available for you at any time for unlimited calls by paying an annual fee ("retainer service" of amerilawyer.com).

- Go to the law library of any Law School - ask for help from the librarian or a law student. They often are more skilled at research than the practicing lawyer because it is a daily part of their academic life.

- Use the Internet information highway – you can surf your way through cyberspace and find all levels of the rules of law. Every major browser such as Netscape and Internet Explorer, as well as search engines such as Lycos, Google and Yahoo, to name a few, have a separate "Law" link that will speed you to your goal. Some helpful Internet addresses are www.law.com, www.findlaw.com, and www.westbuslaw.com. There are legal research databases such as

WESTLAW and LEXIS-NEXIS. Legal forms are available at _www.lawguru.com._ Legislative information is presented at _http://thomas.loc.gov._ _www.law.cornell.edu_ provides a spotlight on legal events, as does _http://jurist.law.pitt.edu._ Even Court TV, which has raised the level of awareness of the legal system for millions of viewers, has a web page at _www.courttv.com._

In the case of _Whirlpool Financial Corporation v. GN Holdings, Inc., 67 F.3d 605 (7th Cir.1995),_ Whirlpool had made a $10 million loan to GN based upon certain false and misleading financial projections contained in a private placement memorandum. (Does this sound familiar in the era of Enron, World Com, and the Arthur Anderson accountants?)

Whirlpool sued for securities fraud three years after making the loan, GN defended based upon the one-year statute of limitations in federal securities law, and both the trial court and appellate court agreed that Whirlpool's claim was barred.

Whirlpool had contended that certain industry trends were concealed from them, extending their time to sue. The court disagreed on the basis that this information was in the public domain and readily available through the Internet. "In today's society, with the advent of the 'information superhighway', federal and state legislation and regulations, as well as information regarding industry trends, are easily accessed."

In the next chapter we will explore the whys and wherefores of choosing the court where you will file your lawsuit if you are the plaintiff, or your possible choices as a lawsuit defendant. This is called jurisdiction.

Remember, if the plaintiff can require the defendant to appear in plaintiff's chosen location that alone may induce a favorable settlement. If however, the defendant is legally able to move the case to his chosen venue, the plaintiff may be forced to settle on the defendant's terms.

The litigation game is all about leverage. Which party has the perceived advantage at any given time? If a party can prevent the other from a desired course of action at any stage of the proceedings, the dispute may be resolved in their favor.

DISCUSSION EXERCISES

1. Discuss any other sources of law that may be available.
2. Discuss any other helpful Internet law sites.

3. Discuss a situation where a court case resulted in a statute.
4. Discuss a situation where a statute resulted in a court case.
5. Discuss your opinions as to which is most important in contract negotiations:
    a. Forum Selection
    b. Choice of Law
    c. Choice of Remedy

CASE EXERCISES

FORUM SELECTION CLAUSE UPHELD

The case of *Carnival Cruise Lines, Inc. v. Shute, 499 U.S. 585 (1991),* involved a dispute regarding whether or not a forum selection clause in cruise tickets was legally enforceable in a ticket holder's personal injury lawsuit.

Mr. and Mrs. Shute, State of Washington residents, were passengers on a cruise between California and Mexico, operated by Carnival, whose principal place of business was Miami, Florida. "The 'passage contract tickets' received by the couple contained a clause (standard in the industry) designating courts located in the state of Florida as the agreed-upon exclusive venue for litigating any disputes arising under the contract between passenger and carrier."

During the cruise, the wife fell and was injured. She claimed the negligence of the cruise line and its employees was the cause, and sued in Washington federal court to recover damages. Carnival successfully moved to dismiss based upon the forum selection clause.

The Appellate Court however reversed, on the grounds that "it would be unreasonable to apply the forum-selection clause of the ticket contract" because of their concerns it was not freely bargained for, it had not been read prior to the voyage, even if it had been reviewed its legalities would not have been understood, and "there was evidence in the record to indicate that the couple were physically and financially incapable of pursuing the litigation in Florida."

Carnival appealed to the U.S. Supreme Court, which accepted the case and decided it in Carnival's favor.

ANALYSIS

The U.S. Supreme Court majority decision in favor of Carnival created a standard for the cruise industry, and similar types of service providers, to specify a forum for suit in their contracts, even though it is not the subject of bargaining between the parties:

"1. a cruise line, which typically carries passengers from many locales, has a special interest in limiting the fora in which the line could be subject to suit,

2. such a clause has the salutary effect of dispelling any confusion about where suits arising under the contract must be brought and defended, thus sparing litigants and courts the time and expense of litigating those issues, and

3. cruise line passengers benefit in the form of reduced fares reflecting the savings which the line enjoys by limiting the fora where it may be sued."

Two Justices dissented. They felt the forum-selection clause was unreasonable, "because only the most meticulous passengers would be likely to become aware of it in the fine print on their tickets . . . the forum-selection clause in question lessened or weakened the couple's ability to recover . . . because it was safe to assume that any witnesses could be assembled with less expense and inconvenience at a west coast forum than thousands of miles away in Florida."

DEFUSE REPLAY

From the viewpoint of the passenger, what could have been done to defuse the time bomb created by the forum selection clause?

The majority decision suggests that the couple, "presumably had the option of rejecting" the clause. As a practical matter, only lawyers, business law professors and their students, and readers of this book would even be aware of the potential problem.

If the clause was removed, the issue of the proper forum to hear the case would have been determined by the "most closely related contact" legal test. Since the injured party was a Washington resident who boarded the cruise in California, the west coast aspect of the case mentioned in the dissent would point to a Washington forum. Florida would be viewed as a "remote alien forum." If that had occurred, the plaintiff may well have been able to induce a favorable settlement in her favor.

If the clause was not removed, the couple could still have continued with their cruise and been faced with the result of this case. The majority and dissenters both recognized that this would probably have removed any leverage they had to settle the dispute, since once rebuffed in Washington they would probably never have filed suit in Florida.

However, a third scenario exists. When the couple bought their ticket, presumably from a travel agent, their demand for a Washington forum could easily have been legally accomplished by inserting it in their reservation and invoice. After all, the agent wants to sell a ticket and would probably let the customer write in anything they want as long as the deal is closed.

Neither the agent (whose acts bind Carnival under the laws of agency) nor Carnival would probably have noticed it or appreciated its legal import. By doing this, the pre-printed forum-selection clause in the ticket would have been revoked.

CONCLUSION

This case has far-reaching effects because it may have become a legal precedent for the entire cruise line industry or other types of customer carriage.

The Court's wording was not limited to legal pronouncements for Carnival alone. In fact, nowhere in its opinion does it refer to "Carnival". Rather it makes continued references to "a cruise line" (rather the 'the' cruise line), and by so doing seems to broaden its impact industry wide.

The same result would no doubt apply for choice of law and choice of remedy clauses, since the specific terms of the contract between the parties will govern any disputes – absent fraud or unfair advantage being taken.

The case also has the effect of putting prospective customers on notice that they should be aware in advance of the contract clauses in their tickets, and this can be easily accomplished by requesting a copy of the standard ticket in advance for review from one's travel agent. If Internet booking is the method of purchase, some carriers are now making their ticket forms available on-line for review and questions.

A. Do you agree with the Court's final decision?
B. How can consumers be protected from adverse forum selection?
C. Should this decision be given industry-wide application?

CASE RESEARCH CYBERCISES

The following cases also relate to the material in this chapter and illustrate the types of disputes that may occur. For each one do the following written assignment:

1. Locate the case using the Internet (Lexis-Nexis, West or any other research cite which provides case transcripts).
2. Briefly summarize what it was about – the nature of the dispute involved.
3. Who won at the trial court level? Who won at the appellate level?
4. Who won if there was a third level of Supreme Court review?
5. What were the legal rules of law and the reasoning used to reach the final decision?
6. Do you agree or disagree with the decision, and explain why?
7. What business law time bomb(s) were involved?

8. Could the time bomb(s) have been avoided by structuring the transaction differently? Discuss.
9. Could the adverse effects of the time bomb(s) have been defused by a different reaction or response by the affected party? Discuss.
10. Replay the facts of the case to achieve a different successful result.

1. *Capital Cities Cable, Inc. v. Crisp, 467 U.S. 691 (1984)(federal law supercedes state law).*
2. *Norgart v. The Upjohn Company, 981 P.2d 79 (Cal. 1999)(statutes of limitations are explained in detail).*
3. *Lipcon v. Underwriter's at Lloyds, London, 148 F.2d 1285 (11th Cir. 1998)(choice of English law clause upheld).*

NOTES

4.

TO SUE OR NOT TO SUE

" We were not born to sue,
but to command."
Shakespeare: King Richard II

Had Hamlet revealed his thoughts in the current commercial marketplace, his famous soliloquy ("to be or not to be") would have been reworded from questioning his existence to trying to decide whether or not to institute litigation ("to sue or not to sue").

Hopefully, you will structure your commercial transaction so skillfully that everything works perfectly. This book will certainly help you. But it is a rare occurrence when a business transaction completes without a dispute. Even the apparently successful ones usually encounter a business law time bomb or two, but the parties are either unaware of the danger, or consciously choose to ignore it because the deal is too good to question.

The objective is always to end the dispute by inducing the other side to accept a resolution favorable to us – the faster, cheaper, and less damaging to future business relationships the better. But we live in a litigious society. When confronted with the inevitable business dispute, most of us have a knee-jerk mentality, and react like this Ziggy cartoon:

Litigation, although sometimes necessary, should be the remedy of last resort after a thoughtful risk-reward analysis of the pending lawsuit. Some of the important factors to consider are:

- The strength of the case based upon applicable rules of law
- The history of court decisions in similar cases
- The monetary amount of damages recoverable
- The type of monetary or non-monetary relief available

Some of the negative aspects are:

- The costs of litigation, including time spent and legal expenses
- The stress involved in the adversarial process
- The possibility of damaging business relationships
- The public nature of the proceedings
- The time to resolve the dispute on crowded court dockets
- The uncertainty of a winning judgment
- The uncertainty of the appellate process
- The uncertainty of collecting a winning judgment
- The negative perception as a litigious party
- The possibility of an opposing counter-suit

Some of the positive aspects are:

- Winning the case and recovering money damages
- Winning the case and receiving a non-monetary remedy
- The public nature of the proceedings can be informative and educational
- The possibility of establishing a legal precedent
- The possibility of clarifying confusing legal issues
- The possibility of setting an example of activism
- The possibility of deterring future improper or unlawful acts
- The power of the right to subpoena witnesses
- The power of discovery of otherwise unavailable information
- The power to prevent imbalances of corporate or governmental power

Sometimes a party to a business dispute is faced with a weak case, either because of adverse rules of law or unfavorable facts. Nevertheless, even marginal cases may have "nuisance value". The filing of a lawsuit in these situations, or the threat of doing so, may be an effective way to induce the other party to settle on a more favorable basis than had previously been available just through verbal or written demands.

One word of caution however. The filing of a completely frivolous lawsuit or sham pleading is frowned upon by the courts, and may result in an award of damages against the filing party for "abuse of process".

Most people think the winning party automatically recovers their reasonable attorney's fees. But this is not so in most states. While a judge may award such fees in the unusual cases where the plaintiff has filed a purely groundless lawsuit, fee reimbursement will usually only be allowed if the lawsuit is based upon a written agreement or a statute that allows such a recovery.

Sometimes the most skillful response to a dispute is to walk away, even though you have legal grounds to sue. What if the defendant, against whom you have a valid claim, is your sole supplier of critical goods? While you might win the lawsuit, you probably would jeopardize your future business. What if your potential expenses of litigation would far exceed the amount due you? What if your lawsuit subjects you to a counterclaim for abuse of process? The best decision in such a case would be not to sue.

The parties themselves, without lawsuits or lawyers, resolve most disputes. This is the broad category called settlement. Trial lawyers will tell you that, "a bad settlement is often better than a good lawsuit," due to the many disadvantages of suing. But it takes two to tango, as the song goes.

Many lawyers express displeasure with the current adversarial system, and are seeking more and more to assume a role as 'counselors at law', who evaluate potential disputes and try to find ways to enable their clients to reach acceptable compromises.

If one of the parties refuses to agree, there can be no settlement, no matter how reasonable the other party's proposals. If that occurs, and the claimant party refuses to let the matter go and walk away, a lawsuit will be filed. Often however, this will be the needed impetus to complete the settlement. The mere threat of litigation may not do the trick, but when legal papers are physically served on you, the possibly expensive message is much louder and clearer.

Against the backdrop in this country of too many lawsuits brought by too many combative lawyers, there has emerged a strong opposition movement called ADR – Alternate Dispute Resolution, where the parties agree, guided by their attorneys, to try to find a way to resolve their differences outside a courtroom.

And what is most interesting is that the legal profession, which itself helped to create the runaway train of litigation through the use of legal advertising, contingency fee arrangements, liberalized discovery rules and use of graphic evidence creating large awards of money damages by juries, is at the forefront of this ADR movement.

The main types of Alternate Dispute Resolution are:

- Arbitration – the parties choose a neutral third party to hear their evidence and decide the dispute. It can be non-binding but usually is agreed to be final. Binding arbitration is commonly used for disputes in labor agreements, building construction and professional malpractice actions.

Advantages include skilled experts, who hear and decide the disputes, that are resolved faster, less expensively and with less animosity than the combat of litigation, and privacy of the proceedings.

Disadvantages are lower awards than would be available with jury trials and the lack of any appellate remedies in the event of erroneous decisions. But recent decisions reflect growing court frustration with rubber-stamping these awards and a developing trend to review their amounts using judicial tests.

Arbitration is the usual remedy to resolve international disputes. Our Congress enacted the Federal Arbitration Act way back in 1925, but in recent times its usage has greatly increased. It validates arbitration only clauses in the contracts of parties in interstate commerce. Similarly, many states have adopted the Uniform Arbitration Act for intrastate commerce, which allows the contracting parties to agree in advance that any disputes must be submitted to arbitration.

Typical disputes resolved by arbitration are labor and employment disagreements, breach of contract cases, tort claims, securities law cases and consumer complaints.

A typical clause reads, "In the event of default, the parties agree to resolve any disputes exclusively by final and binding arbitration, and waive all rights or remedies to sue in a court of law."

The current trend is toward more, rather than less usage of arbitration to resolve disputes, as evidenced by these recent cases:

- Arbitration may be required as a condition to employment. *Johnson v. Circuit City Stores, 148 F.3d 373 (4th Cir. 1998).*

- Deposition discovery does not violate the right to arbitrate. *Merrill Lynch v. Adams, 2001 WL 331976 (Fla. App. 2001).*

- Cost-sharing renders an arbitration clause void. *Perez v. Globe Airport Security Services, 2001 WL 649497 (11th Cir. 2001).*

- Employment arbitration form is binding even though unread by the employee. *Haskins v. Prudential Ins. Co., 230 F.3d 231 (6th Cir. 2000).*

- Contract allowing judicial review of arbitration award is upheld. *LaPine Technology v. Kyocera, 139 F.3d 884 (8th Cir. 1997).*

- Employment contract limiting arbitration remedy to back wages is ruled unconscionable. *Armendariz v. Foundation Health Psychcare Services, 80 Cal.Rptr.2d 235 (Cal. App. 1998).*

- People's Court's Judge Ed Koch has arbitral immunity for alleged slanderous remarks made during court proceedings. *Kabia v. Koch, 2000 WL 1341941 (N.Y. Civ. Ct. 2000).*

- Mediation – the parties choose a disinterested third party to act as an intermediary between their intractable positions and try to lead them to a settlement of their dispute. If the go-between is an interested third party, the proceedings are called conciliation. No binding decisions in either are made without the mutual consent of the parties. The purpose is just to listen and act as an impartial buffer between the conflicting positions of the parties.

- Med-Arb – this is a hybrid combination of the two main forms of ADR, tailored by the parties to their specific needs.

- Minitrial or Rent-A-Judge – this is usually a non-binding lawsuit, where the parties, through their lawyers, agree to a private trial and present their evidentiary case before a retired judge or experienced trial lawyer, who advises them of his informal decision and then encourages them to settle.

- Summary Jury Trial – this is usually a non-bonding mock trial in which the parties, represented by their lawyers, present their opposing positions before a typical civil jury of six persons, and are able to get the reactions to their witnesses and evidence. The reaction of the sample jury may enable the parties to better evaluate their cases and settle their differences.

- Negotiation is the informal give and take bargaining process between the transaction parties that occurs at many stages of planning, creating, performing and enforcing contracts.

Even if the mutually agreed ADR procedures are non-binding on the combatants, their ability to be present and communicate their conflicting positions to an impartial intermediary in each other's presence often softens their conflict and ends the dispute.

The resolution process is assisted by the private and confidential nature of ADR. No dirty laundry is washed in public, unlike most court files, which are open for inspection by the public and the media.

Other countries have long recognized the value of avoiding lawsuits. They note our "sue as a first resort" mentality is reminiscent of the gunslinger battles of the old West. Suing someone is often frowned upon as being dishonorable or uncivilized. And if a lawsuit is necessary, one of the main remedies in a number of Asian countries is a public apology rather than money damages.

Our legal system is also criticized for allowing contingency fee hiring of lawyers, the large awards of our juries in personal injury cases, use of graphic demonstrative evidence, and money damages that can include such nebulous concepts as pain and suffering, mental anguish and loss of consortium. Our remedy of punitive damages, allowed in extreme cases to punish a defendant, and often limited only by the net worth of the defendant, is unique in the United States and is also viewed by outsiders as a flawed concept.

While the ADR movement and settlement mentality is growing in this country, and someday may result in markedly lower levels of litigation, that day has not yet arrived. Our commercial marketplace, with all its potential business law time bombs, produces numerous business disputes that cannot be amicably resolved and require the services of lawyers to evaluate them and file the many lawsuits that often result.

As one of my students so astutely noted after a class discussion of one's choices in resolving a dispute – "suing sucks, but sometimes you have to do it."

DISCUSSION EXERCISES

1. Discuss any other advantages or disadvantages of suing.

2. Discuss any other advantages or disadvantages of ADR procedures.

3. Are there other types of alternate dispute resolution that you think could be effective in resolving personal disputes? In resolving business disputes?

4. Discuss any positive experiences you have had with lawsuits or ADR.

5. Discuss any negative experiences you have had with lawsuits or ADR.

CASE EXERCISES

YOU ARE BOUND TO THE TERMS OF THE CONTRACT YOU SIGN WHETHER YOU READ IT OR NOT

In the Matter of the Arbitration between Mostek Corporation and North American Foreign Trading Corporation, 502 N.Y.S.2d 181(N.Y.App.Div.1986), was a contract dispute between a seller (Mostek) and a buyer (NAFTC) of microchips regarding whether or not its arbitration clause was binding. The parties negotiated the terms of their transaction at the offices of buyer, and then a purchase order was prepared and signed by both.

The front of the purchase order stated that the order was placed under certain conditions set forth on its reverse side. One such condition stated, "Any dispute arising out of this order shall be submitted to arbitration as provided in the terms set forth on the back of this order."

That clause was never specifically discussed by the parties, and seller's agent claimed he never even read the reverse side of the purchase order before signing it. He also claimed that the procedure in the electronics industry was that his order had to be accompanied by a home office sales order confirmation to be binding

ANALYSIS

The trial court ruled for the seller, holding that the arbitration clause was not binding. The appellate court reversed, ordering the parties to proceed with arbitration. It noted that the contract was signed by each of the parties in the presence of each other, and that "buyer and seller are sophisticated corporate entities," and "the intention of the parties can be gathered from the four corners of the signed agreement itself."

The Court also noted that The Federal Arbitration Act governed the transaction because the two parties were involved in interstate commerce, (Seller – Texas/Buyer – New York), that there was a federal policy favoring arbitration, and the Act specifically provides, "a written provision in a contract (for interstate commerce) to settle by arbitration a controversy thereafter arising . . . shall be valid, irrevocable and enforceable."

DEFUSE REPLAY

The two-sided form contract is the standard method of doing business in the commercial marketplace. It is completed in one of two ways in the usual transaction:

(1) After the parties have completed their negotiations for the basic terms of their transaction, the buyer submits its pre-printed purchase order form. The mutually agreed terms are filled in on the front and the reverse contains the standard clauses, commonly called "boiler plate provisions", which are most favorable to and commonly used by the buyer. The seller then sends its pre-printed order acknowledgement form, which also agrees to the basic terms on the front, and contains on the reverse the seller's clauses.

(2) After the parties have completed their negotiations for the basic terms of the transaction, they both sign the same pre-printed form, inserting on the front the specifics of their deal and becoming legally bound to the clauses on the reverse.

Because of the obvious dangers of becoming bound by terms and conditions you have not read, due usually to the lack of time to go over every single word and line of pre-printed forms, contracting parties usually protect themselves by inserting clauses such as:

(1) "In the event of a dispute regarding differing terms of the purchase order and the order acknowledgement, the _____ (p/o or o/a) shall govern." This is what is known as the contract exception to the "Battle of the Forms" rule of the Uniform Commercial Code, which is discussed in the chapter on acceptance of offers.

(2) "The parties are only bound by the terms and provisions appearing on the front page of the contract, and reserve the right to object to boiler plate terms on the reverse side of the contract in the event of a dispute relating to them."

CONCLUSION

One of the fundamental principles of contracts is that you are legally bound by the agreements you sign. Whether or not you read or understand them is immaterial. The exceptions that provide valid defenses to enforcement are the fairness situations where one of the signing parties was coerced, mistaken or deceived. The two universal contract admonitions are, "put it in writing", and "read it before you sign it."

A. Do you agree with the court's final decision?
B. Do you usually read the items that you sign? What types? What parts?
C. Have you ever had a legal dispute regarding a contract you signed?

LAWSUIT PERMITTED FOR INJURIES SUFFERED BY A PRO FOOTBALL PLAYER IN A REGULAR SEASON GAME

Hackbart v. Cincinnati Bengals, Inc. and Clark, 601 F.2d 516 (10th Cir. 1977), raised the legal question of whether an injury from an intentional blow inflicted by one professional football player on another in a regular season game can create tort liability for the offending player and the team that employs him.

The injury occurred when after an interception of a Cincinnati Bengal's pass, Denver Bronco's defensive back Dale Hackbart became an offensive player and attempted to block opposing player Charles "Booby" Clark. While Hackbart lay on the ground after the block, Clark "acting out of anger and frustration, but without a specific intent to injure...stepped forward and struck a blow with his right forearm to the back of the kneeling plaintiff's head and neck with sufficient force to cause both players to fall forward to the ground."

The officials didn't see the incident and no penalty was called. However, the game film showed very clearly what had happened. Plaintiff did not report the incident immediately or seek medical treatment, but he did by the next day when he was in pain. He was treated by the team trainer and cleared to play. He participated in two more Sunday games before he consulted a doctor and it was discovered he had a serious neck fracture.

ANALYSIS

The trial court rejected the plaintiff's claim on legal grounds that he had assumed the risk of known dangers by signing on as a professional football player. It said, "professional football is a species of warfare and that so much physical force is tolerated and the magnitude of the force exerted is so great that it renders injuries not actionable in court."

The trial court suggested the non-legal remedies available for such offenses were a penalty, expulsion from the game, and/or suspension for future games. There was also an implied suggestion that future retaliation by or on behalf of the injured player would also probably occur.

The appellate court reversed and ordered a new trial on the evidence relating to the act that caused the injury. It said, "the game of football is not on trial, but rather, the trial involves a particular act in one game."

It directed the new trial not consider previously introduced evidence of whether or not plaintiff or defendant were dirty players, or other acts of violence between other players and other teams.

It further pointed out the rules of the game prohibit the intentional striking of blows. "All players are prohibited from striking on the head, face or neck with the heel, back or side of the hand, wrist, forearm, elbow or clasped hands."

"Therefore, the notion is not correct that all reason has been abandoned . . . whereby the only possible remedy for the person who has been the victim of an unlawful blow is retaliation."

DEFUSE REPLAY

Although the trial court treated the case as if the plaintiff had no legal right to seek money damages, the rules of the game had no such prohibition.

Under the rules of professional football in effect at the time of the injury, there was no limiting clause or exclusionary provision that limited the legal remedies of a player physically injured by their violation.

Such a waiver of remedy clause could be in both the game rules and the player's standard employment contract. It could read:

> "The undersigned player does hereby agree that professional football is, by definition, a violent contact sport similar to armed combat, and it may be reasonably anticipated and assumed that injuries will occur within the scope of player's employment, including but not limited to regular season games, exhibition games, and team practices. Player acknowledges and agrees that there shall be no legal remedies for such injuries in any court of law, alternate dispute resolution proceeding, or otherwise, and player's sole compensation remedy is any insurance carried by employer and/or employee."

CONCLUSION

Subsequent revisions to the game rules and provisions in the collective bargaining agreement between pro football players and management has addressed the potential legal problem illustrated in this case by limiting the legal remedies of injured players.

The court's ruling also revealed one of the important purposes of our system of laws, as discussed in that chapter:

> "The potential threat of legal liability has a significant deterrent effect. Private civil actions constitute an important mechanism for societal control of human conduct."

    A. Do you agree with the court's final decision?
    B. Should the ruling in this case extend to all sporting events?
    C. What if Hackbart had retaliated and Clark had sued him for damages?

CASE RESEARCH CYBERCISES

The following cases also relate to the material in this chapter and illustrate the types of disputes that may occur. For each one do the following written assignment:

1. Locate the case using the Internet (Lexis-Nexis, West or any other research cite which provides case transcripts).
2. Briefly summarize what it was about – the nature of the dispute involved.
3. Who won at the trial court level? Who won at the appellate level?
4. Who won if there was a third level of Supreme Court review?
5. What were the legal rules of law and the reasoning used to reach the final decision?

6. Do you agree or disagree with the decision, and explain why?
7. What business law time bomb(s) were involved?
8. Could the time bomb(s) have been avoided by structuring the transaction differently? Discuss.
9. Could the adverse effects of the time bomb(s) have been defused by a different reaction or response by the affected party? Discuss.
10. Replay the facts of the case to achieve a different successful result.

1. *Mitsubishi Motors Corp. v. Soler Chrysler-Plymouth, Inc., 473 U.S. 614 (1985)(Sherman Act antitrust claim arbitrable in an international commercial transaction).*
2. *AMF Incorporated v. Brunswick Corporation, 621 F.Supp. 456 (E.D.N.Y. 1985) (agreement to obtain non-binding advisory opinion in advertising dispute is enforceable).*
3. *Gilmer v. Interstate/Johnson Lane, 500 U.S. 20 (1991) (compulsory arbitration of age discrimination in employment claim is upheld).*

NOTES

5.

HIRING A LAWYER

"The First Thing we do, Let's Kill all the Lawyers"
Shakespeare: King Henry IV

It is no surprise that our society holds the legal profession is less than high esteem. Think about the task lawyers are usually hired to do in civil business disputes. Their respective clients have reached a point of disagreement where they both think they are right, and then must have their problems resolved by a legal system which is adversarial, combative and can have only one winner. In the middle of this warfare is the lawyer, advocating the position of his client and seeking to downplay that of his opponent, while seeking to persuade the decision maker to rule in his favor.

Lawyers also serve a very useful function in our business marketplace, aside from their more visible roles in the courtroom. Their main function is not suing or defending lawsuits. Many practicing attorneys never participate in a trial. Their value, equally as important as trial advocacy, is in using their persuasive skills to:

- counsel you as to the real issues in your problem and help solve them
- prioritize your matters where they are not receiving necessary attention
- avoid disputes by advance planning of strategy and techniques
- induce a favorable settlement of a pending dispute
- assist in choosing your best legal remedy if suit may be necessary

These valuable functions are in the lawyers actions as counselors at law, educating their clients in what rules of law govern their particular factual dispute, how their unique facts fit into the applicable law, and then evaluating a probable result.

And while we send a bit of praise to the legal profession, a rare occurrence in our lawyer-bashing society, mention should also be made of the important role of lawyers in providing legal services for the poor.

This is known as pro-bono work, where no fees are charged, or expected to be received. The Bar Associations of most states have implemented these programs to fill the gaps left by cuts in governmental funding for social assistance programs for the financially disadvantaged. They need legal help as much as anyone yet cannot afford to hire an attorney.

In criminal proceedings, the legal system provides an indigent defendant the right to legal counsel through the public defender's office, paid for by the local governmental authority that is bringing the charges.

In civil cases, organizations such as "legal services for the poor" are staffed by lawyers and law firms in each community, who provide this public service with funding provided from a portion of state bar dues of attorney members, cash assessments provided by lawyers who are unable to handle indigent matters, and the IOTA (interest on trust account) program.

One's pending legal dispute is a major drama. It takes center stage in our daily soap operas. It is also like a poker hand being played. Before you place your financial bet on its outcome, you need to know if you are holding four aces or a pair of fives. What are the rules of the game itself? Which are the winning hands? And you need to know how much is the ante you must pay to get the game started.

In most contracts for the sale of goods or services, one of the parties has negotiated a better deal than the other side or subsequent market conditions now make it the better deal.

The advantaged party is holding the high cards now and wants to enforce the contract. The disadvantaged party holds a losing hand and wants to be extricated from it. They both turn to their respective lawyers to accomplish this.

You can represent yourself in court if you wish, but if you do so you have a fool for a client. The legal arena is highly specialized. Lawyers must graduate from an accredited three year law school where they receive a doctoral degree, take and pass a rigorous state bar examination, and then maintain a licensed status in their state by satisfying continuing legal education requirements. They are subject to malpractice actions and state disciplinary proceedings for negligent or criminal conduct.

So, the better procedure if legal problems arise is of course to hire a lawyer. This can be done in a variety of ways limited only by your imagination, ingenuity and bargaining skills, depending upon what action is needed.

What will it take to end the dispute? How can we induce a favorable settlement? E-mail, a phone call, a fax, a lawyer's letter, the filing of a lawsuit and service of the summons on the defendant? Maybe a full-blown lawsuit, and the stubborn adversary won't yield until the jury is on the verge of its decision. Or we might have to reach the point of seizing the judgment debtor's defendant's assets and scheduling their sale at auction before it is over. In all these situations, the lawyer is at the center of the action.

Attorneys are uniquely equipped by training and experience to analyze a hopelessly jumbled set of facts and cut to the heart of the legal problems involved. This is a valuable skill, because lawyers will tell you that one of their most difficult tasks is to get a prospective client to explain in some clear fashion what is their problem? Most people when asked, "what time is it?" will try to tell you how to make a watch.

Legal training enables attorneys to identify the legal issues in a dispute, research the governing rules of law, evaluate whether this particular factual situation will present a strong or weak case, and suggest appropriate action.

The first step is to choose a lawyer to interview. If you have ever used a lawyer in the past, ask for advice regarding your current problem. If you have never dealt with a lawyer, get recommendations from family and friends, talk to business associates, contact your local Bar Association for referrals, and consult the Yellow Pages. Lawyers are now allowed to advertise, and often list their specific experience and specialties in all types of media, including Internet web sites. There is even a reference source in many public libraries called "Martindale-Hubbell" that digests local laws and presents biographical sketches of attorneys, listed by state, specialty and expertise, ranked by their peers.

Don't limit yourself by just speaking to one lawyer. Be a good shopper before you make this important choice. The initial interview with a lawyer is customarily free of charge. Clarify this before making an appointment to discuss your problem.

A. Your Initial Interview

For the initial interview, bring with you all pertinent information. Write out ahead of time as brief a summary of your drama as possible, as if you were writing a newspaper story and were limited in space. Try to remove extraneous facts and get down to the heart of the matter.

Ask the necessary questions at the interview, after you have explained your situation:

1. Do they regularly communicate, promptly return phone calls, and meet deadlines?
2. What is their estimated time frame for your matter?
3. Will you be consulted regarding any settlement negotiations?
4. Will they be sufficiently aggressive for your needs?
5. What is their prior experience in the area of your particular matter?
6. Will they do the work personally or delegate it to associates?
7. Do they have any potential conflicts of interest with other clients?
8. What are the capabilities of support staff and office technology?
9. Have them explain how your funds will be handled?
10. What is their reputation in the legal community?
11. Qualifications aside, do you feel a rapport with this person? Would you trust him or her to be in charge of your important business decisions?

The lawyer should now be able to advise you:

1. The strengths and weaknesses of your case and reasons why.
2. An estimate of the probability of a successful outcome. This should include a summary of what legal papers will be filed, the court procedures, and the anticipated defenses to the action.
3. An estimate of the time it will take to complete the matter.
4. A suggestion as to the type of fee arrangement, and an estimate of fees.
5. The amount of cost deposit or retainer required.

Evaluate the lawyer's responses after the initial interview. Don't make up your mind immediately. Discuss the interview with trusted or experienced family or friends, and then decide.

B. Finalizing the Hiring

After you decide to hire, you should finalize the possible financial arrangements. Again, remember you are in the driver's seat as the buyer of these services. We automatically inquire as to the price of the car, clothing or consumables we are considering buying, but when it comes to our purchase of professional services, most of us are reluctant to ask in advance "how much?"

And the idea that, after we are told the projected cost of the desired services, we can negotiate and structure fee arrangements to suit our needs is equally foreign to our experience.

But that is what we can and should do, especially when we need legal advice. We have many alternatives, and much power as consumers of legal services. The hiring can be structured in any mutually acceptable way. The customary arrangements include the following:

- The free initial consultation – almost all practitioners will give you this if you ask for it. Many use it as an integral part of their advertising. It can let you know whether or not you are holding the high cards in your dispute and should go forward, or just need to let the matter go and walk away.

- The flat fee – matters that require a basic task like drafting a lease, preparing a purchase or sale contract, or resolving a traffic offense are customarily quoted to a prospective client as a fixed amount. Sometimes there is a combination of flat fee for initial work plus time charges thereafter.

- The annual retainer – these fees are agreed in advance to guarantee the availability of legal advice, usually for regular clients with a going business or repetitive legal problems.

The amount payable is usually adjusted annually, based upon the prior year's expenditure of necessary legal time. It is also known as the "eyeball" method.

- The hourly rate – the basic method of lawyer compensation. What attorneys have to sell is their time. Rates may vary depending upon a variety of factors that include the matter's complexity, the lawyer's general level of experience and special expertise, the rates usually charged in the locale, and the big firm / small firm cost factors of the law office you may hire.

- The contingency fee – the no win, no pay arrangement – is common in the United States. It is the main form of attorney engagement in personal injury tort lawsuits. It is also prevalent in malpractice actions, social security benefit disputes, patent litigation, real estate tax appeals, corporate mergers and acquisitions, and public offerings of securities.

  Unique to the American legal system, it enables the financially disadvantaged to have proper access to the courts, and makes the lawyer one's partner in a successful result. The lawyer usually fronts most or all out of pocket expenses for investigation, experts, and legal preparation no matter how costly or time consuming.

  These fees have also been criticized as being financial incentives that encourage lawyers to file unnecessary, unwarranted or unmeritorious lawsuits. There is also the possibility a lawyer will be more inclined to accept the first settlement offer and collect the usual one-third contingent fee, than work harder and go to court for the usual forty percent fee. It really all comes down to properly evaluating the person you hire.

- The equity participation – this usually occurs in start up businesses or new ventures, where there is little capital but great expectations for future profits. The lawyer is gambling that his current investment of time and effort will be rewarded in the future.

- The barter arrangement – sometimes there is a lack of available cash for fees but both lawyer and client have products or other services of mutual benefit that can be traded for each other.

- The combination fee – any or all of the possible fee arrangements mentioned are used combining various aspects, depending upon the negotiation between lawyer and potential client.

- The hybrid fee – creativity of prospective client and lawyer is the key, limited only by their imagination and mutual willingness to make a deal.

Whatever fee arrangement is finally negotiated, it should be put in writing and signed by both parties. It should also cover the possibility of additional work due to an appeal from an adverse decision. Read it like any other binding contract and make sure you understand it and it accurately reflects your prior discussions.

If a retainer / cost deposit is required, clarify how and when it will be used. If the fee arrangement involves any component of time charges, make sure you will receive regular billing statements that include a detailed listing of legal services rendered, who did the work, and the applicable hourly rates. These are computer generated as standard office procedure and should be readily available.

C. Settling Your Case

Trial lawyers will tell you that, in most cases, "even a bad settlement is better than a good lawsuit." Due to all the potential challenges in suing, as reflected in the prior chapter, over 90% of all disputes are settled in various stages of their existence. There are advantages and disadvantages to be considered:

- Disputes may not be finally resolved for years. A fair settlement produces instant cash that is available now, and removes the possibility of losing the case at arbitration, court trial or on appeal.

- Proceeding to arbitration or court trial may result in a much larger award.

- Settlement timing is critical. Sometimes the first offer is the best. Often, waiting until the final moment and 'settling on the courthouse steps' is the most effective bargaining strategy. Many disputes are even settled after a court decision or jury award, due to the uncertainties of the appellate process.

- The legal effect of a settlement should be clearly explained. What will be its effect on past disputes between the parties, if any, or similar pending claims against others? Will it effect future business transactions?

Communication with the lawyer and active participation in settlement negotiations is important. All settlement offers should be made in writing, and copies should be furnished the client.

D. Appealing Your Case

In almost all civil court cases, the losing party has an absolute right to appeal the decision to an appropriate state or federal appellate court. (Normally no such appellate rights exist in alternate dispute resolution procedures such as binding arbitration.)

The notice of appeal must usually be filed within thirty days of the adverse decision of the trial court. Aside from the additional expense involved in an appeal, there is no guarantee of a favorable outcome. Less than thirty percent of civil cases are reversed on appeal. The trial court decision comes to the appellate court with a presumption of correctness. It can only be overturned if there were substantial errors of law. No new facts or evidence may be presented on appeal. The appellate court is limited to a review of the record of the lower court proceedings.

However, your case may be one of the lucky ones. The more time and expense you have already incurred, one more shot at winning may be your best course of action. Since appellate practice is a legal specialty, it may also be necessary to hire a new attorney and make a new written financial arrangement.

E. Changing Your Lawyer

Clients have an absolute legal right to change lawyers at any time. The hiring of a lawyer is like any other employment relationship. Most clients forget this. The attorney is working for you, not the other way around.

Whether the reason for a desired change is a personality conflict, difference of opinion in strategy, unhappiness with the progress of the case, or any other reason, sometimes a change is best for all concerned.

There are, of course, advantages and disadvantages. Bringing in a new lawyer will require a duplication of time and effort, and slow down the progress of the case. Also, any progress made by prior counsel, rapport with other witnesses, parties, insurance persons, judges, arbitrators, etc. will be lost. Finally, changing lawyers is perceived to be a sign of weakness by the other side.

Sometime a breath of fresh air in the form of new counsel will revitalize a stagnant case. A different approach with different parties makes a positive difference in the progress of the matter.

If the reason for a desired change is a concern about your lawyer's professional conduct, another attorney should be consulted for an opinion. Since law is such a specialized profession, what may appear to you as an impropriety may be nothing more than a tactical approach. If however, there are grounds for legal malpractice, your new lawyer will inform you as to your options. In any event, if you are uncomfortable or dissatisfied, by all means consider making a change.

But no matter what your reasons, DO NOT even discuss firing your lawyer until you have found a replacement. Let the lawyers handle all the details between themselves. They are the experts and are familiar with such situations. Do not get involved other than to verify, when asked, that you do in fact want to make a change.

The usual procedure is for you to send a written request that your former attorney forward all your files and related information to your new attorney. If you owe any balances for costs or fees, they must be paid in full. A lawyer has a "charging lien" on client files, and is not required to release them to a new attorney until all pending balances are paid.

So shop wisely before you finalize your lawyer hiring. Combine a prudent Who to Hire? with your wise choices of How to Hire? and When to Hire? and you will greatly improve your chances for a positive outcome to your problem.

DISCUSSION EXERCISES

1. Can you think of any other arrangements to hire a lawyer?

2. For each, what are the advantages and disadvantages?

3. Match the various hiring methods with the types of disputes that would best be suited for each. Discuss your choices.

4. Discuss your personal experiences with lawyers. What was positive? What was negative?

5. Discuss any suggestions to improve the legal profession.

CASE EXERCISES

In *Gisbrecht v. Barnhart, 122 S.Ct. 1817 (2002)*, the U.S. Supreme Court was presented with the legal question of whether or not contingent fee agreements made by social security benefit claimants with their attorneys to recover 25% of the past-due benefits recovered were legally enforceable.

Three claimants, each represented by the same attorneys, brought separate actions in federal court for Social Security disability benefits under the Social Security Act. They won, and their attorneys sought their fee awards to be paid from their client's gross proceeds, per their fee agreements.

The Act provides that, "attorneys who successfully represent Social Security benefits claimants in court may be awarded a 'reasonable fee,' not in excess of 25 percent of the past-due benefits recovered, that is payable only out of those benefits."

The trial court and the appellate court, which consolidated the three cases, refused to honor the contingent fee agreements, ruling that they were replaced under the Act by the "lodestar" method of calculating fees, which required a computation in each case of a reasonable fee based upon the number of lawyer hours spent multiplied by a reasonable hourly rate.

Using the "lodestar" method would have yielded fees of approximately 10% to 50% lower for the attorneys than their agreed 25% contingency.

ANALYSIS

On certiorari review, the majority U.S. Supreme Court reversed, ruling that the Act did not displace contingent-fee agreements as the primary means for representation in such cases, but rather required the amount of fee awards under such agreements be measured on a case by base basis by using the "lodestar" test of reasonableness.

One Justice dissented on the basis that the Act merely required the "lodestar" test of reasonableness to be used to evaluate fee awards. "I conclude that a 'reasonable fee' means not the reasonableness of the agreed-upon contingent fee, but a reasonable recompense for the work actually done."

The majority noted the following points:

"Social Security representation operates largely on a contingent-fee basis".

"The agreements entered into usually specify that, "the attorney's fee will be 25 percent of any past-due benefits to which the claimant becomes entitled."

Congress authorized contingent-fee agreements for agency-level representation in 1990, and "it would be anomalous if contract-based fees expressly authorized at the administrative level were disallowed for court representation."

"The lodestar method (not developed and used until some years after the Act) was designed to govern imposition of fees on the losing party. . . But (the section of the Act applicable here) governs the total fee a successful Social Security claimant's attorney may receive for court representation. Nothing more may be demanded or received."

DEFUSE REPLAY

The practical effect of the majority decision is to make a contingent fee agreement of not more than 25% of the past-due benefits presumptively reasonable in these cases. No proofs by the attorneys seeking such fees need be presented. The agreement will stand by itself.

But what if the contingent fee agreed upon by attorney and client exceeds 25%? Here the "lodestar" test would be used to determine the reasonableness *of the excess*, only. Such agreements, no matter how high the contingency, would not be automatically excluded.

Assuming the attorney used a fair hourly rate, a higher fee that the 25% would certainly be justified in the more difficult, time-intensive cases.

CONCLUSION

This case points practitioners to the important practice of keeping current, accurate and complete time records. As a former managing partner of a law firm, the author can attest to their value, and the importance of establishing a workable procedure to complete them on a daily basis.

The "lodestar" test, which gained a firm foothold in the 1970's as the basis for calculating most attorneys' fee awards, requires lawyers to provide evidence of the time they spent on legal matters. And this same criterion of legal time spent v. hourly rate compared with the cost of business overhead is the basis for analyzing whether or not a lawyer is operating on a profitable basis.

Yet for many law firms, one of the biggest internal problems is recording billable time. "Out of sight, out of mind," the saying goes, and nothing is more difficult than to try and reconstruct billable hours after the fact. Many are invariably lost in the process, and income suffers accordingly.

Another common saying that applies is, "you can't teach an old dog new tricks." One of the author's hardest tasks managing the law firm, and one common to the industry, was to get certain law partners to keep any time records at all. Once they became used to billing by a "seat of the pants" method, flattery, threats, promises of reward and threats of punishment were used at various times to try to get them to change.

Keeping time records is much easier in our age of technology. Rather than manual entries in one's appointment book or time diary, a computer terminal attached to the phone, copier, or fax machine will automatically register billable time, pre-programmed for whatever is the local "reasonable hourly rate". Other time spent on research, court appearances, and client conferences can be electronically entered by the support staff or legal associates, should the lead attorney be one of the reluctant old guard.

A. Do you agree with the Court's majority decision, or the dissent?
B. Can you create a hybrid decision that combines both?
C. When do you think contingent fee agreements should be used?
D. What criteria would you use in determining the "reasonableness" of an award of attorney's fees?

CASE RESEARCH CYBERCISES

The following cases also relate to the material in this chapter and illustrate the types of disputes that may occur. For each one do the following written assignment:

1. Locate the case using the Internet (Lexis-Nexis, West or any other research cite which provides case transcripts).
2. Briefly summarize what it was about – the nature of the dispute involved.
3. Who won at the trial court level? Who won at the appellate level?
4. Who won if there was a third level of Supreme Court review?
5. What were the legal rules of law and the reasoning used to reach the final decision?
6. Do you agree or disagree with the decision, and explain why?
7. What business law time bomb(s) were involved?
8. Could the time bomb(s) have been avoided by structuring the transaction differently? Discuss.
9. Could the adverse effects of the time bomb(s) have been defused by a different reaction or response by the affected party? Discuss.
10. Replay the facts of the case to achieve a different successful result.

1. *Hensley v. Eckerhart, 461 U.S. 424 (1983) (prevailing party can recover attorney's fees under Civil Rights Act).*
2. *Kerr v. Screen Extras Guild, 526 F.2d 67 (9th Cir. 1975) (13 factors used to determine fees under the lodestar method).*
3. *Venegas v. Mitchell, 495 U.S. 82 (1990) (clients may contractually agree to pay more than statutory fee awards).*

NOTES

6

THE LEGAL REMEDY: WHICH ONE IS APPROPRIATE?

"He that will not apply new remedies must expect new evils;
for time is the greatest innovator."
Francis Bacon

There are two basic issues in every civil legal dispute – liability and damages. Liability depends upon whether or not there has been a breach of some legal duty owed by one party to the other. The damages suffered make a breach actionable, creating a necessity to redress the civil wrong by providing an appropriate remedy.

I.   MONEY DAMAGES

The most common civil remedy to the aggrieved party is a claim for money damages. They are commonly classified as follows:

- Compensatory damages – direct amounts necessary to reimburse the injured party for out-of-pocket expenses, such as medical charges, property repairs, value losses and other harms. Also known as reimbursement damages, they are intended to restore the status quo, give back the benefit of the bargain made, and otherwise place the non-breaching party back in the position that would have existed if there had been no breach of duty.

  *Ex: Stella contracts to sell an antique vase to Herbert for $10,000. Herbert refuses to perform, and as a result of his breach, Stella, despite her best efforts, is only able to sell the vase for $6,000. Her compensatory damages for loss of her bargain are $4,000.

  The incidental expenses that are incurred by a non-breaching party are also recoverable, such as monies spent to maintain the status quo or avoid additional loss, additional costs for salvage or liquidation or advertising, and court costs if litigation is required. Note however, that attorney's fees as a general rule are NOT automatically recoverable by the prevailing party in a lawsuit, unless based upon a statute awarding them or a written contract clause, such as the following:

  "In the event of a dispute, requiring the services of an attorney, the prevailing party agrees to pay all reasonable legal expenses and attorney's fees incurred."

In *Jordan v. CCH Inc., 2002 U.S. Dist. LEXIS 19104 (2002)*, a top sales employee who was suddenly fired when he reached age 57 and replaced by a 30 year old with minimal experience sued for violation of the Federal Age Discrimination Employment Act (ADEA), sued and was awarded damages by the jury of $90,000 for contract monies earned, $260,000 in lost future earnings, and $33, 000 to equalize for the "negative tax consequences" of receiving his lost pay in a single tax year.

- Consequential damages – special or indirect amounts to compensate for losses suffered that flow as a foreseeable result of the breach, such as loss of wages, loss of profits, and incidental extra amounts spent after the breach to avoid further losses.

- Personal injury damages – have both compensatory and consequential aspects but, unlike basic contract and sales commercial disputes, include additional categories such as pain and suffering, mental anguish, and loss of sexual consortium.

   In a recent case a paralyzed snowboarder who claimed a ski jump had been negligently designed, requested pain and suffering damages of $10 million, the jury awarded $713,000, and then the judge made a post-trial addition of another $5.3 million to that award, claiming it was inadequate. That additur is now on appeal. *Vine v. Bear Valley Ski Co., Cal.Sup.Ct. Case no. 317766 (2002).*

- Nominal damages – token monetary awards of $1 or $2 made as a matter of principle, when there has been a technical breach of duty creating liability, but little or no corresponding economic loss.

   The comedian, Rodney Dangerfield, bases his humor upon the statement, "I don't get no respect." The Star magazine published a false article about him, headlined, "Vegas Casino Accused Caddyshack Funnyman: Rodney Dangerfield Swills Vodka by the Tumblerful, Smokes Pot All Day and Uses Cocaine." He filed suit for libel, requesting damages to his reputation of $1 million. The trial court found liability against the defendant and awarded "actual damages in the nominal amount of one dollar." It reasoned that the acts complained of, rather than cause him economic loss, conferred a monetary benefit since he now could use it as a real-life example of how he, "don't get no respect." He now uses this case in his nightclub act. *Dangerfield v. Star Editorial, Inc. v. 1996 U.S. App. Lexis 23401 (9th Cir. 1996).*

- Punitive damages – exemplary damages awarded in addition to base damages in tort cases and some contracts cases where the defendant's conduct is so willful, malicious, reckless and outrageous that an expensive financial lesson is needed to deter any such future conduct.

So long as there are even nominal direct damages, an award of punitive damages is possible, though they must be somewhat proportional.

"Although compensatory damages and punitive damages are typically awarded at the same time by the same decision maker, they serve distinct purposes. The former are intended to redress the concrete loss that the plaintiff has suffered by reason of the defendant's wrongful conduct. The latter, which have been described as 'quasi-criminal,' operate as private fines intended to punish the defendant and to deter future wrongdoing." *Copper Industries, Inc. v. Leatherman Tool Group, Inc., 532 U.S. 424 (2001).*

They are only awarded under the American legal system. They also are used as a potent bargaining strategy to gain immediate attention to one's potential claim, and will often induce the opposing party to settle when they are claimed.

They are one of the major reasons that the misconduct of large corporations is held in check. Originally, the amount of punitives recoverable was only limited by the net worth of the defendant. "The bigger their pocketbooks, the harder they will be hit," say plaintiff's lawyers. But as jury awards of punitive damages have reached astronomically high amounts, many state legislatures passed laws capping them to specific percentage multiples of actual damages suffered, or otherwise modifying the defendant's net worth award test. Here are two examples:

Florida Statute 768.73 limits punitive damage awards for each claimant to three times actual compensatory damages or $500,000, whichever is greater. If the injury sued upon results from wrongful conduct motivated by economic gain, the award can be a four times multiple, or $2 million, whichever is greater. If the defendant's wrongful acts are intentional, there is no cap other than defendant's net worth.

Oregon has an unusual statute passed in 1995, which awards 60 percent of any punitive awards to a state fund benefiting crime victims. It was recently legally challenged by a plaintiff who recovered $550,000 in punitive damages in an action for fraudulent transfer of real property against his former attorney, and declared constitutional, so that $330,000 of plaintiff's share now belongs to the state. *DeMendoza v. Huffman, Oregon Supreme Ct. case no. SC S48430 (2002).*

The area of punitive damages during the last few years illustrates how the scales of justice in these damage awards have come almost full-cycle. The news headlines were filled with cases in which huge awards of punitive damages were made, often against target defendants like the tobacco companies, and often involving the same teams of lawyers representing the parties:

- Smoker suffering from lung cancer awarded $850,000 compensatory damages and $28 billion (33:1 ratio) for punitive damages. The largest verdict at the time for a single plaintiff in U.S. history! *Bullock v. Philip Morris, Inc., L.A., CA. Superior Court Case No. 249171 (2002). (reduced to $28M)*

- Forty-year Marlboro smoker with lung cancer wins a $3 billion verdict of punitives. (18:1 ratio) *Boeken v. Philip Morris, Inc., L.A. Superior Court Case No. 226593 (2001).(reduced to $50M)*

The decisions in personal injury and tobacco cases that routinely granted large amounts of punitive damages led to the tort reform movement that arose due to a combination of (1) public outrage at the size of the judgments, (2) adverse publicity about mass tort class action lawsuits, and (3) the corresponding large contingent attorney's fees these lawsuits generated. (For an interesting and entertaining analysis, read "The King of Torts" by John Grisham.)

These awards reached an apex in *Liggett Group v. Engle, 853 So.2d 434 (Fla. App. 2003)*. In that case six named individuals filed a class action complaint on behalf of themselves and 700,000 other Florida smokers against the major cigarette companies and tobacco industry organizations for smoking related injuries. They alleged they were unable to stop smoking due to nicotine addiction and, as a result, developed medical problems ranging from cancer and heart disease to colds and sore throats. They sought over $100 billion in both compensatory and punitive damages.

The trial jury awarded $12.7 million in compensatory damages (offset by comparative fault), and punitive damages of $145 billion, the largest such award in U.S. history, and a bankrupting 18 times the total net worth of the defendants.

The case was appealed and resulted in a reversal and remand and the class decertified. The court commented that the total award exceeded the gross national product of several European countries. "The present case presents a classic example of the inherent dangers that arise when a complex mass tort action is improperly certified ... The fate of an entire industry and of close to a million Florida residents cannot rest upon such a fundamentally unfair proceeding."

(The Florida Supreme Court was asked in late 2004 by plaintiffs to reinstate the punitive damage award and re-establish the class of injured smokers.)

While some states continued to follow the old test that punitive damages were proper up to the amount of the defendant's net worth and others imposed ceilings that limited punitive damages to a stated percentage multiple of proven actual damages, what was needed was guidance from the U.S. Supreme Court in awarding punitive damages.

Finally it arrived in the case of *State Farm Mutual v. Campbell, 538 U.S. 408 (2003)*. In that case the plaintiff insured was involved in a multi - vehicle accident involving a fatality. In the litigation the suing parties had offered to settle within his total policy limits of $135,000 but State Farm rejected their offers and in so doing acted in bad faith. The trial jury entered judgment against Campbell for $185,000 and he became personally responsible for the excess.

He then sued State Farm for failure to settle within policy limits (contract tort of bad faith) and the Utah trial court jury awarded $2.6 million in compensatory damages and $145 million in punitive damages. This award was remitted by the trial judge to $1 million and $25 million respectively, but the punitive damages were reinstated by the Utah Supreme Court to the $145 million figure.

The Supreme Court reversed and remanded the case, holding that the punitive damage award was excessive, being in a 56: 1 ratio to compensatory damages. The court cited with authority its earlier decision of *BMW of North America v. Gore, 517 U.S. 559 (1996)*. That case was a dispute relating to the nationwide policy of the American distributor of BMW automobiles to repair and sell as new automobiles that had been damaged in the course of manufacture and transportation, if the repair costs did not exceed 3 percent of the suggested retail price, without advising their dealers that any repairs had been made.

Gore purchased one of the automobiles, and after discovering it had been repainted, sued the distributor. The trial jury awarded him $4,000 in compensatory damages and $4 million in punitive damages, "based upon its determination that the nationwide policy of nondisclosure constituted gross, oppressive, or malicious fraud for the purposes of Alabama statutes which authorized punitive damages." (1,000: 1 ratio) The Supreme Court of Alabama reduced the punitive damage award to $2 million. (500: 1 ratio)

The U.S. Supreme Court reversed and remanded the case based mainly on the fact that "State Farm was being condemned for its nationwide policies rather than for the conduct directed toward the Campbells," and even the reduced punitive damage award violated the Due Process Clause of the Fourteenth Amendment because the award exceeded the amounts justified under the Court's three "guideposts:

"(1) the degree of reprehensibility of the person's conduct; (2) the disparity between the harm or potential harm suffered by the victim and his punitive damage award; and (3) the difference between the punitive damage award and the civil penalties authorized or imposed in comparable cases.

We apply these three guideposts to evaluate whether "a defendant lacked 'fair notice' of the severity of a punitive damages award and to stabilize the law by assuring the uniform treatment of similarly situated persons."

The *Campbell* Court declared that "in practice, few awards exceeding a single-digit ratio between punitive and compensatory damages, to a significant degree, will satisfy due process" requirements of the 14th Amendment.

This was not a mandatory limitation however. "We decline again to impose a bright-line ratio which a punitive damages award cannot exceed." Even though many awards of punitive damages made prior to the decision have been reduced to be more in line with the 9X guideline, many other decisions with higher multiple awards of punitive damages have been allowed to stand under the *Gore* standards. Here are two examples:

In *Willow Inn, Inc. v. Public Service Mutual Insurance Co., 399 F.3d 224 (3rd Cir. 2005)*, defendant was severely damaged by a tornado in 1998 and defendant, its insurer, unreasonably delayed the damage claim and used "stonewalling tactics" to avoid paying the full amount due. In a non-jury trial, the judge awarded $2,000 in compensatory damages and $150,000 in punitive damages (75: 1 ratio). The appellate court upheld this award as being justified. "Here, the punitive damages award of $150,000 is approximately equal to the value of the (plaintiff's) claim under the policy and the payment that it belatedly received. Because the amount of punitive damages awarded is based on the value placed on the amount of the (plaintiff's) potential harm, the ratio at issue is approximately one-to-one, a ratio that does not 'raise a suspicious judicial eyebrow.'"

In *Williams v. Philip Morris Inc. et al.,48 P.3d 824 (Oregon App. 2002), Philip Morris Inc. v. Williams, 124 S. Ct. 56 (2003)*, plaintiff smoked Marlboro cigarettes for 47 years, died of lung cancer, and his family sued for wrongful death. The trial jury found the parties equally at fault for the fatal lung cancer and awarded the family $800,000 in compensatory damages. In addition, the jury found the tobacco company guilty of common law fraud for its 50 years of lies about the dangers of smoking and awarded $79.5 million in punitive damages, which was then reduced to $32 million by the trial judge.

Both parties appealed to the Oregon appellate court, it reinstated the jury award of the higher sum, and the state's highest court affirmed. The tobacco company then appealed to the U.S. Supreme Court and since it had by then reached the *Campbell* decision, it nullified the decision of the Oregon Court of Appeals.

But after applying the appropriate standards, that court restored the full $79.5 million punitive damages verdict, saying "it is difficult to conceive of more reprehensible misconduct for a longer duration of time on the part of a supplier of consumer products to the Oregon public than what occurred in this case."

II.   LEGAL LIMITATIONS

Damages have to be reasonably ascertainable in amount. The more speculative or conjectural the type and amount of damages, the less likely is a court to grant such a damage award. This is known as the certainty requirement of damages.

Damages also have to be "reasonably foreseeable." If the damages sued upon by a plaintiff are such that a reasonable defendant, in the same or similar factual situation, would not have anticipated them, recovery will be denied or minimized. The loss suffered by the plaintiff must be a "proximate" or foreseeable result of the defendant's wrong, not "remote" or unforeseeable.

In the landmark case, *Palsgraf v. Long Island Railroad Company, 162 N.E. 99 (N.Y. App. 1928)*, taught in all law schools of the land to illustrate the negligence doctrine of causation, Mrs. Palsgraf was standing on a platform in defendant's railroad waiting for a passenger train.

On another platform at the opposite side, a train stopped and two men ran forward to board it while it was starting to move away. One man jumped aboard, and the other man, who was carrying a small package covered by a newspaper, seemed unsteady. Defendant's employee, in an effort to assist the man, negligently knocked the package from his hands.

The package, which contained hidden fireworks, exploded and the shock of the blast threw down some large scales at the opposite end of the platform, which struck and injured Mrs. Palsgraf. She sued the defendant railroad for negligence

After a trial court verdict for plaintiff, the appellate division affirmed, and then this appeal was made to the court of appeals, where the renowned Justice Benjamin Cardozo, writing for the majority of the court, reversed:

"What the plaintiff must show is 'a wrong' to herself, *i.e.*, a violation of her own right, and not merely a wrong to some one else, nor conduct 'wrongful' because unsocial, but not 'a wrong' to any one. . . . Here, by concession, there was nothing in the situation to suggest to the most cautious mind that the parcel wrapped in newspaper would spread wreckage through the station. If the guard had thrown it down knowingly and willfully, he would not have threatened the plaintiff's safety, so far as appearances could warn him. His conduct would not have involved, even then, an unreasonable probability of invasion of her bodily security. Liability can be no greater where the act is inadvertent."

There is also a doctrine called "mitigation of damages." It requires the non-breaching party to use his best efforts to do what is necessary to reasonably lessen the amount of potential damages.

> Ex: Kevin signs a one-year lease to rent an apartment from Stanley. At the end of the third month, Kevin's plans change and he vacates the apartment. Stanley may not automatically claim damages of unpaid rent for the unexpired term. He is legally required to try to re-let the premises. If he is successful and the rental paid will be less, his contract damages are the difference between Kevin's lease and the amount received, plus expenses. If he is unable to find a new tenant, he can recover the full unpaid rent, plus expenses. If he somehow is able to rent for more than required by Kevin's lease, a few states would require him to refund the excess to Kevin and most others allow him to retain this "found money" as damages for his trouble.

Often, the concepts of remedies for breach of contract and mitigation of damages are interconnected in disputes before the courts, as in *Parker v. Twentieth Century-Fox Film Corp., infra,* mentioned in the "How to Sue" chapter.

"Upon the breach of a contract, the party seeking relief has the choice of three remedies: rescind the contract, refuse to treat the breach as a termination of the contract and request that the court compel performance under the contract, or consider the breach to be a termination."

"A basic principle of the law of damages is that one who claims to have been injured by a breach of contract must use reasonable means to avoid or minimize the damages resulting from the breach. . . although the injured party is often spoken of as having a 'duty' to mitigate damages, the term is misleading because there is no liability for failing to take such steps; the party is merely precluded from recovering for avoidable damages." *West Pinal Family Health Center, Inc. v. McBryde, 785 P.2d 66 (Az. App. 1989).*

III. NON-MONETARY REMEDIES

There are also equitable remedies available in those disputes where the non-breaching party cannot be adequately compensated by monetary damages:

- Suppose the parties enter into a contract to perform specialized personal services, or buy/sell unique, one of a kind personal property items such as works of art, custom jewelry, and personal heirlooms, real property, or other special items whose loss could not be replaced by an award of money. The remedy for breach of such an agreement is *specific performance,* in which the judge orders the contract promise(s) to be performed.

In *Okun v. Morton, 203 Cal. App.3d 805 (Cal. App. 1988)*, the litigation concerned a contract dispute for development of the restaurant and commercial enterprises known as the "Hard Rock Café". Plaintiff had been operating a local restaurant and tourist attraction by that name in England, contacted defendant about investing, and ultimately the parties agreed to open the first U.S. operation in Los Angeles, California. The parties signed an agreement in 1982 whereby plaintiff paid $100,000 to the investing limited partnership in exchange for a 20% share in the operating general partnership, including the future right to participate in, "all business opportunities which arise in connection with the business of HRC."

After the initial success of the HRC concept, defendant planned expansion to a number of other cities, but advised plaintiff he could not financially participate, and rejected plaintiff's renewed offer to accept his 20% share.

Plaintiff sued for specific performance of the 1982 agreement. The trial court ruled for plaintiff. On appeal the defendant claimed, "specific performance should not have been granted because enforcement of the contract will require continuous and protracted judicial supervision.
The appellate court rejected this argument, and affirmed the specific enforcement of the rather unique agreement of the parties.

> "Defendant retains the discretion under the terms of the judgment to structure each venture as he pleases so long as he maintains the 20/80 ratio and does nothing to interfere with or burden plaintiff's right to participate in the deal."

Specific performance will not usually be granted however, in cases of alleged breach of contracts to require performance of personal services because it is against public policy to force one party to work for another against their will. But the breaching party can be legally ordered *not* to do so by injunctive relief, as explained below.

Here is a case for you boxing historians. In *Madison Square Garden Corp. v. Carnera, 52 F.2d 47 (2nd Cir. 1931)*, defendant, a professional prize fighter, contracted in his next bout to box the winner of the Max Schmeling-Young Stribling fight for the world heavyweight championship. The agreement prohibited him from any prior fights without plaintiff's permission. He breached it by agreeing to fight Jack Sharkey, and plaintiff sued for an injunction to prohibit the contemplated bout.

The trial court granted the injunction and the appellate court affirmed. "Defendant's services are unique and extraordinary. A negative covenant in a contract for such personal services is enforceable by injunction where the damages are incapable of ascertainment."

- Suppose the parties have entered into a contract and then one of the parties wants to avoid its legal consequences, (probably because he realized he made a bad business deal), and alleges a legally sustainable ground for non-enforcement such as incapacity, illegality, fraud or duress. The remedy to cancel such an agreement is *rescission*.

- The party allowed to legally withdraw is often required to return any benefits received (*restitution*). Notice these four situations:

  > *Ex: Carlton agrees to sell his custom car to Lucy for $15,000. After she makes a partial payment of $5,000, he refuses to complete the sale. She may sue for her deposit, instead of seeking money damages for breach of contract, or suing for specific performance.

  > *Ex: Carlton agrees to sell his custom car to Lucy for $15,000, she makes a partial payment of $5,000, and then she defaults. Carlton then sells the car to Trent for $12,500. Lucy can recover back her $5,000 deposit less Carlton's $2,500 loss of bargain damages. by. If Carlton had been unable or unwilling to sell the car, he could have retained the $5,000 as agreed default damages, so long as his agreement permitted him to do so.

  > *Ex: Carlton agrees to sell his custom car to Lucy for $15,000, she pays the full purchase price, and then he successfully disaffirms the contract on legal grounds of lack of real consent. He may cancel the transaction, but must return any benefits received. He receives his auto back, but must return the money paid by Lucy.

  > *Ex: Carlton agrees to sell his custom car to Lucy for $15,000 under a verbal agreement that is not legally enforceable under the statute of frauds. She improves the car with his permission, prior to the closing. If he decides to cancel, she must be paid the reasonable value of the services she rendered.

- Courts may not make new contracts for the parties, but may in certain situations rewrite them to more accurately reflect their agreement. Suppose there is a significant drafting error in the terms of a contract or clerical miscalculation in sales computations that are not the result of a breach by either party. The remedy to correctly rewrite the contract is *reformation*.

- Suppose you reside in a city that has a local law requiring the adjoining local bar to close no later than 2am, and they fail to comply, disrupting your sleep and general peace of mind. Monetary damages won't help you, but a legal action requesting an *injunction* to stop the prohibited conduct will.

This is also the common remedy in domestic disturbances, where the aggrieved party legally requests a *restraining order.*

In *Beverly Glen Music, Inc. v. Warner* Communications, *Inc., 178 Cal.App.3d 1142 (Cal. App. 1986),* there was an unusual attempt to use the injunction remedy. Then unknown singer Anita Baker signed a recording contract with plaintiff. She later breached that contract by signing with defendant. Plaintiff sued to enjoin defendant from hiring her, rather than suing her directly. The trial court and appellate court ruled against plaintiff, saying:

> "While there are numerous cases on the general inability of an employer to enjoin his former employee from performing services somewhere else, apparently no one has previously thought of enjoining the new employer from accepting the services of the breaching employee."

- Suppose you are unsure of your legal rights relating to a particular situation or contractual provision, and need a judicial ruling so you can know whether or not, or how, to proceed.
  If you have this legal requirement of bona-fide doubt and no other remedy at law, the remedy is called *declaratory judgment.*

- There are many other civil remedies that may or may not include money damages, a few of which are paternity, adoption, divorce and custodial rights, immigration matters, and restorations of legal rights.

IV. CONTRACT TORT OF BAD FAITH

A "tort" is usually defined as a non-contract civil wrong. In the broad category of civil disputes, all must fall in categories of either contract or tort matters. The traditional torts that affect business and the commercial marketplace include, but are not limited to, the following:

1. Theft of trade secrets, formulas and valuable technology - also known as industrial espionage.
2. Infringement of intellectual property rights – patents, copyrights and trademarks.
3. Invasion of privacy – unauthorized viewing of one's files, confidential data, or electronic mail.
4. Defamation – false publication of verbal (slander) or written (libel) matters that injure one's reputation.
5. False imprisonment – unauthorized detention of falsely accused shoplifters.
6. Right of publicity – unauthorized use of one's name, likeness, voice or other personal characteristics, for financial gain.
7. Products liability negligence

With the advent of the Uniform Commercial Code being adopted statewide, thus achieving a uniformity of contract laws and the resultant predictability for planning transactions and resolving disputes involving a "sale of goods", a new form of contract tort has arisen under section 1-203 whereby the transacting parties owe each other a *duty of good faith.*

This has been interpreted by courts and expanded into the *implied covenant of good faith and fair dealing*, which is a broad duty imposed by law on contracting parties, irrespective of the terms of their contract, to assure that they will not take unfair advantage of each other by impeding or preventing the benefits reasonably anticipated from the contractual relationship of the parties.

"It is well settled that, in California, the law implies in *every* contract a covenant of good faith and fair dealing. Broadly stated, that covenant requires that neither party do anything, which will deprive the other of the benefits of the agreement.

Although the precise contours of the covenant depend upon the nature of the contract, where a contract confers on one party a discretionary power affecting the rights of the other, a duty is imposed to exercise that discretion in good faith and in accordance with fair dealing." *Okun v. Morton, supra.*

Breach of this duty to act in good faith and deal fairly with each other creates a remedy additional to the traditional breach of contract, and is treated as a tort. This is significant, because tort actions traditionally result in an award of damages larger than contract actions, and since the essence of this tort is unfairness and misconduct, substantial damages are often awarded.

Areas where the tort of bad faith are applied may be as broad as any contract dispute where one party takes unfair advantage of the other, as well as specific situations such as borrower-lender disputes, employee firings, and failure of insurers to properly service the policies of their customers, including failure to settle within policy limits or promptly pay benefits that are due.

In *Gourley v. State Farm Mutual Automobile Insurance Company, 227 Cal. App.3d 1099 (Cal. App. 1990)*, plaintiff was a passenger in an automobile struck by an uninsured drunk driver. She was not wearing a seat belt, suffered serious injuries that included some permanent disability, and filed a claim under for uninsured motorist coverage under her automobile insurance policy with the defendant, demanding the policy liability limit of $100,000.

Defendant advised plaintiff, their policyholder, they would contest her claim due to her failure to wear a seat belt, although that was not really a valid defense under California law. In addition, defendant only offered a maximum settlement of $25,000. When an arbitrator awarded plaintiff $88,137, defendant paid plaintiff, and she sued for breach of the implied covenant of good faith and fair dealing.

The trial jury awarded plaintiff $15,765 in actual damages for emotional distress and 100 times that amount for punitive damages of $1,576,500. On appeal, the verdict was affirmed. The appellate court decision set forth the law applicable to the tort of bad faith:

"The gist of the bad faith action is to compensate the insured for the angst caused when the insurer willfully refuses to pay under the policy. The primary focus of the tort is the personal wrong done. If it were merely pecuniary, a contract cause of action would suffice. . ."

"There is an implied covenant in every insurance contract that the insurer will do nothing to impair the insured's right to receive the benefit of the contractual bargain that the insurer will promptly pay to the insured all sums due under the contract. A major motivation for the purchase of insurance is the peace of mind that claims will be paid promptly. When an insurer unreasonably refuses to pay benefits due, it frustrates that motivation and a cause of action in tort arises."

The appellate court then explained the legal criteria for an award of punitive damages (similar to the U.S. Supreme Court guidelines set forth in the *BMW case, supra*):

"In making our determination, we look to three factors: (1) whether the amount of the award reasonably reflects the reprehensibility of the defendant's conduct; (2) whether the punitive damages bear a reasonable relationship to the actual damages; and (3) whether the award will have a deterrent effect without crippling the financial existence of the defendant."

In *Dalton v. Educational Testing Service, 663 N.E.2d 289 (N.Y. App. 1995)*, plaintiff, a high school student, took the SAT administered by defendant. When he did so, he signed a statement, which reserved to defendant, "the right to cancel any test score . . . if ETS believes that there is reason to question the score's validity."

Plaintiff took the test twice. Because his score on the 2nd test increased by more than 350 points, his score was considered "discrepant" and the defendant, after a finding that the handwriting differed, notified plaintiff of their intention to cancel his score, stating, "the evidence suggests that someone else may have completed your answer sheet and that the questioned scores may be invalid."

When plaintiff was given the opportunity to provide additional information in his defense, he presented evidence that he had mononucleosis for the first test, his preparatory test scores were consistent with his results on the 2nd test, statements of other students confirmed that he was in the classroom during the 2nd test, and handwriting certification verified that we has the author of both tests. ETS submitted the handwriting again to a new document examiner who again suggested that the tests were in different handwritings.

They did not however, "make even rudimentary efforts to evaluate or investigate the information" submitted by plaintiff. Plaintiff sued, and the trial court ruled in his favor, finding that ETS had breached its duty of good faith. On appeal the case was affirmed:

"Implicit in all contracts is a covenant of good faith and fair dealing in the course of contract performance. . . This embraces a pledge that neither party shall do anything, which will have the effect of destroying or injuring the right of the other party to receive the fruits of the contract. Where the contract contemplates the exercise of discretion, this pledge includes a promise not to act arbitrarily or irrationally in exercising that discretion."

In *Sons of Thunder, Inc. v. Borden, 690 A.2d 575 (Sup. Ct. N.J. 1997)*, defendant, a leading producer of clam products, hired DeMusz to be the captain of one of its four boats used to harvest clams. Later, in order to implement their business project for fishermen to shuck the clams on the boats and thus provide a larger haul, they decided to buy a larger boat for their "Shuck-at-Sea" project.

With defendant's approval, DeMusz formed a company to implement the proposal, bought the boat and leased the necessary equipment for the project. Then defendant orally agreed with DeMusz to assure a long-term supply so that he could buy a second boat, which he did under the name of the plaintiff. This oral contract was for one year with automatic renewals up to five years, allowing either party to cancel by giving 90 days written notice. Plaintiff was unable to buy the boat on its own credit, until defendant intervened with assurances that "they expected the contract to run for five years," and that revenues produced would be sufficient to support the loan.

Soon after the boat was ready defendant's management changed, they refused to honor plaintiff's contract, refused to purchase from plaintiff, acquired a different fishing boat company to perform their clam project, and invoked the 90-day termination clause in the contract. Plaintiff sued for breach of contract and breach of the covenant of good faith and fair dealing.

Demusz and a Borden executive testified at trial that the 90-day termination clause was only to apply after one year. The jury found for plaintiff, awarding $363,292 for lost income during the four months Borden refused to honor the contract, and $412,000 for one year's lost profits.

On appeal, the verdict was affirmed. "A party to a contract may breach the implied covenant of good faith and fair dealing in performing its obligations even when it exercises an express and unconditional right to terminate and the trial court correctly determined that the jury could have reasonably found that Borden breached its obligation to perform its duties in good faith"

"Although the Uniform Commercial code (UCC) governs this case, the obligation to perform in good faith found in the common law exists in every contract, including those with express termination clauses."

V.   INTENTIONAL INTERFERENCE WITH CONTRACT

This is an intentional tort that has come more into legal usage as the commercial marketplace has grown and become more competitive. It is applicable in situations where there is an existing financially advantageous contract, and an outside third party such as a disgruntled bidder for a construction project or business takeover wrongfully induces one of the contracting parties to cancel. Often, the breaching party then enters into a new contract involving the same subject matter with the inducer.

The five traditional elements of this tort, which is sometimes described as "intentional interference with contract", if there is a specific contractual relationship, and "intentional interference with prospective economic advantage", if there is a non-contractual business relationship, are:

1. Existence of a legally enforceable contract involving plaintiff
2. The contract is current, in good standing, and not in default
3. Defendant is aware of the contract's existence
4. Defendant unlawfully induces a contracting party not to perform
5. Plaintiff suffers financial damage

*Ex: Dane and Trent are competing bidders on the chalk and eraser contract with the University. The bid specifications provide that, "all bidders represent and warrant that they are U.S. citizens, if not their bid may be disregarded and this contract will be privately reassigned." This provision is necessary to assure continued federal funding for the University. Dane's bid is lowest and he is awarded the $75,000 contract. Trent is furious, and gives the University forged documents that indicate Dane is an illegal alien, following which they cancel his contract and award it to Trent.

Notice we have all the required elements of the tort reflected in the facts. Element 4 has been clarified by most court decisions to require the inducement to be a separate actionable tort or breach of contract. In this case, providing false written information that damages Dane's reputation is the tort of libel, and supports the 'unlawful inducement' requirement.

In *Buckaloo v. Johnson, et al, 537 P.2d 865 (Cal. 1975)*, plaintiff was a licensed real estate broker who had an exclusive real estate listing on a piece of waterfront property owned by Benioff. Four years after it had expired, she put a sales sign on the property that created an "open listing" whereby any broker who furnished a buyer would receive a commission, unless the owner made a direct sale to an independent buyer, not furnished by the broker.

Plaintiff was approached by the defendants who expressed an interest in that property. He informed them what he knew about the property, and they left, promising to return the next day since he had secured accommodations for them.

When they did not return, plaintiff registered their names with Benioff, informing her he was the "procuring cause" of any later purchase by defendant, thus attempting to protect himself regarding the right to a commission.

Later, plaintiff learned the property had been sold to defendants and his request for a commission was refused. He then sued the seller and the defendants for damages for breach of an implied contract, and for intentional interference with prospective advantage. The trial court dismissed plaintiff's complaint based upon lack of a written agreement required by the statute of frauds.

On appeal, the Court reversed, stating, "Even at this late date defendants fail to comprehend that plaintiff is not alleging interference with contract but interference with prospective advantage. The protected area of activity is not a contractual relationship but an economic relationship with the potential to ripen into contract. Whether the relationship is of sufficient depth to support the tort is a factual question which plaintiff will be put to the burden of proving at trial."

(These proofs include evidence that the defendants conspired, after being made aware of the benefits of a purchase by plaintiff, to purchase directly and secretly, thus eliminating his entitlement to a real estate commission.)

The Court explained the distinction between the two types of tort:

"The great weight of authority is that the tort of interference with contract is merely a species of the broader tort of interference with prospective advantage. Thus while the elements of the two actions are similar, the existence of a legally binding agreement is not a *sine qua non* to the maintenance of a suit based on the more inclusive wrong."

"(Contracts) which are voidable by reason of the statute of frauds, formal defects, lack of consideration, lack of mutuality, or even uncertainty of terms, still afford a basis for a tort action when the defendant interferes with their performance."

DISCUSSION EXERCISES

1. Discuss other types of monetary remedies.
2. Discuss other types of non-monetary remedies.
3. Discuss other types of equitable remedies.
4. Discuss limitations, if any, you would put on actual damages.
5. Discuss limitations, if any, you would put on punitive damages.

CASE EXERCISES

ZSA ZSA LOSES/WINS A DISPUTE FOR HER CANCELLED MOVIES

In *Hollywood Fantasy Corporation v. Zsa Zsa Gabor, 151 F.3d 203 (5th Cir. 1998)*, the plaintiff company was in the business of providing fantasy vacation packages that would allow participants to make a movie with a Hollywood personality and imagine themselves movie stars for one week, for a stated fee. They contracted with the defendant to be one of two celebrities at the event, but she cancelled two weeks before it was to occur.

Plaintiff tried unsuccessfully to replace defendant, and then had to cancel the event, refunding their ticket purchases to the few customers that existed. Shortly thereafter, plaintiff went out of business and brought this action in a Texas federal trial court against defendant for breach of contract and fraud.

ANALYSIS

When defendant failed to appear at the call of the trial docket, the judge entered a default judgment on the issue of liability and the jury awarded damages of $3 million.

She moved to set aside the default judgment on grounds she had not been properly notified. The court granted her motion and ordered a new trial.

At trial, the jury awarded plaintiff $100,000 damages on its breach of contract claim and $100,000 on its fraud claim. In a post-trial order, the court set aside the fraud verdict as being not supported by the evidence, but upheld the contract claim verdict.

Defendant appealed, claiming that there was no valid contract because she had not accepted the plaintiff's offer to perform, but had instead made material changes to it, resulting only in a counteroffer, rather than a legal acceptance of the offer.

The appellate court disagreed with her, and affirmed the trial court judgment, stating, "we find that the modifications Ms. Gabor sought were not material because they did not significantly increase Hollywood Fantasy's financial obligations or significantly reduce Ms. Gabor's performance obligations . . ."

The appellate court then addressed the issue of money damages awarded, and ruled, "The $100,000 damages award cannot be supported as the recovery of lost profits."

It reviewed testimony of plaintiff to the effect that he "estimated" he would have lost $250,000 from future fantasy vacation events and $1 million in future profits from bloopers and outtakes from videotapes of clients acting with the personalities, and found that it was too imprecise and not based upon factual data.

The court discussed the legal requirements for a recovery of consequential damages in the form of lost profits:

"Lost profits must be proved with reasonable certainty . . . at a minimum, opinions or estimates of lost profits must be based on objective facts, figures or data from which the amount of lost profits may be ascertained. Mere speculation of the amount of lost profits is insufficient."

The court then reduced the jury award to $57,500, the defendant's evidentiary out-of-pocket expenses for the celebrity event, which included printing, advertising, film preparation and travel expenses. "The general rule is that the non-breaching party may only recover out-of-pocket expenses incurred after the contract was formed."

DEFUSE REPLAY

Did Zsa Zsa win the battle but lose the war, or vice-versa? The roller-coaster aspects of this case are a real life movie worthy of the publicity she always craved as an "actress".

The plaintiff originally received a $3 million default judgment. When it was set aside, as judges do routinely if the defendant can furnish evidence of lack of notice or excusable neglect, it was a clear signal to the plaintiff that its case needed to be able to support the burden of proof for both liability and damages. It appears it did its homework on liability, but was not prepared to properly prove any damages beyond actual expenses incurred.

The defendant, on the other hand, having survived the default judgment, should have paid attention to the potential damage award she would incur, and settled the case. The ideal time would have been immediately after the trial judge set aside the plaintiff's default judgment. At that moment, defendant had maximum bargaining leverage.

CONCLUSION

According to the many news articles about her, Zsa Zsa Gabor never met a rich man she didn't like, and she was equally enamored with publicity. Give her a forum where she was the center of attention, and she was at her best.

In this case, she was again in the spotlight. She parried questions and answers with the lawyers as well as the judge, and there was a daily pre and post trial news conference for good measure.

Perhaps the reason she allowed the case to continue to its inevitable conclusion was how important it was to her to be in the bright lights of publicity. The pendency of this case was her last real opportunity to play a starring role. If viewed from that perspective, she was successful.

    A. Do you agree with the court's final decision?
    B. Do you think courts apply different standards for celebrities?
    C. Does this case warrant punitive damages?

CASE RESEARCH CYBERCISES

The following cases also relate to the material in this chapter and illustrate the types of disputes that may occur. For each one do the following written assignment:

1. Locate the case using the Internet (Lexis-Nexis, West or any other research cite which provides case transcripts).
2. Briefly summarize what it was about – the nature of the dispute involved.
3. Who won at the trial court level? Who won at the appellate level?
4. Who won if there was a third level of Supreme Court review?
5. What were the legal rules of law and the reasoning used to reach the final decision?
6. Do you agree or disagree with the decision, and explain why?
7. What business law time bomb(s) were involved?
8. Could the time bomb(s) have been avoided by structuring the transaction differently? Discuss.
9. Could the adverse effects of the time bomb(s) have been defused by a different reaction or response by the affected party? Discuss.
10. Replay the facts of the case to achieve a different successful result.

1. *Super Valu Stores, Inv. V. Peterson, 506 So.2d 317(Ala. 1987) (lost profits from an unestablished business recoverable).*
2. *Tamarind Lithography Workshop, Inc. v. Sanders, 142 Cal. App. 3d 552 (Cal. App. 1983) (specific performance and damages granted to compel compliance with motion picture contract by including screen credit).*
3. *Welch v. Metro-Goldwyn-Mayer Film Co., 207 Cal.App.3d 164 (Cal.App.1989) (contract damages of $3M compensatory and $8M punitive awarded to actress Raquel Welch for being replaced by Debra Winger in movie Cannery Row).*

<u>NOTES</u>

7

WHERE TO SUE: THE JURISDICTION OF COURTS

"Scholars dispute and the case is still before the courts."
Horace

More than 90% of transactional disputes are resolved without lawyers, more than 90% of those are settled without a lawsuit being filed, and in 90% of those that are litigated the matters are resolved before there is any final decision by judge or jury.

Yet, there are still an abundance of lawsuits in our knee-jerk "sue-em" reactivity to the challenge of matters not seeming to go our way. So, our focus now turns to the assumption that we will be faced with litigation after we have probably moved through these events in the typical business transaction:

- Preliminary negotiations between the parties
- Mutual agreement is reached either verbally or in writing form
- A material dispute arises
- The parties are unable or unwilling to resolve their differences or invoke formal settlement procedures such as arbitration or mediation
- Threats of legal action are made
- Lawyers are hired
- A lawsuit is filed by one party in a chosen state or federal court

The strategic planning of a lawsuit has been compared to a military campaign. At the very least, it certainly resembles a challenging game of chess. The successful player is usually able to stay one step ahead of his opponent.

Of course, the lawsuit itself is just a final stage of the typical progression of events that has culminated in a business transaction gone bad. At any stage, one of the parties will usually try to induce the other to accept a favorable settlement of some kind. And the deciding factor in such inducement may be, for the purposes of this chapter, the court location where the lawsuit can be brought by the plaintiff or resisted by the defendant.

1. Legal Overview

But where should the plaintiff file suit? What are the choices available? Where must the case be defended? What are the defendant's choices? What strategies are available at this level of the dispute?

A. Forum Selection

If the contract between the parties has a "forum selection clause", it determines in advance by mutual agreement where and in what court any disputes will be heard. It is a part of the advance planning strategy in negotiating commercial transactions.

As we previously discussed in the chapter on sources of law, "choice of law clauses" can be agreed upon in advance by the parties to govern what laws will apply in the event of a dispute.

If for example in a contract for sale of goods, a seller has successfully inserted a requirement that Japanese law will govern (all sales are as-is with no guarantee of performance) rather than the usual UCC law applicable throughout U.S. courts (all sales of goods have warranty protection) - the buyer who successfully requires that any disputes be brought in a New York Federal court, will still be faced with the foreign law being applied by the local forum. The seller would have the advantage in a dispute that occurs, and could probably induce a favorable settlement.

If, however, there were no choice of law clause in the contract, a New York forum selection clause would assure that the buyer had UCC warranty protection because the designated court would be duty bound to apply local law. The buyer would have the settlement advantage if a dispute occurred.

B. Forum Non Conveniens

If there is no forum selection by mutual agreement of the parties, the plaintiff, as the complainant in the lawsuit, will choose where to sue. Sometimes the defendant objects on the grounds that it does not have sufficient legal contacts with the chosen forum to be fairly required to defend there, as required by the due process clause of the U.S. Constitution.

Sometimes the defendant's request for dismissal is based upon the doctrine of *forum non conveniens*. It is a procedural remedy of fairness, derived from 18th century English law, that allows a court to reject jurisdiction over a case if the result would be "vexatious and works unnecessary hardship on the defendant."

This usually occurs in situations where the defendant is a financial "deep pocket", the dispute involves personal injures or large contract damages, important events have primarily occurred outside the United States, but the plaintiff files suit in a U.S. court. The defendant claims the plaintiff is "forum shopping", by using our courts to hope for the unique aspects of our judicial system not available outside the U.S. – large jury awards, unlimited trial discovery, contingent fee hiring of lawyers, punitive damages for extreme conduct, and appellate remedies.

If the parties had agreed upon a forum selection clause in their contract, there could be no "forum shopping" in the event of a contract dispute. But such advance planning often does not occur in contracts, and is not possible in non-contract cases such as alleged negligence of the defendant causing personal injuries to the plaintiff.

In modern times, courts have become wary of the motivations of some foreign plaintiffs in seeking judicial relief in U.S. courts, and have often expressed these concerns:

"(without this) procedural tool . . . Texas will become an irresistible forum for all mass disaster lawsuits. 'Bhopal'-type litigation, with little or no connection to Texas, will add to our already crowded dockets, forcing our residents to wait in the corridors of our courthouses while foreign causes of action are tried." *Dow Chemical v. Alfaro, 786 S.W.2d 674 (Tex. 1990). (dissent)*

The reference to 'Bhopal' comes from probably the most famous application of the forum non conveniens doctrine, to reject the plaintiffs' choice of a U.S. forum. Union Carbide owned a 51% of its Bhopal, India subsidiary, and due to alleged negligence at its chemical plant in 1984, lethal gas was released which severely injured and killed thousands of persons. It was the most devastating industrial disaster in history.

Suit was filed by the government of India against the 'deep pocket' parent company in New York Federal court. Union Carbide contended that the case should be heard in India. The court dismissed the U.S. action, requiring that it be litigated in India. The court's decision was based upon the almost exclusively India based aspects of the dispute:

- All witnesses were in India
- All documents were in India
- Transportation and translation problems
- Plant managed entirely by Indian citizens
- Plant operation regulated by Indian agencies
- No Americans employed at time of accident
- No Americans visited prior to one year before accident
- No communications for 5 years between plant and U.S.

The court said, "the doctrine of forum non conveniens is a rule of U.S. law, which states that where a case is properly heard in more than one court, the one that is most convenient should hear it. Given the facts of this case, the courts of India are the more convenient forums."

Union Carbide settled the case in India before trial, in 1989, for $470M, which was estimated to be one-half of what a jury award would have been in the U.S. *In Re Union Carbide Corporation Gas Plant Disaster at Bhopal, 809 F.2d 195 (2d Cir. 1987).* Notice how the settlement value of this lawsuit changed depending upon where the plaintiff was legally permitted to litigate.

C. Federal or State Court

If there is no such advance selection of the forum, we must examine the applicable rules of law governing jurisdiction of courts. It can be critically important to the outcome of the case but is seldom understood by the general public as a strategic opportunity for advance planning.

Our judicial system is actually dual layers of courts that operate concurrently. There is one Federal system and 50 separate systems within each State. All have three basic levels. While State court judges are usually elected for limited terms, Federal court judges are appointed for life.

The trial court level is where the case is initially presented, presided by a judge as to matters of law and, if either party requests it, heard by a jury that evaluates the factual evidence. At this level, there is presented the testimony of the actual parties and their witnesses, all documentary evidence is introduced, and a final judgement, is entered. State trial courts are numerous, usually being located within each county. There is at least one Federal trial court in each State but there may be more than one since they are located in major population centers.

The appellate level is usually an automatic right of the losing party to try to convince a higher court that there were substantial errors of law in the trial. While there is only one judge on the trial level, there are usually three or more that hear appellate cases. There is no new evidence presented at this level. The judge's are limited to the "record" of the lower court. State appellate courts are located according to each state's population needs, while Federal appellate courts are less numerous, there being only 13 to serve all 50 states.

The Supreme Court of each State, and the U.S. Supreme Court are the highest levels of the court system. These are the "courts of last resort", whose legal decisions are final. Unlike the appellate level, there is no absolute right to appeal a civil case. Whether or not this highest court decides to hear a case usually depends upon its importance to the public and impact on society. Applications to be heard are by "writ of certiorari".

The decision of the higher courts may either be to affirm and leave the trial judgment intact, reverse it, modify it in some manner, or grant a new trial. Unanimous or majority vote determines the appellate decision. Often, majority decisions will include dissenting opinions which may signal critical times when the law may change in a particular area as new cases arise with similar facts.

The typical appellate evolutionary process starts with a case where the trial court decision is unanimously affirmed. Then in a later similar case, there is a majority affirm with one dissenting vote, and later another similar affirm with a smaller majority and more dissents. Finally, one day another related case is decided where the majority vote swings over to the reversal side and we have come full cycle with a new legal precedent.

There are significant practical reasons for a plaintiff to choose to file suit in either the Federal or State court system.

Some of the major advantages and disadvantages are:

FEDERAL

- Judges free from local politics
- Judges more experienced
- Better suited for complex cases
- More time consuming procedures
- More expensive to complete

STATE

- Local interests may prevail
- Judges less experienced
- Uneven levels of judicial expertise
- More flexibility
- Faster resolution of disputes

2. Jurisdiction Over the Subject Matter

Federal Courts have concurrent jurisdiction with State courts, so that a plaintiff has the choice of suing in either place, depending upon its jurisdictional requirements.

Federal courts have exclusive jurisdiction to hear disputes involving certain Federal laws, including immigration, admiralty, bankruptcy, antitrust, and intellectual property rights.

Federal court jurisdiction requires that (1) the dollar amount sued for must exceed $75,000, AND (2) there must be "diversity of citizenship". Diversity legally means that the litigants are both permanent resident citizens of two different U.S. States, a U.S. citizen and a sovereign foreign country, or litigation between U.S. citizens and foreign nationals. For purposes of corporate parties, 'diversity' is governed by their state of incorporation.

If the dispute involves the interpretation or constitutionality of a federal law, suit must be filed in a federal court, but no minimum dollar amount or diversity of citizenship requirements are enforced.

If the Federal court jurisdictional requirements are not met, the plaintiff may be required to sue in the appropriate state court.

Notice how intricate these disputes can be. If the plaintiff files suit in federal court and meets the jurisdictional requirements, the federal procedural law will apply, but the court must use state substantive law, absent a choice of law clause in the contract sued upon. This is the famous *Erie Doctrine*.

But the defendant may still successfully raise an issue of what state law to use depending upon where it is really 'doing business' under the 'minimum contacts' legal test, which in turn depends upon the "choice of law rules" applied by the court, as we see in the next case.

Lazard Freres & Co. v. Protective Life Insurance Company, 108 F.3d 1531 (2nd Cir. 1997), involved a dispute between two large and sophisticated bank debt traders regarding the sale of $10 million face value of bank debt.

Plaintiff, a New York investment bank and broker-dealer, agreed to purchase the bank debt of MCC, and attempted to turn around and sell it to defendant, a Tennessee Corporation, whose principal place of business was in Alabama. After a number of conversations, the transaction was agreed, and reduced to a written "Scheme Report". The defendant had required in the verbal negotiations that "twenty percent of the face amount of the debt was going to be paid (within 60 days), and there were no outstanding litigations against MCC that would reduce the value of the debt." The written document, unread by defendant before signing, did not contain these assurances.

Defendant discovered the problem when the price of the MCC bank debt dropped substantially, and refused to close the deal. Plaintiff sued for breach of contract and defendant asserted fraud as its defense. The trial court granted plaintiff's motion for summary judgment and defendant appealed. On appeal, the summary judgment was vacated, and the case remanded for a trial on the issues raised.

One of the areas of dispute was what law to apply because, "A federal court sitting in diversity must apply the choice of law rules of the forum state," in this case New York:

"Until the latter part of this century, New York courts employed a traditional, 'territorially oriented' approach to choice-of-law issues which applied the law of the geographical place where one key event occurred, such as the place of the wrong in tort cases or where an agreement was entered into or performed in contract cases."

"In contract cases, New York courts now apply a 'center of gravity' or 'grouping of contacts' approach. Under this approach, courts may consider a spectrum of significant contacts, including the place of contracting, the places of negotiation and performance, the location of the subject matter, and the domicile or place of business of the contracting parties . . . The traditional choice of law factors, the places of contracting and performance, are given the heaviest weight in this analysis . . . Under New York conflicts rules, the center of gravity of the MCC transaction was New York."

A number of recent federal court cases reflect disputes as to how the jurisdictional amount required for a case to be heard in federal court is computed.

The disputes take two different forms: (1) plaintiff files suit in state court, defendant requests removal to federal court, and plaintiff files motion to remand back to state court, or (2) plaintiff files suit in federal court and defendant moves to remand.

- Punitive damage claims cannot be added to basic damages to meet the $75,000 jurisdictional amount requirement. *Kirkland v. Midland Mortgage Co., 2001 WL 224776 (11th Cir. 2001).*

- Counterclaim amounts are properly includible in determining jurisdictional amount. *Spectator Mgt. Group v. Brown, 131 F.3d 131 (3rd Cir. 1997).*

- Each diversity plaintiff must have $75,000 at stake. *Leonhardt v. Western Sugar Co., 160 F.3d 631 (10th Cir. 1998).*

- Choice of law rules are based upon a five-point weighing test. *Hughes v. Wal-Mart Stores, Inc., 250 F.3d 618 (8th Cir. 2001).*

- Multiple plaintiffs may not add up the dollar amounts of their claims in order to meet the federal minimum jurisdictional amount. *Sdregas v. Home Depot, 2002 U.S. Lexis 12159 (E.D. PA. 2002).*

State Court jurisdiction has no such limitations, other than the fact that different levels of state courts hear cases in different dollar levels, like small claims courts which usually have a jurisdictional ceiling of $5,000.

Once the plaintiff completes court jurisdictional strategy on either the State or Federal level, the Venue issue arises. It is a procedural rule that requires the plaintiff to file suit in a state or federal court located nearest to:

(1) where the defendant legally resides (primary residence of at least 6 months plus one day, not summer/winter homes or vacation residences), OR

(2) where the dispute legally arose (where contract was signed, transaction was completed, or injuries occurred)

Notice how the legal system again tries to level the scales of justice by directing venue toward the defendant's home base. Plaintiff chooses to sue, chooses a legal remedy, and chooses where to sue – but that "where" involves a requirement that tries to balance any "home cooking" that might benefit plaintiff.

If the plaintiff chooses an improper venue, the defendant may demand a change of venue to the proper court location. This is a mandatory venue change, granted by the court when the defendant files a motion to change venue.

There is also a discretionary venue change rule where a defendant sometimes alleges that a fair trial is impossible due to adverse prejudicial publicity. This rarely is granted by the court in civil business cases, unless a media circus directly impacts the specific issues being litigated.

Now let's play the chess game with a common dispute, and use the rules of proper court jurisdiction and venue to illustrate situations where both of the parties might be able to strategically induce a favorable settlement.

*Ex: Jack and Jill, who respectively reside in Miami, Fl. and Philadelphia, Pa., both decide to visit Disneyworld in Orlando, Fl. Jill drives south on I-95, Jack drives north on I-95, and just as they go up a hill in the Orlando city limits, Jill rear ends Jack. Jack suffers severe injuries and decides to sue Jill for $76,000 in damages. It just so happens that Jack's family has a long history in Miami, streets are named after them, and they know a lot of important local people, so he sues Jill in Miami state court.

1. Is Jack allowed to sue in Miami Federal court? Yes – he satisfies the two jurisdictional requirements of the required amount in dispute (more than $75,000) AND diversity of citizenship (Florida and Pennsylvania). But he could also choose the state court level, since they operate concurrently.

2. Is Jack allowed to sue in Miami state court? Yes – because there are no specific requirements like those imposed by the federal system.

3. Did Jack choose the proper court venue? No – he chose not to file suit where Jill resides (Philadelphia) for obvious strategic reasons. Nor did he sue, as required, where the accident occurred (Orlando). But unless Jill is aware of these venue requirements, and files a "motion to change venue" with the state court judge, nothing will change and she will have to defend in Miami state court. The case will probably settle in Jack's favor shortly thereafter. (Note: A motion is an application to the judge, requesting some type of relief. If no request is made, judges don't do the work of the parties and correct their errors for them.)

4. If Jill filed a "motion to change venue" would she win? Yes – she could have the case moved within the state system to either Orlando, or more probably to the Philadelphia state court, where she resides. The case will probably settle in Jill's favor as soon as her motion is granted.

5. If Jack had chosen the proper venue and sued in Orlando, could Jill still win on a requested venue change on the grounds that she couldn't get a fair trial due to the well-known status in Florida of Jack's family? No – we don't have a media circus here and, like most civil cases, there is not the potential for a lot of prejudicial publicity.

However, what if our dispute in question was a suit for damages brought in Miami Federal Court by the family of Elian Gonzalez against the U.S. Immigration Department for the famous seizing of him by the government swat team and his return to his father for travel back to Cuba? There would have been a three- ring circus in Miami, and the venue would probably have been changed to another less volatile location.

6. If Jack had chosen the proper venue and sued in Orlando, does Jill have any other recourse? Yes – Jill can properly request the case be removed to a federal court having proper venue – her back yard of Philadelphia federal court, and she will no doubt have his case settled as soon as his request is granted. This is due to the "removal rule" of court jurisdiction, which states that a defendant who is sued in state court may remove his case to the federal level if the two federal jurisdiction requirements can be satisfied. Here we have both the required amount in dispute and diversity of citizenship, so Jill would win.

7. Are there ways that Jack can "checkmate" Jill and require her to defend in Orlando state court? Yes: (A) if Jack sues for a jurisdictional amount under $75,000 ($74,999) he will legally prevent Jill from achieving removal to federal court, even with diversity of citizenship. (B) If Jack could also add, in good faith, another Miami defendant, he would destroy diversity and keep the case in state court, even though it met the federal jurisdictional amount threshold.

Notice how the plot thickens as each party to the dispute plans strategy and counters the anticipated moves of the other. Whenever you see a lawsuit that is being heard in either state or federal court, it probably has gone through a similar journey.

3. Jurisdiction Over the Person

Even when the issue of the court's subject matter jurisdiction is resolved, there is another jurisdictional question. Does this court have proper "jurisdiction over the person" of the defendant? In other words, is the defendant properly "in court" so that any rulings are legally binding?

Disputes often arise where a non-resident defendant, especially a corporation, seeks to dismiss the action based upon lack of required "minimum contacts" to constitute it "doing business" in the forum jurisdiction. This is a case-by-case analysis, but the current trend is to allow jurisdiction for most nominal local contacts such as advertisements, phone calls, and business trips.

These recent cases reflect such disputes:

- Legal communications between Germany and Texas establish Texas personal jurisdiction. *Wien Air Alaska, Inc. v. Brandt, 195 F.3d 208 (5th cir. 1999).*

- 40% ownership of Kentucky motel by French corp. not sufficient grounds for personal jurisdiction. *Dean v. Motel 6 Operating L.P., 134 F.3d 1269 (6th cir. 1998).*

- One phone call not enough to establish minimum contacts. *Watertronics, Inc. v. Flanagans, Inc., 2001 WL 942639 (Wisc. App. 2001).*

Jurisdiction over the person usually occurs when an officer of the court delivers the legal papers to the defendant. This is called achieving 'in personam' jurisdiction by "service of process" and the persons who do this are process servers:

A) When a lawsuit is filed in state or federal court, a summons is issued by the court clerk, and copies of both must be legally delivered to the defendant.

   In most states, if the individual defendant cannot be personally served, the papers may be legally delivered to any adult member of the defendant's household. This blunts the games defendants sometimes play to evade service of process. Sooner or later the court papers will properly arrive, so why delay the inevitable? Stop hiding under the bed Mr. Defendant, accept the papers, hire a good lawyer, and get on with it.

B) When the defendant is a corporation or similar legal person, the laws of each state require it to designate a natural person as its registered agent to receive the court papers.
   Service of process on that person legally binds the corporate defendant.

C) Most states also have adopted "long-arm" statutes that allow a non-resident defendant to be legally served if they:

   - Own real estate in the state that is the subject matter of the lawsuit
   - Commit a tort within the state, like automobile negligence
   - Made the contract sued upon within the state
   - Were "doing business" within the state (minimum contacts test)
   - Maintained an "active" website selling goods or services

D) Sometimes, the dispute concerns a piece of land, and 'in rem' jurisdiction is obtained by merely posting the legal notice on the property. Landlord and tenant, mortgage foreclosures, and mechanic's lien disputes fall within this category.

So we now have a dispute that has ripened into full-blown litigation. Attorneys have been hired, the law has been researched, the lawsuit has been filed in a state or federal court of the plaintiff's choosing, and the papers have been served upon the defendant. Let the typical civil lawsuit begin.

DISCUSSION EXERCISES

1. Discuss/create a case in which you as plaintiff would sue in Federal court.
2. Discuss/create a case in which you as plaintiff would sue in State court.
3. Discuss/create a case in which you as defendant would remove from State to Federal court.
4. Discuss arguments you would make to change the venue of a civil case.
5. Discuss any other jurisdictional strategies to induce a favorable settlement.

CASE EXERCISES

LACK OF COMPLETE DIVERSITY PREVENTS FEDERAL COURT REMOVAL

In *Cheskiewicz v. Aventis Pasteur, Inc., 2002 U.S. Dist. LEXIS 15339 (E.D.Pa. 2002)*, a strict liability suit over a child's allegedly adverse reactions to vaccinations manufactured by the defendants was originally filed in Pennsylvania state court.

Plaintiffs were citizens of Pennsylvania, and the named defendants were citizens of other states, except for two Pennsylvania corporate defendants who were allegedly involved in the chain of commerce for production of the allegedly dangerously defective product.

Defendants attempted to transfer the case to Pennsylvania federal court, based upon removal jurisdiction, claiming the two Pennsylvania corporations were "sham defendants", joined solely for the purpose of defeating the diversity requirement. They requested those two defendants be dismissed.

Plaintiff's claimed that the non-diverse parties were properly joined as manufacturers of the vaccines or adulterants that allegedly caused the injuries sued upon, and therefore no required diversity existed and the case would have to be heard in state court. They filed a motion to remand back to state court.

ANALYSIS

The appellate court granted the plaintiff's motion to remand for lack of diversity jurisdiction.

"Removal premised on diversity of citizenship fails where one of the remaining defendants is non-diverse unless: (1) there is a federal question; or (2) the non-diverse defendant was joined fraudulently."

"As there is no federal question, the defendants must show that … the non-diverse defendants have been fraudulently joined."

The legal test of fraudulent joinder was stated to be, "where there is no reasonable basis in fact or colorable ground supporting the claim against the joined defendant, or no real intention in good faith to prosecute the action against the defendants or seek a joint judgment."

The court found the plaintiff's complaint stated allegations against the non-diverse defendants that raised the required "colorable claims", and therefore their joinder which defeated removal jurisdiction was not improper.

DEFUSE REPLAY

This case illustrates an interesting strategy to prevent a defendant from exercising the right to remove to federal court.

If removal was successful, the defendants would have had a distinct advantage simply because they could prevent the plaintiffs from suing where they wanted. By denying removal, the plaintiff's now hold the strategic advantage.

Plaintiffs often employ a checkmate strategy, as stated before, to prevent their defendant(s) from removing to federal court in one of two ways:

- Sue for less than $75,000 in cases where the damages sought are close to that jurisdictional threshold, or

- Join an additional defendant from the same state as one or more of the main defendants.

The latter strategy of creating non-diversity must pass the good faith test, but the path to accomplish this is suggested by this language from the appellate court:

"In deciding whether the non-diverse defendants were properly joined, the court must concentrate on the plaintiff's complaint at the time the petition for removal was filed."

The legal sufficiency of a complaint is whether or not it states a legal cause of action against the defendant(s). This is determined on a motion to dismiss the complaint, by assuming the truth of all its allegations.

CONCLUSION

The appellate court said, "if there is even a possibility that a state court would find that the complaint states a cause of action against any one of the resident defendants, the federal court must find that joinder was proper and remand the case to state court."

Whether or not the plaintiff can later prove the allegations against the added non-diverse defendants is immaterial in questions of proper removal jurisdiction. All that need be done is the stating of facts, which, *if true,* would create reasonable grounds for recovery.

This 2002 case clarifies some of the strategy questions that have previously been raised without any legal confirmation of what can or cannot be done.

It will serve as a guide for the drafting of future complaints and the joinder of non-diverse defendants to thwart issues of removal.

A. Do you agree with the court's final decision?
B. Do you think the creation of non-diversity to prevent removal jurisdiction is an effective strategy? Advantages? Disadvantages?
C. Do you think it is ethical to create non-diversity if the added defendants are not really an important part of the case?

CASE RESEARCH CYBERCISES

The following cases also relate to the material in this chapter and illustrate the types of disputes that may occur. For each one do the following written assignment:

1. Locate the case using the Internet (Lexis-Nexis, West or any other research cite which provides case transcripts).
2. Briefly summarize what it was about – the nature of the dispute involved.
3. Who won at the trial court level? Who won at the appellate level?
4. Who won if there was a third level of Supreme Court review?
5. What were the legal rules of law and the reasoning used to reach the final decision?
6. Do you agree or disagree with the decision, and explain why?
7. What business law time bomb(s) were involved?
8. Could the time bomb(s) have been avoided by structuring the transaction differently? Discuss.
9. Could the adverse effects of the time bomb(s) have been defused by a different reaction or response by the affected party? Discuss.
10. Replay the facts of the case to achieve a different successful result.

1. *Quill Corporation v. North Dakota, 504 U.S. 298 (1992) (out of state mail order house with 3,000 local customers not doing business for purposes of collecting use tax).*
2. *Knowles v. Modglin, 553 So.2d 563 (Ala. 1989) (California defendants did not have sufficient minimum contacts with Alabama for in personam jurisdiction).*
3. *Peoples Trust Company of Bergen County v. Kozuck, 236 A.2d 630 (N.J. Super. 1967) (summons and complaint left outside defendant's home after wife appeared in window and refused to answer door is valid service of process).*

8.

HOW TO SUE:
THE CIVIL LAWSUIT

*"I was never ruined but twice;
once when I lost a lawsuit,
and once when I won one."*
Voltaire

The plaintiff dictates the pace of a civil dispute. Always the moving party, plaintiff has decided to sue after getting input from counsel as to the governing rules of law and the realistic prospects for success. A lawyer has been hired. A legal remedy has been selected which usually is money damages in the typical contracts or sales case. The plaintiff, either in a state or federal court, has also chosen the jurisdiction of the lawsuit.

Let's understand a few more litigation terms:

A). "Filed the lawsuit". We hear the phrase all the time, but what does it really mean? It is deceptively simple. Plaintiff goes to the appropriate courthouse jurisdiction and presents to the clerk's office the necessary legal papers to start the proceedings, together with the required filing fee. The clerk opens a court file with the names of the parties, gives it a court file number, and assigns the case to a judge, using a blind rotating file designation system. Every court document thereafter is docket stamped and goes into this file.

B). "The parties". This refers to the principals in the lawsuit, the plaintiff and defendant. They can be he (male), she (female) or it (a legal entity like a corporation). Others who participate in the giving of testimony or presentation of evidence are called "witnesses". If an appeal is filed from an adverse court ruling or jury decision, the losing party who seeks appellate relief is the "appellant", and the winning party defending the appeal is the "appellee".

C). "Reported cases". Appellate court and supreme court decisions are transcribed and regularly published in various reporting services, such as West Publishing and Lexis-Nexis, to name a few. Trial court proceedings are not usually reported, although some services exist strictly for that purpose. Case citation formats are keyed to the various regional legal reporting services so that any appeal of a lower court case is readily available in a law library that carries those reporter volumes, or more practically with a simple computer keystroke.

When reading a reported case, there is a distinct pattern to their presentation. First there usually is a summary of the action taken by the reporting appellate court, followed by a review of the facts that created the dispute.

Then the rules of law pertaining to that type of problem are stated, often with citations of authority to prior cases.

(The most persuasive authority is recent cases with the same or similar facts decided in the same state.) Finally, the court does its reasoning by applying the facts of the dispute to the governing rules of law so that the necessary decision can be made.

D). "Represented by counsel". Since court proceedings are so specialized, the litigants are usually represented by their respective attorneys, and they speak and act through their lawyers. If however a party wishes to self – represent, it is permissible but tantamount to judicial suicide. How can a layperson, no matter how smart, know all the ins and out of a courtroom? It's like waking up one morning with a rotten tooth and deciding to just take care of matters ourselves with our trusty old pliers.

E). "The pleadings". All the major court documents that the parties to the lawsuit file are called the "pleadings".

F). "The evidence." This consists of all the testimony of the parties and their witnesses and all the documents they are allowed to introduce into evidence.

G.) "Burden of proof." The plaintiff-complainant is always the moving party in a civil dispute, and must satisfy the legal proof test, whereby they establish their case by the "greater weight" or "preponderance" of the evidence. Visualize the scales of justice. If they are tipped, even slightly, in the plaintiff's favor, the burden of proof is satisfied.

H). "Heard by judge or jury". In most civil cases, either party may have a jury trial, by just requesting it in their initial pleading. If this occurs, the judge is in charge of the law and all necessary legal rulings. The judge is also known as "the court" or "your honor". The jury is in charge of the facts, deciding what or who to believe, and how much weight to give the factual evidence.

This is another area where strategy may induce a favorable settlement. Civil juries are usually composed of individuals, just like you and I, chosen at random from the local pool of names for jury service. Jurors are not corporations or other business organizations, and are often hostile to larger organizations since they often are the cause of one's daily problems. So if the lawsuit is a David v. Goliath type dispute, a jury will probably be more receptive to the plight of "the little person".

If ABC, Corp. sues Mr. and Mrs. Macgillicuddy and does not ask for a jury trial, this is a clear signal and opportunity for the defendants to request it. By doing so, they have increased their bargaining leverage and will hopefully achieve a favorable settlement. Again, the judge won't do this for the parties; they have to make the chess moves themselves.

The author was a civil trial lawyer early in his career and spent many a day and night inside courtrooms, and has a special appreciation for the trial process. The scales of justice are a graphic visual metaphor for the ebb and flow of first one party and then the other trying to persuade the decision maker to rule in their favor. The trial is like a fencing contest, a flowing back and forth of thrust and parry, point and counterpoint between plaintiff and defendant. At any stage of a trial, one of the parties may decide to surrender or judge/ jury may seize upon a key aspect of the evidence presented by plaintiff or defendant to turn the scales in their favor.

Here are the chronological steps in a typical civil lawsuit: (Remember, whatever the plaintiff or defendant allege in their pleadings must be proven by the greater weight of the evidence.)

1. The lawsuit starts with the filing of the plaintiff's COMPLAINT, which summarizes the ultimate facts of the dispute, alleges that defendant is at fault, and requests appropriate court relief.

2. The SUMMONS accompanies the Complaint, directing the defendant to appear in court or otherwise respond, usually within 20 days. The court clerk issues it, and then summons and complaint are served by an officer of the court to achieve jurisdiction over the person of the defendant. Service may be made upon resident or non-resident defendants. If the latter, they will often try to resist the disadvantage of having to defend in the plaintiff's back yard by claiming they were not "doing business" within the forum state.

   If the defendant ignores the legal papers served and fails to respond within the required time, a default judgment may be entered by the court in favor of the plaintiff.

3. JURISDICTIONAL MOTIONS are filed by the defendant within the 20-day response time if there is to be a contest of the court's jurisdiction. If they are granted as to improper service of process, faulty venue or removal to a different court, the case may also be settled at this stage.

4. The ANSWER is filed by the defendant after the jurisdictional motions have been decided or if none were filed, again within the initial 20-day period, or later if permitted by the court. The answer summarizes the defendant's case, admits or denies specific allegation of the complaint, and states affirmative defenses claimed by the defendant. These defenses are any legal grounds that would bar the plaintiff's lawsuit.

For example, if Car A is rear-ended by Car B, the law of negligence presumes that Car B is at fault. Car A files a complaint, which alleges that Car B struck it from the rear. In the answer filed by Car B, the collision is admitted but liability may be denied based upon allegations that Car A made a sudden stop, which raises the affirmative defense of contributory negligence.

Another common affirmative defense raised by defendants is the "statute of limitations". Every state has laws that specify the period of time within which the plaintiff must bring a lawsuit. Even if a complaining party has a good case based upon the facts and applicable law, it may be dismissed if not filed in time. Here's an actual case:

> In July 1991, Whirlpool Financial Corp. (Whirlpool) loaned $10 million to GN Holdings, Inc. (GN) to help it acquire another company. To secure this financing, GN furnished to Whirlpool a private placement memorandum with certain financial projections. Three years later, GN defaulted and Whirlpool sued for securities fraud. GN raised the one-year statute of limitations in federal Securities laws as an affirmative defense and won the case. The claim of Whirlpool was time-barred. *Whirlpool Financial Corp. v. GN Holdings, Inc., 67 F.3d 605 (7th Cir.1995).*

5.   COUNTERCLAIMS are sometimes filed by a defendant, as a part of his answer, if he claims a legal injury arising from the same set of facts. This reverses the roles of the parties, whereby the defendant is the cross-plaintiff, the plaintiff is now the cross-defendant, and the original plaintiff must now file an answer (called a reply) to the counterclaim.

6.   DISCOVERY is unique in the American legal system, and is the stage of the proceedings where most settlements are reached. This is due to the fact that now the parties can find out all the details of what really took place in the dispute, rather than the preliminary pleadings, which have just been summaries of events. Additional benefits are that once full disclosures have been made, even if the case continues, there will be no surprises.

- Production of Documents – lists of witnesses, reports of experts, all the relevant correspondence, files, contracts, memorandums, and other items, including e-mail messages and other electronic evidence.

- Mental or Physical Examinations – can be ordered in cases where the parties may claim damages for personal injuries or emotional distress, or their physical and mental conditions are at issue.

- Interrogatories – written questions submitted by the parties which must be answered under oath, and to which documents may need to be attached. This usually elicits information as to who knows about important facts, and where further information might be found.

- Depositions – oral interrogations of parties and witnesses in the presence of their lawyers, transcribed by a court reporter and often videotaped to preserve evidence for future usage at trial if necessary, or for impeachment purposes to protect against a deponent's story being changed at trial.

7. PRETRIAL CONFERENCE is theoretically where the parties appear before the judge in an informal setting to discuss their respective positions, identify the major areas of dispute, agree upon witnesses and documentary evidence, estimate how long it will take to complete their cases, and have the judge set the actual trial date. In actuality, this is used more and more by judges to try and convince the parties to settle their differences, by subtle and not so subtle persuasion. Court dockets are filled to overflowing in our litigious society, and a success from the judge's standpoint is one less open case.

8. PRETRIAL MOTIONS are usually made by the parties once a court date has been set (although they can be made at any stage of the proceedings), in which they try to convince the judge that (a) they should win because the complaint or counterclaim fails to state a cause of action (Motion to Dismiss), or (b) They should win based solely upon the pleadings filed (Motion for Judgment on the Pleadings), or (c) They should win because there are no real issues of fact to be litigated based upon all the evidence and they should win based upon the applicable rules of law (Motion for Summary Judgment).

9. THE TRIAL is non-jury if neither party requested a jury trial. The judge then decides all issues of fact and law. In a jury trial, the judge rules on issues of the law and the jury determines issues of the facts, including the importance of the evidence and believability of the witnesses.

   Let's assume that the plaintiff or defendant has made a jury demand and we will have a jury trial. Notice the symmetry of the trial process in the following steps of a typical jury trial, where plaintiff initiates and defendant responds, as each side tries to tip the scales of justice in their favor: (Remember when we refer to the "parties", their attorneys will really be performing)

- Jury Selection - *voir dire* is the process of selecting potential jurors from the pool of voters who are called for jury duty. They are assembled at the courthouse, assigned to a courtroom, seated in groups usually of 6, and then asked questions by the judge and both parties to determine if they are unbiased and can make a fair and impartial decision. Each party has a number of "challenges", where they can excuse a juror they feel is biased. New potential jurors are then seated in the jury box. The process continues until both sides "accept the panel".

- Opening Statements - this is a preview of their respective cases presented by the parties. The seated jury is told what the parties intend to prove, what witnesses they will hear, what evidence they will see, and what their desired ruling should be.

- The Plaintiff's case – the entire case is presented through the testimony of the plaintiff and witnesses, and all supporting documents are introduced into evidence. As the plaintiff and witnesses "take the witness stand", they are sworn in by the court clerk, they "swear to tell the whole truth and nothing but the truth", and are then questioned by plaintiff's counsel on direct examination. Defendant can then cross-examine about statements and documents covered in direct examination. The plaintiff's task is to satisfy its burden of proof, and convince the jury to decide in its favor. The end of the plaintiff's case is signified by stating, "the Plaintiff rests."

  The defendant usually moves for a directed verdict in his favor at this point, based upon the plaintiff's alleged failure to satisfy the required burden of proof. It is routinely denied if there is any evidence at all on which the jury might rule for the plaintiff.

- The Defendant's case – the same process occurs as previously, just in reverse order, where the entire defense case is presented, and then the plaintiff can cross-examine. The defendant's task is to rebut the plaintiff's case, prove any affirmative defenses raised, and otherwise convince the jury to vote in its favor. When finished, "the defendant rests, "

  Now the plaintiff usually moves for a directed verdict based upon the defendant's alleged failure to prove his case, and again it will routinely be denied. Courts are reluctant to take a case away from the jury if there is any evidence in the record upon which they could rule for the non-moving party.

- Rebuttal – if the plaintiff feels the need to counter or clarify some of the defendant's case, the judge may allow additional related testimony or documents. In most current jury trials however, all necessary evidence is usually presented in the main cases.

- Charging conference – this is the least understood of the jury trial process. Since the jury needs to know what rules of law to apply to the facts they have heard from testimony and seen through the documents in evidence, each party confers with the judge in private chambers while the jury is in recess. Plaintiff and defendant offer the rules of law they believe should apply to the case, called "jury instructions", the judge decides which one or parts of both to use, and then the judge convenes the jury and presents these rules to them for use in their deliberations.

- Closing Statements – the parties summarize to the jury what they have seen and heard in the main cases, and try to convince then one last time to rule in their favor. The jurors will be reminded of what the parties promised to do in their opening statements and then be assured that those promises were kept. The jurors are also told what rules of law the judge will require them to use in deciding the case.

- Jury Instructions – the judge reads to the jurors the rules of law they will be using in this case that he has chosen from the charging conference, and then sends them to the jury room to make their decision.

- Jury Deliberations – the jurors retire to the jury room where they appoint a foreperson, to be in charge of organizing their decision-making process. They are provided with all the items that have been introduced into evidence as well as the written jury instructions. They take a preliminary vote, have discussions, which are sometimes quite heated, and ultimately reach a majority decision.

- The Judgment – the decision of the jury is written, handed to the court bailiff who is on call and then the judge is informed. The court proceedings are reconvened and the judge reads the decision to the parties, and enters judgment in favor of plaintiff or defendant accordingly. If the judgment is for plaintiff, it usually is a two-part award, which declares the (1) *liability* of the defendant and (2) awards a stated dollar amount of money *damages*.

10. POST-TRIAL PROCEDURES:

- The judge may hear post-trial motions of either party. If the losing party feels the amount of damages is excessive it requests a remittitur. If the winning party feels damages are too low it requests an additur.

- If the losing party claims misconduct or bias by the jurors, the attorneys or, in the rare instance, the presiding judge, it files a motion for a new trial.

  In *Minichiello v. The Supper Club, et al, 745 N.Y.S.2d 24 (N.Y. App. Div. 2002)*, plaintiff alleged he was verbally and physically abused by defendants because of his sexual orientation, and then wrongfully fired when he refused to quit his position as late night manager of the restaurant-cabaret owned by defendants.

  The jury awarded him compensatory and punitive damages exceeding $20 million. Defendants appealed, contending that the damages were grossly excessive, based upon misconduct of both plaintiff's counsel and the trial judge, including counsel's analogy references of plaintiff's German boss to Nazi Germany and the Holocaust, as well as other inappropriate comments about African-Americans, Latinos and Jews. The judge also made demeaning remarks in the jury's presence.

  The appellate court reversed and ordered a new trial, saying, "the cumulative effect of the many irrelevant and highly prejudicial comments made by plaintiff's counsel in the course of the trial only served to incite the jury's passion and sympathy and effectively prevented a fair and dispassionate consideration of the evidence."

- The loser may also file a motion for judgment in its favor, notwithstanding the jury decision, called a judgment n.o.v. which is similar to a motion for directed verdict filed before the jury deliberates. It asserts that no "reasonable" jury could have ruled in favor of the winning party. It is rare when this motion will be granted, because it nullifies the jury's verdict.

- The jury is commonly polled by the losing party to verify that its announced judgment is correct. The winning party may also question the jurors as to the reasons for their decision, as a learning experience for future trial technique.

11. COLLECTING THE JUDGMENT:

This area is the subject of much public confusion as to how and when a winning plaintiff gets paid. Contrary to what most people think, you don't automatically get paid when you win a money judgment. At the same time, most winning judgments are paid by the defendants within 10 days of entry. Why? Simply because the compulsion to pay is prompted by the fact that all assets in the name of the defendant are at risk and can be legally seized and sold at auction.

If the judgment is not paid within the required time, which varies from State-to-state, the plaintiff files a request for issuance of a "writ of execution" and the court then orders its civil collection office to enforce the judgment.

What if the defendant becomes judgment-proof by transferring assets out of his name? Since the same court that entered the judgment retains jurisdiction to collect it, and since there is always a paper trail of transfers to evade the claims of judgment creditors, the judge can invalidate them and order the assets back into the name of the defendant so that they are now available for collection by the plaintiff.

What if the defendant really has no collectible assets? The issue here is time. A judgment is legally enforceable, state-to-state, for anywhere from 5 to 20 years, and interest accrues on the balance due like any other indebtedness. Judgment creditors have the right to periodically interrogate defendants under oath as to their current finances. This is called a "deposition in aid of execution". Once assets are discovered, the collection process can be completed. (Note: Before you sue someone, you usually do a preliminary investigation of their financial condition. If they don't have assets, why bother to sue?)

For example, suppose Able sues Baker and recovers a money judgment for $100,000. Able is unable to locate any assets in Baker's name at the present time. The state law provides that money judgments are valid for 10 years. Five years later Able reads in the local paper that Baker just won the lottery. Guess what? Able can now complete the collection process and have the judgment satisfied.

12. APPEAL
is the right of any losing party in most civil cases. Usually a pleading called a "Notice of Appeal" has to be filed within 30 to 90 days after the adverse judgment has been entered. But what most people don't realize is that the mere filing of this notice does NOT automatically stay the process of collection of the judgment. The winning party can still seize and sell any assets found in the defendant's name.

The only way this can be prevented is by the defendant posting an "Appeal Bond" to assure that the plaintiff will be paid if the defendant loses the appeal.

No new evidence or testimony may be presented on appeal. The appellate court reviews the record of the trial proceedings to determine if there were any substantial errors of law, or the factual findings were so faulty that they were unsupported by any evidence. (Remember, the appellate court can affirm the lower court decision, reverse it, or remand and order a new trial.)

A practical problem that often arises in the appellate process is the delay in collection it can cause. Suppose a jury has just awarded $10 million and the losing party immediately announces they will appeal. A defense strategy of dragging out a case as long as possible, especially in the small versus large litigant cases, will often result in a settlement favorable to the losing party, because many plaintiff's and their attorneys cannot afford to wait the year or more it takes for an appeal to be finalized.

Or suppose the losing party at the trial court level wants to appeal, but lacks the necessary funds. Again, this lack often will prevent an otherwise meritorious appeal, and induce a settlement advantageous to the winning party.

There are however alternatives available to the parties. They can try to finance their appeal with banks or other conventional lenders, but often are refused due to the speculative nature of such matters. Or, they can go to a number of private investment companies that specialize in financing appeals on a contingent basis by purchasing for cash a participation in the expected final recovery. They make money by buying at a discount, and provide the needed funds for an appellant to hire an appellate specialist or otherwise be able to complete the appeal. Often, the fact that the appeal will be financed leads to a settlement of the entire matter.

DISCUSSION EXERCISES

1. Discuss in what types of cases, as a plaintiff, you would want a jury trial? In what types would you want a non-jury trial?

2. Discuss in what types of cases, as a defendant, you would want a jury trial? In what types would you want a non-jury trial?

3. Discuss what jurisdictional motions you think most effective.

4. Discuss what pre/post trial motions you think most effective.

CASE EXERCISES

JUDGMENT N.O.V. GRANTED AGAINST WINNING PLAINTIFFS

In *Ferlito v. Johnson & Johnson, 983 F.2d 1066 (6th Cir. 1992)*, plaintiffs filed a products liability action, based upon a failure to warn theory, for injuries suffered by Mr. Ferlito when his Halloween sheep costume made from his long underwear, glue and defendant's cotton batting suddenly ignited as he lit a cigarette and engulfed him in flames. He suffered burns over one-third of his body and underwent several surgeries due to the fire.

The cotton batting is marketed and sold by defendant to clean wounds, apply medication, and for infant care. There were no product use warnings on the product box.

ANALYSIS

Based upon a failure to warn theory, the jury awarded Mr. Ferlito $550,000 and Mrs. Ferlito $70,000 after finding both plaintiffs and defendant equally at fault under comparative negligence for causing the fire.

After the jury returned its verdict, defendant moved for judgment n.o.v. which was granted by the trial court, setting aside the jury verdict, because the plaintiffs "failed to produce any evidence that the failure to warn would have dissuaded them from using the product."

The appellate court affirmed, noting, "When suing under a failure to warn theory, Michigan law requires the plaintiff to prove that if a proper warning had been given, the plaintiff would have taken precautions to prevent injury."

The court did not have to decide if a warning was necessary, but noted the facts of the case appeared to fall within the principle that, "if the risk is obvious from the characteristics of the product, the product itself telegraphs the precise warning."

DEFUSE REPLAY

This case is a rare instance when the trial judge disregards a jury verdict. Judgment n.o.v. is an extreme remedy because the court's granting of the motion takes the case away from the jury as well as denying the usual appellate review of their verdict.

"A judgment notwithstanding the verdict may not be granted unless reasonable minds could not differ as to the conclusions to be drawn from the evidence."

All the plaintiff's had to do was testify, as the court points out, "how their conduct would have differed if there had been a warning on the box of cotton material."

CONCLUSION

The court points out, "Neither plaintiff testified that they would not have used the cotton had they been warned." Incredible, but true. Their case was based upon a failure to warn theory but its essential legal elements were ignored in their presentation.

No questions were asked of them by their counsel to elicit this simple and logical response, so no such evidence was in the court record. Therefore, the jury verdict was clearly unsupported and set aside by the trial judge. This apparent fundamental error of the plaintiff's attorney comes very close to professional malpractice.

This case result is still unusual. Trial judges rarely take cases away from the jury, and even less frequently disturb their verdict once it is rendered. Let the appellate court decide, say most judges, since that is their job and not ours.

An appellate court, if it finds substantial error in the trial proceedings, will usually remand the case to the court below for further proceedings. However, it is also legally authorized to directly enter judgment against a jury-verdict winner, if it determines that the verdict was clearly erroneous.

"Courts of appeal should be constantly alert to the trial judge's firsthand knowledge of witnesses, testimony, and issues; in other words, appellate courts should give due consideration to the first-instance decision maker's 'feel' for the overall case. But the court of appeals has authority to render the final decision." *Weisgram v. Marley Company, 528 U.S. 440 (2000).*

A. Do you agree with the court's final decision?
B. If you were the presiding judge, would you have coached the plaintiff's counsel to ask the crucial questions?
C. Should judges take such a hand-on approach to cases where it appears mistakes are being made?

DON'T MESS WITH SHIRLEY MACLAINE

The case of *Parker v. Twentieth Century Fox Film Corporation, 474 P.2d 689 (Cal. 1970),* involved a dispute between actress Shirley Maclaine (Parker) and her movie studio.

She had contracted to play the female lead in a musical to be shot in Los Angeles, exhibiting her singing and dancing skills, for a fixed fee of $750,000. The studio decided against making that film, and offered her another film at the same compensation, but it was a dramatic western to be shot in Australia. She declined, and sued to recover the agreed contract price. The studio admitted it breached her contract, but defended claiming she failed to mitigate damages by accepting the part in the substitute film. She moved for summary judgment.

ANALYSIS

The trial court granted plaintiff's motion for summary judgment, on the basis that there were no genuine issues as to any material facts and she was entitled to judgment as a matter of law. It awarded her $750,000 plus interest.

On appeal by the defendant, the California Supreme Court affirmed, stating, "defendant has raised no issue of reasonableness of efforts by plaintiff to obtain other employment; the sole issue is whether plaintiff's refusal of defendant's substitute offer of 'Big Country' may be used in mitigation . . . the offer of the 'Big Country' lead was of employment both different and inferior, and that no factual dispute was presented on that issue."

DEFUSE REPLAY

Since a motion for summary judgment requires the judge to assume that all facts in the pleadings are true, the key to prevention is making the necessary factual allegations in the complaint or answer. Whether they can be proved at trial is another issue, but at least their inclusion will thwart summary judgment.

CONCLUSION

Part of the anticipatory thinking in the judicial process is strategic defensive maneuvering. Filing a complaint that is summary judgment proof may well advance the case to the point of meaningful settlement negotiations. Similarly, an answer that raises, for the purpose of that pleading, significant factual issues may well push the negotiating scales in the defendant's favor.

A. Do you agree with the court's final decision?
B. Should the plaintiff be paid the full contract price even if she does nothing?
C. Is it ethical to create factual issues that may never be proven solely to prevent the granting of summary judgment?

CASE RESEARCH CYBERCISES

The following cases also relate to the material in this chapter and illustrate the types of disputes that may occur. For each one do the following written assignment:

1. Locate the case using the Internet (Lexis-Nexis, West or any other research cite which provides case transcripts).
2. Briefly summarize what it was about – the nature of the dispute involved.
3. Who won at the trial court level? Who won at the appellate level?
4. Who won if there was a third level of Supreme Court review?
5. What were the legal rules of law and the reasoning used to reach the final decision?
6. Do you agree or disagree with the decision, and explain why?
7. What business law time bomb(s) were involved?
8. Could the time bomb(s) have been avoided by structuring the transaction differently? Discuss.
9. Could the adverse effects of the time bomb(s) have been defused by a different reaction or response by the affected party? Discuss.
10. Replay the facts of the case to achieve a different successful result.

1. *Mallik v. Jeff Wyler Fairfield, Inc., 2000 WL 1693246 (Ohio. App. 2000) (notice of appeal mailed one day before deadline but received four days after is valid.*
2. *Dolphin v. Wilson, 983 S.W.2d 113 (Ark. 1998) (trial court may not allow new pleadings after a remand).*
3. *Hughes Development Co. v. Omega Realty Co., 951 S.W.2d 615 (Mo. 1977) (two statutes of limitations for contracts are clarified – 10 years for written contracts and 5 years for all others).*

NOTES

9.

CREATING THE CONTRACT

A. BASIC CONTRACT CONCEPTS

"All sensible people are selfish,
and nature is tugging at every contract to make the terms of it fair."
Ralph Waldo Emerson

"To me, party platforms are contracts with the people."
Harry S. Truman

A. LAW OVERVIEW

The commercial transaction is the vehicle of business.

The engine that powers that vehicle in the business marketplace is the contract.

Contracts are created by the legally enforceable *agreements* of the parties to buy, sell or trade goods and services.

The legal existence of any agreement depends upon whether or not the offeror has made a valid offer and the offeree has validly accepted it.

This formula is stated as: OFFER + ACCEPTANCE = AGREEMENT (O+A=AG). Its significance to the world of business is similar to the importance of Einstein's $E = MC(2)$ to the world of physics.

The legal definition of a contract is "an agreement between two or more parties that is legally enforceable in the event of a breach." Thus, the agreement forms the essential foundation of all contracts. (Enforceability depends upon Consideration, Capacity, Legality and Written Form issues examined in later chapters)

Notice the interconnectedness of the O+A elements of the agreement.

If there is no valid offer, there is nothing to accept and there can be no agreement. If there is a valid offer but an invalid acceptance, there still is no agreement. In either situation, if there is no agreement, there can be no contract.

Even if there is a valid agreement, meaning that we have both legal offer and legal acceptance, that agreement must still be legally enforceable if one of the parties fails to properly perform.

* Ex.: Al calls Sylvia and says, "I offer to pick you up at eight, for a date, I won't be late." Sylvia accepts, saying, "I can hardly wait." When Al fails to show up, he has breached their agreement. Sylvia is probably upset, but she has no legal recourse because social arrangements of this type have no legal remedy for the breach.

Many of our daily agreements fall in this category. A party may fail to do what they promised, or do something that they weren't supposed to do. In either case, it usually never occurs to us to question whether or not these broken agreements have legal consequences.

But if we can change the facts of the example just a bit, we reach an entirely different result as to the enforceability of the agreement.

*Ex: Al calls Sylvia and says, "I offer to pick you up at eight, *so you won't be late for your job interview.*" Sylvia accepts, saying, I can hardly wait, *I'm relying on you.*" When Al fails to show up, *Sylvia loses the job to someone else not as qualified as her.* Al's breach of their agreement is actionable under a contract fairness doctrine we'll talk about later called "promissory estoppel".

The key point in time for most agreements is when the parties progress beyond their preliminary negotiations and reach a mutual understanding that involves the exchange of their promises of performance.

"It is hornbook law that the existence of an enforceable contract is dependent upon agreement of the parties, or *meeting of the minds*, upon the terms of that contract." *Smith v. Hammons, 2002 WL 5694 (Mo.Ct.App. 2002).*

There are two basic sources of contract law:

- Common law - these are the legal rules or *precedents* that have been developed by the judiciary from federal, state and local court decisions in contract disputes.

- Statutes – these are legislative enactments on the state and federal levels that relate to contract disputes.

- Uniform Commercial Code (UCC) – this is a body of specialized statutory law that applies to *sales of goods*. It attempts to assist the successful completion of commercial transactions and codifies the different contract laws of the various states in one *uniform* source, so there is uniformity and predictability of the probable outcome of such disputes, no matter where they occur. Every state has adopted it in whole or part.

It often provides a more flexible interpretation in promoting enforcement of contractual agreements than the common law rules, which tend to be more rigid and technical.

In many cases, the ultimate court decision will depend upon whether or not it is applicable. The UCC does not apply to:

1. sale of services
2. sale of real estate
3. sale of intangibles, such as stocks and bonds
4. gifts of goods

Most contract disputes are hybrid, mixing both goods and services. So how do the courts determine whether or not the UCC is applicable?

In *Pass v. Shelby Aviation, Inc., 2000 WL 388775 (Tenn.Ct.App.2000)*, plaintiffs died in a crash of their private plane, and their estate sued the defendant which had performed the annual inspection on the airplane, on a theory of breach of warranty. (warranty recovery is a UCC concept where sellers of goods are legally responsible for defects) The trial court denied defendant's motion to dismiss, holding the matter to be a UCC warranty transaction. The appellate court reversed, holding the transaction to be predominantly the provision of a service, not the sale of goods.

" Most jurisdictions follow one of two different approached to address the problem (of mixed transactions) . . . the first approach, sometimes called the 'gravamen test', looks to that portion of the transaction upon which the complaint is based, to determine if it involved goods or services. The other approach, known as the 'predominant factor' or predominant purpose test', looks at the transaction as a whole to determine whether its predominant purpose was the sale of goods or the provision of a service."

In adopting the 'predominant purpose test' as the law of Tennessee, the court noted it used a weighing test and explained what factors it looks at to make its rulings:

"We examine the language of the parties' contract, the nature of the business of the supplier of the goods and services, the reason the parties entered into the contract (i.e. what each bargained to receive), and the respective amounts charged under the contract for goods and services."

This last factor of cost allocation is the easiest way for parties to identify their transaction as either a sale of goods or services.

*Ex: Sonia goes to her dentist for a check up. He tells her she needs a gold inlay, and the cost will be $1,000. This is a typical mixed transaction. The inlay itself is goods, and its installation by her dentist is services. If this transaction is a sale of goods, Sonia has warranty protection. If it is services, warranty law does not apply.

Normally, this type of professional services would not carry any warranties. However, if Sonia had the dentist allocate a majority of the price on her bill to the inlay ($550 for the gold and $450 for installation), she could create a "sale of goods" and have warranty protection just in case a problem arose.

Let's understand some general terminology of contracts:

- The Offeror makes the initial promise to do or not do something.
- The Offeree receives the offer, and can create an agreement by *acceptance*.
- The Offeree can also *reject* the offer, causing it to terminate.
- The Offeree can also make a *counteroffer*, reversing their roles.
- The Offeror can *revoke* the offer at any time before acceptance.
- An inquiry or question has no legal effect on contract negotiations.

    *Ex: Sam wants to sell his car for $5,000. He tells Herb the basic details. Herb asks if the car has a cd player and an alarm system. When Sam confirms, Herb proposes a price of $4,000. Sam refuses to sell for less than $4,500. While Herb is deciding whether or not to raise his price, Sam agrees to sell the car to Sally for $4,750. Then Herb agrees to pay the $4,000 and Sam tells him he's too late. Herb is mad and wants to sue for breach of contract. He asks your advice.

This is a typical scenario. All contracts start with preliminary negotiations between the parties. At some point they may ripen into a legal agreement (O+A), which, if legally enforceable, may be called a contract.

Let's identify what has happened. Sam and Herb were negotiating. Sam made the initial offer of $5,000. Herb's clarifying question has no legal effect. Herb's proposal of $4,000 is a counteroffer, which rejects the original offer and makes Herb the new offeror. Sam's agreement to sell the car to Sally is a revocation of his $4,500 offer to sell it to Herb. Herb has no legal rights.

There are two basic forms of contracts, depending upon what the offeree does in exchange for the offeror's promise:

- *Bilateral* form is the most common type of contract. It is best described as "a promise for a promise." The contract if formed when the promises are exchanged.

*Ex: Cynthia offers to sell her car to Rita for $5,000 cash. Rita accepts the offer. There is a bilateral contract formed when Rita agrees. The later actions of Cynthia delivering the car in exchange for Rita's payment of money are only relevant if either party fails to perform.

In the case of *D.L. Peoples Group, Inc. v. Hawley, 2002 WL 63351 (Fla.App. 2002),* Hawley was hired by a Florida college to recruit students in Missouri. He had never visited Florida, but was offered the job on a recommendation. He signed the employment contract in Missouri, and then mailed it to Florida where it was signed by the college president. While attempting to recruit a student in Missouri, Hawley was shot and killed. His heirs claimed he was entitled to receive Florida worker's compensation, but the trial judge denied the claim. It was reversed on appeal, the court ruling a bilateral contract existed, and "A contract is created where the last act necessary to make a binding agreement takes place."

- *Unilateral* form occurs in those situations where the acceptance requires the offeree to complete the performance of an act, rather than just promise to perform. It is called, "a promise for an act," and sometimes involves special rules when the parties have a dispute.

  *Ex: Harold hires ABC, Inc. to paint his house. He says, "I offer to pay you $2,000 when you finish the job." This is unilateral form, where the acceptance is an action rather than a mere promise. The wording is critical. If ABC, Inc. had accepted Harold's "... promise to pay you $2,000 to paint my house," we would have a bilateral contract.

- Unless the language of the contract is clearly unilateral, it is presumed to be in bilateral form.

There are also certain classifications of contracts:

- Executed contract – fully completed by both offeror and offeree.
- Executory contract – some required performance remains to be completed.

  *Ex: Sara and Ernest make a bilateral contract for Sara to buy Ernest's computer system for a fixed price, closing in one week. When Sara pays the agreed price and Ernest delivers the merchandise, the contract is executed. After the exchange of promises that creates the contract but before the time to close, it is still executory.

- Valid contract – legally enforceable by one or both of the parties.
- Voidable contract – although it may be valid, one of the parties may have the legal right to elect to cancel it.

- Void contract - has no legal effect and is not enforceable, such as a contract to commit a crime. (Discussed in a later chapter)

Contracts fall into three main types:

- EXPRESS contracts occur when all the essential facts are spelled out, either verbally or in writing. These details usually include a description of the subject matter, the price, payment time and terms such as cash or credit, the quantity and details of delivery if involving goods, and any other important terms.

  *Ex: George goes to the local computer store. He sees a sign that states, "Zip diskettes on sale today." George asks the clerk, "Do you have any Zip 100 disks?" The clerk replies, "Yes sir, we have one six-pack left. You have to buy the whole pack and the price is $55. George says, "sold," hands the cashier his credit card, and when the sale is completed the clerk puts the merchandise in a bag and tells George, "Bye now, have a nice day."

- IMPLIED contracts occur when some of the essential details of the transaction are not expressed, and must be inferred from the conduct of the parties, their past dealings, or the customs of the trade. These are known as "implied-in- fact" contracts. Written and spoken words have provided the essential terms.

  *Ex: Harry wakes up with laryngitis, and slips in the shower injuring his writing hand. He needs some zip 100 computer diskettes, so he drives to the local computer store. He walks in, locates the product, picks up a six-pack, goes to the cashier check-out and puts the diskettes down with a $100 bill. The cashier neither speaks nor writes anything as Harry's disks are put into a bag, he is handed his change, and as Harry leaves the cashier waves goodbye. The essential terms are implied solely from the conduct of the parties – subject matter, quantity, price, terms, and delivery.

  In *Schism v. U.S., 2002 WL 109422 (3d Cir. 2001)*, plaintiffs were retired veterans over 65, who each had more than 20 years of active military service. Their military recruiters had promised them free lifetime medical care benefits, which were later changed by Congress, moving them into Medicare, which is not free. They sued for breach of implied contract. The trial court rejected their claims, but the appellate court reversed, stating,

"An implied-in-fact contract is one founded upon a meeting of minds which, although not embodied in an express contract, is inferred, as a fact, from the conduct of the parties showing, in the light of the circumstances, their tacit understanding."

- QUASI CONTRACTS are called "implied-in-law" because, unlike express or implied contract situations, the parties have no intended dealings with each other.

Normally this would prevent any contractual relationship, but in the interest of fairness to prevent one party from being unjustly enriched at the expense of the other, the law pretends they made a contract and requires payment of the fair value of the goods or services involved. These types of contracts are legal fictions that often arise when one party mistakenly confers a gratuitous benefit on another. The legal cause of action is called *quantum meruit*.

> *Ex: Mr. and Mrs. Jones have a nice home in a suburban housing development where the houses resemble each other. Their front driveway needs re-paving and they call Miami Asphalting Co. for an estimate. Its president, Ernest, offers to do the job for a fair price of $1,000, completion next Thursday, and they accept. On that date, Ernest forgets their address and starts to re-pave their neighbor Jerry's driveway by mistake. Both houses look similar, and both driveways were in poor condition. In fact, Jerry was meaning to do re-paving but never got around to it. Jerry is inside the house when Ernest begins, watches him fully complete the job, and then admires his new driveway after Ernest leaves. Ernest sends his bill to Mr. and Mrs. Jones, they object, Ernest realizes his mistake, and sends his bill to Jerry. Jerry refuses to pay claiming no contract exists. Ernest sues Jerry claiming breach of quasi-contract. Who wins and why? Let's analyze this case.

There certainly was no express or implied contractual relationship between Jerry and Miami Asphalting Co. The key to this dispute is whether or not Jerry was "unjustly enriched". If he was, he is required by law to pay for the work done, even though he never ordered it. Unjust enrichment is another way of saying *unfair benefit*. Certainly Jerry received a benefit from Ernest's mistake. He now has a newly paved driveway. But that is only half the legal test – was it unfair, meaning could he reasonably have prevented the mistake from happening? In this case, the answer is yes. He should have stopped the work as soon as he realized it had started, rather than unfairly taking advantage of it.

If we change the facts of the case just a bit however, we also reach a different result. What if Jerry wasn't home when Ernest re-paved his driveway?

Let's say he was at work in his downtown office, and arrived home to find a brand new driveway. He probably smiled, looked up in the sky, and said, "Thank you. This is my lucky day." And it would be just that because he could not have reasonably prevented the mistake, and therefore was not *unfairly* benefited. He has received a free benefit. This makes sense, because the problem was solely caused by the mistake, not enhanced by any conduct of Jerry.

There is a legal maxim that applies to these mistaken benefit cases. "Where one of two parties must bear a loss, it shall be the party who caused it, or who could have reasonably prevented it.

Quasi contract has also been described as the 'garbage can' for losing claims, because plaintiffs often raise it as a catch-all category of a fairness principle to try and justify their recovery. Courts apply this doctrine carefully however, for that very reason, and try to limit its application only to proper cases.

In *Castillo v. Tyson, 701 N.Y.S.2d 423 (N.Y. App.Div. 2000)*, pay-per-viewers of the heavyweight championship-boxing match between Mike Tyson and Evander Holyfield sued the fight promoters and telecasters for a refund of their money because Tyson was disqualified for biting off part of Holyfield's ear. They claimed various breach of contract theories, including unjust enrichment. The trial court dismissed the suit and the appellate court affirmed.

"Plaintiffs are not in contractual privity with any of the defendants, and their claims that they are third-party beneficiaries of one or more of the contracts that defendants entered into among themselves was aptly rejected by (the lower court) as contrived. Nothing in these contracts can be understood as promising a fight that did not end in a disqualification. The rules of the governing commission provide for disqualification, and it is a possibility that a fight fan can reasonably expect. The plaintiffs paid for what they got: 'the right to view whatever event transpired'."

In *DCB Construction Company, Inc. v. Central City Development Co., 940 P.2d 958 (Colo.App. 1997)*, plaintiff was a contractor that was hired by a lessee to do $300,000 worth of alteration to the building lessee was leasing from the defendant. Defendant notified plaintiff that that it had no legal responsibility for the work. Lessee stopped paying rent, and was evicted by defendant before it had paid plaintiff. Plaintiff sued defendant, claiming unjust enrichment for the work done to defendant's building. The trial court awarded $280,000, but the appellate court reversed, saying, "The mere fact that a benefit has been bestowed on Development Co., and that it appreciated the benefit, is not enough to give rise to a claim for unjust enrichment."

To recover, the plaintiff must show that: 1) a benefit was conferred upon the defendant; 2) defendant appreciated the benefit; and 3) the benefit was accepted by defendant under such circumstances that it would be inequitable for it to be retained without payment of its value."

Examples of proper cases are:

- Plaintiff made valuable improvements to defendant's bar and then was prohibited to operate it because she could not legally hold a liquor license. She had the right to recover the value of non-removable items. *Duncan v. Kasim, 2002 WL 125686 (Fla. App. 2002).*

- Plaintiff paid defendant's real estate taxes due to an error by the tax assessor's office, and then sued to recover the amount of the over assessment on the theory of unjust enrichment. The trial court entered summary judgment for plaintiff. *Partipilo v. Hallman, 510 N.E.2d 8 (Ill. App. 1987).*

- Wife and Husband mutually agreed she would pay for his three years of law school and, when he finished, he would pay for her master's degree. She fulfilled her part of the agreement, but he then initiated divorce proceedings. She claimed entitlement to restitution in quantum meruit to prevent his unjust enrichment because of receiving his education at her expense. The court awarded her reimbursement for the Husband's living and educational expenses she had paid. *Pyeatte v. Pyeatte, 661 P.2d 196 (Az. App. 1982).*

A fourth type of contract category is PROMISSORY ESTOPPEL, which is another fairness doctrine that sometimes binds the parties when the three main types of contracts are not applicable. It applies in circumstances where:

1) the promisor makes a contract promise under circumstances where he knows, or reasonably should know, the promisee will rely upon it, and

2) the promisee does, in fact, reasonably rely upon the promisor's promise, by changing his position, and

3) the promisee suffers financial loss of some kind due to this detrimental reliance.

If all these elements are present, the promisor is *estopped* to deny the legal efficacy of his *promise.*

Like quasi contract, there is no real contractual relationship in promissory estoppel. Rather, the alleged unfairness is urged as the reason to create the fictional contractual transaction. Under these circumstances, although plaintiffs often try to raise it, courts allow its application sparingly.

This doctrine is used in appropriate cases throughout the law of contracts, as a type of legal agreement, a way to prevent revocation of an offer, as a substitute for required consideration, and in any disputes where one party relies upon promises made by another.

In *Charter Township of Ypsilanti v. General Motors Corporation, 506 N.W.2d 556 (Mich. App. 1993),* plaintiff awarded defendant substantial property tax abatements at its local plant, to attract their location and the creation and maintenance of local employment they created. Four years after the last tax exemption award, defendant decided to consolidate its operations because of economic necessity, and moved the operations to Texas. Plaintiff sued for breach of contract and promissory estoppel. While the trial court found the tax abatement did not create a contract between the parties, it did find defendant was bound by promissory estoppel:

"There would be a gross inequity and patent unfairness if General Motors, having lulled the people of the Ypsilanti area into giving up millions of tax dollars which they so desperately need to educate their children and provide basic governmental services, is allowed to simply decide it will desert 4500 workers and their families because it thinks it can make these cars cheaper somewhere else."

But the appellate court reversed, holding that "promissory estoppel requires an actual, clear and definite promise," and "the mere fact that a corporation solicits a tax abatement and persuades a municipality with assurances of jobs cannot be evidence of a promise."

Another key to this case, which at first glance seems to support promissory estoppel, is the failure of the plaintiff to "reasonably" rely upon the alleged promise not to relocate if tax exemptions were granted. There were no guarantees made by the defendant, but they could easily have been required by the plaintiff's inclusion of a clause in the tax abatement that read:

"In consideration for the tax exemptions granted herein, General Motors does hereby agree not to relocate the plant(s) for a period of _____ years, or reduce its local work force below _____ employees. Default in either of these assurances shall require General Motors to reimburse Ypsilanti Township for the full dollar amount of the tax abatements granted."

This clause would have protected plaintiff, but would defendant have agreed to it? Since plaintiff never sought it in the negotiations between the parties, we'll never know.

This use of anticipatory thinking and preventive law could at the very least have produced some concessions from the defendant in exchange for the tax exemptions offered.

A fifth type of contract category has arisen out of the practical legal necessities created by the rise in our society of non-marital living relationships, and is called PALIMONY. While technically a form of implied contract, these types of cases are so distinctive that a separate category is probably warranted.

When traditional marital relationships end, in the absence of pre-agreed financial arrangements between the parties that arise under a pre-nuptial or post-nuptial agreement, the law of alimony customarily allows a temporary rehabilitative award by the court to the less financially advantaged spouse, to provide her or him an opportunity to get back into the work force or otherwise be able once again to self-provide.

But what if there is no marital relationship, yet the parties have been living together as husband and wife for many years? What if the parties produce and raise children as a result of this non-legal union? What if financial promises are made from one to the other regarding lifetime support and/or conveyance of assets?

The old concept of common-law marriage has long been abolished in all states. So the legal rights, if any, of parties in an alleged palimony relationship are based upon contract, and the legal enforceability or lack thereof of the financial promises made.

In *Sopko v. Roccamonte, 787 A.2d 198 (Sup. Ct. N.J. 2001)*, Mary Sopko sued the Estate of Arthur Roccamonte for lifetime support, based upon verbal promises made to her during the course of a thirty year intimate relationship she had with the decedent, while he was married to another, that "I will take care of you", and "You will be taken care of for the rest of your life."

Decedent lived with plaintiff and her daughter in a co-op apartment he purchased even though he was married to Elise. She testified she performed all services for him consistent with that of a housewife. He bought her an engagement ring and wedding band, and otherwise held out their relationship as marital. He lavishly supported plaintiff, and his promises of lifetime support increased in the last ten years of his life when he suffered from throat cancer.

But at the same time he filed joint spousal tax returns with Elise, told plaintiff he could not marry her because Elise would not grant him a divorce due to matters involving the family business, ran that business, kept his assets separate, and refused to make a will setting forth his inheritance wishes. Plaintiff also had her own job, and kept her own assets separate during their relationship.

Upon Arthur's death, he left Mary the co-op and its contents, as well as personal items, a bank cd and life insurance valued over $50,000, but the value of those items would have been far less than a computation of her "lifetime support".

The trial court dismissed plaintiff's suit for lifetime support, on the grounds that she had stated no claim for any contractual relief, including that of palimony, and that the promises in question were vague and indefinite. "It would seem that in New Jersey to allow palimony it must be limited and must be narrowly applied and to be utilized only where there is an express agreement between the parties, almost complete dependency by one cohabitant on the other and the equitable element that one party has 'tossed aside' the other unfairly."

The appellate court reversed and remanded, entering judgment for plaintiff, with the amount of damages for breach of the lifetime support contract to be assessed by the lower court, viewing the trial court's ruling as "overly narrow." "We differ, however, with the trial judge's analysis regarding the legal tests for plaintiff's 'palimony' claim, *i.e.*, her theories of express or implied contract."

"A 'palimony' claim is, by definition, based upon theories of express or implied oral contract. Whether we designate the agreement reached by the parties in 1968 to be express, as we do here, or implied is of no legal consequence. The only difference is in the nature of the proof of the agreement. Parties entering this type of relationship usually do not record their understanding in specific legalese. Rather, as here, the terms of their agreement are to be found in their respective versions of the agreement, and their acts and conduct in the light of the subject matter and the surrounding circumstances."

The case is now on final appeal to the New Jersey Supreme Court. Will the trial court's strict interpretation of palimony prevail, or will the appellate court's more liberal view be upheld? We shall see.

DISCUSSION EXERCISES

1. Discuss your own example of a bilateral express contract.
2. Discuss your own example of a unilateral express contract.
3. Discuss your own example of an implied contract.
4. Discuss your own example of a quasi contract.
5. Discuss situations when you think the courts properly apply promissory estoppel.

CASE EXERCISES

PALIMONY AS A NON-MARITAL CONTRACT

In *Marvin v. Marvin, 557 P.2d 106 (Cal. 1976)*, the concept of a contractual financial obligation existing between unmarried persons, to become known as "palimony", was first judicially recognized, as the California Supreme Court decided what principles should govern distribution of property acquired in a nonmarital relationship.

At the time of this case, the state had conflicting appellate court decisions which either required division of property under its community property laws (50% division of property acquired during the "marriage"), or rejected such nonmarital property rights.

This case involved the living-together relationship of 7 years between actor, Lee Marvin, and his "significant other" Michelle.

She alleged she and defendant had verbally agreed that while "the parties lived together they would combine their efforts and earnings and would share equally any and all property accumulated as a result of their efforts whether individual or combined." In addition, they agreed to "hold themselves out to the general public as husband and wife."

She claimed she agreed to give up her career as an entertainer and singer in order to "devote her full time to defendant . . . as a companion, homemaker, housekeeper and cook." In return defendant allegedly agreed to "provide for all of plaintiff's financial support and needs for the rest of her life."

The parties lived together from 1964 through 1970 and conducted their lives to give the outward appearance they were married, after defendant's divorce in 1967. They often introduced themselves as husband and wife, and described their relationship as one of marriage. Plaintiff used the surname, "Marvin", throughout their relationship.

During this time assets of over $1 million were acquired in defendant's name. In May of 1970, defendant ordered plaintiff to leave the household and continued to support plaintiff until November of 1971, but thereafter refused to provide further support. Plaintiff then sued for a court declaration of her rights pursuant to her contractual agreement(s) with defendant, under which she allegedly was entitled to receive one-half of the marital property.

ANALYSIS

The trial court granted the defendant's motion for judgment on the pleadings, ruling that plaintiff had no legal recognizable claim since there was no marital relationship.

The appellate court reversed and remanded the case back to the trial court to allow her a trial on the merits of her claim. It ruled that the allegations of plaintiff's complaint did state a suitable contractual basis for recovery, whether in express or implied contract:

"Contracts may be express or implied. These terms however do not denote different kinds of contracts, but have reference to the evidence by which the agreement between the parties is shown. If the agreement is shown by the direct words of the parties, spoken or written, the contract is said to be an express one. But if such agreement can only be shown by the acts and conduct of the parties, interpreted in the light of the subject matter and the surrounding circumstances, then the contract is an implied one."

The court considered each of the defendant's four arguments to affirm the lower court and rejected each as follows:

1. The non-marital relationship of the parties is "immoral" and against public policy, so their contracts are not legally enforceable.

   "The fact that a man and woman live together without marriage, and engage in a sexual relationship, does not in itself invalidate agreements between them relating to their earnings, property, or expenses."

2. The alleged contract is invalid as an agreement to promote or encourage divorce.

   "The contract between plaintiff and defendant did not, however, by its terms require defendant to divorce Betty, nor reward him for so doing."

3. The statute that requires that 'All contracts for marriage settlements must be in writing' bars enforcement of the alleged oral agreement.

   "A marriage settlement, however, is an agreement in contemplation of marriage, in which each party agrees to release or modify the property rights which would otherwise arise from the marriage. Our review of the many cases enforcing agreements between nonmarital partners reveals that the majority of such agreements were oral."

4. Enforcement of the contract is barred by the statute that provides, 'No cause of action arises for . . . breach of promise of marriage.'

"Numerous cases have enforced pooling agreements between nonmarital partners."

DEFUSE REPLAY

Lee Marvin found himself in a "damned if you do-damned if you don't" legal dilemma. He didn't deny the verbal promises exchanged regarding the pooling of resources and sharing of assets. Instead, his legal arguments were directed to their alleged non – enforceability. If he had denied them, the plaintiff would have had the burden of proving them, but the other outward manifestations of the 'marital' nature of the parties' relationship, including defendant's willing participation in creating their appearance as a married couple, would have contradicted him and lent support to the alleged oral agreements.

Lee raised the argument that the oral agreement claimed by the plaintiff had to be written, and the court correctly stated it did not due to the fact that it was *not* a marriage settlement. This points us to what he should have done – have a written agreement with Michelle as soon as his divorce from Betty was final - so that there would be no subsequent disputes of a "he said – she said" nature regarding alleged oral agreements.

The written agreement could be a form of pre-nuptial contract for unmarried persons that clearly stated each party claimed no interest in the separate assets of each other. Failing that, it could have set forth a mutually agreed formula for lump sum or periodic payments to Michelle upon the dissolution of their relationship.

There could also have been financial provision for the surviving partner in the event of death, funded by term life insurance. One of the bargaining chips to induce Michelle to sign off on property rights could have been such a term policy on Lee's life, since he was the financially secure older party. It could have named her as beneficiary and been fully paid, so that she was guaranteed additional financial security upon his demise.

By having no written agreements of any kind regarding property rights upon the conclusion of the relationship, combined with the 'marital' conduct of the parties, and residence in a community property state like California - it would appear that Lee intended there to be some financial provision made for Michelle.

CONCLUSION

The law has changed considerably over the years regarding contractual property rights of unmarried couples.

Through the end of the 1800's, when this country was still rural, agrarian, and not well educated in the legal aspects of business and personal relationships, couples who lived together for an extended time were either legally married or had essentially the same rights under the doctrine of common law marriage.

In the event of disputes regarding spousal property rights, the essential evidence would be production of a valid marriage license as an express marriage contract, or implied contract proofs of sufficient surrounding facts and conduct of the parties to substantiate they were living together and holding themselves out to the world as if they were husband and wife.

Then, after the turn of the century, the industrial revolution, the movement of population to the cities, modernizing of education, transportation, communication and, of course, education – a change took place. All states abolished common law marriage, as being the legal sanctioning of an 'immoral relationship', archaic, hard to prove, and a doctrine which encouraged contentious litigation every time the relationship of an unmarried couple ended.

But then, as society became more liberal in thought and actions, the pendulum swung back to a needed legal recognition of the property rights of unmarried couples, and the culmination of the non-spousal legal concept of financial rights became known as "palimony".

The media attention to this case was enormous, both because of the high profile of the defendant as a movie star and the legal consequences involved. Plaintiff's attorney, Marvin M. Mitchelson gained quite a bit of notoriety for his coining of the "palimony" term, and almost overnight became one of the country's best-known and most successful domestic relations lawyers. This case did for him in terms of national publicity, what the O.J. Simpson criminal case did for attorney Johnny Cochran.

Notice how this case involves aspects of all our prior chapters:

- Preventive Law – the strategies employed by plaintiff and not employed by defendant were critical to the case's outcome.

- To Sue or Not? – plaintiff chose to seek judicial relief, even though her case may have appeared questionable to some observers

- Hiring a Lawyer – this case was an opportunity for plaintiff's counsel to make a name for himself on a national scale, and he was employed, according to his later interviews, on a contingency basis.

- Why Laws? – financial rights of unmarried couples reflect how laws and their interpretation and enforcement change as our society evolves.

- We now have a state like Vermont that legally permits same sex marriages, and statutes and case law of other states that provide property rights in same gender relationships.

- Sources of Law – both statutory and case law, as well as reliance on precedent, was used as persuasive authority for the legal arguments made in this case.

- Where to Sue? – the jurisdiction of the court system was clearly an issue, since the California Supreme Court accepted this case to resolve the conflicts that existed in prior decisions of its appellate courts.

- Legal Remedy – this case involved both traditional legal remedies for contract damages and equitable remedy requests relating to the unique aspects of non-marital cohabitation disputes.

- How to Sue? – the presentation of the conflicting arguments of the parties through their complaint and answer, motion for judgment on the pleadings, and the appellate process are all involved in this case.

- Creating the Contract – the legal dispute between the parties is for breach of alleged express or implied contract, and the court bases its decision to remand on the alleged existence of such contracts.

A. Do you agree with the court's final decision?
B. Should the financial rights of "palimony" be allowed for same sex partners? If so, under what circumstances?
C. Does this decision encourage "immoral" cohabitation?

CASE RESEARCH CYBERCISES

The following cases also relate to the material in this chapter and illustrate the types of disputes that may occur. For each one do the following written assignment:

1. Locate the case using the Internet (Lexis-Nexis, West or any other research cite which provides case transcripts).
2. Briefly summarize what it was about – the nature of the dispute involved.
3. Who won at the trial court level? Who won at the appellate level?
4. Who won if there was a third level of Supreme Court review?
5. What were the legal rules of law and the reasoning used to reach the final decision?
6. Do you agree or disagree with the decision, and explain why?
7. What business law time bomb(s) were involved?
8. Could the time bomb(s) have been avoided by structuring the transaction differently? Discuss.

9. Could the adverse effects of the time bomb(s) have been defused by a different reaction or response by the affected party? Discuss.
10. Replay the facts of the case to achieve a different successful result.

1. *Hector v. Cedars-Sinai Medical Center, 180 Cal.App.3d 493 (Cal. App. 1986) (breach of warranty claim for personal injuries from implantation of pacemaker held not a sale of goods under UCC).*
2. *Dines v. Liberty Mutual Insurance Company, 548 N.E.2d 1268 (Mass. App. 1990)(implied contract exists to pay storage charges on police recovery of stolen trailer).*
3. *Rappaport v. Buske, 2000 WL 1224828 (S.D.N.Y. 2000) (alleged oral contract to host TV series held to be only a non-enforceable preliminary agreement).*

NOTES

10.

CREATING THE CONTRACT

B.   IS THERE A VALID OFFER?

" I'll make him an offer he can't refuse."
Mario Puzo: The Godfather

There is a negotiating dance the parties engage in preceding the creation of any offer. In the common purchase or sale transaction these dance steps consist of inquiries, preliminary discussions, invitations for offers, sales talk, soft and hard bargaining, and varied combinations of all of these. Ultimately, a legal offer must be made by the offeror before we proceed with the Acceptance side of the (O+A=Agreement) equation.

The legal disputes are typical.   As in all contract cases, the plaintiff wants to enforce it because he thinks he made a good business deal, and claims breach of contract by the non-performing party. The defendant wants to avoid the legal consequences of the contract because he views the transaction as a bad deal, and asserts whatever legal grounds are available to cancel the contract or otherwise not be legally bound.

I. THE LEGAL REQUIREMENTS

The three required legal elements for a valid offer are:

1.   intention to make a contract
2.   definiteness in the required terms
3.   communication to the offeree

Let's examine them one by one, since all three must be present.

1.   There must be a current and immediate desire to enter into a contract. This "present intention" is not legally judged by the personal or subjective standard that relates only to the specific offeror. The actual intentions of the parties are irrelevant.   Instead, modern contract theory requires the objective test, stated in terms of whether or not the particular facts as viewed through the eyes of a hypothetical reasonable *person* indicate it most likely that the offeror intends to be legally bound.

"A contract has, strictly speaking, nothing to do with the personal, or individual, intent of the parties. A contract is an obligation attached by the mere force of law to certain acts of the parties, usually words, which ordinarily accompany and represent a known intent.

If, however, it were proved by twenty bishops that either party, when he used the words, intended something else than the usual meaning which the law imposed on them, he would still be held, unless there were mutual mistake, or something else of the sort." Judge Learned Hand, speaking in *Hotchkiss v. National City Bank, 200 F. 287 (S.D.N.Y. 1911)*.

Suppose Kim desires to buy a boat from Jim. Assume Jim's response to each of the following statements by Kim is, "I accept your offer." Let's see how the invisible line between preliminary negotiations and the actual offer typically fluctuates:

- "Is the boat for sale?" - no offer, just a beginning inquiry.
- "I'd like to buy your boat." – again just an inquiry in the negotiations.
- "I can't pay more than $500." – sets a bargaining ceiling, but the parties are still dancing.
- Jim replies, "I can't sell for less than $450." – sets a bargaining floor and the dance continues.
- " I'll take it." – the dancing is over and we have an offer.

2. The terms of the offer must be definite, clear and unequivocal, so that the offeree can properly frame an appropriate response. Under the common law definiteness rules, there can be *no gaps* in the essential terms of the offer. These requirements are very strict. If any of the following are missing, there is no valid offer:

- Identity of the parties
- Description of the subject matter
- Price to be paid and terms of purchase
- Quantity
- Time of performance
- Place of delivery
- Special features

In *Gonzalez v. Don King Productions, Inc., 17 F.Supp.2d 313 (S.D.N.Y. 1998)*, Plaintiff, a highly ranked professional boxer, sued to void a "promotional agreement" and"bout agreement" between himself and defendant, for a boxing match with Julio Cesar Chavez, on grounds that they lacked essential terms regarding compensation for future bouts after the Chavez fight, and were just "agreements to agree in the future".

The agreements were poorly drafted, but apparently provided that if plaintiff won the Chavez match, he would receive at least $75,000 for the next fight, and if he lost he would receive at least $25,000 for the next fight, "unless the parties of this Contract agree otherwise."

The Chavez match ended in a draw, and plaintiff, who wanted to get out of having to deal with Don King, claimed the purse for subsequent matches could not be determined with sufficient certainty, and the contract was therefore unenforceable due to indefiniteness. Plaintiff moved for summary judgment.

The court denied the motion, agreeing with defendant, who wanted to hold plaintiff to the contracts, that when read in context, they "could be interpreted as setting a default purse of $25,000 if the parties cannot agree."

"A price term may be sufficiently definite if the amount can be determined objectively without the need for new expressions by the parties; a method for reducing uncertainty to certainty might, for example, be found within the agreement or ascertained by reference to an extrinsic event, commercial practice or trade usage."

(An interesting side note to this case was that it was almost identical to a prior dispute Don King had with Buster Douglas, after his surprise knockout of heavyweight champion Mike Tyson, when he had both under contract. *Don King Productions v. Douglas, 742 F.Supp 741 (S.D.N.Y. 1990)*.

Under the Uniform Commercial Code (UCC), sales of goods transactions are treated more liberally as to required definiteness. The UCC will fill the gaps with what would be *reasonable* under the circumstances. While any missing terms would destroy the alleged offer under the common law, the UCC will keep the potential agreement viable and allow the offer to be valid.

3. The offeree must obviously be aware of the offer in order to respond to it with a question, a rejection, a counteroffer or an acceptance. This awareness requires that the offer be properly communicated to the offeree. Communication can be direct and instantaneous such as a face-to-face conversation or a phone call.

It also can be indirect, such as *receiving* the written offer by regular mail, electronic mail, fax, telegram, the arrival of a messenger or by carrier pigeon. The point is that it is not when the offer is sent that is critical; rather, it is the moment of receipt. And the communicator must be the offeror, or his authorized agent.

> *Ex: Herbert and John have been discussing John's proposed purchase of Herbert's house. John dictates a tentative offer to his secretary. She places it on his desk for review, where John's wife Arleen is awaiting his return from the bank. The phone rings, Arleen answers, Herbert is calling about the house deal, and Arleen reads him the offer. Herbert says, "I accept the offer." John then doesn't want to perform because his price is too high. Herbert likes the deal and demands performance. John claims no valid offer, because it wasn't properly communicated (by him) to Herbert. John wins the dispute because John's wife was acting on his behalf.

Another potential communications problem involves wording that is on the back of offers or is written in *fine print.* The typical dispute involves an offeree who claims not to be aware of certain portions of the offer and, of course, the offeror claims they were binding.

Originally, the cases held that offerees were legally bound by all the terms of the written offer since they should reasonably have read everything before acceptance. However, as business became more intricate and fast paced, and offers became more lengthy and complex, the original rules began to change as offerors often tried to take advantage of offerees by inserting provisions heavily weighted in their favor, hoping that the offeree wouldn't notice. Another fairness principle evolved.

Modern courts recognized this problem and remedied it by the rule that offerees are only legally bound by terms of the offer for which they had actual or reasonable notice. The UCC is similarly critical of non-obvious contract terms.

II. SPECIAL SITUATIONS

A. Statements made in anger, jest or the heat of passion are not valid offers, because a reasonable offeree would understand that the offeror does not really intent to contract. Here we again apply the objective standard to evaluate.

Here's a true story. The author was attending a pro football game in Miami between the Miami Dolphins and Houston Oilers. The winner would clinch a spot in the playoffs. With five seconds to play, Miami was losing by 4 points, but had the ball on the Houston ½ yard line, and had time left for one more play. The ball was handed to the Miami fullback who leaped into the end zone (hooray?), without the ball (Oops!), because he had fumbled. Houston recovered the ball, time ran out, and Miami lost the game.

At that moment, one of the Miami fans (A) jumped up waving his next year's season tickets and yelled, "I've had it. Whoever gives me $20 for these damn tickets (face value $500) gets them." The fan next to him (B) pulled out a $20 bill and said, "I accept your offer." A then told B to forget about it, and B claimed there was a valid contract. If B had sued A for breach of agreement, no problem to pick the winner here. It would reasonably appear that A was not seriously intending to sell because he was angry and frustrated, and B should not have reasonably relied on A's statement as an offer to sell.

In *Leonard v. Pepsico, Inc., 88 F.Supp.2d 116 (S.D.N.Y. 1999),* plaintiff filed suit for specific performance based upon defendant's Pepsi Stuff television commercial that encouraged consumers to collect 'Pepsi Points' from specially marked packages of Pepsi or Diet Pepsi and redeem these points for merchandise.

The merchandise included a U.S. Marine Corps "Harrier Fighter (jet airplane for) 7,000,000 Pepsi Points."

The commercial began talking about basic merchandise that would appeal to "the Pepsi generation" such as t-shirts, leather jackets and 'cool' sunglasses, and then shifted to a military music and a view of the jet plane while a voiceover and print overlay stated, "Drink Pepsi – Get Stuff."

Plaintiff set out to perform the required actions to accept the offer by consuming Pepsi products, but "it soon became clear to him that he would not be able to buy (let alone drink) enough Pepsi to collect the necessary Pepsi Points fast enough."

Plaintiff then noted from the Pepsi gift catalogue that values of promotional merchandise were based upon monetary equivalents of $.10 per point, (it listed 53 items ranging from a jacket tattoo for 15 points to a mountain bike for 3300 points) so he raised the money to buy the necessary Pepsi Points, and submitted a check for $700,000 to defendant to purchase a new Harrier Jet, which would cost $23 million if purchased on the open market. That item was not shown in the catalog.

Defendant's motion for summary judgment was granted, on the basis that:

"First, the commercial was merely an advertisement, not a unilateral offer. Plaintiff's letter with the Order Form and the appropriate number of Pepsi Points, constituted the offer. There would be no enforceable contract until defendant accepted the Order Form and cashed the check.

Second, the tongue-in-cheek attitude of the commercial would not cause a reasonable person to conclude that a soft drink company would be giving away fighter planes as a part of a promotion."

The court went on to state the commercial was evidently done in jest. "The commercial is the embodiment of what defendant appropriately characterizes as 'zany humor'. The implication of the commercial is that Pepsi Stuff merchandise will inject drama and moment into hitherto unexceptional lives. A reasonable viewer would understand such advertisements as mere puffery, not as statements of fact."

B. Advertisements for the sale of goods are generally not considered to be offers, even if they say "special offer". They are regarded as only invitations for offers; a part of the sales dance in the usual situations involving print and visual media ads, mail order catalogues, ad circulars and handouts, price lists and quotation sheets. The rationale for this general rule is based again on the objective standard, where it is not reasonable to believe a seller with limited quantities of goods intends to contract with every person who sees the ad.

*Ex: Pete receives the Cycling USA catalogue that has on page 46 a "Special Offer for our newest 15 speed touring bike, only $175." He calls to accept the offer and pay with his credit card. The seller tells him, "Sorry, we're sold out, so we cannot accept *your offer to buy*." Pete loses the dispute. He should reasonably know the seller would not fill every order.

But Pete is now an unhappy customer; so prudent sellers try to avoid this problem by stating in their ads, "quantities may be limited", or "product availability subject to prior sale".

Sellers also have to be careful of the consumer laws passed by most states, which prohibit "bait and switch" advertising. This unlawful practice involves a seller who advertises an item at a very attractive price, knowing in advance that it is not available. Instead it is used as bait to get the customer into the store, and try to sell him a more expensive item.

*Ex: George reads a newspaper ad where Computer Associates offers to sell one of its Compaq Presario reconditioned computers at a terrific price. In truth, there are none available. When he arrives, the salesperson tells him they are sold out, but "while you're here why don't you look at our new models that just arrived?"

As is the case with most of our general rules of law, there is a fairness exception that applies in factual situations where the ad in question is so definite that the specific item is identifiable, terms of sale are specified, or some special performance by the offeree is required. In both instances, a reasonable offeree would believe the offeror had the present intent to contract.

*Ex: When Peter returns to his car in the parking garage, there is an ad flyer from Downtown Camera Co. on his windshield that offers for sale, "Kodak model 2200 digital camera, serial number #123456, black with silver trim, 1.23 lens, full read out and PC hookups, only $99, first 100 customers guaranteed sale, doors open tomorrow at 9am." Peter is the 50th customer (he waited in line and counted those ahead of him). If the seller refuses to sell, claiming the ad flyer just invited offers, they lose, because it was so specific that customers could reasonably rely on it.

There are cases that illustrate both the general rule and the exception:

• Advertisement mailed to plaintiffs from United States Mint to purchase Statute of Liberty commemorative coins ruled not an offer. "Generally, it is considered unreasonable for a person to believe that advertisements and solicitations are offers that bind the advertiser.

Otherwise, the advertiser could be bound by an excessive number of contracts requiring delivery of goods far in excess of amounts available." *Mesaros v. USA, 845 F.2d 1576 (Fed. Cir. 1988).*

- Kennel club's advertisement to pay $25,000 to party that picked six winners, which was erroneously printed by newspaper as $825,000, was a binding offer. "If a member of the public buys a winning ticket on six races, he has accepted the offer and the parties have a contract." *Jackson v. Investment Corporation of Palm Beach, 585 So.2d 949 (Fla. App. 1991).*

C. Rewards for the return of lost items, or for information leading to the capture of criminals, fall into the category of unilateral form offers. They offer the promise of money or other value to be paid upon the completion by the offeree of the designation action. Disputes in this "promise for an act" type of case arise when the offeree peforms the required act to entitle him to the reward without knowing ahead of time of its existence.

Remember, communication of the offer to the offeree is one of the prerequisites for a valid offer. If the "an act" part of the unilateral offer is done without knowledge of the "promise for" part, most courts will not enforce payment of the reward. The law aside, most people will still "do the right thing" and honor their reward promises. They usually are so grateful that it is not a problem. But from a technical legality point of view, prior knowledge of the reward by the offeree is required.

> *Ex: Mrs. Magillicuddy is very upset because her cat Henry has run away. She posts a notice on her mailbox offering "a $100 reward to anyone who finds my dear tabby Henry and returns him to me." Susan is a jogger, and during her morning run she hears a loud meowing that seems to be coming from above. She looks up and sees an orange cat in a tree, apparently afraid to come down. She tries to do at least one good deed every day, so she climbs up and rescues the cat. It has a collar tag that says, "My name is Henry, and my Mommy live at 123 Main Street." Susan jogs over to that address, and returns the cat to the overjoyed owner. On her way back to the street she sees the reward notice, reads it and then goes back to claim the reward. Mrs. Magillicuddy does not legally have to pay (but hopefully she will also do her daily good deed).

D. Auctions can be both enjoyable and profitable, if you know the legal rules that govern them. They are governed by the UCC. There are two types of auctions, "with reserve" and "without reserve". If the terms of the auction are not specified, it is considered to be "with reserve".

1. If with reserve, the "offer" of the auctioneer requesting bids on an item is really just an invitation for offers. The high bid is the offer. The auctioneer may legally refuse to honor it if the price is too low and withdraw the item.

2. If without reserve, the start of the auction by the auctioneer is a legal offer to sell the item and the high bid, no matter how low, is a legal acceptance.

Here's another true story. When Ed was an active litigator, he would also handle his appellate arguments. They were heard either in Atlanta or New Orleans. On this occasion the argument was in New Orleans at 4pm. In those days, Bourbon Street was asleep during the day, except for a number of auction houses. To pass the time before his oral argument, he wandered into one of them. He noticed that an item to be auctioned was a large English Regulator wall clock, complete with mahogany cabinet and musical chimes. They sold at that time for over $500. When that item was "offered up for bids" by the auctioneer, he raised his hand to ask a question. "Would you please confirm that this auction is without reserve?" The auctioneer seemed confused and didn't respond. "This is an auction without reserve, isn't it? Ed said again, nodding his head and smiling at the auctioneer. "Yes, sure it is," said the auctioneer.

The auction of the clock started and Ed bid $100. No other bids were made. "Come on folks, this is a fine imported Regulator clock, it's worth much more than $100," said the auctioneer. He then began his countdown. "Going once, going twice, last call for any other bids. Sorry, we'll have to withdraw the item." Ed raised his hand again. "Excuse me, mine was the high bid, and you have to sell the clock to me. The auctioneer gave him quite a look. "What are you, a lawyer or something?" "Yes," Ed said. "Why don't you call a short recess and we'll talk about auctions without reserve." That clock still stands in the corner of his office, many years later, keeping perfect time as it chimes the hours.

III. REVOCATION OF OFFERS – BY OFFEROR

The offeror is said to be *master of his offer*. The offeror not only decides to make the offer, but also determines its specific terms, can limit its duration to a specified time period or event, and can even require a particular method and manner of acceptance by the offeree.

If no duration is specified, the general rule is that the offeree has the legal right to withdraw it at any time before it has been legally accepted. This is called the offeror's *right to revoke*. This is an absolute right, and applies even if the offeror has specifically promised to hold the offer open for a stated period of time. The revocation is effective when actually communicated to the offeree, or under circumstances where he knows or reasonably should know it has been withdrawn.

*Ex: Eva decides it's time to buy a new automobile. She goes to the local dealer, test drives a few models, and chooses her particular car. The salesperson, Frank, offers to sell it to her at a "special price", but she needs more time to decide. Frank tells her, "Take 30 days little lady, the car will be here waiting for you." On day 20, Louise sees the car, offers a higher price than the one quoted to Eva, and Frank sells it to her. On day 22, Eva returns to the showroom to complete the purchase. She sees the car on the lot with a sign saying its been sold to Louise. When Eva confronts Frank, he says, "Too bad, you shouldn't have waited so long." The car sale was a valid revocation of Frank's offer before Eva's acceptance.

In *Prenger v. Baumhoer, 914 S.W.2d 413 (Mo. App. 1996)*, plaintiff sought to buy real estate from defendant. After the parties and their attorneys met, seller's counsel prepared a letter suggesting they parties had reached "tentative agreement" about basic terms, including a price of $925,000 contingent upon financing, and included "further contingencies".

Seller then contracted to sell the property to another buyer, for $925,000 on an all cash basis. Plaintiff obtained its financing approval, and sued for injunctive relief to prevent the other sale, and requested specific performance of their contract.

The trial court granted defendant's motion to dismiss, and the appellate court affirmed, stating, "The language itself imparts the notion that this letter was not a final agreement and that more terms needed to be agreed upon and realized." It "is at most an agreement to negotiate a future contract, with a tentative agreement upon some of the terms of the anticipated future contract."

The way an offeree can be protected against the general rule of revocation is to make the offer legally *irrevocable*. There are four major ways an offeree can skillfully do this, each of which shifts the decision-making power from the offeror to the offeree. We'll use the same factual example above to illustrate the first two of these exceptions to the general rule:

1. CREATE AN OPTION - this is a separate contract that has the legal effect of requiring the offeror to hold the offer open for the time specified. It can be verbal or written, has no limitation on its duration, and requires the offeree to pay the offeror something of value in consideration for its creation. The amount of value is immaterial, as long as it is accepted by the offeror.

*Ex: Eva's factual situation is the same as above, to the point when Frank offers it to her at a "special price", but she needs more time to decide and Frank tells her, "Take 30 days little lady, the car will be here waiting for you."

Eva starts to leave but then remembers her business law training, and says to Frank, "Do me a favor, I'm taking a course, let's put this on a business basis, here's a shiny new penny to bind our deal." When Frank accepts the penny, an option is created, and he is legally prevented from revoking his offer for the agreed 30 days.

When Eva decides to proceed she, as the optionee, *exercises* her option. The amount paid for it is retained by the optionor as the price for the option contract, and not credited toward the purchase price unless the parties have agreed otherwise. If she passes on the deal, she has allowed her option to *lapse*. Again the amount paid is forfeited, unless the parties have agreed on a partial or full refund.

2. **CREATE A UCC FIRM OFFER** – this will also make the offer irrevocable, like an option, but differs in these aspects:

- Only applies to a sale of goods
- Seller must be a merchant for these goods (his primary business)
- Offer must be in some type of written form
- Maximum time period is 90 days
- Nothing of value need be exchanged

*Ex: After Frank tells Eva, "Take 30 days little lady, the car will be here waiting for you," she again offers to put the deal on a business basis with her tender of the shiny penny, hoping to create an option. However Frank says, "I can't accept anything from you, don't worry, we have a deal, don't you trust me?" Eva then says, "You know I have a terrible memory and when I return to buy the car, which I'll probably do, I want you to get your sales commission for the sale, and so do you have a business card? Please write on the back the car's description, the price and other terms, my 30 days to think it over, and sign or initial it." Once Frank does this and hands the card to Eva (and there's no reason for him to refuse), she has made the offer legally irrevocable for the 30 days, and it didn't cost her anything.

3. **PROMISSORY ESTOPPEL** – this is another fairness doctrine that applies when one party suffers damages, because they changed their position by relying upon a promise that the other party originally made and now tries to revoke. The promisor is legally prevented (estopped) from withdrawing their promise if:

- Promisor makes the promise
- Promisor knows promisee intends to rely on it
- Promisee does change position, relying on it
- Promisee suffers legal detriment (damages)

*Ex: Able General Contracting intends to bid on the University of Miami's new campus library project. It solicits bids from its subcontractors, telling them, "Give us your lowest bid offers, so we can add our profit and overhead, and make our final submittal to UM. If we get the job, your offer is accepted." Baker Plumbing gives its $50,000 bid offer to do all plumbing work, which Able puts into its final bid. UM announces to the press that Able is low bidder and will get the job. Before Able can accept the plumbing bid, Baker tries to revoke, relying on the general rule.

The law will not allow this. Baker is estopped to revoke its bid promise. Otherwise subcontract bidders could extort higher prices and take unfair advantage of the general contractors. This fairness principle is a relative of the Quasi Contract doctrine of "unjust enrichment" (unfair benefit) that we visited in a prior chapter.

4. UNILATERAL CONTRACT OFFERS – the potential for unfairness in "promise for an act" contracts is that the offeror may wait until 99% of the job is completed, and then announce that he is revoking. He has the legal right to do this under the general rule, because acceptance requires *completion* of the promised action, and revocation is occurring before that occurs. So an exception was created to prevent such an injustice. It provides that once the offeree starts the required act, the offeror's power to revoke is legally suspended for the agreed time to perform. If no time is specified, the offeree must proceed in good faith for the time "reasonably necessary" to complete.

*Ex: Sam offers to pay $1,000 to James, "upon your completion of covering my patio in one foot square Spanish tiles." James begins the job and is down to the last 4 tiles when Sam, realizing he is paying too much, tells James to stop the work because he is revoking his offer.

The inherent unfairness is obvious. Sam is trying to use the general rule of revocation to take advantage of James, who was acting in good faith. The law in this type of situation seeks to protect the innocent party.

IV. REJECTION OF OFFERS – BY OFFEREE

Once a valid offer is made to the offeree, one possible response other than an inquiry or an outright acceptance is a *rejection*. It may be made expressly in verbal or written form ("no, not interested, forget about it"), or the result of the offeree's conduct (shake your head, walk away, ignore it). In either case, it must be communicated to the offeror to be effective.

Once rejected, the original offer is legally terminated, and can no longer be accepted. Any attempt to resurrect it by the original offeree is a counteroffer.

> *Ex: Jones has been looking at an oil painting done by Smith and asks, "How much?" Smith replies, "$5,000." Jones says, "Too high for my budget," and starts to walk away. Jones stops and says, "O.K you drive a hard bargain, but I'll pay your price, I accept your offer." Smith says, "Sorry, the painting is no longer for sale to you." Jones claims they made a legal agreement, and Smith claims no agreement because the offer was no longer on the table. Smith wins.

In *Papa v. New York Telephone Company, 528 N.E.2d 512 (N.Y.App. 1988),* plaintiff signed an order form to place its advertisement in defendant's telephone yellow pages. The form provided that, "Publication of any unit in any issue of the directory specified shall constitute acceptance of this order for such unit with respect to such issue only. The omission of a unit from any issue of the directory shall constitute a rejection by the Company . . ." Plaintiff sued for damages resulting from defendant's failure to include its ad.

The trial court granted defendant's motion to dismiss, and the appellate court affirmed, stating, "The order form therefore constituted a mere offer to make a unilateral offer." Defendant's not performing the required act of publication of the ad was a rejection of plaintiff's offer, and no contractual obligation existed.

If the offeree's response to an offer is to add, eliminate or modify in any material way the basic terms, it is a *counteroffer*. Counteroffers are legal rejections of the original offer and the creation of a new offer.

> *Ex: Jones has been looking at an oil painting done by Smith and asks, "How much?" Smith replies, "$5,000." Jones says, "I'll give you $4,000 for it." Smith does not reply. Later Smith agrees to sell it to another buyer for $3,750. Jones objects, and claims that Smith was legally obligated to sell to him. Wrong – Jones's counteroffer terminated the original offer and was never accepted by Smith.

V. OFFER TERMINATION BY OPERATION OF LAW

Certain external circumstances may arise, having nothing to do with the conduct of the parties, which cause the offer to legally terminate:

> 1. Subsequent illegality - after a valid offer is communicated to the offeree, a law is passed making the subject matter illegal. (A offers to sell to B diet pills containing ephedrine, which are later declared a controlled substance by the FDA and banned from sale.)

2. Destruction of the subject matter – the merchandise offered is destroyed through no fault of either party. (A offers to sell his car to B, and a hurricane, tornado, earthquake, or other natural disaster destroys it.)

3. Death or disability of the offeror – in a personal service offer, the offeror becomes physically or mentally unable to perform due to accident or illness. (Tiger Woods offers to appear for a golf exhibition, and then is involved in an auto accident, which physically prevents him from performing.)

DISCUSSION EXERCISES

1. Discuss how to determine when preliminary negotiations become the intention to make an offer.

2. Discuss how to determine the legal dividing line between fine print and the reasonable communication of an offer.

3. Discuss fairness exceptions that might allow you to claim a reward even though you did not have prior knowledge of it.

4. Discuss the fairness of allowing an offeror to revoke by selling to a higher offeree even though the offer states it will remain open.

5. Discuss whether the law should allow gap filling for missing terms in offers for the sale of goods.

CASE EXERCISES

SELF-STYLED TAX EXPERT GETS TAUGHT A LESSON

In *Newman v. Schiff, 778 F.2d 460 (8th Cir. 1985)*, defendant was a tax rebel who called himself, "America's leading untax expert." He espoused the view that there was no legal obligation to file income tax returns. He wrote books about this, appeared on numerous radio and television programs, and lectured in various cities. He claimed his activities caused over 100,000 people to no longer file or pay income taxes.

He appeared live on CBS News Nightwatch, a nighttime viewer participation phone-in television program, after having served four months in prison for failing to file federal income tax returns. He made this unilateral reward offer, "If anybody calls this show – I have the Code - and cites any section of this Code that says an individual is required to file a tax return, I will pay them $100,000."

Plaintiff, an attorney, did not view the live appearance, but saw a taped segment on a later rebroadcast on the CBS Morning News, believed defendant's statements incorrect, researched the Code, and then contacted CBS verbally and in a letter, stating it represented "performance of the consideration requested by Mr. Schiff in exchange for his promise to pay $100,000."

Defendant claimed this was not proper acceptance of his offer, refused to pay, and plaintiff sued for breach of contract.

ANALYSIS

The trial court ruled in favor of Schiff by finding that Newman's acceptance was not timely. On appeal, that decision was affirmed. The appellate court noted:

"It is a basic legal principle that mutual assent is necessary for the formation of a contract."

"The present case concerns a special type of offer: an offer for a reward . . . In our view, if anyone had called the show and cited the code sections that Newman produced, a contract would have been formed and Schiff would have been obligated to pay the $100,000 reward, for his bluff would have been properly called"

"An offeror is the master of his offer and it is clear that Schiff by his words, 'If anybody calls this show * * *, limited his offer in time to remain open only until the conclusion of the live Nightwatch broadcast. A reasonable person listening to the news rebroadcast could not conclude that the above language – calls this show – constituted a new offer; rather than what it actually was, a news report of the offer previously made, which had already expired."

DEFUSE REPLAY

The case illustrates the power an offeror has to control all aspects of a contemplated transaction. Schiff was "the master of his offer", and could specify all aspects of the necessary acceptance, including what acts would be acceptance, when they were required, and how they had to be completed.

This rule provides legal protection to an offeror to impose a personal, subjective aspect to his offer, so that the objective standard that would ordinarily bring in the outside judgments of hypothetical "reasonable persons" is limited by the offer's express terms.

It is immaterial if the terms of the offer are extreme, bizarre, or otherwise unusual. "I offer to pay you $100,000 if you can continuously stand on one foot for one hour, from 10pm to 11pm on October 1, 2003, at the top of the center span of the Golden Gate Bridge in San Francisco, California," is equally as valid as more conventional unilateral reward offers.

Newman's best strategy to legally obligate Schiff would have been to initiate a new conversation with him that would hopefully lead to a new offer being made by Schiff, that stated "If anyone can find any provision in the U.S. Tax Code making the payment of tax mandatory, I will pay that person $100,000." Notice there is no "call in this show" limitation, nor any time for acceptance limitation. The reward offer is more open-ended and, as such, much easier to legally accept. Given Schiff's talkativeness and sense of self-importance, this may have been easily accomplished.

CONCLUSION

Schiff's checkered career as a tax rebel came to an end shortly after this case, both from increased pressure from IRS for his alleged tax evasion, and as a result of this wording from the court which was widely reported in the media and cast him in a less favorable light to the public than he had previously projected:

"Although Newman has not 'won' his lawsuit in the traditional sense of recovering a reward that he sought, he has accomplished an important goal in the public interest of unmasking the 'blatant nonsense' dispensed by Schiff. For that he deserves great commendation from the public."

    A. Do you agree with the court's final decision?
    B. What do you think was Newman's real reason for suing?
    C. Were the court's remarks about Schiff defamatory?

OUTLAW JESSE JAMES NEVER KILLED - $10,000 SAYS I'M RIGHT

In *James v. Turilli, 473 S.W.2d 757 (Mo. App. 1971)*, the defendant who operated the Jesse James Museum in Stanton, Missouri, went on a nationally syndicated television show and made the following unilateral reward offer:

"The man shot, killed and buried as Jesse James in 1882 was an imposter. In fact, Jesse James lived for many years thereafter under the alias J. Frank Dalton and last resided with me at my museum into the 1950's. I'll pay $10,000 'to anyone who can prove me wrong.'"

Plaintiffs were the widow of Jesse James' son and her two daughters. They presented various affidavits of persons acquainted with the Jesse James family, each stating facts showing that Jesse W. James "was in fact killed as alleged in song and legend on April 3, 1882, by Robert Ford." They claimed the reward on the basis of acceptance of the reward offer, and, after the defendant refused to pay, alleging the offer was too indefinite to be enforceable, they filed suit.

ANALYSIS

The trial jury ruled for plaintiffs and defendant appealed. The appellate court affirmed, allowing plaintiffs to collect the reward.

It stated, "The offer of a reward is a unilateral contract which becomes complete when accepted by performance of the act called for in the offer. A claimant to a reward needs only to show substantial performance."

The court noted that the defendant had virtually made a career out of his contentions, including his museum, publication of a book on the subject, and numerous appearances on radio and television. But he had lost an earlier case when he had tried to effect a name change for his 'friend' J. Frank Dalton to Jesse James.

The case, "hinges on the word 'prove', a word of ordinary meaning. For present purposes, we accept defendant's own definition of the word: 'Under ordinary rules of construction, 'to prove' is to determine or persuade that a thing does or does not exist."

The jury felt that the plaintiff's proofs were sufficient and the court said, "we may not upset the verdict unless it is so palpably unreasonable that reasonable minds can reach no other conclusion about it."

DEFUSE REPLAY

The wording the defendant chose for his reward offer doomed him to the adverse result. "By his alleged offer defendant did not say, as he could have, to whose satisfaction he should be proven wrong."

CONCLUSION

Note the different results in the *Newman* and *James* cases. In both, there were unilateral reward offers and, in both the defendant performed the required act. However in the former the plaintiff lost because he didn't call the live broadcast as required under the terms of the offer. In the latter, plaintiffs won because there were no such limitations on how the offer was to be accepted.

Schiff was master of his offer and protected himself. Turilli was also master of his offer but failed to protect himself. We have a clear lesson in anticipatory thinking and preventive law.

CASE RESEARCH CYBERCISES

The following cases also relate to the material in this chapter and illustrate the types of disputes that may occur. For each one do the following written assignment:

1. Locate the case using the Internet (Lexis-Nexis, West or any other research cite which provides case transcripts).
2. Briefly summarize what it was about – the nature of the dispute involved.

3. Who won at the trial court level? Who won at the appellate level?
4. Who won if there was a third level of Supreme Court review?
5. What were the legal rules of law and the reasoning used to reach the final decision?
6. Do you agree or disagree with the decision, and explain why?
7. What business law time bomb(s) were involved?
8. Could the time bomb(s) have been avoided by structuring the transaction differently? Discuss.
9. Could the adverse effects of the time bomb(s) have been defused by a different reaction or response by the affected party? Discuss.
10. Replay the facts of the case to achieve a different successful result.

1. *Ford Motor Credit Company v. Russell, 519 N.W.2d 460 (Minn. App. 1994) (automobile advertisement to provide 11% A.P.R. financing held not an offer to the general public).*
2. *Stanley v. Bank of El Paso, 847 S.W.2d 218 (Tex. 1992)(alleged offer to provide $500,000 line of credit that had interest rate and repayment terms missing held to fail rule of definiteness).*
3. *Marten v. Estate of Fred J. Marten, 543 N.W.2d 436 (Neb. 1996) (estate's real estate auction was ruled to be 'with reserve', denying nephew's high bid).*

NOTES

11.

CREATING THE CONTRACT

C. IS THERE A VALID ACCEPTANCE?

"The will for deed I do accept."
DuBartas

The creation of an agreement is like watching a tennis match. The offeror serves up what looks like an offer. If it meets the three-pronged test of intention, definiteness and communication, the ball is now in the offeree's court to respond.

- If the response is a question, everything remains suspended once it is answered, awaiting further action by the offeree.

- If the response is an outright rejection, the offer terminates.

- If the response attempts to change or vary any of the terms, it is a rejection of the original offer and a new counteroffer.

- If the response satisfies the legal requirements of an acceptance, a valid agreement is created.

I.   THE LEGAL REQUIREMENTS

Acceptance has its own three-pronged test:

1. intention to make a contract
2. unconditional approval of all the offeror's terms
3. communication to the offeror

Let's examine them one by one, as we did for the validity of the offer.

1. Similar to the offer, there must be a current and immediate desire to make an agreement. It must also be definite, clear and unconditional.

- "I agree to your terms, but I don't like them one bit." This is known as a "grumbling acceptance", which is still legally valid because the key is not why the offeree accepted, but the fact that he did.

- "I agree to your terms, but only if you give me a money back guarantee." This is not a valid acceptance because there are conditions attached. It really is a rejection, and a counteroffer.

The intent to accept is, like the offer, also judged by the objective standard. If it appears to a "reasonable person" that the offeree intends to be bound, the requirement is met.

This objective test is not necessary however, if the offeror has specified the personal manner, method or required details of the offeree's acceptance. As master of the offer, he can do this and require the offeree to subjectively perform exactly as specified.

In *The Private Movie Company, Inc. v. Pamela Lee Anderson, Cal. Sup. Ct. (1997)*, plaintiff sued defendant claiming she breached an oral and written contract to work on a movie project that contained nudity and simulated sexual content. Defendant claimed that while she had preliminary discussions with plaintiff regarding the proposed film project, she never specifically agreed to the manner and method of presenting the sexual content.

In ruling for the defendant that no contractual relationship existed, the court said, "Consent is not mutual unless the parties all agree upon the same thing in the same sense. Ordinarily it is the outward expression of consent that is controlling. Mutual consent arises out of the reasonable meaning of the words and acts of the parties, and not from any secret or unexpressed intention or understanding."

2. All the terms of the offer, no matter how detailed or silly, must be accepted by the offeree. This is called the common-law *mirror image rule*. The acceptance must mirror the offer in all-important respects to be valid. While minor variations are permissible, any major differences in the essentials of the deal cause a rejection of the offer and create a new counteroffer.

"An acceptance of an offer must be absolute and unconditional. All of the terms of the offer must be accepted without change or condition. A change in the terms set forth in the offer, or a conditional acceptance, is a rejection of the offer."

> *Ex: Phil owns a rental home and negotiates leasing it to Mary. He offers it to her for a monthly rental of $500, with a required security deposit of two months rent. She responds saying, "I accept your offer, and I'll pay you a one month deposit, and here's my check." Phil returns her check and rents the house to Gale. Mary objects, claiming that the prior rental agreement was with her. She loses because her response changed the offer's terms regarding security deposits and violated the mirror image rule. She made a counteroffer that was rejected by Phil's conduct in renting to Gale.

"It is well settled in contract law that the failure to accept an offer on the terms proposed constitutes rejection of the offer, which is thereby terminated .. nothing more that a counteroffer, which rejects and terminates the (original) offer, is proposed where an offeree modifies or changes the terms of the offer." *Keryakos Textiles, Inc. v. CRA Development, Inc., 563 N.Y.S.2d 308 (N.Y.App. 1990).*

3. Communication of the acceptance is, like an offer, legally effective when actually received by the offeror. It can occur instantaneously, by dealings in person or on the phone. It can also be indirect, where there is a time delay between the transmittal of the offer and its receipt.

There is an alternative communication rule for indirect communication of the acceptance that can be quite dangerous for the offeror. It was originally known as "the mailbox rule" and provided that an acceptance of a mailed offer could be legally effective when *mailed,* if properly stamped, addressed and dispatched in the mail – even if it was lost and never received by the offeror.

The obvious problem was that if the offeror sent the offer and had no response from the offeree, he would assume the offeree was not interested, and might then enter into a legal agreement with another party, impliedly revoking the offer, or otherwise expressly revoke the offer. Then the original offeree would appear with proof of mailing his acceptance, demanding performance of his agreement.

In *Casto v. State Farm Mutual Automobile Insurance Company, 594 N.E.2d 1004 (Ohio App. 1991),* plaintiff insured two cars with defendant, a Jaguar and a Porsche. She received two separate renewal notices by mail. She then placed payment checks in separate preaddressed envelopes and had them mailed to defendant 7 days before the stated policy cancellation date. The letter renewing the Porsche was timely delivered, but the Jaguar renewal was not, plaintiff had an accident with her Jaguar after the policy cancellation date, and then the envelope for the Jaguar renewal was returned to her by the post office marked "Returned for Postage."

Defendant denied insurance coverage and plaintiff filed a declaratory judgment action seeking a determination that her insurance policy was in effect as of the date of the accident. The trial court ruled for defendant and the appellate court affirmed:

"The well-established general rule of contract formation is that an acceptance transmitted in a form invited by the offer is operative as soon as it is put out of the offeree's possession, regardless of whether it ever reached the offeror. This is the so-called 'mailbox rule' which states that in the absence of any limitation to the contrary in the offer, an acceptance is effective when mailed."

"To be effective upon mailing, however, the acceptance must be properly dispatched. The offeree must properly address the acceptance and take whatever other precautions as are ordinarily observed in the transmission of similar messages . . . the burden of proving coverage was upon the plaintiff and, consequently, plaintiff bore the burden of proving that the envelope was stamped when it was mailed."

In view of the numerous means of indirect communication that now exist, this rule has been updated and is now called "the reasonable medium rule". It allows acceptance to be legally effective when sent, *if* the method of communication used is reasonable under the facts of the case. A "reasonable medium" of acceptance is:

- one that is specified in the offer, or
- one that is the same way the offer was sent, or
- one that arrives as fast or faster than the offer.

> *Ex: Day 1: A mails an offer to B
> Day 2: B receives the offer
> Day 3: A mails a revocation to B
> Day 4: B mails an acceptance to A
> Day 5: B receives the revocation
> Day 6: A receives the acceptance

The offer was legally communicated to B on day 2. A's revocation is not effective until it was received by B on day 5. If the mailing of an acceptance by B on day 4 satisfies the "reasonable medium rule", it is then legally effective, and there is an agreement made before the revocation. If that mailing was not effective, the revocation occurs on day 5, before the acceptance is received on day 6. In this particular case B wins - the offer was dispatched by mail and the acceptance on day 4 was sent via the same medium, so it is effective when sent on day 4.

> *Ex: Day 1 11:59am: A faxes an offer to B
> Day 1 12:01pm: B receives the offer
> Day 2: B mails an acceptance to A
> Day 3: A calls B to revoke the offer
> Day 4: A receives the acceptance

The offer was legally communicated to B on day 1 at 12:01pm. The revocation by A is instantaneous when he calls B on day 3. If B's mailing of the acceptance on day 2 satisfies the "reasonable medium test", the agreement occurs as soon as it was mailed. If it doesn't, the A's revocation preceded receiving the acceptance on day 4. In this case A wins – the acceptance was not sent the same way or faster than the offer, so it is not legally effective until it is actually received.

If the offeror specifies the required manner of communicating the acceptance, the offeree must strictly comply. If the offer is not specific, but the parties had prior dealings or there is a trade practice for the way to communicate that method, it would be required. If none of these apply, then we use the "reasonable medium rule".

There really is no excuse for an offeror to be at the mercy of the rule. As "master of his offer" he can easily *unplug* it simply by stating that "acceptance of this offer is not legally effective until received." This is part of the anticipatory thinking approach to preventive law that is emphasized throughout the book.

Most modern decisions follow these "effective when mailed"rules, but some litigants who will benefit by the "effective when received" rule, make the argument that the Post Office Department has the legal right to recall mail, is therefore the agent of the sender, and that such right coupled with a revocation of the offer prior to receipt of the acceptance voids the acceptance.

In *Soldau v. Organon, Inc., 860 F.2d 355 (9th Cir. 1988)*, plaintiff was fired by defendant, and received a letter in the mail that offered to pay him double normal severance pay in consideration for his signed release of all claims. He dated, signed and deposited the properly stamped and addressed release in a mailbox outside the local post office. On returning home he received from defendant the erroneously mailed severance check, returned to the post office and persuaded them to retrieve his release letter, and then cashed the severance check.

He then sued defendant for alleged Age Discrimination, and the trial court granted summary judgment for defendant, saying, "the release was deemed fully communicated to Organon, and a binding contract was formed, at the time plaintiff deposited the executed release in the mailbox."

Another communication dispute often involves a claim by one of the contracting parties that it is not legally bound by portions of the agreement if they are written in "fine print".

In *Littlefield v. Schaefer, 955 S.W.2d 272 (Sup. Ct. Tex. 1997)*, Walton was killed while participating in a motorcycle race when he struck an uncovered metal rail. Before the race, all participants had signed a "six paragraph release printed in miniscule typeface on the front of a one-page 'Release and Entry Form'."

His widow sued the racetrack operator for wrongful death, and they defended based upon the release. The trial court dismissed the suit, but the appellate court reversed, "because the release is not conspicuous."

The court pointed out that Risk-Shifting clauses must satisfy two fair notice requirements:

"First, a party's intent to be released for all liability caused by its own future negligence must be expressed in unambiguous terms within the four corners of the contract. Second, the clause must be 'conspicuous' under the objective standards defined in the Uniform Commercial Code . . .when it is so written that a reasonable person against whom it is to operate ought to have noticed it."

II.   SILENCE AS ACCEPTANCE

As a general rule, if the offeree fails to respond to the offer within its required time or in its required manner, or in a reasonable time or manner if none is specified, there is a rejection.

In *Durick Insurance v. Andrus, 424 A.2d 249 (Vt. 1980)*, defendant's old fire insurance policy was about to expire. Plaintiff sent insured a new policy, which contained a provision that the insured could cancel the new policy by returning the old policy or a lost policy receipt. Absent that action by the insured, the new policy would be deemed automatically accepted through inaction of the insured.

Insured did not respond, was then billed for unpaid premiums due on the new policy, refused to pay, was sued by the insurance company and the trial court entered judgment against the insured in the amount of the premiums allegedly due.

The Court reversed, saying, "To constitute a contract . . . there must be a meeting of the minds of the parties; an offer by one . . . and an acceptance . . . by the other. The offeror cannot force the offeree to speak or be bound by his silence. 'Silence gives consent . . . only where there is a duty to speak."

But what if the offer states that the offeree's failure to respond constitutes an acceptance?

> *Ex: Victor wants to hire Gloria as a computer programmer. He tells her, "I offer to pay you $500 per week starting next Friday. If I don't hear from you to the contrary by 10pm tonight, I will assume we have a deal." She listens, and then tells him, "I hear what you are saying." When she fails to appear for work on Friday, he claims breach of their agreement. She denies any acceptance of his offer. Gloria wins – the offeror cannot legally impose on the offeree a duty to respond to the offer.

However, the contrary result occurs if the offeree agrees to be bound by silence.

> *Ex: The same offer is made to Gloria as above. Her response is, "I hear what you are saying, and if I don't get back to you by 10am tomorrow, we have a deal." Here Victor wins – the offeree specified that her silence would be acceptance of his hiring offer.

There may also be other "silence as acceptance" disputes when unordered merchandise is received through the mail with an enclosed invoice requiring payment within a specified time. Sometimes, the invoice includes a statement that, "unless the enclosed items are returned at our expense within 15 days from receipt, you will be presumed to have accepted this payment obligation." The failure of the recipient to respond or return the items in these cases does not, as a general rule, create any contractual obligation.

In fact, the *Federal Postal Reorganization Act, Section 3009,* provides that whoever receives unordered mailed merchandise from a commercial sender has the right "to retain, use, discard, or dispose of it in any manner the recipient sees fit without any obligation whatsoever to the sender."

There are three other exceptions to the "silence is not acceptance" rule:

1. Book-of-the-month (or similar) memberships – "if you don't tell us no, we will send you this selection." The offeree has joined the club, and the membership contract expressly states that such a failure to respond is acceptance.

2. Prior dealings between the parties – diamond merchants who for many months deliver a specific quantity and quality every Monday and pick up a check in payment every Wednesday. The customary conduct of the parties creates an implied acceptance.

3. Quasi contract situations – a homeowner who watches the asphalting company mistakenly re-pave her driveway. Since she could reasonably have prevented the mistake but failed to do so, she has been "unjustly enriched" and must pay the fair value for the services performed. Her acceptance of the benefits activates her corresponding duty to pay.

III.   THE UCC BATTLE OF THE FORMS

Most commercial transactions in the business marketplace are conducted by an exchange of pre-printed forms between sellers and buyers of goods. After the customary preliminary negotiations by the parties to reach agreement on the essential terms of their deal, the buyer usually sends out its *purchase order offer* (PO Form).

All the basic negotiated terms of the deal are inserted on the front of this PO offer form as required by the offer rule of definiteness. They include the subject matter, price and terms, quantity, delivery and other essentials.

On the reverse of the form are the pre-printed "boiler plate" provisions commonly used by that party. A buyer of goods would probably have the following terms:

- "All purchases carry full warranty protection in the event of any defects."
- "Buyer may cancel order within 10 days due to labor strikes or adverse market conditions."
- "In the event of a default, buyer may sue in a court of law."

After the seller of the goods receives the PO offer form, it sends out its own form, which also has all the basics of the deal on the front, and its own "boiler plate" of seller's provisions on the reverse. The seller's acceptance form is the *order acknowledgement* (OA Form), and it commonly has on its reverse these terms:

- "Sales are as-is, no express or implied warranties are given."
- "All sales are final."
- "In the event of a default, arbitration is the sole remedy."

Viewing the buyer's offer form and the seller's acceptance form from the standpoint of the common law "mirror-image" rule, there is no agreement because the acceptance has added different terms and caused a rejection of the original offer, thereby creating a new counteroffer.

But the drafter's of the UCC wanted commerce to flourish, not be interrupted by technical rules that invalidate agreements that are intended by the parties to be enforced. Modern business runs on this exchange of forms and they usually contain different terms in their "boiler plate" because the buying and selling parties have differing goals to achieve. This is the *battle of the forms* - if the PO offer and OA acceptance do not mirror each other:

1. Do we have an agreement? If so,
2. Which of the conflicting terms in the offer and acceptance will govern?

1. Under the UCC, if the parties have agreed on the basic terms of their deal (the front of the forms), there is an agreement. Here, either there are no gaps so as to satisfy the common law rule of definiteness, or the gaps are filled under the UCC exceptions to that rule. The rationale is let's not prevent the parties from completing a transaction they obviously desire to make.

2. Which of the conflicting provisions will govern is the area that creates the most difficulty. The UCC's explanation of how to handle this is overly complex, but reduced to its essentials it means that:

- If *both* parties are not merchants, the different terms in the 2nd form are only *proposed additions* to the contract that are not binding unless accepted by the sender of the 1st form.

- If *both* parties are merchants, the different terms in the 2nd form are again only proposed additions that must be accepted, so long as they are "material" changes (important to the transaction). The 1st form (usually the purchase offer) again will govern unless the different terms in the 2nd form are not material, in which event the 2nd form governs. The three buyer's and seller's examples above are all material, like most situations, since they could have a significant financial impact on the transaction.

While the UCC states that, "the additional terms contained in the offeree's form are treated as proposals for addition to the contract," the practical chances of the offeror accepting them are slim and none, because neither party usually reads all the reverse "boiler plate" of their forms, and even if offeror did, there would be no agreement to different terms because they would be disadvantageous.

The parties rarely sit down during the busyness of their days and compare the forms to see if they are identical. So the burden is on the offeree to make sure it reads the entire 1st form, because that is what it is usually legally accepting. The offeror is only concerned with "material" changes anyway, and the merchant-merchant rule that allows the 2nd form to govern for non-material changes has no adverse effect on the offeror. Again, anticipatory thinking and appropriate action here will prevent later business problems.

IV. CANCELLATION OF THE ACCEPTANCE

While offerors usually have the legal right to revoke their offers at any time before acceptance, offerees generally have no such right. The acceptance, once legally made, binds the offeree, even if he made a bad business deal or for other reasons wants to be relieved from the agreement.

There is however another of our fairness doctrines that will allow consumer – buyers of goods on credit to withdraw their acceptances and not be legally bound if they do so within 72 hours of their purchase. This is known as the *3 day right to rescind*, and is created for consumers by the FTC (Fair Trade Commission).

This federal administrative agency requires installment sellers of goods for personal, family or household purposes to place a conspicuous bold-faced legend in their contracts advising their customers of this right. Its purpose is to protect the public from impulse buying due to high-pressure sales.

Notice that a cash purchase has no such protection, only those sales where the buyer is financing the transaction by agreeing to pay the amount due plus interest over a stated time period.

DISCUSSION EXERCISES

1. Discuss any additional legal tests you would use for a valid acceptance.

2. Discuss whether you agree or disagree with *Casto v. State Farm*. Did the insurer take unfair advantage of their insured?

3. Discuss pro's / con's on the "effective when sent" rule.

4. Discuss pro's / con's of the "effective when received" rule.

5. Discuss any "battle of the forms" situations where differences between the forms are not "material".

CASE EXERCISES

HOT DOG!
OSCAR MAYER WIENERS WINS THE BATTLE OF THE FORMS

In U*nion Carbide Corporation v. Oscar Mayer Foods Corporation, 947 F.2d 1333 (7ᵗʰ Cir. 1991)*, a suit for breach of contract was brought by plaintiff, claiming that defendant was legally required to reimburse it for $88,000 in State of Illinois back sales taxes that plaintiff had paid. The reimbursement obligation allegedly arose in a transaction where defendant ordered plastic sausage casings from plaintiff by standard purchase order form. There was an indemnity clause on the reverse side of defendant's order acceptance form that read:

" In addition to the purchase price, Buyer shall pay Seller the amount of all governmental taxes . . . that Seller may be required to pay with respect to the production, sale or transportation of any materials delivered hereunder."

After entering into their contract, another supplier of the sausage casings to Oscar Mayer began charging them a price 1% lower than Union Carbide's, because they accepted orders at an office located outside Chicago and had decided they had no sales tax obligation to collect from their customers. When Oscar Mayer informed Union Carbide of this, plaintiff instructed them to also send their orders to an address outside Chicago, and plaintiff stopped paying the sales taxes and deleted them from the invoices it sent defendant.

Eight years later, the State of Illinois decided these past year sales taxes were due, assessed them, plaintiff paid the amount required, and then filed this suit.

ANALYSIS

The trial court entered summary judgment in favor of Oscar Mayer, and the appellate court affirmed, on the basis that the indemnity provision was a "material alteration" to the agreement of the parties, and was never agreed to by defendant.

The court explained the "battle of the forms" provisions of the UCC:

"Moreover, if it is a contract between 'merchants', in the sense of 'pros', as Union Carbide and Oscar Mayer are, the additional terms become part of the contract. But not any additional terms; only those to which the offeror would be unlikely to object, because they fill out the contract in an expectable fashion, and hence do not alter it materially. If a term added by the offeree in his acceptance works a material alteration of the offer, the acceptance is still effective, but the term is not: that is the contract is enforceable minus the term the offeree tried to add."

It went on to discuss the standards to use to determine "materiality" of such contract changes:

"An alteration is material if consent to it cannot be presumed . . . what is expectable, hence unsurprising, is okay; what is unexpected, hence surprising, is not. Not infrequently, the test is said to be 'surprise or hardship.'"

DEFUSE REPLAY

As a practical matter, most of the "boiler plate" provisions on the reverse of buyer and seller order forms are material to all parties concerned because they have significant financial consequences.

Perhaps they are as clear as having to pay $88,000 of back sales taxes.

Maybe they are more general areas of possible impact:

- remedy choices between litigation or arbitration
- the laws that will apply in event of default
- the forum that must hear such disputes

All are still "material," and therefore the sender of the 2nd form that contains such clauses (usually the seller of the goods) is in danger of them not being legally binding.

The court points us to strategies that could be employed by both the buyer and seller of goods to avoid the adverse consequences of this UCC rule:

"To summarize, a term inserted by the offeree is ineffectual (1) if the offer expressly limits acceptance to the terms of the offer, or (2) if the new term (a) makes a material alteration, in the sense that consent to it cannot be presumed, and (b) there is no showing that the offeror in fact consented to the alteration – whether (i) expressly, or (ii) by silence against the background of a course of dealings."

CONCLUSION

The sender of the 1st form, usually the purchaser, can insulate itself from a "battle of the forms" dispute by inserting a provision that states, "we shall not be legally bound by any statements, clauses, provisions and/or conditions of the (2nd form – offer or acceptance) which in any way, materially or otherwise, alters any of the terms of this (1st form – offer or acceptance).

The sender of the 2nd form, usually the seller, can protect itself if it will:

- Read carefully the 1st form to determine if there is a limitation of acceptance. If so, negotiate it away.

- Read carefully the first form to determine if there are any significant differences in 'boiler plate' terms. If so, negotiate them away.

- Negotiate offeror consent to your 'material' changes.

- Send the 1st form, and reverse the roles of the parties as well as the effects of the UCC rule.

    A. Do you agree with the court's final decision?
    B. How could Union Carbide have changed the result?
    C. What could Oscar Mayer do better in the future?

CASE RESEARCH CYBERCISES

The following cases also relate to the material in this chapter and illustrate the types of disputes that may occur. For each one do the following written assignment:

1. Locate the case using the Internet (Lexis-Nexis, West or any other research cite which provides case transcripts).
2. Briefly summarize what it was about – the nature of the dispute involved.
3. Who won at the trial court level? Who won at the appellate level?
4. Who won if there was a third level of Supreme Court review?
5. What were the legal rules of law and the reasoning used to reach the final decision?

6. Do you agree or disagree with the decision, and explain why?
7. What business law time bomb(s) were involved?
8. Could the time bomb(s) have been avoided by structuring the transaction differently? Discuss.
9. Could the adverse effects of the time bomb(s) have been defused by a different reaction or response by the affected party? Discuss.
10. Replay the facts of the case to achieve a different successful result.

1. *Logan Ranch Karg Partnership v. Farm Credit Bank of Omaha, 472 N.W.2d 704 (Neb. 1991) (real estate buyer denied specific performance, since amendment to purchase agreement created an unaccepted counteroffer).*
2. *Morrison v. Thoelke, 155 So.2d 889 (Fla. App. 1963) (1ˢᵗ impression case with detailed analysis of the rules for deposited acceptance and received acceptance).*
3. *Corbin-Dykes Electric Company v. Burr, 500 P.2d 632 (Az.App. 1972) (no contractual relationship created with subcontractor by general contractor including in his bid for the job the bid of the subcontractor).*

12.

IS THE AGREEMENT LEGALLY ENFORCEABLE?

" Then in the marriage union, the independence of the husband and wife
will be equal, dependence mutual, and their obligations reciprocal."
Lucretia Mott

I.   LAW OVERVIEW

Consideration is the legal requirement that determines whether or not an agreement is legally binding upon its parties. This essential requirement of enforceability is often described as "whether or not the agreement is supported by legally sufficient consideration."

It commonly is viewed as the parties engaging in a mutually bargained for exchange of "something of value", and impliedly saying to each other, "If you do this for me - I'll do that for you."

Even though there has to be a reciprocal exchange of valuable promises, the term "legally sufficient" does not mean the dollar amount of value has to be equivalent. As a general rule, courts will not inquire into the financial adequacy of an otherwise legally binding transaction. Their rationale in avoiding this "how much" analysis is sound – it is not the court's job to save one of the parties from making a bad business deal.

> *Ex: Sophia has accumulated many items over her 75 years and decides to have a weekend yard sale. Arlene, a nurse, loves to spend her off days browsing at flea markets and garage sales. She looks through Sophia's items and notices a pastel painting that appeals to her. "How much? she asks. $10," says Sophia, to which Arlene says, "sold." Arlene takes her purchase to be re-framed and is told there is a valuable under-canvas worth $5,000. Her good fortune is written up in the local paper. Sophia sees the article and sues to cancel the sale, based upon inadequacy of consideration.
>
> Under this general rule, too bad for Sophia – she should have known what her property was worth and priced it accordingly.

However, if the facts of the case reflect that the defendant took unfair advantage of the plaintiff, and there is a wide disparity between the true value of the goods or services sold and the price paid, some courts will set aside the transaction.

In *O'Neill v. DeLaney, 415 N.E.2d 1260 (Ill. App. 1980)*, Mr. And Mrs. DeLaney were married in 1953, acquired a rare Rubens painting in 1958, and later in 1970, after Mr. DeLaney and plaintiff had become close friends, Mr. DeLaney sold the painting to plaintiff "for $10 and other good and valuable considerations", at a time when it was worth

approximately $100,000, without the knowledge of Mrs. DeLaney.
The painting remained for the most part in the home of the DeLaneys.

In 1974 Mrs. DeLaney instituted divorce proceedings, and claimed a special equity of ownership in the painting. Plaintiff sued for declaratory judgment that he was the owner of the painting. The trial court found the sale to plaintiff to be legally unenforceable due to inadequate consideration, and plaintiff appealed. The appellate court affirmed, saying, "Generally, courts will not inquire into the sufficiency of the consideration which supports a contract. However, where the amount of the consideration is so grossly inadequate as to shock the conscience of the court, the contract will fail."

The court noted the questionable circumstances under which the painting was allegedly "gifted" to plaintiff. "Generally, a spouse has an absolute right to dispose of his or her property during marriage without the concurrence of the other spouse. Moreover, the spouse may do so even if the transfer is made for the express purpose of minimizing or defeating the marital interests of the surviving spouse. There is only one exception to this rule: when the transaction is merely 'colorable' or 'illusory' and is tantamount to fraud." (Here, the painting had been acquired by *both* spouses, not just the husband alone.)

Many contracts have standard legalese similar to the *O'Neill* case that states, "In consideration of the sum of ten dollars and other good and valuable considerations." Legal analysis of consideration usually focuses on the reciprocal interactions between the parties. But what if the nominal consideration of $10 is never paid? Does this, in and of itself, invalidate the transaction? The following recent case says no.

In *Bennett v. American Electric Power Service Corp., 2001 WL 1136150 (Ohio App. 2001),* defendant's employee signed a contract that, as a condition of employment, gave defendant complete rights to all inventions made while on the job.

When defendant patented the new invention, the employee would sign a document that read, "In consideration of the sum of One dollar (1.00), and of other good and valuable consideration paid to the undersigned Assignor, by the Assignee . . . the undersigned Assignor by these presents do hereby sell, assign, transfer and set over . . . unto (defendant) the entire right, title and interest in and to that invention."

Plaintiff signed such a document relating to a profitable invention, the stated consideration was never paid, and plaintiff sued to invalidate it on the basis of lack of consideration. The trial court and appellate court ruled for defendant.
"Although ancient, the best authorities on the issue hold that nonpayment of such nominal consideration will not constitute breach, at least in instances where the actual value of the subject of the contract does not, in fact, correspond to the nominal consideration."

If the required Consideration is present, it is said to be "legally sufficient" and the agreement is deemed to be "legally enforceable".

Since any agreement involves an exchange of promises by the parties (offer plus acceptance), the legal tests for Consideration are based on the nature of these reciprocal promises:

A. Each party must receive (gain a benefit) and give up (suffer a detriment) something of value in order for the exchange of promises to be legally effective. The value exchanged is usually money or property, but can also be something less tangible like love, affection or gratitude.

> *Ex: Albert and Jim mutually promise that Albert will buy Jim's car for $1,000. Albert's benefit is his new car and his detriment is his required payment. Jim's benefit is the payment and his detriment is giving up his car.

B. Value can also be the receiving or giving up of the legal right to do or not do something.

> *Ex: ABC law firm promises to pay Larry Litigator a salary bonus if he refrains from his dangerous skydiving hobby until he completes the important trial he is handling. ABC's benefit is Larry's assured presence at the trial and their detriment is the bonus they will pay. Larry's benefit is the bonus and his detriment is giving up his legal right to skydive.

In the unusual case of *Jennings v. Radio Station KSCS, 96.3 FM, Inc., 708 S.W.2d 60 (Tex. App. 1986)*, a penitentiary prisoner sued defendant for breach of an alleged oral contract, relating to defendant's often aired policy that they play "at least three-in-a-row, or we pay you $25,000. No bull, more music on KSCS."

Plaintiff claimed defendant breached this "contract" because it only played three songs, followed by a brief commercial, and then two songs, rather than "three-in-a-row". He contacted defendant and demanded the money, they refused and he sued.

The trial court granted defendant's motion for summary judgment, and on appeal that decision was reversed, and the case remanded for further proceedings:

"It is elementary contract law that a valuable and sufficient consideration for a contract may consist of either a benefit to the promisor or a loss or detriment to the promisee. Thus, when a promisee acts to his detriment in reliance upon a promise, there is sufficient consideration to bind the promisor to his promise."

"In the instant case, appellant's petition alleged he stopped listening to KSCS when appellee refused to pay him $25,000. Implicit in this statement is an allegation by appellant that he listened to KSCS because appellee promised to pay him $25,000 if he could catch the radio station playing fewer than three songs in a row. Appellant thus relied to his detriment."

II.   ILLUSORY PROMISES

The required "mutuality" of the obligations between the contracting parties, which is an essential element of legally sufficient consideration, requires that both must be bound, or neither will be bound.

In *E-Z Cash Advance, Inc. v. Harris, 60 S.W.3d 436 (Ark.2001)*, the business of E-Z was to provide cash loans to persons who presented personal checks that were to be held until the borrower's next payday. The loan agreement gave E-Z the option to sue debtors in court, but required debtors to go to arbitration if they had a dispute.

Defendant gave plaintiff a check for $400 it was to hold, and rather than paying her debt, she kept rolling over the loan and eventually was unable to repay it. She then sued, contending that E-Z's service charges were a hidden form of interest that violated the state's usury law, and therefore prohibited them from collecting her debt.

E-Z moved to dismiss the lawsuit and compel arbitration. The trial court refused, and E-Z appealed. The appellate court affirmed, saying, "There is no mutuality of obligation where one party used an arbitration agreement to shield itself from litigation, while reserving to itself the ability to pursue relief through the court system.

Classic illusory promises lack mutuality because, even though they give the appearance that both parties are bound, the required mutual obligations are not present.

> *Ex: Acme Technology hires Felipe as a computer programmer and the parties sign an employment contract that states in paragraph 1, "We hire you for a term of three years." It also states in paragraph 10, "employer reserves the right to fire employee for any reason, at any time, upon 15 days notice."
>
> The hiring term is just smoke and mirrors. It presents the illusion of a binding definite three year term but really is not. The agreement is unenforceable.

These situations often arise in sale and purchase contracts between businesses, when market conditions change after the agreement is made and one of the parties perceives they made a bad deal. While the courts allow a greater degree of latitude than in personal contracts, the parties often encounter illusory promise disputes that hinge upon specific wording:

- Output contracts – "I agree to sell you my entire production of widgets during 2003." By giving the seller a guaranteed market and the buyer a stable source of supply, these contracts are usually enforceable, since the implied wording is an exchange of promised based upon *need.*

- Requirements contracts – "I agree to purchase from you my entire 2003 production run of widgets." Again, the buyer has a uniform supply and the seller has reduced selling costs and an assured market.

However, if the express wording uses indefinite terms such as *desire, wish, want,* the agreed performance is purely optional, the consideration illusory, and the agreement not legally enforceable.

III.   GIFT PROMISES

The exchange of promises between the contracting parties requires a mutual bargain, where both gain a benefit and suffer a detriment. A gift promise is legally unenforceable, as a general rule, because the required element of detriment suffered by the promisee is missing.

> *Ex: Herbert promises to pay Ann's past due credit card bill. If he then changes his mind and refuses, Ann has no legal recourse. Herbert's promise to pay her bill contains benefit (her gratitude) and detriment (his payment), but Ann is only receiving benefit without the required return detriment promise.

Another basis for non-enforceability of gift promises is that, although most donors honor the moral duty to fulfill their gift promises, donees should not, as a matter of law, reasonably rely on them.

There is an exception to this general rule of non-enforceability of gratuitous promises that applies to charitable pledges. Public policy encourages these gifts for the good of society. But there is a split of jurisdictions as to whether or not to enforce these gifts to charity:

> " Cases throughout the country clearly reflect a conflict between the desired goal of enforcing charitable subscriptions and the realities of contract law. The result has been strained reasoning which has been the subject of considerable criticism. This criticism is directed toward efforts by the courts to secure a substitute for consideration in charitable subscriptions. These efforts were thought necessary to bind the subscriber on a contract theory. Yet, in the nature of charitable subscriptions, it is presupposed the promise is made as a gift and not in return for consideration." *Salsbury v. Northwestern Bell Telephone Company, 221 N.W. 2d 609 (Iowa 1974)(defendant's gift promise to help establish a college is held binding upon the pledgor).*

- They are liberally construed by a majority of states to be legally binding based upon a legal fiction that presumes there is some element of exchanged detriment on the part of the donee.

> " A promise which the promisor should reasonably expect to induce action or forbearance on the part of the promisee or a third person . . . is binding if injustice can be avoided only by enforcement of the promise . . ." *Restatement of Contracts, Section 90.*

- A minority of states take a strict construction that gift promises to charity are not legally enforceable unless there is a demonstrable showing of *reliance* by the charity on the promise, so as to activate the doctrine of promissory estoppel.

In *King v. Trustees of Boston University, 647 N.E.2d 1196 (Mass. 1995),* Dr. Martin Luther King, Jr. named the defendant as the repository of all his papers by letter sent in 1964, delivered his files indexed through 1961, and then annually delivered to them his files of materials until his death. His widow, plaintiff in this case, sued for return of all his papers, claiming his estate, not the defendant, had legal title, because the donor's charitable gift promise was legally unenforceable due to lack of consideration.

The letter in question stated, "I intend each year to indicate a portion of the materials deposited with Boston University to become the absolute property of Boston University as an outright gift from me, until all shall have been given to the University. In the event of my death, all such materials deposited with the University shall become from that date the absolute property of Boston University."

The trial court jury ruled for defendant, on the basis that the gift promise was enforceable.

The appellate court affirmed, while recognizing the strict requirements of the minority rule, found there to have been the required detrimental reliance on the gift promise by the donee-defendant. "The jury could conclude that certain actions of BU, including indexing of the papers, (and making them available to researchers, providing trained assistance staff, holding convocations to acknowledge receipt of papers) went beyond the obligations BU assumed as a bailee of the papers 'with scrupulous care' and constituted reliance or consideration for the promises Dr. King included in his letter to transfer ownership of all bailed papers to BU at some future date or at his death."

IV.   PROMISSORY ESTOPPEL

The fairness doctrine of "Promissory Estoppel" solves the problem of missing detriment in charitable gift promises as we have seen. It also has an even broader application as a legal substitute for missing consideration, in cases involving facts of some types of hardship or inequity, to make the promises of the advantaged party enforceable. It applies to those disputes where the facts present a situation of "detrimental reliance".

Its elements are:

(1)   the promisor makes a gift promise where he knows or should know that the promisee will rely upon it,

(2)   the donee does in fact rely, and acts upon it, and

(3)   this reliance will cause the donee financial hardship.

Under these circumstances, the promisor is *estopped* to deny the validity or enforceability of his *promise.* To allow otherwise, would cause injustice.

> *Ex: James agrees to give Martin an exclusive sales franchise in Miami, if Martin sells his business in Orlando and relocates to Miami. Martin complies with the requirements but James refuses to honor his gift promise. James is legally prevented from denying the legal validity of his promise.

> "Detrimental action or forbearance by the promisee in reliance on a gratuitous promise, within limits constitutes a substitute for consideration, or a sufficient reason for enforcement of the promise without consideration. This doctrine is known as promissory estoppel. A promisor who induces substantial change of position by the promisee in reliance on the promise is estopped to deny its enforceability as lacking consideration."

> "The reason for the doctrine is to avoid an unjust result, and its reason defines its limits. No injustice results in refusal to enforce a gratuitous promise where the loss suffered in reliance is negligible, nor where the promisee's action in reliance was unreasonable or unjustified by the promise."

> " The limits of promissory estoppel are: (1) the detriment suffered in reliance must be substantial in an economic sense; (2) the substantial loss to the promisee acting in reliance must have been foreseeable by the promisor; (3) the promisee must have acted reasonable in justifiable reliance on the promise as made." *Simpson, Law of Contracts, Section 61 (2d Ed. 1965).*

V.   PAST CONSIDERATION

The exchange of valuable promises by the parties must be new. It cannot be based on past actions.

> *Ex: At the conclusion of Mary's retirement party, her employer promises, "Mary, in consideration for your 15 years of faithful service just ended, we will issue you $25,000 worth of stock." If the employer does not honor the promise, Mary has no legal recourse.

> While the employer received benefit (Mary's gratitude) and suffered detriment (the payment), and Mary was benefited by the money - her detriment is lacking. She gave up nothing in order to receive the payment.

> If Mary had, for example, agreed to work one more hour, day, week, or month in exchange for her employer's promise, she could have legally enforced its performance.

In this respect, a promise based upon past consideration is similar to an unenforceable gift promise, and is governed by the same rules.

In *Dementas v. Estate of Tallas, 764 P.2d 628 (Utah App. 1988),* plaintiff was a close friend of Tallas, and had rendered various services for him over a period of 14 years, including picking up his mail, driving him to errands, and assisting with the management of his rental properties. Subsequently, Tallas promised in a written memorandum written in his native Greek, that he owed plaintiff $50,000 for his help over the years, and would change his will to provide for plaintiff in that amount.

Tallas died one year later, had not changed his will as promised, and plaintiff sued to enforce his probate claim for $50,000 based upon the decedent's promise. The trial court dismissed his claim on the grounds that it lacked consideration.

The appellate court affirmed, saying, "Even though the testimony showed that Dementas rendered at least some services for Tallas, the subsequent promise by Tallas to pay $50,000 for services *already performed* by Dementas is not a promise supported by legal consideration. Events which occur prior to the making of the promise and not with the purpose of inducing the promise in exchange are viewed as past consideration and are the legal equivalent of no consideration."

Notice how easily Dementas could have made the promise of Tallas enforceable if he had recognized this potential business law time bomb, by creating a current exchange of a detriment promise, by writing on the same memorandum, or in a separate writing, or in a provable verbal conversation:

" I will continue (for the next day, week, month, year, etc.) to provide mail, errands, management services," or "Here is my antique bouzouki you like so much, in exchange for your promise."

The past consideration rule is also ignored in situations where the payor makes: (1) a current promise to pay a debt barred in bankruptcy, or (2) a current promise to pay a debt barred by the statute of limitations.

VI.   PRE-EXISTING DUTY PROMISES

A pre-existing duty promise is not legal consideration. It usually arises where the parties have made an agreement for the purchase/sale of goods or services at a fixed price, and later the seller wants to change it, for a variety of reasons, by increasing the price.

Even if the buyer agrees to the contract modification, only the original price need be paid if the seller's duty is to perform the same action it was previously bound to do, because there is no reciprocal exchange of a new detriment by the seller for the buyer's new detriment promise that benefits the seller.

*Ex: Mr. and Mrs. Jones hire Miami Catering to render all services for their upcoming 50th anniversary party at an agreed price of $2,000. One week before the event the caterer claims it miscalculated, and demands the price be doubled. The Jones' agree to pay the new price of $4,000. When the party is over and the bill is presented, only the original amount is paid. Miami Catering cannot recover the higher price.

Notice that when the caterer demanded the higher price Mr. and Mrs. Jones did not refuse and threaten to sue for breach of the original contract. What identifies these pre-existing duty cases is that the response to the price adjustment is, "Yes, I agree to pay the higher amount!"

The rationale for the pre-existing duty rule's application in this type of case is to only require the performing party to honor its original promise, and prevent the unfairness of allowing a one-sided modification of previously existing contracts. If a new benefit is granted one party without a corresponding detriment being suffered by the same party, the promisor is, in essence, just making a gift. These cases often involve circumstances of coercion or extortion, like the Jones case, or other situations where the promisee has caused the problem that he seeks to be paid additional for. We are on the legal and moral high ground by refusing to enforce these "tainted" promises.

In *Robert Chuckrow Construction Company v. Gough, 159 S.E.2d 469 (Ga. App. 1968)*, Gough was a subcontractor of Chuckrow on a construction job to build a Kinney Shoe store. The basic contract required Gough to perform carpentry work, including the assembly and erection of wooden trusses, which supported the roof deck on the building. After doing this work, 32 of the trusses collapsed, and Gough claimed there was an oral agreement with Chuckrow to pay extra for their removal, disassembly, rebuilding and re-erection. Chuckrow refused, and Gough sued for breach of contract.

The trial court ruled for Gough, but the decision was reversed on appeal. The underlying contractual agreement between the parties stated, "Subcontractor hereby assumes entire responsibility and liability for any and all damage or injury of any kind or nature whatsoever . . . to all property caused by, resulting from, arising out of, or occurring in connection with the execution of the work provided for in this contract."

"An agreement on the part of one to do what he is already legally bound to do is not a sufficient consideration for the promise of another . . . Where one undertakes to perform for another service or labor for a given sum any amount (agreed to be) paid in excess of that sum, not based upon a new consideration is a mere gratuity."

But many times the party who requests contract modification is in a bind where they are less at fault, such as genuine miscalculations of the job and its location, honest mistakes in bidding or furnishing price quotes, and other situations that may arise after the contract that they have not caused.

There are four exceptions to the pre-existing duty rule, which will allow the performing party to enforce a contract modification price adjustment:

1) The first relates to situations where the need for an upward price adjustment is caused by external conditions such as "acts of God" severe weather, labor strikes, wars and other outside events that greatly increase the performing party's costs. In these cases, the agreed price increase may be justified as a fairness exception if the triggering event is an "unforeseen difficulty".

The legal test is again the objective standard. Would a hypothetical "reasonable person", under the same or similar circumstances as our situation, have anticipated the problem? If so, even though severe problems result that cause the actual costs of performance to greatly increase, it is NOT an event that allows the original contract price to be disregarded. It does not matter if the particular party didn't personally expect it to happen.

A legal test of "foreseeability" often used is, "Did this ever happen before?" The more

often, the more recent, the more regular the occurrence – the more it should have been anticipated and taken into consideration when the original contract price was being negotiated.

Events that would be legally foreseeable:
- A severe earthquake in San Francisco
- A severe winter snowstorm in Montreal
- A hurricane in the Florida Keys
- Another labor strike in the airline industry
- Another war in the Middle East

Events that would be legally unforeseeable:
- An earthquake in Miami
- A snowstorm in Havana
- A war in the Vatican

The practical problem of reliance upon the "unforeseen difficulties" exception by the performing party is that "unforeseen" is an opinion and reasonable decision makers may differ based upon the unique facts of each dispute. Why deal with such uncertainty? Most skillful navigators in the business marketplace insert a clause in their contracts called *force majeure*, which specifically allows the contract price to be modified upwards if specified outside events cause costly delays.

*Ex: "The parties agree that, should completion be delayed by more than ___ days or construction costs increased by more than ___% by causes beyond the control of and through no fault of the parties, such as weather events, strikes, wars, acts of terrorism, or other similar unanticipated problems, the monies due and payable herein shall be adjusted accordingly."

Some states, when presented with such disputes, disregard this exception entirely as being too speculative or conjectural.

In *Crookham & Vessels, Inc. v. Larry Moyer Trucking, Inc., 699 S.W.2d 414 (Ark. App. 1985)*, a contract modification to pay a higher price for "extra ditching" was made in a construction project, because water would not properly drain out of the ditches due to clogged culvert drains, causing the original ditches to collapse. Although the trial court enforced the modification, the appellate court refused.

"The appellee had the duty to acquaint himself before bidding with the conditions, nature, and extent of the work to be performed, and the condition of the culverts in question could have been taken into account. Where one agrees to do, for a fixed sum, a thing possible to be performed, he will not be excused or become entitled to additional compensation because unforeseen difficulties are encountered."

There are three other exception situations in which an otherwise non-binding pre-existing duty contract modification is allowed to be legally enforced:

(2) The original agreement is cancelled and a new one is entered into at the higher price, so there is nothing pre-existing.

> *Ex: Using the Caterer v. Jones situation, when the higher price of $4,000 was agreed, the caterer could have said, "Let's make this simple. Why not just forget about the original $2,000 deal, and we'll just have this new deal for $4,000?" When the Jones' agreed, the new promise became legally unenforceable.

(3) The performing party does something new or different in exchange for the new promise to pay a higher price, thus furnishing the missing detriment to the promisee.

> *Ex: When the caterer's demand for $4,000 was agreed, let's say a request was made that the Jones' cancel the old contract, but was refused. When this happened the caterer said, "Tell you what, I appreciate you agreeing to this and to show my appreciation I'll wash your car." When the Jones' agreed, the new promise became legally enforceable, notwithstanding the difference in value of the exchanged duties. Remember, all that is necessary is the exchange of "something of value". Since the caterer was not previously obligated to perform the new service, it is value.

(4) The subject matter of the modified contract is a "sale of goods", so that it falls within the Uniform Commercial Code provisions that require payment. Remember how tricky this can be because most transactions involve both goods and services. If the majority aspect is tangible personal property, we have the required *goods* to satisfy this UCC exception.

> *Ex: The catering contract made with the Jones' is basically a service agreement, even though it involves items of personalty such as the food, the silverware, the tables, etc. Suppose however that the caterer was skillful enough to have the contract allocate the total price, "$3,000 for all catering supplies and equipment, and $1,000 for labor." That would cause the UCC rules to apply, and protect the caterer against the pre-existing duty rule.

The UCC exception is further tempered by its corresponding legal requirement that the parties act in *good faith*, so that their conduct is consistent with "reasonable commercial standards of fair dealing in the trade."

In *Roth Steel Products v. Sharon Steel Corporation*, 705 F.2d 134 (6th Cir. 1983), defendant agreed to sell steel to plaintiff at prices below its published book prices. Later, Federal price controls to discourage foreign imports, as well as general market conditions caused increased domestic and international demand for steel, resulting in substantial price increases.

Defendant advised plaintiff it was discontinuing all price discounts, unless plaintiff agreed to pay a higher price than originally agreed. Plaintiff agreed, and when a subsequent dispute arose between the parties over late deliveries and unfilled orders, plaintiff sued for breach of the original contract, claiming the modification was unenforceable.

When the trial court ruled for plaintiff, defendant appealed. The appellate court affirmed, acknowledging the applicability of the UCC "sale of goods" exception that would otherwise enforce the contract modification, but ruled that defendant had violated its obligation to act in good faith.

" We believe that the district court's conclusion that Sharon acted in bad faith by using coercive conduct to extract the price modification is not clearly erroneous.

Therefore, we hold that Sharon's attempt to modify the November 1972 contract, in order to compensate for increased costs which made performance come to involve a loss, is ineffective because Sharon did not act in a manner consistent with Article 2's requirement of honesty in fact when it refused to perform its remaining obligations under the contract at 1972 prices."

VII.   DEBT SETTLEMENT

The Debt Settlement cases are another type of pre-existing duty problem that frequently occurs in commercial settings. It arises when a debtor pays the creditor an amount less than invoiced, intending for it to be a release from any further financial obligation.

> *Ex: Stanley hires Alan to perform architectural services for an agreed price of $1,000. Upon completion, Alan delivers his bill. Stanley sends Alan a check for $750 marked "payment in full" and Alan cashes the check.

Whether or not Alan can receive the $250 balance depends upon whether the debt is classified as Liquidated (certain) or Unliquidated (disputed).

If there is a good faith dispute about the debt communicated to the creditor before the debtor makes the payment, the tender of a check for less than the original agreed price with release language is an offer of settlement of the debt. When the creditor cashes the check, that offer has been accepted. An Accord and Satisfaction contract has now been created, which bars further payment to the creditor.

If however, there is no prior good faith dispute, the debtor's tendered release is viewed as a payment on account, and the creditor may recover the balance due.

In *F.H. Prince & Co., Inc. v. Towers Financial Corporation, 656 N.E.2d 142 (Ill. App. 1995),* plaintiff had a disputed claim against United Fire, a subsidiary of defendant, for $1.6 million, which it compromised for $1.2 million by agreeing to release its right to sue United Fire, in exchange for defendant's guarantee of payment.

When defendant refused to honor the guarantee claiming the settlement instruments were unenforceable for lack of consideration, plaintiff sued for breach of contract, and won a jury decision for almost $1 million, that upheld the validity of the settlement.

The appellate court affirmed, saying, "the compromise of a disputed claim will serve as consideration as will a promise to forego legal action . . . the compromise of a disputed claim will provide consideration for the settlement agreement, even if the claim is shown to be invalid, as long as it is asserted in good faith."

VIII.   UNCONSCIONABLE AMOUNT

As previously discussed, the courts will not usually inquire into the adequacy of the amount of exchanged benefits and detriments, as long as they involve "something of value".

However, on rare occasions the courts in some states will come to the rescue of the disadvantaged party invoking a fairness exception that is sometimes applied if the circumstances involving the differential in amounts, relationship of the parties, and related factors may indicate that enforcement of the contract would "shock the conscience of the court."

This usually requires evidence that one of the parties has taken extreme unfair advantage of the other.

*Ex: Let's go back to the garage sale case we discussed at the beginning of this chapter. Suppose that Arlene is not a nurse, but an art dealer. She goes to these homeowner sales hoping to "make a killing" on art that the owner knows little about. When she asked Sophia, "How much?" and was told, "$10", Arlene's superior knowledge and special expertise required her not to take advantage of the situation.

If Sophia was also an art dealer and just sold her property too low, the court would not interfere. Similarly if the amount paid, though low, is still within the guidelines of a hard bargain, the deal will stand.

Differing arguments are made in these situations.

Critics argue: A) If courts can inquire into the amount of value paid, we are disregarding the give and take of the commercial marketplace. No contract will ever be final because a party who made a bad business deal will always "take a shot" at litigation. The courts will be filled with these cases.

B) Owners of property should be required to know its value, at their risk, no matter who is the buyer.

Proponents say there should not be hard and fast rules in this area. Review should be on a case-by-case basis to determine if the value exchanged and the circumstances surrounding the transaction require the court's assistance to right a wrong.

What do you think? Should the parties be allowed to make as good or bad a deal as they can negotiate, assuming that no unfair advantage was taken? Or should the court system be a watchdog, case by case, to make sure each transaction is "fair"? What does fair or unfair really mean, except that reasonable persons may differ in their opinions?

DISCUSSION EXERCISES

1. Discuss why courts allow minimal benefit but always demand detriment.
2. Discuss when you would require inquiry into the adequacy of consideration.
3. Discuss your view as the enforceability of charitable gift promises.
4. Discuss your legal test for application of the unforeseen difficulty doctrine.
5. Discuss legal boundaries you would establish for use of promissory estoppel.

"DON'T YOU WORRY BOUT A THING, CAUSE I'M THE KING"

In *Alden v. Presley, 637 S.W.2d 862 (Tenn. 1982),* the estate of Elvis Presley was sued by the mother of his fiancée to enforce his gift promise to pay off the remaining mortgage indebtedness on her house.

Elvis was engaged to plaintiff's daughter, became aware of plaintiff's desire to divorce her husband, agreed to pay all her expenses, to furnish the money to purchase her husband's equity in their home, and to pay off the mortgage that encumbered it.

She then filed for divorce, and she and her husband signed a property settlement agreement on 8/1/77, subject to later court approval, whereby she would pay her husband $5,325 for his equity in return for a deed conveying her sole title to the house, and release him from any further liability on the mortgage debt which was at that time $39,587.66. Elvis died suddenly on 8/16/77, and on 8/25/77 his estate advised plaintiff it would not assume liability for the mortgage debt.

ANALYSIS

The trial court ruled for defendant on the grounds that his gift promise was legally unenforceable. "Plaintiff and her husband suffered no detriment as she 'wound up much better off after their association with Elvis A. Presley than either would have been if he had never made any promise to Jo Laverne Alden."

The appellate court reversed in plaintiff's favor, applying the doctrine of promissory estoppel to hold that she "had foregone remedies available to her in the divorce petition *in reliance* upon the promise made to her by decedent."

The Tennessee Supreme Court affirmed the trial court's ruling for the defendant, because "plaintiff has failed as a matter of law, to prove essential elements of promissory estoppel, *detrimental reliance,* and a loss suffered as a result of detrimental reliance."

Since the property settlement agreement was not binding until approved by the court, and the estate had denied liability for Elvis' gift promise before it was submitted to the court, "plaintiff's reliance on the promise after August 25, 1977, was not reasonably justified and she suffered no loss as a result of justifiable reliance."

DEFUSE REPLAY

How could Mrs. Alden have converted the non-enforceable gift promise made by Elvis into a legally binding obligation?

- Create an exchanged detriment by promising to do something for Elvis in exchange for his gift promise. "Thank you, Elvis; I'll bake you a cake."

- Create a promissory estoppel scenario. Suppose Mrs. Alden was working after hours to make her mortgage payments. In response to his gift promise, she says, "Thank you, Elvis, now I can quit my night job and spend more time with the family." All requirements of that doctrine would then be present: a promise, knowledge of it and reliance on it, and change of position to her detriment by the promissee.

CONCLUSION

There is no question Elvis would have honored his gift promise had he lived. His heirs, however had a different agenda, as is the usual case in estates. The money to pay Mrs. Alden's mortgage would have come out of their pocket. It is therefore not surprising they refused to pay.

All of us will, hopefully, be in a situation at some time in our lives when a gift promise is made to us. At that moment, the proverbial light bulb needs to be lit in our heads as we recognize this potential business law time bomb, and act skillfully to defuse it.

A. Do you agree with the court's final decision?
B. Was it ethical for the estate to refuse to honor Elvis' promise?
C. Should provable gifts made by decedents be legally binding on their heirs?

"PAID IN FULL" MAY MEAN "PARTIALLY PAID"

In *Pierola v. Moschonas, 687 A.2d 942 (D.C. App. 1997)*, the parties were business associates in the scraping and painting of bridges and other metal structures. They agreed to split profits 60% to Pierola and 40% to Moschonas, although Pierola claimed there was no such contract. They then had a heated disagreement, Moschonas walked off the job, and Pierola delivered to Moschonas a check marked "paid in full" for less than his 40% profit participation, which was cashed.

Then the payee sued for the balance due, Moschonas claiming that the check did not contain that release wording. Pierola raised the defense of accord and satisfaction.

ANALYSIS

The trial court, "troubled by the lack of forthrightness of both litigants", ruled in favor of Moschonas, and rejected the full payment defense raised by Pierola, because his denial of the existence of the contractual agreement between the parties brought him outside the rule that, "there must be a mutual acknowledgement of the underlying debt and a bona fide dispute as to its amount for the cashing of the check to operate as a settlement."

The appellate court reversed, holding that the trial court made a legal error. "It is not necessary for the parties to mutually acknowledge the underlying debt and to dispute only its amount for accord and satisfaction to operate. (It) can operate anytime the underlying claim is disputed *either* as 'to the amount due *or* as to the debtor's liability'."

The court then considered whether there was a bona fide dispute, as required by law.

"The good faith requirement thus is concerned not so much with the subjective moral character of the debtor but rather the requirement of consideration. If there is an objective reasonable basis for the debtor's disputing his obligation to pay, whether in liability or amount, he is giving up something by making a part payment in full satisfaction of the disputed claim and thus provides objective consideration."

"The parties had had a heated disagreement regarding whether to sandblast or scrape the South Capitol Street Bridge, and as a result of that disagreement Moschonas had walked off the job before it was completed and not returned. These facts gave Pierola a legitimate basis to dispute Moschonas' claim to a flat 40% of the profits on both the bridge and tower contracts."

Both parties in the Pierola - Moschonas dispute had a problem telling the truth. The court said, "the requirement that a dispute be legitimate, bona fide or honest focuses not on the propensity of the parties to prevaricate, but rather on the basis for disputing the claim at the time the accord and satisfaction operates."

DEFUSE REPLAY

Debt settlement is a recurring problem in modern business transactions. Most parties assume that the debt is cancelled as soon as the check was cashed. Debtors thus are able to clear their accounts receivable balances, creditors write them off, and then abandon efforts to collect the balances. Creditors don't realize they may be able to treat such partial remittances as payments on account, and properly demand full payment.

The tricky area is the nature of the alleged good faith dispute. It has to be prior in time to the attempted tender. Merely writing on the check additional wording such as, "I dispute this debt", or self-serving words such as, "This payment relates to a prior dispute", will not suffice.

Even if there is a "prior" dispute, it must be legitimate, bona-fide or made in good faith. The debtor's mere refusal to pay does not constitute the required unliquidated debt if it is arbitrary or capricious, and has no legal basis.

*Ex: Anne hires lawyer John to draft some lengthy contracts for an agreed price of $500. Later she has lunch with her friend Susan, tells her about it, and Susan suggests that Anne is overpaying. Anne is taking a Business Law course and studies the debt settlement rule. She contacts John and pretends to disagree on the amount, trying to create the legal requirement of prior dispute. Later, after receiving the bill for $500, she sends him a check for $250 marked "paid in full", and it is deposited with his daily bill collections.

Anne should have to pay the balance due. She had no good faith dispute. This requirement protects creditors from being unfairly disadvantaged by a knowledgeable debtor trying to utilize this debt settlement rule to eliminate an otherwise valid debt.

(Creditor's Perspective)

Most debt settlement problems arise in busy offices where many invoices are sent to debtors, numerous payments arrive daily and there is an automatic bookkeeping procedure to bank payment remittances the same day they are received. If the cashing of some of these payments would create a valid accord and satisfaction, the creditor may have forfeited substantial monies.

Businesses can initiate office procedures to protect themselves. These could include:

(1) Monitor the daily banking procedure.

(2) When the mail is opened, compare all payments to their invoice to determine if they are partial AND examine them for any "full release" or "payment in full" language.

(3) Put the partial payments that contain release language aside, and do not deposit them until the question of whether there is a prior good faith dispute can be answered.

(Debtor's Perspective)

If you are the debtor in this situation, and otherwise qualify for binding debt settlement, a careful creditor that initiates the protective office procedures may thwart your efforts.

However, you may prevail by using a method of payment transmittal that bypasses the creditor's office, such as direct payment to the creditor's bank, certain wire transfers, or payments delivered to an assignee or other designated agent.

If the creditor has not thought ahead far enough to block these types of qualifying payments, you may be successful in discharging the debt.

CONCLUSION

Payments made to settle a debt must be closely monitored by both payor (debtor) and payee (creditor) to determine the possibility of the sequence of events creating a legally binding accord and satisfaction.

As doing business becomes more complex and the technology of e-commerce and instant communication grows, the parties need to be informed of and protect themselves from the danger of unintended cancellation of otherwise collectible account balances.

A. Do you agree with the court's final decision?
B. What if Moschonas had not walked off the job? Who wins then?
C. What if Pierola had bid on another lucrative job without telling Moschonas? Who wins then?

CASE RESEARCH CYBERCISES

The following cases also relate to the material in this chapter and illustrate the types of disputes that may occur. For each one do the following written assignment:

1. Locate the case using the Internet (Lexis-Nexis, West or any other research cite which provides case transcripts).
2. Briefly summarize what it was about – the nature of the dispute involved.
3. Who won at the trial court level? Who won at the appellate level?
4. Who won if there was a third level of Supreme Court review?
5. What were the legal rules of law and the reasoning used to reach the final decision?
6. Do you agree or disagree with the decision, and explain why?
7. What business law time bomb(s) were involved?
8. Could the time bomb(s) have been avoided by structuring the transaction differently? Discuss.
9. Could the adverse effects of the time bomb(s) have been defused by a different reaction or response by the affected party? Discuss.
10. Replay the facts of the case to achieve a different successful result.

1. *Patarek v. Sixty-Six Hundred Ltd., 465 N.W.2d 342 (Mich. App. 1990) (release of liability to play softball on defendant's recreational field held enforceable).*
2. *Maryland National Bank v. United Jewish Appeal Federation of Greater Washington, Inc., 407 A.2d 1130 (Md. App. 1979) (detailed history of the law of charitable gifts).*
3. *Feinberg v. Pfeiffer Co., 322 S.W.2d 163 (Mo. App. 1959) (employer's retirement benefits held enforceable under promissory estoppel).*

NOTES

13.

DEFENSES TO ENFORCEMENT OF THE CONTRACT

A. CAPACITY OF THE PARTIES

" Contract defenses should be used as a protective shield,
not as a cutting sword. "
Legal Maxim

I.   LAW OVERVIEW

Disputes often arise after contracting parties have entered into an agreement that is supported by legally sufficient consideration, and is therefore deemed "enforceable."

Suppose one of the parties wants out of the deal they made, either because they miscalculated, market conditions have changed, or a variety of other reasons? Whether or not they will be legally extricated from their contractual agreement depends upon their ability to prove a legal defense to enforcement.

Like most legal disputes, the scales of justice swing back and forth depending upon the particular agenda of the parties:

1) The party who made the better bargain will always want his contract to be legally enforceable. That same party will sue for "breach of contract" if its terms are not performed. Defenses to enforcement based upon alleged lack of legal capacity will be vigorously opposed.

2) The party whose deal doesn't look as good as when the agreement was made may seek ways to legally be extricated from it. Can their agreement be cancelled, avoided, or disaffirmed? Can that party be allowed to withdraw with no adverse legal consequences?

The party who wants to be relieved of legal responsibilities has the burden of proof. These situations involve *voidable contracts.*

Note the focus of these disputes is on the legal status of the particular party who is seeking judicial permission not to have to perform, rather than the type of business transaction involved.

Even if one of the parties lacks legal capacity, the contract can still be valid and fully enforced by them, if they so desire. If however, they are looking for a way out – their claim and proof of incapacity will free them from legal responsibility.   It is their personal choice whether to accept the contract or seek to cancel it.

The legal remedy to cancel the contract is called *rescission.* The act of cancellation by the party who lacks legal capacity is called *disaffirmance.*

The lack of capacity cases usually involve these two types of situations:

- Plaintiff sues to cancel the contract, and require the return of the value paid to the defendant.

- Defendant is sued for breach of contract by the plaintiff and raises incapacity as a legal defense to its enforcement.

The two main areas of cases involving claims of lack of legal capacity are *Mental Impairment* and M*inority.*

II.   MENTAL IMPAIRMENT

The legal test of mental impairment is whether or not the party in question is capable of understanding the legal effect of their contract – at the time they enter into it. This is an objective test of cognition, whereby the law uses the "what is reasonable?" criteria to resolve disputes.

If the impaired party is allowed to legally cancel their contract, they have the corresponding legal duty to return any value they received, such as deposits or payments when the contract was made. The objective here is to balance the scales of justice again – to place the parties back into the *status quo* where they were before entering into the transaction.

Notice the law focuses on the moment in time when the contract is made, not before or after. Even if the allegedly impaired party was as "nutty as a fruitcake" just prior to making the contract or shortly thereafter, there might have been a *lucid interval* during which the contract was made. If so, the contract is enforceable, even if its terms are disadvantageous, as long as the unimpaired party did nothing wrong.

> *Ex: Groovy was a child of the 1960's and ingested a number of chemicals, which cause flashbacks from time to time. When these incidents occur, he appears to be severely impaired. Groovy has been negotiating with Phil to buy a boat, and they enter into their contract on July 3rd. At the moment the contract is made, Groovy is clear, cogent and fully aware of the nature and consequences of his actions, although shortly before and shortly after he is again in la-la land. Groovy now wants to rescind the contract, claiming incapacity. Phil should win – as long as it was an arms-length transaction. Remember, the marketplace is filled with good or bad deals, depending upon one's side in the transaction.

There are various valid ways that mental impairment disputes may arise:

A) Mental incapacity may legitimately occur due to impairment caused by actual instances of accident or illness, such as concussion, brain tumors, neurological trauma or disease, senility, or other pathologies that impair judgment and cognition, short of a judicial determination of incapacity. These are readily proved by medical testimony, and are not usually litigated for that reason.

B) A legal adjudication of mental impairment may result if there has been a legal proceeding, commonly called guardianship, brought by family or friends to declare someone to be legally incompetent. If such a court order is entered, the person in question loses their legal rights to contract and any such agreements made from its date forward are *void and unenforceable*. Only the court appointed guardian has the right to contract on behalf of the incompetent. If the impaired party later recovers, their competency can be legally restored by another court order, and they are again free to enter into contracts.

C) Voluntary impairments such as drugs, alcohol, and allergic reactions to ingested food, drink, or medicine.

D) Situational impairments, such as inhalation of noxious fumes, atmospheric problems like smog or pollen that interfere with cognition, and severe emotional upsets that create imbalances in judgment.

But what if the party claiming mental impairment appears to be faking, so as to avoid the bad contract bargain they made, or the tests for mental impairment are not so clear? These are the situations that cause most legal disputes, and often involve claims of "I was under the influence of ...." alcohol or drugs or prescription medication or etc.

Originally, most states strictly construed the legal test for impairment, so that even if the complaining party's impairment were self-induced, they would still be allowed to rescind. Their burden of proof was solely to convince the decision maker that "they were legally incapable of understanding the contract at the moment it was created." The reason for their problem, and its surrounding circumstances, was immaterial.

However, parties began to abuse the rule in situations not so clear-cut as verifiable accident or illness and judicial incompetency. Judges became skeptical of their true motivations and whether they were acting in good faith. So the courts met this challenge by adding a fairness exception to the rule in these cases that requires the complaining party to prove that *unfair advantage* was taken – they were victimized by the non-impaired party. This is a fault vs. no-fault test.

This has greatly reduced litigation in this area, but close cases can still occur where the alleged impairment was self created, but there are mixed aspects of fault:

*Ex: Sidney is an experienced businessman with an unusually high alcohol tolerance. He often uses this "gift" as a negotiating tactic as the parties sit around the table, having a few drinks. When the other party is sufficiently drunk, Sidney then completes the contract on very favorable business terms. Assume that Sidney has just completed such a contract with Karl, who also has business experience. Later, Karl claims mental impairment and seeks to have the contract cancelled. Sidney would argue:

- "Karl chose to drink himself into financial oblivion."
- "He should have thought about the consequences of his actions."
- "I didn't hold a gun to his head."
- "Business is business."

Karl would argue that Sidney didn't act in good faith, and victimized him by using his alcohol tolerance as a means to that end.

Under the old rule, Karl would probably win, since he could satisfy the legal test if impairment at the moment of contracting, and that was the sole factor to consider.

Under the new rule, Karl would lose unless he had some additional facts, such as, "When Karl went to the restroom between drinks, Sidney placed a drug capsule into his drink," so that he could prove that Sidney took unfair advantage of him, and was therefore at fault.

A case analysis of the "impairment" defense reflects how these rules are interpreted and implemented by the courts. Some analyze whether or not the facts of their particular dispute meet the "capable of understanding at the time of contract" test. Others, like the case below, allow enforcement by the non-impaired party, even if there was the legally required mental incapacity.

In *Hedgepeth v. Home Savings and Loan Association, 361 S.E.2d 888 (N.C. App. 1987)*, Cora Haith signed a power of attorney that authorized her son to sign for her a promissory note and deed of trust in favor of the defendant, in connection with mortgage refinancing for the remodeling of her house. She was adjudicated incompetent *after* the papers were signed, her daughter (plaintiff) was appointed her guardian, and then sued to invalidate the power of attorney and resulting papers due to the mother's alleged mental impairment at the time of signing.

Defendant argued the documents were legally valid, it had made previous loans to Mrs. Haith in which similar powers of attorney were used, and it was unaware of any problems with her mental state.

The trial court ruled for defendant, upholding the validity of the note and deed of trust, despite the fact that the signer was mentally impaired. On appeal, the court affirmed, stating the applicable law:

"It is well established in our state that a contract by an incompetent prior to being so adjudicated, is voidable and not *void ab initio*. The party contracting with an incompetent may nevertheless enforce the agreement if the following requirements can be established: (1) ignorance of the party's mental incapacity; (2) lack of notice of the incapacity such as would indicate to a reasonably prudent person that inquiry should me made of the party's mental condition; (3) payment of a full and fair consideration; (4) that no unfair advantage was taken of the incompetent; and (5) that the incompetent had not restored and could not restore the consideration or make adequate compensation."

Notice how the plaintiff would first have the burden of proving mental incapacity at the time of signing the documents. That being done, the burden of proof would shift to the non-impaired party seeking enforcement of them, to prove the five-pronged test of enforcement.

Other cases, often involving alleged intoxication, are decided on more traditional lines of whether or not there was mental impairment, and if so, did the impaired party timely demand cancellation.

In *First State Bank of Sinai v. Hyland, 399 N.W.2d 894 (S.D. 1987),* defendant's son borrowed money from the bank in the form of promissory notes. When they became past due, the bank required defendant to co-sign, as a condition to their renewal. Defendant did so in the son's presence, and also gave him a check for the past due loan interest of $900. The bank and the defendant had prior dealings over the last 15 years, in which defendant had signed and paid off approximately 60 promissory notes.

When the note came due, the son filed for bankruptcy, and defendant refused to pay, claiming he was "incapacitated through the use of liquor when he signed the note." The evidence showed that defendant had been involuntarily committed to hospitals for his alcohol problems five times over the last few years. But it also showed he had transacted business with the bank between the periods of these commitments.

The trial court ruled for defendant, and the bank appealed. In reversing the lower court's decision the court enforced the defendant's note because, "he did not show that he was entirely without understanding when he signed the note . . . and his subsequent failure to disaffirm (lack of rescission) and his payment of interest (ratification) then transformed the voidable contract into one that is fully binding upon him."

The conduct of the defendant was consistent with a legally enforceable obligation. He paid the interest arrearage. Why do this if he was allegedly alcohol impaired when he signed the note? What if he also claimed, which he didn't, that he was impaired when he wrote out the interest check? Why not promptly notify the bank that he refused to be legally bound? Instead, he sat back and did nothing until the bank was forced to sue him for payment.

In *Diedrich v. Diedrich, 424 N.W.2d 580 (Minn. App. 1988),* the marriage of the parties was dissolved in January of 1981, and the court's judgment provided that wife's remarriage would trigger a sale of the homestead which she occupied. In August of 1981 the parties signed a post-judgment agreement contingent upon wife's anticipated remarriage, which provided, among other things, that if she were divorced within five years, maintenance of $350 per month previously being paid by husband would be reinstated.

Wife remarried, was divorced within five years, and demanded enforcement of the maintenance payments under the post-judgment agreement. Husband opposed this demand, and "alleged he did not remember signing the agreement and that at the time of the signing, he had experienced blackouts due to alcoholism."

The trial court found the agreement valid, and the appellate court affirmed.

"Appellant took no action to have the agreement declared invalid for over five years. A contract is voidable but not automatically void if a party was too intoxicated to comprehend the terms of the agreement. In order to repudiate a contract entered while intoxicated, the party must act promptly."

The longer the alleged incompetent waits to assert his incapacity, the more it appears to the decision maker that this is just another case of someone making a bad business deal and then wanting to be judicially rescued. Where the non-impaired party did nothing wrong, the contract will stand.

However, if the requisite "unfair advantage" is taken of the impaired party, the scales of justice are out of balance, and court assistance is necessary to prevent injustice.

In *Smith v. Williamson, 429 So.2d 598 (Ala. App. 1982),* plaintiff was an attorney who had previously successfully represented defendant in an action to recover her residence that had been conveyed to a party named Matthews when she lacked legal capacity due to her habitual alcoholism. When he learned of a threatened foreclosure against her, he appeared at her home and was hired to represent her again.

While in his office where he was preparing to file this lawsuit, he "advanced $500 to Ms. Williamson and took back a note and mortgage on her home." When she later defaulted, he began foreclosure proceedings on her home, and she "obtained a temporary restraining order to prevent the attorney's actions."

The trial court invalidated the mortgage given to plaintiff and prohibited him from foreclosing on it by permanent injunction. The appellate court affirmed, and questioned the conduct of the plaintiff:

"Smith appeared unsolicited at Ms. Williamson's home and assured her that he could help her with her legal problems . . . the record indicates that Ms. Williamson executed the note and mortgage on her home to Smith . . . the following morning. The record further shows that Ms. Williamson had consumed a pint of one hundred proof vodka and that she remained in an agitated state over the sale of her home. To hold that Ms. Williamson was incapable of understanding the nature of the transaction with the Matthewses and then to hold that she was able to comprehend the nature of her dealings with Smith would be to reach illogical results, especially in light of the facts presented at trial."

III. MINORITY

The law tries to protect underage parties from the legal consequences of their contracts on the theory that they lack sufficient maturity, education and experience to protect themselves.

Under the common law, persons were classified and referred to as infants until they reached the age of 21 years.

"The dominant purpose of the law in permitting infants to disaffirm their contracts is to protect children and those of tender years from their own improvidence, or want of discretion, and from the wiles of designing men." *McCormick v. Crotts, 153 S.E. 152 (N.C. 1930).*

Most states have statutes that specify the age of 18, or older, as when a person has attained *majority status,* and is treated as an adult in their contracts and related business transactions.

Since the law presumes that adults have both the ability and the inclination to take advantage of minors, it declares most of their contracts to be *voidable* at their election.

1)   The general rule, still followed by a majority of the states, is unchanged since earlier times, and causes adults to contract with minors at their peril.

It is very one-sided and allows a minor to rescind (cancel, dissafirm, avoid, withdraw from) his or her contracts at any time, and in any way whether verbally or in writing, as long as it takes place before reaching the age of 18, *plus a reasonable time thereafter.*

A) Adult's unlimited duty of restitution – requires the competent party to return to the disaffirming party all the money or other value paid, with no deduction or offset for use, wear and tear, depreciation or needed repairs due to non-intentional damage. The objective is to return the minor back to the pre-contract state.

B) Minor's limited duty of restoration – requires only that the disaffirming minor return the property received from the adult in its then existing condition. If the property has been totally destroyed, the minor need not return anything but can still receive full restitution. If the damage or destruction of the property is caused however by the intentional acts of the minor, full reimbursement to the adult for these expenses is required.

2) A smaller number of states view the general rule as archaic in these more sophisticated times. They consider it too harsh on the adult that does not take advantage of the minor, where the terms of the business deal are reasonable and fair. They equate the minor's participation in the business marketplace with an acceptance of its adult rules.

While they allow the minor the same right to disaffirm as the general rule, they attempt to restore the status quo for *both* parties by requiring the minor to reimburse the adult for the reasonable use, wear and tear, and cost of repairs related to the period of the minor's ownership. This is usually deducted from the value originally paid, and the net amount is then returned to the minor.

*Ex: Susan has just received $5,000 from her wealthy aunt for her 17th birthday. She lives in a state where the driving age is 16. Susan decides to buy a used car from Miami Motors. She chooses a red Ford because it looks "cool". She inquires of the salesperson, "how much?" and is asked in return, "how much do you have to spend?" When she tells about the money from her aunt, she is informed, "That certainly is an amazing coincidence, because you can drive that Ford out of here today for $5,000 cash." She buys the car. As she drives it off the lot, she turns the radio to her favorite music station, is distracted, and accidentally slams the car into a utility pole. She is not hurt but the car is totaled. She decides to disaffirm the transaction and requests her money back. The car dealer refuses. Who wins this dispute?

Susan prevails, since Florida is one of the majority rule states, Susan satisfied all the legal requirements, and is legally entitled to receive back her full $5,000:

- She was a minor at the time of the transaction.
- She cancelled before reaching age 18.
- She didn't intentionally cause the accident.
- She has nothing to return because the damage is total.

*Ex: Assume that the facts are the same, except Susan drives the car away from the dealership and is on the road for six months. She drives north to Maine, west across the country to Washington, down to southern California, and then back east all the way to Miami. By the end of her trip, the car is dinged, dented, and dusty. She drives back into Miami Motors, declares her disaffirmance, again demands the return of her full $5,000 and the dealer again refuses. Same result – full restitution is required with no deduction for the usage or damage.

However, if this transaction had taken place in one of the "restore status-quo" states, Susan could still disaffirm, but would receive back the difference, if any. between her $5,000 and the reasonable costs of repair, salvage and/or replacement in the first example or the reasonable value of depreciation, wear and tear and damage in the second.

3) The California rule attempts to re-balance the scales in favor of the innocent adult. It will refuse to allow disaffirmance by a minor in local cases where the minor has voluntarily contracted with an adult, there are no circumstances of unfair advantage taken, and now the minor seeks to use the minority doctrine *to victimize the adult.* "Nor should infants be allowed to turn that protective shield into a weapon to wield against fair dealing adults." *41 Indiana Law Journal 829 (1948).*

*Ex: Walter has a produce trucking business in Bakersfield. His son, Tommy, is a 17-year-old high school junior, who keeps pestering him about learning the business. This reaches a point where Walter finally says, "O.K., you want to do this so bad, I'm going to give you the opportunity. I have bought you a truck and let's see how well you operate." To Walter's pleasant surprise, Tommy is a born entrepreneur, and is very successful. One of the contracts he makes is to buy fruit and vegetables at a current fixed price from Merle Farms, for future delivery. Due to a crop surplus, that price is way above current market, so Tommy attempts to disaffirm the contract. Merle Farms objects. Who wins this dispute? Merle Farms is successful.

When Tommy placed himself into the world of adult commerce, its rights and duties bound him, and since Merle Farms is an innocent party that acted in good faith, they are protected and Tommy loses his legal right to use the minority doctrine.

4) Legal exceptions to the minor's right to disaffirm are also based upon fairness. The legal pendulum swings back and forth using fairness doctrines to try to maintain the scales of justice in balance. There are four areas to discuss:

A) Under many state statutes, certain categories of transactions may not be disaffirmed by minors in the interests of public policy:

- Contracts made by a married minor
- Student loans
- Child support and alimony agreements
- Health, disability and life insurance contracts
- Agreements to provide medical services

B) Ratification of the minor's contract occurs if it is not disaffirmed within the required time. That time as we have seen under the general rule is based upon the objective standard of "what is reasonable under the facts of the particular case." But can we be more precise than this when the disaffirmance occurs after age 18?

In various factual situations, a reasonable time period for disaffirmance can be the same day as the minor's 18th birthday, one day later, one week later, one month later, and in the most bizarre of possible scenarios – one year later:

*Ex: Remember our friend Susan, who bought her Ford at age 17 for $5,000 cash? Suppose she was one day short of her 18th birthday when she drove her car off the lot, was distracted by her radio, and crashed into the utility pole, but she didn't walk away from the wreck. Let's assume Susan injured her head and is in a deep coma. Day after day in the hospital, surrounded by family and friends who try to summon her back into the world of consciousness with words of encouragement and love, she slumbers on. This continues for one year and one day. Then, as the family sings happy 19th birthday, Susan's eyelids start to flutter, her limbs begin to tremble, and she suddenly opens her eyes, sits up and says, "Mom, Dad, let's call Miami Motors so I can cancel my car purchase."

Under the general rule, and these unique facts, this really was Susan's first reasonable opportunity to disaffirm. She would win the case.

In *In Re: The Score Board, Inc.*, 238 B.R. 585 (N.J. Dist. 1999), the federal bankruptcy court was presented with a dispute involving professional basketball player Kobe Bryant.

While 17, and before he achieved superstar status, he had signed a licensing contract with the debtor, which obligated him to make personal appearances and sign autographs in exchange for $10,000 base compensation and other benefits. Three days after turning 18, he deposited debtor's check for $10,000 and performed his contractual duties for about a year and a half, until he questioned the validity of the contract on grounds of infancy, and sent a "cease and desist" letter to stop debtor from using his name, likeness or other publicity rights.

Debtor went into chapter 11 bankruptcy, and its valuable assets were ordered sold, including the Kobe Bryant contract. Plaintiff objected to no avail, as the bankruptcy judge ruled, "the parties subsequent conduct demonstrated their acceptance of the contractual obligation by performance, thereby creating an enforceable contract."

The appellate court affirmed. The right to disaffirm a contract is subject to the infant's conduct which, upon reaching the age of majority, may amount to ratification . . . Performance of a contract's executory obligations can serve as acceptance even in the absence of any writing . . . Bryant's acceptance of the $10,000 check and the parties subsequent performance were more than adequate to satisfy the offer and acceptance requirements of the contract formation."

C) Age misrepresentation by the minor, under traditional rules of law, still allows the minor to disaffirm the contract. Originally, there was not even a duty to restore the innocent adult back to status quo. This evolved to the current rule of most states, which confers on the minor the right of disaffirmance but requires the corresponding duty of full restoration. Some states take a more extreme position and totally deny the right to cancel, viewing the minor's conduct in not being truthful about his age as a serious breach of duty.

What constitutes misrepresentation of age must also be judged by the objective reasonableness standard. Certain situations clearly violate the rule, such as furnishing false identification documents or lying when asked one's age.

For other verbal exchanges, there are no hard and fast yes or no guidelines. Each case is determinative. Let's assume that Rose is 17 years old and has entered Acme Electronics to buy a laptop computer. The salesperson asks, "You are over 18 aren't you?" Rose's replies and their legal effect are the following:

- "How old do you think I am?" No misrepresentation.
- "I hear you loud and clear." Probably no misrepresentation.
- "Would I be paying you this money if I wasn't?" Misrepresentation.

D) Necessaries are those items that are deemed essential to one's existence - food, shelter, clothing and medical attention.

The minor's age, lifestyle, upbringing and family background are considered in determining whether or not a particular item is a necessity or a luxury. This determination is determined by the unique facts of each case.

This difference in category is legally significant:

(1) If the subject of the transaction is deemed a necessity of life, the minor must pay its fair market value, under the related contract doctrine of quasi contract discussed in an earlier chapter. The law encourages adults to provide these necessities to minors and not be impeded by worries about possible disaffirmance of the transaction.

But the minor still receives protection under this law to the detriment of the adult, because most of the time the adult negotiates a contract price that exceeds the current fair market price, representing the profit margin. Even if the transaction is a necessity, the required payment by the minor merely covers the adult's marketplace cost.

(2) If however, the subject of the transaction is deemed a luxury, the general rules of minor's contracts apply and the adult is again at full risk of disaffirmance.

*Examples for Food: Basic food groups like breads and grains, vegetables, dairy, produce and beef, and the foods created from them are usually necessaries. Basic beverages like milk, tea, coffee, beer and table wines are the same. The fancier the item or its preparation, and the higher it's cost the more it approaches the luxury category.

- Fried chicken vs. Pheasant under glass
- Hamburger vs. Filet Mignon
- Fresh cherries vs. Flaming cherries jubilee
- Fried eggs vs. Eggs benedict
- House domestic wine vs. Vintage imports.

*Examples for Shelter: Harvey, 17, is orphaned when his parents are killed in a plane crash. The family had been living in a rental house whose lease expires in 10 days. Harvey leases an apartment for an additional year. This is a necessity for him. If however, his parents are alive, and while living at home he rents an apartment for romantic liaisons with his girlfriend, or runs away from home during a heated argument and has the right to return, it is a luxury.

*Examples for Clothing: There are basic articles of apparel, such as shoes, underclothing, shirts, trousers, dresses, blouses, ties, scarves, etc. that sell for reasonable prices and those that are specialty or expensive brands like Gucci, Versace or Zegna. The former can be necessaries, while the latter are luxuries.

*Examples for Automobiles: Our friend Harvey needs a job to support himself. He is offered a job at a restaurant making home deliveries that requires him to use his own car. If he buys a reasonable means of transportation, the purchase is treated as a necessity. If however, he is sold a top of the line new and expensive sports car, the adult suffers the risks of the infancy doctrine.

5) A practical observation about the minority doctrine is appropriate. Businesses have done studies to determine what is its real impact. How often is a claim of rescission or disaffirmance made? How much in marketplace dollars is lost by adults when they are required to make restitution in a cancelled transaction? How much in sales is lost to competitors if a business refuses to do business with minors?

Most adults do not know their legal rights, and are unfamiliar with the doctrine and its intricacies. Most minors are in a similar predicament, with an added factor – even if they know their rights to disaffirm, few minors are skilled enough in communicating with adults and asserting themselves to complete a disaffirmance.

At the same time, the purchasing power of minors is substantial, and they will do business with whoever provides them the least complicated way to complete their transaction. The more roadblocks in their path in the form of identification/verification procedures regarding their age, the less likely they are to spend their money.

Try this practical exercise:

*Ex: Picture the busiest shopping mall in your city. Every weekend hordes of teenagers descend to shop, their pockets bulging with cash. Notice the types of businesses. Music, books, clothing, electronics, toys, food – the variety is limitless. And most all stores in one end of the mall have direct competitors located at the other end of the mall. If you owned a store in the mall, what procedures, *if any*, would you implement to protect against the legal problems caused by the minority doctrine?

The possible negative financial impact of the minority doctrine increases in direct proportion to the price of the goods or services sold in your store. The more costly the transaction, the more you are at risk. But if you make it a "hassle" to shop in your store, the affluent teens will go to your competition. What should you do?

Many commercial organizations and business consultants suggest the best procedure is to do nothing to impede the underage customers.

This is good advice, up to a certain dollar amount of purchase. If all your items are relatively low ticket, like selling books, CDs and DVDs, no problem. But what if you sell the more expensive items?

Various suggestions have been made that age verification procedures should apply to transactions of $300, $500, $1,000 or more. Would you draw a dollar line? If so, where would it be and how would you implement it?

DISCUSSION EXERCISES

1. Discuss the criteria you would use to evaluate mental impairment defenses to contract enforcement.

2. Discuss any distinctions you would make between intoxication, drugs, injury, disease, or other types of mental impairment.

3. Discuss whether the minority doctrine is still necessary to protect underage contracting parties.

4. Discuss which of the minority doctrine rules you favor, and why.

5. Discuss your view of what sales situations for goods or service should constitute a necessity of life.

CASE EXERCISES

IS THE MINOR VICTIM OR VICTIMIZER?

In *Dodson v. Shrader, 824 S.W.2d 545 (Tenn. 1992)*, the 16-year old plaintiff paid defendant $4,900 cash for a used truck he intended to use for recreational purposes. No inquiry of his age was made by defendant, nor did plaintiff make any age misrepresentations.

Nine months after the purchase, the truck developed mechanical problems, and after a mechanic advised plaintiff that there appeared to be valve problems, he nevertheless continued to drive it until the engine blew up. He parked the vehicle in front of his parent's home and contacted defendants to rescind his purchase, tendering the car and requesting a full refund. When they refused, he sued them.

Before the trial court could hear the case, the vehicle, still parked in his front yard, was struck by a hit-and-run driver, further reducing its value to $500 salvage.

The trial court granted rescission, based upon the long-standing legal rules of a majority of the states, allowing minor's to cancel their contracts. The appellate court affirmed this decision.

ANALYSIS

On further appeal to the State's highest court, the decision was reversed, and remanded to determine the proper amounts to be charged plaintiff for usage and damage liability, as well as the current fair market value of what was left.

In doing so, Tennessee adopted the so-called "restore status quo"rules of a minority of jurisdictions. These rules hold "that the minor's recovery of the full purchase price is subject to a deduction for the minor's 'use' of the consideration he or she received under the contract, or for the 'depreciation' or 'deterioration' of the consideration in his or her possession."

The Court recognized how times have changed from the early days when the courts first created the minority doctrine.

"There is, however, a modern trend among the states, either by judicial action or by statute, in the approach to the problem of balancing the rights of minors against those of innocent merchants."

" This rule is best adapted to modern conditions under which minors are permitted to, and do in fact, transact a great deal of business for themselves, long before they have reached the age of legal majority ... Further, it does not appear consistent with practice of proper moral influence upon young people, tend to encourage honesty and integrity, or lead them to a good and useful business future, if they are taught that they can make purchases with their own money, for their own benefit, and after paying for them, and using them until they are worn out and destroyed, go back and compel the vendor to return to them what they have paid upon the purchase price."

DEFUSE REPLAY

Comparing the conduct of the plaintiff and defendant in this case unbalanced the scales of justice. Plaintiff was irresponsible and caused or contributed to the damage to the automobile. Defendants fit the legal profile of the "innocent merchant", and under the modern view adopted by the Court, should be restored as much as possible to their business position prior to the sale.

Plaintiff could argue that defendants could have protected themselves by determining his age and then either choosing not to do business with him, or more likely, requiring the joinder of a responsible adult. The traditional rule of minor's contracts makes the adult an insurer of the transaction, absent the presence of the legal exceptions that protect adults who deal with minors.

"This rule is based upon the underlying purpose of the 'infancy doctrine' which is to protect minors from their lack of judgment and 'from squandering their wealth through improvident contracts with crafty adults who would take advantage of them in the market-place.'"

Defendants would counter this argument by stating they had no legal obligation to make age inquiry, they were innocent and the minor was the party at fault, and the "restore status quo" rules by which they are benefited supply adequate legal protection for both parties.

"If there has been any fraud or imposition on the part of the seller or if the contract is unfair, or any unfair advantage has been taken of the minor inducing him to make the purchase, then the rule does not apply."

CONCLUSION

This case illustrates another area of our law that is evolving. Soon, the majority of states will, no doubt, recognize some combination of the "status quo" and "benefit" rules in all cases where the adult is not attempting to take advantage of the minor.

The law will have come full cycle to protecting the adult from the crafty minor, rather than vice-versa.

"At a time when we see young persons between 18 and 21 years of age demanding and assuming more responsibilities in their daily lives; when we see such persons emancipated, married, and raising families; . . . when we see such persons engaged in business and acting in almost all other respects as an adult, it seems timely to re-examine the case law pertaining to contractual rights and responsibilities of infants to see if the law as pronounced and applied by the courts should be redefined."

    A. Do you agree with the Court's final decision?
    B. What are the advantages and disadvantages of the traditional rule?
    C. What are the advantages and disadvantages of the modern rule?

IS AN EMPLOYMENT AGENCY A NECESSITY OR A LUXURY?

In *Gastonia Personnel Corporation v. Rogers, 172 S.E.2d 19 (N.C. 1970)*, the nineteen-year-old defendant (minority under that state's law was 21) was married, and his wife was expecting their first child. His wife was employed as a computer programmer and the couple was living in a rented apartment. He had graduated high school, and was close to obtaining his college degree in applied science, but had to quit school and go to work.

For assistance in obtaining suitable employment, he went to the plaintiff's office and signed a standard contract that provided, "If I accept employment offered me by an employer as a result of a lead from you within twelve (12) months of such lead even though it may not be the position originally discussed with you, I will be obligated to pay you as per the terms of the contract."

Under the contract, defendant was free to seek employment on his own and was only obligated to plaintiff for their employment referral. It further provided he would pay a service charge of $295.00 if his annual starting salary exceeded $4,680.00.

Defendant was subsequently employed through plaintiff's referral at a salary that obligated him to pay them the service charge. He refused to pay; on the grounds the contract was not enforceable against him due to the infancy doctrine. Plaintiff sued him for breach of contract, claiming the liability under the "necessity" rule.

ANALYSIS

The trial court granted defendant's motion for nonsuit at the conclusion of plaintiff's evidence, holding the minor's contract to be a "luxury" and thus fully cancelable. The first appellate court affirmed that decision. Then the North Carolina Supreme Court granted *certiorari* accepting jurisdiction, reversed, and remanded the case for submittal to a jury, because a genuine issue existed as to whether or not the contract in question was a "necessity", and therefore would require defendant to pay the reasonable value of the services rendered.

"In general, our prior decisions are to the effect that the 'necessaries' of an infant, his wife and child, include only such necessities of life as food, clothing, shelter, medical attention, etc. In our view, the concept of 'necessaries' should be enlarged to include such articles of property and such services as are reasonably necessary to enable the infant to earn the money required to provide the necessities of life for himself and those who are legally dependent upon him."

The majority Court took a "change the law if necessary" approach to this problem: "The nature of the common law requires that each time a rule of law is applied it be carefully scrutinized to make sure that the conditions and needs of the times have not so changed as to make further application of it the instrument of injustice."

DEFUSE REPLAY

There were two dissenting opinions favoring a "strict construction" of the law approach, and questioning the propriety of the majority court expanding the legal definition of "necessaries" to include a contract for services of an employment agency.

"This is not my conception of the nature of the common law, nor is it my understanding of the authority conferred upon the Court by the people of North Carolina. The authority of the people, through their representatives in the State Government, to change the common law when conditions and needs have so changed as to render the law unjust or unwise is clear. They have, however, seen fit to vest this authority in the Legislature and not in us."

There was also a concern that the majority was creating a situation that would be harmful in the future to minors, because adults would be reluctant to deal with them.

"The reason for this rule (limiting 'necessaries' to the traditional categories) is the desire of the law to protect the infant. His liability to pay for necessaries is not imposed so as to protect an adult supplier against a shrewdly scheming infant. It is imposed solely because otherwise the infant, honest or not, might be unable to acquire that which he must have for the support of himself and his dependents."

CONCLUSION

One of the dissenting opinions also raised the obvious concern, whenever a long-established legal doctrine, like the definition of "necessaries", is broadened, that the courts would face a chaotic situation.

"Inferentially, this modification of the common law rule applies only to 'older minors,' although what age group this embraces is not clear . . . Thus with respect to contracts with minors, it now becomes impossible for the legal profession to advise clients with any degree of certainty. What is a 'necessary' in any given case is largely unknown until the jury speaks. Furthermore, what factual situation a trial judge should non-suit at the close of the evidence and what he should submit to the jury under appropriate instructions becomes a judicial game of chance."

A. Do you agree with the majority or dissenting opinions?
B. Under current business conditions, should the innocent adult face any legal restrictions in dealing with minors?
C. How would you handle the legal problems raised by this statement of one of the dissenting judges, "What was a necessary in 1770 may not be so in 1970, and vice versa."
D. Contrast the *Dodson* and *Gastonia* cases regarding their holdings that protect innocent adults.

CASE RESEARCH CYBERCISES

The following cases also relate to the material in this chapter and illustrate the types of disputes that may occur. For each one do the following written assignment:

1. Locate the case using the Internet (Lexis-Nexis, West or any other research cite which provides case transcripts).
2. Briefly summarize what it was about – the nature of the dispute involved.
3. Who won at the trial court level? Who won at the appellate level?
4. Who won if there was a third level of Supreme Court review?
5. What were the legal rules of law and the reasoning used to reach the final decision?
6. Do you agree or disagree with the decision, and explain why?
7. What business law time bomb(s) were involved?
8. Could the time bomb(s) have been avoided by structuring the transaction differently? Discuss.
9. Could the adverse effects of the time bomb(s) have been defused by a different reaction or response by the affected party? Discuss.
10. Replay the facts of the case to achieve a different successful result.

1. *In the Matter of Adoption of Smith, 578 So.2d 988 (La. App. 1991) (written document for surrender of children for adoption held invalid due to mental impairment).*
2. *Pankas v. Bell, 198 A.2d 312 (Pa. 1964)(minor's non-compete is voidable, but he is enjoined from violating it).*
3. *Fletcher v. Marshall, 632 N.E.2d 1105 (Ill. App. 1994)(minor tenant's actions held to be ratification of his lease agreement).*

NOTES

14.

DEFENSES TO ENFORCEMENT OF THE CONTRACT

B. LEGALITY OF THE TRANSACTION

"All the things I really like to do are either immoral, illegal, or fattening."
Alexander Woollcott

I. LAW OVERVIEW

Agreements are considered to be *void*, and not legally enforceable if they (1) violate a statutory law, or are (2) contrary to public policy.

Unlike the prior chapter on capacity, where *voidable* contracts allow the affected party to choose whether or not to disaffirm, there is no choice process involved here. Courts usually refuse to enforce these contracts. They take a *hands-off* approach that leaves the parties exactly where it finds them and refuse to assist them in any way, because the parties are *in pari delicto* (having equal fault).

Therefore, in the usual cases of illegality, neither party can sue the other for breach, or recover for any partial payments received or part performance rendered. The familiar contractual fairness doctrines of our legal system such as quasi contract (unjust enrichment) and promissory estoppel (detrimental reliance) do not usually apply.

Non-enforcement language used in these cases often is, "since the subject matter violates (the law in question), this transaction is declared void, illegal and unenforceable."

The two categories of contracts contrary to law or public policy are related, because the laws enacted by the legislative bodies of various levels of government are presumably to protect the public and promote its general health, safety and welfare.

The three major categories of disputes where the enforceability of a contract is in question because it allegedly violates a law are:

1. Licensing Laws
2. Lending Laws
3. Gambling Laws

Often, disputes arise which, while not contrary to specific laws, are nevertheless governed by prevailing codes of conduct, acceptable behavior, and political considerations.

These are all lumped into a general title of the prevailing "public policy". This category often changes with the times we live in, but three major categories of these cases have become well-established law:

1. Non-Competition Agreements
2. Exculpatory Clauses
3. Unconscionable Contracts

II.   AGREEMENTS THAT VIOLATE A LAW

The rules of acceptable conduct that govern our everyday lives and our transactions in the commercial marketplace are provided to a large extent from statutory sources. Each session of a state legislature yields new laws, changes some existing ones, or eliminates others that are no longer useful.

While most of these laws are relevant and contemporary, there are many laws still on the books in each state that are outmoded and rarely enforced. They serve as humorous footnotes of the past, and can be found on any web search engine under a heading of "crazy laws" or "weird laws." They include the following legal prohibitions:

- Alaska – it is illegal to provide alcoholic beverages to a moose
- California – it is illegal to ride a bicycle in a swimming pool
- Kentucky – it is illegal to carry an ice cream cone in your pocket
- Maine – it is illegal to exit an airplane while it is in flight
- Washington – moving goldfish in bowls may not ride city buses

The typical commercial dispute in this section arises when the subject matter of the contract the parties have entered into is prohibited by a particular law, one of the parties breaches the contract, and then the breaching party raises the violation of that statute as a defense to enforcement of their agreement on the grounds that it is void.

A. LICENSING LAWS

(1) Revenue-raising laws are primarily for the purpose of collecting money for the local or state government that imposes them. They often are laws that require purchase of an occupational license before one can open a store in a particular location, or require buying seasonal recreational licenses for hunting, fishing or camping. Anyone who pays the fee is granted the license. But can the failure to obtain such a license by one of the contracting parties be used to invalidate their contract?

*Ex: Brad leases a store for his new cellular phone business. The city has an occupational licensing law requiring payment of $100 before opening for business.

Before he is able to buy the license, his "grand opening sale" swamps him with customers. One of them, Craig, contracts to buy a complete phone planning system for his company for $1,000. Later, Craig realizes he overpaid, discovers that Brad was unlicensed at the time of the contract, and demands cancellation based upon violation of this licensing law.

Brad can still enforce the contract. Violation of a revenue-raising law does not invalidate contracts made by a non-complying party, because its primary purpose is the income it produces, rather than harming the public welfare. The only party allowed to complain is the licensing government, which usually imposes a fine for non-compliance.

(2) Regulatory laws are the opposite of revenue-raising laws. They are laws that license various professions. Their primary purpose is the protection of the public. There is only an incidental collection of money to signify licensing compliance.

These laws are created so that unscrupulous or unqualified practitioners will not harm the general public. Such regulation is punitive, carrying criminal and civil sanctions. The offending parties can be fined or imprisoned, and they are legally prohibited from enforcing their contracts.

*Ex: Harry is the top law student in his class, graduating with the highest GPA in the history of the school. He takes the bar examination required by his state, is sure he passed it, but is awaiting the results. Sally has a legal problem and seeks Harry's advice. He tells her not to worry, it is a matter he can solve for her, and "I'll only charge you $300 to handle it." She accepts his offer. He completes the work successfully and sends her a bill. She discovers he is not yet legally licensed as an attorney, and refuses to pay.

Sally wins – Harry cannot enforce his illegal contract and must suffer the consequences. If Sally complains to the Bar, he might also be sanctioned for "unauthorized practice of law".

The annual Bar dues that Harry must pay to remain licensed raise revenue for the state. But the contracts that Harry makes, even while in default of his duty to keep his annual dues current, are still valid. He runs the risk however of having his license to practice law revoked if the dues aren't paid by a certain date.

In *Gutfreund v. Demian, 642 N.Y.S.2d 294 (N.Y.App.Div. 1996),* plaintiff was acting as an unlicensed insurance broker who sought to receive from the defendants a percentage of insurance commissions earned for procuring new insurance carriers for defendant's clients.

The New York Insurance Law prohibited insurers from, "paying any money or giving any other thing of value" to unlicensed brokers. Plaintiff sought to circumvent this law by having a friend of his who was a licensed broker send the bill for monies due, collect it and then pay him.

The trial court granted defendant's motion for summary judgment and the appellate court affirmed. "To allow plaintiff, as an unlicensed broker, to evade the statutory scheme by receiving payments from another broker, rather than directly from an insurance carrier, would violate the legislative intent. A party who contracts to violate a statute enacted for public protection may not sue for a breach thereof."

In *Hydrotech Systems, Ltd. v. Oasis Waterpark, 803 P.2d 370 (Cal. 1991)*, plaintiff contracted with defendant to design and construct a large 'surfing pool' using their wave equipment. The total contract price was $850,000 and defendant was allowed to hold back specified portions pending satisfactory completion and operation of the pool. After making full payment for plaintiff's construction services, defendant "retained" more than $110,000. Plaintiff sued for breach of contract and defendant alleged it had no obligation to pay because plaintiff lacked a California contractor's license.

The California statute provided that an unlicensed contractor could not, "bring or maintain any action in a California court to recover 'compensation for the performance of any act or contract for which a (contractor's) license is required."

The trial, appellate and Supreme Court all rejected the plaintiff's contract claims, which included promissory estoppel claims and allegations that the defendant has fraudulently induced them to perform while knowing they were unlicensed. "The purpose of the licensing law is to protect the public from incompetence and dishonesty in those who provide building and construction services . . . Thus, an unlicensed contractor cannot recover either for the agreed contract price or for the reasonable value of labor and materials . . . It follows that an unlicensed contractor may not circumvent the clear provisions and purposes of (the statute) simply by alleging that when the illegal contract was made, the other party had no intention of performing."

As a practical matter, *Oasis* could have refused to pay all or any portion of the contracted price and *Hydrotech*, as an unlicensed contractor, would have had no legal recourse.

B. LENDING LAWS

Lenders make money in their loan contracts by charging interest to their borrowers. State usury laws govern the allowable maximum rates of interest charged. A usurious loan is one that charges in excess of the allowable statutory rate.

The sanctions are severe for this unlawful contract, to protect the public from being victimized and to deter lenders from engaging in such prohibited conduct in the future.

The maximum allowable interest rates and penalties for violation vary from state to state. There are often criminal penalties as well as civil sanctions, depending upon the severity of the offense. Florida Statute Chapter 687 is illustrative:

"All contracts for the payment of interest…at a higher rate than 18 percent per annum simple interest are hereby declared usurious" However, if such "…obligation exceeds $500,000 in value, then no contract to pay interest thereon is usurious unless the rate of interest exceeds (25 percent per annum)."

Loan sharking is defined to mean extracting interest over 25 % per year. Charging interest from 25% to 45% per year is a criminal misdemeanor and taking interest over 45% per year is a felony.

"Any person, or any agent, officer or other representative of any person, willfully violating the provisions of s. 687.03 shall forfeit the entire interest so charged."

Florida's statute is typical. Other states are more severe, requiring a forfeiture of double the interest paid. A few states are totally punitive – they require the forfeiture of all interest *plus the entire principal.*

*Ex: Jules desires to borrow $100,000 from Matthew. When Jules is told the only way the loan can be made is at maximum interest, he says, "That's fine. I need the money now and I don't care what interest rate I have to pay." Matthew sees the lack of resistance and charges interest of 2% per month for the two-year loan term. Jules agrees, and later refuses to pay, claiming usury.

Even though it looks like Jules might have induced Matthew into this position with his "no resistance" approach, the law is clear – the usurious lender is penalized to the extent of the laws of the state where the loan took place.

C. GAMBLING LAWS

Wagering agreements are, as a general rule in all states, void, illegal and unenforceable. They carry civil and criminal penalties.

We are not talking here about lawful risk transfers in the form of property, casualty or liability insurance.

And we are also excluding the numerous revenue-raising exceptions such as the Florida pari-mutual industry that allows legal betting on horse racing, dog racing, and the game of Jai-Alai. Within the past 10 years there has also been a huge increase nationwide in state sponsored lotteries, scratch-off games and related lawful gambling that raises needed revenue for their states of operation.

Gambling law prohibitions try to protect the public and deter offenses by allowing the participants in games of chance to legally refuse to honor their bets. This can impact both winners and losers in a betting dispute.

*Ex: Ted, a Miami resident, wants to bet on the outcome of the 2003 World Cup soccer final. It is illegal in his home state, but legal under Nevada law in the city of Las Vegas where his friend Bill lives. Ted asks Bill to bet $500 for him on Brazil to win the game, and says, "Don't worry about the money. When I win, you just get a bank check and send it to me, deducting the bet and your commission of 20%. If I lose, I'll reimburse you." When Ted loses the bet, he refuses to pay back the money that Bill advanced.

Bill is out of luck. The underlying transaction is a private gambling contract, void and unenforceable in both Florida and Nevada. Suppose Bill gets creative and claims this was really a loan agreement? No dice Bill – again a court would look to the true subject matter – the purpose of the loan – and reach the same result.

In *Ryno v. Tyra, 752 S.W.2d 148 (Tex. App. 1988),* Ryno owned a BMW automobile dealership and discussed a sale to Tyra of a 1980 M-1 auto for $125,000. When Tyra hesitated, Ryno suggested a "double or nothing coin flip". Tyra agreed, won the coin flip, and Ryno handed Tyra the car keys plus the title to the auto, and provided paper dealer's tags so it could be licensed for street use.

Later, Tyra was convinced by Ryno to loan the car back to the dealership for display at an auto show, and Ryno then took the car and sold it himself to a third party. Tyra sued for conversion of his property, and Ryno defended on the grounds that the original transaction was an illegal gambling contract.

The trial court jury awarded Tyra $125,000 conversion damages and $10,000 punitive damages. On appeal, the decision was affirmed.

"We agree with appellant that his wager with Tyra was unenforceable. The trial court could not have compelled Ryno to honor his wager by delivering the BMW to appellee. However, Ryno did deliver the BMW to appellee and the facts incident to that delivery are sufficient to establish a transfer by gift of the BMW from Ryno to the Tyras."

What about Internet gambling? Its proliferation in the last few years has been dramatic. Some states, like California, specifically prohibit it by statute, while others like Florida allow it until there is a legislative prohibition:

"The Internet is the first truly global communications network, utilizing both interstate and international wire communications to link users around the world. Therefore, any effort to regulate use of the Internet is better suited to federal regulations than to patchwork attention by the individual states. Evolving technology appears to be far outstripping the ability of government to regulate gambling activities on the Internet and of law enforcement to enforce such regulations. Thus, resolution of these matters must be addressed at the national, if not international level." *Florida Attorney General Opinion Number: AGO 95-70 (October 18, 1995).*

*Ex: Ted goes on-line to an offshore gambling site and deposits $500 to start making bets on sporting events with Cyberspace Gaming. He is very successful and builds a credit balance of $10,000. He then requests a check for $9,000 from his winnings and Cyberspace refuses. Can Ted legally enforce this contract?

This collection problem rarely occurs due to the intense competition between Internet gambling sites and their need to maintain credibility. Their advertisements provide a large source of revenue for local media, and they are rated by gaming services as to their payout reliability. However, potential enforcement problems could certainly occur, since they legally do not have to pay these private gambling agreements under U.S. law.

Ted is probably out of luck. Even though millions of dollars are wagered every day on-line in similar transactions, if the gaming companies decided not to pay, there is nothing he could legally do. Firstly, his site and unpaid winnings are located offshore in a foreign jurisdiction. Secondly, even if a foreign lawsuit was filed and service of process legally made, the court deciding the case would apply the general rule and declare the gaming contract invalid. Thirdly, the time, expense and stress of such litigation, as well as admitting to the world he had been gambling illegally, would cause Ted to probably walk away from the dispute and learn an expensive lesson. Internet gamblers beware!

The same type of practical collection problems arises in casino gambling. Aside from the non-legal aspects of whether a debtor would risk bodily harm by non-payment to the casino, and the public relations problems that would arise by a casino defaulting in its payment obligations, the same rules of non-enforceability of gambling contracts apply.

In *Metropolitan Creditors Service of Sacramento v. Sadri, 19 Cal. Rptr.2d 646 (Cal. App. 1993)*, defendant incurred gambling debts of $22,000 at a Lake Tahoe, Nevada casino.

He wrote the casino two personal checks for the amount, signed two matching promissory notes, received gambling chips in exchange and lost all playing baccarat. He later stopped payment on the checks, which were drawn on his California bank.

A Nevada statute made credit instruments evidencing gambling debts owed to licensed casinos valid and enforceable. Caesar's Tahoe did not, however sue defendant on his debts. Instead they assigned them to plaintiff for collection, and suit was filed against defendant in California. The trial court ruled for defendant, under the established rules of non-enforceability of gambling debts in California. The appellate department affirmed and certified the case for transfer to the appellate court where the judgment was affirmed.

Plaintiff contended that, "under the constitutional doctrine affording full faith and credit to the public acts, records, and judicial proceedings of other states, (the court was) required to enforce Sadri's gambling debts pursuant to the Nevada statute . . ."

The court said, "The pivotal question is whether such enforcement is against the public policy of the State of California . . . California has always had a strong public policy against judicial enforcement of gambling debts, going back virtually to the inception of statehood. This prohibition is deeply rooted in Anglo-American jurisprudence . . ."

The court then distinguished the proliferation of legalized gambling now present in California, and in most states, in the form of pari-mutuel racing, poker clubs, charitable bingo games and the state lottery, from prohibited "gambling on credit."

"There is a special reason for treating gambling on credit differently from gambling itself. Gambling debts are characteristic of pathological gambling, a mental disorder which is recognized by the American Psychiatric Association and whose prevalence is estimated at 2 to 3 percent of the adult population. Characteristic problems include extensive indebtedness and consequent default on debts and other financial responsibilities, and financially motivated illegal activities to pay for gambling. Having lost his or her cash, the pathological gambler will continue to play on credit, if extended, in an attempt to win back the losses."

Plaintiff could not enforce the debt by a direct lawsuit in California, but the court told it what should have done instead. "If a licensed owner of a Nevada casino wishes to recover on a check or memorandum of indebtedness given by a California resident under such circumstances, the owner will have to obtain a Nevada state court judgment, which will then be entitled to full faith and credit in California regardless of our public policy."

This legal time bomb exploded in plaintiff's face because of their failure to employ anticipatory thinking and prevent their losing outcome.

III.   AGREEMENTS THAT VIOLATE PUBLIC POLICY

Our courts have consistently recognized the importance of invalidating contracts that are adverse to the best interests of the general public and are considered to negatively impact society.

However, the judicial and legislative definitions of morality, acceptable conduct and the public welfare constantly have changed over the years. So an agreement that may be declared pornographic in one era (Nathaniel Hawthorne's *The Scarlet Letter* or Henry's Miller's *Tropic of Cancer*) may be recognized as a literary masterpiece in another time. The contract to publish that book would be unenforceable in the first instance, and perfectly valid in the latter.

Certain common business situations arise so frequently and are of such importance to commercial transactions that a body of law to govern them has grown from the many disputes that ripened into lawsuits decided by various courts. They involve the three areas of:

(A) Non-Competition agreements
(B) Release of Liability agreements
(C) Unconscionable agreements

A. NON-COMPETITION AGREEMENTS

One of the oldest public policies we have is our common law principle that contracts in restraint of trade are unlawful, because they limit the free competition that is the essence of our commercial marketplace.

Federal and state antitrust laws echo these sentiments. Nevertheless, two major types of contractual restraints on competition are skillfully used in everyday business, and are held to be valid and enforceable so long as they (1) serve to protect a legitimate business interest as part of an otherwise valid contract, (2) are not harmful to the general public, and (3) are reasonable in time restricted, geographic area involved, and scope of activity protected.

1. PURCHASE OF AN EXISTING BUSINESS

The value of a going business is primarily in the customers that shop there and produce its income stream. This is called goodwill. It applies to businesses that sell goods, and especially to those that are service oriented.

When a prospective buyer is reviewing the flow of income the business currently produces and is projected to produce in the future, a key consideration is guaranteeing that the former owner will not open a competing business and lure away the former clientele.

The price paid for such a business is based upon that income, and a new owner needs transition time for existing customers to feel comfortable with new management.

*Ex: Nick has owned and operated the Mykonos restaurant for 15 years in a South Miami Beach shopping center, growing from one storefront to the entire west side of the center. As that area has grown over the years, so has the restaurant. His customers are treated like family, and the food and service are consistently excellent. Nick decides it is time to retire, advertises the business for sale, and contracts to sell it to Neal & Mike. The purchase price is based upon a multiple of existing sales revenue. The buyers require a clause in the purchase contract that states, "Seller agrees not to enter into a competing restaurant or food service business in Miami Beach for 3 years." After the sale is completed and one year goes by, Nick is driving his wife crazy being around their house, and opens a restaurant called Zorba's in North Miami Beach, 20 miles away from the old location. Neal & Mike claim breach of contract and sue for damages. Nick claims the non-compete is legally unenforceable.

Let's play judge and decide who should win. Firstly, the non-compete was a part of a valid contract to buy the restaurant, and (1) serves a legitimate business purpose to protect the buyer's customer base. If the facts were different and rather than buying Nick's business, Neal & Mike had an existing location and contracted to pay him not to expand into their area, such a restriction would be viewed as void and against public policy. The difficulty arises in deciding (2) whether the critical terms of the non-compete are *reasonable*.

- Scope - this is a restaurant business that primarily serves Greek food specialties. The restraint is therefore reasonable as to, "restaurant or food service." If it had said, "any restaurant serving any type of food," it would have been unduly restrictive, and unenforceable.

- Time - the restraint of 3 years seems reasonable. It will probably take the buyers at least one year to stabilize the new management situation, and at least another year to have everything running smoothly. If the duration of the non-compete exceeded 5 years, it probably would be excessive.

- Area - here lies the main problem. Miami Beach is a large city, spanning over 20 miles. Did most of Nick's customers come from the immediate area? If so, the restraint on the entire city seems too large.

  If however, the clientele came from all over, due to the restaurant's reputation, status and other factors – the area of non-compete would appear reasonable. The unique facts of each case will govern.

We may also have another practical problem with non-competes that involves the *no resistance* situation we looked at previously in usurious loans. What if Nick was desperate to sell his business, the buyers told him they would require the standard "reasonable" non-compete, and Nick had said, "Do whatever you like. I am burned out and have to get away from this place. I'll sign anything you put in front of me."

Let's suppose the non-compete he signed was for "any business involving food", "for 10 years", in "all of southeastern Florida". The restrictive agreement is obviously unreasonably broad, void and unenforceable as an illegal restraint. If Nick could have induced such an agreement, he could have opened a competing restaurant next door the day after his sale closed, and effectively put the new buyers out of business.

Caveat emptor – let the buyer (of an existing business) beware!

In *Thermatool Corp. v. Borzym, 575 N.W.2d 334 (Mich. App. 1998)*, a case of first impression, *defendant* sold his business to plaintiff, and as a part of the sale, the buyer agreed to pay him 5% of annual sales above $2.5 million, as a royalty "in return for assets such as good will, technological expertise, patents and trade names, as well as the agreement not to compete" for a period of five years after the sale. The seller collected in excess of $1 million royalties.

Before the end of the 5-year term, the seller filed a declaratory judgment action claiming the agreement was unreasonable and therefore unenforceable. Thermatool counterclaimed that he had violated the agreement by forming a competing consulting company.

The trial court ruled that the non-competition agreement was reasonable and enforceable, and the buyer moved for a judgment awarding damages for Borzym's alleged breach of the agreement. The court agreed with the buyer, awarded damages of $30,040 and extended the term of the non-compete an additional 18 months. Borzym appealed and that aspect of the decision was affirmed.

"In cases where a party has flouted the terms of a non-competition agreement, the court should be able to fashion appropriate equitable relief despite the fact that the parties did not expressly provide for such relief in their agreement."

Thus, the court in effect rewrote the agreement for the parties; a result that is allowed in some states and not permitted in others. The critical factors usually involve the extent to which the seller of the business has breached its competition restriction and the resultant damage suffered by the buyer.

2. EMPLOYMENT CONTRACTS

When a person decides to buy a business they are making an investment. It is a calculated choice rather than a necessity. One's employment however is more of an emergency situation. Finding a job provides the financial resources for acquiring food, shelter and clothing, and some luxuries too if it succeeds. It pays the bills and allows the employee to survive and hopefully thrive in the world of work.

For this reason, the legal tests for the validity of an employment non-compete are stricter than those imposed by the sale of a business. The allowable scope, term and area are smaller. People must be allowed to work.

1. the scope of restraint must be specific and not industry wide
2. the time of restraint should not exceed the term of the hire
3. the prohibited territory should be reasonably limited
4. the employee who leaves voluntarily or is fired with cause is usually not protected

Many states treat employment non-competes as legally unenforceable, even if voluntarily created, unless the employer can show that the employee has access to or has been entrusted with trade secrets, technological details, and other valuable confidential information that would give a business rival (new employer) a distinct competitive advantage. In California they are totally prohibited by statute.

The more training and expertise possessed by the employee, or the higher up the ladder his position, the more reason exists to enforce his non-compete when he leaves employment. And this is especially true in this era of the Internet, because the downloading of a company's client or customer list and the transmission of trade secrets can take place literally in the blink of an electronic eye.

Courts may also refuse to enforce a violated employment non-compete and allow the breaching party to work for his new employer, but can issue a permanent injunction to prevent disclosure and use of the trade secrets of the former employer.

Often the employee signs both an agreement not to compete and an agreement to maintain confidentiality of company information, or these are separate clauses in the non-competition agreement.

Some employers that once limited non-competition covenants only to high level executives, top salespersons and research and development personnel are now routinely asking rank-and-file workers to also sign them as a condition of their employment, because of the high tech nature of many businesses and the current level of industrial espionage.

Disputes involving employment non-competes are not easily decided and the law is in a state of flux.

- California bans employment non-competes. *California Civil Code sec. 16600.*

- New York does not favor them, but will enforce them if reasonable and necessary to protect a valid business interest. But there is an important exception called the 'employee choice doctrine': "New York courts will enforce a restrictive covenant without regard to its reasonableness if the employee has been afforded the choice between not competing (and thereby preserving his benefits) or competing (and thereby risking forfeiture). *Post v. Merrill Lynch, 397 N.E.2d 358 (N.Y. 1979).*

- Non-compete of a cardiovascular surgeon earning $300,000, with 18 months to become an equal owner of the practice, "for a period of two years following the date of termination", "within a 75 mile radius of Albany, Georgia", was upheld.

  "Keeley was to become an equal owner of CSA within 18 months, which means this covenant was not subject to the strict level of scrutiny accorded normal employment contracts, but to the middle level of reduced scrutiny accorded professional contracts where the parties are considered as having equal bargaining power." *Keeley v. Cardiovascular Surgical Associates, 510 S.E.2d 880 (Ga. App. 1999).*

- Non-compete of general manager of a company engaged in the manufacture and sale of roofing and insulation products, "within three hundred (300) miles of Allentown, Pennsylvania", "for a period of three (3) years after the date of termination of Employee's employment hereunder", was held to be "both broader than necessary to protect the employer's business interests and unduly oppressive on the former employee." *Insulation Corporation of America v. Brobston, 667 A.2d 729 (Pa. Super. 1995).*

- Non-compete of vice-president employed "at-will", in charge of the content of employer's websites. Their business provided online products and services to information technology professionals who managed computer systems.

The restraint that "prohibits Schlack from working for any person or entity that directly competes with Earthweb for a period of twelve months after the termination of employment with Earth Web," was ruled too broad.

"As a threshold matter, this court finds that the one-year duration of EarthWeb's restrictive covenant is too long given the dynamic nature of this industry, its lack of geographical borders, and Schlack's former cutting-edge position with EarthWeb where his success depended on keeping abreast of daily changes in content on the internet . . . When measured against . . . the Internet environment, a one-year hiatus from the work force is several generations, if not an eternity." *EarthWeb v. Schlack, 2000 U.S. App. Lexis 11446 (2000).*

In *Gomez v. Texas Aries Medical Society Services, 814 S.W.2d 114 (Tex. App. 1991), a* temporary injunction to prevent a former employee from competing with the employer's business of assisting hospitals in recovering money for medical services provided to indigent patients was dissolved, even though he was fired for alleged performance problems and discovery of his plan to create a competing business.

His duties, which included soliciting hospitals to become customers of his employer, were deemed to be personal services, and under the state law the employer had the burden to prove the restraint, "contains reasonable limitations as to time, geographical area, and scope of activity to be restrained that do not impose a greater restraint than is necessary to protect the goodwill or other business interest of the promisee."

The non-competition covenant barred Gomez "from competing in an 'existing marketing area' and a 'future marketing area of the employer begun during employment.'"

"The covenant not to compete would cover virtually every major metropolitan area in the State of Texas. Non-competition covenants with such a broad geographic scope have generally been held unenforceable, particularly when no evidence establishes that the employee actually worked in all areas covered by the covenant."

In *Varsity Gold, Inc. v.Porzio, 45 P.3d 352 (Az. App. 2002),* plaintiff's business was to provide materials for fund-raising programs used by schools throughout the United States, through a network of independent sales agents. The sales agents would contract with schools to provide "Gold Cards", entitling the holder to receive discounts at local businesses. The students would sell the cards to consumers, and the schools would keep a portion of the sales proceeds.

Defendant was hired on a month-month basis, and signed a 'Sales Representative Agreement' that prohibited him, "for a period of three years after termination of the agreement, from competing with Varsity in the State of Pennsylvania or any contiguous state." It also forbid him to solicit Varsity's customers or divert its business during the stated term.

The agreement further provided that, "the court may reform the geographic area and time restrictions if it finds them to be unreasonable and unenforceable."

Defendant violated the terms of the agreement and plaintiff sued for breach of the covenant not to compete, an injunction and money damages.

The trial court ruled that the covenant was unenforceable as written because the geographic area was too broad and the time constraint too lengthy. It then modified the restrictions, per the reformation clause, deciding "the covenant not to compete could be enforced in the south Pittsburgh area (where Porzio had worked) for a period of one year."

The appellate court reversed. "While Arizona courts may 'blue pencil' a restrictive covenant by eliminating grammatically severable, unreasonable terms, the court cannot add provisions or rewrite them." The attempted strategy of plaintiffs in trying to cover themselves with a "safe-harbor" clause to allow judicial rewriting of an objectionable restriction failed. They should have been more careful in limiting the reach of their non-compete to only protect their legitimate business interests.

You try to be the judge on this one:

*Ex: Norman is hired by Kentucky Fried Chicken (KFC) as executive vice president, in charge of their Atlanta, Georgia regional office, for a term of three years, at an annual salary of $150,000. One of the conditions of his employment was his signing an agreement "not to enter into a competing business for five years anywhere in the southeastern United States." Two years later, Norman resigns and goes to work for Popeye's Chicken in Jacksonville, Florida in a similar position for a comparable salary. KFC sues for breach of the non-compete agreement. Norman defends, claiming it is unreasonably broad and unenforceable.

Certainly KFC's "secret seasonings" that make its taste unique are a valuable trade secret that requires protection. As an executive, Norman would have more access to such confidential information than a lower level employee. Popeye's is in a related food enterprise and fits the definition of "a competing business".

The time of the restraint of 5 years exceeds the 3 year hire, and would therefore appear to be invalid, but this might be offset by the executive position and compensation received.

The "southeastern U.S." restriction appears on its face to be too broad. However when considering the fact that KFC is a worldwide company and both Atlanta and Jacksonville are within the restriction, this may not be the case.

B. EXCULPATORY CLAUSES

To exculpate is, "to free from blame, liability or responsibility." As our lives have become more complex and business relationships more litigious, it is almost essential for businesses to protect themselves against liability.

The use of an exculpatory clauses with its customary language of *not responsible for loss or damage* covers the entire business spectrum from damaged autos in parking garages and injured spectators at sporting events to liability claims for accidents in hazardous outdoor recreational activities.

Originally, such clauses were an absolute bar to recovery by the injured party under the legal theory of *volenti non fit injuria* – he who consents cannot be injured. This is the basis for the legal defense known as "assumption of the risk".

As our laws and their judicial interpretation turned more toward protecting the public, the blanket protection of these release clauses has changed to one that denies or allows enforcement based upon the following scenarios:

- A minority of states allow them to release ordinary negligence
- A majority of states refuse to allow release of any negligent acts
- Most states allow release of liability in athletic or sporting events for ordinary negligence, but not gross negligence
- All states refuse to allow release of liability for intentional torts, willful misconduct, fraud or acts of gross negligence

*Ex: Lois decides to go bungee jumping off the 200-foot Capilano Bridge in Vancouver, B.C. In order to participate she is required to sign a form that states, "the undersigned agrees to release the operator from any and all liability for any and all claim, loss or damage suffered by me resulting from this activity." The employee strapping her into the elastic harness miscalculates her size and weight, so that she hits her head on the riverbank at the bottom extension of her jump. She sues for damages, and the release form is offered as a defense to liability.

Most states would uphold the exculpatory agreement and rule in favor of the operator, if bungee jumping were considered an athletic or sporting event. Although the operator's breach of care caused the loss, the act in question was still within the bounds of ordinary or simple negligence.

If however, the injuries to Lois were caused by the bungee cord breaking, this would be gross negligence and invalidate the protection of the release.

Courts will also usually require that the exculpatory clause be clearly written and conspicuously placed in the contract, so that a "reasonable" person would be aware of its liability limitations. Also if the party seeking to enforce the limitation has abused superior bargaining power and forced the limitation on the agreeing party, non-enforcement usually results.

California has gone the farthest in refusing to enforce exculpatory clauses:

- Residential tenant who tripped on a rock in a common stairway in his apartment building and was injured is not bound by a blanket exculpatory clause in his lease. The case was not decided on a theory of negligence, but rather a 'public interest' ruling that "exculpatory clauses in residential leases violate public policy." *Henrioulle v. Marin Ventures, 573 P.2d 465 (Cal. 1978).*

- Hospital admission form that released liability for future negligence was invalid as an "exculpatory clause affecting the public interest." *Tunkl v. Regents of University of California, 383 P.2d 441 (Cal. 1963).*

- Auto repair order form contained the clause in bold letters, "Not responsible for loss or damage to cars or articles left in cars in case of fire, theft or any other cause beyond our control," which the court refused to enforce. Porsche owner's car brought to his dealership for repair was stolen while parked at the repair garage. "The modern citizen lives-and all too frequently dies-by the automobile . . . An out-of-repair automobile is an unreliable means of transportation. . . It follows that clauses which exculpate repair firms for ordinary negligence in handling and securing vehicles under repair are invalid as contrary to public policy." *Gardner v. Downtown Porsche Audi, 180 Cal. App. 3d 713 (Cal. App. 1986).*

Other states are not so stringent, and will enforce exculpatory clauses in appropriate cases:

- 17 year old skydiver signed a covenant not to sue which included an exemption from liability that stated, "whether such loss, damage, or injury results from the negligence of the Corporation, its officers, agents, servants, employees, or lessors or from some other cause," who was injured in an airplane crash due to alleged negligence, was not allowed to recover due to its specific terms. *Jones v. Dressel, 623 P.2d 370 (Colo. 1981).*

- ADT Security provided a fire alarm monitoring system for plaintiff's plant, and extensive damage resulted due to alleged defects in the system. The contract, which specifically limited the liability of ADT to a maximum of $1,000, was upheld. "Both parties had equal bargaining power.

Chicago Steel declined the opportunity to pay for an allocation of additional liability to the fire alarm service." *Chicago Steel Rule and Die Fabricators Co. v. ADT Security Systems, Inc., 763 N.E.2d 839 (Ill. App. 2002).*

- Health and fitness facility had members sign a standard exculpatory clause, which included a negligence release. Plaintiff was injured while doing a series of tests to evaluate her physical condition. Summary judgment was granted in favor of the defendant based on the release clause. *Seigneur v. National Fitness Institute, Inc., 752 A.2d 631 (Md. App. 2000).*

C. UNCONSCIONABLE CONTRACTS

We previously discussed contracts that might "shock the conscience of the court" when we talked about the garage sale cases that raised the legal issue of whether or not the dollar equivalent amount of consideration paid was adequate. The key factor was if the buyer took unfair advantage of the seller. We were talking about exploitation.

We now revisit this concept. It is not to be used as a legal excuse for one party's bad bargain. Rather it is a balancing principle to prevent extreme unfairness or severe injustice.

If the following elements are proven, a contract will be declared void, illegal and unenforceable, on grounds of unconscionability:

1) There is a great disparity in the bargaining power between the parties
2) The stronger party misuses its advantage to oppress the weaker party through extremely unfair contract terms
3) The weaker party has no reasonable alternative

In *Williams v. Walker-Thomas Furniture Company, 350 F.2d 445 (D.C. Dist. 1965)*, plaintiff signed a contract requiring installment payments for the purchase of residential furniture where title and foreclosure remedies would be retained by the seller until the total of all payments for all items even though individual items were paid in full. In refusing to enforce the contract, the court said, "Unconscionability has generally been recognized to include an absence of meaningful choice on the part of one of the parties together with contract terms which are unreasonably favorable to the other party."

"In many cases, the meaningfulness of the choice is negated by a gross inequality of bargaining power. The manner in which the contract was entered is also relevant to this consideration. Did each party to the contract, considering his obvious education or lack of it, have a reasonable opportunity to understand the terms of the contract, or were the important terms hidden in a maze of fine print and minimized by deceptive sales practices."

The following example is based on the case of *John Deere Leasing Company v. Blubaugh, 636 F. Supp. 1569 (D. Kan. 1986)*:

Jed is a wheat farmer, with limited formal education. His crop is in the ground when his Caterpillar brand tractor dies. He needs a new one at once for his harvest. He goes to his local dealer, and is presented a rental contract for a new tractor. He is told to "take it or leave it", with no modifications allowed.

It is printed on lightweight paper, in complex, legalistic language, and the reverse has fine print which provides that if he defaults in payment, Caterpillar had the right to repossess the tractor, sell it, keep the sales proceeds, and still be able to recover from him a complex formula of termination damages. When he defaults after paying two annual payments that total $31,000, they seize the tractor, re-sell it for $42,000 and then sue him for an additional $12,000. He defends on the grounds that the default clauses were unconscionable.

Jed wins this case. Notice the telling factors that individually and collectively add up to the blatant unfairness of the lessor in exploiting their lessee. As we mark them off, one by one, we feel that Caterpillar should not be allowed to do this. It just isn't right. Public policy requires non-enforcement of the offending clauses.

These types of agreements are often called *contracts of adhesion*. They are preprinted on standardized forms that require the weaker party to "adhere" to their terms on a "take it or leave it" basis, with no opportunity to negotiate, and the circumstances are such that they appear to be trapped with no reasonable way out of their predicament.

Parties who have made a poor business deal are often tempted to try and find a legal doctrine that will extricate them from their self-created problems. Unconscionability is often alleged in these commercial contract cases, but is rarely upheld by the courts unless the conduct complained of is extreme, way beyond the line of reasonable business conduct.

In *Iwen v. U.S. West Direct, 977 P.2d 989 (Mont. 1999)*, plaintiff signed an order with defendant for advertising in the telephone yellow pages. The order form prepared by defendant was a standard preprinted form that read as follows:

"Any controversy or claim arising out of or relating to this Agreement, or breach thereof, *other than an action (at law) by Publisher for the collection of the amounts due under this Agreement, (emphasis added)* shall be settled by final, binding arbitration in accordance with the Commercial Arbitration Rules of the American Arbitration Association . . ."

When the directory was published, plaintiff noticed his phone number was incomplete and his address was missing. He advised defendant he would not pay the bill until the parties had resolved the negligent errors. Defendant received a disconnect notice, and after several unsuccessful attempts to resolve the matter, he filed suit for damages. Defendant moved to stay litigation and compel arbitration per the clause in the advertising order.

The trial court ruled the arbitration provision valid and enforceable. Plaintiff appealed and the Court reversed, holding, "that the arbitration provision at issue in this case is unconscionable."

"Drafted as such, the weaker bargaining party has no choice but to settle all claims arising out of the contract through final and binding arbitration, whereas the more powerful bargaining party and drafter has the unilateral right to settle a dispute for collection of fees pursuant to the agreement in a court of law."

The legal claim of "unconscionability" also arises in situations where one party has signed a surgical medical release, which either seeks to disclaim liability for malpractice, or more commonly requires the patient to arbitrate a dispute before a medical board, rather than litigate for personal injuries in a court of law.

In *Broemmer v. Abortion Services of Phoenix, Ltd., 840 P.2d 1013 (Az. 1992),* plaintiff was a 21 year old, unmarried high school graduate who was 16 weeks pregnant, with a minimal $100 a week job and no medical benefits. The father-to-be insisted she have an abortion, her parents insisted she do not, and she was conflicted, confused and emotionally upset.

Plaintiff's mother made an appointment with defendant clinic, and upon arrival plaintiff was asked to complete a series of preprinted forms, one of which was an agreement to arbitrate, which stated, "any dispute arising between the Parties as a result of the fees and/or services" would be settled by binding arbitration and "any arbitrators appointed by the AAA (American Arbitration association) shall be licensed medical doctors who specialize in obstetrics/gynecology."

She completed the forms in five minutes without reading them, and the clinic staff made no attempt to explain them before or after she signed, nor was she provided copies. Her pregnancy termination procedure was scheduled the following morning, and unfortunately she suffered a punctured uterus, requiring separate medical treatment. She filed a malpractice complaint in a court of law and the defendant moved to dismiss based upon the agreement to arbitrate.

The trial court ruled for the defendant, holding that although the arbitration agreement was a contract of adhesion, it was not unconscionable and therefore enforceable against plaintiff. The appellate court affirmed, but the Arizona Supreme Court reversed.

"An adhesion contract is typically a standardized form offered to consumers of goods and services on a 'take it or leave it' basis without affording the consumer a realistic opportunity to bargain and under such conditions that the consumer cannot obtain the desired product or services except by acquiescing in the form contract."

"To determine whether this contract of adhesion is enforceable, we look to two factors: the reasonable expectations of the adhering party and whether the contract is unconscionable."

"Plaintiff was under a great deal of emotional stress, had only a high school education, was not experienced in commercial matters, and is still not sure 'what arbitration is.'"

Some text writers have suggested that all surgical medical releases are, by definition and surrounding circumstance, legally unconscionable. What do you think? Should distinctions be made based upon the severity of the patient's injury or illness and/or the medical risks of the contemplated procedure? What about cosmetic surgery? It is purely voluntary but can sometimes be very dangerous.

IV. SPECIAL SITUATIONS

(1) What if all or a part of the purchase price is paid in an illegal contract? If the contract is not enforceable, does the paying party get their money or property back?

*Ex: Perry buys a house in Coconut Grove, surrounded by plants, trees and all types of undergrowth. While exploring his property he notices that a large area of apparent weeds at the rear of his land is really marijuana. He is welcomed to the neighborhood by Duane who makes him this business proposition. "Howdy dude, you've got a cash crop growing in your back yard. I'll pay you $10,000 to harvest it tomorrow night at midnight. Here is $5,000 as a good faith deposit." Perry agrees and takes the money. When Duane returns, Perry refuses to allow him on the property and also refuses to return the money. Duane sues for breach of contract and Perry defends based on illegality.

The contract here is obviously void. But should Perry be allowed to profit? Under the general rule of illegal contracts, he would because courts do not interfere with such contracts other than to refuse to enforce them. Should the fact that Perry did not grow the marijuana himself be a factor in his favor? What if he didn't even know the plant was growing on his property at the time Duane made his offer? Since Duane initiated the contract, should he suffer the greater loss? What if Duane's offer included the purchase of Perry's car for a fair price?

Notice how changing a fact or two in this dispute could change the persuasive arguments to be made.

When we talked about the types of contracts in an earlier chapter, we discussed the fairness concepts of quasi contract (unjust enrichment) and promissory estoppel (detrimental reliance). Is not this the case if the court adopts its "hands-off" policy in illegality cases and leaves the parties where it found them?

While most states strictly enforce the illegality doctrine and refuse to assist either party to such a transaction, others are more lenient, and have created exceptions to the general rule in these situations:

a) the recovering party was less at fault than the other
b) the recovering party was excusably ignorant of the governing law
c) the illegal act was never performed
d) the illegal act can be separated from the lawful activity

- Plaintiff, as a knowing and willing participant in a promotional stocks and bonds pyramid scheme of defendant, prohibited by New York law, could not recover any part of his investment. "It is the settled law of this State (and probably of every other State) that a party to an illegal contract cannot ask a court of law to help him carry out his illegal object. For no court should be required to serve as paymaster of the wages of crime, or referee between thieves." *Ford v. Henry, 598 N.Y.S.2d 660 (N.Y. App. 1993).*

- Employment contracts that guaranteed county employees salary merit increases violated the state's "pay as you go" law, and "any reliance on promises made by the county was unreasonable and could not form the basis for promissory estoppel." *Weese, et al v. Davis County Commission, 834 P.2d 1 (Utah 1992).*

(2) What if illegality occurs or is discovered after the contract is created? In such a case, the parties have entered into a valid and enforceable agreement. The subsequent illegality prevents its enforcement and discharges the parties, but they should be restored to their prior status quo position or otherwise made whole.

In *Duncan v. Kasim, 2002 WL 125686 (Fla. App. 2002)*, plaintiff contracted to run a bar owned by defendant, made substantial improvements to the property, and then could no longer perform because she had failed to reveal she was a convicted felon, contrary to the liquor licensing law. She sued for unjust enrichment due to the value of the improvements she had made.

The trial court dismissed her case and she appealed. The appellate court reversed, recognizing that her contract to manage the bar was illegal, but this fact did not preclude her legal action.

"The fact that the contract is illegal does not mean that Kasim has the right to keep the property Duncan placed in the bar when she was in possession of it. Anything she brought to the premises she can remove. She also has the right to receive the value of fixtures not removable from the premises that enhance its value."

(3) What if the parties have contractually agreed in advance as to the dollar amount of damages payable in the event of a breach? This is known as a *liquidated damages clause*. It is commonly used in construction agreements to prioritize the project and give the builder an added liability incentive to complete on time.

Similar to our discussion of non-competes, these damage agreements are a skillful way to transact one's business when it may be difficult to determine actual damages, and they are legally valid so long as the amount of the default damages are "reasonable". This has been interpreted to mean they must bear some proportionate relationship to the actual damages that would be suffered by the customer if the builder did not perform within the required time.

However, if the amount of agreed damages are unreasonably high, based on the facts of the case, they are deemed to be a *penalty*, and are void, illegal and unenforceable on public policy grounds.

Here is another true story:

*Ex: Martin is a young law school student in the 1960's. He and his wife contract with Southwest Construction (SC) to construct their new house for a total price of $24,000. (Yes, that's what it cost way back then). Martin, whose wife is expecting their first child, discusses with the builder his desire to specify a date of completion and also to set a cost for each day of delay.

The builder approves the completion date, laughs and says, "No problem kid, put in any dollar amount you like, we always finish our jobs on time." Martin notices no resistance from the builder and puts the following clause be in the contract: "SC agrees to complete this job in all respects, including issuance of certificate of occupancy by Dade County, no later than 7/1/61, and for every day SC is late in said completion it shall pay liquidated damages of $1,000 per day." SC completes 10 days late. Martin wants to deduct $10,000 from his agreed purchase price.

Sorry Martin – this clause is really a penalty because it is unreasonably high. Suppose the cost of renting a similar house in those days was $300 per month, and suppose there would be additional expenses to re-route furniture purchases, duplication of moving costs, and other damages directly caused by the delay of $500. The maximum allowable per day charge should have been $100. Martin was not as smart as he thought. (By the way, his wife never let him hear the end of it either.)

In *Luminous Neon, Inc. v. Parscale, 836 P.2d 1201(Kan. App. 1992)*, defendant leased outdoor advertising signs from plaintiff, which were custom designed for her needs. The lease contained a liquidated damages clause that required her, in the event of a breach, to pay damages equal to 80% of the remaining payments due. She had originally been offered the signs for $5,600 on a purchase basis but declined. This computation was based upon plaintiff's expenses incurred in manufacturing, installing and financing the signs, plus their profit.

Later, street construction by the City of Topeka adversely affected plaintiff's business and she was forced to close, at a time when 41 monthly payments remained due under the lease, resulting in a computation of liquidated damages due of $6,951.04, which defendant refused to pay, so plaintiff sued to collect it.

The trial court granted plaintiff's motion for summary judgment and the appellate court affirmed, finding that there was a reasonable relationship between the expenses of the plaintiff and the amount charged the defendant.

"The contention that only the original sale price of the signs constitutes reasonable damages is not persuasive. There are advantages to be weighed when one considers leasing rather than purchasing an item ... The damage clause of the lease was not a penalty."

The following case is controversial, since the computation of liquidated damages far exceeded actual damages, and resulted in the recipient party receiving an apparent monetary windfall. What do you think?

California and Hawaiian Sugar Co. v. Sun Ship, Inc., 794 F.2d 1433 (9th Cir. 1986), involved a contract given by plaintiff to defendant to built for it a custom 'integrated tug barge' for the shipping of the raw sugar it harvested from the Islands during the six month sugar season from Hawaii to its California refinery.

The contract price was $25,405,000, and provided that, "if 'Delivery of the Vessel' was not made on the 'Delivery Date' of June 30, 1981, Sun would pay C and H 'as per-day liquidated damages, and not as a penalty' $17,000 per day as a 'reasonable measure of damages.'"

Sun did not complete the vessel until March 16, 1982, thus triggering damages under the contract clause of $4,413,000. But during the 1981 season plaintiff was able to arrange for purchasing another vessel for shipping the sugar crop, so that its actual damages were only $368,000.

C and H sued to collect the liquidated damages. Sun claimed they were a penalty, "unreasonably disproportionate to the actual damages," and not due. The trial court upheld the contract clause and the appellate court affirmed:

"The anticipated damages were what might be expected if C and H could not transport the Hawaiian sugar crop at the height of the season. The damages were clearly before both parties . . .

Given the anticipated impact on C and H's raw sugar and on C and H's ability to meet the demands of its grocery and industrial customers if the sugar could not be transported, liquidated damages of $17,000 a day were completely reasonable."

"Contracts are contracts because they contain enforceable promises, and absent some overriding public policy, those promises are to be enforced. 'Where each of the parties is content to take the risk of its turning out in a particular way' why should one 'be released from the contract, if there were no misrepresentations or other want of fair dealing? Promising to pay damages of a fixed amount, the parties normally have a much better sense of what damages can occur. Courts must be reluctant to override their judgment."

V. STRATEGIC PLANNING

Notice that agreements that restrain trade, limit liability, require adherence to their terms, or specify damages in advance are all legally enforceable IF they are drawn and utilized properly. However public policy considerations are increasingly used to question their enforcement, and the laws continually bend to assist the consumer or perceived weaker party in any bargain.

An improperly drafted agreement, that goes beyond the bounds of reasonableness, may be effective in intimidating the other party from violating it or seeking legal recourse to invalidate it. Most parties don't know their legal rights and the express terms of these agreements bar any attack upon them.

However, more and more persons are questioning these agreements notwithstanding their terms, and the best strategy is to anticipate they will be legally attacked, and then prepare them in such a way that they are enforceable.

What should the drafting party do to help withstand a claim that the agreement or clause is "unreasonably restrictive?"

1) Non-competition agreements – determine what at first appears to be the most conservative time, area and scope of restraint, and then limit these areas even further, to try and assure validity. There must be legitimate business concerns for reasonably worded restrictions, not arbitrary categories inflated by the other party's lack of resistance. In fact, that willingness to sign whatever the document says, "because I must have the job" or "because I have to sell the business", is a sure sign that perhaps the employer or purchaser is being set up for failure.

2) Exculpatory clauses – recognize that one's own negligence or the negligence of one's agents cannot legally be waived.

Instead of wording that obviously overreaches, such as releasing "any and all acts of our negligence", the limitation should be directed more toward a dollar amount of recovery if negligence is proven.

3) Unconscionable contracts – continue to use take-it-or-leave-it contracts of adhesion on preprinted forms, but make sure that the restrictive language is in bold type, and there should be an opportunity offered to the bound party both before and after signing for a full and complete explanation of the legal and practical effect of the document. Their clear choice then is to knowingly sign it or refuse the services or goods offered.

4) Liquidated damages – the same constraints of non-competition restrictions apply here. Don't be induced by non-resistance or enthusiastic acceptance to provide for payment of damages that will exceed actual loss. These clauses are not like punitive damages, and should be limited to the compensatory and consequential aspects of the loss suffered by delays in completion.

DISCUSSION EXERCISES

1. Discuss what usury sanctions you think appropriate.
2. Discuss the advantages v. disadvantages of the forms of legalized gambling that are available in your state.
3. Discuss the enforceability guidelines you would create for non-competes.
4. Discuss whether the California restrictions on use of exculpatory clauses should be followed or modified.
5. Discuss any other public policy arguments that should render contracts unenforceable.

CASE EXERCISES

FUTURE EMPLOYMENT RESTRICTED WITHOUT A NON-COMPETITION CONTRACT

In *Doubleclick, Inc. v. Henderson, Dickey and Alliance Interactive Networks, 1997 N.Y. Misc. LEXIS 577 (N.Y. 1997)*, Henderson was hired to an executive position in plaintiff's business of selling internet advertising through a network of websites. It agreed with the owners of the sites to sell advertising space and solicited advertisers to participate in its network. Customers would click-on posted advertising banner links and learn about the advertiser's products.

When Henderson was hired as an executive to hire, train and manage plaintiff's sales force, he became their highest paid employee.

Like other executives, including Dickey, the person who recruited him, he signed a confidentiality agreement, but unlike the others who had signed one-year non-competes, he signed no such agreement.

After about one year, Henderson and Dickey were dissatisfied with the direction of plaintiff, resolved to start their own company (Alliance), and began to draft a business plan and talk to some fellow employees about going with them. When the company president received a tip, he confronted them, and then plaintiff brought suit to enjoin them from launching a new company or taking employment with a competitor – claiming (1) misappropriation of trade secrets, (2) breach of duty of loyalty, and (3) unfair competition.

ANALYSIS

The court ruled against the defendants and granted injunctive relief to plaintiff narrower than originally sought:

Plaintiff's initial injunction request was to, "enjoin defendants for a period of at least twelve months from launching a competitive business or from working for a direct competitor of DoubleClick."

The court reviewed all the evidence and balanced the equities in favor of the plaintiff, finding that defendants

"1) used DoubleClick's proprietary information to prepare for the launch of alliance and to position it to compete with DoubleClick,

2) worked on their plans for their new company during working hours at DoubleClick and used resources given to them by DoubleClick to do so, and

3) sought customers and financing for Alliance without regard to their duties to their current employer."

But the court felt the one-year time period was too long, "given the speed with which the Internet advertising industry apparently changes," and ruled that:

"Defendants are enjoined, for a period of six months from the date of this opinion, from launching any company, or taking employment with any company, which competes with Doubleclick, where defendant's job description(s) or functions at said company or companies include providing any advice or information concerning any aspect of advertising on the Internet."

The decision can be attacked on two legal grounds:

1) The injunction seems to be a prohibited industry-wide restraint. DoubleClick's business is Internet advertising, the defendant's business tasks involved Internet advertising, and they are both prohibited from "launching any company or taking employment with any company" involving "any aspect of advertising on the Internet". What other field of work is available to them?

2) Dickey signed a non-competition agreement. It appears to be an unreasonable restraint upon him because it is overly broad as to scope, and thus unenforceable. As to Henderson, the argument is much stronger because *he never signed a non-competition agreement.* The court attempts to reform the confidentiality agreements signed by the defendants so that the usual prohibitions against disclosure of trade secrets while working for the new employer are broadened into a restraint against working at all for the next six months.

CONCLUSION

This case has had far-reaching implications in the everyday business world, because it began a trend that now exists toward a more common usage of non-competition restraints among all workers, whether entry level, midlevel or executive managerial.

Today's predominantly high-tech marketplace is an atmosphere of intense competition for the consumer dollar; predatory hiring practices to lure valuable employees and their intimate knowledge of the internal workings of competitors, and increasingly sophisticated techniques of industrial espionage.

But media reports indicate that non-competes are being required in many non-tech businesses, running the gamut from medicine, law, architecture, securities, and insurance to tattoo parlors, body-piercing shops and your friendly neighborhood Starbucks restaurant. *Be loyal or see you in court, employers warn workers. U.S. News & World Report, December 18, 2000.*

Management strategy is to require non-competes from most all employees, even clerical staff. The restraints are drafted as broadly as possible and are legally unenforceable on their face. However, few employees faced with such restraints have the resources or inclination to challenge them. Strict compliance with the non-compete is the usual course of employee conduct.

They often obey these unreasonable contracts out of ignorance, or the intimidation presented by this perceived threat to their jobs.

Even successful attacks may result in the plaintiff being perceived as a "litigious" person and cost them new job opportunities. The actual court proceedings are also so draining financially and emotionally, that few employees are willing to file suit. The message to other employees is don't rock the boat.

And the impact of *DoubleClick* is to raise the stakes even higher, since employees whose conduct threatens company trade secrets are legally bound by non-competition restraints implied by the court, without the necessity of then signing a specific non-competition agreement.

    A. Do you agree with the Court's final decision?
    B. Should Henderson have been restrained in the same way as Dickey?
    C. Would the court have ruled the same way if there was no confidentiality agreement?

CASE RESEARCH CYBERCISES

The following cases also relate to the material in this chapter and illustrate the types of disputes that may occur. For each one do the following written assignment:

1. Locate the case using the Internet (Lexis-Nexis, West or any other research cite which provides case transcripts).
2. Briefly summarize what it was about – the nature of the dispute involved.
3. Who won at the trial court level? Who won at the appellate level?
4. Who won if there was a third level of Supreme Court review?
5. What were the legal rules of law and the reasoning used to reach the final decision?
6. Do you agree or disagree with the decision, and explain why?
7. What business law time bomb(s) were involved?
8. Could the time bomb(s) have been avoided by structuring the transaction differently? Discuss.
9. Could the adverse effects of the time bomb(s) have been defused by a different reaction or response by the affected party? Discuss.
10. Replay the facts of the case to achieve a different successful result.

1. *Ray v. Stroman, 923 S.W.2d 80 (Tex. App. 1996) (insurance agent's 5 year – entire county employment non-compete held unenforceable).*
2. *Milligan v. Big Valley Corp., 754 P.2d 1063 (Wyo. 1988)(liability release upheld in skiing death of Ironman Decathlon competition).*
3. *Graham v. Sasson-Tail, Inc., 28 Cal. App. 3d 807 (Cal. App. 1981) (arbitration clause held unconscionable in Bill Graham/Leon Russell rock concert contract).*
4. *Kemper Family Farm Partnership v. Dakota Industrial Development, Inc., 603 N.W.2d 463(Neb. App. 1999) (payment of additional $10,000 on $600,000 road construction contract not completed on time is enforceable).*

5. *BDO Seidman v. Hirschberg, 712 N.E.2d 1220 (N.Y. App. 1999) (accountant employee's non-solicitation of firm's clients clause for 18 months after termination with formula liquidated damages held enforceable).*

NOTES

15.

DEFENSES TO ENFORCEMENT OF THE CONTRACT

C. REAL CONSENT: WAS THE ASSENT VOLUNTARY AND KNOWING?

"It is true that you may fool all the people some of the time;
You can even fool some of the people all the time; but
You can't fool all of the people all the time."
Abraham Lincoln

I.   LAW OVERVIEW

In the types of commercial disputes we have previously examined one of the parties to the alleged contract seeks to avoid its enforcement by claiming that:

- No legal agreement was made because of lack of a legal offer or lack of a legal acceptance, or

- The agreement is not legally enforceable due to a failure of consideration, or

- Even though the required agreement between the parties was reached and is supported by consideration, it is nevertheless legally unenforceable due to incapacity (voidable) or illegality (void).

Now we examine a new area of business disputes where the complaining party agrees that they made an otherwise legally enforceable agreement, they do not claim incapacity or illegality, but still want to be legally excused from having to perform because of a claim that their consent given to the contract was not genuine.

They claim that there was a lack of voluntary and knowing assent due to the particular factual circumstances, and therefore the contract made should be legally cancelled.

Our commercial marketplace requires that contracting parties be able to enforce their contracts. But if that contract was obtained by threat or force or mistake or deception it should not, in fairness, be allowed to stand. The victimized party should be legally allowed to raise such unfair circumstances as a legal defense to enforcement.

This assumes that the offending party will receive an unfair benefit in the form of a more advantageous business deal than would have been otherwise available through an arms-length transaction. So equitable principles demand that the scales of justice be re-balanced to prevent one party from taking unfair advantage of the other.

Typically, the plaintiff sues for breach of the contract and the defendant seeks to have it cancelled and demands rescission based upon one of the following defenses:

1. Duress – coercion
2. Undue Influence – persuasion
3. Mistake - error
4. Fraud - trickery

If rescission of the contract is granted, the reciprocal duties of restitution and restoration that we previously examined in the chapters on Capacity and Illegality apply. The party who is allowed to cancel is entitled to receive back anything of value previously given as consideration, but must correspondingly return anything received. This restores the parties to the status quo. If there is an imbalance in the valuations upon completing these rights and duties, courts will typically assess damages to equalize.

The complaining party has a further duty to act promptly. As soon as the offending circumstances occur, the decision must be made and announced in a clear and convincing way. Any unreasonable delay or attempt to retain the benefits of the contract while avoiding its burdens will be interpreted as a "ratification" of the contract and require its full enforcement.

II.   DURESS

Duress is wrongful coercion. One of the parties commits an unlawful act by which the other party is forced to enter into the contract against their will.

If this occurs, that contract is voidable at the option of the victimized party. Typical testimony in such a dispute is, "I was forced to sign the contract. I had no choice. He held a gun to my head, literally or figuratively."

The duress is actual force or, more commonly, the threat of force and the victim is placed in a "no way out" situation, with no reasonable alternative other than agreeing to the proposed contract.

In these types of disputes, courts determine whether or not the plaintiff will prevail using the personal "subjective" standard. The fact that the conduct in question would or would not be actionable coercion to the hypothetical reasonable person of our law's "objective" standard is not applicable. The particular plaintiff is evaluated, with his existing background, station in life, level of experience, and unique personal characteristics to ascertain if he may be excused from the agreement in question on grounds that it was procured by duress.

*Ex: Clint, a 6-foot tall bodybuilder wants to buy mild-mannered Gene's watch and offers $100. Gene says, "I really am not interested in selling, so sorry." Clint says in a menacing tone, "People usually don't refuse me friend, my final offer is $150, and here is a bill of sale for you to sign." Again Gene says no deal. Then Clint grabs one of Gene's arms, twists it behind him, pulls the watch off his wrist, and says, "Sign the paper or I'll break your arm." Gene signs and then promptly sues to rescind the sale and recover his property.

This is a case of actual physical duress, a clear violation of the requirement of voluntary consent to the contract, and Gene would win. The contract here would be void because it was obtained illegally. Clint committed an offense of extortion and battery upon Gene. Often such conduct is met with criminal charges filed against the offender as well as a civil action for contract rescission.

Duress disputes are usually much more subtle. These involve threats that induce the contractual agreement rather than actual physical contact.

*Ex: Assume the same basic Clint and Gene transaction. When Gene says no deal, Clint pulls a gun from his coat, points it at Gene, and says, "This is a 357 magnum, the world's most powerful handgun, and unless you give me that watch and sign the paper right now I will blow you away." Gene complies and then promptly sues to cancel the sale.

Again this is clearly duress by Clint and Gene would win. Although there was no physical force exerted, the circumstances clearly show lack of genuine assent by Gene, and Clint would still be subject to criminal charges for his unlawful actions.

Modern legal requirements for duress are more liberal. Rather than the threat situation having to involve conduct that is clearly illegal, most states allow duress claims in situations where the complainant successfully proves the contract was entered into "improperly". This is a matter of opinion that again is judged based upon the objective standard of reasonableness.

- The threat to file criminal charges is usually held to be duress
- The threat to file a civil lawsuit is usually not duress

The differences in the severity of penal versus civil sanctions is given as the reason for these different results.

In addition to the conduct complained of by the victim being "improper" to the degree required by law, the victim must not have any reasonable "out" and thus be forced to comply.

*Ex: Audrey needs repairs to her car, takes it to the dealer in the morning for an estimate and is quoted $500 as the offer to perform the work. She accepts the offer and authorizes the work. When she returns to the dealership late that afternoon with a cashier's check for $500 to pick up her car, she is told at the cashier's desk that the bill is $750. When she objects she is told, "Sorry miss, there is no one here at this hour but me, and unless you pay the charges I can't release your car to you." Audrey pays the additional cash and then demands return of the excess cost.

Audrey's claim of duress would be sustained. Although she technically "accepted" the higher contract, the mitigating circumstances would allow it to be cancelled.

A practical way that Audrey could avoid such a dispute is by paying with a credit card. Aside from the basic plastic money advantage of up to 60 days of "free money" - you buy the item on day 1, are billed on day 30, and don't have to pay until day 60 – Audrey is protected by consumer laws against improper deliveries, faulty workmanship, or breach of agreement.

She receives her car and then tries to work out the problem with the auto dealer. If unsuccessful, when she pays the credit card bill she just circles the disputed item on the front, writes her explanation on the back, and her vendor is then required to justify its item. If they can't, it is removed from Audrey's account, along with any finance charges incurred while the dispute was in process.

The raising of the duress defense in current business or commercial transactions is often known as *economic duress*. This occurs when the financial vested interest of one party is improperly threatened to force them to enter into a new contract, modify an existing one, or waive valuable contract rights.

Hurd v. Wildman, et al., 707 N.E.2d 609 (Ill. App. 1999), disallowed a claim of economic duress by a fired lawyer who signed a release and separation agreement to receive his last paycheck, and then sued for benefits due him under the law firm's partnership agreement. The court recited the basic law of duress:

"Economic duress is a condition where one is induced by a wrongful act or threat of another to make a contract under circumstances that deprive one of the exercise of one'' own free will. To establish duress, one must demonstrate that the threat has left the individual 'bereft of the quality of mind essential to the making of a contract.' The acts or threats complained of must be wrongful; however, the term 'wrongful' is not limited to acts that are criminal, tortious, or in violation of a contractual duty. They must extend to acts that are wrongful in a moral sense as well."

"In terms of 'economic duress,' also known as 'business compulsion,' the defense cannot be predicated upon a demand that is lawful or upon doing or threatening to do that which a party has a legal right to do. Furthermore, it has long been held that where consent to an agreement is secured merely because of hard bargaining positions or financial pressures, duress does not exist."

Economic duress involves the traditional profile of a stronger party seizing an opportunity to take extreme unfair advantage of a weaker party that we have seen previously in the "take it or leave it" cases of unconscionable contracts.

*Ex: CBZ Inc. is a small construction company that bids on a million dollar apartment building project of Mega Corp. They are low bidder and get the job, which will be their biggest venture. As the job moves forward, they routinely submit their draw requests and receive progress payments. They then pay their subcontractors and suppliers from these funds.

They lack liquidity to carry their creditors more than 30 days. This is known to Mega Corp. CBZ Inc. completes construction and submits their final draw request for the $200,000 balance due. Mega Corp. never denies owing the money but plays games delaying payment, such as "the check is in the mail," "our computers are down," "we just lost our bookkeeper and our records are a mess." CBZ, Inc. is desperate. Its creditors are threatening lawsuits and worse.

Mega offers to pay $100,000 out of its petty cash, "as a favor to you, while we attempt to straighten out our financial records, so long as you sign a release indicating you are paid in full. Take it or leave it." CBZ, Inc. signs, receives the money, and then sues for the balance, claiming it signed the release under economic duress.

This is classic economic duress, a case of financial abuse of bargaining power, where Mega Corp. engaged in a predatory business practice once it sensed the vulnerable position of its adversary.

Mega Corp. will claim it was just engaged in "hard bargaining", which is an everyday fact of the commercial marketplace. This is an effective defense to a claim of duress, and modern courts are more prone to denying recovery in questionable cases because the basic motivation of the party raising this defense is to be relieved from what they perceive as a bad business deal. Courts will not usually substitute their judgment for the business risks assumed by the parties.

In *Strickland Tower Maintenance, Inc. (STM) v. A T&T Communications, Inc., 128 F.3d 1422 (10th Cir. 1997), (ATT)*, Plaintiff contracted with defendant to provide supervision services in the burying of 46 miles of fiber-optic cable, was to be paid a set percentage of the total project cost, and had management responsibility.

After the project began, defendant demanded that they assume project management, and implied that if plaintiff would not agree, defendant would deny future business.

When a dispute arose about the computation of amounts due STM, it sued for breach of contract and "asserted that AT&T used economic duress to force STM to agree to use inspectors and hand control over the project to AT&T."

The trial jury awarded STM $470,601 in restitution damages on the economic duress claim. On appeal, that award was reversed. The court said, "A litigant cannot, therefore, make out a claim of economic duress by alleging merely that the opposing party took advantage of her weak negotiating position or because of 'business necessities'. The assertion of duress must be proven by evidence that the duress resulted from defendant's wrongful and oppressive conduct and not by plaintiff's necessities."

In *Aldrich & Company v. Donovan, 778 P.2d 397 (Mont. 1989)*, defendant was a building contractor who purchased merchandise from plaintiff and signed a promissory note for his open account debt. Due to nonpayment, plaintiff sued.

"Donovan admits he executed the note, but asserts that he did so under economic duress. He alleges duress in that Aldrich would not extend him further credit unless he signed the note."

Summary judgment was entered against the defendant and, on appeal, the judgment was affirmed, because the court felt he was not forced to incur the debt.

"A claim of economic duress requires a showing that the contract at issue was made under circumstances evincing a lack of free will on the part of the contracting parties. It is not sufficient to show that consent was secured by the pressure of financial circumstances, or that one of the parties merely insisted on its legal right."

"The note at issue here evidenced an existing debt owed by Donovan to Aldrich . . . Aldrich had a legal right to require security of some sort before extending credit to Donovan. He was therefore 'pressured' only by his need for further credit, not by any duress imposed by Aldrich."

There are occasions however, where a claim of economic duress will be sustained, often in situations where a release is signed in settlement of a disputed claim and the non-signer is the party who caused the dispute.

In *International Underwater Contractors, Inc. v. New England Telephone and Telegraph Company, 393 N.E.2d 968 (Mass. App. 1979)*, plaintiff contracted with defendant to assemble and install conduits under the Mystic River for a fixed price of approximately $150,000.

The defendant required major changes in the project to be done in the winter months, which caused delays in the work. This generated extras of over $800,000 that defendant assured plaintiff would be paid. When defendant refused to honor its alleged promises, settlement discussions ensued and dragged on. Plaintiff by now had exhausted its bank credit, its cash position was overdrawn, and its creditors were demanding immediate payment. When defendant offered $575,000, plaintiff "was forced to take it 'on a take-it-or-leave-it basis'".

The trial court entered summary judgment for defendant on the economic duress issue, and plaintiff appealed. The appellate court reversed, ruling that the issue should be fully litigated.

"A release signed under duress is not binding. Coercion sufficient to avoid a contract need not, of course, consist of physical force or threats of it. Social or economic pressure illegally or immorally applied may be sufficient."

"Merely taking advantage of another's financial difficulty is not duress. Rather, the person alleging financial difficulty must allege that it was contributed to or caused by the one accused of coercion. The assertion of duress must be proved by evidence that the duress resulted from defendant's wrongful and oppressive conduct and not by plaintiff's necessities."

"If the assertions of the plaintiff are true, the defendant did more than assert a legal right (settling the dispute instead of litigating), as its acts created the financial difficulties of the plaintiff, of which it then took advantage."

III.   UNDUE INFLUENCE

Undue Influence is closely related to duress. The difference in its disputes is that the abusive bargaining and wrongful pressure are exerted in a more subtle manner. Rather than outright coercive action, there is unfair persuasion of someone who, because of advanced age or illness or health conditions is weak and vulnerable. The typical elements are:

- A special relationship of trust and confidence exists, such as legal fiduciary relationships of attorney-client and doctor-patient, or personal caretakers, nurses or attendants.

- There is a strong party who has a dominant position over a weaker party.

- The strong party takes financial advantage of the weak party, usually in the form of asset transfers from them called "gifts".

    *Ex: Winifred is a 90-year-old widow, living alone in a large house. She is mentally alert but physically frail. Her needs are attended to by Cleo, her live-in companion and nurse.

Winifred has a grown son and daughter who live in a distant city. Winifred owns a large Cadillac automobile she no longer drives that is parked in her garage. One day Cleo tells her, "My car just died and I need a new one. Why don't you give me yours, since you no longer use it?" Cleo declines saying, "Sorry dear, but I'm saving it for my children." Then Cleo says, "If you don't sign over that car to me, I may forget to give you your medicine, or I may decide to leave you all alone tonight." Winifred is frightened and signs the title transfer.

Clearly this is Undue Influence and the transfer can be cancelled. All the required elements of abuse of special relationship for personal advantage are present. Cleo's motives are clearly improper and we have no sympathy for her. But what if we change the facts just a bit?

*Ex: After Cleo's initial request for the car, instead of making those threats, she merely asks Winifred to reconsider before declining. Winifred now says, "You know dear, you are correct. You take such good care of me, and the children are far away and you need the car and they don't, so it is yours with my gratitude."

Here the transfer of the asset to Cleo is clearly voluntary, knowing, and Winifred obviously intends that the transfer occur.

But what if Winifred never tells the children about this gifting, and then dies? They expect it to be a part of their inheritance and when they find it was transferred to Cleo, they will suspect some impropriety. But they weren't present at the time of the transfer so they really don't know Winifred's true intentions.

This is a practical dilemma that has caused most states to change the traditional burden of proof required in Undue Influence cases.

If Winifred wanted to cancel the gift transfer during her lifetime, she would seek rescission on the grounds of Undue Influence, and testify as to the surrounding circumstances. She knows better than anyone whether her act was free and voluntary. She could easily sustain her burden of proving her lack of real consent with her personal assertions.

But when she dies and her heirs bring a rescission action to cancel the transfer because of their suspicions, they cannot sustain their burden of proving it was improper because they have no personal knowledge of what actually occurred. Did Cleo abuse the personal relationship with Winifred for personal gain, or did Winifred voluntarily give the item in question to Cleo? There is the appearance of improper conduct, but the heirs don't really know.

Therefore, in Undue Influence actions, the complaining heirs need only prove that: (1) a special relationship of trust and confidence existed between the stronger and weaker parties, and (2) the stronger party received the so-called "gift" benefit. This raises a *presumption of undue influence* and the burden of proof shifts to the benefited party to prove that they *didn't commit undue influence.*

This is a total reversal of the usual proof requirements, in the interests of fairness, because of circumstances that give the appearance that someone has taken unfair advantage of another.

A decision maker in such a dispute must objectively evaluate the circumstances under the "reasonableness" test, without the benefit of personal subjective testimony of the alleged giver, and the shifting burden of proof is a great disadvantage to the recipient of the gift.

Rather than the criminal proof test of "innocent until proven guilty", the gift donee is faced with "guilty until you prove your innocence." And such proof is extremely difficult unless there were independent witnesses to the gift transfer, or other evidence of its voluntary nature.

"Where one party stands in relation of trust and confidence to the other, such as is here involved, attorney and client, trustee and cestue que trust, where the dominant party – and in this relation the attorney or trustee is regarded as the dominant party – receives or derives a benefit or advantage from a transaction during the existence of such relation, the party reposing the confidence, on seasonable application to a court of equity, may obtain relief from the burden of such transaction, by showing the transaction and the confidential relations, unless the person receiving the benefit overcomes the presumption of undue influence by evidence which reasonably satisfies the judicial mind that the transaction *was in every respect just, fair, and equitable.*" *Verner v. Mosely, 127 So. 527 (Ala. 1930).*

This shift of the burden of proof in Undue Influence cases has had the practical effect of putting most situations of gifts between non-family members at legal risk. It requires an intended gift donee to anticipate the potential legal problems and try to create the necessary protective testimonies that the donor was not subjected to any unfair persuasion, the transfer was purely voluntary, and no improper advantage was taken. This is not an easy task, but it is essential to prevent unfair advantage being taken of susceptible donors.

Here are three types of typical undue influence court disputes:

1) Sometimes, the plaintiff in an undue influence dispute is available to testify regarding whether or not the document in question, which usually transfers valuable property rights to another, was freely and voluntarily signed.

In *Goldman v. Bequai, 19 F.3d 666 (D.C. App. 1994)*, the plaintiff, an 80 year old widow, alleged that her attorney and long-time family friend had unduly influenced her to convey substantially all her property to him three months after her husband's death. She executed two transfer documents to her residence condominium and her partnership interest in a commercial property, creating joint tenancies with right of survivorship between herself and the defendant. The latter was later sold, and her proceeds were placed in a joint account with defendant.

Plaintiff had been treated by a doctor with antidepressant drugs during her husband's last illness and thereafter, and had no legal counsel or independent advice when making the transfers. There were no witnesses to the transactions, and she also claimed defendant did not fully explain the transactions to her.

Plaintiff stated her 'first inkling' that defendant had 'deceived' her came after she sold the commercial property. "He put his name on my half. His name was on everything I had: my checking account, my savings account. The other half he put in his name and his wife's name and I couldn't understand that."

After she had an argument with defendant stemming from the transfers, she fired him as her attorney, but did not sue him to cancel the transfers until five years later when she sold the residence and learned she received only one-half of the proceeds. Defendant claimed no liability on the plaintiff's claims due to the running of the three-year statute of limitations. She asserted the statute was equitably tolled by the defendant's improper conduct.

The trial court rejected the plaintiff's claims, ruling by summary judgment that they were barred by the statute of limitations. It also noted that plaintiff's psychiatrist testified she was not mentally incompetent.

The appellate court reversed and remanded for a trial on the merits, noting this was a case of first impression on the issue of whether or not, "if a plaintiff proves undue influence, the statute of limitations is equitably tolled so long as the influence continues."

"Undue influence is a contract doctrine which serves to equitably toll the statute of limitations. Appellant has presented evidence sufficient to raise a material question of fact as to this theory . . . undue influence in its essential elements has no real relation to mental incapacity."

"Undue influence is sometimes treated as a species of duress, as both doctrines address situations in which the will of one party to a contract is overcome by the improper acts of another party. Situations amounting to undue influence vary widely and are fact-specific, but in general undue influence may be found when 'a party in whom another reposes confidence misuses that confidence to gain his own advantage while the other has been made to feel that the party in question will not act against his welfare."

2) More often, a defense of undue influence is raised by the estate of an alleged lifetime transferor of valuable property, complaining about the appearance of improper conduct when a particular asset has been previously conveyed by the decedent and is no longer available for distribution to the heirs as an estate asset.

In *Rea v. Paulson, 887 P.2d 355 (Or. App. 1994),* the plaintiff, as personal representative of his mother's estate, sued to set aside a deed conveying her former home to defendant, who was the plaintiff's half-brother, and the deceased's son by a second marriage.

Decedent died leaving four children, including plaintiff and defendant. Her will left all her property to them in equal shares. During the last years of her life, she suffered from arthritis, renal failure, heart failure and diabetes, was taking several strong medications, and was undergoing daily dialysis treatments.

Defendant did not originally reside near his mother, but one year before her death moved in with her, expressed admittedly false concerns to her that she was in danger of losing her house to the state due to improper Medicaid payments (although she did not receive Medicaid), and convinced her to transfer the house out of her name. Defendant did not mention the transaction to his half-sisters or half-brothers until months later, after they learned of her death, a fact that he had also not communicated to them.

He obtained a form warranty deed from a local title company, and filled it out in his handwriting, conveying the residence to him. His mother had previously moved in with him in a rental residence, her former house was rented out and the income it produced was deposited in her savings account, to which defendant had power of attorney and did, in fact, use for his personal expenses.

The trial court ruled in favor of the estate, and the appellate court affirmed, concluding that the transfer in question, "was the product of undue influence exerted by Larry on his mother . . . We conclude that there was a confidential relationship between decedent and Larry and that, under the circumstances, he held a position of dominance over her; he was, literally, in the driver's seat."

The court noted the various factual indicia of Larry's undue influence:
- She was completely dependent on him in her daily life
- He helped with her finances and held her power of attorney
- He wrote all her checks and signed her name for her
- He drove a wedge between the rest of the family and the decedent
- The rest of the family was not welcome in his house
- He procured the deed, prepared it, and assisted in its signing
- It was his false idea to transfer the house out of her name
- She had no independent advice

3) Sometimes, what appears to be voluntary valid gifting to charitable religious organizations is really the result of the donee taking unfair advantage of a wealthy and susceptible donor.

In *Dovydenas v. The Bible Speaks, 869 F.2d 628 (1st Cir. 1989),* plaintiff, the multimillionaire heir to the Dayton-Hudson department store fortune estimated at $19 million, moved with her husband to Massachusetts and joined the defendant's church, known as TBS. They attended services and after she left a very generous contribution of $500 in the collection plate, she was contacted by Carl Stevens, the fundamentalist preacher and founder of TBS.

The church had grown from a small group of 50 members in Maine, to a large organization centered in Lenox, Massachusetts having 1,300 members, a large campus with many outbuildings, and a radio and television ministry.

A series of private meetings with Stevens ensued, at which he asked for and received increasing donations for his church, until plaintiff started attending bible classes, became a part of his inner circle of friends, was a devout member of TBS, abandoned her prior friends, and had little to do with her family.

Plaintiff testified she had daily private meetings with Stevens. "In these private meetings, she was given advice on religious, financial and personal matters. She was told she had to obey Stevens because he was the highest authority on earth. She was also told to listen to tapes of Stevens' speeches over and over and to take notes of all Stevens told her and then study those notes. She was to inundate her mind with Steven's words. She disclosed her net worth to him, and he told her that her mission in life was to give and that her gifts could cause great events."

Plaintiff became friendly with Baum, Stevens' future wife, who suffered from migraine headaches, and was concerned about their effect on their forthcoming marriage. Before the wedding, plaintiff was driving with Stevens and heard a voice telling her to donate $1 million to TBS, which she did in Dayton-Hudson stock. She told him, she was going to give TBS $1,000,000 and that she believed by doing so it would cure Baum's headaches." Stevens told her the headaches were cured after the gift, even though they continued, and "plaintiff believed that large gifts from her to TBS could affect events on earth."

Plaintiff's husband opposed the $1 million gift, and after it was made, Stevens told him "he would not take any more money without Jonas' consent." Later, she told Stevens she heard God tell her to give $5 million to TBS. He advised her not to tell her husband about it, and plotted a strategy for it to be paid by her company, whereby she signed a letter he had drafted which stated that, "God had spoken to her, which was why she was making the gift, that no one from TBS had asked her for the gift or knew about it and that Stevens was to administer the gift."

Plaintiff also made another gift of $500,000 under similar questionable circumstances, when she wrote a check on her brokerage account, with a note attached that said she had been led by God to make the gift.

Plaintiff was subsequently tricked away from Stevens and the church by her relatives, deprogrammed from her "cult" experience, relieved of the "mind-control" to which she had been subjected, and then sued to rescind the gifts on the grounds of undue influence and fraud.

The trial court ruled in her favor and the defendant appealed. The appellate court ruled that the $1 million gift was valid, finding no undue influence when it was made, but invalidated the $5 million gift. "Any species of coercion, whether physical, mental or moral, which subverts the sound judgment and genuine desire of the individual, is enough to constitute undue influence. Its extent or degree is inconsequential so long as it is sufficient to substitute the dominating purpose of another for the free expression of the wishes of the person (who gives)."

"Because undue influence is often practiced in 'veiled and secret ways,' its existence may be inferred from such factors as disproportionate gifts made under unusual circumstances, the age and health of the donor, and the existence of a confidential relationship. Two other factors are also important under Massachusetts's case law. One, attempts by the recipient to isolate the donor from her former friends and relatives can be considered undue influence. Two, a court can also consider that she (the donor) acted without independent and disinterested advice."

IV. MISTAKE

Defending enforcement of a contract on the basis of mistaken circumstances does not involve situations where there are claims of unfair advantage taken by one party at the expense of the other. Instead, after the contract is made, one of the parties wants to avoid it based upon allegations that there was a serious misunderstanding regarding material, existing facts that are essential to the bargain made.

A mutual or bilateral mistake of a material fact made by both parties allows either to rescind. If however, the mistake was unilateral, where only one of the parties was mistaken, no rescission is allowed and the contract will stand, regardless of how disadvantageous its terms.

Therefore, the party who made a bad deal and wants out will claim "mutual mistake" and the party who has the economic advantage will defend on the basis of "unilateral mistake".

These types of disputes are complicated by the legal nature of what in fact is a legal mistake, and how courts should evaluate them:

- It is not a simple error in judgment or miscalculation
- It is not a matter about which reasonable people would not differ
- It does not relate to facts that may arise in the future
- It must involve fact(s) that are important to the transaction like existence, identity, quality, price, time, quantity, delivery, and the like
- It must concern present facts, where reasonable people do not differ, such as the existence or identity or essential nature of the subject matter of the transaction
- It cannot primarily relate to a matter of opinion – where reasonable people may differ – such as the value or inherent worth of the transaction, although value always underlies every business deal

*Ex: Vincent and Carlos go wilderness hiking. Carlos finds two amber stones along the bank of a river. Neither has any training in gemology. Carlos and Vincent both believe the stones to be topaz, semi-precious gems only worth about $30 each. Vincent offers Carlos $50 for them and Carlos accepts. When they return, Vincent shows the stones to his friend who is a gem collector, and is informed they are really yellow diamonds worth $4,000. An article appears in the local paper about Vincent's good fortune, Carlos sees it, and sues to cancel the sale on the grounds of mutual mistake. Vincent defends the sale as an arms-length transaction, stating he did nothing wrong, and Carlos is just upset because he made a bad business deal.

Let's analyze the problem. One complication in these mistake cases is that value underlies all such disputes. Value is an opinion, not a fact, and therefore cannot be the basis of a rescission claim based upon Mistake of Fact. Carlos wants to rescind because he sold too low – but is the case really about value? No – both parties believed the stones to be a definite "something", topaz, and in actuality the stones were a different "something", diamonds. So they are mutually mistaken about the identity of the subject matter and therefore either party may cancel.

*Ex: Same factual pattern, but neither party believes the stones to be anything other than yellow rocks. Since their identity is in fact what both parties believed them to be, there is no mistake and no cancellation is allowed.

*Ex: Same basic factual pattern, but what if Carlos believes the stones to be topaz and Vincent believes them to be yellow diamonds? Unless Vincent has superior knowledge, like a gem expert, when Vincent's belief proves accurate he is allowed to profit. The unilateral mistake of Carlos does not allow cancellation.

In *North Grand Mall Associates, LLC v. Grand Center, Ltd., 278 F.3d 854 (8th Cir. 2002)*, the plaintiff leased rental space to the defendant. The lease contained an option to buy the property, whose purchase price was to be computed by "dividing the average sum of the rent paid for the last three years prior to the purchase by seven percent."

A dispute arose after the defendant exercised its option to purchase, arriving at a purchase price of $500,000 based upon the average rent for the last three years of $35,000 divided by seven percent. Plaintiff sued, claiming the method of computation was based upon a mutual mistake, and such computations were usually done in a different way.

The trial court ruled for plaintiff, and reformed the contract to result in a higher purchase price. Defendant appealed and the court reversed, saying, "The language in the lease, which even included an example, was unambiguous. The fact that industry custom is to use another method to establish commercial real estate prices is irrelevant since the parties to the original contract made their intention clear. The terms established by the contract do not indicate mutual mistake, so the contract stands"

Contrast the above case of no mutual mistake in a lease agreement with the following case of *Phil Bramsen Distributor, Inc. v. Mastroni,et al., 726 P.3d 610 (Az. App. 1986)*, where the opposite result occurred.

A commercial building was leased for twenty years, where plaintiff was tenant and the defendants were landlord. The lease had a monthly base rental plus an escalation clause to be applied every five years, based upon "the Consumer Price Index for Phoenix, Arizona." Unfortunately, there was no such index.

The defendants sought to invoke the escalation clause, and plaintiff filed suit to enjoin its enforcement based upon mutual mistake. The trial court ruled for defendants, reforming the rent escalation clause by replacing the faulty index with the "metropolitan Phoenix consumer price index prepared by the Bureau of Business and Economic Research, Arizona State University." Based on this reformation, the monthly rent would be increased from $4,150 to $6,848, and the court entered judgment for approximately $178,000 in back rent.

Plaintiff appealed, arguing, "there was no mutual mistake but rather a unilateral mistake on the part of appellees," because of the lack of the subject cost of living index. The court disagreed, and affirmed the reformation of the lease.

"In the present case, the parties agreed to an escalation clause based on the rate of inflation. It was a mistake of fact that caused the clause to fail. The draftsman, (defendant's) attorney, inserted the term 'cost of living index for the city of Phoenix prepared by the Bureau of Labor Statistics.'

There is no evidence that either appelles or appellants Bramsen had any independent knowledge of such an index or relied on anyone's word but the attorney's. Therefore, by mutual mistake the parties believed they had a workable formula."

What follows is another case of mutual mistake. As you read it, consider how easily the Bank could have avoided the dispute, which fortunately for them was decided in their favor, if they had just properly inspected the estate residence before they sold it, or specified that plaintiff could only keep "miscellaneous personal property having no significant monetary value."

In *Wilkin v. 1ˢᵗ Source Bank, 548 N.E.2d 170 (Ind. App. 1990)*, a world famous artist and sculptor died, and defendant was appointed personal representative of the estate. Defendant contracted to sell the deceased's residence to plaintiff. The purchase and sale agreement included the real estate and its appliances, and standard built-ins, such as drapes, curtains and sconces.

After the closing, plaintiff complained that the premises had been left in cluttered condition, and requested a cleanup. Defendant proposed two options: it would retain a rubbish removal service or "Wilkins could clean the premises and keep any items of personal property they wanted." Plaintiff chose the latter, and during their clean-up efforts found eight drawing and a plaster sculpture made by the deceased, for which ownership was claimed. Even though neither party knew of the existence of the art, defendant objected, and filed a petition with the probate court to determine title to the artwork.

The probate court determined the artwork was the property of the estate, and ordered the items returned to the bank. Plaintiff appealed and the court affirmed.

"Mutual assent is a prerequisite to the creation of a contract. Where both parties share a common assumption about a vital fact upon which they based their bargain, and that assumption is false, the transaction may be avoided if because of the mistake a quite different exchange of values occurs from the exchange of values contemplated by the parties. There is no contract, because the minds of the parties have in fact never met."

"The parties in the instant case shared a common presupposition as to the existence of certain facts that proved false. The Bank and the Wilkins considered the real estate which the Wilkins had purchased to be cluttered with items of personal property variously characterized as 'junk,' 'stuff' or 'trash'. Neither party suspected that works of art created by Ivan Mestrovic remained on the premises."

Cases of unilateral mistake usually result in the denial of requested cancellation of a contract unless the non-mistaken party has taken unfair advantage, but few have such a financial impact as *Wells Fargo Credit Corporation v. Martin, 605 So.2d 531 (Fla. App. 1992),* which we'll call "The $100,000 Bidding Error."

Wells Fargo obtained a judgment of real estate mortgage foreclosure, and at the foreclosure sale, it was represented by its attorney's paralegal. She was experienced, having attended more than 1,000 of these sales. She brought a form instruction sheet to the sale that informed her to bid $115,500 for the property, which was its tax appraised value. Martin attended the sale because his home had been destroyed by fire, and he needed a new residence. This was the first such foreclosure sale he had ever attended.

When the sale began, the paralegal misread her instruction form and opened the bidding at $15,500. Martin then bid $20,000. After giving ample time for any other bids, the clerk announced, "$20,000 going once, $20,000 going twice, sold to Harley --." At that point the paralegal screamed, "Stop, I'm sorry I made a mistake." The clerk took the matter to a judge, who ordered the clerk to issue title to Martin, as the high bidder.

Wells Fargo moved to set aside the sale, on grounds of mistake. The trial judge declined, finding that, "the $20,000.00 bid was grossly inadequate, but that there was no evidence of fraud or any type of misconduct on the part of Mr. Martin."

The appellate court affirmed. "We accept the trial court's conclusion that the amount of the sale was grossly inadequate. This inadequacy, however occurred due to an avoidable, unilateral mistake by an agent of Wells Fargo. As between Wells Fargo and a good faith purchaser at the judicial sale, the trial court had the discretion to place the risk of this mistake upon Wells Fargo."

The court considered two prior Florida cases where bidding errors were made at foreclosure sales and the sales were set aside, but in one the mortgagee's agent failed to appear at the sale, and in the other the property owner's attorney was not present at the sale – both no-show situations being a result of alleged mistake. Those cases were distinguished by the court, "because the mortgagee never had an opportunity to bid at the sale, and because the prevailing bid was essentially nominal."

A. Was the court's decision too harsh on the Bank?
B. Would your answer be different if the bank's paralegal had failed to appear?
C. Do you think the paralegal and/or her attorney-employer were fired by the bank as a result of this case?

V.   FRAUD

The relief granted in proper cases of Duress, Undue Influence and Mistake is a cancellation of the contract made without real consent, and the attempt to restore the parties to their positions prior to the transaction. No money damages are usually allowed to punish wrongdoing.

Fraud, however, is a more serious matter, since its very nature involves an intentional act of deception. In addition to the contract remedy of rescission, the courts often award monetary damages for the non-contract tort of deceit, to compensate the injured party for losses sustained. In the more severe cases that satisfy the textbook categories of conduct that is "willful, malicious, reckless and outrageous," an award of significant punitive damages is often made to punish the wrongdoer.

The three most common fraud situations are:

1) Inducement - the fraud is *why you sign* the written contract or verbally enter into the transaction (consumer scams, sales of goods or services for unfairly inflated prices). These transactions are voidable.

2) Inception - the fraud relates to *what you sign*, and relates to the identity of the transaction (you sign a promissory note thinking it is an autograph). These transactions are void.

3) Nondisclosure – the fraud is in concealing valuable information that you have a legal duty to disclose (you buy a used car and are not told about its prior repairs that cause dangerous hidden defects). These transactions are also voidable.

There are four required legal elements that all must be proven to sustain a claim of fraud:

1. Defendant misrepresents a past or current fact that is important to his decision to enter into the contract.
2. Defendant knows that fact is false, thus intending to deceive
3. Plaintiff reasonably relies on the misrepresentation
4. Plaintiff suffers monetary damage as a direct result

Many fraud cases arise regarding investment transactions. When they have adverse financial results, the losing party often cries, "I was defrauded," and seeks to cancel the transaction and recover their losses. Their complaints often fail, because they must not only prove damages but also that the conduct of the defendant was intentional and not just a negligent failure of business judgment.

*Ex: Hal is a securities salesperson who has gained a reputation as being able to make money for his clients with his stock picks. Josh is a young professional who decides to makes his first market investments with him. Hal makes two statements to Josh: (1) "My sources tell me that Acme Radium is a terrific buy at its current values," and (2) My sources also tell me that Acme Radium should double in price within 90 days." Hal really has no information at all about Acme Radium. He just wants to unload his excess inventory of that stock. Josh buys $10,000 of the stock based upon Hal's recommendations. In 30 days, the price has dropped by half. Josh claims he was defrauded, and sues to cancel the transaction and recover his money.

Let's analyze the dispute for the required elements of fraud:

Hal did misrepresent the Acme Radium investment. He intended to deceive Josh, to induce him to invest because Hal knew his statements were false. Josh relied upon both statements as a material inducement and suffered monetary loss. But were they statements of fact and did he reasonably rely?

Statement (1) is a present opinion, rather than a fact. Reasonable people could differ about it. The use of adjectives, such as "terrific" is a sure sign of opinion rather than fact. Reasonable people do not normally rely upon opinions. However, there is a fairness exception for fraud cases when experts or those with superior knowledge, like Hal, state opinions. Utterances by such persons are treated the same as misstatements of fact and can be fraud. Courts inquire not only into *what* was said, but *who* said it.

Statement (2) looks like an opinion, but is really a prediction about the future. Under the law, reasonable persons never should rely upon predictions because of their unreliability, no matter who expresses them.

Therefore, Hal's (1) statement is fraud, but (2) is not.

There is also a long line of fraud cases involving dance studios that have sold their customer's lessons that far exceed their ability and potential, with regard only to how much of their money can be spent.

In *Vokes v. Arthur Murray, Inc., 212 So.2d 906 (Fla. App. 1968)*, plaintiff, a widow of 51 years, lonely and without family, desired to be "an accomplished dancer" with the hopes of finding "a new interest in life." She attended a dance party at defendant's local franchisee where she was complimented on her grace and poise, and her future as "an excellent dancer", and signed up for eight 1/2-hour dance lessons to be used with the next month.

She was then sold a total of fourteen "dance courses", in separate contracts, totaling an aggregate of 2,302 hours of dancing lessons for a total cash outlay of over $31,000. These contracts were procured by "false representations to her that she was improving in her dancing ability, that she had excellent potential, that she was responding to instructions in dancing grace, and that they were developing her into a beautiful dancer, whereas in truth and in fact she did not develop in her dancing ability, she had no 'dance aptitude', and in fact had difficulty in 'hearing the musical beat'."

She eventually sued to have the dance contracts declared null and void, cancelled based on fraud in the inducement, and she sought a recovery of damages in the dollar amount of her unused dance lessons. Defendant asserted that no fraud existed, because any statements and misrepresentations made were not "as to a material fact, (but) rather . . . an opinion, prediction or expectation, and (they) were in the category of 'trade puffing', within its legal orbit."

The trial court dismissed her complaint for failure to state a cause of action, and she appealed. The appellate court reversed and remanded, stating that while "it is true that 'generally a misrepresentation, to be actionable, must be one of fact rather than opinion,' . . . it does not apply where there is a fiduciary relationship between the parties, or where there has been some artifice or trick employed by the representor, or where the parties do not in general deal at 'arm's length' as we understand the phrase, or where the representee does not have equal opportunity to become apprised."

"A statement of a party having superior knowledge may be regarded as a statement of fact although it would be considered as opinion if the parties were dealing on equal terms . . . It could be reasonably supposed here that defendants had 'superior knowledge' as to whether plaintiff had 'dance potential' and as to whether she was noticeably improving in the art of Terpsichore . . . Even in contractual situations where a party to a transaction owes no duty to disclose facts within his knowledge or to answer inquiries respecting such facts, the law is if he undertakes to do so he must disclose the *whole truth*."

Here is another interesting fraud case; let's title it, "Finding Your Guru – Inner Peace for You or Wealth for Him?" Notice the similarity to the *Dovydenas v. The Bible Speaks* case previously discussed in the section on Undue Influence.

In *Dushkin v. Desai, 18 F.Supp.2d 117 (D. Mass. 1998),* fourteen former devotees of the self-proclaimed yoga guru Amrit Desai sued to recover losses suffered when he was revealed to be a charlatan.

They had resided for many years at the Kripalu Ashram, a 350-acre yoga retreat center in Lenox, Massachusetts.

It was here that the defendant presented himself as a "true and authentic guru, promoting a celibate and ascetic lifestyle with vows of poverty, and providing on a large-scale a facility for the paying public to attend for a fee, "to relax, take yoga classes, meditate, have massages, and otherwise take a break from the routine of their daily lives.".

Plaintiff's and others, some for as long as 20 years, had operated the facility, working for room and board and a small monthly stipend in exchange for the opportunity to live there as defendant's "disciples." They also had, at defendant's urging, donated literally all their material wealth and possessions to the ashram.

Plaintiff's alleged that defendant, behind his carefully cultivated public image, was a fraud, and had entered into a series of privately lucrative contracts with the ashram as an independent contractor, providing him annually hundreds of thousands of dollars, and had also engaged in a series of secret sexual relationships with several female "disciples".

When there were public disclosures of defendant's conduct, he resigned and moved to Florida. Plaintiff's suit included a count for fraud and misrepresentation. Defendant moved to dismiss for failure to state a cause of action, arguing that, "his alleged misrepresentations did not concern matters of fact – that they were merely promissory in nature, or simple expressions of opinion – and therefore could not form the basis of an action for fraud."

The court allowed the fraud claims to continue, denying the defendant's motion. "In short, plaintiffs have offered sufficient allegations from which the court reasonably may infer that Desai made false representations with respect to his status with the intent to induce plaintiff's reliance, and that plaintiffs in fact relied on defendant's representations, as evidenced by their significant donations of time, labor and money to the facility."

The essence of fraud is a misrepresentation of material fact, as stated above. But what if the defendant says nothing? Can his silence be fraud? Rather than actively hiding important information the defendant fails to volunteer it. The issue here is whether or not the defendant has a duty to disclose information if not asked specifically about it.

The general rule of law followed by most states is that silence is usually not fraud, because defendants are not mind readers, and can't know what facts are important to the plaintiff unless they are asked specific questions. There are fairness exceptions, however, which create a duty to speak and require disclosure of hidden facts if:

- There is a fiduciary relationship between the parties
- Hidden defects may adversely affect the buyer's health or safety
- The private information may materially affect property value

*Ex: Harriet goes to Gotham Motors looking for a good buy in a used car. She finds a late model Volvo that looks fine and meets her price range. She test drives it and is satisfied with its performance. She buys it, and later almost has a serious accident when the brakes fail coming down a hill. She discovers that the seller had the car repaired by the same mechanic she now uses, and there was a hidden leak inside the brake lining at the time she purchased that the seller did not disclose to her. She sues for fraud and wins.

What if the withheld information concerned a cosmetic problem such as the original color of the car, rather than a mechanical defect? Probably not fraud, unless Harriet had discussed it as a part of her negotiations, such as, "I am assuming this dark blue is the original color." No response to her statement would reasonably be interpreted as an affirmation. If the color had been changed, it was obviously material to her, and nondisclosure of that fact by the seller would be fraud.

Here are two bizarre fraud cases, both of first impression, involving the alleged duty to disclose that residential real estate being sold: (1) was haunted by poltergeists, and (2) was the site of a multiple murder. With apologies to Charles Dickens, we will call this saga "A Tale of Two Houses".

In *Stambovsky v. Ackley, 572 N.Y.S.2d 672 (N.Y. App. Div. 1991)*, plaintiff discovered after he had contracted to purchase a $650,000 house from defendant in the Village of Nyack, New York, that it was widely reputed to be haunted by poltergeists. When he learned of this set of facts prior to the closing, he sued to rescind the transaction on grounds of fraud, and sought return of his $32,500 down payment. Defendant moved to dismiss the complaint, and sought specific performance of the purchase agreement.

The trial court dismissed the complaint, but the appellate court reversed, holding that plaintiff had a cause of action for cancellation. The court noted that the "defendant-seller deliberately fostered the public belief that her home was possessed," by widely reporting that fact, and had otherwise sought to capitalize on the attendant publicity.

The court went on to say, "Whether the source of the spectral apparitions seen by defendant seller are parapsychic or psychogenic, having reported their presence in both a national publication and the local press, defendant is estopped to deny their existence and, *as a matter of law, the house is haunted.*"

"However, with respect to transactions in real estate, New York adheres to the doctrine of caveat emptor and imposes no duty upon the vendor to disclose any information concerning the premises unless there is a confidential or fiduciary relationship between the parties or some conduct on the part of the seller which constitutes 'active concealment'."

The court further noted that the doctrine of "let the buyer beware" deals with the physical condition of the premises, not the type of situation encountered in this case. "(Plaintiff) met his obligation to conduct an inspection of the premises and a search of the available public records with respect to title. It should be apparent, however, that the most meticulous inspection and the search would not reveal the presence of poltergeists at the premises or unearth the property's ghoulish reputation in the community."

"In an action seeking rescission of a contract to purchase a house widely reputed to be haunted, nondisclosure of that reputation constitutes a basis for relief as a matter of equity where the condition was created by the seller, it materially impairs the value of the contract, and it is peculiarly within the knowledge of the seller or is unlikely to be discovered by a prudent purchaser."

In *Reed v. King, 145 Cal. App.3d 261 (Cal. App. 1983)*, plaintiff purchased a house from defendant, and learned from a neighbor after the sale that a woman and her four children were murdered there 10 years earlier. Neither the seller nor his real estate agents had mentioned this prior to the closing.

Plaintiff sought to rescind her purchase and recover the purchase price. The trial court granted defendant-seller's motion to dismiss. On appeal, judgment was reversed, and plaintiff was allowed to proceed at law to prove her case of alleged fraud due to nondisclosure. "Reed paid $76,000, but the house is only worth $65,000 because of its past."

"Concealment is a term of art which includes mere nondisclosure when a party has a duty to disclose . . . In general, a seller of real property has a duty to disclose: 'where the seller knows of facts materially affecting the value or desirability of the property which are known or accessible only to him and also knows that such facts are not known to, or within the reach of the diligent attention and observation of the buyer, the seller is under a duty to disclose them to the buyer."

"The murder of innocents is highly unusual in its potential for so disturbing buyers that they may be unable to reside in a home where it has occurred. This fact may foreseeably deprive a buyer of the intended use of the purchase. Murder is not such a common occurrence that *buyers* should be charged with anticipating and discovering this disquieting possibility."

Even more bizarre, and worth noting in our contemporary society that values celebrity and sensationalism, was the quantifiable effect that murder had in raising, not lowering, the market value of two other houses:

- Lizzie Borden was tried and acquitted in 1892 for the alleged hatchet murders of her father and stepmother in the family home in Fall River, Massachusetts. The case attracted such attention that it was popularized in verse: "Lizzie Borden took an axe and gave her mother forty whacks, and then when all was said and done, she gave her father forty-one."

- Charles Manson and his 'family' of followers have been serving life imprisonment, for the brutal Tate/LaBianca murders that they committed in 1969 in actress Sharon Tate's Beverly Hills, California residence. The case attracted worldwide attention, was described in detail by the prosecuting attorney Vincent Bugliosi in his book "Helter – Skelter", and was the subject of a Beatles song of the same name.

Both of these houses were eventually sold for a premium over their current market value due to their notoriety, and are now sightseeing attractions, and operated on a bed and breakfast basis, with the rooms where the murders took place commanding the highest nightly rentals, especially on Halloween.

Fraud is also the basis of many consumer laws and is enforced by state and federal regulatory agencies. The legal requirements for a fraud prosecution are the same as those for rescinding a contract – their essence is the defendant's conduct of intentional deception that victimizes the complainant.

DISCUSSION EXERCISES

1. Discuss how to separate valid claims of business duress from efforts to avoid the consequences of a bad business deal.

2. Discuss how you would protect yourself, as a gift donee, from a claim of undue influence.

3. Discuss how you would differentiate between the mistake liability rules.

4. Discuss whether you would assess higher damages for fraud by misrepresentation or nondisclosure.

5. Discuss whether punitive damages deter fraud.

CASE EXERCISES

GIFTS FROM CLIENTS – "ACCEPT" OR "REJECT"?

In *Klaskin v. Klepak, 534 N.E.2d 971 (Ill. 1989)*, the administrator of Woodruff's estate sued to recover title and remove defendant from possession of a condominium unit which the decedent held in a land trust.

The trust had been created 11 years before his death, and provided that he reserved a life estate and the property would belong to the defendant, his long-time attorney and "special" friend at the time of his death, or to his estate if she predeceased him.

When Woodruff died at the age of 54 without a will, he had never married, had no children, and his only legal heirs were two maternal aunts and one maternal cousin.

The professional relationship of attorney-client between decedent and defendant began 10 years before he bought the condominium, when she first represented him in a criminal misdemeanor matter. She continued to represent him thereafter in various business matters, and "although their relationship began as attorney and client, it developed into one of friendship. They dined, attended operas and vacationed together. Klepak testified that she and Woodruff socialized about once a month until three years before Woodruff's death."

When Woodruff purchased the property, he relied upon defendant to review the contract, she advised him to proceed, assisted in the creation of the land trust, personally loaned him money for the down payment, returned all the signed documents to the trustee bank, and performed all services to complete the sale, although she didn't personally attend the closing.

Although defendant repeatedly denied that she legally represented Woodruff when he bought the condominium, she testified that, in addition to the above matters to assist in the transaction, the land trust was signed by Woodruff and notarized by defendant while they dined at a restaurant.

ANALYSIS

The trial court reviewed all the evidence, some conflicting, and entered judgment in favor of plaintiff, and ordered defendant to assign her beneficial interest in the property to the estate, holding that the presumption of undue influence created by the deceased's transfer to his attorney was not successfully rebutted by the defendant.

On appeal, the judgment was reversed, basing its holding on evidence that Woodruff "was not enfeebled by age or health", thus not lacking mental capacity, and that, "she and Woodruff shared a close relationship for 17 years; that it was Woodruff's expressed intent to give her the trust res as contingent beneficiary; and that the trust was in existence for 11 years prior to Woodruff's death."

The state's highest court reversed, affirming the trial court ruling that invalidated the transfer to defendant due to her failure to overcome the legal presumption that it was obtained by her exercise of undue influence.

"Transactions between attorneys and clients are closely scrutinized. When an attorney engages in a transaction with a client and is benefited thereby, a presumption arises that the transaction proceeded from undue influence. Once a presumption is raised, the burden shifts to the attorney to come forward with evidence the transaction was fair, equitable and just and that the benefit did not proceed from undue influence."

DEFUSE REPLAY

What could, and should defendant, the gift grantee, have done to protect herself from the estate challenge that usually occurs when a decedent's estate does not contain property that was transferred to a fiduciary, friend, acquaintance or other family member during the deceased's lifetime without the knowledge of the complaining heirs?

The Court provides help. "Some of the factors which this court deems persuasive in determining whether the presumption of undue influence has been overcome include a showing by the attorney (1) that he or she made a full and frank disclosure of all relevant information; (2) that adequate consideration was given; and (3) that the client had independent advice before completing the transaction."

Some courts will also add the following additional requirement where, as in our case, there was no monetary consideration paid because the property transfer was a gift, "(4) that the legal document(s) to complete the transaction be signed in the presence of disinterested witnesses," to verify the transferor understands the nature and legal effect and proceeds voluntarily and knowingly.

Here is another practical suggestion for Ms. Klepak. Even if she failed to satisfy all the legal factors set forth above, since the presence of full monetary consideration removes much of the thrust of an undue influence claim, why not pay full value to Woodruff for the condominium by borrowing the money from him? She could have given him a demand promissory note secured by a first mortgage on the property, with a provision that, "any balances due and owing by my dear friend Ralla Klepak at the time of my death shall be forgiven."

CONCLUSION

Klepak argued that the presumption of undue influence should not apply where "the attorney has a close, personal relationship with the client." Notwithstanding the nature of their non-professional relationship, she should have known the perilous nature of this transaction. "An attorney who maintains a close advisory relationship with a client has a duty not to abuse that relationship and an obligation to avoid even the appearance of impropriety."

As a practical matter, most gift grantees, whether fiduciary or not, are not going to decline to accept an offered gift. The problem is what will happen when the donor dies? Even if the three required legal elements of a completed gift are present,

- Intent to make a gift by the donor
- Delivery of the gifted property to the donee
- Acceptance of the gift by the donee

the mere fact that the property is missing from "Uncle Harry's" estate raises the suspicion that whoever received it did something wrong to induce its transfer.

The more evidence that is available to substantiate the willing, knowing and voluntary aspects of these transactions, the better it is for all parties concerned.

1. Do you agree with the Court's final decision?
2. Is the legally created presumption of undue influence too harsh on innocent gift grantees?
3. If you were to create exceptions to the presumption of undue influence rules in gift cases where there was a pre-existing "friendship" between the parties, would they apply to:

- Fiduciary relationships, like attorney-client, doctor-patient, financial advisor-customer, etc.?
- Non-intimate personal friendships? Of what duration?
- Intimate personal friendships? How intimate? Of what duration?
- Intra-family transfers?
- Transfers to health care providers or caretakers?
- Gifts to charities?
- Gifts to minors?

CASE RESEARCH CYBERCISES

The following cases also relate to the material in this chapter and illustrate the types of disputes that may occur. For each one do the following written assignment:

1. Locate the case using the Internet (Lexis-Nexis, West or any other research cite which provides case transcripts).
2. Briefly summarize what it was about – the nature of the dispute involved.
3. Who won at the trial court level? Who won at the appellate level?
4. Who won if there was a third level of Supreme Court review?
5. What were the legal rules of law and the reasoning used to reach the final decision?
6. Do you agree or disagree with the decision, and explain why?
7. What business law time bomb(s) were involved?

8. Could the time bomb(s) have been avoided by structuring the transaction differently? Discuss.
9. Could the adverse effects of the time bomb(s) have been defused by a different reaction or response by the affected party? Discuss.
10. Replay the facts of the case to achieve a different successful result.

1. *Lesher v. Strid, 996 P.2d 988 (Or. App. 2000)(mutual mistake –both parties believed a 4-acre water right adjoined property being purchased - can cancel).*
2. *Oh v. Wilson, 910 P.2d 276 (Nev. 1996)(unilateral mistake in signing auto accident release –but insurer took unfair advantage –can cancel).*
3. *City of Salinas v. Souza & McCue Construction Company, 424 P.2d 921 (Cal. 1967)(actionable fraud – silence of City in concealing unstable subsoil conditions resulting in increased job costs).*

NOTES

16.

WRITTEN FORM:
WILL A VERBAL AGREEMENT BE ENFORCEABLE?

"A verbal agreement isn't worth the paper it's written on."
Samuel Goldwyn

" An honest man's word is as good as his bond."
Don Quixote

"Put it in writing!" These four words are one of the basic commandments of business law. If followed consistently in everyday commerce, they will insulate most transactions from serious legal problems, and lessen the situations where one of the contracting parties is provided an "out" if their business deal has become less attractive than originally negotiated.

(1) **The first reason to comply is practical.**

We know by definition that a contract is the result of a series of negotiations between the parties that culminates in a final legally enforceable agreement. The best and only way to preserve that agreement, with all its unique aspects, is by reducing it to written form.

The writing memorializes what the parties intended to say, and the rights and duties to which they agree to be bound. When the inevitable business dispute arises and one of the parties to the agreement wants to avoid its enforcement, it is interesting how that party's memory of the terms of a verbal contract suddenly becomes different than that of the party seeking to enforce it.

We are talking about financial self-interest here, and faulty recollections often become misunderstandings or outright lies when the stakes are high enough. Why allow any opportunity for faulty memory or perjured testimony? "Put it in writing", and there is a document at either party's disposal as a reminder, reference and evidence as to what the agreement is, what performance is required and where one's legal obligations lie.

(2) **The second reason to comply is legal.**

THE STATUTE OF FRAUDS, passed in England in 1677, which has been adopted in one form or another by all states, requires certain types of contracts to be in written form or they are not legally enforceable. If a particular type of verbal agreement is "within" the Statute, writing is required and verbal form, even if proven by witnesses, may not be enforced. If it is "outside" the Statute, verbal form is legally acceptable and enforceable.

Although it is advisable to put ALL one's agreements in writing so there will be no dispute as to essential terms, most verbal agreements are legally enforceable if their terms can be sufficiently proven. But the following main categories of transactions covered by the Statute are deemed too susceptible to potential problems to be enforced in verbal form:

- Contracts for the sale of any interest in real property (land and anything permanently affixed to the land)
- Guaranty contracts to pay someone else's debt
- Contracts for a definite performance term of one year or more
- Contracts for the sale of goods for a price of $500 or more
- Special situations – promises to make a will, inheritance promises, finder's fee agreements, marriage contracts, real estate brokerage contracts and certain service agreements such as assisting the completion of the sale of a business.

In *Whitman, Heffernan, Rhein & Co., Inc. v. Griffin Company, 557 N.Y.S.2d 342 (N.Y. App. 1990)*, plaintiff was a financial advisor, assisting in the defendant's (Merv Griffin) acquisition of Resort's International, Inc. (Donald Trump), by analyzing and considering various alternatives in the proposed transaction and assisting in arranging necessary financing.

The parties verbally negotiated payment to plaintiff of performance fees, including some based upon a percentage of the total purchase price. A draft agreement was prepared incorporating this agreement, but was never signed by the defendant. (Danger ahead for plaintiff!)

Once defendant completed the purchase, it refused to pay the fees to plaintiff, citing the New York Statute of Frauds which, "provides that an agreement is void, unless evidenced by a writing signed by the party to be charged, 'if the agreement is a contract to pay compensation for services rendered in negotiating the purchase of a business.' The term 'negotiating' includes assisting in the consummation of the transaction."

Plaintiff sued to enforce the verbal agreement and lost at the trial court level and on appeal. "The services to be rendered by plaintiff, in assisting (defendant) in evaluating and analyzing the proposed acquisition and providing consultant services, fall within the ambit of the Statute of Frauds, and plaintiff's claims are, therefore barred."

There is also a curious legal requirement regarding the signing of written contracts. Most people would automatically assume that all parties to the agreement must sign it. This is the best procedure of course. But it is not required under the Statute – if signed by less than all its parties, the contract must at least be properly signed by "the party to be charged", as stated in the New York law above.

This means the party against whom the contract is being enforced, which in all disputes is the defendant.

 *Ex: Sean wants to buy Tom's boat. The parties have been negotiating the terms of the deal, and have finally verbally agreed on all aspects, including the price of $50,000. Sean signs a confirming letter that repeats the terms of the transaction and sends it to Tom, requesting he sign and return it. Tom never signs it. Later there is a dispute when Sean realizes he has agreed to buy at a price far above market value and refuses to perform. Tom sues for breach of agreement. Sean claims non-compliance with The Statute of Frauds (sale of goods for over $500).

 Tom wins the case. The confirming letter was the required writing, and the defendant, against whom it is being enforced, signed it.

 *Ex: Same facts except the dispute occurs when Tom realizes he has agreed to buy at a price far above market value. He refuses to perform and Sean sues for breach of contract. Tom claims non-compliance with the Statute.

 Sean loses the case. Even though we have the writing required by the Statute, Tom, who is the party to be charged, did not sign it. This renders it legally unenforceable.

 In addition to WHO must sign the writing, issues sometimes arise as to HOW one must sign. Any signature or mark that expresses the intention of a party to be bound is sufficient. This includes one's legal name, nickname, signatures with either hand, initials, a seal or stamp, a symbol or making one's mark (X), or having someone else sign for you as your agent. And any medium for signing can be used, such as pencil, pen, ashes, blood, or even crayon, as the next case suggests.

 In *Rosenfeld v. Basquiat, 78 F.3d 84 (2nd Cir. 1996),* the dispute centered around an alleged sales contract for three paintings made by neo-expressionist artist Jean-Michel Basquiat to the art dealer plaintiff. Basquiat was talented and eccentric, rising to fame and a premature death at age 27. Plaintiff alleged she had visited the artist's apartment, agreed to buy the paintings for $4,000 each and gave the artist a $1,000 cash deposit.

 "When she asked for a receipt, he insisted on drawing up a 'contract,' got down on the floor and wrote it out in crayon on a large piece of paper, remarking that 'some day this contract will be worth money.'" The document listed the paintings, stated the terms, and she and the artist both signed it. She later returned to pick up the paintings, but claimed the artist convinced her to wait at least two years so he could show the paintings at exhibitions.

When the artist died, plaintiff sued his estate for delivery of her paintings. It denied her ownership rights, claiming, among other grounds, that the alleged contract violated the New York Statute of Frauds because it lacked a delivery date.

After the trial jury ruled in plaintiff's favor, the estate appealed, and even though the case was ordered retried due to certain discretionary evidence rulings by the trial judge, the contract written in crayon was validated.

"Any question regarding the Statute of Frauds is governed by the U.C.C.; section 2-201 (contract for (sale of goods) $500 or more is unenforceable 'unless there is some writing sufficient to indicate that a contract for sale has been made between the parties and signed by the party (charged). Under the U.C.C., the only term that must appear in the writing is the quantity. Beyond that, 'all that is required is that the writing afford a basis for believing that the alleged oral evidence rests on a real transaction. The writing supplied by the plaintiff indicated the price, the date, the specific paintings involved, and that Rosenfeld paid a deposit. It also bore the signatures of the buyer and seller. Therefore, the writing satisfied the requirements of section 2-201."

Technological advances have also expanded the concept of what is a signature, as noted in the controversial case of *Parma Tile, Mosaic & Marble Company, Inc. v. Estate of Short*, 663 N.E.2d 633 (N.Y. App. 1996), where plaintiff was a material supplier on a building project, and refused to deliver tile to a designated subcontractor unless the general contractor guaranteed payment.

The general contractor sent a 2-page unsigned fax that said, "MRLS would guarantee payment for goods delivered to the Nehemiah project in the event Sime Construction does not pay within terms." Its transmission was not preceded by or accompanied with any cover letter. The name MRLS was printed across the top of each page of the unsigned fax, together with its phone number, date, time and page number. Plaintiff then began furnishing quantities of tile to the subcontractor.

When the subcontractor, plaintiff sued in 1992 demanding payment under the guarantee. MLRS refused, arguing that a guarantee contract fell within the writing requirements of the Statute of Frauds, and since the writing was unsigned, it was not legally enforceable. Defendant also argued that the transmission was, at best, an unsigned guarantee proposal. The trial court entered summary judgment for plaintiff and allowed enforcement of the unsigned guarantee, ruling that "the heading automatically imprinted by the fax machine on plaintiff's copy of the document satisfied the subscription requirement (of the Statute) because an intent to be bound had been demonstrated."

"The Statute of Frauds was not meant to be utilized to evade an obligation intentionally incurred. MRLS should not be permitted to evade its obligation because of the current and extensive use of electronic transmissions in modern business transactions."

After the appellate division affirmed this ruling, it was noted by the legal profession and found its way into many business law texts as a new exception to the Statute of Frauds based upon such unsigned fax transmissions.

However, leave for further appeal was granted, and the Court of Appeals set aside the summary judgment, ruling that defendant's mere sending of an unsigned guarantee document and its programming of its fax machine to automatically imprint its name across the top of all transmitted pages, "does not, by itself constitute a signing authenticating the contents of the document for Statute of Frauds purposes."

Many of the legal authorities from the 1992 decision are still not modified to reflect this final ruling. The same research resources mentioned in the prior sources of law chapter can be used to verify and update the accuracy of cited decisions. Beware of cases that are no longer good law.

WHAT form must be used for the writing is equally flexible. Again we are seeking a lasting memorial of the terms of the transaction, so one can use almost anything: parchment, paper, a tee shirt, toilet tissue, the back of an envelope or the bark of a tree. Any form is acceptable, so long as the writing is legible and lasting.

"Any signed memorandum is sufficient to satisfy the Statute of Frauds so long as it (1) identifies the subject matter of the agreement, (2) establishes that a contract has been made, and (3) states the essential terms with reasonable certainty. The memorandum may be written after the alleged oral promise occurred. It does not have to be a formal memorial of the agreement." *Busler v. D&H Manufacturing, Inc., 611 N.E.2d 352 (Ohio App. 1992).*

The legal disputes that occur in this chapter are typical of all contract disputes. They involve the parties entering into an oral agreement and then, when one of them perceives they made a bad business deal, that party seeks to avoid enforcement of the agreement on the legal ground of non-compliance with the writing requirements of the Statute. This raises critical comments like the following, which comes from a case involving breach of an oral promise for lifetime employment:

"Whatever may be the fact with regard to the history of the statute, and whatever may have been the difficulties arising from proof that all sides agree brought about the enactment of the statute of frauds over 300 years ago, it is an anachronism today. The reasons that prompted its passage no longer exist. And, far from serving as a barrier to fraud—in the case of a genuinely aggrieved plaintiff barred from enforcing an oral contract—the statute may actually shield fraud." *O'Hanian v. Avis Rent A Car System, Inc., 779 F.2d 101 (2nd Cir. 1985).*

1. CONTRACTS FOR THE SALE OF ANY INTEREST IN REAL PROPERTY

Real estate contracts are treated with the highest degree of legal sanctity. Land has always been a traditional source of wealth and financial security. Real property transactions can involve vacant land, improved property with residential dwellings, commercial offices, mercantile shops and any other permanent improvements that are made on or to the land.

In *Hoffman v. S V Company, Inc., 628 P.2d 218 (Idaho 1981)*, the Court was faced with a dispute based upon the refusal of defendant to convey real property under an alleged contract with plaintiff. The real estate "writing" consisted of plaintiff's signed letter confirming terms of their purchase negotiation, which defendant did not sign, and plaintiff's deposit check which defendant endorsed and deposited into its account.

In agreeing with the trial court that the agreement was not enforceable by the plaintiff, the majority of the Court noted the rationale of the basic law regarding real property transactions, and the Idaho exception to the general rule that the defendant need only sign writings:

"The purpose of the statute is commonly thought to be the prevention of fraudulent assertions of oral contracts for the sale of land. . . The statute effectively insulates from litigation nearly all completely oral transactions involving the sale of land, thus contributing to the stability of title and marketability of land generally. The statute may also stimulate the use of formal written contracts, certainly an advisable practice for transactions as important as land sales."

"An agreement for the sale of real property is invalid unless the agreement or some note or memorandum thereof be in writing and subscribed by the party charged or his agent. Failure to comply with the statute of frauds renders an oral agreement unenforceable both in an action at law for damages and in a suit in equity for specific performance . . . Although the majority of jurisdictions require that the memorandum be signed only by the party against whom enforcement is sought, this Court (in a 1912 case) has construed the Idaho statute to require both parties to a bilateral contract to sign the memorandum."

Often there are disputes concerning whether a particular piece of property is real or personal because of how differently they are treated in our legal system:

- The UCC rules apply only to goods, tangible personal property – real property is specifically excluded.

- Municipalities raise the majority of their revenues by imposing taxes on one's real property. Certain types of personal property are taxed at much lower rates. Again, the laws and procedures differ.

- Owners of property often use it as collateral for borrowing. These loans are usually secured by a mortgage that encumbers the property and is foreclosed by the lender if the borrower defaults. Laws and procedures differ for real or personal property.

A. FIXTURES

Items that are personal property, such as cabinets, bookcases, air conditioning units and printing presses, can legally become part of the real estate where they are permanently attached. If so, they are called "fixtures" and lose their character as personalty. Often this requires a legal interpretation of the intention of the parties and what is reasonable under the circumstances.

What if a property owner borrows from two different secured lenders, one having a mortgage encumbering real property and the other encumbering personalty, and the borrower defaults? Often both lenders will claim the same item of property as a part of their mortgage lien, and the court must decide the priorities.

*Ex: John and Marsha own a nice home in suburbia. They borrowed part of the purchase money from CityBank, which has a real estate first mortgage on the property, "and all items of personal property later permanently affixed to it." The owners later borrow additional sums from StateBank, securing that home contents loan with a personal property chattel first mortgage that states, "encumbering all tangible personalty located within the residence of the borrowers." Lining the walls of the home's living room are built-in bookshelves of fine Philippine mahogany, that are bolted to the supporting struts of their load bearing walls.

When John and Marsha default on both loans at the same time, both lenders seek to foreclose on the bookshelves.

An analysis of the case leads to a reasonable conclusion that it was the intention of the owners that the bookshelves become fixtures. Any type of personal property is removable, but the more difficult to remove or more damage to the surrounding property in accomplishing the removal, the more it appears that the item is a part of the realty. Bolting the bookshelves to the superstructure of the walls of the house is more consistent with a permanent attachment.

B. REAL PROPERTY INTERESTS INCLUDED

Verbal agreements involving the following transactions are "within" the Statute and must be in required written form:

- Purchase or sale of any interest in real property
- Mortgages encumbering any interest in real property
- Easements that allow the use of one's real property
- Leases of real property for a term of one year or longer
- Real estate brokerage listing and commission payment agreements

*Ex: Hank verbally agrees to sell Joe his farm property located on 50 acres of land, which includes (1) a 5 bedroom house, (2) separate outbuildings including barn, silo and livestock enclosures, (3) 10 apple trees, (4) 10 bushels of apples from the trees, and (5) 100 chickens, for $150,000, and to (6) lease an additional 10 acres of adjoining land for 6 months at a fixed price of $10,000. Joe wants out of the deal. What is the result?

Items 1, 2 and 3 are clearly real property, requiring a writing. Item 5 are clearly personal property, so the oral agreement is legally enforceable. Item 4 could be a bit tricky – we need more facts. If the apples are to remain attached to the trees, they retain the character of their source and remain part of the land. If however, they are picked or have fallen on the ground, they are personalty. Item 6 is "outside" the Statute and enforceable because the verbal lease is under one year.

Here are two cases where what appear to be verbal real estate contracts are ruled outside the Statute, and enforceable:

In *Pardoe & Graham Real Estate, Inc. v. Schulz Home Corp., 525 S.E.2d 284 (Sup. Ct. Va. 2000),* the defendant builder promised to pay plaintiff real estate broker a 2.5% commission when they built a custom home on a lot already owned by the home buyer. This promise was in the form of an amendment to a written agreement whereby defendant agreed to pay plaintiff a 6% commission on the sale of any speculative homes that they had built. The amendment was never signed by the defendant.

When a lot owner hired defendant to build their home, plaintiff claimed its 2.5% commission. Defendant refused to pay on the basis of failure to comply with the Statute of Frauds. The trial court ruled for the defendant - builder, and the plaintiff – broker appealed. The appellate court reversed.

"The Statute of Frauds covers a contract for the sale of real estate. Real estate does not include a building that is unattached to land. Since construction of the Carlton home had not begun at the time of the oral contract between Pardoe and Schulz, the home was not included in the definition of real estate under Virginia law."

The court viewed the oral agreement as one for the performance of services, and thus enforceable as being outside the Statute.

"An oral contract providing for a sales commission is not subject to the statute of frauds when that contract is based on the sale of a house to be affixed to land that does not include a contemporaneous sale of the land to which the house will be attached."

In *Firth v. Lu, 49 P.3d 117 (Wash. 2002)*, plaintiff verbally agreed to buy the stock ownership of defendant in cooperative apartment unit #2 for $180,000, and paid a $3,000 deposit, closing to be in October. Defendant requested a three-month extension of time to close. Plaintiff demanded the original closing date and sued for specific performance. Defendant moved to dismiss on the basis of the failure of the alleged verbal real estate contract to satisfy the Statute of Frauds.

The trial court held the verbal agreement valid and ordered specific performance. The appeals court reversed. The Supreme Court reversed again; upholding the trial court decision, based on the distinction between real estate such as a condominium where the property owned is real estate, and a cooperative where the ownership is personal property.

"The corporation owns the land and building that contains 19 apartments. Each apartment is associated with a block of shares in the corporation. The corporation rents the units to the shareholders under long-term leases. One may become a resident only by buying a block of stock associated with apartment 2."

"Stock in a corporation whose only asset is real property is not an interest in real property; it is ownership in a corporation."

C. THE PART PERFORMANCE EXCEPTION

Like most areas of business law, there are numerous fairness exceptions to the applicable general rules that seek to maintain the scales of justice in balance. Part performance is an equitable doctrine that courts use to accomplish this in the area of real property contracts.

In an oral real estate sales contract, if the buyer has made partial payment of the agreed consideration, some states will take the agreement outside the Statute and allow its enforcement.

Other states require additional facts that show the buyer has paid a deposit and has also been allowed by the seller to take early possession of the property.

The majority of states take a harder line before they will allow the part performance doctrine to enforce a verbal real estate contract. In addition to the part payment and the granting of occupancy, they also require facts that show the buyer has made valuable improvements to the seller's property with the seller's knowledge and consent. This is our old friend again in disguise, the fairness doctrine we call *promissory estoppel.*

*Ex: Ross owns 10 acres of fertile land in the Mississippi delta. Amos is a poor, hardworking farmer who has always dreamed of owning his own property. The parties reach a verbal agreement whereby Amos will buy the land for $15,000, payable in 5 yearly installments of $3,000 from the sale of the crops he cultivates on the land. Amos pays a deposit of $100 and starts to clear the property and farm it. Six months later, Ross receives an offer from Delta Sugar Co. to buy his 10 acres for $50,000, accepts it and tells Amos his oral purchase agreement has been cancelled.

You can almost feel the blatant unfairness of this situation if Ross is allowed to avoid the contract with Amos. Ross has a verbal agreement to sell to Amos, Amos has changed his position in reasonable reliance upon it by paying the deposit and improving the vacant land, and Ross should be legally prevented (estopped) to deny the legal enforceability of his verbal (promissory) contract.

What if no deposit was paid by Amos? What if he cleared the land, prepared it for planting, put the seeds into the ground and grew some crops? Should Ross be allowed to escape liability because of the lack of this technical requirement? Probably not. Most states would create a legal fiction for fairness purposes by "pretending" that the work done by poor Amos that improved Ross's property was the same as an implied deposit.

In *Sutton v. Warner, 12 Cal. App. 4th 415 (Cal. App. 1993),* Warner inherited a residence and some other properties. To afford the mortgage payments, Warner verbally agreed to allow Sutton to purchase the property by paying a $15,000 down payment toward the $185,000 purchase price and making all required mortgage and real estate tax payments. Sutton also made valuable improvements to the property, relying upon the oral purchase agreement.

When the market value of the property greatly increased, Warner offered to sell the property to Sutton for $250,000, following which Sutton sued for specific performance. The trial court ruled for Sutton on the grounds of the part performance exception, and the appellate court affirmed:

"The doctrine of part performance by the purchaser is a well-recognized exception to the statute of frauds as applied to contracts for the sale or lease of real property.

Under the doctrine of part performance, the oral agreement for the transfer of an interest in real estate is enforced when the buyer has taken possession of the property *and either* makes a full or partial payment of the purchase price, *or* makes valuable and substantial improvements to the property."

The longer the period of allowed occupancy of the property under the verbal purchase agreement by the buyer, and the more improvements they make that benefit the seller, the more likely courts are to uphold the buyer's rights under part performance.

2. GUARANTY CONTRACTS TO PAY SOMEONE ELSE'S DEBT

A. LEGAL OVERVIEW

Your verbal promise to pay your own debt is a direct, original and primary obligation that is "outside" the Statute. It is legally enforceable against you by your creditor without legal writing requirements (unless required by another section of the Statute).

A secondary, collateral or guaranty promise is "within" the Statute and must satisfy written form. It typically is a promise you make, not to initially obligate yourself to pay, but only to be responsible if the other party who has the primary obligation to pay fails to do so. The Statute refers to these as, "promises to pay the debts of another".

> *Ex: Len is a hard-working young man who needs a computer for his work. He and his best friend Alan, a wealthy doctor, go to Miami Motors where Alan is a long time customer. Len chooses his purchase (let's assume it is under $500), but is short of cash to close the deal. Alan says, "Give my pal Len the item, send him your bill, don't worry about it, if he doesn't pay you, I will." Later, after Len fails to pay the bill for the computer, the seller demands payment from Alan on his verbal guarantee.
>
> Alan does not have to pay. While Len's promise to pay was primary and verbally enforceable, Alan's is a secondary guarantee promise and "within" the Statute. The lack of a writing prevents enforcement against Alan.
>
> *Ex: What if Alan's response after Len came up short of cash was, "Give Len the item, don't worry about it, put it on my bill."
> Now Alan is liable. He made a primary promise to pay.
>
> Notice how easy it would be for the seller in the guarantee situation to protect itself if it were aware of this potential problem of enforcement. As soon as Alan made his verbal guarantee promise, the seller could have simply had Alan sign the purchase invoice or other written receipt for the transaction. That would be a sufficient writing to comply with the Statute.
>
> These disputes often involve insurance companies, such as in *Carter v. Allstate Insurance Company, 962 S.W.2d 268 (Tex. App. 1998)*, where plaintiff's had an auto accident with defendant's insured, and then sued defendant for failure to honor an oral pre-suit settlement agreement.

Defendant claimed enforcement was barred by the Texas statute of frauds, under its "suretyship provision", as "a (secondary) promise by another person to answer for the debt, default, or miscarriage of another person."

The trial court granted summary judgment for defendant, and the appellate court reversed, distinguishing the nature of Allstate's obligations:

"Had Allstate only assumed responsibility to pay damages whenever its insured became legally responsible, it would have assumed the role of a surety. When Allstate took the initiative to settle the claim for which its insured had not yet become legally responsible, however, it was settling not only its insured's potential liability but its own possible obligation to pay and its own duty to defend its insured."

B. THE MAIN BENEFIT EXCEPTION

A verbal guaranty promise often benefits the guarantor as well as the primary obligor. In the guarantee example above, Alan was assisting Len, but he was also motivated by their friendship. At what point does the amount of benefit to the guarantor convert his non-binding verbal promise into a legally enforceable obligation?

If the guarantor will receive financial benefit from his verbal guarantee promise, it will be treated like a primary promise for enforcement purposes. How much benefit will tip the scales from incidental to significant? The state law involved and the facts of each dispute are critical – the guarantor will claim non-liability because of lack of written form, and the seller / creditor will claim this fairness exception. Again the objective standard of reasonableness is used by the courts to resolve these disputes.

> *Ex: Let's assume that Len works as the general manager of a business for which he needs the computer. If Alan were an owner of that business, or Len's boss, even if he has no separate friendship with Len, the main purpose of the guarantee would appear to be to benefit the business. If so, Alan is liable.

In verbal guarantee cases, courts will usually ask and seek to answer three questions:

1. Who made the primary promise to pay?
2. Who made the guarantee of the primary promise?
3. What was the underlying purpose of the guarantee?

In *Power Entertainment, Inc. v. National Football League Properties, Inc.,* *151 F.3d 247 (5ᵗʰ Cir. 1998),* plaintiff alleged defendant had verbally agreed to transfer it a license to sell its collectible cards. This was in return for plaintiff's promise to assume an $800,000 debt for unpaid royalties from card sales owed to Defendant by its former licensee that had filed for bankruptcy.

When defendant refused to honor the oral agreement, plaintiff sued for breach of contract. The trial court granted defendant's motion to dismiss on the grounds of failure to comply with the statute of frauds writing requirements for plaintiff's guarantee promise.

The appellate court reversed, since "the Texas courts have adopted the "main purpose doctrine," which, broadly speaking, removes an oral agreement to pay the debt of another from the statute of frauds 'wherever the main purpose and object of the promisor is not to answer for another, but to subserve some purpose of its own...'"

Some states, like New York, claim they do not recognize this exception, but in actuality do the same thing on a type of estoppel exception when a verbal guaranty promise, "is supported by a new consideration moving to the promisor and beneficial to him and that the promisor has become in the intention of the parties a principal debtor primarily liable." *Martin Roofing v. Goldstein, 469 N.Y.S.2d 595 (N.Y. 1983).*

The "guarantee" disputes that present the most problems of judicial interpretation are those involving promises of indemnity, such as in the case of *Feiler v. Rosenbloom, 416 A.2d 1345 (Md. App. 1980),* where the parties were directors of a corporation that manufactured buttons and needed additional financing to sustain itself.

The bank loaned it $250,000, and to assure repayment the defendant and others signed as loan guarantors. Plaintiff did not want to sign, but he nevertheless orally agreed to be responsible for, "a pro rata one-sixth share of the loan payable to the five signatory guarantors who would be required to pay in the event of default by the corporation," and the others signed in reliance upon his promise.

When the corporation defaulted on its debt to the bank, the guarantors were required to pay off the amounts due. They demanded the agreed share from plaintiff, who refused to pay, and sued him to enforce his oral promise of indemnity. The trial court ruled against the plaintiff, entering judgment against him for $42,666.67 plus interest.

On appeal, the judgment was affirmed. "Feiler's promise to pay, by way of indemnity, was a contract with the appellees. No third party was involved, ergo, the Statute of Frauds, past or present, does not apply."

"The type of indemnity contract which has produced the divergence in cases is the four party situation in which it is alleged that the promisor induced the promise to become surety for P by promising to save him harmless or indemnifying him. The decided preponderance of judicial opinion is that a promise to indemnify is not within the statute." *Simpson, Handbook on the Law of Suretyship, sec. 39 (1950).*

"The first and most fundamental reason underlying the majority decisions is that it is a horrid injustice to let the defendant escape his duty to indemnify after inducing the plaintiff to undertake the suretyship obligation for another person." *Corbin, A Comprehensive Treatise on the Rules of Contract Law, sec. 385 (1950).*

4. CONTRACTS FOR A DEFINITE TERM OF ONE YEAR OR MORE

A. LEGAL OVERVIEW

The resolution of these disputes is often complicated by the convoluted wording of the Statute itself. The Massachusetts statute is typical:

"No action shall be brought: . . . upon an agreement that is not to be performed within one year from the making thereof; unless the promise, contract or agreement upon which such action is brought, or some memorandum or note thereof, is in writing and signed by the party to be charged therewith or by some person thereunto by him lawfully authorized." *Doherty v. Doherty Insurance Agency, Inc., 878 F.2d 546 (1st Cir. 1989).*

What in the world does this mean? Reduced to its essence, if the verbal agreement has a stated time period for performance of anything less than one year, it is "outside" the Statute and verbal form is enforceable. Conversely, a definite time period of one year or more requires written form.

Courts are only required to look at the literal wording of the agreement itself, NOT events that happen afterward or any surrounding circumstances, in computing whether or not the one-year or more term exists. The running of the required time begins at the inception of the contract.

Fortunately, it can be simplified as "the one year rule". If the specific terms of the verbal agreement state a fixed duration of anything less than one year, it is "outside" the Statute and verbal form is enforceable. Conversely, a definite time period of one year or more requires written form.

In *Iacono v. Lyons, 16 S.W.3d 92 (Tex. App. 2000)*, plaintiff and defendant were long time friends. Defendant invited plaintiff to join her on a trip to Las Vegas, and would also pay all expenses, including providing money for gambling, since Defendant believed plaintiff was lucky. Before the trip plaintiff had a dream about winning the jackpot of a particular Las Vegas slot machine.

Defendant also offered "to split 50-50" any gambling winnings. Plaintiff accepted the offers and the parties went to Las Vegas, where they played slot machines at Caesar's Palace. After losing $47, the defendant wanted to leave, but plaintiff begged her to stay. Defendant agreed so long as she could put the coins into the machines because it took plaintiff, who suffered from rheumatoid arthritis and was in a wheel chair, too long. Plaintiff agreed and noticed a $1 dollar machine that looked like the one in her dream. They played it once with no payoff. On the second play however, it hit a jackpot of $1,908,064, to be paid out over a period of twenty years to the winner.

Defendant told Caesar's she was the sole winner, denied her oral agreement to split the winnings with the plaintiff, and refused to share the winnings she received. Plaintiff sued for breach of contract and defendant moved for summary judgment. The trial court ruled for defendant, based upon failure to comply with the one-year rule.

On appeal, the case was reversed and the plaintiff's right to 50% of the winnings was enforced. The trial court mistakenly believed the agreement could not be performed within one year because of the 20-year payout of winnings, rather than looking only at the specific terms of the agreement that did not specify any duration.

"(The statute of frauds) does not apply if the contract, from its terms, could possibly be performed within a year—however improbable performance within one year may be . . . To determine the applicability of the statute of frauds with indefinite contracts, this Court may use any reasonably clear method of ascertaining the intended length of performance. The method is used to determine the parties' intentions at the time of contracting. The fact that the entire performance within one year is not required, or expected, will not bring an agreement within the statute."

Employment contracts are often the subject of these cases:

*Ex: Disney hires Cruise and Hanks to work as actors in their movie studio under two separate verbal contracts: The Cruise contract states, "we hire you for a term of six months, with our option to renew for a term of one year." The Hanks contract states; " we hire you for a term of one year, subject to our right to cancel after 6 months." Cruise and Hanks both work at Disney for 2 years, and are then fired. They both sue for breach of contract. Disney defends saying their verbal agreements are legally unenforceable.

This is not as complicated as it looks. The Cruise contract term was 6 months, so it is verbally enforceable. The fact he actually worked there longer than one year is immaterial.

If Disney verbally exercised their option and renewed for one year, that would violate the Statute. The Hanks contract is really of 6-month duration due to its limiting terms. It, like the Cruise contract, is verbally enforceable, regardless of how long Hanks was actually employed.

B. THE 'FOR LIFE' CONTRACTS EXCEPTION

What if a verbal employment contract states, "We hire you for life," or words of similar import, indicating a promise of lifetime employment? Is this to be treated as governed by the Statute's writing requirements or not? The test remains whether or not there is a "fixed period of one year or more".

A definite time period such as 6 months or 6 years leaves no room for speculation. The 6-year contract is "not possible of performance within one year" because its express terms state otherwise. Its duration exceeds the one-year rule and therefore must be in writing.

But a "for life" contract can last one second or 100 years. It is impossible to determine its ultimate duration from its stated terms. In almost all states, it is "outside" the statute and may be verbally enforced, the same as any other contingent agreement. Whether it states, "you are hired for the remainder of your life", or "the term of this agreement will continue until the Miami Dolphins win the Super Bowl", we still lack the required definitive term of one year or more to be apparent from the specific wording of the agreement.

Currently only a few states such as New York require "lifetime employment" contracts to be in writing. They reason that this wording should be treated the same as if it referred to a lengthy specific term because such situations are usually accompanied by circumstances of changing existing jobs, moving to different areas, or other instances of detrimental reliance.

The counter argument is more sensible. If you want to require a written agreement in these situations, simply specify a definite term of one year or more, and then keep renewing it until the end of the person's life.

In *Hodge v. Evans, 823 F.2d 559 (D.C. Cir. 1987)*, plaintiff was hired as vice president and general counsel of defendant's company, based on oral promises of lifetime employment arising from this dialogue:

Hodge: "No. 1, the job must be permanent. Because of my age, I have a great fear about going back into the marketplace again. I want to be here until I retire."

Evans: "I accept that condition."

Plaintiff moved from his former company in Pittsburgh, Pa. to Washington, D.C. and began work in September of 1980. He was fired in May of 1981. Plaintiff sued for breach of his verbal contract of permanent employment, and defendant raised failure to comply with the one –year rule of the statute of frauds requiring written form.

After a jury trial and award to plaintiff of $175,000 in damages for breach of the oral agreement, defendant appealed. On the fact that the lifetime employment agreement in question was outside the statute of frauds, and enforceable without being in writing, the court affirmed:

"Hodge argues that . . . a permanent or lifetime employment contract does not fall within the statute because it is capable of full performance within one year if the employee were to die within that period. Hodge's view of the statute's applicability to lifetime or permanent employment contracts has, in fact, been accepted by an overwhelming majority of courts and commentators."

"The enforceability of a contract under the statute does not depend on the actual course of subsequent events or on the expectations of the parties. Instead, the statute applies only to those contracts whose performance could not possibly or conceivably be completed within one year. The statute of frauds is thus inapplicable if, at the time the contract is formed, any contingent event could complete the *terms* of the contract within one year."

5. CONTRACTS FOR THE SALE OF GOODS FOR $500 OR MORE

A. THE BASICS

This is by far the largest category of commercial transactions, and is governed by Section 2-201(1) of the UCC. All contracts for the sale (not gifts or leases) of goods (tangible personal property – not real property or personal services) that have an agreed price of $500 or more are "within" the Statute and must be in writing to be legally enforceable:

"Except as otherwise provided in this section a contract for the sale of goods for the price of $500 or more is not enforceable by way of action or defense unless there is some writing sufficient to indicate that a contract for sale has been made between the parties and signed by the party against whom enforcement is sought or by his authorized agent or broker."

Efforts are made annually in various states to adjust the dollar limit upward to reflect the needs of the current commercial marketplace. It is argued that only "expensive" transactions should have to be the subject of written contracts, and that the protection of the consumer by a required writing is not needed for common transactions of a lesser amount. But what should be the dollar threshold?

What about $1,000 or more? $5,000 or more? So far, all states retain the $500 or more threshold.

*Ex: Diane and Jill are antique collectors with different specialties. Diane collects art pottery and Jill collects rare books. They verbally agree that Diane will buy Jill's 12-volume set of Dickens for $600 and Jill will buy Diane's 10-piece Royal Doulton tea set for $1,000. When the required performance date arrives, Diane or Jill declines because they believe they made a bad bargain.

If both transactions are viewed as two separate oral contracts, neither is legally enforceable due to lack of the required writing. If however, they are viewed as individual agreements to buy and sell each item in the set(s), with no individual items costing over $500, which is probably not likely in these facts, no writing is required. The specific wording of the agreements will be crucial to the outcome.

B. THE NON-SIGNER EXCEPTION

We have previously discussed how the parties often follow their period of verbal negotiations with some form of writing that sets forth the essential terms of their agreement. It can be a formalized contract, but is often some type of confirming letter or memorandum that acknowledges their intention to be bound.

Though usually signed by all parties to the agreement, this contract writing need only be signed by the party against whom it is to be enforced (the defendant), to be legally enforceable against that party.

But what if enforcement of a transaction for the verbal sale of goods of $500 or more is sought against a non-signing party? It is usually not enforceable. However, we have another fairness exception under Section 2-201 (2) of the UCC:

"Between merchants, if within a reasonable time a writing in confirmation of the contract and sufficient against the sender is received and the party receiving it has reasons to know its contents, it satisfies the requirements of subsection (1) against such party unless written notice of objection to its contents is given within ten days after it is received."

Between merchants, means they both specialize in the subject matter of the particular transaction, or it represents their primary business enterprise. The legal test involves whether or not a majority of their business time is spent in the particular activity.

- A rare book dealer who contracted to buy a car would not be considered a merchant in that matter, although the auto dealer selling the car would.

- A transaction between merchants for the purchase of a car would require that both seller and buyer be in the automobile business in one form or another, as their main commercial enterprise.

If both S and B are contracting merchants, and S signs a confirming memorandum of the deal and sends it to B, and B receives it and does not object to its terms within 10 days of receipt – B is legally bound even though he never signed it.

The reason for this exception to the signing rule is that merchants, by virtue of their experience and expertise, are held to a higher standard by the law. Sales of goods between them which are governed by the UCC are to be encouraged, rather than legally limited.

*Ex: Fun, Inc. a toy manufacturer, verbally agrees to sell 5,000 of its Mr. Macho action figures to Toys Miami, Inc., a toy retailer, for $1 each. Five days later, it personally delivers to the buyer its signed memo confirming the details of the sale, requesting the buyer's signature and return. Toys Miami, Inc. puts the memo in its file and does not sign it. Thirty days later they phone Fun, Inc. to cancel their order because Mr. Sensitivity figures are now the rage and Mr. Macho will not sell and say, "Besides, we never signed anything." Fun, Inc. refuses to cancel and demands enforcement of the agreement.

Fun, Inc. will win. Both parties are in the toy business. The signed confirming memo was received and not objected to by Toys Miami, Inc. As a merchant, they should have known about this exception to the general rule. Since they didn't protect themselves by a timely objection to the memo, they are bound by it.

In *Thomson Printing Machinery Co. v. B.F. Goodrich Co., 714 F.2d 744 (7th Cir. 1983)*, plaintiff met with defendant to discuss the purchase of used printing machinery for a price of $9,000. Four days later, plaintiff sent defendant a purchase order for the equipment with a $1,000 deposit check. Hearing no objection, plaintiff called defendant weeks later to arrange to remove the machines and was told they had been sold to someone else. Plaintiff then sued for breach of contract, asserting the applicability of the merchant non-signer rule.

Defendant asserted by way of defense that no contract had been formed, and "that in any event the alleged oral contract was unenforceable due to the Statute of Frauds . . .

Thomson's writing in confirmation cannot qualify for the 2-201(2) exception because it was not received by anyone at Goodrich who had reason to know its contents. Goodrich claims that Thomson erred in not specifically designating on the envelope, check, or purchase order that the items were intended for Ingram Meyers or the surplus equipment department. Consequently, Goodrich contends, it was unable to 'find a home' for the check and purchase order despite attempts to do so ..."

Notwithstanding a jury verdict for plaintiff, the trial court entered judgment for defendant based upon plaintiff's failure to satisfy the Statute of Frauds "signed by the party to be charged" requirement. The appellate court reversed:

"Even if we go beyond the literal requirements of 2-201(2) and read into the 'receipt' requirement the 'receipt of notice' rule of 1-201(27)*, we still think Thomson Printing satisfied the 'merchants' exception.

*is effective for a particular transaction ... from the time when it would have been brought to (the attention of the individual conducting that transaction) if the organization had executed *due diligence.*"

Notice the court's wording that clearly indicates that a business law time bomb exploded in the face of the defendant, which they could easily have defused:

"If Goodrich had exercised due diligence in handling Thomson Printing's purchase order and check, these items would have reasonably promptly come to Ingram Meyers' attention. First, the purchase order on its face should have alerted the mailroom that the documents referred to a purchase of used printing equipment. Since Goodrich had only one surplus machinery department the documents 'home' should not have been difficult to find. Second, even if the mailroom would have had difficulty in immediately identifying the kind of transaction involved, the purchase order had Thomson Printing's phone number printed on it and we think a 'reasonable routine' in these particular circumstances would have involved at some point in the process a simple phone call to Thomson Printing. Thus, we think Goodrich's mailroom mishandled the confirmatory writings. This failure should not permit Goodrich to escape liability by pleading nonreceipt."

C. THE SPECIAL MANUFACTURE EXCEPTION

When the parties enter into a purely verbal sales agreement for the creation of a unique, specialized or custom item costing $500 or more, another fairness exception applies which eliminates the writing requirements, under UCC 2-201(3)(a):

"If the goods (are) to be specially manufactured for the buyer and are not suitable for sale to others in the ordinary course of the seller's business and the seller, before notice of repudiation is received and under circumstances which reasonably indicate that the goods are for the buyer, has made either a substantial beginning of their manufacture or commitments for their procurement."

Once the seller substantially begins the manufacture of the specialty item, the buyer is estopped to cancel based on the Statute because the item usually cannot be sold to anyone else. If the buyer could cancel due to lack of the required writing, injustice to the seller would result since he would totally lose the time, effort and costs expended.

*Ex: Charles, a lawyer, verbally contracts with Miami Printing for all his customized office stationary for a total price of $700. The printer begins the job, has finished the business cards and envelopes, and is halfway through the print run of letterheads when Charles calls to cancel. He doesn't give a reason, but the printer suspects he founds someone to do the work at a lower price. The printer demands full payment for the finished work.

To allow cancellation by the buyer would result in a severe injustice. Miami Printing would be unable to find anyone else to assume payment of the job or purchase the specialty items because they are one of a kind.

Even if Charles argues that the transaction is really a sale of services rather than goods, and therefore not governed by the UCC or the Statute, he still is faced with a legally enforceable verbal contract.

In *LTV Aerospace v. Bateman, 492 S.W.2d 703 (Tex. App. 1973)*, LTV needed to buy a quantity of special export shipping crates to deliver a number of its all-terrain vehicles to Southeast Asia. It circulated a detailed sheet of specifications to prospective bidders, and Bateman's proposal exceeding $500 to sell 8,000 crates was accepted after extensive verbal discussions. Though there were written bid and purchase order communications exchanged by the parties, none were ever fully signed.

After Bateman had delivered approximately 653 crates, LTV's Tyler, Texas plant closed and it refused to pay for any additional crates. Bateman sued for breach of contract and demanded damages for lost profits of $25,000.

The trial jury ruled for Bateman, and on appeal that decision was affirmed:

"These shipping crates or containers were manufactured by appellee to detailed specifications required by appellant, and they were to be used for shipping overseas an all-terrain vehicle manufactured by appellant. They were not suitable for sale to others in the ordinary course of appellee's business.

The record discloses that appellee had made a substantial beginning in manufacture of the goods, and it was done for appellant's benefit before any notice of repudiation was given or received."

Notice that this exception allows enforcement of a verbal agreement for the sale of goods of $500 or more with no writing of any kind, not even a confirming letter or memorandum.

C. THE PART PAYMENT OR PART DELIVERY EXCEPTION

This type of partial performance in a verbal sale of goods contract takes it outside the Statute and allows enforcement because that conduct is a clear expression of the intention of the parties to be legally bound, under UCC 2-201(3)(c):

"With respect to goods for which payment has been made and accepted or which have been received and accepted."

Some states reason that such partial performance is a ratification of the contract; others use estoppel reasoning in allowing enforcement.

E. THE COURTROOM ADMISSIONS EXCEPTION

UCC 2-201(3)(b) also validates a contract that does not otherwise satisfy the "sale of goods of $500 or more" requirements of the Statute:

"If the party against whom enforcement is sought admits in his pleading, testimony or otherwise in court that a contract for sale was made, but the contract is not enforceable under this provision beyond the quantity of goods admitted."

These situations of courtroom admissions of a contract are based upon the contract doctrines of waiver of defenses, ratification of otherwise legally invalid contracts, and estoppel to deny the enforceability of such agreements.

6. SPECIAL SITUATIONS

- A verbal promise to make or modify a will for the financial benefit of another must be written. Estate laws are highly technical, and the specific legal formalities surrounding the creation of testamentary documents are very detailed. There is too much risk of wrongdoing in allowing verbal inheritance agreements because the party creating the contract is now dead and cannot state their true intentions.

- A verbal agreement to pay a fee to another contingent upon them finding a person or a business opportunity, or rewarding them for specific actions, or agreeing to compensate them for some required performance, must also be written. Again, any and all such unusual arrangements must be documented in written form to assure the intentions of the parties are followed.

This also applies to fee-splitting agreements between attorneys, as was the case in *Chambers v. Kay, 2002 Cal. LEXIS 7396 (Cal. 2002),* where Chambers was serving as a co-counsel in a sexual harassment action Kay had previously filed on behalf of his client, Rena Weeks. A dispute arose between the parties regarding settlement efforts, and Kay then sent a letter to Chambers removing him from the case.

This letter also confirmed that he would receive the compensation previously agreed upon, "that is: in the event the case was settled before depositions, '16.5% of the attorney's fees called for under my agreement with (Weeks), which is 40% of the monies recovered'; thereafter, 'an increase to 28% of the fees specified under the agreement with Weeks; and reimbursement of the costs (Chambers) advanced to date." Chambers accepted the compensation.

After the Weeks case resulted in a large award of compensatory and punitive damages for her, Kay offered to pay Chambers only $200 per hour for his rendered services. Chambers sued for breach of contract, the trial court granted summary judgment to Kay, Chambers appealed, and the appellate court affirmed:

"(California Rule of Professional Conduct 2-200, patterned after the Statute of Frauds) provides: (A) a member shall not divide a fee for legal services with a lawyer who is not a partner of, associate of, or shareholder with the member unless: (1) The client has consented in writing thereto after a full disclosure has been made in writing that a division of fees will be made and the terms of such division."

Here is another liability time bomb that detonated, right in the wallet of attorney Chambers. All he had to do was confirm that Weeks had consented to his fee-splitting arrangement. She most certainly would have done so, since it had no effect on the total contingent fee she had agreed to pay.

- Agreements to marry were at one time common in this country, and still are in other venues. Because of their highly specialized nature and the sanctity of the relationship, written form is required. The same holds true for antenuptial and postnuptial agreements, where the parties agree before or after marriage on the financial arrangements to be made in the event of divorce or death.

7. THE EQUITABLE ESTOPPEL EXCEPTION

In situations where the parties have made a verbal agreement that falls within any of the categories of the Statute of Frauds that require adherence to its writing and signing requirements, they may nevertheless be excused from this formality if they satisfy the elements of equitable estoppel:

As related to the party estopped, they are: "(1) conduct which amounts to a false representation or concealment of material facts, or, at least, which is calculated to convey the impression that the facts are otherwise than, and inconsistent with, those which the party subsequently attempts to assert; (2) intention, or at least expectation, that such conduct shall be acted upon by the other party; (3) knowledge, actual or constructive, of the real facts."

As related to the party claiming the estoppel, they are: "(1) lack of knowledge and of the means of knowledge of the truth as to the facts in question; (2) reliance upon the conduct of the party estopped; and (3) action based thereon of such a character as to change his position." *First Interstate Bank of Idaho, N.A. v. West, 693 P.2d 1053 (Idaho 1984).*

8. INTERPRETING WRITTEN CONTRACTS

We know that "put it in writing" is the basic commandment of doing business successfully. Equally as important is "read it before you sign it." Parties are presumed to know the content and legal import of their contracts. Once you sign it, you are bound by its terms, good or bad.

THE PAROL EVIDENCE RULE encourages written agreements because it bars from legal consideration any prior written or verbal communications between the parties that seeks to alter, vary or contradict their signed written contract. This law recognizes the inherent unfairness and potential danger of one of the parties trying to escape from a transaction and succeeding because they are more believable in the false story they concoct to justify such action.

The four corners of the writing are the best evidence of the final completed agreement of the parties, and it usually cannot be modified by outside matters, unless to explain prior dealings of the parties, supply missing information, clear ambiguities, or correct obvious clerical or typographical errors. All prior negotiations are deemed to be merged into the final contract. Thus, a fully integrated contract is the best evidence of what agreement was made and intended by the parties.

> *Ex: Robin applies for an employment position with Samaritan Hospital as a physical therapist. She signs a contract that states, "employer may terminate employment at any time with or without cause by 14 days written notice," and begins work.

When she is fired six months later, she sues for breach of contract, claiming there were prior verbal discussions whereby the employer had said in response to her questions about job security, "you cannot be fired without cause, you are guaranteed a hearing, and even if fired it is not effective for 30 days." The employer denied this conversation.

Robin loses. The written contract is binding. It is presumed to include all prior negotiations. It is clear and unambiguous in this case. Robin could easily have protected herself by proof reading the written contract and continuing negotiations until it said exactly what she claim the parties agreed. If you sign a writing without reading it, you usually do so at your peril.

*Ex: Robin negotiates to buy Tina's car. A final written contract is signed by the parties which states, Robin agrees to buy Tina's 1999 blue Chevrolet 2-door sedan for $5,000, payable in cash no later than 15 days from today." A dispute occurs because Tina has two blue Chevvies, a Corvair and a Camaro. Robin claims she was buying the Camaro, and Tina claims she was selling the Corvair.

In this case, we have an ambiguity as to the subject matter of the transaction. Parol evidence of the prior negotiations or other outside circumstances may be introduced to resolve the dispute. The objective here is to help the court interpret the true contract intended by the parties, not to contradict it.

Ambiguity is the reason most commonly raised in cases to justify the judge looking beyond the four corners of a written agreement. The case of *Idaho Migrant Council, Inc. v. Warila, 890 P.2d 30 (Wyo. 1995)*, is typical. IMC leased property from Warila for use as a Migrant Head Start Center. The written lease agreement, prepared by IMC, contained a clause allowing IMC to terminate without penalty, under certain conditions.

One year after beginning the lease, IMC invoked the termination clause. The parties then attempted to negotiate a settlement of their differences through their attorneys, relating to whether or not the conditions for termination had in fact been reached. A verbal settlement was reached, a written agreement was prepared, but the Warila's refused to sign it.

IMC sued to enforce the oral settlement agreement that allowed it to terminate upon payment of two year's rent to the lessor. The trial court ruled the termination clause in the written lease to be ambiguous, construed it against IMC, and enforced the settlement. The appellate court affirmed, and noted, "We have repeatedly held that a contract will be construed most strongly against the party who drafted the contract."

"Contract interpretation is the process of ascertaining the meaning of the words used by the parties to express their intent. We generally look to the 'four corners' of an instrument to determine the intent of the parties. However, this rule is only applicable where the language clearly and unambiguously expresses the intent of the parties. If the meaning of a provision in a contract is not readily apparent, the court may resort to competent evidence of extraneous circumstances to explain the ambiguity."

Written agreements commonly have "integration clauses" at their conclusion, located immediately above the signatures of the parties, that literally caution the parties against seeking to alter the clear terms of the final agreement they have made.

A typical integration clause was present in *Malmstrom v. Kaiser Aluminum, 187 Cal. App.3d 299 (Cal. App. 1986)*, a case where Kaiser was granted a summary judgment in a dispute between it and a former employee about an alleged oral promise of lifetime employment that conflicted with a subsequent written contract that said the employment was terminable at will. It read as follows:

Paragraph 1 – "Employer employs and shall continue to employ Employee at such compensation and for such a length of time as shall be mutually agreeable to Employer and Employee."

Paragraph 6 – "This agreement shall supersede all previous agreements by and between Employer and employee and shall be retroactive to the date on which Employee commenced his employment."

In *Leitz v. Thorson, 833 P.2d 343 (Or. 1992)*, plaintiffs leased commercial space from defendant to open a flower shop. Before the lease was signed, the defendant allegedly told plaintiffs they could have a freestanding sign. The signed lease however had a standard clause that said, "Tenant shall not erect or install any signs or advertising media . . . without written consent of the Landlord," as well as an integration clause.

Plaintiffs later learned they could not place a sign along the highway to advertise their business, because the local zoning code allowed only one freestanding sign per property, and a sign advertising a business partly owned by defendant was already in place.

Plaintiffs sued for breach of oral contract and fraud. The trial jury ruled for plaintiffs, saying "there are many appendixes that are referred to (in the lease), none of which were completed or attached to the document – that being the contract. Based on the testimony that I heard and I believe that this is not a fully integrated contract and that the additional evidence concerning the terms is not inconsistent with the written contract."

The defendant appealed, based in part upon a violation of the Parol Evidence Rule by the trial judge admitting into evidence testimony about the oral signage agreement. The appellate court affirmed:

"No provision of this lease prohibits a freestanding sign. The disputed parol evidence was not inconsistent with the written agreement."

"If the parties did not intend the writing to represent their entire agreement, the agreement is only partially integrated, and prior consistent additional terms not evidenced by the writing may still form part of the entire agreement."

A. Do you believe the defendant intended to deceive plaintiffs?
B. If the defendant was unaware of the prior sign, do you think the court would have allowed parol evidence of the prior oral signage promise?
C. Notice how courts sometimes reach a fair result by applying to the facts of the case the legal rule or legal exception that will accomplish it?

Some courts have differing interpretations of how the Parol Evidence Rule's "ambiguity" exception should be used. The traditional approach, prohibiting reference to outside matters when the writing is clear and specific, followed by a majority of states is called the *plain meaning rule.*

A more recent approach, which may signal a trend in the law, allows reference to outside sources for help in determining the intent of the parties even if there is no ambiguity, and is called the *context rule.*

In *Berg v. Hudesman, 801 P.2d 222 (Wash. 1990),* the Court allowed outside evidence to assist in understanding how to apply a rent payment clause in a lease ruled by the trial court not to be ambiguous. "We reject the plain meaning rule and expressly adopt the context rule as the applicable rule for ascertaining the parties' intent and interpreting written contracts."

"The Plain Meaning rule states that if a writing, or the term in question, appears to be plain and unambiguous on its face, its meaning must be determined from the four corners of the instrument without resort to extrinsic evidence of any nature."

"A trial court may, in interpreting contract language, consider the surrounding circumstances leading to execution of the agreement, including the subject matter of the contract as well as the subsequent conduct of the parties, not for the purpose of contradicting what is in the agreement, but for the purpose of determining the parties' intent."

A similar result to the *Berg* case took place in *This is Me, Inc. v. Taylor, 157 F.3d 139 (2nd cir. 1998)*, where actress Cicely Tyson, through her personal service company, successfully sued to collect a $750,000 "play or pay" guarantee due her for the lead role in a Broadway play and later anticipated television tapings.

Actress Elizabeth Taylor and Broadway producer Zev Bufman had formed a theater group to produce live performances of plays on the legitimate stage and video and television versions of the same plays. Their second production, "The Corn is Green", cast Tyson in the lead role, but soon closed and the video was never made.

Tyson, at the height of her career, had turned down other opportunities to do this project, and a series of contracts for the stage performances and the video performances guaranteed payment of $750,000 by defendants if the show closed before she had earned that amount in salary.

"Considering all the circumstances, we believe that (A) the several agreements should be read together, and that (B), when they are so read in the light of all the evidence, they are capable of sustaining the jury's conclusion that Bufman and Taylor were bound by the $750,000 guarantee set forth in the video contract."

THE STANDARDS OF ANALYSIS RULES assist in determining what words, phrases and terms the parties intended in their written contract if they are not available at the time of a dispute to testify. This non-availability, though sometimes voluntary, is usually in cases of accident, illness, disability and often death. In a preprinted form agreement, there often are conflicts between the original content, added typewriting and added handwriting. If the contracting parties are unavailable, the law presumes that the proper order of interpretation is:

1. handwriting
2. typewriting
3. preprinting

The rationale is that we are seeking the last expression of the intent of the parties. It is reasonable to assume that once the preprinted agreement is presented for signature, some additional changes may have been negotiated as reflected by the typewritten additions, and then at the final moment of completion the handwritten changes probably were inserted.

If the parties are members of a particular trade or profession, or the agreement concerns a specialized subject matter – the wording will be interpreted consistent with that specialty and the specific terminology used. For example, the number "86" has a special meaning in the restaurant and food business signifying cancellation. "Stet" in the printing business means let it stand. "Prima facie" in the legal profession means the fact is established. "Feed corn" means food for cattle.

DISCUSSION EXERCISES

1. Discuss the advantages/disadvantages of a verbal one - year lease from the standpoint of the Landlord. What about the Tenant?

2. Discuss how you would determine when the main benefit exception to the guaranty contract rule should apply.

3. Discuss whether oral lifetime employment contracts should be enforced.

4. Discuss what dollar minimum you would require for the sale of goods writing requirement.

5. Discuss any additional statute of frauds exceptions you would implement, other than the ones already discussed.

CASE EXERCISE

IS THE RONETTES' $15,000 RECORDING CONTRACT OF 1963 THAT IS NOW WORTH MILLIONS STILL BINDING?

In *Greenfield, et al v. Philles Records,et al, 2002 N.Y. Lexis 3146 (N.Y. App. 2002)*, an unknown singing group known as "The Ronettes" met the legendary rock and roll producer and composer Phil Spector in 1963, who signed them to a five-year "personal services" music recording contract with the defendant, his production company.

The agreement was a two-page contract, widely used in the 1960's by music producers signing new artists, was signed by plaintiff's without the benefit of counsel, and provided for the artists' transfer of full ownership rights to the master recordings of their musical performances for a cash advance of $15,000.

It specified defendants' "right to make phonograph records, tape recordings or other reproductions of the performances embodied in such recordings by any method now or hereafter known, and to sell and deal in the same . . ."

The Ronettes recorded 28 songs for defendant, including *Be My Baby*, which became a number one hit and sold over one million copies. Despite the group's popularity, it disbanded in 1967, and no other monies were paid to plaintiffs.

Defendants began to capitalize on a resurgence of public interest in 1960's music by using new recording technologies, non-existent at the time of the contract, to use master recordings of the Ronettes' vocal performances for "synchronization licensing" in the 1980's.

This was done in movies such as, "Dirty Dancing" and "Goodfellas", and the television series, "Moonlighting", to yield over $3 million in licensing proceeds, none of which was paid to plaintiffs.

ANALYSIS

Plaintiffs sued for breach of contract in 1987, alleging that the 1963 agreement did not grant defendants the right to license their masters for the new synchronization process, and demanded the industry's standard 50% royalty fee.

The trial court ruled in their favor and awarded approximately $3 million in damages. The appellate division affirmed, "concluding that defendants' actions were not authorized by the agreement with plaintiffs because the contract did not specifically transfer the right to issue synchronization and third-party domestic distribution licenses."

The Court of appeals accepted the case, and ruled for the defendants, following the strict, plain meaning rule of contract interpretation:

"Despite the technological innovations that continue to revolutionize the recording industry, long-settled common-law contract rules still govern the interpretation of agreements between artists and their record producers. The fundamental, neutral precept of contract interpretation is that agreements are construed in accord with the party's intent. The best evidence of what parties to a written agreement intend is what they say in their writing. Thus, a written agreement that is complete, clear and unambiguous on its face must be enforced according to the plain meaning of its terms ... Thus, if the agreement on its face is reasonably susceptible of only one meaning, a court is not free to alter the contract to reflect its personal notions of fairness and equity."

DEFUSE REPLAY

The court stated the central issue in this case: "Does the contract's silence on synchronization and domestic licensing create an ambiguity that opens the door to the admissibility of extrinsic evidence to determine the intent of the parties?

Their answer was, "We conclude that it does not and, because there is no ambiguity in the terms of the Ronettes contract, defendants are entitled to exercise complete ownership rights, subject to payment of applicable royalties (at 3%, not 50%) due plaintiffs."

The author would respectfully suggest this ruling is wrong, from both a legal and ethical standpoint.

"AMBIGUOUS: 1. Having two or more possible meanings. 2. Not clear; uncertain or vague." *Webster's New World Dictionary(1969).*

There was most certainly an ambiguity in the 1963 agreement. The technology for synchronization licensing that produced the revenue in question was not in existence until well after it had expired in 1968. By definition, it was impossible to include in the agreement because these concepts were unheard of at the time. Therefore, outside evidence should be admissible, such as the current standard industry royalties paid for such types of licensing.

If we apply the context rule of interpretation, referred to in *Berg v. Hudesman, supra,* the existence or non-existence of an ambiguity is irrelevant, and all outside factors necessary to clarify the true intentions of the parties are admissible.

The trial court and appellate division rulings make more sense. How could plaintiffs have protected themselves in the 1963 agreement against truly unforeseeable future events? Many fairness doctrines exist in our contract law to protect innocent parties from such a result. The plaintiffs are the victims, and the defendants the victimizers in the final court result.

CONCLUSION

This case had a number of other interesting aspects:

- Plaintiff Ronnie Greenfield, then known as Veronica Bennett, was married to Phil Spector from 1968 to 1974.

- The 1963 agreement did not restrict the ability of The Ronettes to earn income from appearances in concerts, on television, or in movies, and they re-formed briefly to do so after their renewed 1980's popularity.

- This litigation spanned a period of 15 years until its final conclusion.

- The Recording Industry of America was a strong defendant's advocate during the case, as was the Recording Artists Coalition for the plaintiffs.

A. Do you agree with the court's final decision?
B. Does this case set a precedent to enforce all similar recording agreements from the 1950's, 1960's and 1970's that are now significantly more valuable due to technological advances?
C. What legal standards would you use, and what factors would you consider to determine such disputes?

CASE RESEARCH CYBERCISES

The following cases also relate to the material in this chapter and illustrate the types of disputes that may occur. For each one do the following written assignment:

1. Locate the case using the Internet (Lexis-Nexis, West or any other research cite which provides case transcripts).
2. Briefly summarize what it was about – the nature of the dispute involved.
3. Who won at the trial court level? Who won at the appellate level?
4. Who won if there was a third level of Supreme Court review?
5. What were the legal rules of law and the reasoning used to reach the final decision?
6. Do you agree or disagree with the decision, and explain why?
7. What business law time bomb(s) were involved?
8. Could the time bomb(s) have been avoided by structuring the transaction differently? Discuss.
9. Could the adverse effects of the time bomb(s) have been defused by a different reaction or response by the affected party? Discuss.
10. Replay the facts of the case to achieve a different successful result.

1. *Levin v. Knight, 780 F.2d 786 (9th Cir. 1986) (issue of fact exists regarding the enforceability of a three page handwritten memorandum for sale of the L.A Clippers professional basketball team).*
2. *Cantell v. Hill Holiday Connors Cosmopulos, Inc., 772 N.E.2d 1078 (Mass. App. 2002) (verbal finder's fee contract to provide job candidates held unenforceable).*
3. *Briggs v. Sackett, 418 A.2d 586 (Pa. 1980) (part performance allows enforcement of verbal agreement to buy a house occupied and improved for 14 years).*
4. *Golden State Porcelain v. Swid Powell Design, 37 U.C.C. Rep. Serv.2d 928 (N.Y. 1999) (verbal agreement to special manufacture Gucci porcelain products upheld).*
5. *Allied Grape Growers v. Bronco Wine Company, 203 Cal. App.3d 432 (Cal. App. 1988) (verbal contract to purchase grapes enforceable by promissory estoppel to prevent buyer from canceling due to drop in market prices).*

NOTES

17.

RIGHTS OF THIRD PARTIES:
CAN OUTSIDERS TO THE CONTRACT ENFORCE IT?

"Who is the third who walks always beside you?
T. S. Eliot

A. LEGAL OVERVIEW

We now shift our focus from disputes between the original contracting Parties, to situations where a third party outsider to the contract claims legally enforceable rights. Let's look at the legal principles governing these situations, and then some actual cases that illustrate typical disputes.

The original contracting parties create their own legal bargain, with its unique terms and provisions. They usually are the only ones who have corresponding legal rights and duties. They are said to be in *privity of contract*. If one of the parties fails to properly perform its duties, the other has the legal right to enforce it by suing for breach of contract.

The early common law prohibited any transfer of contract rights or duties on the grounds that they were unique and personal to the original parties. There was little or no movement of capital beyond the real property based economy. The extension of credit was viewed as a solemn bargain. In those days, the failure to pay one's debt was subject to possible incarceration in debtor's prison, because it was considered a form of theft.

As our society became more complex, the needs of the commercial marketplace required a broader based system of obtaining credit and ways to trade in intangible assets such as debt obligations. Transfers of these obligations are encouraged in appropriate situations and assisted by the fact that they carry no legal writing or consideration requirements to be valid. As long as the intention of the parties to convey third party rights or duties is clear, the courts will honor them.

There are three basic situations which grant to parties who were not part of the original contract the same rights of legal enforcement that belong to the original participants.

- Assignment transfers of legal rights (usually to collect debts)
- Delegation transfers of legal duties (usually to perform services)
- Third party beneficiary cases - (no assignment or delegation made)

The legal effect of these exceptions is to cancel the rights and duties of the original performing parties to each other, and confer them instead upon the third party outsider.

B. DIRECT ASSIGNMENT OF THIRD PARTY RIGHTS

The transfer of a legal right to another is called an *assignment*. The Party who is legally obligated to perform is called the *obligor*, and owes this duty to the *obligee*. When the obligee transfers that right to receive the performance to a third party outsider, the obligee-transferor is called the *assignor* and the third party transferee is called the *assignee*.

The following diagram should be helpful. It illustrates a typical assignment situation, where the original creditor (A) assigns to a third party (C) its right to collect the obligation owed to it by the original debtor (B):

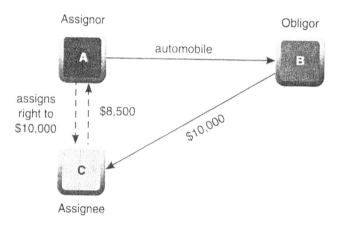

Though these assignment situations commonly involve loans of money or the creation of accounts receivable from the sale of goods to another, they may also take other factual forms.

There are also a number of reasons why the creditor (A) would transfer its right to collect to (C), rather than directly receive the funds due on the contract obligation:

- A owes C money on an unrelated matter and assigns this valuable contract right in full or partial payment

- A desires to make a gift to C (perhaps a friend, family member or charity) of this valuable contract right

- A contracts with C to obtain financing for a project, and assigns this valuable contract right as its collateral security

By far the most prevalent third party assignment situation is one which is commonly known as *factoring*, or accounts receivable financing, which satisfies the needs of business to convert future pay assets into current cash:

- A sells goods or services to B on delayed payment basis (A gains an account receivable and B owes an account payable), needs current liquidity and then sells it for cash to C at a discounted price.

There are a number of legal factors that determine whether or not the assignee can legally claim rights and enforce the obligations assigned.

In the typical dispute, a third party outsider seeks to enforce rights against the obligor, who denies the validity of the assignment.

1. Does the contract itself prohibit assignments to third parties?

The wording of any contract determines the rights and duties of its parties. Under common law rules of most states, a contract is presumed assignable unless it specifically states otherwise. The UCC takes a different position regarding sales of goods, declaring that even though there is an antiassignment clause in the contract, it is binding as to delegation of duties but not as to assignments of rights.

There are good, practical reasons for these prohibitions against assignment in residential and commercial lease situations. The landlord has negotiated the deal with a particular tenant, and created the important lease terms that include rental payments, security deposits, and all other aspects of the transaction.

An antiassignment clause is designed to protect a landlord and the other tenants from undesirable new tenants, who have bypassed whatever screening procedures are required before a lease is finalized. Sudden occupancy by strangers to the original lease contract is frowned upon by most states.

To allow the named tenant to assign (new party assumes the lease and pays the landlord) or sublease (new party pays directly to tenant) at any time they wish may seriously jeopardize the finances and security of the transaction and the property itself.

*Ex: Jacob owns a 24-unit apartment building near the local University. He enters into a lease agreement with student Emily, where he agrees, "to rent to Tenant unit number 12 for one year at a monthly rent of $500, first month and two months security deposit payable in advance. No assignment or sublease allowed. Breach of lease entitles Landlord to declare immediate default and collect full remaining rental for entire term plus expenses and legal fees, if any." Emily is homesick after 2 months and decides to leave. Since her unit is the only one available in the vicinity, she is able to sublease it to Chad for $650 per month, thus making a $150 monthly profit for herself. Jacob finds out, demands Chad vacate, and sues Emily for the 10 months of rent remaining under the lease.

The prohibition against transfer in this case raises another practical advantage to the landlord. The original lease may be a very good deal for the tenant due to a skilled negotiation or the supply and demand factors that change over time.

If Emily wants to assign or sublease in this case, she needs Jacob to give his consent, and their discussion will reveal the profit possibility that exists in a new rental.

Probably, they will agree to share the profit in some mutually agreeable proportion, where in exchange for Jacob releasing Emily from any further lease obligations, he receives a larger share of the new rental. If the opposite situation exists where Emily is unable to find a new tenant, she will negotiate a buy out of her lease obligations with Jacob. In either instance, Jacob makes a profit that would not exist if assignment were allowed.

*Ex: Suppose Emily contracts to buy the apartment building from Jacob at a very low price of $250,000, due to a combination of her skilled negotiating, his desire to retire, and the fact she offers an all cash deal with a 60 day closing. Chad has been looking for this type of investment property which he estimates is worth $350,000, finds out Emily has the contract right to buy at the low price, and contracts for her to assign her interest to him now for $100,000.

This assignment of rights situation is known in real estate terms as "flipping the contract". It highlights the respective practical interests of the original contracting parties. If you are a seller of real property, you always want to use an antiassignment clause to protect yourself against selling below the current market price. If you are a buyer, you always want to be allowed to assign just in case your deal has the potential for a market profit.

Most states, faced with a specific prohibition on transfer in a lease or sale of real property, will interpret it according to a rule-of-reason standard to say, "no assignment allowed without my consent, *but such consent shall not be unreasonably withheld.* Then each dispute is evaluated to determine what is reasonable using this objective test. Some of the relevant factors are the third parties general reputation, credit rating, financial position, past history of similar dealings, effect on the property and/or its tenants, and profit or loss involved in granting or denying the assignment.

2. Is the assignment contrary to a law or public policy?

The legality of the assignment is sometimes at issue. Most states prohibit an assignment of future employment wages to protect against impulsive decisions created by illness or addiction, compulsive disorders such as gambling, and related situations.

Assignments for the benefit of particular creditors at the expense of others are also frowned upon, and often invalidated as unlawful preferential transfers.

The discounted cash sale of life insurance benefits by terminally ill policy holders, called "viatical settlements", caused such a legal problem when Aids became an unfortunate part of our everyday reality. Most life insurance contracts at that time did not prohibit assignment. These transactions were initially viewed as beneficial to all parties. The seller received immediate cash to provide for medical and related expenses, allowing current gifting to loved ones as an accelerated inheritance. The third party buyer was making a profitable short-term investment and assisting the seller with the funds paid. The insurance company was merely changing beneficiary to be paid upon death of their insured.

Publicity about these assignments raised public concern that insureds were being victimized by unscrupulous buyers who preyed upon their weakened physical and mental condition. The insurance companies were also criticized for allowing such transfers to take place.

As a result, new life insurance policies contained clauses prohibiting such assignments, even though many holders of policies publicly voiced their support for the financial flexibility these assignments allowed them. These conflicting positions became moot as the life expectancy of Aids patients greatly increased due to improved treatment options. The uncertainty of when such life insurance policies will now "mature", and the negative public perception of them, has resulted in these assignments essentially disappearing from the marketplace.

Public policy arguments were also involved, as the reader will recall, in the chapter on illegal contracts, concerning the enforceability of non-competition agreements. Even if a particular non-compete satisfies the "reasonable" tests for time, area and scope – is it assignable and enforceable?

In *Special Products Manufacturing, Inc. v. Douglass, 553 N.Y.S.2d 506 (N.Y. App. Div. 1990),* defendant was employed by Page-Wilson Corp. to service hardness-testing machinery, pursuant to two employment contracts, one of which protected intellectual property and customer lists and the other prohibited employment competition.

Canrad Corp bought all the assets of Page-Wilson, including defendant's two employment agreements, and plaintiff was their wholly owned subsidiary for whom defendant worked until he resigned to work in a competing business he established, violating the restrictions of his employment contract.

Plaintiff sued defendant to enforce the non-compete, defendant failed to respond on time, a default judgment was entered against him, and then his motion to extend the time to answer the complaint was denied by the trial court.

On appeal by the defendant, the appellate court affirmed:

"We perceive no merit in defendant's claims that the employment agreements are not binding because consideration therefor is lacking or not recited. Nor are we persuaded by the contention that because defendant entered into the agreements with Page-Wilson, they are unenforceable by plaintiff . . . Defendant's consent was not required to effectuate this transfer. When the original parties to an agreement so intend, a covenant not to compete is freely assignable." (unless it contains a non-assignment clause).

3. Is notice of the assignment required to be given to the obligor?

*Ex: Michael loans Hannah $50,000 on July 1, payable in 90 days on October 1. Hannah signs a promissory note agreeing to these terms. Due to liquidity needs Michael sells the note to Xavier on August 1, receiving $40,000 cash in exchange for his assignment transfer. Michael tells Xavier, "Don't worry about contacting Hannah, I'll tell her to make all payments to you." Before Michael can notify Hannah, she calls him to say she wants to prepay her debt. He says, "Great, bring cash and I'll give you a paid in full receipt." She pays Michael on August 15; he never mentions the assignment, takes the money and runs off to the jungles of Brazil. On October 1 Xavier calls Hannah requesting full payment of her note. She says, "I don't know you and for your information I already paid it in full back on August 15. Leave me alone." Michael sues Hannah to enforce the note.

Sorry Michael, you goofed. The law in this area clearly states that the validity of an assignment is not affected by the failure to give notice of it to the payment obligor. Hannah is obligated to pay someone at the due date, and whether the payee is the original creditor Michael or the assignee Xavier is immaterial. She is not prejudiced in any way by having to pay someone else.

From a practical standpoint however, notifying the obligor of an assignment of her debt is of great importance to avoid the predicament encountered by Xavier. He has lost $40,000, unless he can locate Michael, sue him for the loss, recover a judgment and collect it. Hannah cannot be forced to pay her debt twice; unless it could be proven she was notified of Xavier's ownership interest before she paid Michael. The party who should notify the obligor is always the assignee, not the assignor, who may be a scoundrel in waiting like Michael in our example.

Disputes often arise in these notice situations because the parties confuse the obligatory *must notify* with the discretionary *should notify*. The assignee doesn't have to, but it certainly is the most skillful way to proceed.

4. Is the consent of the obligor to the assignment required?

There is no legal requirement, as a general rule, that the obligor must Approve an assignment for it to be valid. Especially when the obligation to be performed is the payment of money.

> *Ex: Suppose that notice of the assignment in the above example had been properly given to Hannah (obligor) by Michael (assignor) or more probably Xavier (assignee)? Let's pretend that Hannah's response was, "I don't know you Xavier, I signed a promissory note to Michael and he is the only person I will pay. I don't consent to the sale of my note to you." Xavier says, "I'm not asking for your consent, I'm just telling that you now are legally obligated to pay me on the due date."

> Xavier is correct under the general rule. Hannah is not disadvantaged in any way by paying him instead of Michael.

There are some fairness exceptions where the prior consent or approval of the obligor is required for an assignment of their rights to be valid. They all relate to a legal test of whether or not the obligor is adversely affected in a significant way by the desired assignment. If it causes a "material hardship" on the obligor, their consent is legally necessary.

- Legal claims of a personal nature – if I have a claim against you for alleged misconduct that injured me, it is not assignable to a stranger. Similarly, I cannot assign my insurance contract to a stranger without the consent of the insurer who is obligated to pay for losses incurred under its terms.

- Personal service/relationship contracts – if I am hired as your personal physician or attorney, or your portrait painter or acting teacher - to perform specialized services for you, I may not legally transfer (delegate) them to a stranger who is less qualified or experienced.

- Personal employment situations – when employers sell a business, some of their significant assets that create value for the deal are their valuable employment contracts. When an employee is notified of the assignment of his contract, and is requested to report for work to the new owner, his response is often, "heck no, I won't go." Are such contract rights assignable without the employee's consent?

> *Ex: Marlon is a talented actor under 10 year employment contract with MGM Studios in Hollywood, California, where he has a house, family, children in school and is a local city commissioner.

The MGM parent company sells its entertainment division to Disney Studios based in Miami, Florida in year 7, and assigns to them his contract. Disney notifies Marlon to report for work in 10 days. He refuses, claiming he never approved the sale.

Marlon's consent is required. He would suffer financial hardship through moving expenses, relocation costs and related monetary considerations. Even if Disney agreed to reimburse for these items, there are non-monetary hardships in having to adjust himself and his family to a new location, including personal associations, schooling, weather, population demographics, language and culture considerations, and related matters.

What if the move was from MGM in Hollywood to Universal Hollywood located two miles away? Here Marlon could still argue hardship, citing emotional factors of being uprooted from his long personal relationship with MGM, new surroundings, personnel, possible changes in employment duties, and the like.

These employment cases rarely involve disputes in professional sports contracts, even though identical factors exist that would satisfy the prior consent test of hardship. This is because there are specific provisions in these contracts between owners and players that allow the purchase and sale of contracts without employee's prior approval. Some sports have collective bargaining labor agreements that allow a player to veto a contract trade or sale after a required minimum number of years in the league, or for other special aspects of free agency.

The unique facts of each dispute will determine whether or not the obligor's consent to assignment is required:

- In *The Munchak Corporation v. Cunningham, 457 F.2d 721 (4th Cir. 1972)*, Billy Cunningham was under contract to play professional basketball for the Philadelphia 76ers during the late 1960's until his option year of 1970-1971, and signed a contract to play for The Carolina Cougars commencing when his prior contract ended. The new contract included a bonus to be paid him, part cash and part deferred, due in full before 10/1/71 which was his critical reserve clause date to either renew his 76ers contract or be paid at 75% of his last year's pay. In it he also agreed that the Cougars could "enjoin him from playing basketball for another team" during the contract term

  When the note payment was not made he advised the new team that the contract was breached, and contracted with the 76ers for an additional five years at more than double the money to be paid him under the Cougars contract. Plaintiffs (owners of the Carolina team) sued for an injunction to prevent him from violating his contract.

The trial court denied the injunction, due to the "unclean hands" of plaintiffs in luring defendant away from his former team. On appeal, the decision was reversed, and remanded for entry and enforcement of the injunction prohibiting defendant from playing for the76ers.

"Cunningham was under no obligation, option or restraint with respect to the 76ers after October 1, 1971, and the Cougars had a lawful right to bid and contract for his services to be rendered after that date."

Notice the court's reasoning to remove contracts of athletes from the "consent rule", unless they specifically prohibit assignment. "The policy against assignability of certain personal service contracts is to prohibit an assignment of a contract in which the obligor undertakes to serve only the original obligee. This contract is not of that type . . ."

(As an interesting sidelight, Cunningham was on the other side of the fence in later years as a part owner of The Miami Heat professional basketball team.)

- In *Aslakson v. Home Savings Association, 416 N.W.2d 786 (Minn. App. 1987)*, the purchase of plaintiff's mobile home was contingent upon the buyers' assumption of their loan with the approval of defendant. Defendant twice rejected the credit of two contract buyers from plaintiff, thus preventing their sale from taking place.

  Plaintiff sued for the tort of "wrongful interference with contract", and the trial court granted summary judgment for defendant. The appellate court affirmed, examining the applicable law regarding a party's right to delegate contractual duties, such as taking over the payments on a mortgage obligation:

  "We believe the trial court correctly determined that a contract between appellants and a subsequent buyer could not arise absent performance of a condition precedent: respondent's approval of the subsequent buyer's assumption of the loan. Under the provisions of (the state's UCC law), which must govern here, appellants were prohibited from delegating their contractual duties if respondents had a substantial interest in having appellants perform or if an assignment would materially increase respondents' burden or risk or impair its chance of obtaining return performance."

One of the additional areas where the "consent" defense is raised pertains to efforts of an assignee of a guaranteed debt to enforce that guarantee after the primary obligor has defaulted.

Courts have made distinctions between the types of guarantees involved, and factual situations where the assignment was made prior to or after default, and whether or not the assignee also extended credit to the obligor.

Notice the typical process of how courts analyze a complicated legal problem. In *New Holland, Inc. v. Trunk, et al, 579 So.2d 215 (Fla. App. 1991)*, *plaintiff* was the assignee of a contract from Sperry, the seller of equipment on credit to Trunkline. Defendant guaranteed payment of the specific Trunkline debt directly to Sperry. The assignment was made at a time that the debt was not in default, and plaintiff continued to extend credit to Trunkline thereafter.

Later, when Trunkline defaulted, plaintiff sued defendant on its debt guarantee. Defendant claimed that it was a "special guaranty" that was not enforceable by plaintiff, because it was not activated by a default of the debtor prior to its assignment. Plaintiff claimed its assignment was valid, and its extension of credit created a type of estoppel that prevented defendant from denying its claim.

The trial court ruled for the defendant, but the appellate court reversed in favor of the plaintiff, and discussed the legal principles involved as well as the split of authority in different states on the question of whether a special guaranty was assignable:

"A 'general' guaranty is one addressed to all persons generally and may generally be enforced by anyone to whom it is presented who acts upon it. A 'special' guaranty is one addressed to a particular entity and under it ordinarily only the named or specifically described promisee acquires rights."

"Generally, contract rights can be assigned unless they involve obligations of a personal nature or there is some public policy against the assignment or such assignment is specifically prohibited by the contract."

"Under the common law which Florida follows, a general guaranty is assignable while a special guaranty is generally not assignable because extending credit constitutes the exercise of discretion and a guaranty agreement naming a particular creditor as promisee implies special trust and confidence placed by the guarantor in the named creditor and the assignment of the guaranty to another prospective creditor materially alters the guarantor's undertaking."

So at this point of the court's opinion, it looks like the trial court will be affirmed. But now notice how the focus of reasoning is changed as the court, after agreeing that a special guarantee is involved in this case, examines the four conflicting legal rules and then decides in favor of enforcing the special guarantee after all:

"Some courts hold that the assignment of a special guaranty is effective to collect obligations existing at the time of the assignment, others hold that whether a special guaranty can be enforced to collect debts accruing after the assignment is a question of fact to be resolved by reference to the intent of the parties, while still others hold that whether a special guaranty is assignable depends on whether the undertaking of the guarantor has been materially altered by the assignment. Others steadfastly adhere to the common law rule precluding assignment of special guaranties."

Now the court completes its analysis focusing on the distinction between original debt of the primary debtor that was guaranteed (enforceable) versus new debt created by the assignee's post-assignment advances (not enforceable):

"There is a principle of law that the assignment of a principal obligation also operates as an assignment of the guaranty of the obligation so that the guaranty is effective to collect the obligation which existed at the time of the assignment. This principle seems eminently fair, permitting an assignee to enforce the guarantor's obligation as it exists at the time of the assignment, but not subjecting the guarantor to liability for (additional) extensions of credit made by the assignee."

"The assignee of a special guaranty cannot enforce the special guarantee as to debt the assignee has created by extending credit to the debtor. An assignee of debt and of a special guaranty relating thereto can enforce the guaranty as to debt resulting from credit extended by the original creditor to the debtor, whether or not that assigned debt is due or past due at the time of the assignment."

5. What if the obligor has a legal defense to payment?

This raises the fundamental principle of third party rights which is the basis of all sales of contract rights to an outsider. It is called the "stands in shoes" rule. Simply stated, it provides that the assignee stands in the shoes of his assignor, and takes subject to any and all claims or defenses that the obligor could assert against the assignor.

This rule makes it essential that a potential purchaser - assignee of an existing contract debt verify in writing with the *obligor-payor* the following matters after negotiating the financial terms of his deal with the obligee – assignor but *before* paying any of the agreed price:
* Is there an existing contract between the parties?
* What are its terms?
* Have there been any prior payments made?
* Are there any defenses to payment that may be raised?
* Are there any counter claims or set-offs due?
* Obligor will pay the assignee after being notified.
* Obligor will consent to the assignment.
* Obligor's is solvent and able to pay.

Notice that the due diligence of the buyer-assignee is directed to the obligor, not his potential assignor. The assignor wants to sell the contract right and therefore has a financial agenda that may include bending the truth to suit his needs. The key party is the obligor, who will be ultimately called upon to pay. Once the obligor signs off on these matters, and the buyer has otherwise verified outside factors like the credit standing of the obligor, the purchase of the account may be completed.

*Ex: Computers, Inc. sells $100,000 worth of laptops to Florida Stores (F) on a net-180, 6-month payment basis, on March 1. It sells that account receivable to Southern Investors (S) shortly thereafter on March 15 for $80,000, and notifies (F) of the assignment to them. On the due date of September 1 (S) contacts (F) to arrange payment to it of the $80,000. The obligor says, "We will not pay you because after you notified us, we inspected all the laptops and they don't work. They are defective." The assignee demands payment, saying, "That's not our problem. Take it up with your seller."

This is a classic "stands-in-shoes" case and Southern Investors loses. The account they bought from Computer, Inc. carries the right to collect its face amount but is also burdened with the risk of any valid defenses to payment. Faulty merchandise, deviation from contract specifications, and other transactional defenses that may be asserted against the assignor are also binding upon the assignee.

Southern Investors should not have completed their purchase of the account until *after* all verification was completed, including requiring the obligor to inspect the merchandise and waive any defects or other claims.

6.   What if rights are assigned more than once?

Situations of successive multiple assignments are thankfully rare, but when disputes arise the courts are unable to agree how to handle them. This raises another potential problem to be avoided before it occurs.

These cases do not involve transfers of interests in real estate, mortgages and other financing arrangements or accounts that are required to be recorded in the official records of the state involved. When a prospective purchaser-assignee of such accounts does the necessary verifying, a search of the public records would reveal their existence and prior transfer to another, and he would decline to proceed.

But what if an unscrupulous obligee-assignor holds a valuable debt or account that is not customarily recorded, like most accounts receivable and unsecured promissory notes, and sells it more than once to unsuspecting assignees?

Assume the obligor agrees to the obligation and wants to pay somebody. But who has the payment priority as between multiple assignees?

Here is a typical dispute:

*Ex: Scoundrel sells goods to Buyer-Obligor on open account, with payment due in 90 days. Scoundrel sells the account to 1st Assignee 45 days later at a discount for cash. 1st Assignee does not notify Buyer-Obligor. Scoundrel then sells the same account again to 2nd Assignee 15 days later, falsely certifying that there were no prior assignments. 2nd Assignee verifies with Buyer-Obligor that there was no prior notice of transfer of the account received from anyone. On the due date both Assignees demand payment. Buyer-Obligor pays the money due into the court registry saying, "here is the money I owe to somebody, let the judge decide who gets it."

Most states follow the *American Rule* that states that first in time wins, regardless of notice. Its reasoning is that a party can only transfer what they own. Once Scoundrel sold the account to 1st Assignee there was nothing left for another sale. Its strict interpretation has been criticized as contrary to the numerous other fairness doctrines in our legal system, thus prompting some authorities to call it the "unfairness rule".

A growing number of states follow the *English Rule* that states that the party first to notify wins. The 2nd assignee who promptly notified and had no way to know of the prior assignment did everything required by the law, and in fairness should prevail. The 1st Assignee could have prevented the situation if it had notified the buyer-obligor when it bought the account.

A compromise position is the *Symbolic Delivery Rule* that applies in cases where the contract right purchased has a tangible form such as a promissory note, documentary draft, stock certificate, or bank account passbook. When the 1st Assignee buys such an account, the physical delivery to him of the symbolic item establishes the legal right to receive payment. If however, that token is not demanded by the 1st Assignee and allowed to be transferred to a subsequent buyer who is also the first to notify, the later assignee wins.

Class surveys conducted by the author overwhelmingly favor the English Rule due to its inherent fairness. It is hoped the law in this area will be soon codified with one rule of law that will lead to a predictable result in future disputes.

C. DIRECT DELEGATION OF THIRD PARTY DUTIES

A contracting party may, as a general rule, designate someone else to perform required duties. Such a transfer is called a Delegation of Duties.

The original party owing the performance is called the Delegator, and the new party who is to perform the services is called the Delagatee. The Promisee receives the services and is obligated to pay for them.

Notice in the diagram of a typical Delegation of Duties, the respective positions of the parties:

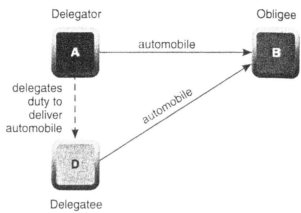

Similar to an assignment of legal rights, no writing or other legal formalities are required for creation. The intention of the parties is determined from the facts and surrounding circumstances of each case.

The parties may also specifically prohibit delegation in the wording of their contract. These clauses are legally treated the same as assignments, and are usually enforced, unless there is a highly personal relationship or the services to be performed are of a unique or specialized nature. Whether or not a duty is non-delegable depends upon similar considerations of relationship, hardship and detriment as those found in the legal tests of "consent to assignment".

A few major differences between assignments of rights and delegation of duties do exist:

- The assignment of rights cancels the assignor's right to enforce the subject debt and transfers that right to the third party

- The delegation of a duty does *not* cancel the continuing liability of the delegator in the event of a breach in the required performance by the delegatee.

*Ex: Joshua and Madison are newlyweds who buy a 3-bedroom 2-bath residence from Ram Builders. They pay 20% cash and the balance with a purchase money mortgage loan and promissory note with Local Bank. Three years later they sell the house to Jeanette, who assumes and agrees to pay the existing mortgage and note. Four years later she sells the house to Francine, with a similar assumption. Later, Francine defaults and declares bankruptcy.

Since the value of the property has substantially declined due to a changing neighborhood, Local Bank sues both of the prior owners for the remaining note indebtedness. They defend saying they have no liability due to their sales to new owners and the resulting assumptions of the mortgage and note.

This is one of the least understood and most dangerous liability situations. Most persons who sell mortgaged property to another believe they are released from liability if their buyer legally takes over the payments. Not so! An assumption does not release the delegator-payor from liability unless there is a three party *novation,* whereby the creditor-bank agrees to release the original debtor and substitute in their place the assuming party.

"An assignment is an expression of intention by the assignor that his duty shall immediately pass to the assignee. Many a debtor wishes that by such an expression he could get rid of his debts. Any debtor can express such an intention, but it is not operative to produce such a hoped-for-result. It does not cause society to relax its compulsion against him and direct it toward the assignee as his substitute." *4 Corbin on Contracts sec. 866.*

As we have discussed before, creditors hardly ever grant a novation and release a party from liability unless they are paid for this privilege, or it is part of the original negotiations for the first financing that creates the debt.

In *Rosenberg v. Son, Inc. and Pratt, 491 N.W.2d 71 (N.D. 1992),* plaintiffs contracted to sell their Dairy Queen business to Pratt for $10,000 cash and $52,000 installment payments due over a 15-year period. Pratt then assigned her rights and delegated her duties to Son, Inc. by assignment agreement, which obligated the assignee to assume all her obligations, as well as indemnify and hold her harmless, "against all claims, demands and actions by reason of the failure . . . to observe and perform the said agreement."

Plaintiffs then signed, at defendant's request, a "consent to assignment" clause that read, "the undersigned, Harold Rosenberg and Gladys E. Rosenberg, sellers in the above described Contract of Sale, do hereby consent to the above assignment."

Son, Inc. then assigned the sales contract to Merit Corporation. There was no consent clause in that assignment, but plaintiffs were aware of the assignment and later accepted a prepayment from Merit that reduced the outstanding debt to $25,000.

Ultimately Merit defaulted and went into bankruptcy leaving an unpaid balance due plaintiffs of approximately $17,000. Plaintiffs then filed this suit against the defendants to collect the indebtedness.

The trial court granted summary judgment for the defendants, ruling that "once Pratt assigned her contract she became a guarantor," and was exonerated due to alterations in her original obligation.

The appellate court reversed, and remanded the case for a full trial:

"It is a well-established principle in the law of contracts that a contracting party cannot escape its liability on the contract by merely assigning its duties and rights under the contract to a third party ... No delegation of performance relieves the party delegating of any duty to perform or any liability for breach ... This rule of law applies to all categories of contracts, including contracts for the sale or lease of real property, service contracts, and contracts for the sale of goods, which is present in the facts of this case."

"It is not however, a legal impossibility for a contracting party to rid itself of an obligation under a contract. It may seek the approval of the other original party for release, and substitute a new party in its place. In such an instance, the transaction is no longer called an assignment; instead it is called a novation."

Defendant Pratt claimed she was released from liability when the plaintiffs consented to her assignment to Son, Inc. She thought the consent was enough to free her from future problems. Wrong! The court reminded her of this legal time bomb which had just exploded:

"The Rosenbergs did sign a consent to the assignment at the bottom of the agreement. However, by merely consenting to the assignment, the Rosenbergs did not consent to a discharge of the principal obligor—Pratt. Nothing in the language of the consent clause supports such an allegation. A creditor is free to consent to an assignment without releasing the original debtor."

D. THIRD PARTY BENEFICIARY CASES

These are situations where there has been no specific assignment of rights or delegation of duties to the third party outsider. If this direct linkage to outsiders is missing, their interest nevertheless derives in an indirect way, from the facts and circumstances of the transaction that clearly shows they are its *intended beneficiary*. If so, they have legally enforceable rights though not the original contracting parties or specific assignees or delagatees.

Their beneficial interest is often shown by the fact they are identified as such by name in the contract. If not specifically identified by name, they may still occupy a class of persons who are clearly to receive the benefits of the agreement.

In *Cherry v. Crow et al, 845 F.Supp. 1520 (M.D. FL. 1994),* Eddie Cherry was booked into the Polk County jail to begin serving a 30-day sentence for drunk driving. He and his wife informed the authorities he was an alcoholic.

He had a history of delirium tremens, and repeatedly requested medical attention for symptoms related to alcohol withdrawal. When he was found in his cell hallucinating and shaking violently, he was taken to the infirmary and shackled to the bed. Later that night, he either walked or jumped off the bed and, because of the leg restraints, fell on his head, and died five days later.

His wife, as personal representative of his estate, sued the county and Prison Health Services, Inc., medical contractor in charge of the county's prison system for breach of contract and wrongful death based upon the negligence of county employee's.

The contract between the county and the health provider stated:

"Whereas, the Sheriff, is desirous of contracting with PHS and PHS is desirous of contracting with the Sheriff to provide total health care services *for the inmates/detainees* (including federal and state prisoners) housed within the county correctional system facilities described above . . ."

The trial court denied defendants' motions to dismiss and the appellate court affirmed, holding that, the Court finds sufficient evidence of an intended third party beneficiary relationship to withstand this motion to dismiss."

"Where, therefore, it is manifest from the nature or terms of a contract that the formal parties thereto intended its provisions to be for the benefit of a third party, as well as for the benefit of the formal parties themselves, the benefit to such third party being the direct and primary object of the contract, or amongst such objects, such third party may maintain an action on the contract even though he be a stranger to the consideration."

There are two basic categories of third party beneficiary contracts:

1. Donee Beneficiary - the clear intent of one of the parties is to make a gift to the third party outsider, who has legally enforceable rights in the event of default in receiving what is due them. The most common example is life insurance contracts.

*Ex: Ann contracts with Dial Insurance Co. to buy a $100,000 life insurance policy in which her friend Charlie is to receive the policy benefit upon her death. She perishes in a fire. The insurer fails or refuses to pay him, claiming he is not a blood relative. He sues to recover asserting his legal status as an "intended third party beneficiary" of the insurance contract.

Charlie wins the case. He did not pay anything because his interest is gratuitous. He is a donee beneficiary. He is its intended recipient because he is specifically named as such.

The policy wording does not require any blood relationship for his beneficial status. He has legally enforceable third party rights.

2. Creditor Beneficiary – a party becomes a debtor by borrowing money from a third party creditor to purchase some type of property. The creditor's lien encumbers the property. When the debtor later sells the property, the new buyer legally promises to pay the creditor. If they default, the creditor has legal rights to enforce it against them. The usual examples are "take over the payments" transfers of property.

The harder cases are those where a plaintiff claims legally enforceable third party rights because, while not specifically named in the main contract by name or category of persons intended to be included, they will still receive some type of benefit from the contract performance. This potential "fall-out" benefit, they feel, gives then a legally enforceable right to sue in the event of default. Unfortunately for them, they occupy the legal status of *incidental or indirect beneficiaries*, and have no legal rights.

*Ex: AA Corp. owns a small shopping center across the street from the local University. ZZ Corp. is a tenant in the center, operating a book and music store. AA Corp. contracts with Mcdonalds Restaurants to lease to them the vacant corner of the center. ZZ corp. is delighted by this news, anticipates increased business at their site from the restaurant customers, and spends $20,000 to remodel its store. One month later, Mcdonalds decides not to proceed, and ZZ Corp. sues it for breach of the lease agreement with AA Corp., claiming rights as a third party beneficiary of that contract.

ZZ Corp. has no legally enforceable rights. Through they would receive financial benefit from the increased customer traffic generated by the Mcdonalds lease, such advantage is merely incidental, a by-product of the lease which was created for the primary benefit of the names landlord and tenant parties.

But what if we change the facts a bit to state that the lease had a clause that said, "all existing tenants of this center shall receive a 20% discount on all store purchases." Now the case is not as clear. ZZ Corp. could argue they are an "intended beneficiary" since they occupy the stated class of parties to be benefited. What do you think?

The cases that present claims for enforcement of contracts by third party "incidental" beneficiaries involve some of the most novel requests for relief by obviously remote claimants. They cause the reader to question how in the world such "bizarre" cases were ever filed, and are a commentary on our litigious society:

- The Big Ten athletic conference hired Bain as a college basketball referee. He called a foul on a U. of Iowa player, permitting the free throws that gave Purdue a last second victory, and denied Iowa a championship. Gillispie operated a sports memorabilia store in Iowa City, and would have profited greatly by an Iowa victory. He sued for the alleged malpractice of Bain, claiming enforceable rights. The trial court and appellate court agreed that summary judgment was correct, denying the claim. "It is beyond credulity that Bain, while refereeing a game, must make his calls at all times perceiving that a wrong call will injure Gillispies' business or one similarly situated and subject him to liability. Heaven knows what uncharted morass a court would find itself in if it were to hold that an athletic official subjects himself to liability every time he might make a questionable call. The possibilities are mind boggling . . . There is no tortious doctrine of athletic official's malpractice . . . *Bain v. Gillispie, 357 N.W.2d 47 (Ia. App. 1984).*

- Defendant had a contract with the owner of a Days Inn motel to treat it monthly for pests, including insects. When plaintiff was bitten by a brown recluse spider while spending the night at the motel, she sued for negligence, claiming severe injuries and having beneficial rights under the contract. Both courts also granted summary judgment against plaintiff. "The risk of being bitten by a spider is a general risk we all face . . . The motel's desire to reduce that risk by utilizing Admiral's pest control services does not create a negligence cause of action in favor of every guest at the motel." *Copeland v. Admiral Pest Control, Co., 933 P.2d 937 (Ok. App. 1996).*

- Plaintiff was injured when she slipped on an icy public sidewalk abutting Bank's property. Bank had contracted with Fox for snow and ice removal from the public sidewalk as required by local ordinance. Plaintiff sued for negligence, as a third party beneficiary of that contract, claiming it was "intended to benefit pedestrians who were using the public sidewalk to patronize Peoples' business establishment." Again summary judgment for defendants was upheld. "There is no language in the contract before us to generate an issue of Peoples' intention to create in plaintiff enforceable rights as an intended beneficiary." *Denman v. Peoples Heritage Bank, Inc. and Fox, 704 A.2d 411 (Maine 1998).*

DISCUSSION EXERCISES

1. Discuss assignment strategies of buyer and seller in real estate contracts.

2. Discuss due diligence strategies of a potential assignee.

3. Discuss boundary rules to determine when obligor consent to an assignment or delegation should be legally required.

4. Discuss boundary rules for differentiating between intended and incidental beneficiaries.

5. Discuss your preference of legal theories to govern the problem of multiple assignments.

CASE EXERCISE

IF YOU STAND IN THIS BANK'S SHOES, YOU LOSE $50,000

In *Royal Bank Export Finance Company LTD. v. Bestways Distributing Co., 229 Cap. App.3d 764 (Cal. App. 1991)*, E.R.S. sold to Bestways ten "night Clerk" electronic units to be used in hotels and motels to register guests without the need for a clerk in attendance, at a unit price of $4,997, payable on a deferred basis as accounts payable.

E.R.S. then assigned these purchase order receivables to the Bank as a means of raising financing capital. When the Bank sued Bestways to collect the balances due, it declined payment on the grounds that the products they bought were defective and not merchantable. The Bank claimed it purchased the accounts "free and clear of any defenses."

ANALYSIS

The trial court entered judgment in favor of Bestways, based upon the conclusion that the accounts were nonnegotiable instruments under the California UCC, and therefore "subject to any defenses Bestways had against E.R.S."

"(The trial court) determined that because of the failure of consideration by E.R.S., Bestways was not obligated to pay for the products."

The appellate court affirmed, based upon the "stands in shoes" rule of assignments:

"The question in this case is not whether there has been an effective transfer or assignment of the debt instruments from E.R.S. to Bank or whether Bank's title to the papers has priority over other claims of title. Rather, the issue in this case is whether the title transferred to Bank is subject to defenses Bestways has against the transferor."

"The assignment merely transfers the interest of the assignor. The assignee 'stands in the shoes' of the asignor, taking his rights and remedies, subject to *any defenses* which the *obligor* has against the assignor prior to notice of the assignment."

The court's last remarks highlight how incredibly inept the Bank was in this case. Before any prospective assignee of accounts receivable purchases them from the original creditor, verification of the various due diligence factors previously mentioned is absolutely essential. Remember, "5. What if the obligor has a legal defense to payment?"

In addition, no Bank that wishes to remain in business very long ever buys instruments that are non-negotiable, because they are by definition not protected from the stands-in-shoes rule. Purchasers of any types of commercial instruments would never provide the liquidity business demands if they had to worry about problems in the transactions that underlied the creation of those instruments.

That is the reason for the negotiable instruments provisions of the UCC, which provide that:

(1) If an instrument is in *negotiable form*, and
(2) If it is properly held by a *holder in due course*,

that holder-assignee circumvents the 'stands in shoes rule' and takes free of all transactional defenses that may be otherwise asserted by the original debtor-obligor against the original creditor-assignor.

"A non-negotiable written contract for the payment of money or personal property may be transferred by indorsement, in like manner with negotiable instruments. Such indorsement shall transfer all the rights of the assignor under the instrument to the assignee, *subject to all equities and defenses existing in favor of the maker at the time of the indorsement.*"

CONCLUSION

Investors in the factoring industry, who buy accounts receivable, and banks, insurers and other purchasers of any types of commercial paper have basic rules that their financial lifeblood depends upon:

* Before completing the purchase, get written certifications of all facts from the debtor, including assurances that there are no transactional defenses.

* Verify negotiable form of any commercial instruments purchased.

* Verify legal ownership of commercial instruments as a true 'holder' and 'in due course' status.
A. Do you think the Bank was aware of the legal distinctions between 'stands in shoes' and 'holder in due course'?

B. Why wasn't the Bank aware of the problems with the goods experienced by Bestways?

C. What should the Bank have done in this transaction to protect itself?

CASE RESEARCH CYBERCISES

The following cases also relate to the material in this chapter and illustrate the types of disputes that may occur. For each one do the following written assignment:

1. Locate the case using the Internet (Lexis-Nexis, West or any other research cite which provides case transcripts).
2. Briefly summarize what it was about – the nature of the dispute involved.
3. Who won at the trial court level? Who won at the appellate level?
4. Who won if there was a third level of Supreme Court review?
5. What were the legal rules of law and the reasoning used to reach the final decision?
6. Do you agree or disagree with the decision, and explain why?
7. What business law time bomb(s) were involved?
8. Could the time bomb(s) have been avoided by structuring the transaction differently? Discuss.
9. Could the adverse effects of the time bomb(s) have been defused by a different reaction or response by the affected party? Discuss.
10. Replay the facts of the case to achieve a different successful result.

1. *Trient Partners I LTD. v. Blockbuster Entertainment Corporation et al, 83 F.3d 704 (5th Cir. 1996) (Blockbuster not an intended beneficiary of its licensee's 43 Superstore leases, and was denied the right to acquire them).*
2. *Krass v. Joliet, Inc., d/b/a Harper Food Center, 593 N.W.2d 578 (Mich. App. 1999) (security guard service contract with supermarket owner did not extend legal benefit to estate of patron shot and killed in property parking lot).*
3. *Portland Electric and Plumbing Company v. City of Vancouver, 627 P.2d 1350 (Wash. App. 1981) (contractor's assignment of collection of balance due from City to pay its debt to assignee, ruled not enforceable against debtor due to contract antiassignment clause).*

NOTES

18.

LEGAL EXCUSES FOR NON-PERFORMANCE

"He who excuses himself accuses himself."
Gabriel Meurier

*"I should have been clearer if I had desired to be excused from it,
as a thing against my conscience."*
John Woolman

At the heart of contractual agreements is certain required performance by one or both of the parties. The timing of when this action must be completed distinguishes the two basic forms of contracts.

In the *unilateral* form, one party exchanges a promise (usually to pay) for the act of the other. The agreement itself is not legally made until performance of the act is completed.

In the *bilateral* form, the contract is formed when the parties exchange reciprocal promises, one to pay and one to perform an act. The agreement is legally made when the promises are given, prior to the actual performance of the designated act.

Disputes often arise when one of the contracting parties wants to be legally excused from having to perform and the other party demands strict adherence to the agreement. In cases of discharge by "breach", "operation of law" and "impossibility", the factual circumstances that surround the agreement determine whether or not adherence to it is legally required. In "discharge by agreement" and "conditional contracts", legal non-performance is based upon the wording of the agreement.

1. DISCHARGE BY BREACH

A contract requires the parties to perform certain agreed actions. If there is a failure to do so by one party, they have breached.

The legal consequences of a minor breach are usually an award of money damages to compensate the non-breaching party for his loss. The required performance is still due from him, but it may be delayed until the breach is remedied. In construction contracts these are usually cosmetic touch-ups or other superficial deviations from the agreement.

If however, there is a major deviation from the contracts requirements, called a *material breach*, the injured party can collect damages as well as being legally excused from his required performance.

Some states allow the breaching party to be paid the reasonable value of any partial performance that benefits the other party, while others deny any recovery to the breaching party. In construction contracts these are usually major structural problems.

> *Ex: Mr. and Mrs. Newlywed contract with Quality Builders to construct their new residence for $200,000. The construction contract is of the usual type, where the builder receives a 10% deposit at contract signing, submits draw requests for progress payments as the job moves through its stages of foundation, walls, roof, plumbing, electric and finishing, and the owners holdback 20% until the final walk-through to assure that the job has been successfully completed. The final inspection reveals structural, non-cosmetic construction problems that would cost $25,000 to correct, plus an additional $5,000 for incidental expenses. The builder wants payment in full and the owners refuse.

> In most states, the structural defects would be considered a material breach. The owners could deduct the actual repair costs plus the related expenses of completing the job from the contract price. Thus, the owners who have retained $40,000 as their holdback, are discharged from any further payment obligations once they pay $10,000 to the builder.

Florida is one of the states with the highest dollar amount of new construction annually. It has numerous disputes between builders and their customers regarding their respective performance obligations. In determining what should be paid to a builder in cases where there are defects in construction its courts often use a four-pronged computation formula based upon two factors:

A) If the defects are minor, the builder has substantially performed (SP). If the defects are major, there is NO SP.

B) If the builder did the best he could, he has acted in good faith (GF). If the builder intentionally covered up problems or was grossly negligent, he has acted in bad faith (BF).

1) SP + GF = builder receives the contract price less the cost of repairs
2) SP + BF = builder receives the fair market value less repairs (assume the builder negotiated a higher price that similar marketplace comparables)
3) NO SP + GF = builder receives the reasonable value of what was properly completed
4) NO SP + BF = builder is penalized and receives nothing

Another form of material breach occurs when one of the contracting parties notifies the other, before the required date, that he will not perform.

This is called *anticipatory repudiation* and while the non-breaching party is immediately discharged from performance, he also has a number of alternate remedies against the offending party that may include:

- Immediately declare a default and sue for breach of contract
- Wait until the performance date to see if the other party will perform
- Use the breach and threat of legal action to renegotiate a better deal

In *Lucente v. International Business Machines, 2002 WL 31478458 (N.Y. App. 2002)*, the dispute between the parties was the violation of an employment non-competition covenant (discussed previously in the Illegality chapter), but also included allegations by the plaintiff of anticipatory repudiation, and the court presented a good summary of the applicable law:

"Anticipatory repudiation occurs when, before the time for performance has arisen, a party to a contract declares his intention not to fulfill a contractual duty. When confronted with an anticipatory repudiation, the non-repudiating party has two mutually exclusive options. He may (a) elect to treat the repudiation as an anticipatory breach and seek damages for breach of contract, thereby terminating the contractual relation between the parties, or (b) he may continue to treat the contract as valid and await the designated time for performance before bringing suit."

2. DISCHARGE BY OPERATION OF LAW

Contracting parties can usually assume as a general rule that their valid agreements will be legally enforceable. However, there are three common exception situations where specific rules of law allow a party to be discharged from having to perform their contractual duties:

1. *Bankruptcy* proceedings are governed by federal law, and allow a debtor that has been granted an order of discharge to be forever excused from having to pay valid debts owed to unsecured creditors.

The philosophy of these laws is to provide a "fresh start" to a debtor who has suffered financial reverses and is now insolvent. Because of the risks involved, many creditors are reluctant to extend substantial amounts of unsecured credit in the form of open account purchases of goods and services, or make outright loans unless there is some form of collateral or other collection protection.

2. *Statutes of limitations* are legal time periods established by the laws of each state during which a plaintiff is required to file suit on a particular type of claim, including most contracts and sales transactions. If a lawsuit is not timely filed by the plaintiff, a defendant may raise this failure as an absolute defense that will cause dismissal of the case and forever excuse the defendant from having to perform, even though the plaintiff has an otherwise successful case.

Contracting parties are presumed to know their legal rights (even though we know this is often not the case), ignorance of the law is no defense, and a potential plaintiff must file suit within the time frames specified. For example, the UCC requires its breach of contract cases to be brought within 4 years from when the breach occurs, most states require medical malpractice cases to be filed no later than 1 year after the plaintiff is first reasonably aware of the problem sued upon, and negligence cases seeking recovery for personal injuries have limitation periods of from 3 to 7 years, depending upon the state law where the dispute arose.

3. *Intentional contract alteration* is a little known but very effective way for a party to be legally excused from having to perform. The alteration must be material, relating to one of the essential terms such as subject matter, price, quantity and terms of payment. The wrongdoer is penalized by not being allowed to enforce any part of the contract. The innocent party is given the choice to disregard the contract, enforce it under its original terms, or require enforcement per the altered terms – whichever is best.

> *Ex: Gertrude is a wealthy woman, but is elderly and in poor health. Her only debt is a 5-year promissory note for $100,000 payable to Andrew, a private lender, which provided the investment capital 3 years ago for her financial holdings. She dies and Andrew, thinking she didn't keep a copy of the note, skillfully alters it to read $400,000. He then files a creditor's claim in her estate proceedings for payment of that amount. Unfortunately for Andrew, Gertrude had saved a copy of the original note in her personal papers, and her Executor now claims the estate has no payment obligation whatsoever due to Andrew's unlawful conduct.
>
> Andrew loses the entire unpaid principal of the promissory note, plus any accrued interest due. This sanction is similar in its punitive nature to the forfeiture of principal or interest in the Usury cases or the NO SP + BF construction cases.

3. DISCHARGE BY IMPOSSIBILITY

Sometimes events occur after the formation of a contract that make one party's required performance impossible. These are no-fault events, usually unforeseeable and outside the control of the party who now wants to be legally excused from having to perform. If the complaining party could reasonably have prevented the problem or is the cause of it, he is legally bound under its terms.

Occasionally, one of the contracting parties seeks to be released from performance claiming their inability to financially perform, caused by circumstances beyond their control, such as bad weather or bad luck. This "I can't pay" defense is known as *subjective impossibility*", and is uniformly rejected by the courts.

In *Christy v. Pilkinton, 273 S.W.2d 533 (Ark. 1954),* Christy agreed to purchase an apartment house from Pilkinton for $30,000 (remember, this was 1954!). When the time came to close, Christy was unable to raise enough money to complete the transaction, and Pilkinton sued for specific performance. The defense raised was that Christy's used car business had declined and he could not borrow the unpaid balance of $29,900 (only a $100 deposit was paid).

The trial court ordered Christy to perform, and on appeal, the ruling was affirmed. "Proof of this kind does not establish the type of impossibility that constitutes a defense. There is a familiar distinction between objective impossibility, which amounts to saying, 'The thing cannot be done,' and subjective impossibility – 'I cannot do it.' The latter, which is well illustrated by a promisor's financial inability to pay, does not discharge the contractual duty and is therefore not a bar to a decree of specific performance."

The situations recognized by the courts as allowing one party to be released from their contractual obligations are called *objective impossibility,* as mentioned above in the *Christy case,* meaning that, "the thing cannot be done," rather than the personal subjective test where the party individually chooses not to perform.

- Subsequent illegality – the required action is legal at the time of contracting, but barred afterwards by statutory or case law, or factual circumstance.

- Destruction of the subject matter – after making the contract, an outside no-fault event, such as fire or windstorm, destroys the property on which it is based, or factual circumstance also prevents its completion.

- Personal service contracts – where the party who is supposed to perform is unable to do so because of accident, illness, or other incapacity suffered through no fault of their own. In the event of death, their estate is discharged from any continuing liability, such as a party who had contracted to give a golf exhibition. If however, the contract were just to buy the golf clubs, their estate would be liable since no unique personal services are involved.

You will recall we discussed these same scenarios in an earlier chapter as legal grounds for termination of a contract offer.

Some disputes are a bit different, but so closely related to these categories of objective impossibility that they are treated the same way:

- To resolve a prior title insurance dispute with another party, defendant agreed to buy an easement for access to highway 95 across plaintiff's property.

Later defendant claimed the easement transfer was rendered impossible because the State Department of Transportation would not approve such access. Plaintiff sued to enforce the purchase agreement, the trial court ruled in his favor, and the appellate court reversed:

> "The doctrine of impossibility operates to excuse performance when the bargained-for performance is no longer in existence or is no longer capable of being performed due to the unforeseen, supervening act of a third party." *Haessly v. Safeco Title Insurance Company of Idaho, 825 P.2d 1119 (Id. 1992).* (similar to destruction of the subject matter)

- Plaintiff, a college-educated bachelor, signed up with defendant for a series of 75 dancing lessons at an agreed price of $1,000, after he was told he had "exceptional potential to be a fine and accomplished dancer" during the free lessons introductory phase of defendant's sales plan, and signed additional contracts thereafter for a total of 2,734 hours of lessons for which he paid in advance $24,812.80. The contract plaintiff signed stated in bold print, "Non-Cancellable Contract: I understand that no refunds will be made under the terms of this contract."

  Plaintiff was severely injured in an auto accident that rendered him incapable of continuing his dancing lessons, and he demanded return of the unused portion of his lessons based upon impossibility. Defendant declined based upon the wording of the contract. Plaintiff sued to rescind the contract.

  The trial court granted rescission and the appellate court affirmed:

  > "Defendants do not deny that the doctrine of impossibility of performance is generally applicable to the case at bar. Rather they assert that . . . the contract indicates a contrary intention. Such bold type phrases as (No Refunds, etc.) manifested the party's mutual intent to waive their respective rights to invoke the doctrine of impossibility. This is a construction which we find unacceptable . . . plaintiff never contemplated that by signing a contract with such terms as 'Noncancellable' and 'No Refunds' he was waiving a remedy expressly recognized by Illinois courts." *Parker v. Arthur Murray, Inc., 295 N.E.2d 487 (Ill. App. 1973).* (similar to disability in a personal service contract)

- Plaintiff hired defendant to install a sewer lateral for the home it was building. Defendant did not complete the job, claiming it had relied on plaintiff's representations regarding the depth of the foundations and subsurface soil, which proved to be materially different and thus made their performance impossible.

Plaintiff hired a new contractor to complete the job, and then sued for breach of contract. The trial court granted plaintiff summary judgment, denying the impossibility defense, and the appellate court affirmed:

"The record reveals that the subdivision plat which showed the actual depth of the sewer main was on file in 1994, prior to the execution of the contract. Defendant, who held itself out as an expert excavator, could have taken reasonable steps to determine the depth of the subsurface soils and sewer main ... Impossibility excuses a party's performance only when the destruction of the subject matter of the contract or the means of performance makes performance objectively impossible. Moreover, the impossibility must be produced by an unanticipated event that could not have been foreseen or guarded against in the contract." *Comprehensive Building Contractors, Inc. v. Pollard Excavating, Inc., 674 N.Y.S.2d 869 (N.Y. App. Div. 1998).*

Another apparent form of "objective impossibility" recognized by the UCC and most states, though technically different, involves situations where, although a party could actually perform, he chooses not to do so because the no-fault events complained of have so damaged him financially he claims it is no longer economically feasible:

- Frustration of purpose – excuses performance when the contract benefits are rendered worthless by outside events, such as a lease of your vacant lot to park cars for the upcoming Super Bowl and then having the game cancelled. These cases are rarely litigated because the contract objective can no longer be attained and courts will allow the parties to be returned to the status quo.

"Under the doctrine of commercial frustration, if the happening of an event not foreseen by the parties and not caused by or under the control of either party has destroyed or nearly destroyed either the value of the performance or the object or purpose of the contract, then the parties are excused from further performance. The doctrine of commercial frustration is close to but distinct from the doctrine of impossibility of performance. Both concern the effect of supervening circumstances upon the rights and duties of the parties; but in cases of commercial frustration, performance remains possible but the expected value of performance in the party seeking to be excused has been destroyed by the fortuitous event which supervenes to cause an actual but not literal failure of consideration." *Werner v. Ashcraft Bloomquist, Inc., 10 S.W.3d 575 (Mo. App. 2000).*

In *Chase Precast corporation v. John J. Paonessa Company, Inc., 566 N.E.2d 603 (Mass. 1991)*, a case of first impression, defendant general contractor agreed with the Massachusetts Department of Public Works to resurface and improve portions of Route 128, and subcontracted with plaintiff for the replacing of the grass median strip with concrete median barriers.

After the project began, angry residents objected to the removal of the grass median and its replacement with the concrete barriers. In response, the Department entered into a settlement agreement with the protestors stating that no additional concrete barriers would be used, and deleted them from their contract with defendant, who in turn notified plaintiff to stop production.

Plaintiff sued for breach of contract. Before stopping production, plaintiff had produced and delivered one-half of the required median barriers, and was paid in full for those items. Defendant claimed it was excused from performance by virtue of the defense of "frustration of purpose", although this argument also involved aspects of impossibility due to destruction of the subject matter and subsequent illegality.

The trial court ruled for Defendant, and the Court affirmed:

"This court has long recognized and applied the doctrine of impossibility as a defense to an action for breach of contract . . . the parties shall be excused . . . (when) performance becomes impossible from the accidental perishing of the (basis of their bargain) without the fault of either party."

"On the other hand, although we have referred to the doctrine of frustration of purpose in a few decisions, we have never clearly defined it . . . when an event neither anticipated nor caused by either party, the risk of which was not allocated by the contract, destroys the object or purpose of the contract, thus destroying the value of performance, the parties are excused from further performance."

Do you think the Court's ruling would have been the same if Chase had not been paid yet for its production and delivery of concrete median barriers? Should application of the 'frustration of purpose' defense be limited by the amount and type of damages allegedly suffered by the plaintiff suing for breach of contract?

- Commercial impossibility – is the first cousin of the "unforeseen difficulties" doctrine that we previously visited in our discussion of legal consideration, as an exception to the rule that pre-existing duty promises are legally unenforceable. It is used in this new context for cases where outside events that occur after making the contract have a serious adverse financial impact and the disadvantaged party wants to be excused from having to perform.

It is also used as a companion rule with 'frustration of purpose', because its definition in the UCC is almost identical to the 'frustration' definition in the Restatement of Contracts:

"Where, after a contract is made, a party's principal purpose is substantially frustrated without his fault by the occurrence of an event the non-occurrence of which was a basic assumption on which the contract was made, his remaining duties to render performance are discharged, unless the language or the circumstances indicate the contrary." (Frustration of Purpose) *Restatement of Contracts, Section 265.*

"Delay in delivery or non-delivery in whole or in part by a seller . . . is not a breach of his duty under a contract for sale if performance as agreed has been made impracticable by the occurrence of a contingency the non-occurrence of which was a basic assumption on which the contract was made . . ." (Commercial Impossibility) *Uniform Commercial Code, Section 2-615.*

In *Northern Corporation v. Chugach Electrical Association, 518 P.2d 76 (Alaska 1974),* plaintiff was the low bidder and awarded a contract by defendant for the repair and protection of the upstream face of the Cooper Lake Dam. It required plaintiff to quarry and haul gravel rock from a site on the opposite end of the lake to the dam in winter, by "transport across Cooper Lake to the dam site when such lake is frozen to a sufficient depth to permit heavy vehicle traffic thereon."

During repeated attempts by plaintiff to commence the transport beginning in December of 1966, the ice conditions were unable to support their trucks and some equipment was damaged. When plaintiff complained about the unsafe conditions, defendant threatened default unless performance took place. Plaintiff continued to attempt transport, but ultimately ceased in March of 1967.

When defendant again threatened default unless performance was completed by April 1, 1968, plaintiff returned to Cooper Lake again, and "started hauling with half-loaded trucks; but within the first few hours, two trucks with their drivers broke through the ice, resulting in the death of the drivers and loss of the trucks." Plaintiff then ceased operations and notified defendant it considered the contract terminated due to impossibility of performance.

Plaintiff sued for its reasonable costs in attempting performance, less sums already received. Defendant counterclaimed for damages, claiming it had overpaid. The trial court "discharged the parties from the contract on the ground of impossibility of performance."

On appeal, the decision on discharge was affirmed. "Discharge of a party for impossibility of performance abates the severity of the old common law doctrine that not even objective impossibility excused performance; . . . the Restatement of Contracts has departed from the early common law rule by recognizing the principle of 'commercial impracticability'.

Under this doctrine, a party is discharged from his contract obligations, even if it is technically possible to perform them, if the costs of performance would be so disproportionate to that reasonably contemplated by the parties as to make the contract totally impractical in a commercial sense."

But isn't there an apparent legal inconsistency in not excusing from performance a party like *Christy* who says, "I cannot do it," because his business suffers financial reverses, but excusing *Northern* who also says, "I cannot do it," because "it can only be done at an excessive and unreasonable cost"?

'Impossibility' is further defined as, "not only strict impossibility but impracticability because of extreme and unreasonable difficulty, expense, injury or loss involved." *Restatement of Contracts, Section 454.* But how much is "extreme?" How much is "unreasonable?" How costly must the anticipated loss be? What if the amount of loss to be suffered by a small company will impact it much more severely than a greater loss to be incurred by a larger company?

A party faced with an unprofitable transaction will always answer these questions in a way that justifies being excused from performance, so the commercial impracticability doctrine as a convenient excuse from performance is difficult to properly apply and dangerous in the marketplace.

The *Northern* Court recognized this problem of application when it said:

"The doctrine ultimately represents the ever-shifting line, drawn by courts hopefully responsive to commercial practices and mores, at which the community's interest in having contracts enforced according to their terms is outweighed by the commercial senselessness of requiring performance . . ."

The more 'reasonably foreseeable' are the underlying circumstances that create the commercial difficulties, the less likely is a court to allow a party to escape its contract obligations.

> *Ex: Acme Oil contracts to buy 100,000 barrels of crude oil over the next 6 months from Saudi Arabia at a fixed price of $30 per barrel for its chain of nationwide gas stations. 30 days after making the contract, a Middle East peace agreement is signed by all the previously warring countries, and the worldwide price of crude oil drops to $10 per barrel. Acme Oil says it will go broke if it has to pay the $30 per barrel contract price, and sues to rescind the contract based upon "commercial impossibility".
>
> Tough luck, Acme Oil. Yes the events that occurred after making your contract have had a negative financial impact, but they are not unforeseeable.

There have been past hostilities in the region that caused oil shortages and higher prices, as well as peaceful periods where oil prices dropped. If it happened before, it could happen again.

Acme Oil could reasonably have protected themselves by a *force majeure* clause in the contract that would allow price adjustments in the event of specified outside events such as Acts of God involving severe weather events, and/or disruptions in oil supply or demand caused by the changing politics of the region.

4. DISCHARGE BY AGREEMENT OF THE PARTIES

No matter what the provisions of their contract, the parties may mutually agree to modify them in whole or part, or cancel them entirely so long as they are executory.

- Mutual rescission – the contract is cancelled and performance is no longer required by either party.

- Waiver – one of the parties voluntarily gives up the legal right to complain and agrees to excuse the other party's non-performance.

- Modification – certain of the required performance promises of the existing contract are changed, but the basic agreement remains intact.

- Substitution – the old contract is cancelled and a new one is created which takes its place.

- Novation – by mutual agreement, one of the parties to a contract is released from performing and an outside third party is substituted in their place. This often is sought by a mortgage debtor who wants to be released from liability when he sells the encumbered property to another party with comparable financial credit who has agreed to assume the payment obligation.

"A substituted contract, or a novation, in which the sole participants are the parties to the original agreement or obligation not only creates a new agreement or obligation, but also rescinds the former one. It is not unlike the emergence of a butterfly from a chrysalis. It is the two-fold character of the transaction, that is, the rescission and substitution, which constitutes the supporting consideration for both phases of the transaction." *Dorsey v. Tisby, 234 P.2d 557 (Oregon 1951).*

5. DISCHARGE IN CONDITIONAL CONTRACTS

Usually the required performances in a binding contract and the terms stating them must be clear, definite and unequivocal. If however, a party's required performance is dependent upon the occurrence of an uncertain, future event, the contract is conditional, and disputes arise as to when one's performance is legally required:

- Condition precedent – the legal duty to perform does not arise until the happening of a future, uncertain event. If you promise to buy a parcel of land, subject to it being rezoned to allow business usage, you are not required to perform until this outside event occurs. Notice the root word is "precede", meaning to come before.

  Usually the existence of a condition precedent is based upon the wording of the contract and will be denied in questionable cases:

- Franklin's will stated that her estate was to go to the Waltman's, "in case I die on my way to & from Jersey." Franklin made the trip safely. When she died six years later, a will contest ensued, and the trial court ruled the will contained a condition precedent – dying on the trip to New Jersey – and since she didn't, that will was ineffective and her earlier will was in effect. The appellate court reversed:

  "A conditional or contingent will is one that takes effect only upon the satisfaction of a certain condition or happening of a specified contingency. If the condition is not satisfied, or the contingency fails, the will is rendered inoperative and void." However, courts do not regard a will as conditional when it is reasonable to infer that the testator was merely expressing a reason to make a will (because she was concerned about her pending trip). *In re Estate of Franklin, 2001 WL 896635 (Tenn. App. 2001).*

- Condition subsequent – the legal duty to perform currently exists, but may be excused in the future if the specified event occurs. If you lease a college bookstore and promise to pay monthly rental, so long as the University exists across the street, you are legally obligated unless and until that future event occurs to discharge you. Notice the root word is "subsequent", meaning to come after.

The key to determining whether or not a contract is conditional is its specific wording, because that is the best expression of the intention of the parties. Courts will examine these disputes on a case-by-case basis since the legal effect of condition precedent (no contract obligation yet) and condition subsequent (contract currently exists with possible future discharge) are exactly opposite.

The words commonly used to indicate the existence of a conditional contract are usually conjunctions, connective words signaling something before or after the stated performance may affect its enforcement:

- Conditioned upon
- Subject to
- On condition that
- When
- If
- As soon as
- For so long as
- Provided that
- After

In *Pace Construction Corporation v. OBS Company, Inc., 531 So.2d 737 (Fla. App. 1988),* Pace, as general contractor, agreed with Shumann Investments to construct for them a commercial building. OBS was the dry wall subcontractor, and the contract between it and plaintiff stated, "Final payment shall not become due unless and until the following conditions precedent to Final Payment have been satisfied: . . . c) receipt of final Payment for Subcontractor's work by Contractor from Owner . . ."

After OBS completed their work, they were unable to collect payment from Pace because it had been refused payment by Shumann. OBS sued Pace for the monies due, and was granted summary judgment. On appeal, the decision was reversed and remanded, the court agreeing that, "the subcontract agreement expresses a clear intent to shift the risk of nonpayment by the owner from Pace to OBS and that, therefore, OBS is not entitled to recover final payment from Pace or pursue its claim against the payment bond until Pace receives such payment from the owner."

"In most subcontract agreements, payment by the owner to the contractor is not intended to be a condition precedent to the contractor's duty to pay the subcontractor . . . most subcontractors are not willing to assume the risk of owner nonpayment because they cannot afford to remain in business without prompt payment for their completed work . . . a subcontract agreement may nevertheless contain valid provisions which shift this risk to the subcontractor."

This was one of those cases. OBS allowed this legal time bomb to blow up in their face. Do you think they did so consciously, as part of the process of negotiating their business deal with Pace, or did they simply overlook the clear and unambiguous wording that shifted the payment risk to them?

If, however, a party is improperly prevented from performing their required condition precedent, they are excused from their contractual obligations and the party at fault suffers the loss.

In *Barrows v. Maco, Inc., et al, 419 N.E.2d 634 (Ill. App. 1981)*, plaintiff, a roofing contractor, hired defendant as a commission salesperson to work a designated territory securing roofing contracts and doing public relations work with his customers.

Plaintiff's employment agreement provided that his basic commission on jobs was 26% of the net profit, and, "To qualify for payment of the commission, the Salesman must sell and supervise the job; the job must be completed and paid for; and the Salesman must have been in the continuous employment of the company during the aforementioned period . . . In such case that Salesman's employment shall be terminated for any reason prior to the complete supervision and installation of a job, the Salesman shall not be entitled to and shall not receive credit for any commission on the said job."

One of plaintiff's roof repair contracts was with the Cook County School District, with whom Defendant had done business for many years. Plaintiff testified that he was present at the job site 60 to 90 times, to help explain the jobs progress to various school district personnel. After various problems between defendant and its subcontractor on that job that caused the school to stop paying before completion of the job, defendant notified plaintiff that his employment was terminated and he would not receive any commissions.

Plaintiff sued defendant to recover his commissions due under his employment contract. They denied liability on the grounds that, he was not entitled to commissions because all the conditions of that provision had not been satisfied. Plaintiff claimed defendants own actions prevented its subcontractor from completing the job.

The trial court entered judgment for plaintiff, and the appellate court affirmed:

"A party to a contract may not complain of the nonperformance of the other party where that performance is prevented by his own actions. A party cannot take advantage of a condition precedent the performance of which he has rendered impossible."

The rationale for this fairness principle is similar to the rule we examined in an earlier chapter on Offer, to the effect that the offeror is legally prohibited from terminating a unilateral offer (promise in exchange for an act) while the offeree is in the process of proceeding in good faith to complete the required performance.

Conditional contracts can also be used to protect parties against uncertain future events if and only if they are anticipated to the extent that a conditional clause addresses them.

The specific events may not be specified, but general areas of concern need to be anticipated as potential problems, so the parties can protect themselves accordingly. Here is an actual dispute that took place:

*Ex: Major league baseball teams customarily sell the exclusive broadcast rights to the highest bidder. This is done annually. The Florida Marlins baseball team entered into annual contracts with the same Miami radio station starting in the early 1990's. They became champions of major league baseball in 1997 by winning the World Series. The winning bid for the next year was much higher than previous years in anticipation of their new status as defending champions. However, to the dismay of players and fans and the broadcast station, the owner decided to dismantle the team for alleged financial reasons and not permit it to defend its title. The radio station sued to rescind its now greatly overpriced contract, but had no legal grounds to do so because the contract left no "out" for their problem and the owner could do whatever he wanted with his team.

The radio station could have defused this time bomb if the winning bid for the broadcast rights had been:

"Conditioned upon ownership not engaging in any business practices or conduct, intentional or unintentional, that have the effect of substantially reducing the following, audience, appeal to advertisers or other broadcast of value of the broadcasts, and if such practices or conduct occurs, then the amount to be paid for the broadcast rights shall be adjusted downward (like a force majeure clause) to reflect the loss suffered by the broadcasting party."

As a practical matter, following this unique dispute, most all companies bidding for broadcast rights of sports teams now include similar condition precedent clauses in their contracts.

6. THE ENGAGEMENT RING CASES

One of the more interesting type of disputes that involve the rules of conditional contracts are the cases to determine ownership of an engagement ring following termination of the engagement, and refusal of the donee to return it to the donor.

Some states decide these disputes based upon who is "at fault," meaning the party that broke the engagement. The other party is deemed to be "not at fault," and gets to keep the ring.

But the inherent difficulties and unpleasantness in this process of blaming one party over another, the "he said/she said" finger pointing argument which probably was a part of the engagement break up in the first place, causes most states to now follow a no-fault approach. They treat engagement rings as conditional gifts in contemplation of marriage, which must be returned to the donor no matter who caused the end of the relationship, *if* the condition precedent of marriage does not take place.

These are the same reasons that most states have changed their domestic relations laws for the termination of a marriage from a rather complicated process of fault divorce that required the plaintiff to prove specific grounds such as extreme cruelty, habitual intemperance or adultery, to the simplified procedures that now exist for no-fault dissolution of marriage.

In *Meyer v. Mitnick, 2001 WL 171453 (Mich. App. 2001)*, a case of first impression, plaintiff gave defendant a custom-designed engagement ring he bought for $19,500 when they became engaged. Three months later plaintiff asked defendant to sign a prenuptial agreement, and when she refused the engagement was broken. Both parties claimed it was the "fault" of the other.

When defendant refused to return the ring, plaintiff sued, alleging it was a conditional gift, and defendant counterclaimed alleging it was an unconditional gift and that, because plaintiff broke the engagement, she was entitled to keep the ring.

The trial court granted summary judgment to plaintiff, holding that he was entitled to return of the ring, "Because an engagement ring is given in contemplation of marriage, the marriage itself is a condition precedent to the ultimate ownership of the ring." It ignored the issue of who ended the engagement.

The appellate court affirmed, noting that, "While there is no Michigan law regarding ownership of engagement rings given in contemplation of marriage where the engagement is broken, the jurisdictions that have considered cases dealing with the gift of an engagement ring uniformly hold that marriage is an implied condition of the transfer of title and that the gift does not become absolute until the marriage occurs."

"Once we recognize an engagement ring is a conditional gift, the question still remains: who gets the gift when the condition is not fulfilled?

The court than analyzed the history of how courts have handled these situations and adopted the no-fault rule:

Generally, courts have taken two divergent paths. The older one rules that when the donor has unjustifiably broken an engagement, the donor shall not recover the ring. However, if the engagement is broken by mutual agreement, or unjustifiably by the donee, the ring should be returned to the donor . . .

The other rule, the so-called 'modern trend,' holds that because an engagement ring is an inherently conditional gift, once the engagement has been broken the ring should be returned to the donor. Thus, the question of who broke the engagement and why, or who was 'at fault,' is irrelevant."

In *Lindh v. Surman, 742 A.2d 643 (Pa. 1999)*, also a case of first impression, plaintiff proposed marriage to defendant and presented her with a diamond engagement ring he purchased for $17,400. Two months later, plaintiff broke the engagement and asked for the ring back. Defendant did in fact return it, the parties reconciled, and again plaintiff proposed marriage and gave defendant the same ring for the second time.

Five months later, plaintiff again called off the engagement and this time, after he requested return of the ring, defendant refused. Plaintiff then sued, seeking recovery of the ring or a judgment for its equivalent value. The case then went to an arbitration panel that ruled for defendant. Plaintiff appealed that decision where a non-jury trial resulted in a judgment in his favor for $21,200, the fair market value of the ring, based upon the application of no-fault rules of law.

The Pennsylvania Supreme Court accepted final appellate jurisdiction, and affirmed the decision for the plaintiff, thus answering the two basic questions before it:

"(1) What is the condition of the gift (i.e., acceptance of the engagement or the marriage itself), and (2) Whether fault is relevant to determining return of the ring. Janis (defendant) argues that the condition of the gift is acceptance of the marriage proposal, not the performance of the marriage ceremony. She also contends that Pennsylvania law, which treats engagement gifts as implied-in-law conditional gifts, has never recognized a right of recovery in a donor who severs the engagement."

"This theory (1) is contrary to Pennsylvania's view of the engagement ring situation . . . This court, however, has not decided the question (2) of whether the donor is entitled to return of the ring where the donor admittedly ended the engagement. In the context of our conditional gift approach to engagement rings, the issue we must resolve is whether we will follow the fault-based theory, argued by Janis, or the no-fault rule advocated by Rodger."

"A ring-return rule based on fault principles will inevitably invite acrimony and encourage parties to portray their ex-fiancées in the worst possible light, hoping to drag out the most favorable arguments to justify, or to attack, the termination of an engagement. Furthermore, it is unlikely that trial courts would be presented with situations where fault was clear and easily ascertained and, as noted earlier, determining what constitutes fault would result in a rule that would defy universal application."

Would you consider the following transfers by Rodger to Janis during their relationship as completed or conditional gifts?

- A diamond ring prior to announcing their engagement.
- Additional jewelry such as rings, earrings, bracelets and necklaces given prior to announcing their engagement.
- Additional jewelry items given after announcing their engagement.
- Gift items such as computers, television sets, and clothing given before or after the engagement.
- An automobile titled in Janis' name when the engagement is announced.

7. THE SATISFACTION CONTRACT CASES

The most difficult disputes are those that involve "satisfaction contracts". These are condition precedent contracts where the obligation of one party to pay for the specified goods or services is conditioned upon prior approval.

The most obvious practical question they raise is why any party would agree that he need not be paid unless the other is satisfied? Perhaps this was required in their negotiation, or the ego involved does not anticipate anyone could be less than thrilled with the work to be done or goods to be delivered. In any event, these cases have given rise to two legal tests used in determining their result:

- Personal satisfaction test – if the required performance involves personal taste, individual comfort, aesthetics or similar factors the courts are subjective. No matter whether outside parties consider the required performance acceptable, it must satisfy the party involved. Examples are personal portraits, photographs, paintings, artistic creations, individual hairstyles, custom clothing and cosmetic surgery.

*Ex: Brad, the famous actor, contracts with Salvador, the famous artist, to paint Brad's portrait, "subject to my approval", for a price of $5,000. After a number of sittings, the painting is completed. Brad goes to Salvador's studio where 10 other famous artists eagerly await the finished product. When the cover is removed from the painting, the artists all declare it to be the best work Salvador has ever done. Brad looks at it and says, "I don't like it. I'm not paying one cent for it." Salvador sues for breach of contract.

Brad wins. The nature of the work was purely personal and should be judged by the subjective test of satisfaction. No one forced the artist to agree to a satisfaction contract. He assumed the risk if his customer was not pleased. The opinions of the third parties are immaterial.

- Industry standard test – if the required performance involves mechanical fitness, construction and repairs, the courts are objective. If the work involved is completed reasonably well by meeting the prevailing industry standards, as attested by outside expert witnesses, payment is required no matter whether or not the party involved is personally satisfied. Most basic commercial contracts for property repair, improvement or construction fall into this category.

*Ex: Brad contracts with Salvador to paint Brad's Beverly Hills residence for an agreed price of $5,000, "subject to my approval". After several weeks, during which Brad was out of town, the job is completed. 10 other house painters that admire Salvador's work are present to view the finished product. Brad takes one look at it and says, "No way, this is not what I wanted, I won't pay." The 10 house painters all say the work is excellent, exceeding industry standards. Salvador sues for breach of contract.

Brad loses. The nature of the work to be done is outside the realm of a personal or custom artistic creation. Instead, it is commercial work and must therefore be judged objectively under that industry's standards.

What about this case, where the line between subjective and objective considerations are not so clearly drawn?

*Ex: Brad, a famous actor, hires Salvador, a famous artist, to paint Brad's Beverly Hills residence for an agreed price of $5,000, "subject to my personal specifications and approval". The job consists of painting each room of the house a different color requiring the blending of common primary colors to achieve a unique new color. In addition, Brad's swimming pool is to be painted with a laughing likeness of him on it, to achieve a visual image from his diving board of launching yourself into his face. When the job is completed, amidst much publicity and media attention, 10 other area artists declare it to be fabulous and the best work of its kind. Brad doesn't like it and refuses to pay.

Pretend you are deciding this dispute. What would you argue in support of Brad's legal position? What arguments would you make in favor of Salvador? Who should win and why?

Here are some cases in which satisfaction contracts were involved and the legal principles discussed.

In *Indiana Tri-City Plaza Bowl, Inc. v. Estate of Glueck, 422 N.E.2d 670 (Ind. App. 1981)*, the parties had a lease agreement that required Glueck, as Lessor, to provide plaintiff with adequate paved parking and a building for their bowling alley.

For the first 11 years of the lease, plaintiff used parking from the adjacent shopping center owned by Glueck. When the center went into receivership, the parties had a dispute over parking which they attempted to resolve by settlement agreement, which required Glueck to build a parking lot after submitting the plans to plaintiff for *prior approval.*

When Glueck submitted his architect's plans to plaintiff for approval, it failed to reply for four months and eventually responded without approval or disapproval. Glueck claimed it was acting in bad faith.

Plaintiff sued for specific performance of the lease and damages. Defendant counterclaimed for damages. The trial court ruled for defendant, applying the "reasonable person" standard of approval, and plaintiff appealed. The appellate court affirmed on the issue of prior approval.

"Although Indiana has not previously discussed the situation of a party to a contract having his duty of performance *conditioned upon his own satisfaction,* other jurisdictions have. A minority of jurisdictions use one standard, which gives the party to be, satisfied an unqualified right of rejection in all circumstances unless he acts fraudulently. The majority of jurisdictions use two standards, reasonable person and good faith, to determine if a party has been satisfied."

- Reasonable Person standard: "Satisfaction is said to have been received if a reasonable person in exactly the same circumstances would be satisfied. The reasonable person standard is employed when the contract involves commercial quality, operative fitness, or mechanical utility which other knowledgeable persons can judge."

- Good Faith standard: "The recipient of the work must be genuinely satisfied; which includes a subjective satisfaction. However, the mere statement by the recipient that he is dissatisfied is not conclusive. The majority of jurisdictions will recognize the recipient's dissatisfaction only when he is *honestly,* even though unreasonably, dissatisfied and acts in good faith. The standard of good faith is employed when the contract involves personal aesthetics or fancy."

  "We conclude that Indiana should follow the majority view ... In the case before us, the construction of the parking lot concerns commercial value and operative fitness rather than personal aesthetics. Therefore, the good faith standard is not applicable to the facts before us."

In *Beverly Way Associates v. Barham, 226 Cal. App.3d 49 (Cal. App. 1990),* defendant contracted to sell a residential building to plaintiff for $3.9 million.

The agreement provided that, "Buyer's obligations to purchase the Property shall be conditioned upon 'approval by the buyer of a number of specified inspections and documents, and delivery of clear title and conveyance documents at the close of escrow." One of these requirements was "a certified ATLA survey of the property."

When the buyer received the survey, it did not approve it due to a perceived problem regarding the number of available parking spaces, and proposed "some alternatives to keep the deal alive." There were no further communications between the parties, until the buyer advised, "We are prepared to waive our objections to such items and to proceed to close escrow within 45 days . . ." When the defendant refused to go forward with the original sales transaction, plaintiff sued for specific performance.

The trial court ruled that, "By disapproving the survey on December 12, 1988, plaintiff buyer terminated the contract and cannot sue on same." The appellate court affirmed:

"Both sides to this appeal treat the buyer's right of approval under paragraph 5 of the contract as a condition precedent in favor of the buyer. They are quite correct in that characterization . . . There can be no question but that the buyer exercised its power of disapproval in this case . . . This rejection, communicated to the seller, terminated the contract. It left the buyer with no power to create obligations against the seller by a late 'waiver' of its objections and acceptance of the proffered documentation."

In *Morin Building Products Company, Inc. v. Baystone Construction, Inc., 717 F.2d 413 (7th Cir. 1983)*, defendant was hired by GMC to build an addition to their Chevrolet factory, and, in turn, hired plaintiff to furnish and erect the aluminum walls for the structure for a contract price of $23,000.

The main contract required that the exterior siding of the walls be of a specific aluminum type, "with a mill finish and stucco embossed surface texture to match finish and texture of existing metal siding." It further provided, "that all work shall be done subject to the final approval of the Architect or Owner's (GM's) authorized agent, and his decision in matters relating to artistic effect shall be final, . . . should any dispute arise as to the quality or fitness of materials or workmanship, the decision as to acceptability shall rest strictly with the Owner . . ."

After plaintiff erected the walls, the exterior siding appeared in bright sunlight to lack a uniform finish and was rejected by GM's representative. Plaintiff claimed the defect was trivial, and GM's rejection was unreasonable. Defendant removed plaintiff's siding, hired another subcontractor to replace it, and GM approved the replacement siding. Defendant then refused to pay plaintiff for the original aluminum siding, and it sued for the balance.

The trial jury ruled for plaintiff, and the appellate court affirmed based upon its conclusion that the governing standard should be objective rather than personal:

"The general rule applying to satisfaction in the case of contracts for the construction of commercial buildings is that the satisfaction clause must be determined by objective criteria. Under this standard, the question is not whether the owner was *satisfied in fact*, but whether the owner, as a reasonable person, *should have been satisfied* with the materials and workmanship in question."

"The building for which the aluminum siding was intended was a factory – not usually intended to be a thing of beauty. That aesthetic considerations were decidedly secondary to considerations of function and cost is suggested by the fact that the contract specified mill-finish aluminum, which is unpainted."

In concluding its opinion, the court tells us, in so many words, how the inexact wording of the approval clause by GM created the financial time bomb that blew up in their face, and also suggests how it could have easily been defused:

"We repeat that if it appeared from the language or circumstances of the contract that the parties really intended General Motors to have the right to reject Morin's work for failure to satisfy the private aesthetic taste of General Motors' representative, the rejection would have been proper even if unreasonable. But the contract is ambiguous because of the qualifications with which the terms 'artistic effect' and 'decision as to acceptability' are hedged about, and the circumstances suggest that the parties probably did not intend to subject Morin's rights to aesthetic whim."

DISCUSSION EXERCISES

1. Discuss any additional situations where a contract party should be discharged by Operation of Law.

2. Discuss any additional situations that should constitute Objective Impossibility.

3. Discuss how much contemplated financial loss renders a contract Commercially Impracticable.

4. Discuss your preference of what rules should govern Engagement Ring disputes.

5. Discuss your preference of the rules governing Satisfaction Contract disputes.

CASE EXERCISES

THE IMPORTANCE OF WORDING "PAY-WHEN-PAID" CLAUSES

In *Power & Pollution Services, Inc. v. Suburban Power Piping Corporation, 598 N.E.2d 69 (Ohio App. 1991)*, Suburban was the general contractor on a construction job who contracted with the property owner, LTV Steel Corporation. Suburban had a separate subcontract with P&P Services that contained a "pay-when-paid" clause, that read:

"Company (Suburban) shall not be required to pay any such monthly billing of the subcontractor prior to the date Company receives payment of its corresponding monthly billing from the Owner."

ANALYSIS

When LTV filed for Chapter 11 Bankruptcy, Suburban claimed it was excused from having to pay P&P. P&P sued for monies due under the contract. The trial court granted summary judgment for P&P, and that decision was affirmed on appeal, rejecting Suburban's argument that the clause was a condition precedent to its obligation to pay.

DEFUSE REPLAY

"Ohio courts have not previously addressed the issue of how 'pay-when-paid' clauses should be interpreted and enforced . . . (Suburban) cites (a prior case) which held that a promise to pay 'if and when funds are available' was conditional and did not impose any obligation to pay until funds were available. The use of the conjunction 'if' in the payment provision evidenced that party's intention to condition receipt of payment by the subcontractor upon receipt of payment from the owner and is, thus, distinguishable from the present case."

CONCLUSION

The contract wording is absolutely critical in these cases. The more definite, clear and unequivocal the intention of the parties is expressed, the easier it is for them to place themselves within the law's protection. Here are two additional clauses:

- For the General Contractor: "The parties recognize and acknowledge the existence of a construction contract between the Property Owner and the General Contractor establishing specific rights and duties between them, including the payment of monies for work performed.

The receipt of such payment(s) by General Contractor from the Property Owner IS an absolute condition precedent and prerequisite to any payment obligation owing to Subcontractor, and must first occur before the General Contractor is required to pay the Subcontractor."

- For the Subcontractor: "The parties recognize and acknowledge the existence of a construction contract between the Property Owner and the General Contractor establishing specific rights and duties between them, including the payment of monies for work performed. The receipt of such payment(s) by General Contractor from the Property Owner is NOT a condition precedent or prerequisite to the payment obligations due to Subcontractor; rather, the General Contractor shall pay the sums due hereunder to Subcontractor promptly and without regard to its receipt of payment funds from the Property Owner."

AN OUNCE OF PROTECTION WORKS

In *Architectural Systems, Inc. v. Gilbane Building Company, 760 F. Supp. 79 (Dist. Ct. Md. 1991),* plaintiff entered into a construction subcontract to provide drywall and tile work on defendant – general contractor's construction project with Carley Capital Group for conversion of their warehouses into condominiums.

The main contract and subcontract provided, "It is specifically understood and agreed that the payment to the subcontractors is dependent, as a condition precedent, upon the contractor receiving contract payments, including retainer from the Owner."

When the Owner became insolvent during construction and ceased making payments to defendant, it ceased paying plaintiff.

ANALYSIS

Plaintiff sued to recover the $348,155 remaining unpaid under the subcontract. Defendant claimed it had no liability due to the condition precedent clause. The trial court granted Gilbane summary judgment, and the appellate court affirmed:

"Although Gilbane acknowledges that in the construction business the general contractor incurs the owner's credit risk, it maintains that the risk of insolvency was transferred explicitly by the condition precedent in the Trade Contract. ASI argues that it did not assume the credit risk simply by the inclusion of the statement 'as a condition precedent' in the Trade contract, and that the subcontract does not address owner insolvency specifically."

DEFUSE REPLAY

The court noted a simultaneous similar case the defendant had won that has also contained, as here, "both a pay-when-paid provision and an unambiguous precedent provision." *Gilbane Building Co. v. Brisk Waterproofing Co., 585 A.2d 248 (Md. App. 1991).*

In agreeing with the defendant that the condition precedent was a defense to its liability to ASI, the court noted that the subcontractor had assumed that business risk. "It may not be sound business practice to accept such a business proposal but that is what occurred. The provision unambiguously declares that Gilbane is not obligated to pay ASI until it first received payment by the Owner. The cause for the Owner's nonpayment is not specifically addressed and could be due to a number of causes, including insolvency."

CONCLUSION

The court's opinion clearly delineates the boundaries of when the general contractor may enforce a "pay-when-paid" clause, and when the subcontractor may disregard it.

Perhaps the critical wording of such clauses is part of the business negotiations between the parties, and one or the other makes a conscious decision to trade off advantages / disadvantages. More often, the parties simply are unaware of these legal distinctions and fly blindly into their agreements, hoping for the best result, but sometimes receiving the worst, like ASI.

CASE RESEARCH CYBERCISES

The following cases also relate to the material in this chapter and illustrate the types of disputes that may occur. For each one do the following written assignment:

1. Locate the case using the Internet (Lexis-Nexis, West or any other research cite which provides case transcripts).
2. Briefly summarize what it was about – the nature of the dispute involved.
3. Who won at the trial court level? Who won at the appellate level?
4. Who won if there was a third level of Supreme Court review?
5. What were the legal rules of law and the reasoning used to reach the final decision?
6. Do you agree or disagree with the decision, and explain why?
7. What business law time bomb(s) were involved?
8. Could the time bomb(s) have been avoided by structuring the transaction differently? Discuss.

9. Could the adverse effects of the time bomb(s) have been defused by a different reaction or response by the affected party? Discuss.
10. Replay the facts of the case to achieve a different successful result.

1. *Eagle Industries, Inc. v. Tucker, 900 P.2d 475 (Ore. 1995)(three party agreement whereby judgment debtor was released from paying judgment creditor and agreed to pay their lawyer to satisfy their fee obligation to him held to be a binding novation).*
2. *Alimenta (U.S.A.), Inc. v. Cargill, Incorporated, 861 F.2d 650 (11th Cir. 1988)(failure of peanut crop due to severe drought excuses seller from having to deliver goods on grounds of commercial impracticability).*
3. *Harmon Cable Communications of Nebraska Limited Partnership v. Scope Cable Television, Inc., 468 N.W.2d 350 (Neb. 1991)(discusses the law of conditional contracts regarding contracts to buy cable television systems predicated upon sellers' delivery of specified number of subscribers).*

NOTES

19.

SPECIAL RULES FOR SALES OF GOODS

"I will buy with you, sell with you, talk with you, walk with you."
Shakespeare: The Merchant of Venice

"The buyer needs a hundred eyes, the seller not one."
George Herbert

"Don't sell the stock; sell the sizzle."
Elmer Wheeler

In our examination thus far of commercial transactions, we have been primarily concerned with the common law general rules and fairness exceptions that have been in existence for many years. They govern how business transactions are created and enforced. They are historically the main source of contract law, and govern most transactional disputes in the business marketplace, including the sale of goods and services.

We have also been introduced to specialized rules of more recent origin that pertain solely to *sales of goods*. They are codified by statutory law in the form of the Uniform Commercial Code (UCC), in Article 2. It streamlines and encourages the modern flow of commerce by seeking to affirm the existence of contracts and enforce them, rather than provide technical and sometimes outmoded loopholes for avoiding them.

The UCC also codifies existing law and provides an orderly framework for planning sales transactions and predicting the outcome of commercial disputes. Rather than having to face differing laws of the 50 U.S. states and adapting transaction jurisdiction to which venue would work best for buyer or seller, it provides the parties with a national forum for their transactions.

Stated in its own words, its underlying purpose and policy is, "to simplify, clarify, and modernize the law governing commercial transactions." *UCC 1-102.* All states have adopted the UCC provisions except for Louisiana, which has approved portions of the UCC, and whose laws based upon the French civil law should be separately examined for local disputes.

The UCC applies to "sales" of movable, tangible personal property known as goods. These are transactions where title or ownership of the items in question pass from seller to buyer. It does not apply to gifts.

It also does not apply to real property or intangibles such as money, marketable securities and legal rights. Nor does the UCC apply to transactions whose main component is the sale of services.

Since most business transactions have mixed aspects of both goods and services, the legal test to be decided on a case-by-case basis is, "what is the main or dominant aspect of the transaction?"

This distinction is critical in many disputes where the plaintiff claims they are damaged financially or personally by defects in the "goods" they purchased, and therefore subject to warranty protection under the UCC that requires sellers of "goods" to stand behind their transactions.

While the UCC applies to all sales of goods, it also in certain cases requires higher standards of conduct from a party who has the legal status of a *merchant*, who is defined to be someone who deals primarily in the type of goods involved or is considered to be an expert regarding them.

In *Cook v. Downing, 891 P.2d 611 (Ok. App. 1994)*, plaintiff had dentures made for her by defendant, a dentist, who devoted less than 50% of his practice to fitting and making dentures. She had resulting mouth problems that she attributed to ill-fitting dentures, and complained to Defendant. He referred her to oral surgeons who ruled out the possibility that her sore spots were caused by denture fitting problems, and suggested a generalized condition due to allergies or autoimmune reactions.

Plaintiff sued for breach of warranty under the State's UCC law, was awarded damages by the trial court, but the appellate court reversed, holding that the UCC did not apply. The appellate court noted the dispute as a case of first impression:

"Finding no Oklahoma law on point, we . . . hold that . . . a dentist is not a merchant, and dentures, furnished by a dentist, are not goods under the UCC."

The dissenting opinion stated the applicable law in these types of transactions:

"The transaction of a patient being fitted for and purchasing dentures from a dentist is actually a hybrid. It is not purely a sale of goods by a merchant, nor is it purely the providing of a service by a health care professional. Whether implied warranties under Article 2 of the U.C.C. apply to such a transaction should depend on whether the predominant element of the transaction is the sale of goods or the rendering of services."

In *Central District Alarm, Inc. v. Hal-Tuc, Inc., 886 S.W.2d 210 (Mo. App. 1994)*, plaintiff was in the business of selling security systems and defendant operated retail lingerie and novelty stores. Plaintiff sold and installed one of their systems, but it was a used instead of a new VCR as required by the contract between the parties.

When this was discovered by defendant due to scratches on the unit, plaintiff offered to replace it with a new unit, "as soon as one arrived, which would take one or two months." Defendant refused, and demanded return of their deposit.

Plaintiff sued for breach of contract, claiming their right to cure defects under the UCC. Defendant denied that right, and claimed it had been defrauded.

The trial court entered judgment for defendant, and the appellate court affirmed, first stating that the transaction was a sale of goods, and therefore governed by the UCC:

"In a contract which calls for both goods to be furnished and services to be performed, the test for whether the UCC applies is whether the predominant purpose of the contract is to render services with goods incidentally involved, or to transact a sale, with labor incidentally involved. CDA supplied and installed security equipment pursuant to a 'Sales Agreement'. The contract did not include ongoing maintenance or services other than installation. Under the predominant purpose test, this was a sale of goods ..."

1. DIFFERENCES BETWEEN CONTRACT LAWS

In many disputes that involve a sale of goods, the result may differ depending upon which body of law applies. There may be a common law rule that favors one party, a UCC exception that favors the other. In the case of such a conflict, the UCC will govern.

There is also a body of law known as the United Nations Convention on Contracts for the International Sale of Goods, known as the CISG, which is a treaty ratified by more than 50 of the countries engaged in a large proportion of the world's commercial business transactions, including the United States. It governs all non-domestic contracts for the sale of goods between parties located in different countries that have ratified the treaty.

The CISG allows treaty parties to "opt-out", or non-treaty parties to "opt-in", depending upon the strategies involved in a particular transaction and the laws that will benefit the parties most. Since a treaty is a federal law, the CISG supercedes the UCC in disputes where either could be applied.

These differences can be critical factors in planning a contractual transaction and evaluating disputes. Though we have examined many of them in prior sections, with text and case studies, here is a helpful summary of the differences between our common law rules, UCC provisions and the CISG:

COMMON LAW v. UCC v. CISG

A. Application

The common law applies to all sales transactions. This includes services, tangible personal property, intangibles such as rights of legal action, stocks and bonds and money used as a medium of exchange, and real property. The UCC applies only to sales of tangible personal property, known as goods, and can be used in products liability cases. The CISG applies to all commercial/business sales of goods, but not to consumer sales of goods for personal, family, household and auction purposes, and is not applicable in products liability disputes.

B. Merchants

Under the common law, a merchant is generally described as a person engaged in a type of commercial activity. Under the UCC, a merchant is a person who deals in goods of the kind involved in the particular transaction, or who has special skills or expertise relating to the transaction. Under the CISG, a merchant is broadly defined as anyone who has a place of business. Thus, if the author sold you his old laptop computer at a garage sale, he would be a merchant under the CISG, but not under the UCC.

C. Terms of the Offer

Under common law rules of definiteness, if any of the essential contract terms such as subject matter, price, terms, time, and quantity are missing – there can be no valid offer.

The UCC will fill all the gaps created by open terms, except quantity, and declare the offer valid using an objective standard of what appears reasonable under the facts and circumstances of each case. Aside from a reasonable price, terms of payment and time for payment, there are two other UCC rules that seek to achieve a balance between buyer and seller where gaps exist in contract terms:

- Place of delivery – seller's place of business, or if none, then seller's residence
- Assortment of goods – buyer's choice will be binding

The CISG will not fill contract gaps for either price or quantity.

D. Advertisements as Offers

The common law and UCC consider advertisements as a general rule to be invitations for offers, rather than offers, even if they describe themselves as offers.

The exception is if the ad's wording is so specific that a reasonable offeree would assume the ad to be an offer. The CISG presumes that advertisements that call themselves offers are, in fact, offers, and imposes no specific wording requirements.

E. Revocation of the Offer

Under the common law, an offer may be revoked at any time before a legal acceptance occurs, even if the offeror agrees to hold it open for a stated period of time. It is up to the offeree to protect himself by creating one of the exception situations that render the offer legally irrevocable, such as an option or the detrimental reliance doctrine of promissory estoppel.

This unlimited power of revocation held by the offeror is also limited by the UCC firm offer rule. It makes the offer irrevocable for a maximum time of three months, if it is in a writing that is signed or initialed by a merchant, and grants an additional time for acceptance.

The CISG follows the firm offer exception to the common law revocation rule, but allows such offers stated by a merchant to be verbal, as well as written.

F. Form of Acceptance

The common law Mirror-Image rule requires a valid acceptance to clearly match all the terms and provisions of the offer. If the acceptance does not mirror the offer, but changes it in any material way by modification, addition or deletion, it is only a counteroffer.

Under the UCC Battle of the Forms, the purchase order offer and the order acknowledgement acceptance usually contain different pre-printed terms tailored to benefit either the buyer or the seller. In such a case, if the parties have agreed on all the basic terms (the detailed front page of their form), thus expressing their mutual intent to be bound, there is a valid acceptance. Disputes as to which of two differing clauses in the standardized part of the form (the reverse boiler plate sections) are then usually decided in favor of the first form, so long as the changes are of a material nature.

The CISG follows the common law mirror-image rule, and deems any changes in the purported acceptance to be a counteroffer.

G. Time of Acceptance

Under the common law receipt rule - offer and revocation, counter offer, acceptance and rejection, are all legally effective from a communication standpoint when actually received. Acceptance also may be legally effective when sent, under the Mailbox Rule, if the acceptance is transmitted the same way as the offer. (Regular mail offer and regular mail acceptance)

The Mailbox Rule is used more liberally under the UCC. Acceptance is legally effective when sent, so long as it is done through any reasonable medium, properly stamped and addressed, and is sent either the same way as the offer was received, or in any other way that results in faster communication. Thus, an offer sent by fax and an acceptance sent by regular mail would not satisfy the rule).

The CISG rejects both the mailbox rule and the reasonable medium rule, requiring the acceptance to be actually received before it is legally effective.

H. Pre-Existing Duty

Under the common law, a contract modification based upon a new promise by one of the parties to do what he was originally legally bound to do is unenforceable due to lack of legally sufficient consideration. Under the UCC, if a merchant makes the modification payment promise, either verbally or in writing, it is enforceable. Under the CISG, the modification payment promise is enforceable whether made by a merchant or not, bit it must be in writing.

I. Writing and Signing Contracts

The Statute of Frauds requires contracts for the sale of goods for the purchase price of $500 or more to be in written form. The UCC allows enforcement of these contracts in purely verbal form in certain situations:

- Sale of custom goods, where the seller has substantially started manufacture
- Partial delivery of the goods by the seller
- Partial payment for the goods by the buyer
- Admission in court by the parties that they have a contract

The basic Statute of Frauds requires written contracts to either be signed by all the parties or, if less than all, the signing party in any dispute must have been the defendant.

Under the UCC Non-Signer Rule, if there is a verbal agreement between two merchants for the sale of goods and its terms are confirmed by a written memorandum or other writing signed by one and sent or delivered to the other – the non-signing merchant is legally bound if he does not object within 10 days after receiving the confirmation.

Under the CISG, there is no basic writing requirement in contracts for the sale of goods. Each dispute is governed by its own facts, and the parties involved have the burden of proving verbal agreements – a difficult task when they have conflicting agendas as to who made the better business deal.

J. Warranties

The common law has no separate rules that require sellers of goods to perform properly, other than basic breach of contract situations where the parties are legally required to perform their promises.

The UCC imposes implied warranty requirements on sellers of goods, merely from the act of selling the goods to the public. The implied warranty of merchantability requires a merchant seller to furnish goods that will perform their usual and customary purpose. The implied warranty of fitness for a particular purpose, applicable to all sellers whether they are merchants or not, requires that the goods are suitable for a special usage of the buyer.

The CISG recognizes the implied warranties, but only allows them in transactions between a merchant seller and a merchant buyer.

K. Seller's Breach

The seller's basic duty is to make timely delivery of conforming goods. If the buyer claims a default, the common law requires giving the seller a "timely" notice of breach, after he has inspected the shipment. The UCC requires the giving of "reasonable" notice of breach. No exact time periods are specified, and the unique facts of each case will govern. If the requires notice is not given at all, or not made within the time parameters, the buyer may lose its default rights. The seller's legal right to cure defects expires, under both the common law and the UCC, once the contract delivery date arrives, unless the contract states otherwise.

The CISG allows notice of default to be given as long as two years after the goods are delivered, if the goods are not conforming and there was some reasonable explanation for the long delay in inspection. If the seller gives a "Nachfrist" notice to the buyer prior to delivery of the goods, the seller is allowed an additional grace period to cure defects after the normal cure time has expired.

2. IMPERFECT TITLE CASES

In the normal UCC sale of goods, the seller has legal title to what is sold to the buyer. A buyer cannot usually acquire good title if the seller's title is imperfect in any way. But what if the buyer of the goods satisfies the legal definition of a "good faith purchaser for value" (GFP), by paying a fair price, having no knowledge of the title imperfection, and reasonably believing their seller to have good title? Does a GFP gain any special ownership rights to the goods?

A) The Void Title Rule: If the seller of the goods to the GFP was a thief or finder of stolen goods – no better title can be conveyed, and the GFP must return the goods on demand of the true owner. Since the seller has void title, no better title can pass to another, even if they are a GFP.

The only recourse of the GFP is to locate the thief or finder (highly unlikely) and sue them for the return of their purchase price of the goods.

> *Ex: Matty owns an expensive laptop computer with a personalized encoded security chip that emits a retrieval signal to locate the item if lost or stolen. He is working on it in his office, goes to the restroom for a few minutes leaving his door open, and returns to find his computer missing. During his absence, Thief entered the office and took it. Thief then offers it for sale to Sammy for a fair price. Sammy knows nothing about how Thief acquired it. In the meantime, Matty activates his retrieval device, locates Sammy, and demands return of his computer. Sammy refuses.
>
> Sammy must return the computer to Matty. Sammy's seller had void title, and could not pass any better title in the transaction. The only recourse for Sammy, since he will never find Thief, is to try to find facts that will support a claim that Matty somehow voluntarily delivered the computer to Thief.

B) **The Voidable Title Rule:** If the goods are *voluntarily delivered* to another by the true owner under circumstances where he has assented to the transfer, even though it would constitute fraud by the recipient, such as misrepresentation, impersonation, or a dishonored check – the party in possession of the goods has voidable title, and may pass good title to a GFP.

> In these cases, the true owner may not legally reclaim their goods from the GFP, and their only recourse is an action for money damages against the party to whom they delivered the goods for their fair market price or replacement value.
>
> *Ex: Max owns a large screen projection television set that needs repair. He calls National TV Sales and Service (National) for a "pick up and repair" because they make house calls for such large items. Travis is fired by National the day Max's order comes in and decides to get his revenge. He falsifies the repair order with his own name, goes to Max's house and picks up the TV set by impersonating the correct employee. He than sells it to Agatha, who knows nothing about the fraud, for a fair price. When Max doesn't hear back from National, he inquires and they discover the problem and verify the sale to Agatha. Max demands the
>
> Agatha may keep the TV set. Travis had voidable title, since the true owner intentionally delivered it to him, and he can pass good title to her as a GFP. Max now has a claim against National for their negligent conversion of his property, and hopes they are still in business and solvent to pay his damages.

In order for Max to prevail against Agatha, he would have to find facts to prove either (1) the TV set was stolen from his possession, or (2) she was not a GFP, because she knew or should have known of the questionable circumstances due to paying a price far below fair market value.

C) The Merchant Entrustment Rule: If the true owner of the goods delivers them into the possession of a merchant (usually for repair or modification), the merchant has voidable title and can pass good title, by mistake or otherwise, to a buyer of those goods in the ordinary course of the merchant's business.

In these cases, which are the most bizarre of all, the buyer has legal title to the goods and is not required to return them to the true owner, who now has a claim for conversion of his property and damages for replacement against the merchant.

The rationale in these cases that protects the GFP is that the merchant is held to a higher standard of care. The GFP did nothing wrong. Max was in the best position to prevent the problem and failed to do so.

*Ex: Changing the above case a bit, Travis is the employee of National who goes to Max's house, properly picks up the TV set, and brings it back to their shop for repair. They complete their work and place it on the floor in an area where used TV sets are sold. Agatha is a customer during regular hours who is mistakenly sold that item for a fair price by a salesperson before it is re-delivered to Max. When he finds out about the problem and contacts Agatha, she refuses to return his TV set.

Agatha wins again. She satisfies all requirements of the merchant entrustment rule. The only way for Max to recover his property would be to prove that either (1) National is not a merchant for such merchandise, such as selling these items as a hobby or (2) the sale to her was outside the ordinary course of regular business, because it was after hours or otherwise not authorized.

D) The Pawnshop cases present an interesting issue of whether or not they can ever be a GFP? The legal argument is sometimes made by the true owner of goods sold under the voidable title or merchant entrustment doctrines that pawnshops are known to sometimes deal in merchandise of questionable origin and therefore, they should not be allowed GFP status.

While a few states adhere to this extreme view, most do not, and apply the same standards of "intentional or voluntary delivery" to establish the voidable title necessary for conveyance of "good title" to a GFP.

Although each of these disputes is closely evaluated on a case-by-case basis, they often are governed by statutes that require owners of stolen property to timely file police reports, and thus preserve recovery rights if the items have not yet been sold to good faith purchasers in the ordinary course of business.

The cases in this A-D section are entertaining and sometimes unusual, presenting various interpretations of the general rules of imperfect title set forth above.

VOID TITLE RULE: In *Johnny Dell, Inc. v. New York State Police, 375 N.Y.S.2d 545 (N.Y. 1975),* a New York auto theft ring stole a car in Canada, and using stolen registration forms transferred it ultimately to Elmer, a good faith buyer. He then sold the auto to plaintiff, a car dealer. When that dealer attempted to transfer the vehicle to another dealer, defendant impounded it, and plaintiff sued for an order directing release of the vehicle.

The trial court denied the request, and the Court affirmed, holding that, "it would appear that Elmer purchased from a thief, thereby obtaining no title at all. Plaintiff, in turn, in purchasing from an individual, Elmer, could obtain no better title than Elmer possessed, to wit: none.

The court also noted the factual circumstances that could have been defused this time bomb, but didn't. "Plaintiff, having failed to show that it purchased from a dealer in the ordinary course of business, did not obtain good title. At this point, plaintiff, being a dealer in the goods, *could have* transferred to an innocent bona fide purchaser for value good title by means of a completed sale."

The imperfect title rules of UCC 2–403 are explained: "A purchaser of goods acquires the title which the transferor had or could transfer. A person with voidable title has power to transfer a good title to a good faith purchaser for value. Entrusting of possession of goods to a merchant who deals in goods of that kind gives him power to transfer good title to a buyer in the ordinary course of business. However, absent (these circumstances), one may not obtain title from a thief, nor may such purchaser assert a claim against the true owner."

VOIDABLE TITLE RULE: In *Greater Louisville Auto Auction, Inc. v. Ogle Buick, Inc., 387 S.W.2d 17 (Ky. App. 1965),* defendants sold the vehicles in question to Caylor, who paid with checks totaling $12,500 which had been supplied to him by plaintiff as advances to finance his acquisition of autos for them to be sold through their auction. They stopped payment on the checks, so they were returned as uncollectible and the defendant sellers received nothing. Defendants sued for the monies lost, the trial court ruled in their favor, and the appellate court affirmed.

The court recognized that the defendant had voluntarily delivered the vehicles to Caylor, thus passing 'voidable title', which, in turn, enabled him to pass 'good title' if the case fell within either: (1) the merchant entrustment rule, or (2) the good faith purchaser rule.

"Certainly Auction (was not) a 'buyer in the ordinary course of business or other good faith purchaser'' from Caylor, since it did not purchase from him but merely acted as his agent in selling the cars to others . . . Auction knew that for the past two or three weeks Caylor's checks had been bouncing like rubber balls, from which it was bound to realize that other checks given by him to other people would likewise be dishonored, particularly after the stop orders."

In *Al Saud v. Fast Forward, Inc., 672 N.E.2d 568 (Mass. App. 1996)*, plaintiff, a member of the Saidi royal family, imported into the U.S. four luxury automobiles valued at $430,000 he had purchased in Saudi Arabia – a Ferrari, two Aston Martins, and a Lamborghini.

The vehicles were required to conform to U.S. safety and emissions standards, so plaintiff shipped them to Pereira, who was recommended to him to do the necessary work, although he was not licensed as either an auto dealer or broker. Pereira transferred the vehicles to dealer Stoehr, who then transferred them to defendant, dealer Fast – without either a certificate of origin or a certificate of title.

When plaintiff saw an advertisement in an automobile magazine for his Ferrari, he realized there was a problem, hired a private investigator, and recovered three of his vehicles. The Ferrari had been sold by defendant, a car dealer, in the ordinary course of business, and thus legally belonged to its new buyer, so plaintiff sued for money damages.

The trial jury found that, "plaintiff had entrusted those vehicles to Pereira who was not a merchant dealing with merchandise of the type involved in the instant case, (and) that, in dealing with Pereira, Fast and Stoehr were neither buyers in the ordinary course of business of any of the vehicles nor good faith purchasers for value, and that the plaintiff was entitled to damages from Fast in the amount of $430,000."

The trial judge accepted the jury's findings, and penalized Fast by doubling the award of damages to $860,000, based upon testimony proving that Fast had knowingly purchased counterfeit certificates of origin to transfer title to plaintiff's vehicles.

In *The Creggin Group, LTD. v. Crown Diversified Industries Corp., 682 N.E.2d 692 (Ohio App. 1996)*, the following more conventional dispute, the buyer from a purchaser who had voidable title qualified as a good faith purchaser for value, and was therefore accorded good title and allowed to keep the goods.

Defendant sold its Cessna aircraft to Duke, who paid with a non-certified Check and delivered him possession. He advertised it for sale in a trade journal, and then sold it to plaintiff with a forged bill of sale, for a fair price. When defendant reported the plane stolen, the FBI ultimately traced it to plaintiff and had it returned to defendant. Plaintiff sued to recover the plane, claiming it was a GFP for value from Duke, who had voidable title. The trial court agreed with plaintiff and the appellate court affirmed:

"The 'voidable title' doctrine evolved to ameliorate the harshness of the basic rule that a seller can convey no greater title than that seller has to convey. This doctrine attempts to reconcile the rights of a 'true owner' who was fraudulently induced to transfer title in goods to a 'wrongdoer' with the rights of an innocent purchaser from the wrongdoer. Title in the wrongdoer is 'voidable' because the true owner is entitled to rescind the transaction and recover the goods from that individual. The right of rescission is cut off, however, by a transaction to a 'good faith purchaser.'"

UCC 2-403(1) sets forth the voidable title doctrine, and specifically states, "A person with voidable title has power to transfer a good title to a good faith purchaser for value, when goods have been delivered under a transaction of purchase, . . . even though:
> (1) the transferor was deceived as to the identity of the purchaser, or
> (2) the delivery was in exchange for a check which is later dishonored, or
> (3) it was agreed that the transaction was to be a 'cash sale.' Or
> (4) the delivery was procured through fraud . . .
> The voidable title doctrine only applies where there is a 'transaction of purchase.' (as opposed to theft)"

Here are various merchant entrustment situations:

- Plaintiffs were grain farmers who delivered their grain to a trucker to take to the defendant grain elevator for them as their agent so they could complete its sale. The trucker had also engaged in the past in the practice of buying grain directly and reselling it to defendant. On this occasion the trucker improperly listed his name as the owner of the grain, and was directly paid $288,000 by the defendant. Plaintiffs never were paid by the trucker and sued for the unlawful conversion of their property.

  The trial court entered summary judgment for the defendant and the appellate court affirmed, holding that, "the trial court properly granted summary judgment to the elevator because the undisputed facts show the farmers entrusted their grain to an independent trucker who was also a merchant, thereby empowering him to transfer ownership to the elevator as a buyer in the ordinary course of business." *Schulter v. United Farmers Elevator, 479 N.W.2d 82 (Minn. App. 1991).*

- Plaintiff owned three paintings it displayed at the home of the artist, after he declared bankruptcy and it bought them from the Trustee. It allowed the artist to continue to possess and display the paintings. The artist sold them to defendant for $50,000, after defendant had viewed them and noted that there were no tags or labels on them to indicate in any way the artist no longer owned them. The price paid was more than appraised value, and defendant received a bill of sale from the artist. Plaintiff sued to recover possession of the paintings from defendant.

The trial court ruled for defendant and the appellate court affirmed. "Under (UCC 2-403), a buyer in the ordinary course of business will prevail over the claim of a party who entrusted such items to the merchant. In order for McKean to be protected by (UCC 2-403), DeWeldon, Ltd. must have allowed Felix DeWeldon to retain possession of the paintings (they did). McKean must have bought the paintings in the ordinary course of business (he did). He must have given value for the paintings, without actual or constructive notice of DeWeldon Ltd's claim of ownership to them (he did). Finally, Felix DeWeldon must have been a merchant as defined by (UCC 2-104) (he was)." *DeWeldon, LTD. V. McKean, 125 F.3d 24 (1ˢᵗ Cir. 1997).*

In *Alsafi Oriental Rugs v. American Loan Company, 864 S.W.2d 41 (Tenn. App. 1993),* plaintiff allowed Bradley to take three of his oriental rugs out on consignment with the understanding that she would return them if her customer was not interested. She never returned, but plaintiff did not report the rugs to the police department as stolen.

She was really working for another rug dealer, Salaam, and turned the rugs over to him. He took them to defendant's pawnshop, completed the necessary pawn of goods paperwork and received $5,000. He never returned to redeem the rugs. Five months later, plaintiff learned his rugs were in defendant's shop, and filed suit to regain possession of them.

The trial court ruled for plaintiff, on the basis that his rugs had been stolen, and the void title rule protected his claim of ownership.

The appellate court reversed, noting one of its earlier decisions where a tractor and blade was delivered to a buyer based upon a promise to return the next day, which never occurred. "In the present case, the plaintiff voluntarily relinquished possession to Rickman. As one commentator has pointed out, '(a) thief who wrongfully takes goods is not a purchaser . . . but a swindler who fraudulently induces the victim to voluntarily deliver them is a purchaser . . .'"

The court also noted the Tennessee Pawnbrokers Act, which is a typical statute that protects owners of stolen property that winds up in such stores: "The statute gives such a person a right of recovery if he notifies the 'proper authorities' of the theft and the location of the property purported to be stolen within 30 days after acquiring such knowledge."

Plaintiff failed to file a police report and forfeited his pawnshop recovery rights. Again, knowledge of the laws that protect or harm our business transactions enables us to anticipate potential problems and avoid them.

3. RISK OF LOSS IN REGULAR SALES

There is a timeline in UCC sales transactions that usually starts with the creation of the contract and ends with the delivery of the goods. What if at some point while the goods are in transit in this timeline they are lost, damaged or destroyed through no-fault of either seller or buyer? As between the two contracting parties who should bear the risk of loss? That party must pay for the goods. Usually insurance is carried by the parties to cover such losses, but what if there is none, or what if policy exclusions deny coverage?

There are two basic types of these transactions with different rules of law that answer these questions:

- Two party direct sales between seller and buyer
- Three party shipping cases involving seller, carrier and buyer

A. Two Party Direct Sales-No Fault Loss

The risk of loss rules in these transactions are different depending upon whether or not the seller is a merchant.

- A non-merchant seller has risk of loss until "tender of delivery" to the buyer is made. This means the seller has done all he can do short of actual delivery, and he notifies the buyer he is holding the goods for him.

- A merchant seller, being held to a higher standard, does not relinquish risk of loss until the goods are actually received by the buyer.

*Ex: Andrew goes to ShopperMart to buy a freezer. He chooses the floor model he wants, pays for it at the cashier, and then is directed to the warehouse behind the showroom to pick up his purchase. When it is wheeled out for him he realizes the truck he brought is too small, and decides to return the following morning. That evening a fire of unknown origin burns the warehouse and destroys all the merchandise, including his item. Who has risk of loss?

ShopperMart retains the risk of loss. They are a merchant seller, and the no-fault loss event occurred before they completed actual delivery to their buyer.

If the freezer had been bought at a garage sale or under other circumstances where his seller was not in the primary business of selling such items, Andrew would suffer the risk of loss. The freezer was being held overnight in the seller's warehouse solely for his convenience – tender of delivery had been made.

In *Martin v. Melland's, 283 N.W.2d 76 (N.D. 1979)*, plaintiff contracted with defendant, a farm equipment dealer, to buy a new truck with attached haystack mover for $35,389 and trade in his old one for $17,389, leaving a balance due of $18,000. He delivered his certificate of title to the old unit, but was allowed to retain and use it until his new one was ready in about two months due to some needed modifications. The contract was silent as to allocating risk of loss.

Fire destroyed the trade-in unit, due to no fault of plaintiff, while it remained in his possession, and his insurance had lapsed. Plaintiff sued to require defendant to bear the loss and it refused. The trial court ruled for defendant, and the appellate court affirmed: "Thus, the question in this case is not answered by a determination of the location of title, but by the risk of loss provisions in (UCC 2-509) . . . It is clear that a barter or trade-in is considered a sale and is therefore subject to the Uniform Commercial Code. It is also clear that the party who owns the trade-in is considered the seller."

"It is undisputed that the contract did not require or authorize shipment by the carrier pursuant to (UCC 2-509(1)); therefore the residue section, subsection 3 is applicable: 'In any case not within subsection 1 or 2, the risk of loss passes to the buyer on his receipt of the goods if the seller is a merchant; otherwise the risk passes to the buyer on tender of delivery.' Martin admits that he is not a merchant; therefore it is necessary to determine if Martin tendered delivery of the trade-in unit to Melland's (UCC 2-503) . . . It is clear that the trade-in unit was not tendered to Melland's in any case. The parties agreed that Martin would keep the old unit 'until they had the new one ready.'"

B. Three Party Indirect Sales-No Fault Loss

These transactions are commonly known as the shipping cases. The distance between shipping and delivery points as well as the length of time involved in the shipment is immaterial. The risk of loss rules in these transactions are different depending upon what type of legal contract is created between the parties?

- In a "shipment contract", risk of loss passes from the seller to the buyer upon completed delivery of the goods to the designated carrier. Until this occurs, the seller remains responsible for any no-fault loss events.

Completion of such delivery is usually signified by a receipt issued by the carrier called a bill of lading. These contracts are more favorable to sellers.

- In a "destination contract", risk of loss remains with the seller until the goods are tendered to the buyer at their specified destination. Actual physical delivery to the buyer is not required in all cases. These contracts are more favorable to buyers.

The rule that should apply to a risk of loss dispute in these shipping cases may be specifically negotiated by the parties as part of their transaction and mentioned in the contract by stating, "This is a shipment contract," or "This is a destination contract."

Often however, the parties are not equally aware of their legal rights. If you are a seller, you might insert "shipment contract" into your proposed terms and the buyer might not question it, thinking, "of course, the goods are being shipped to me." Similarly, a buyer might insert "destination contract", and an uninformed seller might let it stand thinking, "of course, I have to ship the goods to the stated destination." In either case, the premium, as always, is on advance knowledge of the governing rules of law.

UCC 2-509 Risk of Loss in the Absence of Breach states: "(1) Where the contract requires or authorizes the seller to ship the goods by carrier (a) if it does not require him to <u>deliver them at a particular destination</u> (emphasis added), the risk of loss passes to the buyer when the goods are duly delivered to the carrier even though the shipment is under reservation (2-505); but (b) if it does require him to deliver them at a particular destination and the goods are there duly tendered while in the possession of the carrier, the risk of loss passes to the buyer when the goods are there so tendered as to enable the buyer to take delivery . . . (3) (In direct sales), the risk of loss passes to the buyer on his receipt of the goods if the seller is a merchant; otherwise, the risk passes to the buyer on tender of delivery."

The parties can insert any terms they choose in their proposed contract of course, and perhaps they will gain an advantage due to inattention or ignorance of the other party. In the best of all sellers' worlds, that clause would state, "risk of loss passes to the buyer at the time the contract is signed." Its counterpart for a buyer would read, "risk of loss passes to the buyer 30 days after the goods are received, inspected and approved."

The UCC also specifies trade terms that determine not only who is required to make transit arrangements and who pays freight charges, but also who bears risk of loss in shipping cases, the most common of which is FOB:

- FOB seller or seller's city – seller makes all arrangements and pays all costs, including risk of loss prior to delivery of the goods to the carrier. This is a shipment contract.

- FOB buyer or buyer's city – seller makes all arrangements and pays all costs, but has risk of loss up to the time of tender of delivery to the buyer. This is a destination contract.

- Contract is silent as to these terms – it is considered a shipment contract for risk of loss purposes. The seller is favored.

*Ex: Ashley is a New York lawyer who has an important trial in Boston. While in Boston, she contracts with Red Sox Motors (RSM) to buy a new Mercedes automobile, "FOB Boston", for a prepaid price of $35,000. RSM hires Auto Carriage, Inc. to deliver the auto to her. After the car is delivered to them, their driver has an accident on the Massachusetts Turnpike en route to New York caused by wet weather, which totally destroys the shipment. None of the parties have insurance to cover the loss. Ashley demands the return of her money and RSM refuses.

The facts of the case identify the transaction as a three party sale, and the FOB seller's city trade term as a shipment contract. The risk of loss passed to Ashley as soon as RSM completed delivery of the auto to the carrier. Since the loss event took place afterwards, Ashley has the risk of loss and cannot recover her money.

If the contract specified, "FOB New York", it would have been a destination contract and Ashley would have won.

In Morauer v. Deak & Co., Inc., 26 UCC Rep. 1142 (Sup. Ct. D.C. 1979), the plaintiff contracted to buy investment bags of gold and silver coins for $35,000 from the defendant, a D.C. dealer. He took personal delivery of the silver coins, but chose to have the gold coins shipped to his Maryland residence to avoid the D.C. tax on the sale of gold.

The defendant shipped the gold coins in two packages, uninsured via U.S. registered mail, relying upon its own commercial insurance policy to cover any risk of loss. The plaintiff received one package and, thinking it contained the entire order, didn't open it for inspection until two years later when he discovered a portion of the coins were missing. When he notified the defendant of the problem, it was discovered that the post office records had been destroyed and the defendant's insurance had expired.

Plaintiff sued to recover the value of the missing coins. The court ruled in favor of the defendant, holding that, "the risk of loss of the gold coins in question passed from the defendant Deak to Morauer upon Deak's delivery of the coins to the Post Office for shipment to Morauer."

The agreement between the parties was silent as to the type of risk of loss contract, but the court determined that "shipment contract" rules governed:

"The fact that the parties had agreed that Deak would ship the coins to Morauer's residence in Maryland is not dispositive of this controversy. A 'ship to' term in a sales contract has no significance in determining whether the agreement is a 'shipment' or 'destination' contract. Moreover, there is a preference in the UCC for 'shipment' contracts."

B. Regular Sales – Loss Due to Fault

The no-fault risk of loss rules change if one of the parties breaches their duties under the sales contract. The breaching party always has risk of loss, no matter whether or not the no-fault rules would have a different result.

The required duties of the parties are:

- Seller - to deliver conforming goods. This means the completion of required actual or tendered delivery of the goods in an undamaged condition, with no material defects or deviations.

- Buyer – to accept and pay for the goods. This means receipt of the goods, inspection of them within a reasonable time, prompt notification of any material problems in type or condition, and completed payment in good funds.

*Ex: Let's go back to Ashley's automobile purchase, via carrier, from RSM, "FOB Boston". In this shipment contract, since the no-fault loss occurred while the auto was in possession of the carrier, the buyer had risk of loss. But what if when the wreckage of Auto Carriage, Inc. was inspected it was discovered that the wrong auto was shipped to Ashley? This non-conformity would constitute a breach of contract by the seller, and shift risk of loss back to RSM.

If it was a destination contract due to terms of, "FOB New York", the seller would have retained no-fault risk of loss. But what if at the time the auto was destroyed the buyer's check had bounced due to insufficient funds? This breach by the buyer would shift the risk of loss back to Ashley.

4. RISK OF LOSS IN CONDITIONAL SALES

Many sales of goods are made in the commercial marketplace where the buyer has the privilege of returning all or part of the items to the seller for credit or refund. What if a no-fault risk of loss event occurs while the goods are in the buyer's possession, before the return option has been exercised? Who bears risk of loss?

These transactions, sometimes known as trial sales, fall into two categories:

- Sale on approval - a condition precedent purchase contract based upon buyer's satisfaction - where there is a current transfer of possession of the goods to the buyer, but no transfer of ownership or obligation to pay until the buyer accepts the goods. The buyer has a return privilege until the goods are accepted. Acceptance may occur if:

    a) buyer expressly indicates acceptance verbally or in writing
    b) buyer ratifies by failing to return the goods on time
    c) buyer impliedly accepts by conveying the goods by sale or gift

  Since ownership of the goods remains with the seller while the goods are in the buyer's possession, the seller retains their risk of loss. They are also not subject to the claims of buyer's creditors, nor claimable for loss under the buyer's insurance.

  *Ex: Joseph wants to get those washboard stomach muscles that he sees in the television infomercials and orders the "Super Ab Cruncher" from Steel Man, Inc. for $99 "on 90 day approval". He tries it immediately, but then gives up in 15 days because of the muscle soreness in his initial workouts. He puts it back in the box, addresses it for return to the seller, and intends to mail it the next morning. That night lightning strikes his roof, a fire starts, and his house and all its contents burn to the ground. When Joseph informs Steel Man, Inc. they demand payment and he refuses. Who has risk of loss?

  Joseph does not have to pay. Ownership of the goods remained with the seller at the time of no-fault loss. They can file a claim with their insurer if they have coverage.

In *Prewitt v. Numismatic Funding Corporation, 745 F.2d 1175 (8th Cir. 1984),* plaintiff responded to defendant's ad and bought Morgan silver dollar collector coins valued at $3,400 on terms that stated, "Everything is available to you on a 14 day approval basis." When the coins arrived, plaintiff didn't like them, and since there were no specific instructions how to return unwanted items, plaintiff returned them via Federal Express within the required time.

Plaintiff then agreed on the same terms for a second shipment of coins, valued at $20,000. They were again returned via either Federal Express or the U.S. Postal Service within the required time.

A third shipment on the same terms was made, valued at over $61,000, and they were returned on time via certified mail in two packages, with the maximum amount of insurance available - $400 per package. Defendant never received the packages, demanded payment, and plaintiff brought a declaratory judgment suit to determine his nonliability.

The trial court ruled that the transaction was a "sale on approval", and the defendant had to bear the risk of loss. The appellate court affirmed on the basis of the UCC, section 2-327(1), which provides:

"(1) Under a sale on approval unless otherwise agreed
(a) although the goods are identified to the contract the risk of loss and the title do not pass to the buyer until acceptance; and
(b) use of the goods consistent with the purpose of the trial is not acceptance but failure seasonably to notify the seller of election to return the goods is acceptance, . . .
(c) after due notification of election to return, the return is at the seller's risk and expense, but a merchant buyer must follow any reasonable instructions."

Notice how simple it would have been for the seller to avoid this liability time bomb, by merely providing specific instructions for a method or manner of returning items. All the defendant had to say was, "any returns shall be made via Federal Express, U.S. Registered Mail, or any other means whereby the shipment value as reflected by the payment invoice price enclosed is fully insured."

Also consider the fact that millions of dollars of goods are sold daily on 'approval' basis, where sellers are happy to accept the potential risk of no-fault loss while the goods are in the buyer's possession, banking on the fact that most persons will never get around to returning them on time, even if not interested in buying.

- Sale or return – a condition subsequent contract that grants the buyer a future right to return unsold inventory for refund or credit within a specified time. There is a completed sale where the buyer has legal title to the goods as soon as they are delivered and paid for. The buyer has risk of loss, an insurable interest in them, and the goods are subject to seizure by his creditors.

    *Ex: Sarah owns a women's clothing boutique in a local mall. She orders 100 of the latest sports outfits from Gals R Us, for $99 each "with 90 day right of return" and no payment due until 45 days.

After delivery and sale of one-half of the shipment in 30 days, she prepares to return the unsold items. They are boxed for mailing, but overnight her sprinkler system malfunctions and they are ruined. When she informs the seller and requests a credit for their loss, they refuse and demand full payment for the entire shipment.

Sarah owns the entire shipment as soon as they arrive and bears the risk of loss for all remaining in her possession. She must pay the full amount. Hopefully, she is insured for this type of loss.

A consignment sale, where the owner of goods (consignor) entrusts them to a merchant (consignee) for the purpose of trying to sell them, is legally treated for risk of loss purposes as a sale or return. If the consignee is successful, they usually receive an agreed percentage of the sales proceeds, with the balance to be paid to the consignor.

They are dangerous to parties unaware of this legal status, because the consignee is generally presumed to be the owner of goods in its possession, and subject to the claims of its creditors. These may include lenders who have liens against the contents of the consignee's store, or a bankruptcy trustee if the consignee seeks the financial protection of that Court.

The UCC provides protection for the owner-consignor if he complies with state law, which usually requires that he record a security interest in the goods with his Secretary of State, or otherwise mark the goods with a conspicuous notice of his ownership interest.

In *Auclair v. Jackson, 15 U.C.C. Rep. Serv.2d 1212 (B.C. Ala.1991)*, the Auclair's operated a gun shop and convenience store in Alabama, to which Jackson delivered 70 firearms for them to sell on consignment, per an agreement between the parties that had an attached listing of all the guns.

The Auclairs filed for bankruptcy, Jackson removed his guns from the store without the permission of the bankruptcy trustee, and the trustee sued to have the guns returned as a part of the bankruptcy estate of the Auclairs, available for sale to pay off their creditors. The court ruled in favor of the trustee:

"(UCC 2-326(3) regarding consignments applies to the facts of this case. Under that subsection, goods delivered on consignment are 'deemed to be on sale or return.' Thus, by deeming the consignee a purchaser of the goods, the consignor is precluded from asserting an ownership claim to the goods vis-à-vis the consignee's creditors."

SPECIAL RULES FOR SALES OF GOODS

"Jackson is precluded from asserting his ownership of the firearms vis-a-vis the trustee. However, the subsection is not applicable to a consignor who – (a) complies with an applicable law providing for a consignor's interest or the like to be evidenced by a sign, or (b) established that the person conducting the business is generally known by his creditors to be substantially engaged in selling the goods of others, or (c) complies with the filing provisions of the article on secured transactions (UCC Article 9)."

Jackson's guns exploded here, in a financial liability sense, because he was unaware of these legal requirements. Such is usually the case, as we have seen, throughout this book. How simple it would have been for him to attach small hang tags to the trigger guards of each weapon, noting his name, address, phone number, and that the items were, "consignment goods – the property of Luke Jackson."

5. NON-PERFORMANCE OF SALES CONTRACTS

As previously stated in our discussion of risk of loss, the seller must deliver conforming goods and the buyer must accept and pay for them. Failure of either party to render this performance constitutes a breach, for which the UCC provides a number of different remedies, in addition to the fact that the risk of loss remains with a party who breached its contract duties.

These remedies are based upon the fairness principle of restoring the injured party to his pre-breach position, so that the business scales are returned to a position of balance. The UCC statute of limitations is 4 years to file suit for an alleged breach of a sale of goods contract.

The usual remedies for the non-breaching party include the right of rescission to cancel the contract, the privilege of being excused from performance, and the recovery of damages:

- Compensatory - to reimburse for out-of-pocket expenses incurred as a result of the breach, and the effort to restore the status quo

- Consequential – to cover damages, like loss of future profits, that flow as a reasonable result of the breach

- Punitive – to punish the wrongdoer with additional damages in extreme cases of willful and malicious wrongdoing

A. Assurance of Performance

If either party to the contract is reasonably concerned that there *may be a default in performance* by the other party, they may make written demand for assurance, and the party receiving the demand must give a positive response within 30 days or the demanding party may treat the contract as cancelled.

This is a valuable strategic tool. Perhaps the buyer who makes the demand has a legitimate concern whether a strike at the seller's plant will delay delivery. Rather that waiting for an ultimate default, which could be months later, the "assurance" procedure speeds up matters and allows the demanding party to plan accordingly to find alternate sources of goods.

It also is of practical benefit if one of the contracting parties realizes, due to a change in market conditions or by virtue of being out negotiated, that they made a bad business deal. They would love to be legally excused from having to perform. This "assurance" procedure gives them that opportunity. It is relatively easy to give a reasonable explanation for their concern, thus satisfying the UCC requirement that the parties act in good faith. Once their demand for assurance is received, the recipient is on the clock, and has the burden of responding with a timely good faith positive answer that they will perform, or the contract may be nullified.

B. The Perfect Tender Rule

If the goods delivered by the seller are nonconforming *in any way*, the buyer has the right to:

- Reject the entire shipment , treat the contract as cancelled, and recover any damages sustained (especially if the buyer made a bad deal), or

- Ignore the default, accept the shipment and proceed with the transaction, (especially if the buyer made a good business deal), or

- Accept the correct portion of the shipment, reject the part that is non-conforming, and recover any partial damages sustained

This Rule is very hard on sellers if applied literally. What if their shipment was 99% perfect and only 1% non-conforming? They would still be in violation of the Rule and subject to its sanctions.

Therefore parties to these transactions usually limit its application by inserting appropriate wording in their contract to handle these situations in a more equitable manner, relating to the seller's right to cure defects, as discussed later in this chapter. Of course, if no such limiting wording is present, the Perfect Tender Rule will still apply, to the advantage of the buyer.

In *Moulton Cavity & Mold Inc. v. Lyn-Flex Industries, 396 A.2d 1024 (Maine 1979),* plaintiff agreed to manufacture and sell to defendant twenty-six innersole molds, after defendant had approved the sample molds. Upon delivery to the buyer, the molds were rejected because they allegedly did not 'exactly' satisfy the required specifications.

The seller sued for breach of contract alleging wrongful rejection. The buyer contended that the 'perfect tender rule' allowed it to reject, regardless of whether or not the seller had substantially performed. After the trial court ruled for the seller, the buyer appealed and the decision was reversed in the buyer's favor.

The court first noted that the perfect tender rule has been criticized because, "it allowed a dishonest buyer to avoid an unfavorable contract on the basis of an insubstantial defect in the seller's tender." But UCC Section 2-601 continues the application of the rule because it, "states that, with certain exceptions not here applicable, the buyer has the right to reject 'if the goods or the tender of delivery fail *in any respect* to conform to the contract.'"

The burden is put upon the seller to limit the right of the buyer to reject nonconforming goods in their contract, and thus protect itself.

C. Buyer's Rights to Inspect, Reject, Accept and Revoke

The buyer has the right/duty to make a good faith inspection of the shipment for any defects or deviations within a reasonable time after they arrive, before the legal duty to accept or reject the goods arises. The time for inspection varies with the type of goods sold – one generator in a wood carton can be unpacked and viewed at once, whereas an order of one thousand men's suits demands much more time and attention to detail.

The good faith factor applies in situations where a buyer realizes he has made a bad business deal and decides to claim some questionable defect or deviation so that a seller's default can be declared and the contract cancelled. If the buyer acts in bad faith, he is in default and the seller's remedies apply.

If a preliminary inspection does not reveal any defects or deviations, but a later inspection does, and the problem was not easily discoverable and will substantially impair the value of the goods, the buyer may revoke a prior acceptance.

This right to revoke acceptance is especially important in C.O.D. shipments, where the buyer is required to accept and pay for the goods *before* inspecting them. In these cases. inspection is required within a reasonable time *after* arrival. If problems are revealed, the buyer has the legal right to revoke his acceptance within a reasonable time after discovery.

Acceptance occurs when the buyer expresses it in words, implies it by conduct such as reselling the goods to another, or by default if the buyer fails to reject within a reasonable time.

In *Graaf v. Bakker Brothers of Idaho, Inc., 934 P.2d 1228 (Wash. App. 1997)*, Bakker Brothers agreed to buy Graaf's onion seed crop, under contract that stated, "deliver all the seed F.O.B. as directed . . . buyer can reject the crop if the germination rate is less that 85%, 'or if the seeds cannot be cleaned to contain less than one per cent (1%) inert (material)' . . ."

When the buyer began processing the seed and tested samples for germination, it found rates below the required 85% and told Graaf that the seeds had failed the contract requirements, were unmarketable, buyer would not pay for them, and seller should pick them up.

Graaf then sued Bakker for breach of contract, both parties moved for summary judgment, and the trial court ruled for Bakker, finding that the seller had breached the contract and the buyer had timely rejected the shipment.

On appeal, the decision was affirmed.

On risk of loss under 2-510 (1): "The seller by his individual action cannot shift risk of loss to the buyer unless his action conforms with all the conditions resting on him under the contract. Therefore, even if we assume that the contract's use of F.O.B. passed the risk of loss, the term became operative only when Mr. Graaf tendered conforming goods."

On right to reject under 2-513(1): "A buyer has a right before acceptance to inspect delivered goods at any reasonable place and time and in any reasonable manner. The reasonableness is again a question of trade usage, past practices between the parties, and the other circumstances of the case."

The appellate court determined that Bakker acted reasonably and effectively rejected the shipment.

In *Fortin v. Ox-Bow Marina, Inc., 557 N.E.2d 1157 (Mass. 1990)*, plaintiffs purchased a new 32 foot power boat from the defendant, and there was to be work done including, "installation of the cabin top and pulpit, installation of special equipment and optional items, and electrical work."

After early delivery, the buyers inspected the boat and noted problems including, "ill-fitting engine latches, marred gel coat in the cockpit, a missing bow eye, and numerous scrapes on the hull near the water line." The defendant's sales representative assured them all the defects would be cured and the special work completed by the closing date in two weeks.

On the day of the closing, the buyers again inspected and found nothing further had been done. They were assured that the boat would be shortly made completely ready, and went ahead with the closing.

About a week later, at defendant's request, they made a check list of all the items to be repaired or corrected, which now included additional problems to the marine toilet.

Three weeks later, the boat was re-delivered to them for their maiden voyage, on which they had additional problems with the depth finder, marine radio, one engine and the electronic equipment. Again, they were assured that repairs would be completed within a few days.

The buyers attempted again to use the boat and the problems persisted, to the point that they hired counsel, notified the seller they were revoking their acceptance (four months later), and sought a refund of their purchase price and related damages, including loan interest they had paid on the financed portion of the purchase price. The seller refused, suit was filed, and the trial court ruled for the buyers.

On appeal, the decision was affirmed, based upon UCC Article 2:

"There is no dispute that the Fortins, having inspected the boat on several occasions earlier and after noting a number of defects, did not reject the boat, as they would have been entitled to do under (2-602). However, a buyer may revoke an acceptance providing that he or she can show that the 'nonconformity' in the goods that the buyer has purchased 'substantially impairs (their) value to him (or her), (2-608) (1); that the buyer has accepted the goods on the 'reasonable assumption that (their) non-conformity would be cured and it has not been seasonably cured, (1) (a), and that he or she revoked acceptance 'within a reasonable time after the buyer discovers or should have discovered the ground for it."

As to the issue of whether or not the revocation of acceptance was made within a 'reasonable time', the court said, "Many courts have held that any delay on the part of the buyer in notification of revocation of acceptance is justified where the buyer is in constant communication with the seller regarding nonconformity of the goods, and 'the seller makes repeated assurances that the defect or nonconformity will be cured and attempts to do so.'"

"Thus, the defendant errs when it looks solely at the length of time it took the Fortins to revoke acceptance – four months – in asserting that the notice of revocation was untimely. Delays of longer than four months have been held to be reasonable, when regular complaints from the buyer and assurances and repair attempts from the seller filled the gap between acceptance and revocation."

D. Seller's Right to Cure

After the goods arrive and the buyer's inspection reveals any defects or deviations that are properly communicated to the seller, the general rule is that the buyer may reject and cancel the transaction.

This is desirable when the buyer made a bad business deal and seeks a way to be legally excused from performance, especially by using the "out" provided by the perfect tender rule of rejection where the seller has not limited its application.

But what if the seller wants to be given an opportunity to correct the defects and complete the transaction? This is the case when the seller made a good deal and hates to lose it. The UCC Section 2-508 (1) provides an exception that limits the buyer's right of rejection, and grants the seller the *absolute* right to cure defects:

"Where any tender or delivery by the seller is rejected because non-conforming and the time for performance has not yet expired, the seller may seasonably notify the buyer of his intention to cure and may then within the contract time make a conforming delivery."

If however, there is no advance time to cure due to delivery on the due date or late delivery, the seller's right to cure is *discretionary* on the part of the buyer and is not guaranteed. "

The skillful seller should therefore always try for early delivery so as to preserve "cure" rights:

*Ex: Boris buys an old hotel on South Beach and remodels it in the Art Deco style for sale as a 12-unit condominium. He orders glass and chrome furnishings from Hialeah Manufacturing with a delivery date of October 15th, so that he can have his grand opening on November 1st for the upcoming winter season. The seller delivers on October 10. Boris inspects the next day and finds that the bedroom furnishings have the wrong color upholstery. He checks other sources and finds another local supplier who would sell him the items for less than he originally agreed to pay. When he notifies the seller of the problem, he advises he is canceling the contract. They demand the right to cure.

This case illustrates how the different agendas of the parties dictate the remedies they seek. If the seller can clearly cure and complete the corrected delivery by November 1st it has the legal right to do so. But what if the time is tight like our case, where although the problems were discovered before November 1st, it may take a few days beyond that date to complete the cure? When should the time for performance by the seller expire?

The seller will argue that the cure can be effected within a reasonable time, and fairness requires it be allowed. The buyer will argue to the contrary and seek all default remedies. What do you think? What is reasonable? Should any cure at all be allowed after the due date? One day late? One week late?

Another "cure" possibility is available to the seller under UCC Section 2-508 (2), after the time for performance has expired, that will circumvent the requirement of getting the buyer's approval:

"Where the buyer rejects a non-conforming tender which the seller has reasonable grounds to believe would be acceptable with or without money allowance the seller may if he seasonably notifies the buyer have a further reasonable time to substitute a conforming tender."

*Ex: ABC Co. orders 50 current model 5960 laptop computers from Dell Co., to be delivered no later than July 1. They are delivered on time, but don't work properly and are rejected. Dell Co. suggests it can immediately furnish last years model 5959 which lists for 10% less, and deliver the order at a 15% discount below the contract order price. ABC Co. first accepts the proposal, but then rejects it. Dell Co. then promptly notifies the buyer that it will re-ship conforming current model 5960's. It has a reasonable time after the July 1 deadline to do so.

E. Buyer's Right to Cover

If the seller fails to deliver, or it appears delivery will be delayed beyond the performance date, the buyer may protect itself by trying to purchase substitute goods in the marketplace in good faith and without delay, and thus complete the contract.

This often occurs in situations where the goods are being purchased for resale by the buyer for existing orders to its customers. The buyer, faced with competition in these situations, cannot afford to lose the potential business relationships. Often a premium must be paid in these last minute market purchases to locate the necessary goods.

The buyer's measure of damages is the difference between the original purchase price and the amount actually paid for the replacement goods, plus additional damages such as out of pocket costs and loss of future profits.

The *right* to cover differs from the *duty* to mitigate damages, in that the buyer is not required to cover, while the non-breaching party must always act reasonably to try to lessen the amount of ultimate damages it suffers.

Using the "Cure" example, the facts told us that Boris had set a grand opening for his Art Deco Hotel on November 1st, so he could catch the winter season. If his seller defaulted on delivery, it would make no sense for him to just file suit for breach of contract and nothing else. He would probably seek another seller-manufacturer who would be paid a premium for expediting the order, so that the hotel could open on time. Then he would determine the full extent of his damages and sue his defaulting seller.

Other common "cure" cases are seasonal goods such as Thanksgiving turkeys, Easter bunnies, July 4th fireworks and Christmas trees:

*Ex: Kayla sets up a large tent every holiday season and sells Christmas trees. She has done this for the past 10 years in the same location, and her business is comprised mainly of repeat customers. She orders her trees, as usual, from Wisconsin Arbors, Inc., specifying November 15th as the delivery date. On November 17th Kayla still has no trees, calls her seller and learns that due to a clerical error, they sent her trees to another customer. When she requests a duplicate shipment to her she is told that all the trees are sold. She locates another supplier who fills her order at a 25% premium, which she pays together with additional costs for shipping, insurance, and advertising.

Kayla can recover all the damages that are reasonably related to the failure of her seller to timely perform.

In *Red River Commodities, Inc. v. Eidsness, 459 N.W.2d 811 (N.D. 1990)*, defendant agreed in two contracts to grow and sell to plaintiff a total of 350,000 pounds of confection sunflowers at a floor price of 11.25 cents per pound. Defendant made no deliveries to plaintiff, and it later learned he was selling sunflowers to a competitor at 22 cents per pound. Plaintiff sued for anticipatory breach of contract, and urged defendant to perform.

When he refused, the trial court found that, "in an attempt to mitigate damages (RRC) purchased 'cover' at $26.00 per hundred weight.' Implicitly, this determined that RRC's substitute purchases at 26 cents per pound were reasonable."

The trial court ruled for plaintiff, and the Court affirmed, citing UCC Section 2-712:

"Cover – Buyer's procurement of substitute goods.
1) After a breach . . . the buyer may 'cover' by making in good faith and without unreasonable delay any reasonable purchase of or contract to purchase goods in substitution for those due from the seller.

2) The buyer may recover from the seller as damages the difference between the cost of cover and the contract price together with any incidental or consequential damages . . . , but less expenses saved in consequence of the seller's breach.

3) Failure of the buyer to effect cover within this section does not bar him from any other remedy."

F. Other Remedies for Breach

Aside from the basic remedies of contract cancellation, seller's cure and buyer's cover, and the recovery of money damages from the breaching party - the UCC provides additional remedies to the injured party depending upon the stage of the transaction where the breach occurs.

1. Seller's Remedies - Buyer defaults

- Stop processing the order, withhold delivery, and sell it for scrap
- Withhold delivery, complete the order, and re-sell for the best available price
- If the goods are in transit, stop delivery and reclaim the goods
- If the goods are in buyer's possession, demand their return

This is called the "right of reclamation" and is not a very practical remedy. The UCC requires the seller to send the defaulting buyer a 10 day written notice before being allowed to sue for return of the goods. Why bother? If the buyer has the goods and defaults by failing to properly pay the seller, that means insolvency and the buyer has already sold off his available assets.

The best procedure for a seller is to receive all or a large portion of the purchase price, or some security to assure payment, *before* releasing possession of the goods. This protects against most buyer defaults.

2. Buyer's Remedies – Seller defaults

- Retain and store rejected goods awaiting seller's return instructions
- Resell rejected goods if seller doesn't arrange their return in a reasonable time
- Resell perishable goods as seller's agent
- Sue for specific performance of the contract if the goods are unique
- Recover goods from an insolvent seller

This is the impractical buyer's counterpart of the seller's right of reclamation. The UCC provides a buyer who has made a partial payment the right to recover the goods if the seller's insolvency occurs within 10 days of the first payment, and the buyer tenders the balance of the purchase price.

What buyer, in his right mind, would pay additional sums to a financially distressed seller? And what insolvent seller would voluntarily relinquish possession of partially paid goods that could be sold to others for emergency cash?

Like every other step of commercial transactions, both parties need to anticipate the potential problems that can occur, and seek to plan accordingly to avoid them or at the very least minimize their financial impact.

DISCUSSION EXERCISES

1. Discuss areas of the law involving international sales of goods where you believe the UCC rules should govern rather than the CISG.

2. Discuss situations where the void title rule causes an unfair result.

3. Discuss situations where the voidable title rule causes an unfair result.

4. Discuss whether a buyer of goods from a pawnshop should ever be considered a good faith purchaser.

5. Discuss whether the shifting of risk of loss to a buyer of goods before delivery causes an unfair result.

6. Discuss whether sale on approval or sale or return is the fairer type of trial sale from the standpoint of the seller or buyer.

7. Discuss whether a seller that delivers non-conforming goods should have any right to cure defects after the required performance date.

CASE EXERCISES

CAN A USED CAR BUYER WHO DOES NOT RECEIVE A CERTIFICATE OF TITLE BE CONSIDERED A GFP?

2 CASES – TWO RESULTS

In *Thorn v. Adams, 865 P.2d 417 (Ore. 1993)*, the defendant bought a car and her son-in-law took it into the car dealer for repairs. Several days later, plaintiff saw the car on the dealer's lot next to several cars marked for sale. The dealer allowed her to take it for a test drive and later mistakenly sold it to her without also delivering to her a certificate of title.

When the defendant learned of the sale, return of the car was demanded. The plaintiff refused and filed suit to require the defendant to deliver the title to her. Defendant counterclaimed for an order requiring plaintiff to surrender possession of the car, or pay for its fair market value. Both parties moved for summary judgment.

In *Alamo Rent-A-Car, Inc. v. Mendenhall, 937 P.2d 69 (Nev. 1997)*, Clark rented a 1994 Lexus auto from plaintiff using an alias, obtained a 'California quick title' using forged signatures of fictitious parties, advertised the car in the Las Vegas newspaper, and sold it to defendants for a price of $34,000 cash. They then had it registered, licensed and titled in their names.

After the car was seized by the Nevada Department of Motor Vehicles, the defendants sued to recover it as good faith purchasers for value from Clark, who they claimed had voidable title. Alamo was substituted as the defendant, and it claimed that Clark was a thief with void title and could not pass good title to the buyers.

ANALYSIS

In *Thorn,* the trial court ruled for the buyer's claim of ownership, finding it was a purchaser in the ordinary course of business from a merchant with voidable title to whom the goods were entrusted. The Oregon Supreme Court affirmed:

"Defendant argues that it is unfair to place motor vehicle owners at the mercy of the entrustment principle . . . (But) the entrustment principle promotes one of the basic goals of commerce:

In most cases the equities between the entruster-owner and the buyer in the ordinary course are equal, and the balance is tipped in favor of the latter because that frees the marketplace and promotes commerce. This goal, called 'security of transactions,' is an ideal of the commercial law. The protection of property rights . . . is not an ideal of the commercial law . . . On the assumption that both the entruster and buyer have been equally victimized by the dishonesty of the merchant-dealer, section 2-403(2) resolves the issue so as to free the marketplace; rather than protect the original owner's property rights."

In *Alamo,* the trial court also ruled for the buyer and awarded it ownership and possession of the automobile. But the Nevada Supreme Court reversed, equating the manner and method of how Clark obtained the auto as that of a thief and thus applying the void title rule:

"The issue of whether a thief can convey voidable title is one of first impression in Nevada. In Cooper (a prior case), an original owner/seller gave title to a buyer who purchased the car with an invalid cashier's check. Thus, the buyer had fraudulently obtained the vehicle from the owner, as did Clark; however; the owner had actually transferred the vehicle's title to the buyer . . . Because Alamo still had possession of the Lexus' title, Clark could not have had voidable title simply by fraudulently obtaining a facially valid California title."

CONCLUSION

Which case makes more sense? While the merchant entrustment cases sometimes cause an unfair result for the entruster-owner, possession of the certificate of title is really not relevant to the issue of whether the auto seller has a voidable title. *Thorn* recognizes the usual procedure in the purchase of an automobile, where the buyer first takes possession and then later receives the title after the necessary paperwork is completed.

Contrast the circumstances that occurred in *Alamo.* The buyer argued that the renter-owner really caused its own problems when it, "did not verify the validity of Clark's driver's license." If it had, the automobile would never have been delivered to Clark, and there would have been no court dispute. In addition, before the buyers paid the cash purchase price to Clark, they verified his signatures on the California title and his driver's license, and otherwise did everything a good faith purchaser could do.

Was Clark a thief with void title, as the Court ruled, or did he satisfy the definition of having voidable title because the Lexus had been 'voluntarily delivered' to him as a result of the fraud-like deception of Clark?

A. Do you agree with the Court's final decision in either or both cases?
B. How should a court deal with the issue of possession of the certificate of title in these automobile sale cases?
C. What legal test(s) would you create for determining the difference between void and voidable title?

CASE RESEARCH CYBERCISES

The following cases also relate to the material in this chapter and illustrate the types of disputes that may occur. For each one do the following written assignment:

1. Locate the case using the Internet (Lexis-Nexis, West or any other research cite which provides case transcripts).
2. Briefly summarize what it was about – the nature of the dispute involved.
3. Who won at the trial court level? Who won at the appellate level?
4. Who won if there was a third level of Supreme Court review?
5. What were the legal rules of law and the reasoning used to reach the final decision?
6. Do you agree or disagree with the decision, and explain why?
7. What business law time bomb(s) were involved?
8. Could the time bomb(s) have been avoided by structuring the transaction differently? Discuss.

9. Could the adverse effects of the time bomb(s) have been defused by a different reaction or response by the affected party? Discuss.
10. Replay the facts of the case to achieve a different successful result.

1. *Gulash v. Stylarama, Inc., 364 A.2d 1221 (Sup. Ct. Conn. 1975)(contract to "furnish and install swimming pool with vinyl liner complete with built-in fence and stairs" was a sale of services, with no UCC warranty protection).*
2. *Executive Financial Services v. Pagel, 715 P.2d 381 (Kan. 1986)(sale and leaseback of three tractors which were then sold to third parties who did not take possession, were nevertheless sales in the ordinary course of business under merchant entrustment doctrine).*
3. *Joc Oil v. Consolidated Edison, 434 N.Y.S.2d 623 (N.Y. 1980)(seller of fuel oil with required .5% maximum sulphur content was allowed to cure 1% sulphur content defect after required delivery date by substitution of conforming shipment).*

NOTES

20.

SPECIAL RULES FOR PRODUCT LIABILITY

"Consumption is the sole end and purpose of all production;
and the interest of the producer ought to be attended to only so far
as it may be necessary for promoting that of the consumer.
Adam Smith

1. LEGAL OVERVIEW

In addition to the duties of a seller/manufacturer of goods to deliver conforming goods to the buyer, there is an additional duty owed to assure that the goods are not defective.

Product defects may cause out-of-pocket economic loss to the buyer, such as the purchase price paid, costs of replacement, loss of future profits and the possible loss of customer relationships. If so, the seller has UCC contract liability under the law of warranty.

If product defects cause personal injuries, the seller incurs common law and statutory tort liability under the laws of negligence or strict liability.

This entire area of seller's liability for damages due to defective merchandise is aptly called "Product Liability". Often the same set of facts in a dispute may result in multiple claims of breach of warranty, and damages due to negligence and/or strict liability.

The historical perspective tracks the evolution of consumer's rights in the business marketplace. Up to the late 1800's, in our agrarian, rural society, sellers/manufacturers were favored by the law. The prevalent legal doctrine was *caveat emptor - let the buyer beware.* Unless a seller specifically guaranteed the performance of the goods sold in a separate promise that was part of the contract, the buyer had no right to sue for damages caused by product defects.

In both contract and tort cases, a direct contractual relationship called "privity of contract" was required between the parties due primarily to the fact that the buyer-plaintiff usually purchased the goods directly from the seller-defendant. If remote parties were damaged by product defects, they had no legal recourse.

Then, the industrial revolution that started in the early 1900's brought massive changes to society, with large segments of the population moving into the larger cities to work in factories to produce the goods demanded by the consuming public, lengthening the lines of product distribution.

Injured consumers usually did not deal directly with the seller/manufacturer responsible for defects in the products they purchased. The laws gradually changed to protect the consuming public under the new doctrine of *caveat venditor – let the seller beware.* Sellers of goods were better able to absorb the increased costs of doing business, and product liability claims were permitted by remote injured parties.

2. NEGLIGENCE – FAULT LIABILITY

The largest number of civil lawsuits filed in both federal and state courts is personal injury tort claims arising from alleged negligent conduct of the defendant that results in damages suffered by the plaintiff.

Negligence is an unintentional non-contract wrong. The plaintiff is required to prove that the defendant was at fault, through these three legal elements:

1. Defendant had a duty to maintain a certain standard of care
2. Defendant breached this duty by falling below the standard
3. Plaintiff was injured as a direct result of defendant's breach

In the usual negligence disputes there is no transactional relationship between the parties. They are usually total strangers, as often occurs in automobile collisions, plane crashes, industrial accidents and related commercial or non-commercial involvement where the defendant has unintentionally injured the plaintiff due to conduct which meets the legal tests of elements (1) and (2) above.

On the other hand, in products liability negligence disputes a seller and buyer have transacted for the goods in question and they prove defective in some way, injuring the buyer or others who are legally entitled to recover for their damages.

Products liability negligence claims typically involve allegations of:

- Negligent manufacture of the goods causing injury
- Negligent design of the goods causing injury
- Failure to inspect for defects causing injury
- Failure to warn of defects causing injury

The defendant in such claims will attempt to avoid liability by proving any or all of these traditional legal defenses:

- Assumption of the risk - the plaintiff's injury was caused by a known and foreseeable danger that plaintiff exposed himself to, thereby causing his own loss:
    - Plaintiff is hit by a hockey puck or baseball
    - Plaintiff is injured skiing or skydiving

- Plaintiff becomes ill from drinking outdated milk
- Plaintiff is knowingly treated by an unlicensed doctor

- Product misuse - the plaintiff's inappropriate or incorrect usage of the product causes his injury (the following are actual cases, believe it or not):
    - Hammering a nail with the barrel of a loaded revolver
    - Cleaning your teeth with a steak knife
    - Drying a pet in your microwave

- Comparative Negligence – the plaintiff's own negligence caused a part of the loss. Originally "contributory negligence" was an absolute bar to a plaintiff's claim even if the defendant was mostly at fault. The courts gradually recognized the unfairness of this approach and modified it so that the plaintiff's proven damages are just mathematically reduced by the percentage of the loss he caused.

- Statute of Limitations - each state has laws that proscribe the time period in which negligence suits must be commenced, running from one year in professional malpractice cases to four years in some situations that involve the sale of defective merchandise. Even if the plaintiff could prove the required legal elements of negligence, his failure to sue on a timely basis is an absolute bar to recovery.

Often the alleged negligent conduct of the defendant involves more than one of these categories of claim and defense in the same factual pattern. The damages sought by a plaintiff are the usual categories found in personal injury cases:

- Compensatory - to reimburse for actual expenses or damages.
- Consequential - to cover resulting damages, such as loss of wages from one's employer or lost profits from one's business.
- Incidental – costs of the claim/lawsuit process
- Pain and suffering, mental anguish and loss of companionship

An injured plaintiff also commonly seeks punitive damages, especially where the conduct of the defendant in its manufacture or sale, design, inspection, or concealment of the product defects is considered willful, malicious, reckless and outrageous.

Let's analyze the following typical dispute:

*Ex: Curtis buys an electric coping saw at Sears, manufactured by Sheffield Co. Its operating instructions state, "not to be operated at speeds higher than 1,000 rpm's or used to cut metallic or other non-wood based objects."

The saw is equipped with a detachable blade guard as standard equipment, because some woodworking functions cannot be performed while it remains in place. Due to a production flaw, the bolts holding the saw blade in place are sheared in half. Curtis detaches the blade guard to do intricate wood carving with the saw, starts it and then when it is running at 1,100 rpm's the blade shatters, severing two of his fingers. He sues Sears and Sheffield Co. for product liability negligence and they raise all available defenses. Who wins and why?

Curtis would allege the negligence of Sheffield Co in shearing the blade bolts constituted defective manufacture, design and failure to properly inspect. If in fact Sheffield Co. knew about the problem and allowed sales to take place, they also breached their duty to warn of defects. This negligence was the proximate cause of his injury. Since privity of contract is no longer required, Curtis can sue Sheffield Co. even though he did not deal with them directly.

One of Sheffield's defenses would be that Curtis assumed the risk by detaching the blade guard. He would successfully counter by arguing the product contemplated such removal and was produced to allow it. This was not a case of him removing permanent blade protection.

Sheffield would also argue that Curtis was contributorily negligent by operating the saw in excess of the stated rpm limit and should not recover any damages. He would counter that, at best, he was only negligent to the extent of 5% to 10%, and the blade would probably have broken by prolonged use under 1,000 rpm's. Under the comparative negligence doctrine now followed by most states, his award would just be reduced by the applicable amount, rather than being barred completely.

Decision for Curtis against Sheffield Co.

The claim against Sears is different. Curtis probably sues them hoping to induce a nuisance settlement. They are considered a "deep-pocket" defendant, due to their financial resources, but would still have to spend large sums for attorney's fees and related expenses. (That same "deep-pocket" may also cause Curtis to settle because his financial resources are much more limited.) Let's assume they refuse to settle.

They will win and be dismissed as a defendant because they were only the retail intermediary in the chain of commerce, committed no acts of negligence, and were not at fault.

There are an enormous number of successful product liability negligence cases due both to the sheer volume of manufacture and sale of goods to consumers and the litigious society in which we live, where an injury from a defective product is usually the subject of a claim for damages.

There is also the occasional bizarre case in which recovery is denied:

In *Daniell v. Ford Motor Company, 581 F. Supp. 728 (Dist. Ct. N.M. 1984)*, the plaintiff was despondent and attempted to commit suicide by locking herself inside the trunk of her Ford LTD automobile, which had been manufactured by the defendant. She promptly changed her mind about the suicide attempt once she was locked inside, but remained there for nine days until she finally was rescued.

Plaintiff sued the defendant in product liability negligence for negligent design in not having an internal trunk release, and for failure to warn consumers that the trunk could not be unlocked from inside. The defendant moved for summary judgment.

The court granted defendant's summary judgment:

"Under negligence, a manufacturer has a duty to consider only those risks of injury which are foreseeable. A risk is not foreseeable where a product is used in a manner which could not reasonably be anticipated by the manufacturer and that use is the cause of the plaintiff's injury . . . The court holds that the plaintiff's use of the trunk compartment as a means to attempt suicide was an unreasonable use as a matter of law."

"Nor did the manufacturer have a duty to warn the plaintiff of the danger of her conduct, given the plaintiff's unforeseeable use of the product . . . There is no duty to warn of known dangers."

This was an unusual case that could be criticized as nonsense litigation, but it still had a beneficial result to consumers. After it was decided auto manufacturers tried to brainstorm factual scenarios where a different result would occur and the language of the case pointed them in the direction of a potential problem due to the possibility of children crawling into auto trunks. This is called "an attractive nuisance" in the law of negligence, and remedial design was needed.

"The design features of a trunk make it well near impossible that an *adult* intentionally would enter the trunk and close the lid. The dimensions of a trunk, the height of its sill and its load floor, and the efforts to first lower the lid and then to engage its latch, are among the design features which encourage closing and latching the trunk lid while standing outside the vehicle."

This problem could also exist for an adult. What if you lived on the ocean, where strong gusts of wind were a common occurrence? And what if your car had a large trunk? And what if your bags of groceries overturned so that you had to crawl completely into your trunk to retrieve them? Get the picture?

Since this 1984 case, all auto manufacturers have changed the design of their cars to provide an internal trunk locking mechanisms.

Now compare the following case of a successful recovery based upon failure to warn the consumer:

In *Dunne v. Wal-Mart Stores, Inc., 679 So.2d 1034 (La. App. 1996)*, the children of the plaintiff bought their 500 pound mother an Aero Cycle exercise bike to help her lose weight. The second time she used it, beyond a short trial run, it collapsed under her weight; she fell off the bike backwards, and was severely injured.

Although the AeroCycle was not designed to be used by persons weighing over 250 pounds, the owner's manual and other safety information had no statement or warning regarding that weight-use limit.

The plaintiff sued Wal-Mart and the manufacturer of the bike under the Louisiana Products Liability Act that read:

"The manufacturer of a product shall be liable to a claimant for damage proximately caused by a characteristic of the product that renders the product *unreasonably dangerous* when such damage arose from *a reasonably anticipated use* of the product by the claimant or another person or entity (emphasis added)."

The trial court ruled for the defendant, holding that, "the use of this exercise bike by a woman of 500 pounds was not reasonably anticipated."

The plaintiff appealed and the appellate court reversed:

"There was no issue of misuse of the product by plaintiff in this case. In fact, the record demonstrates that plaintiff used the product in a manner wholly consistent with its intended use . . . Plaintiff had no reason to know that the AeroCycle would not sustain her weight as she previously had used a similar exercise bike for several years without incident . . . Here, there is absolutely no evidence contained in the record that the danger was obvious or that plaintiff knew or should have known of the danger."

Since we are all graduates of the school of Anticipatory Thinking by now, it is incredible that the bike manufacturer did not include a one sentence statement in its materials that said, "WARNING: THIS PRODUCT IS NOT TO BE USED BY ANYONE WEIGHING MORE THAN 250 POUNDS – SUCH USE MAY RESULT IN SEVERE INJURY!" If there had been such a warning, the defendant would have won the case.

4. STRICT LIABILITY – NO-FAULT RECOVERY

As commerce expanded and the laws changed to accommodate consumers who bought and used goods in their everyday business, product liability disputes sometimes arose where a party suffered a severe negligent injury but was unable to prove who caused it.

If this were the case, the injured parties would be unable to win a negligence claim because they could not sustain their required burden of proving the defendant was at fault.

In the 1960's, as more and more courts allowed these claims in the interest of fairness, states began to pass public policy laws recognizing the no-fault doctrine of "strict or absolute liability". They reasoned that the sellers of defective goods could best absorb the costs of litigation through insurance and increased prices for their products. Now, almost all states recognize it.

The doctrine provides that all the parties in the chain of distribution of a *dangerously defective* product, from first manufacturer to final retailer, may be sued by anyone who is injured by that product – without regard to whether or not they were at fault.

In order to recover, a plaintiff or his legal representative need only prove that (1) the seller is a merchant engaged in the business of selling such a product or in the chain of distribution, (2) it was sold to plaintiff, and (3) it was dangerously defective because the plaintiff suffered a severe injury or died.

The Restatement, Second of Torts states strict liability will be imposed if:

"(1) the defendant was engaged in the business of selling a product such as the defective one;
(2) the defendant sold the product in a defective condition;
(3) the defective condition made the product unreasonably dangerous to the user or consumer or to his property;
(4) the defect in the product existed when it left the defendant's hands;
(5) the plaintiff sustained physical harm or property damage by using or consuming the product; and
(6) the defective condition was the proximate cause of the injury or damage."

This raises a presumption of strict liability, and shifts the burden of proof to the defendant to prove the product was not defective at the time it left their control. As hard as it would be for a plaintiff to prove the fault of the defendant, that's how hard it is for the defendant to prove non-fault. Most all such cases are ultimately settled by the defendants and their insurers in the plaintiff's favor.

The Curtis v. Sears and Sheffield Co. case we discussed in the negligence section also has facts that would allow a claim for strict liability. The electric saw was "dangerously" defective as evidenced by Curtis's severe injury. Sheffield Co. was a merchant seller/manufacturer who sold it to Curtis. Curtis prevailed against Sheffield Co. for negligence but lost against Sears since he could not prove they were at fault. In a separate count for strict liability against them, he would win against both. Sears cannot escape liability here because they were the retail seller in the chain of distribution of the product.

Here is an example of the usual type of strict liability case, based upon an actual incident that occurred a few years ago in Miami, Florida:

*Ex: Juan is a construction worker who buys a cold soda on noon break at a nearby local convenience store. He drinks the soda while standing outside the store. After a few minutes, he feels ill, convulses, and collapses. The store calls 911, Juan is rushed to the hospital emergency room and dies. His autopsy reveals a large amount of pure cocaine in his stomach, which is traced back to the can of soda. A search of the store reveals three other cans similarly tainted.

The seller of the soda received the soda from his distributor. They received it from their jobber, who received it from the importer, who received it from the manufacturer in Colombia. No one knows who put the cocaine in the soda. The executor of Juan's Estate sues all the parties in the chain of commerce for strict liability.

Plaintiff will win against everybody. The burden of proving the three required elements of strict liability will be easily satisfied, and the defendants will be unable to prove where the problem arose. They will all be presumed liable to the plaintiff for all legally recoverable damages.

The unusual cases also occur in this category, causing much discussion and debate as to whether the strict liability doctrine goes too far in protecting the rights of consumers:

In *Greene v. Boddie-Noell Enterprises, Inc., 966 F. Supp. 416 (W.D. Va. 1997),* the plaintiff purchased hot coffee at the drive-through window of a Hardees restaurant. The cup she was holding in her hand splashed hot coffee on her legs when "the lid came off" as her vehicle hit a dip in the road as it exited the restaurant. She was treated at a hospital emergency room, missed 11 days of work and suffered permanent scarring to her thighs.

Plaintiff sued defendant, claiming the product she purchased was "unreasonably dangerous" as required by the Virginia statute for strict product liability. The defendant restaurant operator moved for summary judgment, which was granted.

On appeal, the decision was affirmed:

"The plaintiff argues that the mere fact that she was burned shows that the product was dangerously defective, either by being too hot or by having a lid which came off unexpectedly. But it is settled in Virginia that the happening of an accident is not sufficient proof of liability, even in products cases."

The court also noted, somewhat critically, the prior 1984 McDonald's hot coffee case that received world-wide attention, in which an 81 year-old customer burned in a similar manner as this case, sued the fast food chain for her injuries and received a jury verdict of $160,000 in compensatory damages and $2.7 million (later reduced to $480,000) in punitive damages.

It certainly appears that this Hardees case was a copycat of the McDonalds case. Unfortunately for the plaintiff, the result was not the same. As a practical matter however, similar to what happened after the "attempted suicide in the automobile trunk" case, after the McDonalds and Hardees cases, all fast-food sellers of coffee have reduced its temperature and placed "danger of burning" warnings on their cups.

5. BREACH OF WARRANTY

While negligence and strict liability theories of product liability are tort-based, warranty law is a contract concept. A warranty can be defined as a guarantee or assurance that the goods sold will measure up to a certain standard of quality or performance. If they do not work, are defective in some material way so that they can't be used, or such defects cause personal injury to the buyer or end user, damages for breach of warranty may be recovered from the seller.

These damages may include:

- Refund of the purchase price and cancellation of the sale
- Repair or replacement of the defective goods, and completion of the sale
- Recovery of the value differential between the warranted & sold goods
- Money damages awardable in usual personal injury cases

The warranty sued upon by a buyer of the goods must be an important factor in his decision to buy, called *basis of the bargain.*

The UCC does not go so far as the "detrimental reliance" test of liability in promissory estoppel contract cases, but still requires some degree of an inducing connection between the warranty and the decision to buy.

While the privity of contract defense that limited a buyer of defective goods to suing only his direct seller has been abandoned by our courts in tort actions, it remains to a limited extent in warranty cases. There are three alternatives provided by Article 2A of the UCC:

1. Most states grant warranty protection to the buyer, *and* other natural persons in his family or household or who are a guest in his home.

2. Others extend it even further to include "any natural person who may reasonably be expected to use, consume or be affected by the goods.

3. The most liberal alternative, allowed by a few states, expands coverage to all persons, both natural and corporate, who were injured either financially or physically so long as the damage was "reasonably foreseeable".

The UCC statute of limitations time period for filing suit for breach of warranty is 4 years from when the goods were delivered to the buyer.

A. Express Warranties

Express warranties are verbal or written factual representations by the seller that the goods will conform to a certain quality or performance standard. They can take many forms:
- Statements of fact about the goods – "This car has 8 cylinders."
- Descriptions of the goods – "This is a Buick LeSabre model."
- Performance promises - "This auto will give you 30 mpg."
- Advertisements/signs – factual statements, not just sales talk
- Purchases made from a sample or model of the item
- Custom or trade – relying upon past or local business practices

Sellers of goods are not legally required to furnish express warranties, but competition in the business marketplace demands it. Think of the largest shopping center in your local community. There are usually at least two stores that sell the same type of goods at the same level of prices. What if one store had a "no warranty - what you see is what you get" policy and another similar store said, "full warranties on all sales - we stand behind our goods"? Where would you shop? The consumer wants the best deal and will purchase from the seller providing it.

Disputes sometimes arise in express warranty cases when defendants deny liability on the grounds that the verbal or written statements in question were merely expressions of opinion rather than factual assertions.

*Ex: Jeffrey goes to Glen's Clothiers to buy a tuxedo for his upcoming wedding. The salesperson directs him to the correct department where there is a sign that reads, "finest Italian silk tuxedos", and tells Jeffrey, "I have been in this business for many years and these are the best values in formal wear you could find anywhere." Jeffrey buys one of them for the sale price of $300. After the wedding he goes to clean the tux and is informed that it is made in China of a cheap synthetic material and will probably fall apart if cleaned. He claims breach of express warranty and the seller denies liability.

This looks like a fraud case and could probably be decided in Jeffrey's favor *if* he could prove the seller knew of the problem and intended to deceive him. Let's assume there is no such prior knowledge, just a mistaken assertion by the seller's agent.

Was there an express warranty? Yes, the sign had factual statements of "Italian silk" that were breached. But what if the sign only said, "finest tuxedos". The word finest is an opinion – reasonably people might differ – normally not a warranty. The salesperson's statement was one of value – an opinion –more sales talk, and normally not a warranty.

But, like fraud cases, the UCC has a fairness exception to the "statement of fact" rule in factual circumstances like this one where the buyer would reasonably rely upon the opinion statements due to the superior knowledge or expertise of the seller. Jeffrey wins his claim for breach of warranty.

In *Felley v. Singleton, 705 N.E.2d 930 (Ill. App. 1999)*, the plaintiff purchased a used 1991 Ford Taurus automobile, with 126,000 miles on the odometer, from the defendants for $5,800. After a test drive, the defendants told him the car was in good condition, answered all his questions with positive responses, and plaintiff bought the car.

Within the first month of use, plaintiff experienced problems with the clutch pedal and the brakes costing almost $2,500, and then sued for breach of express warranty. The trial court entered judgment for the plaintiff, and the appellate court affirmed. The issue before the court was whether the statements made by the defendants were an express warranty or just sales puffery of an as-is sale:

"Section 2-313 of the (UCC) governs the formation of express warranties by affirmation in the context of a sale of goods such as a used car. Section 2-313 provides, in relevant part:

Express warranties by the seller are created as follows: (a) any affirmation of fact or promise made by the seller to the buyer which relates to the goods and becomes part of the basis of the bargain creates an express warranty that the goods shall conform to the affirmation or promise"

"We agree . . . that, in the context of a used car sale, representations such as the car is 'in good mechanical condition' are presumed to be affirmations of fact that become part of the basis of the bargain."

Louisiana has an unusual statutory law called "Redhibition" that allows a buyer of goods that have hidden defects to rescind the transaction and recover the purchase price paid.

In *Crow v. Laurie, 1999 WL 99069 (La. App. 1999)*, the plaintiffs bought a used 17-foot fishing boat and trailer for $2,500. After one use, plaintiffs discovered that the boat's transom forming the stern of the boat was rotten and the boat should not be used. The condition was not visible under its outer layer of fiberglass.

After plaintiffs unsuccessfully tendered the boat and trailer to defendant, requesting a "full and complete repair or refund of the purchase price", they filed suit. The trial court ruled in favor of the defendants, ruling that the plaintiffs "had a heightened duty of inspection" as purchasers of a 19 year-old boat.

The appellate court reversed based upon the doctrine of Redhibition:

"Redhibition is the avoidance of a sale on account of some vice or defect in the thing sold which renders it either absolutely useless, or its use so inconvenient and imperfect, that it must be supposed that the buyer would not have purchased it, had he known of the vice

In a suit for rehhibition, the plaintiff must prove: 1) the seller sold the thing to him and it is either absolutely useless for its intended purpose or its use is so inconvenient or imperfect that, judged by the reasonable person standard, had he known of the defect, he would never have purchased it; 2) the thing contained a non-apparent defect at the time of sale; and 3) the seller was given an opportunity to repair the defect."

B. Implied Warranties

In its effort to protect the consumer, the UCC grants to every buyer of goods *from a merchant* the following two implied warranties. They arise as a matter of law, without any verbal or written statements from the seller, solely from the transaction itself:

1. Merchantability

This implied warranty assures that the goods purchased are fit for their normal or customary purposes of use. This would mean a pen or pencil writes, a watch keeps time, an alarm clock rings, a computer will perform its standard functions, and so on.

The merchant seller's obligations include the goods being properly contained, packaged and labeled, as well as being of consistent quality and quantity if more than one item.

The thrust of this implied warranty is that the buyer-consumer relies upon his merchant-seller and gets what he reasonably expects to receive. It is another of our fairness rules.

*Ex: Stephen, an accountant, decides to retire, and sell his electronic equipment. He has a high quality Texas Instruments printing calculator that performs many bookkeeping functions including 12-digit three-color printing of numbers, tax calculations, and also addition, subtraction, multiplication and division. He sells it to Smith Office Supply. They then sell it to Riley, a young auditor.

When Riley puts it in use he discovers that it will only print in black & white, and while it performs all the mathematical computations, it will not do the tax rate conversions. He demands return of his money from Smith Office Supply who, in turn, demands the return of their purchase price from Stephen.

The ordinary and customary usage of the calculator in this case is to compute and color print calculations that include tax functions. That is presumably the basis for the bargain when it was bought by Smith Office Supply as well as their customer, Riley. The calculator clearly fails to perform as required and is therefore considered defective.

But the key issue here is the legal status of the respective sellers. Is Stephen a merchant with respect to the goods sold to his buyer? No, he is retired and no longer engaged in his profession, so he no longer is viewed as a merchant seller. He is not liable for breach of the warranty for that reason.

Smith Office Supply, while having no legal recourse for breach of warranty against Stephen, is a merchant actively engaged in its primary business that includes the sale of items such as the calculator. Therefore it is liable to Riley.

2. Fitness for Human Consumption

The "consumables" warranty cases are an outgrowth from implied warranty of merchantability. If the goods sold by a merchant not only fail to function properly but have harmful side effects resulting from their use, the buyer is also legally protected. Over the years, these cases have evolved into a separate implied warranty category and are decided on a case-by-case basis. The broad category of sellers includes bars and restaurants, package stores, licensed food sellers, public vending machines, and take-out services. Whether the items are consumed on premises or off premises is immaterial.

Originally there was a factual distinction based upon only two factors:

- Foreign object test – consumer always wins - "cutting your mouth on a piece of metal in your fish chowder"

- Natural object test – seller always wins – "cutting your mouth on a fish bone in your fish chowder"

If the cause of the damage was *reasonably related* to the food or drink in which it was found, it was considered a natural object and no recovery was allowed by the consumer. This would include situations like a chicken bone in fried chicken, orange seeds in orange juice and meat gristle in a hamburger.

As the law became more attuned to the rights and needs of the consuming public, and the ability of businesses to absorb legal risks through insurance and pricing policics, a shift in emphasis took place in a majority of states in these cases.

All states hold that damage from a foreign object subjects the merchant-seller to liability. But what about those cases where the damage is caused by what is technically a natural object, but one that the buyer-consumer did not expect to encounter?

Most states now judge these disputes based upon a *reasonable expectation* test. If the object encountered in the food or drink was normal or customary (notice the wording similar to merchantability), and thus expected by or foreseeable to the consumer, it is treated as a natural object. But if reasonable people would not expect it under the same or similar circumstances (the objective test we have used time and again), it is treated as a foreign object and creates seller liability.

*Ex: Ricky takes his girlfriend Mia to the Om Natural Eats restaurant for lunch. They both order veggie burgers. When their food arrives she takes a big bite and says, "Wow, it's delicious." He takes a big bite and says, "Ouch, I cracked my tooth on this large uncooked carrot in my burger." He sues for breach of food warranty. The seller denies liability, claiming it was just a natural object.

Certainly carrots are part of the usual veggie burgers served in health food restaurants. But would the consumer "reasonably expect" to encounter what caused Ricky's problem? If so, you could not eat a veggie burger without carefully looking through it before each bite. That is not reasonable for food in general, and especially when it comes to a hungry diner biting into a fresh, juicy burger. The burden is upon the food seller to properly prepare it. Ricky wins.

3. Fitness for Special Use

This warranty applies to *all* sellers of goods, whether merchants or not. It includes garage sales, barters or exchanges, and any other transfers of title to goods. This broad application of warranty protection is limited by the legal requirements for its application:

- Seller knows or reasonably should know of buyer's desired use
- Seller knows or reasonably should know buyer is relying upon him
- Buyer does rely upon seller to deliver the correct goods
- Seller breaches by failing to provide the correct goods
- Buyer suffers damage due to seller's breach

Notice how similar these five elements are to the doctrines of fraud and promissory estoppel that we have previously discussed. Their basis is fairness, and again the law is seeking to balance the scales to protect the consumer.

This warranty protection does not relate to the merchantability situations of the goods being fit for their normal usage. It only applies to a failure of the seller to meet the special needs of the buyer.

It also requires that the buyer is not on the same level of knowledge or expertise as the seller, and is thus depending upon the seller to provide what is needed. The reasonable reliance factor is missing if the buyer is able to tell at a glance whether or not the correct goods are being furnished.

"Section 2-314 of the (UCC) provides that every sale of goods by a merchant includes an implied warranty that the goods are fit for the ordinary purposes for which they are used unless the warranty is modified or excluded. Section 2-315 of the code states that a sale of goods also includes an implied warranty of fitness for a particular purpose if a seller knows of the buyer's particular purpose for the goods and the buyer relies upon the seller's skill or judgment to select suitable goods. However, 2-316 of the code states that no implied warranties apply when a buyer examines the goods or a sample as fully as he desires, or refuses to examine the goods, prior to the purchase." *Trans-Aire International, Inc. v. Northern Adhesive Co., Inc., 882 F.2d 1254 (7th Cir. 1989).*

*Ex: Zachary is a 1st time scuba diver who seeks to find the wreck of an old Spanish galleon off the Florida coast. He needs a pen that will write on land, in the water, and at pressure depth so he can make notes on his dives. He goes to DEF Stationers, and tells the salesperson he wants a good pen, "that will write in all kinds of weather." He buys the pen provided. On his next dive trip, it is raining and the pen writes fine, but it won't write underwater and he is unable to record important location coordinates. As a result, he loses his salvage and sues DEF Stationers for breach of warranty.

It appears that the pen Zachary bought was merchantable, since it did function properly in "all kinds of weather" rain or shine. His problem was underwater writing, not just being able to work when wet. There are special pens that divers use for this purpose, but since he was a first-timer, he would not notice whether or not he had received the right model. If he were experienced, he would be aware of any discrepancy and could correct it.

The seller gave him what he asked for. Zachary is at fault because he didn't specify his special needs and particular usage. The seller was not a mind-reader and therefore is not at fault.

But what if Zachary walked into the store wearing a scuba diving tee shirt, or was carrying some of his apparatus so that it would reasonably appear what he needed the pen for?

Then we would have a different result because he could successfully argue that the seller "should have known" his special use.

Here are four implied warranty cases:

MERCHANTABILITY: In *Denny v. Ford Motor Company, 639 N.Y.S.2d 250 (N.Y. App. 1995)*, the plaintiff purchased a Ford Bronco II SUV manufactured by the defendant for her every-day use. It was advertised in their marketing manual as being 'considered fashionable' for suburban driving and, 'particularly appealing to women who may be concerned about driving in snow and ice with their children.'"

While driving on a standard road, she slammed on the brakes to avoid a deer and the vehicle rolled over, severely injuring her. She sued for breach of implied warranty of merchantability, claiming the vehicle's high center of gravity, short wheelbase and suspension design created a higher risk of rollover accidents than customary passenger vehicles. Ford claimed the car was an off-road vehicle, not designed for use as a conventional passenger automobile on paved streets.

The trial court ruled for plaintiff and awarded damages of $1.2 million. On appeal, the decision was affirmed:

"The law implies a warranty by a manufacturer that places its product on the market that the product is reasonably fit for the ordinary purpose for which it was intended. If it is, in fact, defective and not reasonably fit to be used for its intended purpose, the warranty is breached . . . routine highway and street driving was the 'ordinary purpose' for which the Bronco II was sold and that it was not 'fit' – or safe – for that purpose."

FITNESS FOR HUMAN CONSUMPTION: In *Yong Cha Hong v. Marriott Corporation, 3 UCC Rep. Serv.2d 83 (D. Md. 1987)*, the plaintiff purchased take-out fried chicken from a Roy Rogers Family Restaurant owned by defendant. While eating a chicken wing, she bit into an object she thought was a worm and became ill. She sued the deep-pocket defendant for $500,000, claiming breach of implied warranty of merchantability.

After the defendant introduced evidence that the object in the chicken wing was a worm-like part of the chicken's aorta or trachea, it moved for summary judgment based upon the natural object test.

The court denied the defendant's motion:

"The reasonable expectation test has largely displaced the foreign-natural test adverted to by Marriott . . . The court cannot conclude that the presence of a trachea or an aorta in a fast food fried chicken wing is so reasonably to be expected as to render it merchantable, as a matter of law . . . Thus, a question is presented that precludes the grant of summary judgment."

In *Goodman v. Wendy's Foods, Inc., 142 S.E.2d 444 (N.C. 1992)*, plaintiff bought a double hamburger sandwich at a Wendy's restaurant and bit into a small bone that broke three of his teeth. He sued for breach of the implied warranty of fitness for human consumption.

Plaintiff claimed the 'expectation test' was the basis for recovery. The defendant claimed that the 'natural object test' precluded recovery. The trial court directed a verdict for the defendant, and the plaintiff appealed.

The court reversed based on the fact that; "a consumer should not reasonably have anticipated the substance's presence . . . notwithstanding the injury-causing substance's naturalness to the food . . ."

"Surely it is within the expectation of the consumer to find a bone in a T-bone steak; but just as certainly it is reasonable for a consumer not to expect to find a bone in a package of hamburger meat."

As an interesting sidelight to this case, a story in the news last year mentioned an unreported case where a Wendy's customer sued for breach of implied food warranty when he allegedly became ill when he saw that one of the chicken wings in his order looked like the head of a chicken. If you were the judge, how would you rule? Hint – the customer certainly did not reasonably expect this, but he never "consumed" anything.

FITNESS FOR SPECIAL USE: In *Mack Massey Motors, Inc. v. Garnica, 814 S.W.2d 167 (Tex. App. 1991)*, the plaintiff desired to buy a vehicle that was able to tow the 23-foot Airstream trailer she had ordered. When she went to defendant to inquire about buying a Jeep Cherokee, the sales manager investigated the Airstream's specifications and recommended the Jeep "as being suitable for the purposes Mrs. Garnica was seeking – that of towing the Airstream trailer she had on order."

After she bought the vehicle she had difficulty with slipping transmission when pulling the trailer, and eventually the drive shaft on the Jeep twisted apart. She then sued for breach of the implied warranty of fitness for a particular purpose. The jury returned a verdict in her favor and the defendant appealed.

The appellate court affirmed:

"A claim of warranty of fitness requires that the goods serve their particular purpose. The evidence supported the jury determination that the Jeep Cherokee simply was exceeding its towing capacity and that Massey Motors had misrepresented the fact that this was the proper vehicle suitable for towing the Airstream trailer."

The purchase of motor vehicles, which creates a large number of sales transactions and an equally large number of products liability claims, has an alternative warranty remedy provided by the statutory "Lemon Laws" of most states.

These laws provide procedures and remedies for consumers that have recurring problems with their vehicles, so that litigation can be avoided and their disputes decided by an administrative panel established for that particular purpose. The remedies can include refund of repair costs, reimbursement of expenses, incidental damages, rescission of the transaction and return of the purchase price, and in some cases the requirement that the dealer substitute a new vehicle.

Florida's *Chapter 681 Motor Vehicle Sales Warranties* is representative:

"Consumer means the purchaser, other than for purposes of resale, or the lessee of a motor vehicle primarily used for personal, family or household purposes.

Lemon Law rights period means the period ending 1 year after the date of the original delivery of a motor vehicle to a consumer or the first 12,000 miles of operation, whichever occurs first.

Motor vehicle means a new vehicle, . . . and includes a vehicle used as a demonstrator or leased vehicle, . . . but does not include vehicles run only upon tracks, off-road vehicles, trucks over 10,000 pounds gross vehicle weight, the living facilities of recreational vehicles, motorcycles, or mopeds.

After three attempts have been made to repair the same nonconformity or a motor vehicle has been out of service by reason of repair of one or more nonconformities for 20 cumulative calendar days, the consumer shall give written notification, by registered or express mail to the manufacturer, of the need for repair . . . in order to allow the manufacturer a final attempt to cure the nonconformity or nonconformities.

If the manufacturer, or its authorized service agent, cannot conform the motor vehicle to the warranty by repairing or correcting any nonconformity after a reasonable number of attempts, the manufacturer, within 40 calendar days, shall, in consideration of its receipt of payment of a reasonable offset for use, replace the motor vehicle with a replacement motor vehicle acceptable to the consumer, or repurchase the motor vehicle from the consumer and refund to the consumer the full purchase price, including all reasonably incurred collateral and incidental charges, less a reasonable offset for use. However, the consumer has an unconditional right to choose a refund rather than a replacement."

4. Seller's Disclaimers of Liability

A full product liability disclaimer is a contract clause that the seller inserts to release it from any liability. It is a form of exculpatory clause, similar to the "not responsible for loss or damage ..."cases we looked at in the chapter on illegality. A partial disclaimer limits the amount, procedures and type of recovery.

When we buy new merchandise, especially appliances, we find inside the carton a cellophane enclosed package of papers containing the product warranty. We rarely open it, but know it should be saved. We usually throw it in a kitchen drawer and never look at it again unless we have a problem with a product defect.

One of my class exercises involves the students each bringing in one of these warranty cards. They usually cover a wide spectrum of small low priced items to large expensive ones. They often include household appliances, home furnishings, sporting goods, apparel, jewelry and computer products. They may even include automobiles, with the booklet on "lemon law" protection provided by the State Department of Motor Vehicles.

They are all express warranties of one form or another, but upon inspection most all talk about *limitations* on how they are applicable and the seller's duties to repair or refund or pay damages.

Sellers of goods in today's commercial marketplace realize that their customers expect some form of express warranty, so they give it to them. But as they giveth, they taketh away in the limitations they impose. Consumers either don't mind or more probably don't even notice because these warranty cards are rarely read.

These disclaimers of liability by the seller usually impose certain requirements on the buyer to notify of defects and return goods within a specified time. They also list common exclusionary situations of non-liability:

- Product misuse or abuse
- Acts of god or other accidental damage
- Failure to follow instructions
- Improper installation
- Cosmetic damage
- Unauthorized repairs
- Costs of product removal or re-installation

Since competition requires these express warranties and buyers expect them, Sellers often protect themselves sometimes by limiting the express warranties by time and type and exclusions. But sellers also usually completely disclaim any legal responsibility for the implied warranties.

The UCC allows such disclaimers of liability for implied warranties so long as they are conspicuous and easy to understand, but imposes certain legal requirements:

- Merchantability – may be verbal or written, but must contain the word "merchantability"

- Fitness for special use – must be written, but no specific wording is required so long as its intent is clearly expressed

Do you think non-merchant sellers of goods should have any implied warranty liability? Do you think merchant sellers should be allowed to disclaim legal responsibility for implied warranties? Are the scales of justice evenly balanced with our current warranty laws?

DISCUSSION EXERCISES

1. Discuss where you would draw the liability dividing line of foreseeability in the four areas of products negligence.

2. Discuss areas where "caveat emptor" should be the governing law.

3. Discuss areas where "caveat venditor" should be the governing law.

4. Discuss the arguments pro and con regarding the doctrine of strict liability.

5. Discuss types of "natural objects" found in consumables that should and should not result in seller's liability.

CASE EXERCISES

THE LITTLE ENGINE THAT COULDN'T

In *Leavitt v. Monaco Coach Corporation, 616 N.W.2d 175 (Mich. App. 2000),* the plaintiff bought a new motor home from the defendant. While shopping for it he "informed defendant of his plans to use the coach extensively for travel in mountainous areas and of his wish to avoid problems he had experienced with rented vehicles that lacked sufficient engine and braking power."

"Almost immediately upon receiving the vehicle, and for the years leading up to this lawsuit, plaintiff complained that his coach could not maintain ordinary highway speeds going up steep hills and that the brakes were prone to overheating while going down."

Despite many warranty repairs, plaintiff concluded that the engine and brakes were not suitable and he sued for breach of implied warranty of fitness for a particular purpose.

ANALYSIS

The trial jury found for plaintiff and awarded damages of $33,730, after the judge denied defendant's motion for directed verdict. The appellate court affirmed, rejecting as not supported by the evidence the defendant's arguments that, "plaintiff did not explain his special needs for engine power with sufficient particularity to establish a warranty of fitness for a particular purpose."

"Where the seller at the time of contracting has reason to know any particular purpose for which the goods are required and that the buyer is relying on the seller's skill or judgment to select or furnish suitable goods, there is ... an implied warranty that the goods shall be fit for such purpose."

DEFUSE REPLAY

Sellers of goods have a continuing problem of when non-actionable preliminary sales talk becomes possible warranty liability. Most of the cases for breach of either express or implied warranty are caused by an overzealous seller trying to close the deal.

Because of the litigation risks when problems result from the goods that are sold, many sellers are now using disclaimers to protect themselves. If the defendant in this case had inserted the following clause in the sales contract with the plaintiff, the case of the plaintiff would probably not have survived a motion to dismiss:

"SELLER MAKES NO WARRANTY, EXPRESS OR IMPLIED, CONCERNING THE PRODUCT OR THE MERCHANTABILITY OR FITNESS THEREOF FOR ANY PURPOSE CONCERNING THE ACCURACY OF ANY INFORMATION PROVIDED BY THE SELLER."

CONCLUSION

Consider the multitude of legal principles that now protect the consumer-purchaser of defective goods. Alternate counts in the lawsuit could include:

I.   Breach of Contract
II.   Breach of Express Warranty
III.   Breach of Implied Warranty of Merchantability
IV.   Breach of Implied Warranty of Fitness for Human Consumption
V.   Breach of Implied Warranty of Fitness for a Particular Purpose
VI.   Strict Liability
VII.   Product Negligence

It is no wonder that the sales price of goods in this country has to factor in the potential liability expenses of damage claims, and that defendant-sellers lobby for tort reform while plaintiff-buyers seek even broader judicial protection.

CASE RESEARCH CYBERCISES

The following cases also relate to the material in this chapter and illustrate the types of disputes that may occur. For each one do the following written assignment:

1. Locate the case using the Internet (Lexis-Nexis, West or any other research cite which provides case transcripts).
2. Briefly summarize what it was about – the nature of the dispute involved.
3. Who won at the trial court level? Who won at the appellate level?
4. Who won if there was a third level of Supreme Court review?
5. What were the legal rules of law and the reasoning used to reach the final decision?
6. Do you agree or disagree with the decision, and explain why?
7. What business law time bomb(s) were involved?
8. Could the time bomb(s) have been avoided by structuring the transaction differently? Discuss.
9. Could the adverse effects of the time bomb(s) have been defused by a different reaction or response by the affected party? Discuss.
10. Replay the facts of the case to achieve a different successful result.

1. *Daughtrey v. Ashe, 413 S.E.2d 336 (Va. 1992)(express warranty was created by a diamond expert's quality appraisal).*
2. *In Re L.B. Trucking, Inc., 23 UCC Rep. Ser.2d 1093 (U.S. Bankr. Ct. 1994) (multiple express and implied warranties were breached in the furnishing of improper herbicides that destroyed plaintiff's harvest).*
3. *Rauscher v. General Motors Corporation, 905 S.W.2d 158 (Mo. App. 1995)(recurring problems with plaintiff's new Buick automobile that continued for five years and resulted in the stalled car being struck by another vehicle stated a proper claim of strict liability to be heard by a jury).*

NOTES

SPECIAL RULES FOR E-COMMERCE AND CYBERLAW

"Anyone with access to the Internet may take advantage of a wide variety of communication and information retrieval methods. These methods are constantly evolving and difficult to categorize precisely...Taken together, these tools constitute a unique medium – known to its users as 'cyberspace' – located in no particular geographical location but available to anyone, anywhere in the world, with access to the Internet."
Reno v. ACLU, 521 U.S. 844 (1997).

1. LEGAL OVERVIEW

We have experienced dramatic technological advancements during the last century in every area of human involvement, including but not limited to population movement (rural country to urban city), transportation (trains, planes and automobiles), basic communications (telephone, radio, television, and movies), life comforts (air conditioning, paper copiers, faxes, cell phones), medicine (antibiotics, surgical techniques, organ transplants), alternative medicine (holistic health), nutrition (vitamins, food supplements), food supply (agribusiness) and many others.

As these innovations changed the structure of our society the legal system slowly responded with laws, rules and regulations adapted to the areas where disputes occurred so as to try to maintain the orderly framework of legally permissible, predictable and enforceable acts, usage and behavior.

But nothing prepared us, our legislators, or the judicial system for the way our lives have changed and our need for governing laws due to the Internet revolution. Seemingly isolated technology links resulted in our current computerized world. It is an interesting story of how the wheels of progress were set in motion:

- In the late 1960's the U.S. Defense Department researched military communication using massive computers in their DARPA network.

- In the early 1980's they joined with the National Science Foundation to extend this capability to the scientific community, resulting in the NSFNET that joined the scientific and academic communities.

- These two networks merged in the late 1980's and we had the earliest version of the Internet.

- Then in mid 1990 Congress authorized use of this network for commercial purposes.

- In the early 1990's a Swiss scientist designed the technical protocols, coding languages and hyperlinks necessary for creation and linkage of informational and commercial web sites, birthing the World Wide Web.

This chain of events led in the late 1990's to an explosion of usage resulting in our current global and instantaneous method of communication and commerce that is accessible to everyone through a network of millions of computers. It is truly mind-boggling!

We call it the Internet (interrelated network), and it operates in an area we call Cyberspace. It is the superhighway of electronic communication, information gathering and dispersal. It is the worldwide office for merchants and non-merchants to conduct their business, and the marketplace of the world for electronic commerce.

"The Internet is the world's largest computer network (a network consisting of two or more computers linked together to share electronic mail and files). The Internet is actually a network of thousands of independent networks, containing several million 'host' computers that provide information services. An estimated 25 million individuals have some form of Internet access, and this audience is doubling each year. The Internet is a cooperative venture, owned by no one, but regulated by several volunteer agencies." *MTV Networks v. Curry, 867 F.Supp. 202 (S.D.N.Y. 1994).*

With the advent of the Internet, our legal system found itself totally unprepared for its unique needs. Our existing laws on contracts and sales, though refined over the years and usually effective in normal transactions, were inadequate in many areas of this new way of doing business electronically. New laws were needed and, as e-commerce disputes began to be litigated, court decisions were rendered in many areas that changed the old rules. In addition, the unique domain of Cyberspace required a uniform set of laws to govern nationwide, rather than a series of inconsistent state laws. This also took time and effort.

Many disputes also arose because the business community is historically slow to react to technological advances, such as paper copiers, fax transmission of documents, office computerization, and especially the potential opportunities for paperless contracts, continuous worldwide selling, and marketplace presence through Web sites.

Internet Law alone can be the current subject of an entire book, running the gamut of legal issues from business torts to intellectual property rights to electronic speech rights to consumer protection to securities, taxation and Cybercrime. It is in a process of early evolution, as rules of law for off-line transactions are gradually adapted to its needs.

Therefore, the purpose of this chapter is just to highlight some of the important areas of electronic commerce and Cyberlaw that relate to our focus on contracts and sales law. Since Internet laws and court decisions are so new, the examples used in this chapter will be based upon current legislation and recently decided cases, rather than hypothetical situations.

Some of the major areas of digital abuse that have caused legal disputes and generated legislative and judicial Cyberlaw responses are:

- **Cybersquatting** – the bad-faith registration and resale of a popular or brand-related domain name. Also known as cyber kidnapping and cyber extortion.

- **Typosquatting** – intentional mis-typing of high-volume website names to divert Internet traffic and generate ad revenue for the typo-site.

- **Deep Linking** – creating a link that bypasses a website's home page to confuse consumers, divert traffic to rival websites and infringe copyright, trademark and database rights.

- **Cybersmearing** – negative portrayal of an organization, product or trademark by a disgruntled competitor, employee or customer. Also known as cyber-defamation.

- **Counterfeiting** – creation of copycat websites to market unauthorized products at discounted prices, infringing logos and distinctive brands.

- **Hyperlinking** – linking websites without authorization, violating exclusive rights to market, distribute or display designated files to the public.

- **Meta Tags** – tag a website's distinctive catch phrases in header and/or body codes designed specifically to be picked up by search engines to divert customers from legitimate websites to competitive or defamatory locations.

- **Keying** – banner ads offered by search engines on well-known websites that attempt to attract users to the advertiser's unrelated site.

2. RECENT ORIGIN OF CYBERLAW

Reno v. ACLU, 521 U.S. 844 (1997), was the first case to be heard by the U.S. Supreme Court that tested governmental limits to regulate the Internet. The legal question before it was whether the Communications Decency Act, which created criminal liability for the on-line transmission of 'indecent' and 'offensive' material to minors, violated First Amendment free speech protection.

The Act created a defense if defendants took effective action to block the offensive material. The practical problem that resulted in this test case was that available technology was unable to differentiate between filtering out the material to minors or adults, so that the law restricted both proper and improper transmissions.

The trial court found the Act unconstitutional under the First Amendment. The Court affirmed the lower court, and in the process accurately predicted what had proved to be the Internet revolution:

"(T)he Internet . . . provides a relatively unlimited, low-cost capacity for communication of all kinds. The Government estimates that 'as many as 40 million people use the Internet today, and that figure is expected to grow to 200 million by 1999.' This dynamic, multifaceted category of communications includes not only traditional print and news services, but also audio, video, and still images, as well as interactive, real-time dialogue. Through the use of chat rooms, any person with a phone line can become a town crier with a voice that resonates farther then it could from any soapbox. Through the use of Web pages, mail exploders, and newsgroups, the same individual can become a pamphleteer."

2. SURFING THE NET

Let's briefly review how we travel in cyberspace. Internet addresses are constructed using a domain name system (DNS) that allows users to enter a word alias electronic name that has been previously licensed to an individual or a company, and be forwarded to that specific numeric Internet address. We navigate the web by first "going online". This requires the user to register with one of the many online service providers (ISP). This provides the opportunity for electronic mail communications (e-mail) of a personal or business nature between the individual addresses created by the parties, coded to their ISP.

Companies and individuals now routinely create their own Web sites, which may be passive for informational purposes or actively used as their commercial stores or personal offices located in Cyberspace and accessible 24-7 throughout the world. These Web sites consist of Web pages created by the parties that may also contain links to other Web pages and Web sites, thus creating a continual sub-network of flowing information and commerce within the worldwide web.

We can access information and visit Web locations by entering the information category or desired domain name in one of the commercial search engines, or enter the specific hyperlink address in our computer browser.

3. DOMAIN NAMES

Trademark issues on the Internet first arose with domain names. They are the technical identifying names for a Website's Internet electronic address.

They identify the name and location in cyberspace of a particular user, and are critical in e-commerce. The domain name is how the public identifies and finds the user on the World Wide Web. It is the offline equivalent of one's Trademark.

The objective of domain name licensing is to register the prefix name most easily recognizable to the public, such as ge (general electric), gm (general motors), and ibm (international business machines). This is accomplished through many domain registries created with identifying suffixes such as .com, .net (commercial use), .edu (educational /research facilities), .gov (governmental facilities), .org (non-profit groups/trade associations), .info(resource site), .biz (small-business sites), .name (individuals), .aero (aviators), and .pro (professionals).

Since the Internet began as a governmental project, the assigning of domain names was originally under federal control. However, in the late 1990's, assigning and management of domain names was privatized to the Internet Corporation for Assigned Names and Numbers (ICANN), which oversees the entire system even though there are many private registries for licensing domain names.

As we entered the new millennium of 2000, the exploding popularity of the Internet led to lack of domain name availability under the traditional addresses and many additional suffixes were made available by ICANN to registrants.

DOMAIN NAMES MUST COMPLY WITH REGISTRY STANDARDS

*Ex: In the case of *National A-1 Advertising, Inc. v. Network Solution, Inc., 121 F.Supp.2d 156 (N.H. Dist. Ct. 2000)*, the plaintiff (National) sought to register 30 domain names with the defendant (Network), the then sole domain registry company. Network had a decency policy for these second-level domain names that prohibited the usage of the profanity that comedian George Carlin made famous – the 7 words banned by the FCC in broadcast media.

Their registration process automatically filtered out and rejected these "disapproved names" submitted by National because they contained the restricted strings of letters. National claimed they were entitled to 1st amendment rights of free speech because Network was performing a "governmental" action. Network countered claiming its actions were purely as a private business and thus valid.

ANALYSIS

The court first presented a detailed historical analysis of the Internet and how it works under headings of, "I. Government's role in the Evolution of the Internet," "II. The Cooperative Agreement and Network Solutions' Authority," and "III. Navigating the Internet."

It then attempted to apply legal tests from traditional disputes:

SPECIAL RULES FOR E-COMMERCE AND CYBERLAW 403

"Because of the relative novelty of the Internet, there is very little precedent applying traditional and familiar legal principles to its operation." The court ruled in favor of Network, allowing it to reject the registration applications, notwithstanding the fact that the rejection might adversely affect the business of the applicant.

"Standing alone, however, the mere fact that plaintiffs might, as a result of Network solutions' conduct, realize less Internet traffic to their sites by people typing in assumed domain names, does not convert an otherwise invalid claim into one of constitutional significance . . . the First Amendment does not guarantee anyone a profit."

The court also noted how the government's role in the Internet was intentionally being reduced and turned over to private businesses, so that under this current trend of how the business is conducted, Network was not a government actor and not subject to the claims made by the plaintiff.

DEFUSE REPLAY

When National was advised of the rejection of their application, what did they do? They reacted with a "let's sue them" approach, and spent thousands of dollars in lawyer's fees and countless hours of their own time, not to mention the stress and bad publicity surrounding the matter, in misguided constitutional litigation.

They should have just changed the wording of their domain names a bit – enough to avoid the rejection filters of Network, but still leave the phonetic name intact. For example, the offending s-h-i-t could be s-h-m-i-t; the prohibited f-u-c-k could be f-o-r-k, and so on. A play on words is often more effective than the actual words anyway, and just a little bit of creative thought could have defused this problem.

The registration procedure is simple. With an on-line visit to a domain Registry - name availability, cost and duration information, and completion of the process is a click of the mouse away. The cost is so nominal now (as low as $3.95 for one year per assigned name) anyone can register one or more names.

In the early days of the Internet, before mainstream businesses understood the commercial advantages of this new technology, the registration of domain names was on a "first come – first served" basis. Many young and enterprising persons who realized the tremendous potentialities of doing business in cyberspace became "cyber-millionaires" by engaging in the then lawful practice of "cybersquatting." It was the domain name registration of well-known trademarked companies with the intention to sell the names back to their business users for as large a profit as possible. Unlike traditional trademark law that required the names to be actually used in commerce by the registrants, early Internet law had no such requirement.

These people were called cyber-squatters because they were not doing anything with the names except sitting on them, and engaging in cyber-extortion by kidnapping the well-known names while waiting for their real owners/users to pay the premiums demanded. There were no legal prohibitions because the non-existent Internet laws lagged far behind the emerging world of high-tech. Registered trademark name owners were researched, used as a basis for domain name registrations by young entrepreneurs, such as gm.com, exxon.com, jerryseinfeld.com, and wallstreetjournal.com , and then assigned back to the actual companies for large windfall profits. .

In late 1999, Congress finally addressed the problem by passing the "Anti-Cybersquatting Consumer Protection Act (ACPA), which legally prevents do main registration of well-known names of companies or persons if done in *bad faith*. It was specifically aimed at parties who register Internet domain names of famous people/companies and then hold them hostage by demanding ransom payments. A claim of trademark infringement under offline laws was unavailable because either the name in question had never been formally registered or there was no distribution of goods or services as required by law. That aspect of the intention of the registrant reflects the view of the legislators that the prohibited parties were cyber-pirates who were extorting money to free the names they had kidnapped.

Factors tending to show bad faith are:

- Multiple registrations by one registrant
- Solicitation of sale or assignment by the registrant for an inflated price
- Lack of name similarity with the name registered
- Lack of an active related business or personal connection

The legal sanctions imposed by the Act included money damages and injunctive relief, but questions arose as to the problems of civil lawsuits that would be public, time-consuming and very costly.

A Uniform Dispute Resolution Policy (UDRP) was adopted by ICANN limiting the legal recourse of all its domain name registrants to arbitration before the World Intellectual Property Organization (WIPO), an agency of the United Nations, and several private dispute resolution companies.

FIRST REGISTRATION OF A DOMAIN NAME MAY NOT BE BINDING

In its first ruling under the UDRP, styled *World Wrestling Federation v. Bosman,* the WIPO heard a complaint filed by the WWF, claiming that defendant had registered "worldwrestlingfederation.com"in bad faith as a cybersquatter, and solicited its sale to them. The WWF owned a prior registered trademark for that name under federal law for a number of years prior to Bosman's domain name registration. WWF demanded cancellation of Bosman's rights in the name and its transfer to them.

ANALYSIS

The arbitrator ruled in favor of the WWF, stating that no legal ownership rights existed in the defendant, and assigned the name to them, citing the various factual indicia of bad faith that included the solicitation and the fact that defendant had no personal or family connection to the registered name. He was merely trying to take advantage of the economics of the situation.

DEFUSE REPLAY

Interestingly enough, had Bosman registered prior to passage of the Act he would have faced no legal impediment to his scheme, and the WWF would no doubt have paid his price. Bosman would have won under the priority doctrine of "first in time, first in right". After the Act, a domain name registration that is valid on its face may still be cancelled on grounds of cyber-squatting, but the complaining party must prove the required legal aspects of "bad faith".

But there still appears to be a loophole in the Act. While it clearly protects names of well-known persons and companies, there is no prohibition on using generic names. If each time a specific name is registered, its class or category name were also registered, there would be an effective back-up position. Examples are kraft.com with cheese.com, pepsi.com with soda.com, and budweiser.com with beer.com. If Bosman would have registered "wrestling.com" with his specific domain name, he might have been counting profits instead of losses.

Examples: After passage of ACPA, the domain name juliaroberts.com was successfully recovered by the famous actress who sued the registered holder. However the singer Sting found sting.com already registered he was unable to reclaim it because the word "sting" is generic and can be found in the dictionary, thus disqualifying it from protection under the Act.

There may also be a jurisdictional loophole in the Act:

In *Harrods Ltd. v. Sixty Internet Domain Names, 302 F.3d 214 (4th Cir. 2000)*, plaintiff sued under the Act, alleging that the defendant Argentinean company registered with Virginia based Network Solution, Inc. (now VeriSign) 60 domain names such as "harrodsbank", harrodsshopping" and "harrodsvirtual" in bad faith, infringing upon and diluting its U.S. registered "Harrods" trademark.

The trial court found that 54 of the names were registered in bad faith, and ruled they were therefore forfeited and returned to the plaintiff. The appellate court affirmed and expanded the lower court's ruling, so that now the Act's jurisdiction provisions may be used not only to stop bad-faith Internet domain name registration, but also to combat trademark infringement.

Rather than having to obtain personal jurisdiction over the offending party in Argentina, the court allowed the in-rem filing of infringement and dilution claims by going to the U.S. jurisdiction where they were registered.

In *Mattel, Inc. v. Barbie-Club.com, 310 F.3d 293 (2nd Cir. 2002)*, plaintiff sued to cancel 57 Internet sites that allegedly sought to "cybersquat" on their "Barbie" trademarks. Because it could not obtain personal jurisdiction over the defendants, it sought (similar to the *Harrods Case*) to invoke the Act's in-rem jurisdiction in the U.S. venue of New York where it had deposited its trademark registration certificates.

The trial court and appellate court dismissed the suit, and ruled that individual lawsuits would have to be filed in each jurisdiction where the registering domain-name authority was located. In this case, unlike the *Harrods case*, most of the contested domain names were registered in states other than New York.

"Rather, it is the presence of the domain name itself … in the judicial district in which the registry or registrar is located that anchors the in rem action and satisfies due process and international comity."

The loophole that needs to be closed in utilizing in-rem jurisdiction to avoid the necessity of acquiring personal jurisdiction is that of multi-state domain name registries. Since separate lawsuits have to be brought in each state of registration, the economics of that litigation prevents effective action.

Why not amend the Act to provide, "in cases of multiple domain name registrations, suit for claims of bad-faith domain name registration and/or trademark infringement/dilution may be properly filed in any one of the registry jurisdictions and be binding upon all registrations that are found to have violated the Act."

The Anticybersquatting law applies only to disputes that occur after its enactment in 1999. However, it was deemed to have retroactive application in the unusual Pennsylvania case of *Schmidheiny v. Weber, 319 F.3d 581 (3rd Cir. 2003)*, where a billionaire sued an alleged cybersquatter who offered to sell him the Internet domain with the billionaire's name followed by dot-com.

The trial court dismissed the lawsuit because the offending name had been registered by Weber more than nine months before the law took effect. But the appellate court reversed due to the fact that Weber had re-registered the name in June' 2000, "an action within the purview of the Anti-Cybersquatting Act."

But in the case of *TMI, Inc. v. Maxwell, 368 F.3d 433 (5th Cir. 2004)*, a website designed to be critical of a company that specifically used its name was ruled not to violate the company's trademark and was not considered cybersquatting because there was no "commercial intent" by the creator of the site.

TMI built homes under the name TrendMaker Homes and had a corresponding domain name. Defendant was an unhappy customer who created a website with the company name and used a similar logo. His site shared his negative experience and asked site visitors to share their information about dealings with the company. But he never tried to sell the site to TMI and didn't accept any ads or financial contributions. It unsuccessfully sued him for allegedly violating the Lanham Act and the ACPA.

Another prohibited domain name practice is "Typosquatting". This involves the intentional misspelling of words in domain names to siphon off Internet traffic from its intended destination to another site.

In *National Association of Professional Baseball Leagues, Inc. v. Zuccarini (WIPO 2003)*, the defendant intentionally registered "minorleaugebaseball.com, and the commonly made misspelling caused Internet traffic for the correct site (professional baseball's farm clubs in U.S. and Canada) to be directed to defendant's pornographic Web site. Plaintiff had registered "minorleaguebaseball.com and "minorleaguebaseball.org" in 1996 and 2000 respectively, and received various trademark registrations in 2001.

Defendant had a lengthy history of registering domain names using the trademarks of others with slight misspellings, to increase Internet traffic to his sites. A WIPO arbitration panel ruled for plaintiff, and directed that defendant transfer the disputed domain name back to plaintiff.

"Typosquatting is inherently parasitic and of itself bad faith" because the intent is to "siphon off traffic from its intended destination, by preying on Internauts who make common typing errors."

The panel also noted that bad faith was further reinforced by the defendant's past conduct of directing traffic to his pornographic sites, and his "porn squatting" where he registered websites under a porn star's name without authorization.

4. INTERNET STATUTES & CONTRACT LAW

There are two Uniform statutory laws created in 1999, governing the formation, performance and enforcement of certain aspects of electronic contracts:

- UCITA (Uniform Computer Information Transactions Act of 1999) - regulates agreements to create, transfer or license computer information and software.

- UETA (Uniform Electronic Transactions Act of 1999) – accords electronic signatures and electronic records the same status as written signatures and paper contracts.

- E-SIGN (Electronic Signatures in Global and National Commerce Act of 2000) upgrades UETA, so that e-contracts cannot be denied legal enforceability because of electronic delivery or signatures, and electronic signatures can be legally notarized.

The first two statutes do not actually replace existing contract law and do not officially become the law of a state until formally adopted. (UCITA has currently been approved in Virginia and Maryland, UETA in 18 states, and E-SIGN in 40 states). But they nevertheless are guidelines that may be followed on a case-by-case basis, similar to the Restatement of Contracts and the UCC before it achieved statewide adoption. E-SIGN is also a federal law that has nationwide application.

While they usually follow the Common Law or the UCC rules for off-line contract transactions, the main differences in the Internet statutes are:

- Electronic acceptance of an offer is not effective until received – the reasonable medium rule is not applicable

- Counteroffers are not effective against electronic agent's offers, like voice mail, and Web page order systems - a contract is formed upon placing the basic order and any additional conditions imposed are to be disregarded

- Electronic records of a transaction may be clarified by prior dealings or trade usage – not restricted by the parol evidence rule

- Electronic records of a transaction are in compliance with the Statute of Frauds writing and signing requirements

- Transactions for $5,000 or more (and licenses for one year or more) must be electronically authenticated – less than the Statute of Frauds dollar limit of $500 or more

- Tender of performance of an electronic document occurs when it is available for download from the licensor's Web site

- Unilateral electronic contracting mistakes do not bind the consumer if there is prompt notification to the other party of the error - contrary to the non-cancellation of such off-line contracts. But this does not apply to relieve consumers if the other party requires a click-on or similar method to confirm the order before it is finalized, and the consumer erroneously approves

- Electronic self-help stated in the agreement can be used after 15 days prior notice in the event of a licensee breach in the usage or payment for licensed information or software, through the activation of embedded disabling commands.

But if software is improperly disabled, the licensor may be liable for damages. The judicial remedies are mandatory in non-electronic commercial transactions.

- Statute of limitations for breach of a licensing agreement is one year from discovery, but not more than 5 years from the actual breach event – most UCC limitation periods are shorter.

- Warranties of non-infringement, non-interference and informational accuracy apply to a license of informational rights – in addition to the implied warranties of non-electronic transactions

- Disclaimer of electronic warranties is allowed by the licensor-seller if they specify by individual name, or collectively by using the words, "as-is", "with all faults", or similar language

- Licensor's breach of a software licensing agreement may be "cured" without the licensee's needed consent:

  1. Before expiration of time for contract performance
  2. After expiration, if completable within a reasonable time
  3. If completed before licensee cancels the contract

  Notice that (1) above is the same rule as the UCC, so long as the cure can be completed before the expiration date. (2) and (3) differ from UCC cure after the required date that requires the buyer's permission whether or not the seller actually completes the cure.

- Licensee has the right to "cover" the licensor's breach by entering into a substitute electronic transaction, and recover as damages the value of the promised performance, or the difference between it and the cover cost – this is essentially the same protection as the UCC.

5. CLICK-WRAP CONTRACTS

Computer software programs are an essential part of today's e-commerce. They have been created for most all aspects of everyday business and are customarily offered for sale and usage with a requirement that the customer first accept and agree to the terms of their licensing agreement.

When retail software is purchased and delivered, the licensing agreement is usually referred to on the exterior carton and enclosed with the software disks inside a plastic or cellophane package – a shrink-wrap license.

This license is also encoded on the software disks and scrolls out on the user's screen when the program is opened, requiring a mouse click-on "I accept", before usage is allowed. The acceptance click creates the legal contract, "wraps" around all the terms, and the user is legally bound whether or not they were read or understood.

License agreements customarily include the common contract dispute clauses for (1) forum selection (where to sue), (2) choice of law (what rules that court must apply), (3) choice of remedy (arbitration rather than litigation), and (4) disclaimers of liability (no warranties or money damages).

Even if the user is able to add additional requests, instructions or conditions, under UCITA they do not create a counteroffer, as would be the case under the UCC in non-electronic contracts.

ALL TERMS IN SHRINKWRAP LICENSES ARE BINDING

In the case of *ProCD Inc. v. Zeidenberg, 86 F.3d 1447 (7th Cir. 1996),* the plaintiff compiled information from more than 3,000 telephone directories into a computer database that it sold on CD-ROM discs. It spent considerable sums to create and maintain this product, which was sold at a high price to commercial users. It marketed a low price version to the general public for personal, non-commercial usage only, as specified in the use restrictions encoded and detailed in its shrink wrapped disks, which appeared on the computer screen every time the program ran.

"The database in SelectPhone (trademark) cost more than $10 million to compile and is expensive to keep current." The product package stated the software was subject to restrictions included in the enclosed license. The license terms were in the printed manual inside the product box as well as encoded on the disks.

Defendant bought the consumer product but then violated the restrictions by forming a company and reselling the information to the public on the Internet at a price below what plaintiff charged its commercial customers. ProCD sought an injunction to prevent the illegal usage. Zeidenberg defended saying he was not bound by the license since the product was sold to him without requiring his specific acceptance.

ANALYSIS

"The 'shrinkwrap license' gets its name from the fact that retail software packages are covered in plastic or cellophane 'shrinkwrap,' and some vendors, though not ProCD, have written licenses that become effective as soon as the customer tears the wrapping from the package."

The court ruled in favor of the Plaintiff, based upon principles of basic contract law, stating that the defendant's conduct in using the product knowing it was subject to some license restrictions bound him to its terms. This was acceptance by conduct. The defendant's argument was rejected by the court, which mentioned by analogy other common purchases of consumer goods like computers, where the buyer makes the purchase, brings the merchandise home and then reads the enclosed shrink-wrapped information for the first time.

"Transactions in which the exchange of money precedes the communication of detailed terms are common . . . (insurance, airline tickets, concert tickets, drugs, consumer goods) To use the ticket is to accept the terms, even terms that in retrospect are disadvantageous . . . And that is what happened. ProCD proposed a contract that a buyer would accept by *using* the software after having an opportunity to read the license at leisure. This Zeidenberg did. He had no choice, because the software splashed the license on the screen and would not let him proceed without indicating acceptance."

Note that this case did not involve a click-wrap, "I accept" situation, and was decided pre-UCITA. Most computer software is now coded so that the opening of the program accesses a license agreement that must be scrolled from beginning to end and clicked-on for acceptance before it will function. This is a more direct expression of acceptance of all the terms, and the user is bound. Read the terms and if they are not acceptable, don't click your approval.

DEFUSE REPLAY

Let's update this case to post UCITA –1999, and change the facts to include a click-wrap acceptance feature that does not require the user to first scroll through all the terms. Under these modified facts, Zeidenberg could win, arguing that UCITA's requirement for these types of contracts that the user "manifest his assent" requires a *knowing acceptance of the terms.* He could argue that since the software seller allowed usage without scrolling the terms, he never assented to them, and the seller had waived its rights. He could also claim that the "acceptance by conduct" rules for off-line contracts were not applicable under UCITA.

Most Internet license disputes involving "click-wrap" and "shrink-wrap" licenses seem to uniformly enforce the agreements in question:

- A forum selection clause contained in the on-line subscriber contract of MSN was enforceable, where the plaintiffs clicked on the "I agree" prompt at the end of the scrolled agreement. *Caspi, et al v. Microsoft, 732 A.2d 528 (N.J. 1999).*

- The purchaser's use of defendant's software that contained a limitation of recoverable damages to only the purchase price was enclosed in a shrink-wrap license accompanying the software.

This was acceptance of the limitation and it was enforceable against the purchaser. *Mortenson v. Timberline Software Corporation, 998 P.2d 305 (Wash. 2000).*

The following recent case is, however, reminiscent of the *ProCD Inc. Case*, in its use of "browse-wrap", rather than "shrink-wrap" or "click-wrap" licenses, and its result favoring the customer.

In *Specht v. Netscape Communications Corp, 306 F.3d 17 (2d Cir. 2002)*, the plaintiff and others sued Netscape and its parent company, America Online, Inc., alleging that usage of its free SmartDownload plug-in software transmits private information about the user's file transfer activity. The plaintiffs claimed this transmission, which included other downloads made from the Internet, violated Federal laws, including the Electronic Communications Act and the Computer Fraud and Abuse Act.

The defendants moved to compel arbitration, pursuant to a binding arbitration clause in their license agreement that also required the losing party to pay all court costs. They asserted that "the mere act of downloading" indicated assent, because the user was not required to click-on or view the license to proceed.

The trial court ruled for the plaintiffs on the arbitration issue and the appellate court affirmed. It found the license to be more like a "browse-wrap" license, in which only an icon notice appears on the Web site for download, and this could be accomplished without viewing or even being aware of the existence of the license.

"Where consumers are urged to download free software at the immediate click of a button, a reference to the existence of license terms on a submerged screen is not sufficient to place consumers on inquiry or constructive notice of those terms ... We disagree with the proposition that a reasonably prudent offeree in plaintiff's position would necessarily have known or learned of the existence of the SmartDownload license agreement prior to acting ... Reasonably conspicuous notice of the existence of contract terms and unambiguous manifestation of assent to those terms by consumers is essential if electronic bargaining is to have integrity and credibility."

6. PERSONAL JURISDICTION IN CYBERSPACE

The filing of a lawsuit against a non-resident defendant invariably results in a motion to dismiss filed on grounds that the court lacks jurisdiction over the person of the defendant. This is especially true when the defendant is a corporation formed in a foreign state and doing business nationwide. Courts try to determine if there is a physical presence of some kind within the forum state.

If the defendant loses, it must incur the time, expense and inconvenience of defending itself in a foreign court. Often this risk of non-local court jurisdiction will induce the defendant to settle on terms favorable to the plaintiff. If however the motion is granted, and the plaintiff must bring suit in the defendant's home court, settlement will often occur in the defendant's favor.

The minimum contacts test of doing business that is used to determine if a non – resident defendant is subject to the jurisdiction of a local court is complicated when the business contacts involve a web site presence in the state. Distinctions are made depending upon the type of business conducted:

- Active web site – sales of goods are offered and can be completed on-line
- Partially active web site – interactive usage with password access
- Passive web site – the user is a viewer/listener of information content posted on a site with unlimited access

The more active the web presence in the state, the easier it is for a court to allow jurisdiction over the person of the defendant. Operating a website for profit, whether it be via direct sales or links to other web sites, will subject the site owner to jurisdiction in the home state of a plaintiff-customer. However, there are still conflicting court decisions on these issues. Try to differentiate the original landmark cases of *Zippo and Bensusan*.

In *Zippo Manufacturing Company v. Zippo Dot Com, Inc., 952 F.Supp 1119 (W.D.PA. 1997)*, the plaintiff-maker of the famous Zippo lighters was a Pennsylvania Corporation that sued a California Corporation protesting its sale of domain names using the word "zippo". Suit was filed in Pennsylvania, and the defendant argued that personal jurisdiction was lacking because they owned no property, had no employees and maintained no physical presence in that state.

The court ruled that it had personal jurisdiction over the defendant, using a "sliding scale test" of the extent of contacts with Pennsylvania (active to passive) that resulted from the activities of the defendant. It noted that, "the likelihood that personal jurisdiction can be constitutionally exercised is directly proportionate to the nature and quality of commercial activity that an entity conducts over the Internet."

"At one end of the spectrum are situations where a defendant clearly does business over the Internet (personal jurisdiction granted) . . . At the opposite end are situations where a defendant has simply posted information on an Internet Web site which is accessible to users in foreign jurisdictions (personal jurisdiction denied) . . . The middle ground is occupied by interactive Web sites where a user can exchange information with the host computer. In these cases, the exercise of jurisdiction is determined by examining the level of interactivity and commercial nature of the exchange of information that occurs on the Web site."

In reaching its decision that the defendant was clearly operating an active Web site, the court noted, "It is undisputed that Dot Com contracted to supply Internet news services to approximately 3,000 Pennsylvania residents and also entered into agreements with seven Internet access providers in Pennsylvania."

In *Bensusan Restaurant Corporation v. King & The Blue Note, 937 F.Supp. 295 (S.D.N.Y. 1996),* the case involved two blues clubs that both used the name "The Blue Note". Defendant used it first in 1980 in Missouri when he opened his small club. Plaintiff used it in 1985 when it opened its much larger New York club and registered the name as a federal trademark. Both parties maintained web sites.

Defendant's site was posted on a computer server in Missouri to promote his club. It had a disclaimer that stated, "The Blue Note's Cyberspot should not be confused with one of the world's finest jazz clubs, the Blue Note, located in the heart of New York's Greenwich Village." It also had a hyperlink to the New York site.

Plaintiff sued in New York for trademark infringement, and the defendant moved to dismiss for lack of personal jurisdiction. The trial court granted defendant's motion, and the appellate court affirmed on the grounds that the defendant did not conduct business in New York.

"An act of infringement (if one existed) would have occurred in Missouri, not New York . The mere fact that a person can gain information on the allegedly infringing product is not the equivalent of a person advertising, promoting, selling or otherwise making an effort to target its product in New York."

"King, like numerous others, simply created a Web site and permitted anyone who could find it to access it. Creating a site, like placing a product into the stream of commerce, may be felt nationwide – or even worldwide – but, without more, it is not an act purposefully directed toward the forum state . . . There is in fact no suggestion that King has any presence of any kind in New York other than the Web site that can be accessed worldwide."

The court also distinguished the case of *Compuserve, Inc. v. Patterson, 89 F.3d 1257 (6th Cir. 1996),* in which the court found personal jurisdiction proper in Ohio over an Internet user from Texas who subscribed to an Ohio based network service.

The user had "reached out" from Texas by entering into a separate agreement with the Ohio service to sell his software over the Internet, and filled a number of orders there.

This personal jurisdiction test of being active in soliciting business was also used in *Minnesota v. Granite Gate Resorts, 568 N.W.2d 715 (Minn. App. 1997),* where a Nevada Internet gaming company was subject to in personam jurisdiction in Minnesota in a lawsuit for consumer fraud.

Its Web site claimed to "provide sports fans with a legal way to bet on sporting events from anywhere in the world, 24 hours a day!" and listed a toll-free phone number to call for information which, when accessed, confirmed to the caller that it was legal to place bets in Minnesota. The court ruled that the defendant's active solicitation of local consumers furnished sufficient minimum contacts for in personam jurisdiction.

A later series of cases further refined the rules regarding whether or not a non-resident Internet defendant can be sued in the particular jurisdiction chosen by the plaintiff in a Cyberlaw dispute. No longer is the legal distinction one of whether the website in question is an active commercial site or a passive informational site:

1. In *Molnlycke Health Care v. Dumex Medical Surgical Products, 64 F. Supp.2d 448 (E.D.Pa. 1999)*, a Swedish Corporation with a subsidiary in Pennsylvania sued a Canadian corporation in Pennsylvania for alleged patent infringement of a wound care invention that it advertised and sold in the U.S. through its Internet commercial website. Defendant moved to dismiss asserting lack of personal jurisdiction because, "it does not have a regular place of business in Pennsylvania and that less than one per cent of its sales occurred in Pennsylvania. Dumex also states that it has never sold the allegedly infringing product in Pennsylvania."

The court denied defendants' motion to dismiss. After reviewing the "sliding scale of jurisdiction" established in the *Zippo* case, discussed in our text, it went on to say: "This court, however, disagrees with plaintiff's more fundamental premise (that doing business over the Internet confers worldwide jurisdiction) and holds that the establishment of a website through which customers can order products does not, on its own, suffice to establish general jurisdiction... The court believes that Dumex's websites are akin to (a) general advertising campaign: while the websites are available in every state, they are not necessarily targeted towards every state. Plaintiff has made no showing that defendant's websites targeted Pennsylvania."

2. In *Hurley v. Cancun Playa Oasis, 1999 U.S. Dist. LEXIS 13716 (1999)*, plaintiff filed suit in Pennsylvania for personal injuries suffered as a result of defendant's alleged negligence at its hotel in Mexico, against a Georgia Corporation claimed to be the hotel's agent. It maintained a website called "ReservHotel" and a 1-800 phone number but plaintiff didn't allege he visited the website or used the phone to make his reservations in Cancun.

In addition, it was not registered to do business in Pennsylvania, had no asset, offices, officers or employees there, and had never made any contact with a customer or travel agent in the state. The motion to dismiss was granted.

"The use of a 1-800 telephone number by a nonresident corporation does not create the 'extensive and pervasive' contacts with the forum state needed to assert general jurisdiction over a corporation..."

"General personal jurisdiction, however, requires more than a recognition that a nonresident corporation has an 'interactive' web site. Rather, the nature and quality of the commercial contacts usually conducted over the Internet must be continuous, systematic, and substantial. In other words, there must be some proof that ReservHotel 'purposefully availed itself of the privilege of conducting activities within the forum state...'"

3. In *Gator.Com, Inc. v. L.L. Bean, Inc., 341 F.3d 1072 (9th Cir. 2003),* defendant was a Maine corporation that sells outdoor equipment through its stores located in 5 various states and primarily through its mail order Internet website, totaling over $1 billion annually to consumers in 150 different countries. Plaintiff was a California corporation that develops and distributes software that stores computer user passwords, credit card information and related personal information in a digital wallet.

When a user visits an Internet website, it recognizes certain URL's associated with that web page, and the program displays a pop-up window offering a coupon for a designated competitor. "Gator users who visit L. L. Bean's website are offered coupons for one of L.L. Bean's competitors, Eddie Bauer, via a pop-up window that at least partially obscures L.L. Bean's website."

Defendant sent plaintiff a "cease and desist letter" threatening trademark infringement litigation, and plaintiff brought this suit for declaratory judgment in California requesting a judgment that there was no infringement. Defendant filed a motion to dismiss based on lack of personal jurisdiction which the court granted. On appeal, that dismissal was reversed and the case reinstated since the court felt that L.L. Bean had sufficient contacts with the state to create jurisdiction.

"L.L. Bean is not authorized to do business in California, has no agent for service of process in California, and is not required to pay taxes in California. However, in the year 2000 alone, L.L. Bean sold millions of dollars worth of products in California (about 6 percent of its total sales) through 'its catalog, its toll-free telephone number, and its Internet web-site.'"

"It is increasingly clear that modern businesses no longer require an actual physical presence in a state in order to engage in commercial activity there. With the advent of e-commerce, businesses may set up shop, so to speak, without ever actually setting foot in the state where they intend to sell their wares. Our conceptions of jurisdiction must be flexible enough to respond to the realities of the modern marketplace."

7. ONLINE SERVICE PROVIDER LIABILITY

Companies providing Internet access to customers, such as AOL, Bell South, MSN and Juno are financial "deep-pockets".

In the early days of the Internet, they were traditionally targeted by plaintiffs who alleged that defamatory statements, infringement of trademarks and unlawful domain name use were legally attributed to the ISP that provided the information platform. The fact that the guilty parties could usually not be located in cyberspace caused such vicarious claims to be numerous and potentially disastrous.

Congress responded in 1996 by passing the Communications Decency Act (CDA) to provide federal immunity from such third-party liability suits, and many states have enacted similar legislation. The Act provides in section 230:

"No provider or user of an interactive computer service shall be treated as the publisher or speaker of any information provided by another information content provider."

Courts consider the ISP's to have a qualified privilege that protects them from liability, so long as they did not know of the offending transmissions. Once a customer goes online, there is normally no control over message content, and therefore no corresponding liability.

Cases are still filed, however, seeking to impose ISP liability:

- Crank e-mail falsely attributed to plaintiff was sent through the Prodigy e-mail server. Plaintiff's defamation suit was dismissed due to qualified privilege, with the court saying, "Just as the phone companies are not responsible for defamatory messages sent over phone lines, e-mail servers are not responsible for the content of messages they do not control." *Lunney v. Prodigy Services, Co., 683 N.Y.S.2d 557 (Sup.Ct.App.Div N.Y. 1998).*

- Plaintiff's name and phone number were posted on an AOL bulletin board with a false message that he was selling t-shirts with offensive Oklahoma City bombing slogans. The ISP was sued for the online equivalent of defamation which is called "cybersmearing". The court ruled that CDA immunity extended to all ISP's, regardless of their classification as publishers or distributors. *Zeran v. America Online, Inc., 129 F.3d 327 (4th Cir. 1997).*

- Negative comments about plaintiff's books were posted on Amazon's site. Suit against it was dismissed under the Act. *Schneicer v. Amazon.com, Inc., 31 P.3d 37 (Wash. App. 2001).*

- NSI, the main registrar of domain names does not monitor whether or not they infringe registered trademarks. Plaintiff contended its registration of offending marks violated the Anticybersquatting Act of 1999. Suit was dismissed. Only the infringer is liable. *Lockheed Martin Corp. v. Network Solutions, Inc., 141 F.Supp.2d (N.D.Tex. 2001).*

- Gucci sued the offending website and its ISP for alleged trademark infringement. They had notified Mindspring on several occasions of the problem but it did nothing to stop the infringement. The court ruled the ISP was not protected by the Act under these facts. *Gucci America, Inc. v. Hall & Associates, 2001 WL 253255 (S.D.N.Y. 2001).*

- Plaintiff's copyrighted clip art was posted on a website for free download. It sued the provider of the host computer for infringement. The court indicated that while the ISP could not be sued for direct or vicarious infringement, possible contributory infringement could be proven if the ISP had prior knowledge of the violation. *Marobie-FL, Inc. v. Nat'l. Assn. of Fire Equipment Distributors, 983 F.Supp. 1167 (N.D. Ill. 1997).*

- The Children's Online Privacy Protection Act of 1988 (COPPA) was passed to protect children under thirteen from commercial websites that collect, store and distribute their personal data. It required the operator of the website to post notice of what information was collected, how it was to be used, and to obtain parental consent for such practices. It was updated in 2000 as the Children's Internet Protection Act (CIPA), requiring all federally funded schools and libraries to have filter and blocking technology on all computers with Internet access, and its constitutionality upheld in the case of *U.S. v. American Library Association, 123 S. Ct. 2297 (2003).*

- Pennsylvania copied the idea of CIPA to protect children from the massive amount of pornography on the Internet and was the first state to pas an Internet Child Pornography Act that imposed criminal liability on ISP's providing a platform for pornography. The law was struck down in *Center for Democracy and Technology v. Pappert, 337 F.Supp.2d 606 (E.D. Pa. 2004),* because it violated 1st Amendment rights of ISP's, Internet users and Web site operators because it effectively forced blocking access to more than 1.1 million innocent Web sites in a effort to target a few hundred illegal sites.

- One of the fastest growing areas of offline tort liability is identity theft. The online equivalent occurs through "phishing" e-mails. They are fake messages that appear to be from legitimate business users such as banks, credit card companies and ISP's, but are really from imposters. They ask recipients to verify or update personal data and often state that, "failure to verify information will cause account closure." Then when the information is sent, identity theft occurs. Congress is considering The Internet Spyware Prevention Act, passed unanimously by the House in October, 2004, to outlaw software that quietly monitors the activities of Internet users.

    The FTC filed the first case in the country to enjoin software companies from selling intrusive spyware in *FTC v. Seismic Entertainment Productions and Smartbot.net, 2005 U.S. Dist LEXIS 21899(N.H. Dist. Ct. 2004).*

The defendants allegedly secretly installed the softwa re, causing systems to be overwhelmed by pop-up ads, and then sending alarming messages saying they needed to buy "Spy Wiper" or "Spy Deleter" for $30. Defendant's motion to dismiss was denied in September, 2005 and the case is pending.

8. ONLINE COPYRIGHT DISPUTES

Copyright protection against infringement of creative works has been traditionally provided offline by the Federal Copyright Act, including recent extensions of protection to computer programs. The Internet's rapid growth made is possible for infringements to occur on a massive scale and resulted in the passage of the following laws:

- No Electronic Theft Act of 1997 (NET) – closed a loophole in the federal law which allowed infringers to pirate copyrighted works willfully and knowingly so long as they didn't do so for profit.

- Digital Millennium Copyright Act of 1998 (DMCA) – amended the federal law to implement the World Intellectual Property Organization Copyright Treaties.

- Digital Theft Deterrence and Copyright Damages Improvement Act of 1999 – amended the federal law to increase statutory infringement damages.

The music industry has been the most active area of conflict involving electronic Distribution of copyrighted works. The emergence of MP3 compression file technology provided the oppo rtunity for millions of users to download compact disk quality music via the Internet. Because these exchanges were usually created between computers through the World Wide Web, ISP's were an original liability target, but they were essentially granted lia bility immunity for third-party infringement by the DMCA. The focus of potential liability then shifted to end users who downloaded copyrighted material and the Websites that facilitated the MP3 peer-peer downloads.

The popular Napster Website was the initial target of infringement litigation. In *A&M Records, Inc. v. Napster, Inc., 239 F.3d 1004* and *A&M Records v. Napster, 284 F.3d 1091 (9th Cir. 2001)*, Napster was found liable for contributory and vicarious infringement to the extent that it was aware that the copyright works were available on its servers and had failed to prevent their free exchange by users. The music industry, through its trade association RIAA, kept the pressure on Napster and eventually forced it to shut down. Part of the litigation s trategy included suing the investors who had bankrolled Napster, claiming they had maintained hand-on management and control and were liable for copyright infringement that their company's service had enabled.

But other companies remained in active existence, providing the same platform for user for free user downloads of copyrighted music. Pressures were now exerted on suspected music swappers through subpoenas of their ISP's records of user activity, lawsuits against individual persons who downloaded the protected files, and the acceleration of litigation against owners of the download Websites. Companies such as the new Napster were formed for the purpose of selling music downloads, as the public became conditioned to buying their copyrighted music rather than facing the legal consequences of continuing the practice of illegal downloads.

Napster and other websites that facilitated free music downloads relied upon the landmark case of *Sony Corp. of America v. Universal Studios, 464 U.S. 417 (1984),* where the U.S. Supreme Court had ruled that the sale of videocassette recorders did not create copyright infringement liability even though the defendant-manufacturers knew that customers were using the machines to copy protected creative works.

Some U.S. trial and appellate court rulings supported their position, as well as decisions in Canada, Australia, and other countries. This included *In re: Charter Communications, 393 F.3d 771 (8ᵗʰ Cir. 2005),* where RIAA had identified various infringing subscribers to ISP Charter who were infringing on copyrighted music by sharing the files. It sought to enforce subpoena's to produce personal information about more than 200 of defendant's subscribers. The court ruled that the DMCA did not authorize subpoenas of subscribers when their ISP was merely performing a transmission function, rather than a storage or linking function.

Ultimately the question of whether or not website enabled peer-to-peer free downloads of MP3 files could be allowed in the U.S. was answered in the negative by the Court in *Metro-Goldwyn-Mayer v. Grokster and Stream Cast Networks, 125 S. Ct. 2764(2005).* That case was brought against a popular music download website and a distributors of Morpheus, a software program that facilitated Internet file-sharing. In ruling for the defendants, the 9ᵗʰ Circuit *(04 C.D.O.S. 7624)* relied on the Sony case, as well as distinguishing the facts that while Napster used a centralized index to tell users where to look for files to download, the newer programs didn't, thus exerting less control over the traded content.

But the Supreme Court reversed, holding that:

"One who distributes a device with the object of promoting its use to infringe copyright, as shown by clear expression or other affirmative steps taken to foster infringement, going beyond mere distribution with knowledge of third-party action, is liable for the resulting acts of infringement by third parties using the device, regardless of the device's lawful uses."

9. THE FUTURE OF INTERNET LAW

We are now into the second decade of litigating and legislating Cyberspace disputes. More laws will be passed to address Internet issues. Input from other countries will result in their own versions of laws to be further assimilated. Cases will be decided at all court levels to add layers of precedent to various concepts. As the saying goes, "time will tell," but here are a few probable areas of interest:

1. Internet giants Microsoft Corp. and Sun Microsystems will probably continue their history of competitive disputes:

A. Sun sued Microsoft in 1997 for allegedly violating its license to use its Java programming language. Microsoft produced and promoted a version of Sun Microsystems' Java programming that would only run on the windows operating system, contrary to its licensing agreement. That case was settled by Microsoft for $20 million and an injunction issued that barred Microsoft from distributing nonstandard Java.

B. Sun also joined others in 1998 to lobby the Department of Justice to sue Microsoft under the Sherman Antitrust Act for monopolizing the Internet browser market. That lawsuit ultimately led to a ruling against Microsoft that initially required a breakup, and then was limited to a finding of antitrust violations due to its jamming of Java. These issues were settled 2001.

C. Sun currently is pursuing a private antitrust case against Microsoft, alleging that Microsoft has gained an unfair competitive advantage by shipping Windows, used by more than 90% of the world's personal computers, with an outdated version of Java that is inconsistent for its users.

2. Questions remain to be answered regarding Internet contracts and sales transactions, and how our traditional concepts of the law and the legal system will be changed by technology. These influences are being felt with ever-increasing frequency as more and more Cyberlaw disputes are being decided. Some questions of practical daily importance to the consumer are:

- If licensed software is installed in the computer you sell, does it's "no sale or transfer" restriction apply to you? Does it apply to the buyer? Does the software have to be removed from the desktop before sale?

- Do license restrictions apply to used software purchases? Is there a legal difference between off-line retail purchases from computer stores or garage sale purchases and on-line Web site transactions?

- Can licensed material be copied or quoted for scholarly or academic purposes by the licensee, even though prohibited by terms of the license agreement?

3. Of broader application are the types of current cases, of which the following are a representative sample:

- State taxing authorities that are seeking increased revenue sources are now trying to tap into the Internet revenue stream by trying to collect use taxes from online sellers of goods that are delivered in their jurisdictions.

- Alternate dispute resolution is strongly urged for Internet related disputes. One option is to mediate a dispute online through The Online Ombuds Office. Another is negotiation through one of the many online websites offering ADR remedies. An example is the resolving of insurance claims online through Cybersettle, the first company of this kind, the exclusive grantee of the Computerized Dispute Resolution System and Method Patent, through which over 475 insurance companies have settled over $80 million in claims in the last few years.

- Courts are adopting electronic case filing in civil matters, to allow 24-hour access to case files from any location, remote document filing, immediate e-mail notification of case activity and electronic service of court filings. Most courts are also creating their own Web sites.

  Once a judge designates that a case can be handled electronically, attorneys can file documents over the Internet and bring a diskette to the clerk's office for entry into the system. The public will have access to most of the systems, except for sealed documents. Criminal cases are excluded currently, because of issues of privacy.

  Electronic data discovery (EDD) is the wave of the future in our technology oriented business environment. More than 90% of documents produced since 1999 were created in digital form. Information technology specialists will be used to ease the burdens of production of documents and related factual discovery. In the recent case of *Residential Funding Corp. v. DeGeorge Fin. Corp., 2002 WL 31120098 (2nd Cir. 2002)*, the trial court was ordered to impose discovery sanctions when the plaintiff failed to produce e-mail evidence in time for trial.

  Federal courts are beginning to install technology courtrooms where monitors, screens and digitized evidence are projected to reduce the length and cost of trials dramatically. This project is expected to spread to state courtrooms and eventually be a modern way of conducting trials.

  But critics point to "jammiesurfers", those nosey souls who could check out the details of divorces and other highly personal cases anonymously from their home desktop. The balancing of the public's right to access v. the litigant's right to privacy is still to be resolved.

- Under the Sarbanes-Oxley Act of 2002, the deadline for SEC filings of insider transaction has been reduced from 40 to two business days, and all companies now have to electronically report.

- Mistrials are being sought in cases where jurors are doing Internet research on legal terminology and other factors involved in their lawsuits, contrary to the judge's instruction when he charges them with the law. The traditional sanctions for juror misconduct, such as being held in contempt of court, are not easily applied because it is almost impossible to monitor their conduct outside the courtroom as a case progresses to its conclusion. Attorneys faced with an adverse verdict now routinely question the jurors about Internet usage.

- The Federal Trade Commission's Mail or Telephone Order Merchandise Rule has been held to also apply to orders by computer. The Rule spells out the ground rules for sellers of goods making promises about shipments, notifying customers about unexpected delays, and refunding consumers' money. Time for shipping must have a reasonable basis. If the shipping time is not specified, delivery must be made within 30 days. If that time cannot be met, the customer must be promptly notified and given the opportunity to cancel and receive a full refund. For delays up to 30 days, the customer's silence is consent, but for longer delays the customer's consent is required. If orders can't be filled in a timely manner, the seller may cancel if the customer is promptly notified and given a refund.

- Spam (electronic junk mail) on the Internet reached such a problem level that Congress finally enacted the Federal Can-Spam Act of 2003 that became effective January 1, 2004. It preempts state laws on the subject, allows for injunctions, imposes a civil fine of $250 per e-mail violation with a cap of $2 million, and carries a possible criminal sanction of 5-years. Opponents of the Act point out that it allows Spam so long as the e-mails have the sender's postal address and a working link for the recipient to opt-out, rather than prior state laws that prohibited it outright unless the recipient authorized its transmittal.

  The Act does, however, allow states with stricter laws to pursue criminal (not civil) charges against violators. But Spam is still a major problem and the nations leading ISP's are pro-active and have filed successful civil lawsuits against major spammers under the Act. Monies collected to satisfy their court judgments are being donated to charity to raise public awareness of the problem.

DISCUSSION EXERCISES

1. Discuss the five main areas of your Internet usage.
2. Discuss the amount of time you spend daily in Cyberspace.
3. Discuss the types of purchases or sales you have made on the Internet and any business law problems you have encountered.
4. Discuss the consumer liability rules you would create for click-wrap, shrink-wrap and browse-wrap software licenses.
5. Discuss the rules you would create for personal jurisdiction in Internet disputes.

CASE RESEARCH CYBERCISES

The following cases also relate to the material in this chapter and illustrate the types of disputes that may occur. For each one do the following written assignment:

1. Locate the case using the Internet (Lexis-Nexis, West or any other research cite which provides case transcripts).
2. Briefly summarize what it was about – the nature of the dispute involved.
3. Who won at the trial court level? Who won at the appellate level?
4. Who won if there was a third level of Supreme Court review?
5. What were the legal rules of law and the reasoning used to reach the final decision?
6. Do you agree or disagree with the decision, and explain why?
7. What business law time bomb(s) were involved?
8. Could the time bomb(s) have been avoided by structuring the transaction differently? Discuss.
9. Could the adverse effects of the time bomb(s) have been defused by a different reaction or response by the affected party? Discuss.
10. Replay the facts of the case to achieve a different successful result.

1. *Hotmail Corporation v. Van Money Pie, Inc., 1998 U.S. Dist. LEXIS 10729 (N.D.Ca. 1998) (click-wrap service agreement prohibiting the sending of "spam" e-mails is binding, and violators are enjoined).*
2. *Earthweb v. Schlack, 71 F.Supp 2d 299 (S.D.N.Y. 1999) (employment non-competition agreement of one-year duration was ruled too long and unenforceable, due to the dynamic nature of the Internet industry).*
3. *Kelly v. Arriba Soft. Corp., 280 F.3d 934 (9th Cir. 2002) (search engine was allowed to display thumbnail-size images of copyrighted photographs as fair use, but display of full-size images by clicking on the small image is infringement).*

22.

BUSINESS ETHICS

"Ethics and science have their own domains,
which touch but do not interpenetrate.
The one shows us to what goal we should aspire,
The other, given the goal, teaches us how to attain it."
Poincare

"Beauty is in the eye of the beholder."
Margaret Wolfe Hungerford

Webster's Dictionary defines an *oxymoron* as "a figure of speech in which contradictory ideas or terms are combined (e.g. sweet sorrow)." To this we might add "jumbo shrimp", "military intelligence", and especially "business ethics."

The question of whether or not a particular act or non-act is "ethical" or "moral" and therefore in compliance with a proper standard of conduct cannot be definitively answered since we are dealing with opinions about which reasonable people may differ, rather than facts. Our pronouncements of good or bad change from moment to moment, depending upon a multitude of subjective and objective factors including but not limited to the following:

- one's personal background, education, upbringing, experience - philosophy, psychology, theology, and
- the changing external forces shaping one's life such as societal values, laws, politics, and experiential learning.

Behavior acted out based upon a moving party's beliefs will of necessity change as those underlying beliefs are modified. And the shifting sands of personal and business life in our modern society are characterized by periods of sudden and dramatic change. Companies may continually weave their way between the ethical polarities of good and bad as they complete business transactions, being viewed as hero or villain at any given point in time.

When commercial transactions ripen into a dispute and the parties decide to seek a judicial remedy, the decision-maker is faced with a similar dilemma. Most business disputes are evaluated using the "objective standard" of *reasonableness* by asking, "What would a hypothetical reasonable person do under the same or similar circumstances?"

Large corporations are financially powerful, politically influential, and often insulated from popular opinion.

While they often have a positive influence in the benefits they create through employment, products and services, tax revenues, education, and philanthropy - they sometimes overstep the boundaries of permissible conduct in their quest for profitability. There are numerous historical examples including:

- Automobile manufacturing and engineering defects
- Drug products with dangerous side-effects
- Toxic industrial chemical leaks affecting land and water supplies
- Oil spills and natural gas leaks
- Tainted foods and other consumables
- Anti-competitive trade practices by large retailers
- Securities and business fraud
- Tobacco, alcohol and firearms injuries

We also now live in an age of more corporate accountability, courtesy of the above- listed areas as well as the various financial scandals that have run the gamut from the Savings & Loan bank failures, to the Enron bankruptcy to the imprisonment of corporate millionaires such as Martha Stewart.

The legal system, like the world of nature, abhors a vacuum. Abuses of power and flagrant misconduct that boils to the surface of media attention generates public outrage that often results in legislation and litigation to prevent the now-prohibited conduct from being repeated in the future.

One of the most effective ways to make sure companies do business in a proper manner is the ethical oversight furnished by federal and state "whistle-blower" laws that provide protection against retaliation and compensation for employees of companies who report unlawful business practices, especially attempts to defraud local, state or federal governmental customers.

Another example of such legislation is the Sarbanes-Oxley Act of 2002 (SOA), also known as the "Public Company Accounting Reform and Investor Protection Act." Its main purpose is to improve accuracy and reliability of corporate financial reports and protect the public through management accountability by regulating:

- Corporate governance
- Financial disclosure
- Public accounting

The Act was a direct legislative response to the widespread corporate fraud and accounting and legal complicity uncovered in early 2002 in the Enron, WorldCom and Tyco scandals and subsequent bankruptcies.

Our judicial system has three of its own unique deterrents to corporate wrongdoing:

1) Punitive damages are awarded to financially punish a defendant and set an example for others, so that similar actions will not occur in the future. They may be awarded if the plaintiff proves that the defendant's conduct was willful, malicious, reckless and outrageous – in reckless disregard for the rights of others.

They were originally limited only by the upper limits of the defendant's net worth. As the size of these awards escalated to huge amounts in various cases where the defendant's conduct was particularly objectionable, the tort reform movement came into existence to try and put limits on punitive damages. In many states they are now limited to a specified multiple of compensatory damages suffered. The U.S. Supreme Court has suggested in its *State Farm v. Campbell* decision that punitive damages should usually not exceed nine times actual damages.

2) Class action lawsuits may be certified in situations where a large group of plaintiffs have claims arising from the same event or act of alleged misconduct. The relatively small amounts of their individual damages would make it cost-prohibitive to file separate lawsuits, and difficult to get quality legal representation. But if one class of hundreds or thousands of persons "similarly situated" is allowed to be the collective plaintiff, the economies of scale and bargaining power change dramatically. Lawyers hired on a contingent-fee basis flock to these types of cases, since liability is often admitted or easily proved, and the only real issue is the dollar amount of damages to be awarded. Tort reformers also have targeted class actions in their efforts to reduce the size of court judgments.

3) Contingent fee hiring of lawyers allows persons to hire lawyers who may not otherwise be able to afford them and pay for representation on the standard flat-fee or hourly rate basis. The usual contingent fee arrangement is no-win / no-pay. The lawyer fronts all or most of the out-of-pocket expenses of court costs and litigation expenses, sometimes running into the thousands of dollars. If the case is won, the lawyer usually receives a percentage of recovery between one-fourth and one-third, with the client receiving the remainder.

So where does that leave us regarding ethics in the commercial marketplace? Are businesses ethically self-regulated by current laws? Should companies have affirmative duties to conduct their business in a socially responsible manner? How can this be done and still achieve financial profitability? And what does the term "socially responsible" really mean?

Is it really possible to reach a consensus as to what conduct is ethical and what conduct is not? Probably not, other than to note that these difficult questions arise each time an important decision is made in one's personal or business life.

The questions are probably best answered on an individual / transactional basis by educating ourselves as to the issues involved through examining (a) historical theories of ethics, (b) real-life examples of the ethical implications of doing business,

(c) self-tests to filter business decisions through a critical lens of ethical conduct, and
(d) crisis management planning at the corporate level.

A. SOME THEORIES OF ETHICS

1. **Ethical egoism** – decisions as to right and wrong are based upon what promotes one's own long-term self-interest. The focus is internal and subjective – "my way or the highway." Even though society may benefit from such acts such as the recall of a defective product, its real motivation is personal gain – improved public relations, fending off lawsuits or legislation, blunting stockholder dissent, and related ways to achieve one's personal view of proper conduct.

2. **Ethical fundamentalism** – decisions as to right and wrong are based upon outside sources of authority. These sources can range from the different personal teachings of individuals (e.g. Albert Schweitzer, Mother Teresa, Adolph Hitler and Karl Marx), gurus and religious figures (e.g. Paramahansa Yogananda, Dalai Lama, Billy Graham and Pat Robertson), and universally known written works (e.g. Bible, Koran, Torah, and Book of Miracles). The focus is external and objectified; what is "reasonable" is defined by how conduct is portrayed in the particular sources relied upon.

3. **Ethical experientialism** – decisions as to right and wrong, whether initially influenced by one's emphasis on internal or external sources, are ultimately determined by the life experiences encountered by the decision-maker. This is a philosophical middle ground between egoism and fundamentalism that seeks input from both in reaching a final decision, but is not mutually exclusive.

4. **Utilitarianism** – moral authority is determined by the consequences of one's actions. Jeremy Bentham and John Stuart Mill expressed this theory of ethics as requiring choice of a course of action that provides the greatest good to society. Individual benefits are secondary to societal results. Mathematically speaking, an act is morally right if its net benefits to society exceed its costs. Applied literally, this could read, "The end justifies the means," and could be a way to rationalize improper acts that lead to a satisfactory result, like vigilantism.

5. **Ethical deontology** – moral duties owed by persons are based upon universal rules, the most universal of which is Immanuel Kant's suggested categorical imperative commonly known as The Golden Rule: "do unto others as you would have them do unto you."

Almost every organized religion has the Rule at its base in one form or another. Even the Hippies of the 1960's social revolution incorporated it into their lexicon as creating good karma or bad karma by each conscious act.

It also can be viewed as the circle of life – "there is a destiny that connects us, none go their way alone, all that we bring into the lives of others comes back into our own."

Here are some other similar religious prescriptions for ethical interpersonal and business relationships:

- Judaism - "Thou shalt love thy neighbor as thyself."

- Christianity - "Therefore all things whatsoever ye would that men should do to you, do ye even so to them."

- Islam – "No one of you is a believer until he loves for his brother what he loves for himself."

- Hinduism – Good people proceed while considering that what is best for others is best for themselves."

- Buddhism – Hurt not others with that which pains yourself."

- Confucianism – What you do not want done to yourself, do not do to others."

6. Corporate business responsibility – whether or not a company's conduct is described as good or bad may depend on its internal philosophy of doing business as set forth by its board of directors and carried out on a daily basis by its officers and employees. The three general polarities of corporate social responsibility are:

- Maximize profits for the shareholder-owners of the company. So long as laws are not broken along the way, no duty exists to assist society other than the residual benefits received through the company's direct profit-oriented acts.

- Profits are desired as a primary focus, but there is a corresponding moral minimum duty to either avoid or financially correct social harms that occur. This duty "not to harm" helps to balance the excesses of the profit-only way of doing business.

- Corporations must be good citizens. They have an affirmative duty to make society a better place by "doing good." This corporate citizenship theory would prevent a company from producing toxic chemicals, selling armaments or engaging in environmentally destructive activities.

  It would also require contributing a portion of business profits to charitable, educational and other humanitarian causes.

Critics of increasing corporate social responsibility and broadening the ethical duties owed by businesses to their consuming public make a number of arguments:

- Inept Custodian: Corporate executives lack the expertise to make non-economic decisions. If they are permitted to do so, society will be materialized rather than moralized.

- Hand-of-Government: Governmental regulation is required to keep in check the natural inclination of companies to financially enrich themselves at the expense of society.

- Invisible Hand: Contrary to the need for public oversight of business, the profit-making focus of corporations will itself result in the greatest good for society.

Those who favor broadening corporate duties of social responsibility suggest that it is a fair exchange for legally allowing the corporate form of business, complete with its legal entity status, insulated personal liability of shareholders, and other legal advantages of doing business in that form. In return, society has the right to expect corporations not to harm to society, to be accountable for their conduct if they do harm, and to point their activities in the direction of promoting the common good.

As a practical matter, notice how almost any corporate decision you can think of could arguably involve some or all of these theories of ethics at any point of the business transactional process.

B. ETHICS, OR THE LACK THEREOF, IN ACTION

In almost all companies, especially large businesses, management choices in the area of ethical behavior constantly present themselves. Mistakes of judgment will occur from time to time due to ignorance or bad luck because, after all, business managers are human beings. But sometimes they are not inadvertent. What if they are repeated, covered up, or are a part of a calculated intentional course of unethical conduct that suggests an arrogant disregard of the rights of others?

Though a company so inclined to unethical conduct may get away with it for a period of time, ultimately the legal system steps in and the guilty are punished and substantial monies are awarded. This is the common pattern of most of the well-known instances of questionable corporate conduct. What follows are six of the most famous or infamous, depending on one's ethical perspective.

1. McDonald's Sale of Scalding Coffee

When the news of the "hot coffee" case appeared in visual and print media as a short headline that read, *Customer spill burns woman, Jury awards $29 million,* the general consensus was that this was just another frivolous lawsuit brought by a greedy client and her shady lawyers. Most agreed it was evidence the legal system was out of control. But as in most of these situations when all facts were disclosed, the truth was quite different. Here's what really happened.

In 1992, Stella Liebeck, a 79-year old retired sales clerk, was a passenger in a car driven by her grandson, and ordered 49-cent cup of coffee at a McDonald's drive-through in Albuquerque, New Mexico. As she placed the cup between her knees and removed the lid to add cream and sugar, the entire contents of scalding hot coffee spilled out on her lap. The sweatpants she was wearing absorbed the coffee and held it next to her skin. She suffered third-degree burns on her groin, inner thighs and buttocks.

She was hospitalized for eight days, during which time she underwent skin grafting and removal of dead tissue. The burns left her scarred and disabled for more than two years. She notified McDonald's of her injuries and asked that it pay her medical bills that totaled $11,000. It countered with an offer of $600. She then decided to sue, claiming McDonald's was negligent in selling such super-heated coffee to the public and failing to warn of its known dangers. She sought to settle her claim at that point for $20,000 but that offer was refused.

During discovery it was revealed that McDonald's held the temperature of its coffee at 180-190 degrees, based on a consultant's advice that it would maintain optimum taste although that temperature produced third degree burns in less than three seconds exposure. Other establishments in the area sold their coffee at least 20 degrees cooler, and it was also determined that coffee served at home is usually 135-140 degrees. It was also revealed that the company had received more than 700 coffee claims of burns from scalding coffee, including some to the third degree, during the prior ten years. Many of these claims were settled, amounting to more than $500,000.

Prior to the trial plaintiff offered to settle for $300,000 and the judge ordered both sides into a mediated settlement conference, where the mediator who was a retired judge recommended that McDonald's settle for $225,000. McDonald's refused all settlement offers.

The trial lasted seven days. McDonald's own testimony was very damaging to its case Its quality assurance manager testified that even though the company knew a burn hazard to throat and mouth existed with coffee served at 140 degrees or above, the company actively enforced its requirement that the coffee be held in the serving pot at 180 – 185 degrees. A company executive testified that the company knew its coffee sometimes caused serious burns, but hadn't seen the need to reduce the temperature, consult burn experts to remedy the situation, or warn customers. A company human factors engineer testified that the number of hot-coffee burns was "statistically insignificant" compared to the billion cups of coffee sold annually, even after he was shown graphic photographs of the plaintiff's burns.

The jury awarded Mrs. Liebeck $200,000 compensatory damages, reduced to $160,000 because she was found to be 20% at fault in the coffee spill. The jury also awarded her $2.7 million in punitive damages, equaling two days of company sales, finding that the company's conduct was willful, wanton, reckless and malicious.

After the trial the judge reduced punitive damages to $480,000, or three times the compensatory damages. After this remititur, the parties entered into a post-verdict private settlement. Post-verdict investigation disclosed that coffee temperatures at local McDonald's had dropped to 158 degrees.

Jurors polled after the case said that although at the beginning they considered it just a nuisance claim for a coffee spill, they changed their minds when hearing the testimony. One juror remarked that the conduct of the company demonstrated "a callous disregard for the safety of the people."

Question: You are the new CEO of McDonald's and have an opportunity to turn back the clock and properly handle this matter. What management errors were made, what ethical aspects should have been considered, and how would you have done things differently?

2. Ford's Exploding Pinto Automobile

In 1965, Ralph Nader was a young lawyer working for General Motors Corp. who discovered a company cover-up of defects in the Chevrolet Corvair. He became the first high profile whistle blower when he reported the problems in his book *Unsafe at Any Speed*. That brought public attention to the issue of automobile safety and resulted in Congress beginning to actively regulate the industry.

At the same time, in the late 1960's, Lee Iacocca was president of Ford Motor Company, had successfully created and marketed the Ford Mustang, and now sought a repeat performance. Since consumer demand for sub-compacts was rapidly increasing, he championed the new Ford Pinto. "The Pinto was not to weigh an ounce over 2,000 pounds and not cost a cent over $2,000." The company was anxious to get it to market.

But there was a problem. During design and early production, crash tests revealed a serious defect in the fuel tank that caused it to rupture and burst into flames in moderate-speed rear end collisions that exceeded 25 miles per hour. Nevertheless, with much sales and marketing fanfare the car went into full production.

As accidents happened and Pinto gas tanks exploded, word began to spread that these were not just isolated incidents and a real problem existed. But the company made no official statements and did not order a product recall. When Congress considered regulations on auto fuel tanks, company lobbyists were at the forefront of a successful effort to delay governmental regulations for another eight years.

Whether or not Chairman Iacocca was personally aware of the defective design is fairly debatable. What is clear however is the fact that any delay in bringing the Pinto to market was out of the question. Executives and managers at all levels did not dare to raise the subject, and there was a massive cover-up that lasted until 1978 when Ford finally agreed to recall 1.5 million vehicles.

The impetus for the recall came from a combination of factors. In 1974, the Center for Auto Safety started to receive reports from attorneys of deaths and serious injuries in Pinto gas tank explosions and petitioned the National Highway Traffic Safety Administration to order a recall. It refused, and did nothing until 1977. In that year an investigative story exposing the hazard was published in Mother Jones News Magazine, using documents found in the Center's files.

The story cited internal Ford documents that proved it knew of the weakness in the fuel tank before the car was placed on the market, but an internal cost-benefit study suggested to management it would be cheaper to cover up the problem and pay death and injury claims than order a recall and modify the fuel tanks. According to Ford's estimates the unsafe tanks would cause 180 burn deaths, 180 serious burn injuries, and 2,100 burned vehicles each year. It calculated that it would have to pay $200,000 per death, $67,000 per injury, and $700 per vehicle, for a total of $49.5 million. However the cost of saving lives was higher, $11 per vehicle for alterations which added up to $137 million per year, so the cover-up continued.

Shortly after publication of the article, national publicity was focused on the California case of *Grimshaw v. Ford,* on which the movie "Class Action" with Gene Hackman was later based. In it the jury awarded Richard Grimshaw $125 million in punitive damages for injuries he sustained while a passenger in a 1971 Pinto, which was struck by another car at an impact speed of 28 MPH and burst into flames. Although the award was later reduced to $3.5 million by the trial judge, the jury's reason for the large award (the largest in history at the time) was that Ford had marketed the Pinto knowing that injuries and deaths were inevitable. The award of $125 million was equivalent to the profit Ford had made on the Pinto since its introduction.

With the publication of the Mother Jones article and the publicity surrounding the *Grimshaw* case, the Center for Auto Safety re-submitted its petition for a defects investigation to the NHTSA and a formal defect administration case file was opened. Based upon crash tests performed which verified its preliminary findings of serious gas tank defects, and the tremendous publicity being generated, Ford agreed to recall all 1971-1976 Pintos.

Between the time that recall notices were mailed and parts were available at dealers to modify the defective fuel tanks, six more people died in Pinto fires after a rear impact. This caused an Indiana grand jury to take the unusual step of returning indictments against Ford Motor Company for criminal negligence, but a jury found the company innocent of the criminal charges. Even so, it suggested a possible additional remedy to be used in the future in cases involved extreme corporate misconduct.

Question: You are the new CEO of Ford Motor Company and have an opportunity to turn back the clock and properly handle this matter. What management errors were made, what ethical aspects should have been considered, and how would you have done things differently?

3. A.H. Robin's Defective Dalkon Shield

A.H. Robins was a small family-owned Virginia pharmaceutical firm in the 1960's. Some of their popular products were Chap Stick lip balm, Sergeant's flea and tick collars and Robitussin cough medicine. Then it heard about a new intrauterine device known as the Dalkon shield that was being tested at the Johns Hopkins Hospital birth-control clinic by the clinic director, Dr. Hugh Davis. The device was a plastic, nickel-sized, crablike instrument to be inserted into a woman's uterus as a way to prevent pregnancy.

Dr. Davis had reported in the February, 1970 issue of the *American Journal of Obstetrics and Gynecology* that use of the Dalkon Shield reduced the rate of pregnancy to 1.1%, a similar result to using the birth-control pill. His article did not disclose, however, that he was past-owner of the Dalkon Corporation that manufactured the IUD device.

By mid-1970, A.H. Robins sensed a business opportunity, acquired legal rights to the Dalkon Shield, and hired Dr. Davis as a consultant. Within two weeks of the purchase, it began to hear of potential difficulties for use of the product since its tail shield design, unlike that of other IUD's on the market, was open at one end and the exposed nylon filaments could potentially attract bacteria and cause infection. It essentially ignored the warnings.

The company made some minor design changes, conducted no more research on the possible problem, and rushed to bring their product to market, launching a massive marketing campaign that included reprints of the Davis study.

Rigorous testing of the device and approval by the Food and Drug Administration was not required before release because it was classified as a medical device rather than a drug. Within one year, the Dalkon Shield had captured 60% of the IUD market.

As sales and profits increased, more news of adverse results appeared. It was reported that the pregnancy rate for the device was closer to 4.3% than the 1.1% advertised. In addition, some users were developing pelvic inflammatory disease infections and others were being hospitalized for perforated uteruses. If a pregnancy did occur, users complained of ectopic pregnancy, septic abortions, and premature labor and delivery. Some users became sterile and some died from using the Dalkon Shield.

Finally, in 1973 the FDA ordered the company to stop selling the product due to health concerns. It promptly withdrew the device from the U.S. market, but waited another year before banning international sales.

Lawsuits were also being filed against the company for damages suffered by users. Between 1974 – 1979 the company refused to cooperate, denied liability, and essentially played hardball, finally settling many cases for an average of $11,000 each. But then a Colorado jury awarded an injured user $6.8 million in damages, including a large punitive component, and the financial handwriting was on the wall. By 1984 the company had paid out $314 million in 8,300 lawsuits, still faced 3,800 pending suits, and new cases were being filed against it daily.

The trial judge in one of the pending cases summoned the top A.H. Robins executives, including its CEO, severely criticized them for their lack of cooperation and hard approach with their injured customers, and demanded they take some type of protective action on behalf of the many women who still wore the Dalkon Shield.

Finally, in October, 1984 the company launched an advertising campaign telling users that it would pay for removal of their Dalkon Shields. It also established a litigation reserve fund of $615 million to pay for pending and future claims, which was the largest of its kind for liability concerning use of a medical device. But the company never issued a formal recall of the product and continued to claim that the Dalkon Shield was not defective or dangerous.

By August, 1985 it was obvious the company's litigation cost estimates were too low. The sum of $530 million had already been lost by A.H. Robins and its insurance company Aetna Life & Casualty in 9,500 completed lawsuits, there were an additional 5,200 cases pending, and new cases were being filed at the rate of 400 per month. The company also had been sued by its own shareholders for its actions that resulted in the severe diminution of the company's value, and settled those claims for $6.9 million. With no prospects for financial recovery the company filed for Chapter 11 bankruptcy, automatically stopping all pending litigation, preventing new suits, and limiting amounts of compensation to be paid to injured users of the Dalkon Shield.

(A Historical note: A.H. Robin's financial meltdown and subsequent Chapter 11 filing was similar to Johns-Manville's asbestos insulation, Dow Chemical's Agent Orange herbicide, and Corning Glass's silicone breast implants.)

Question: You are the new CEO of A.H. Robins Co. and have an opportunity to turn back the clock and properly handle this matter. What management errors were made, what ethical aspects should have been considered, and how would you have done things differently?

4. Occidental Petroleum's Toxic Love Canal

Love Canal is a residential neighborhood in Niagara Falls, New York. Its name came from the last name of William Love who owned the land in the 1890's. He began construction of a canal to divert water from the upper Niagara River for an electric power plant, but the economic depression left only one mile of the canal dug.

The land was sold at public auction in 1920 for unpaid taxes to the City of Niagara Falls, who began using it as a petroleum chemical waste disposal site. Later the U.S. government began using the same site to bury waste from its military chemical experiments. In 1942 Hooker Chemical Co., a subsidiary of Occidental Petroleum, bought the land and used it for burial of more than 20,000 tons of its own toxic chemicals. When the site was filled to capacity in 1952, it was closed for further waste disposal and the canal was back-filled.

The time of closure coincided with the housing demands of the expanding Baby Boom generation of the 1950's. The City of Niagara Falls needed to expand to satisfy these residential needs, and sought to buy the portion of the land not previously used for waste disposal and use it to build an elementary school. But Hooker Chemical wanted to only sell the entire property and the parties ultimately agreed on its sale to the Niagara Falls Board of Education for $1 dollar, with the sales agreement containing a warning clause that explained the dangers of building on the site, and an exculpatory release of the seller from liability.

The school was opened in 1955, and in 1957, the City sold the land to private developers for a 16-acre rectangular housing development and constructed sewers on land adjacent to the landfill site. The new owners of the land were not warned about its dangers. After the houses were built and sold to individual owners, a number of them began to complain about strange odors and foreign substances oozing into their basements. City inspectors were brought in to investigate, but nothing further was done to solve the problems.

By 1977 the residents of the neighborhood where the school was located had an unusually high incidence of cancer and their children had a similarly alarming level of birth defects. The Love Canal Homeowner's Association actively investigated and discovered the chemically dug canal and learned of the origins of the toxic dump site. Complaints were made to government officials but they refused to intervene.

Hooker Chemical also denied liability, claiming that any toxic chemicals had come from areas other than their disposal site, but agreed to demolish the school that was on their former property.

The homeowners felt trapped because they had no public agency to defend them and their sickness levels increased since they could not sell their properties and move away. By 1978 the Love Canal had become a national media event. Responding to the overwhelming evidence of a severe problem and massive cover-up by local governmental officials and the corporate property owner, and activist activity that included taking two EPA representatives hostage, President Jimmy Carter used disaster relief authority to declare a federal emergency. But he claimed there were not enough federal funds available to move affected residents away from the hazardous area without congressional action.

After extensive geological tests conclusively established that the underground toxic chemicals had leached into household basements, polluted household air, and were the cause of the severe health problems, and public outrage continued to escalate, the Environmental Protection Agency filed suit in 1979 against Occidental Petroleum. Bills were finally passed by Congress to allow the Federal Government to fund initial cleanup efforts, evacuation and relocation of almost 900 Love Canal residents, reimbursing them for the cost of their now abandoned homes.

As a result of the pending litigation and the attendant publicity about the dangers of other toxic dumpsites that existed in various locations around the country, Congress created the Superfund Law in 1980. It provided federal funds for cleanup of the most hazardous toxic waste sites around the country and required waste dumpers to pay the costs. The federal judge hearing the case against Occidental declared it to be a "responsible party" under the Superfund Law.

After passage of the Law, the federal government worked in tandem with the State of New York to clean up the Love Canal site. Dioxin was removed from creeks and sewers adjacent to the Love Canal so fish would not be contaminated, and a leachate collection system was put into operation to prevent contaminated groundwater from spreading outward from the Canal.

In 1988 the state and federal governments declared that most of the area was again suitable for residential use, and the Love Canal Revitalization Authority began selling 200 abandoned homes north of the canal to new families. The FHA provided mortgage insurance for the re-inhabited homes.

Finally in December of 1995, the Justice Department and the EPA succeeded in negotiating a settlement with Occidental under which it would repay the federal government all of the $101 million it spent on cleanup, $28 million in interest, and an additional $102 million would be paid to the EPA Superfund, and $27 million paid to the Federal Emergency Management Agency (FEMA) for its funding of the cleanup and relocation prior to enactment of the Superfund Law.

The U.S. responded to Occidental claims that it should bear a part of the costs because it also dumped at the site by agreeing to pay $8 million of the total cleanup costs.

Question: You are the new CEO of Occidental Petroleum Company and have an opportunity to turn the clock back and properly handle this matter. What management errors were made, what ethical aspects should have been considered, and how would you have done things differently?

5. Exxon's Alaska Oil Spill

In March 23, 1989 the Exxon Valdez, a supertanker owned by Exxon Corporation and carrying more than 53 million gallons of crude oil (1,260,000 barrels), left the trans-Alaska pipeline terminal in Valdez, Alaska heading for Long Beach, California. The run was a standard route, having been traversed by various oil tankers thousands of times in the twelve years since 1977, when the oil pipeline opened.

The ship's captain was Joe Hazelwood, who had a known history of alcohol abuse, had lost his automobile license for drunk driving, and later admitted to having has several drinks on the fateful evening of March 23, 1989. Icebergs had been encountered in the shipping lanes, so around midnight when the Captain retired to his quarters, he turned the ship over to his third mate who was not certified to take the tanker into those waters, and ordered the helmsman to steer around the icebergs and then return to the shipping lanes.

The mate steered the ship too far south, and as it entered Prince William Sound it crashed into Bligh Reef at a speed of 12 knots and ran aground, rupturing 8 of its 11 cargo tanks and spilling 11 million gallons of crude oil (260,000 barrels) into the pristine landscape. It was at the time the biggest environmental disaster in U.S. history.

The response to the disaster was far from satisfactory. The Alyeska Service Company, a consortium of seven oil companies led by Exxon, was primarily responsible for quick response. When its ranking executive was called within one-half hour of the spill in the early hours of the morning he sent a subordinate to check out the situation and went back to sleep. The required disaster contingency plan Alyeska had previously submitted to the Alaskan government stipulated that any disaster site could be reached with necessary equipment within five hours. In fact, the first Alyeska barge did not reach the spill site until fourteen hours after the spill, was unprepared to deal with a disaster of such magnitude, and didn't scoop up floating oil in the first two days before it reached the shoreline.

In addition, Exxon officials at the urging of their counsel refused to comment on the incident for almost one week at which time its CEO refused to acknowledge the extent of the problem and didn't even visit the scene of the accident for three weeks after the spill.

Initially Exxon blamed state and federal officials for delays in containing the oil spill which had spread into a 12 square mile slick in the first two days.

The spill ultimately grew to 100 square miles, and eventually soaked over 1,400 miles of coastline, killing untold birds, fish and wildlife and destroying unique habitat. Then when asked how it would pay for the massive cleanup costs a company spokesperson said it would raise gas prices. The public was further upset when the company claimed it was misquoted and blamed the media.

Finally the company launched a massive newspaper ad campaign ten days after the spill apologizing for it but still refusing to accept any responsibility. The public was unimpressed and remained outraged as the facts about the incident became public knowledge.

Eventually Exxon put together a full response team and worked continuously for six months to remedy the oil spill as best they could, employing more than 12,000 local residents who could no longer fish because of the spill. It then left the scene, claiming it had done all it could and had met its social responsibilities. The State of Alaska and the Federal government filed civil and criminal lawsuits against Exxon and its principals that were finally settled in 1991 as follows:

- Civil charges: Exxon agreed to pay the State of Alaska and the U.S. $900 million over a ten-year period for restoration.

- Criminal charges: Exxon would pay a fine of $250 million. Two restitution funds of $50 million each were established, one state and one federal. $125 million of the balance was forgiven, over strong objection of many Alaskans, due to Exxon's "cooperation" during the cleanup and upgraded safety procedures to prevent a reoccurrence. The remaining funds were divided between the Victims of Crime fund and the North American Wetlands Conservation fund.

In 1994 a federal jury awarded $287 million in compensatory damages to 15,000 fishermen and also returned a $5 billion punitive damages verdict against Exxon. (The punitive award was overturned by an appellate court in 2001.) Captain Hazelwood was assessed $5,000 in punitive damages by the jury, acquitted of operating the ship while drunk, but convicted of a misdemeanor offense of illegally discharging oil. He was also required to spend 1,000 hours of community service picking up garbage along Anchorage area highways. The Exxon Valdez was renamed the SeaRiver Mediterranean and is still carrying oil around the world, but is forever barred from entering Alaskan waters again.

There were some positive results of the disaster, other than the monetary awards. It resulted in Congress passing the Oil Pollution Act in 1990. It strengthened safety standards and emergency-response planning requirements.

It also imposed tighter environmental regulations on tanker ships that included the requirement that they must be built with double hulls to protect against leakage. The actual cleanup experience also produced a workable step-by-step procedure for future cleanups.

The massive publicity that surrounded the incident highlighted its cause as well as the less than cooperative early efforts of Exxon officials to realize its magnitude and offer needed assistance. This also resulted in a group called the Coalition for Environmentally Responsible Economies (CERES) creating a set of ten corporate commitments to help companies behave in a more socially responsible manner called the *Valdez Principles*. Many of the largest companies in the world have adopted them in principle, although whether or not they are applied on a day-day basis is still an open question. The ten points are as follows:

1. Protection of the Biosphere
2. Sustainable use of Natural Resources
3. Reduction and Disposal of Waste
4. Wise Use of Energy
5. Risk Reduction
6. Marketing of Safe Products and Services
7. Damage Compensation
8. Disclosure
9. Environmental Directors and Managers
10. Assessment and Annual Audit

Question: You are the new CEO of Exxon Corporation and have an opportunity to turn back the clock and properly handle this matter. What management errors were made, what ethical aspects should have been considered, and how would you have done things differently?

These first five examples of ethical predicaments have a number of common aspects. The companies were actively involved in either causing the problems, covering them up, failing to be cooperative, adopting postures of dirty tricks, playing hardball to resist prompt and proper resolution, trying to obscure the real facts, and generally behaving in what could be described as an unethical manner. When faced with no other alternatives due to relentless media, legislative or judicial pressure they ultimately were brought to a point of accountability for their misconduct at a cost of millions to billions of dollars to their stockholders.

At the same time, as occurs in most instances of massive corporate misconduct, when the smoke clears and the guilty are punished society eventually benefits because corrective laws are passed and judicial decisions are rendered in response to the situations so that we are better equipped to deal with situations like this in the future.

Our legal system does not usually act in an anticipatory or preventive law manner. Rather, it treats problems after they arise instead of before, and uses the past as prologue for the future.

For our final real-world study, here is a famous incident of product tampering that shows us how a large company can behave properly and do the right thing when faced with a potentially disastrous situation. It is a positive example of socially responsible corporate behavior.

6. Johnson & Johnson's Tylenol Murders

In the fall of 1982 seven people in Chicago died after ingesting an Extra-Strength Tylenol capsule that had been laced with cyanide. The Tylenol bottles had been purchased at different store locations. Initially the incidents were thought to be isolated and the causes of death were listed as unknown. But in a short time public officials were able to link them together, and media attention was focused on the deaths.

Law enforcement and company officials were able to confirm that no tampering could have occurred in the production plants due to their strict quality control procedures and the fact that the poisoned capsules were from four different manufacturing lots. Since the tainted capsules only showed up in the Chicago area, it was determined that the perpetrator bought some bottles of the product, tampered with their contents by inserting cyanide into some capsules, and then placed the tainted bottles back on the shelves of five different randomly selected local stores.

A national and local panic was imminent as three major television networks reported the deaths on their evening news broadcasts, and police drove through Chicago broadcasting Tylenol warnings on loudspeakers. A Chicago hospital received 700 telephone calls about Tylenol in one day. Many people in cities across the country complained of various symptoms and were admitted to hospitals on a general suspicion of cyanide poisoning.

Company officials at Johnson & Johnson's McNeil Consumer Products subsidiary immediately burst into action together with the parent company's CEO who demanded quick action in accordance with the company's 1940's social consciousness credo which puts customers first and stockholders last.

A massive and costly three-phase campaign was launched by the company to protect the public from product tampering and, at the same time, protect the company's reputation with the consuming public and its most profitable product which was Tylenol.

(1) The first phase was the actual handling of the immediate crisis. Along with the nationwide alert, Johnson & Johnson established working relationships with the Chicago police, the FBI, and the Food and Drug Administration.

The company wanted to assure a continuing active participation in the criminal investigation. It also immediately put up a $100,000 reward for the killer.

(2) The second phase, upon which the company's future hinged, was its public relations plan. The company immediately alerted consumers across the nation and worldwide, via the media, not to consume any type of Tylenol product until the extent of the tampering was determined. All production and advertising of Tylenol was stopped, and all Tylenol capsules were recalled from the market within one week of the incidents. This recall involved more than 31 million bottles of Tylenol with a retail value of over $100 million. The company also offered to exchange all Tylenol capsules already purchased, estimated at several million bottles, for new bottles of Tylenol in tablet form. It went even further in addressing attention to the general problem of product tampering by developing at its own cost a revolutionary new triple-tamper-resistant package, the first of its kind in the industry.

(3) The third phase was a comeback plan to bring the company in general and Tylenol in particular back to its former market-leading position. Directly following the incident the company's stock fell sharply as its market share of the non-prescription pain-reliever market dropped from 35% to 8%. An extensive marketing and advertising campaign was now focused on restoring public confidence in the following areas:

- Reintroduction of Tylenol capsules with the new triple-seal packaging
- Providing discount coupons for all Tylenol products through print media and toll-free telephone
- Launching new consumer ad campaigns
- Instituting retailer stock and shelf-level discounts
- Having company personnel make presentations to the medical community

The efforts by Johnson & Johnson were successful. Media articles about the Poisonings, the company's response, and its new packaging applauded its efforts, in a sense providing free advertising. From the inception of the crisis, the company had decided to fully cooperate with the press, radio and television. As the situation unfolded, the media then was able to do much of the company's work in rebuilding itself. The major news services estimated that the story was given the widest U.S. news coverage since the Kennedy assassination.

The company was also praised for resisting the temptation to disclaim responsibility because of its non-fault in this incident of a criminal outsider doing product tampering. Many other large companies have not behaved in such an ethical manner, including our first five "ethics in action" examples in this section.

The event also resulted in federal legislation that responded to the problems that arose and sought to prevent them in the future. In May, 1983, Congress passed the "Tylenol Bill," making malicious tampering with consumer products a federal offense.

In 1989 the Food and Drug Administration established a uniform national requirement for tamper-resistant packaging of over-the-counter products. When the smoke cleared, the company had regained their former market position and surpassed it. Tylenol is currently the number one over-the-counter analgesic in the country.

What about apprehending the poisoner? No one was ever charged with the Tylenol murders. But the main suspect, James Lewis, was convicted of attempting to extort $1 million from Johnson & Johnson by sending its McNeil Products subsidiary a ransom demand that threatened more deaths if payment was not made. He received a 20-year sentence and was released in October, 1995 after serving 13 years of his sentence.

Question: you are the new CEO of Johnson & Johnson and have an opportunity to turn back the clock. Is there anything you would have done differently in dealing with this incident?

C. ETHICAL SELF – TESTS

The Center for Business Ethics at Bentley College suggests these six questions be asked before the decision-making process is completed in pending transactions:

1. Is it right?
2. Is it fair?
3. Does it harm anyone?
4. What if it is reported on the front page of your local newspaper?
5. How would you explain it to your wife, son or daughter?
6. Is there any intuitive internal resistance to it?

Classical ethical self-tests suggested by various experts in the field include:

1. The Test of Reciprocity – ethical conduct to others brings it back to you. This is the equivalent of the Golden Rule we previously discussed as a theory of ethics.

2. The Test of Common Sense – think about the consequences of your actions before you act. If a contemplated act doesn't make sense, reconsider or restructure it.

3. The Test of Communication – discuss the situation with people whose opinions you respect on both sides of the issue before making a final decision.

4. The Test of Image – consider whether the proposed decision is compatible with your best view of yourself. If it isn't you, don't do it.

5. The Test of Fallout – what will be the ripple-effect of the contemplated decision? Look at it in the same way as throwing a pebble into a still forest pool. The ripples first cycle outward and then return back to the point of impact.

In the final analysis, parties are guided in their decision-making process by a multitude of factors that are easier to identify after the transaction is completed and its full impact felt than before it has been made.

What is your own self-monitoring ethical decision-making process?

D. DEVELOPING CORPORATE CRISIS MANAGEMENT

Whether or not a company can withstand a crisis is usually dependant on how it responds when the crisis arises. Once a crisis occurs, the company becomes an immediate target of the media, especially in this age of instant communication. The public's perception is usually that involved companies try to obscure the truth and avoid responsibility for their acts or failures to act. Silence and denials at the corporate level only confirm this perception. Because of this basic skepticism in believing in the good intentions of corporations involved in crisis situations, and the assumption that there are misdeeds or cover-ups, positive response-time is accelerated and a workable crisis plan is essential.

Here are some of the suggested steps in preventive crisis management:

1. Establish an advance Crisis Management Team within the company composed of a cross-section including expertise in areas of public relations, management, security, personnel, financial, legal and internal industry specialists.

2. Develop an advance Crisis Response Plan based upon a worst-case scenario so that all potential problem areas can be considered and planned for. These would include everything from the death or resignation of the CEO to allegations that company products or services are killing people.

The plan should include the who, what, when, where and how of dealing with a crisis. It should also produce in advance many of the possible materials necessary if a crisis occurs, including press releases, company statements, fact sheets, background information, scientific reports and communication flow-charts. In addition, the plan should be regularly updated and practiced with crisis simulations.

3. Practice information gathering through using available technology. This could include:
- on-line discussion groups, message boards and chat rooms,
- off-line focus and discussion groups,
- communications through cell phones, e-mail and wireless technology,
- media outlets and news clipping services

23.

TRENDS IN THE LAW

"The future is now."
<u>George Allen</u>

"All the ages are linked together by a chain
of causes and effects which unite
the existing state of the world with all that has gone before."
<u>Anne-Robert-Jacques Turgot</u>

"The only reason people want to be masters of the future
is to change the past."
Milan Kundera

The process of change can be considered positive or negative depending on the viewpoint of the observer. A legal principle or business procedure that ceases to exist or one that newly arrives is viewed by some as progressive and by others as regressive.

The law never really stands still. It may only give that impression from time to time since the gears of change usually grind slowly. And then sometimes there are sudden bursts of change energy that literally take our breath away.

What may have been declared as "final" legal precedents at a given point in time may then be modified by virtue of new court decisions from various judicial levels until a Supreme Court pronouncement puts the subject apparently to rest – until the Court changes its own prior decision as times and society change and new topical disputes are brought before it for consideration. The same process holds true for constitutional amendments, legislative enactments, regulatory rules, and local ordinances.

The scales of justice are continually being balanced by the diligent efforts of plaintiffs to locate, develop and legally test new causes of action, and the equally diligent efforts of defendants to resist.

And there may also be instances where the process of legal change comes full circle, back to where it started in the first place. Indeed, it may truly be said, "the only constant in law (and life) is change."

So, rather than label the following areas where the law seems to be reshaping itself as good or bad, we shall just note them in summary fashion and allow a bit more time to go by before we view their significance as major, minor, or marginal in the overall scheme of things. Let us just consider them to be food for thought and discussion:

Let's start with predicted Trends for the basic text material in Contracts and Sales. Here are 25 guesses, listed in no particular order other than their stream of consciousness journey from the author's mind to his computer keyboard:

1. Requiring the losing party in a lawsuit to pay the reasonable attorneys fees of the winner.

2. Limiting contingency fee attorney hiring to a maximum percentage of successful awards.

3. Lowering the amount of punitive damages that may be awarded and limiting them to specified types of lawsuits.

4. Increasing alternate dispute resolution and decreasing litigation.

5. Setting limits on the availability of jury trials.

6. Making the right to appeal an adverse judgment discretionary rather than mandatory.

7. Expanding remedies available to defendants victimized by bad-faith litigation.

8. Clarifying the doing-business and minimum-contacts tests of in personam jurisdiction to provide clear legal application tests for suits against non-residents.

9. Codifying the laws of the states to provide more uniformity and predictability.

10. Modifying Louisiana's French civil law system in favor of the basic common law rules and statutory exceptions that prevail in most states.

11. Reducing the permissible uses of procedures such as summary judgment and directed verdict that remove cases from jury determination.

12. Greater application of the fairness doctrine of promissory estoppel.

13. Elimination of the mailbox rule of offer acceptance.

14. Restructuring of the pre-existing duty rule of consideration.

15. Reversing the majority and minority views of minor's contracts.

16. Unifying the sanctions for usurious contracts.

17. Making the rules for garage sale purchases and unconscionable contracts more precise and practical.

18. Expanding the award of monetary damages in cases of lack of real consent to areas other than fraud.

19. Clarifying the confusion regarding permissible gifting and undue influence.

20. Raising the Statute of Fraud's $500 limitation for sale of goods contracts.

21. Adoption of the "first to notify" rule for cases of multiple assignments.

22. Reduction of the right of sellers of goods to limit implied warranties.

23. Shortening of statutes of limitation for commercial lawsuits.

24. Limiting the allowance of class action lawsuits.

25. Codifying state civil laws in areas beyond the UCC to create a more uniform and predictable legal framework

Next, here are 25 more potential legal Trend areas with an expanded focus on the overall commercial marketplace, based on what appear to be significant legislative and judicial developments:

1. The electronic courtroom is rapidly expanding as litigants use technology to gather their evidence and present it to hearing examiners, arbitrators and mediators, and courts and juries. In addition, paperless electronic procedures are also being adopted by many courts as the preferred way of filing and administering pending lawsuits. The federal judiciary has also recognized the challenges of litigating in a world of digital data, and has published a set of proposed rules for e-discovery. Public comment on the rules was open until February 15, 2005 and their scheduled effective date is December 1, 2006.

2. Innovations in Science and Technology are impacting other legal areas:

- Convicted felons are now allowed to file legal challenges to request DNA testing to prove their innocence. A number of states, including Florida, have commenced "Innocence Projects" to review capital felony cases before 1995 (when DNA testing of criminal defendants started), to verify legitimacy.

- The Federal Trade Commission's "do-not-call" registry directed against telemarketers elicited "yes" advance registrations from 50 million consumers.

- Junk faxes are regulated by the Telephone Consumer Protection Act of 1991 that entitles each recipient of an unsolicited, faxed advertisement to sue and recover damages of from $500 to $1,500 per fax. Affected consumers are using class action lawsuits to maximize their recoveries.

- Downloading of popular music pits the innovations of computer technology against the law of copyright infringement, as the recording industry trade association (RIAA) continues to vigorously pursue offenders (including attempting to subpoena the records of ISP's to reveal the name of subscribers suspected of downloading and circulating bootleg recordings) while at the same time trying to educate the public to accept the idea of paying for downloads.

    The trend is definitely toward legal protection of this creative material. In *MGM Studios v. Grokster, (U.S. 2005)*, the Supreme Court ruled for the first time that Internet file-sharing services Grokster and StreamCast Networks were liable under U.S. copyright law for user's illegal downloads of music and movies using their software. In September, 2005 an Australian federal court judge ruled that song-swapping service Kazaa must install filters to prevent its software from being used for unauthorized sharing.

- Worldwide software piracy of DVD's and videotapes has also become a multi-million dollar business. The top three international counterfeiting countries are Vietnam, China and Russia. Diplomatic pressure and the threat of retaliatory economic sanctions is being exerted to stop this practice. The motion picture trade association (MPAA) is using the same strategy as RIAA to force compliance.

- Anti-piracy copy protection technology is quietly being added to e-books, CD's, DVD's, and other products, known in the industry as Digital Rights Management (DRM).

- The new Wi-Fi technology, known as wireless Internet, is expanding. Popular bookstores, restaurants, hotels and motels are now routinely offering it to customers and newer laptops include wireless capability as its availability grows. Ethernet bridges are also offered to convert older laptops to wi-fi.

- Cell phone technology has changed the way we live. Laws have been passed prohibiting the use of cell phones while driving, although few are enforced, unless an accident results. Right of privacy issues have surfaced as health clubs have recently begun to ban cell phones from locker rooms due to the current "cell-cameras" that can also shoot photos as well as transmit them by e-mail or upload them for online viewing. Digital voyeurism is another trend requiring legal protection.

- Pornography on the Internet – legal challenges are being heard to prevent enforcement of regulations requiring public libraries to use an adults-only screening system on grounds of violation of 1st Amendment freedoms. At issue is the Child Online Protection Act of 1998 (COPA). It provides sanctions of up to six months in jail and $100,000 fines for companies that "make obscene material available to any minor ... by means of the World Wide Web."

  The "Indecency" Act raised maximum fines against broadcast licensees from $27,500 to $500,000 per incident and raised top fines against individual performers from $11,000 to $500,000 – causing a zero-tolerance policy by major broadcasting companies. The "Amber Alert" Law passed in April 2003 by Congress as an amendment to the Truth in Domain Names Act, makes it a federal crime with up to four years imprisonment to use misleading Internet addresses to lure children to pornographic sites.

- Spam on the Internet – the Federal Can-Spam Act of 2003 (effective January 1, 2004) was passed by Congress to finally address the problem. It preempts state laws as to civil penalties, imposing a fine of $250 per e-mail violation with a cap of $2 million, and a maximum 5-year prison sentence.

- Whether or not an employer commits an invasion of privacy when searching a worker's e-mails to ostensibly determine the status of pending business matters and verify trade secret protection is another legal issue. The employer-employee sensitivities in this area also led to congressional passage of (ECPA), banning interception of messages at time of transmission, but otherwise allows employer monitoring of employee emails and exempts the innocent owner of the e-mail system from liability.

- Online gambling is a multi-million dollar business that is essentially unregulated in Cyberspace. While most states have laws prohibiting gambling, only a few like California also declare online gambling illegal. The practical problem, of course, is how to locate and punish the offenders? The casino and sports betting sites pay off winning customers because the competition demands it. Legally however, if a customer demands payment of account balances and the betting site refuses, there is no legal recourse. The Justice Department announced in November, 2004 that it will crackdown on Internet gambling advertising. Critics suggest it violates 1st Amendment free speech.

- Internet mash-ups involve mixing data from different websites to create all sorts of new offerings – the tech equivalent of the sandwich. Links to most of the map mashups are found at: www.googlemapsmania.blogspot.com

3. The tort reform movement's attack on large jury awards of punitive damages against big corporate defendants, malpractice claims against doctors and hospitals, and other actions alleging willful, malicious and reckless conduct of the defendant is registering gains. Wyoming, Oregon, Nevada and Florida approved constitutional amendments in the November, 2004 elections limiting medical malpractice awards and contingent attorney's fees. (Florida's Amendment 3 capped contingency fees in medical liability lawsuits at 30% of the first $250,000 in damages, and 10% of the excess.) The Class Action Fairness Act was enacted in February, 2005 to eliminate or restrict the use of state class action lawsuits in mass torts and related cases over $5 million where 2/3 of the plaintiffs are out-of-state by requiring them to be heard only under the more restrictive procedures of federal court.

The U.S. Supreme Court's 2003 *State Farm v. Campbell* decision suggested for the first time that in most cases the ratio of punitive damages to actual damages should not exceed nine to one. Many state courts are now following that guideline for jury awards and in some cases, overturning prior awards of larger amounts.

Some states have split-award laws that require a percentage of civil punitive damage awards to be placed in public benefit trusts or be awarded to victims of crimes. In some states nursing homes have succeeded in new laws that limit punitive damages and raise the standard of proof in abuse/neglect cases to require the plaintiff to prove "a conscious disregard of life, health, or safety or intentional misconduct. There are also renewed suggestions that a "loser pays" rule be followed whereby the prevailing party in civil lawsuits should in all cases be entitled to recover their reasonable attorneys fees and court costs from the losing party.

Advocates of this rule say that it would reduce the number of "nuisance" tort lawsuits that are filed for the purpose of trying to induce settlement of questionable claims. Interestingly, those opposed to the rule say it will have the opposite effect and cause the filing of more marginal cases, rather than reducing their number. What do you think?

4. Despite tort reform, class action mass tort lawsuits are still being litigated in record numbers in situations where catastrophic injuries have been suffered by a large group of similarly affected persons. They may lack the financial strength to sue individually, but if a class action is certified by the court joining all claimants into one action, the stakes are raised to the highest level, the finest legal representation is available on a contingent-fee (no win/no pay) basis. Some examples of these mass tort actions are:

    a) revival of asbestos cases related to automobile brake linings and the World Trade Center cleanup, and new claims by workers alleging exposure without showing any caused impairment

b) claims against non-profit hospitals brought by non-insured patients who were either denied care, received an inferior level of service, or were charged more than insured patients

c) obesity lawsuits against fast-food vendors (States are passing "Baby McBills" to ban personal injury obesity suits against fast food chains)

d) tobacco litigation against deep-pocket manufacturers

e) alcohol litigation that copies the tobacco claims

f) live-television reality or talk show torts

g) automobile tire-tread separation claims

h) continuation of drug and product litigation concerning Fen-Phen diet pills, Benlate fungicide, Dalkon Shield IUD's, Dow-Corning silicone breast implants, Agent Orange herbicide, and Baycol cholesterol reducer

i) new claims concerning women's hormone replacement therapy

j) new claims arising from recall of the Vioxx anti-inflammatory drug that allegedly can cause strokes and other heart problems. The first case ended in a Texas jury award to plaintiff August, 2005 of $24.4M in actual damages and $220M in punitive damages in *Ecarol A. Ernst v. Merck & Co., Inc.* One week after this decision, over 5,000 similar lawsuits for damages against Merck & Co. were pending in state and federal courts.

k) new claims against Coca-Cola for violating the Unfair Trade Practices Act by using non-nutritive sweeteners in its fountain drink syrups

l) new claims by third-party payor health funds who had to issue refunds to insureds and beneficiaries when Baycol was withdrawn from sale

m) new claims for sexual discrimination in hiring/promotion against Wal-Mart stores involving up to 1.6 million current and former female employees

n) new claims against Dupont for failing to warn consumers about Teflon-related cancer dangers of PFOA, allegedly in coated cookware

o) new claims against Taser stun gun manufacturers by police departments for falsely claiming they are non-lethal

p) new claims against Medtronic by heart patients for recalled defective implantable defribillators

q) new claims for silicosis damages

r) new claims from clinical drug trials ranging from wrongful death damage claims to actions to enforce the right to continue receiving the drugs

5. Separation of Church and State will continue to be constitutional issues and will be tested in courts. Some of the questions to be answered will be: Should the pledge of allegiance contain the words "under God?" Should a prayer be allowed before athletic competitions? Should schoolchildren be required to sing the National Anthem daily? Should a sculpture of the Ten Commandments be allowed in front of a state courthouse? Should scholarship assistance be allowed for students who plan to go into the ministry?

- *McCreary County, KY. V. ACLU of KY. and Van Orden v. Perry (Texas) (U.S. 2005)* ruled that displaying framed copies of the 10 commandments text inside two Kentucky courthouses was not permissible, but allowed a six-foot granite outside display monument in the Texas state capitol as one of 17 historical displays on the 22-acre lot as a legitimate historical tribute.

- *Elk Grove Unified School District v. Newdow(U.S. 2004)* ruled against the atheist plaintiff seeking to ban the Pledge of Allegiance "under God" wording from public schools nationwide on procedural grounds, but he refiled his complaint and a federal judge ruled in September, 2005 that reciting the Pledge was unconstitutional and entered a restraining order preventing its recitation until a higher court decides the matter. The court's order was based on a 2003 Ninth Circuit case that found teacher-led recitation of the Pledge to be "coercive" because it "places students in the untenable position of choosing between participating in an exercise with religious content or protesting."

- *The Circle School v. Pappert (381 F.3d 172 (3rd Cir. 2004)*, a federal court affirmed a lower court ruling that struck down a Pennsylvania law that required state schoolchildren to recite the Pledge of Allegiance or sing the National Anthem daily, unless they declined for political or religious reasons with parental notification. The legal issue in these cases is whether the pledge is a patriotic activity or promotion of religion.

- *Rose v. Planned Parenthood of S.C. (4th Cir. 2004)* overturned a 2001 state law that allowed issuance of "Choose Life" license plates. It ruled that they violated the 1st Amendment because abortion rights supporters were not given a similar forum to express their beliefs. The U.S. Court declined to hear the case in January, 2005. (Many other states including Florida still offer such plates.)

6. Damage claims against the Catholic Church for alleged sexual abuse will probably find their way into the courts in those instances where out-of-court settlement is not completed. One of the legal questions to be answered will be how far back in time may a claimant go? Is there a limitations period on such claims? So far courts have said no. Some church defendants are declaring bankruptcy as a legal strategy to avoid having to pay large civil damage claims in pending lawsuits.

7. Assisted suicide is a legal issue that gained national headlines some years ago through the case of Dr. Death - Jack Kevorkian and later with Oregon's assisted suicide law that took effect in 1998. It is the only state to legally allow mercy killing. The law gives Oregon doctors authority to prescribe controlled substances to competent, terminally ill patients who are within six months of dying. In *Ashcroft (now Gonzalez) v. Oregon*, the government sought to invalidate the law as violating the 1970 controlled Substances Act. The Federal 9th Circuit disagreed, but the Supreme Court announced in February, 2005 that it would hear the case.

In Florida, the Terri Schiavo case gained international attention. She remained in a vegetative state for over 14 years without a living will or other health care directive, while her husband and family fought over the legal right to let her die. A Florida lower court ordered removal of her feeding tube, the legislature passed "Terri's Law" prohibiting it, the Florida Supreme Court overturned the law, and the U.S. court refused to hear the case in January, 2005. Teri Schiavo died March 31, 2005.

8. International trade law will remain in the headlines as the European Union and other foreign trading blocs flex their economic muscles and have disputes with the United States over the issues of protecting local jobs and domestic industries through tariffs, quotas, subsidies and other trade barriers versus free trade.

9. Environmental law will continue to be important as the search for wasting resources such as oil, natural gas, minerals and lumber, and general continued industrialization creates conflict with persons living in the natural areas involved. In June, 2005 the EPA announced final guidelines for states to curb industrial emissions that cause haze in 156 national parks and wilderness areas by year 2007. The relentless increase in gas prices and the nation's dependence on foreign oil led to the August, 2005 Energy Bill. The legislation includes tax breaks and loan guarantees for new nuclear power plants, clean coal technology and wind energy. For consumers, the law will provide tax credits for buying hybrid gasoline-electric cars or making energy conservation improvements in new and existing homes.

10. Criminal laws are constantly being tested in the courts:

- *Miranda v. Arizona (U.S. 1966)* Police questioning procedures.
- The death penalty and, possible "humane" methods of execution.
- *Apprendi v. New Jersey (U.S. 2000)* ruled that "aggravating"or enhancing factors to increase penalties for a crime must be determined by a jury, rather than the judge alone. *Ring v. Arizona (U.S. 2002)* ruled that all judge-imposed sentences were unconstitutional. *Schriro v. Summerlin (U.S. 2003)* ruled that the jury sentencing requirement was not retroactive.

- *Blakely v. Washington (U.S. 2004)* made it unconstitutional for judges to impose sentences above state guidelines but still below statutory maximums on facts not found by a jury. *U.S. v. Booker (2005)* threw out federal mandatory sentencing guidelines, essentially making them advisory rather than mandatory, and subject to the rule of "reasonableness" in each case. *Guzman v. U.S. (2nd Cir. 2005)* ruled "Booker"not retroactive to cases finalized before it was issued, and *Schardt v. Payne (9th Cir. 2005)* also ruled "Blakely" not retroactive.

- *Atkins v. Virginia (U.S. 2002)* held that execution of the mentally retarded violated the 8th Amendment's prohibition against cruel and unusual punishment, leaving to the states the right to define it and decide how to apply it.

In an ironic twist – the plaintiff was later found mentally competent by a Virginia jury on August 12, 2005 and was scheduled for execution December 2, 2005 for the robbery and slaying of an Air Force enlisted man.

- *Roper v. Simmons (2005)* ruled that executing juvenile offenders (under the age of 18 when they committed the crime) violated the 8th Amendment.

- *Deck v. Missouri (U.S. 2005)* forbids the use of visible shackles during a capital trial, unless the use is justified in the interests of courtroom security, flight risk, or other similar factors.

- *Batson v. Kentucky (U.S. 1986)* barred racially discriminatory use of peremptory challenges in criminal jury selection, usually by striking black jurors in a case involving a black defendant.

- *Rompilla v. Beard (U.S. 2005)* expanded the doctrine of ineffectiveness of counsel when it set aside the death penalty of a Pennsylvania man because his lawyers failed to search files of past convictions for mitigating evidence – such as mental retardation or a "traumatic upbringing" to be used in the sentencing phase of the trial, even if the defendant was not interested in getting a lighter sentence. *Wiggins v. Smith (U.S. 2003)* previously faulted lawyers for "inattention" in investigating records.

- Regarding Fourth Amendment search and seizure in traffic stop cases, the Court expanded the doctrine in *Caballes v. Illinois (U.S. 2005)* by ruling that drug-sniffing dogs can be used to check out motorists stopped for traffic violations even if officers have no reason to suspect they may be carrying narcotics. Normally, police can't search cars for drugs without having specific probable cause. But in *Rabb v. Florida (U.S. 2005)* the use of a drug-sniffing dog outside the suspect's home was ruled a 4th Amendment violation. And in an earlier 2002 case, the Court rejected police use of devices to detect heat emanating from home where it was suspected that marijuana was being grown.

- Usage of medical marijuana has been growing as a legal issue as various state laws permit it and others prohibit it. *Gonzalez v. Raich (U.S. 2005)* ruled that federal anti-drug laws can be enforced against users of medical marijuana as a Schedule I banned substance in California (The Compassionate Use Act of 1996) and nine other states if the federal government chooses to do so. But those state laws were not overturned by the case and remain in effect. This area of the law remains confused.

- Oregon was concerned with the rise in labs that can produce illegal methamphetamines using over-the-counter cold and allergy medicines containing pseudoephedrine. It enacted a law August 16, 2005 making it the first state to require prescriptions for these items. It had previously required consumers to show ID and sign a log when buying them.

11. Abortion rights have always been a sensitive issue and the pro-life v. pro-choice debate will continue to rage until the U.S. Supreme Court decides to revisit the issue again in a challenge to its landmark 1973 ruling in *Roe v. Wade*. That case ruled that a woman had a constitutional right to abortion before the fetus is viable, and to terminate her pregnancy if it poses a risk to her health. In *McCorvey v. Hill (5th Cir. 2004)* the original case plaintiff known as Jane Roe (Norma McCorvey) unsuccessfully sued to vacate the original ruling in her favor thirty years after it had been decided.

Other related issues are:

- Whether or not the parents of an abortion patient must be notified of the procedure, or consent to it before it takes place.
- Legal definitions of when a fetus is "viable."
- Legality of so-called late-term abortions. The Partial-Birth Abortion Ban Act of 2003, prohibiting pregnancy termination in the second or third trimester, was ruled unconstitutional in 2004 because it lacked exceptions for rape, sexual battery and mother's health risks.
- Legal standards for the degree of health risks or medical emergencies allowing abortion procedures.
- Recent wrongful death tort cases against fertility clinics that allegedly negligently discarded fertilized egg "embryos", focusing on the legal question of whether or not a pre-embryo is a human being.
- Stem cell research to treat juvenile diabetes and Parkinson's disease, requiring destruction of aborted embryos.
- Whether protests outside abortion clinics violate Federal racketeering or extortion laws. In 1998 the Court imposed a nationwide ban on protests that interfere with abortion clinic business, barring demonstrators from trespassing, setting up blockades, or behaving violently. The ban was lifted in 2003, but then the 7th Circuit Federal Appeals court questioned whether the ban should be imposed again. The Supreme Court will decide in *Scheidler (and Operation Rescue) v. National Organization for Women.*

12. Gay and lesbian rights are currently the most dramatic area of legal change. While most legal scholars assumed other areas of legal change would gather most of the public's attention, the issue of legal rights of gays exploded in 2004 and continues to be front-page news. The questions asked include: Should we legalize gay marriage, or gay civil unions, or legislate the same legal rights as married couples for same-sex partners in a long relationship through domestic partnership laws? Or should all non-heterosexual unions be outlawed? Should gays be allowed to be foster parents and/or legally adopt?

- Forty-three states have Defense of Marriage laws or similar statutes that define marriage in terms of "a union between a man and a woman." Some of these laws have been ruled unconstitutional by state lower courts as violating the equal protection clause of the state constitutions, and await appeal.

The Federal Defense of Marriage Act was signed into law in 1995, and a Federal Bankruptcy judge ruled August, 2004 that it was constitutional. Gay couples are ineligible for federal benefits like social security, Medicaid health care, and estate tax spousal exemptions.

- 4 states have Domestic Partnership Acts or Domestic Relations Laws that grant same-sex couples most of the same legal rights as married couples.

- Same-sex civil unions are legal in Vermont (2000) and Connecticut (2005).

- Same-sex marriages are legally allowed to residents of Massachusetts by virtue of the 2003 case of *Goodrich v. Dep't. of Public Health*. Sister states do not give them "full faith and credit." The state legislature rejected in September, 2005 a proposed constitutional amendment banning the marriages. Same-sex marriages are also legally allowed in Belgium, the Netherlands, and as of July, 2005 in Spain and Canada.

- Lawsuits are pending in 20 states to challenge state bans on gay marriages.

- *Forum for Academic and Institutional Rights v. Rumsfeld (3rd Cir. 2004)* ruled that Congress cannot force law schools to allow U.S. armed forces recruiters on campus, by threatening to cut - off all federal funding – since the military policy of excluding gays and lesbians conflicts with anti-discrimination policies. The case overturned the 1994 Solomon Amendment. In an ironic twist, the ruling was based in part on the 2000 Supreme Court case that allowed the Boy Scouts to exclude gay scoutmasters. Law schools were said to have the same exclusionary 1st Amendment rights of expression. In May, 2005 the U.S. Supreme Court agreed to review that case.

13. Voting issues surfaced in the last two closely-contested presidential elections of 2000 and 2004 including electronic versus paper balloting, requiring add-on printers to leave a paper trail for computerized voting machines, issues of missing absentee ballots, electoral vote splitting based on popular vote, right of ex-felons to participate, and limits on financial contributions and media saturation.

14. Domestic relationship issues continue to arise in the legal areas of pre-marital agreements, "palimony" financial rights of unmarried couples, community property versus rehabilitative alimony laws, and grandparent visitation. In *Peck v. Peck*, Dallas' 5th Court of Appeals ruled for the first time that it is within a judge's discretion to "permanently" enjoin both parents from having a person of the opposite sex stay overnight while the parent was in possession of the couple's child.

15. Tribal legal rights – the financial revenge of the native peoples for their exploitation by the federal government and its citizen-settlers, broken treaties, confiscation of lands, relocation of tribes, and other abuses is finally being achieved through skillful legal maneuvering.

In issues of tribal gaming, since the native tribes are legally considered to be sovereign nations on their own federally-designated reservation land, they are not subject to local gaming laws and have become immensely prosperous through their casino-hotel properties.

16. Corporate finance reform – the Wall Street scandals involving Enron, WorldCom, Tyco, Martha Stewart and others, concerning financial irregularities, dissemination of false and misleading information, and fraud on investors led to passage, after years of failed attempts, of the Sarbanes-Oxley Act of 2002.

The mutual fund industry that originally escaped the scandals was itself targeted for its market timing tactics that "churned" short-term profits in excessive trading activity by exploiting time-zone differences. And now the SEC has passed new rules effective in 2006 that regulate hedge funds with assets of more than $25 million. These funds were previously unregulated because of the financial sophistication of the client base, but now will have to comply with new oversight rules to protect investors. The insurance industry has also been targeted for alleged fraud, bid-rigging, illegal steering, other anti-competitive practices, and overcharging of premiums for property casualty, health and workers' compensation insurance.

17. IRS tax reform - shelters that allowed investors to avoid paying billions of dollars in taxes have been slowly removed from the financial markets by attacking selling companies and their investors. IRS announced as of year-end 2003 that it will target lawyers and accountants who devise illegal tax shelters and issue advisory opinions on which investors rely.

18. Campaign finance reform – the McClain-Feingold Campaign Finance Reform Act of 2002 was judicially upheld in December 2003. It prohibits unlimited "soft money" contributions from wealthy contributors and bans use of corporate or union funds for electioneering communications. But the loophole for "hard money" smaller contributions of up to $2,000 per contributor remain, and partisan ads are placed by so-called political action groups that claim to be independent of the candidates themselves.

Whether or not states may limit campaign spending by political candidates is also being legally tested. Vermont passes a law in 1977 that would cap the dollar amounts candidates for state office could spend in a 2-year election cycle. The law has been in limbo as litigation has moved through various court levels up to the U.S. Supreme Court. It has announced it will decide campaign spending issues soon.

19. Tobacco company personal injury liability lawsuits continue to evolve. They have run a circular course through the courts from total non-liability based on the product liability defense of "assumption of the risk", to huge plaintiff judgments including punitive damages, back to more defense victories than losses.

Additional tobacco issues are those relating to:

- Class action lawsuits under state unfair competition laws for allegedly targeting teens with provocative and deceptive ads such as "Joe Camel", the "Marlboro Man", and their "B-Kool" campaigns. The legal question is whether they are pre-empted by the Federal Cigarette Labeling and Advertising Act. *In re Tobacco Cases II (Cal. 2004).*

- Whether the "first-brand" tobacco company is liable for a smoker's subsequent lung cancer after smoking other cigarette brands. *Rosen v. Brown & Williamson Tobacco Corp. (N.Y. 2004).*

- The damage claims of flight attendants for inhalation of secondhand smoke were partially resolved in a 1997 industry-wide settlement between the tobacco industry and nonsmoking attendants for cabin smoke before its 1990 ban in domestic flights. A system of mini-trials are being heard to decide whether each flight attendant deserves compensatory damages.

  Other secondhand smoke litigation that involves landlord – tenant issues includes these state cases:
  Harwood Capital Corp. v. Carey (Mass. 2005) – eviction of condominium tenants smoking inside the premises and bothering neighbors, even though their lease didn't have a non-smoking clause and they were told by the landlord that smoking was permissible.

  Dworkin v. Paley (Ohio 1994) – secondhand smoke that drifted into an apartment through the ventilation system from the unit below breached that tenant's right to "quiet enjoyment."

- Does the California statute of limitations for suing tobacco companies begin to run when the plaintiff is first diagnosed with a health problem, or much earlier when he should have known of the potential dangers of smoking? *Soliman v. Philip Morris, 311 F.3d 966 (9th Cir. 2002) ruled for the defendant, but Grisham v. Philip Morris will now be decided by the California Supreme Court to resolve the issue in that state.*

- Tobacco grower settlements with cigarette makers: In 1999 tobacco companies agreed to pay growers and quota-holders $5.1 billion over 12 years to compensate for reduced demand, as part of the $206 billion settlement of anti-smoking lawsuits filed by 46 states against the four largest cigarette makers. In 2004 Congress agreed to pay the growers $10.1 billion to end price supports begun in the 1930's.

- State laws banning smoking in indoor workplaces, food service areas, public auditoriums-arenas-stadiums, and related commercial and recreational facilities.

- Consumer fraud class action lawsuits alleging fraudulent marketing of "light" cigarettes as posing less health risks than other cigarettes.

20. Gun industry lawsuits have been filed based on the success of the tobacco cases, but the results have been far different. The two types of actions are product liability claims that handguns are unreasonably dangerous, and negligently allowing them to fall into the hands of street criminals. Although some favorable settlements were reached, most cases failed.

The new Federal Gun Law passed October, 2005 requires separate child safety locks to be sold with each handgun and imposes a penalty for violation of loss of license and/or a $10,000 fine. The key aspect of the new law for the gun industry is a liability shield in favor of firearms manufacturers, dealers and importers against lawsuits brought by victims of gun crimes.

21. Legal rights of the disabled: *Spector v. Norwegian Cruise Line (U.S. 2005)* ruled for the first time that the Americans with Disabilities Act of 1990 (ADA) protecting the disabled from discrimination in public places and transportation also covers cruise ships that operate under foreign flags but stop in U.S. waters. (The 11th Cir. had previously ruled yes while the 5th Cir. had ruled no as to applicability.) *Tennessee v. Lane (U.S. 2004)* authorized lawsuits by disabled persons whose physical access to courts was hampered by courthouse design. *Goodman v. Georgia* will also be heard by the Court on the issue of whether disabled inmates can sue states over prison conditions under the ADA.

22. *Granholm v. Heald,* decided by the Supreme Court in May, 2005 struck down as discriminatory laws in New York and Michigan allowing only in-state wineries to sell to state residents but disallowing wine shipments to state residents by out-of-state wineries. The decision has the potential to open up direct access to out-of-state wineries for residents of 24 states. 26 other states plus D.C. already allow these direct sales.

23. Whistle-blower lawsuits under the federal False Claims Act are increasing for alleged Medicare fraud against state governments committed by the drug and pharmaceutical industry involving price manipulation. State-led civil actions accuse the biggest drug makers of inflating drug prices so that state reimbursements to pharmacists, doctors and clinics serving low-income Medicaid clients were overstated. These hidden benefits were to induce use of the drug company's products.

Federal whistleblower laws also prohibit retaliatory firing of employees who report violations. This was extended in *Willy v. Adm. Review Board, U.S. Dep't of Labor (5th Cir. 2005)* to in-house counsel who blew the whistle on their employers. The attorney-client privilege between the lawyer and his company did not require exclusion of key evidence of the violations.

24. The 1970 Racketeer Influenced and Corrupt Organizations Act (RICO) was ostensibly created to apply only to traditional Mafia-style criminals as a way to force them to pay for their criminal enterprise. But, over the years, its interpretation has been a tug of war between the U.S. Supreme Court allowing its use in civil disputes and the more restrictive views of the federal appellate courts. RICO is a favored remedy in civil disputes. Since it was modeled on antitrust law, successful private plaintiffs may recover treble (3X) damages. Discovery is allowed going back as much as 10 years. And, it has a longer four-year statute of limitations.

In *U.S. v. Philip Morris USA Inc., 396 F.3d 1190 (D.C. Cir. 2005)*, the government sued Big Tobacco based upon RICO, seeking disgorgement of the $280 billion it earned through alleged fraud by lying to the American people about the dangers of smoking. The appellate court eliminated that remedy from the massive lawsuit, conflicting with prior decisions of other federal circuits, so a final ruling to resolve these conflicts by the U.S. Supreme Court was necessary. *U.S. v. Carson, 52 F.3d 1173 (2nd Cir. 1995)* and *Richard v. Hoechst Celanese Chem. Group, 355 F.3d 345 (5th Cir. 2003)* had both authorized disgorgement of tainted profits as a RICO remedy. But the High Court affirmed the appellate court in October, 2005.

25. The U.S. Supreme Court, for the first time in many years, has vacancies due to the death of Justice Rehnquist and announced retirement of Justice O'Connor. New justices are now on the bench and since most recent cases have been decided by a 5-4 vote, the effect on future cases is yet to be determined. Key cases to be heard by the newly constituted Court's for its 2005-2006 term are:

- *Ayotte v. Planned Parenthood of Northern New England* – tests the constitutionality of a New Hampshire law that prevents physicians from performing abortions on under-18 girls until 48 hours after a parent is notified because it lacks an exception for health emergencies.

- *Rumsfeld v. FAIR* – tests the constitutionality of the Solomon Amendment that requires the withholding of federal funds from colleges that deny military recruiters the same access to campus as other employers.

- *Gonzalez v. Oregon* – tests the power of the U.S. attorney general under federal drug laws to block enforcement of Oregon's "Death With Dignity Act" which allows physicians to help terminally ill patients end their lives.

- *U.S. v. Georgia* – tests whether the states are shielded from lawsuits brought by disabled prisoners who allege violations of the ADA.

- *Randall v. Sorrell* – tests whether states can restrict the spending of political candidates without violating their 1st Amendment freedom of speech rights.

- *Gonzalez v. O Centro Espirita* – tests whether the Religeous Freedom Restoration Act of 1993 requires the federal government to waive drug-control laws to permit importation of hallucinogenic tea for use by a religious group founded in Brazil that now practices in the U.S.

- *Hudson v. Michigan* – tests whether police with a search warrant who fail to knock and announce themselves before barging into a home where they suspect drug activity can use at trial any drug evidence they find.

Now that these 50 Trend areas have been presented for your consideration, are there any others in the specific area of Contracts and Sales or the broader overall Business Marketplace that you see developing?

24.

THE BUSINESS LAW SURVIVAL GUIDE
CHAPTER CASE UPDATES

1.
THE PREVENTIVE LAW METHOD:
THE POWER OF ANTICIPATORY THINKING

The business marketplace reflects continuing emphasis on using the anticipatory thinking approach to identify and defuse potentially damaging business law time bombs in commercial transactions. If they can be prevented, minimized or effectively re-structured, one's chances for success are dramatically improved. By asking "what if?" when a transaction is in its early stages and exploring alternate legal planning scenarios, the chances of a successful outcome are greatly enhanced.

Every executive business decision has legal implications, so the focus must be on skillfully managing this legal factor. Therefore many companies are now creating separate legal risk-management departments that focus on the preventive law considerations discussed in the text, and experts in the field predict that within the next five years this advance legal analysis and planning concept will become the recommended way of doing business.

In addition, the long-standing legal maxim, "ignorance of the law is no defense," has new meaning in our current Internet cyber-world of instantly available information. There is absolutely no practical or legal excuse these days not to know the rules of law governing proposed future action and the judicial results of failing to do this simple research. More and more business people understand that they can become instant experts on almost any subject just by a few keystrokes on a computer keyboard that will access them to one of the many excellent search engines currently available.

The business community finally pays attention and "gets the message" when our litigious society imposes more and more costly lessons on the losing party in contracts or sales disputes who are blown-up financially by one of those pesky avoidable business law time-bombs. So, the best indicator of *what to do* is often those cases that illustrate to us *what not to do*. What happened in the past can guide our future if we pay attention.

A.   Let's first look at an example of a litigant who paid the price for not knowing the law governing their telemarketing business practice of faxing unsolicited advertisements to prospective customers, resulting in a costly damage award against the sender, because the defendants failed to follow the requirements of the Federal Telephone Consumer Protection Act of 1991 which makes it unlawful "to use any telephone facsimile machine, computer, or other device to send an unsolicited advertisement to a telephone facsimile machine."

It also provides a private right of action whereby "for each violation a person is entitled to the greater of actual monetary loss or $500 in damages."

In the case of *Hooters of Augusta v. Nicholson, 537 S.E.2d 468 (Ga. App. 2000),* the national restaurant chain sent out 7,825 unsolicited faxes through its hiring of the Value-Fax telemarketing company. Nicholson was a recipient of one of the faxes and filed a class action against both parties on behalf of himself and all other recipients, seeking injunctive relief to stop the transmittals and substantial money damages. The trial resulted in a $12 million judgment in favor of the plaintiffs.

The defendants objected to the class action certification and the resultant judgment claiming that no private right of action for damages existed under Georgia law. They were unsuccessful and the judgment was affirmed.

Notice how easily the whole problem could have been avoided. Can you imagine a telemarketing company, like Value-Fax that either doesn't know or doesn't care that its daily business is illegal? And what about a large company like Hooters hiring them without making sure that their marketing plan is lawful?

B.   Lack of anticipatory thinking often occurs in disputes where a party forfeits contract rights by failing to give notice in a timely manner.

1. In *Sensormatic Electronics Corp. v. First National Bank, 2005 U.S. App. LEXIS 18868 (3rd Cir. 2005),* plaintiff had a buy-back option at the end of its 20-year franchise lease with James Winner, inventor of the Club auto anti-theft device. It had that option to terminate the franchise agreement 11 times during the lease term as well as the right to buy-back the franchise for $1 million by giving 90-days written notice. It delayed sending its notice of buy-back to Winner until just 47 days before the lease was to conclude, and he then declared a default. Litigation ensued for five years, resulting in judgment in favor of Winner, awarding him $32.6 million in unpaid franchise fees and interest.

2. In *Aspro Mechanical Contracting, Inc. v. Fleet Bank, N.A., 805 N.E.2d 1037 (N.Y. App. 2004),* the bank made $12.5 million in construction loans for a New York City Housing authority project and was the disbursing agent. When the project was finished, the bank repaid itself. Plaintiff and other subcontractors who were not paid sued, alleging that the bank wrongfully diverted trust assets in violation of the state lien law. A $1.9 million judgment against the bank was affirmed on appeal. The bank could have avoided liability by filing a Notice of Lending that would have "served as adequate notice to beneficiaries of its status as a trustee and its depletion of trust assets to repay its loans."

C.   Wal-Mart Stores, Inc. is one of the world's largest retailers with approximately 4,500 stores worldwide and over 100 million shoppers weekly.

It is also one of the most sued defendants, having to face an estimated 5,000 lawsuits annually. It had a long history of refusing to negotiate with plaintiffs and this hardball strategy resulted in huge expenses for legal fees paid to outside counsel, as well as an adverse reputation in the business community. Recently, a new management team decided to shift litigation strategy to a more preventive approach by (1) moving from strict fee arrangements with outside lawyers to creation of an in-house legal department, (2) making an affirmative effort to settle disputes rather than litigate, and (3) creating a new executive post of executive vice-president for legal and corporate affairs.

This change is company policy has significantly reduced legal expenses, but there are still many disputes that ripen into litigation. Often, such cases are classics of failure to use the preventative law method, like *Griggs v. Wal-Mart Stores, Inc.,* an unreported 2002 case. In that case, a Mississippi jury awarded $8.5 million to a former employee truck driver who was fired after being falsely accused of shoplifting chewing tobacco. He had gone in the store and picked up the item when he remembered he had to call in to his supervisor, left the store seeking a phone and informed the "greeter" at the door that he had the tobacco but would be right back.

Before he could re-enter the store he was stopped by the defendant's loss prevention people, questioned, and then fired, causing a revolt by other truck drivers. In order to quell the rebellion, defendant's supervisor claimed plaintiff was a thief and lied that there had been prior wrongdoing and a videotape of the theft.

At the time of his firing, plaintiff was earning $70,000 per year but was unable thereafter to find another trucking job. He then filed suit. Prior to trial the defendant offered to settle for $30,000 and the plaintiff countered with $750,000.

Microsoft Corp. also found itself drowning in legal expenses. It drastically reduced the army of more than 100 law firms it used to a "preferred provider list" of a chosen 20 firms who were required to renegotiate their billing structure, provide detailed data on diversity and staffing, and otherwise comply with new uniform guidelines established by Microsoft.

D.   In *CGB Occupational Therapy Inc. v. RHA/Pennsylvania Nursing Homes Inc., 357 F.3d 375 (3rd Cir. 2005),* an appellate victory backfired when a federal jury awarded $30 million in punitive damages in the retrial of a case where the first jury had awarded just $1.3 million. Plaintiff had claimed that defendant tortiously interfered with its contracts by inducing by inducing two Philadelphia – area nursing homes to terminate it and then hire away five of its therapists. The trial jury had awarded $685,000 in compensatory damages, reduced to $109,000 on appeal by the defendant, and the new trial was limited to the issue of punitive damages. In hindsight, if the trial decision had not been appealed, the defendant would have saved almost $29 million. Defendant rolled the appellate dice in this case and lost.

E.   The SESAC (Society of European Songwriters, Authors and Composers) music copyright infringement case in 2002 illustrates how an adverse result is often caused by the stubborn refusal of a party to follow good common sense. That organization, together with ASCAP and BMI, comprises the three main music performing rights companies in the U.S. Though it is smaller and less-well-known, SESAC is the copyright home of such well-known artists Bob Dylan and Neil Diamond. All three companies sell a "blanket license" costing about $5,000 per year allowing radio stations to play any of the music covered by their copyrights.

WPNT Inc., owner of radio stations in the Pittsburgh and St. Louis areas, were originally licensed to perform SESAC works. But they decided for some reason to stop purchasing the licenses, yet continued unlawfully to play the protected works and sued for statutory willful copyright infringement damages. Proofs at trial showed that defendant was warned many times not to play songs of unlicensed artists, had promised in a consent decree not to play the songs, and had violated that decree over 244 times. The jury returned a judgment for plaintiff of $1,263,000. (The cost of the annual license fees in question that defendant had refused to pay were no more than $170,000.)

F.   Failure to follow preventative law principles also affects large and otherwise successful companies:

1. In *Sporn v. Home Depot, Inc., 24 Cal. Rptr.3d 780 (Cal. App. 2005)*, plaintiff sued an unknown person for stealing his identity to apply for credit at defendant, claiming that after the theft became known the company still checked on him so frequently with a credit reporting agency that his credit was damaged.

After plaintiff served the court papers on defendant, it failed to respond and a default judgment for $930,000 was entered against it. Trying to set the judgment aside, the company blamed its tardiness on plaintiff's lawyer, claiming that it never received notice of the default judgment hearing.

The claim proved false because plaintiff's lawyer had sent a letter giving defendant an extra two weeks to respond to the complaint before he'd seek a default judgment. That letter had also been ignored by the defendant. In addition the defendant presented no valid excuse to the court that would constitute excusable neglect. In affirming the default judgment, the court said, "There is no statement that the papers (served on defendant) were lost, stolen, forwarded to the wrong person or eaten by the dog."

2. Blockbuster Inc. was also involved in a similar costly "asleep at the switch" situation in early 2005. Faced with increased competition from online video seller Netflix, it launched a new "No Late Fees" policy to bring back its eroding customer base.

But in implementing the policy, customers were subjected to hidden "restocking fees" and charged the full price of rented movies if they were retuned a week after the original due date – contrary to the "customer-friendly" image the company sought to create. Forty-seven states sued Blockbuster for violating consumer protection lawsuits, and it cost the company $630,000 to settle those claims.

3. Yahoo Inc. hosted online auctions for Nazi memorabilia, and was sued in France in 2000 by France's Union of Jewish Students to ban such sales on any Internet site viewable in France. French law bars the display or sale of racist material. Yahoo had stripped such items from its French subsidiary, Yahoo.fr, but did not remove them from its more popular site Yahoo.com that is accessible worldwide. The French court ordered Yahoo to take down the items and began to levy fines of more than $13,000 per day starting in February, 2001. Yahoo then announced in January, 2001 that it will no longer allow Nazi and other hate memorabilia to be displayed on its Web sites and implemented a monitoring or filtering system to assure compliance.

Yahoo at the same time sued in U.S. Federal court to invalidate the court order on grounds it violated the First Amendment, but the trial court refused, ruling that the company assumed the risk of violating laws of countries where it allowed it items to be sold. *Yahoo Inc. v. La Ligue Contre Le Racisme Et L'Antisemitsme, Case No. 00-21276 JF N.D.Cal. (2000).*

G.   Movie star Steven Seagal was involved in an unusual off-screen legal drama, *Nasso v. Seagal, 263 F.Supp.2d 596 (E.D.N.Y. 2003).* He had collaborated with Julius Nasso on many of his hits. In 2000 Seagal ended the partnership and declined to appear in four Seagal-Nasso films. Nasso sued in federal court in 2002 alleging Seagal's breach of contract had cost him between $21 and $39 million in anticipated profits.

Before the case went to trial, Nasso hired a Mafia soldier to threaten Seagal with harm if he didn't pay. Nasso was then indicted for extortion and pleaded guilty to the felony. This is obviously not the way to try to prevent a legal claim from succeeding.

H.   Liability of guarantors and indemnitors can often be skillfully limited by inserting time limitations so their obligations are not open-ended. Here are two examples of failure to do so:

1. In *Louis Dreyfus Energy Corp. v. MG Refining and Marketing, Inc., 780 N.Y.S.2d 110 (N.Y. 2004),* the case involved a dispute over the interpretation of a guaranty agreement. It recited a date of expiration for the guarantee, but was silent as to whether it would apply to an obligation incurred prior to its creation, but payable after the guaranty expired. As a result, the guarantor was bound.

Stated simply, there was no anticipatory thinking by the guarantor to prevent this liability possibility and therefore the case was lost.

2. In *County of Delaware v. J.P. Mascaro & Sons, Inc., 830 A.2d 587 (Pa. Super. Ct. 2003)*, defendant waste disposal company contracted with plaintiff in 1975 to haul away residue from an old garbage incinerator to a landfill. That contract stated that defendant, "shall defend, indemnify and save harmless Delaware County from and against all suits for claims that may be based upon any alleged injury to any person or property that may be alleged to have occurred in the course of the performance of this contract."

Twenty years later Delaware was sued for environmental problems caused by the waste defendant had hauled and dumped, and settled the case for $300,000. Defendant had refused to participate, claiming that its indemnity obligation ended when the work was completed. Delaware sued defendant under its indemnity and won the case. "The clause here says Mascaro will indemnify against "all suits" related to the performance of the contract. Since it made the decisions where to dump the residue, it is responsible for indemnity in this case."

I.	Governmental units can also fall into the liability traps caused by lack of anticipatory thinking. One of the most graphic examples is *Charter Township of Ypsilanti, Michigan v. General Motors Corp., 506 N.W.2d 556 (Mich. App. 1993)*. The facts of that dispute are that defendant had operated two automobile plants in the town for many years employing, as many as 10,000 local workers. In the 1970's plaintiff created special industrial development taxing districts for defendant and in the 1980's voted to approve sizable tax abatements totaling more than $13 million, allegedly in return for defendant's promises to continue local operations of its Willow Run plant. Later, in 1991 when defendant announced its intention to consolidate operations by closing the local plants and moving to Arlington, Texas, plaintiff sued for breach of agreement and promissory estoppel, and secured a trial court injunction preventing the move.

The trial court said, "there would be a gross inequity and patent unfairness if General motors,, having lulled the people of the Ypsilanti area into giving up millions of tax dollars which they so desperately need to educate their children and provide basic governmental services, is allowed to simply decide it will desert 4500 workers and their families because it thinks it can make these same cars cheaper somewhere else."

On appeal that order was reversed because, contrary to plaintiff's assertions, there never were any actual promises made by defendant that could support plaintiff's claims.

"Turning to the case at bar, almost all the statements the trial court cited as foundations for a promise were, instead, expressions of defendant's hopes or expectations of continued employment at Willow Run."

"... the acts cited by the trial court were acts one would naturally expect a company to do in order to introduce and promote an abatement proposal to a municipality. The acts did not amount to a promise and, as course-of-conduct evidence, showed only efforts to take advantage of a statutory opportunity. They did not constitute assurances of continued employment."

Note how easy it would have been for the plaintiff to require defendant to make written and binding assurances of a continued local presence at the time plaintiff had the greatest power to demand such promises – when defendant was seeking the tax abatements.

2.
THE PURPOSE OF LAWS:
WHY DO WE HAVE THEM?

Societal events sometimes signal the need for laws to change. In other instances the times change only after the governing laws are modified. Therefore the social and political climate existing when legal decisions and their judicial review by a particular state or federal court occur is critical.

Traditionally speaking, a liberal jurist is at times an activist who may interpret the Constitution broadly to effect social change when deemed necessary. A conservative jurist, on the other hand, generally interprets rights under the Constitution narrowly and believes that society's problems should be the domain of elected officials, rather than judges.

A.   These conflicting philosophies frequently appear as majority and dissenting opinions in recent 5-4 rulings of the U.S. Supreme Court. The most notable of these was *Bush v. Gore*, discussed in the text. It judicially decided the Florida 2000 presidential election and gave Mr. Bush the necessary electoral votes to become President, although Mr. Gore received almost 500,000 more popular votes. The majority in that case required strict construction of the Federal Constitution's 14th Amendment and prohibited continuation of the vote recount ordered by the Florida Supreme Court.

The Massachusetts Supreme Court, on the other hand, demonstrated judicial activism in their 4-3 landmark decision granting the legal right of marriage for the first time in the United States to gay and lesbian couples in *Goodridge v. Department of Public Health, 798 N.E.2d 941 (Mass. 2003)*. In that case seven gay and lesbian couples in committed relationships of long-standing attempted to obtain marriage licenses and were denied on the ground that Massachusetts does not recognize same-sex marriage. The denial of the licenses effectively denied them the right to marry.

They filed suit claiming that the denial was unconstitutional discrimination and a denial to them of equal protection under the law. The trial judge dismissed their claim but it was reversed on direct appeal to the state's highest court. "The Massachusetts constitution affirms the dignity and equality of all individuals. It forbids the creation of second-class citizens. In reaching our conclusion we have given full deference to the arguments made by the Commonwealth. But it has failed to identify any constitutionally adequate reason for denying civil marriage to same-sex couples."

The three dissenting judges expressed their strict interpretation viewpoint: "What is at stake in this case is not the unequal treatment of individuals or whether individual rights have been impermissibly burdened, but the power of the Legislature to effectuate social change without interference from the courts. . . The power to regulate marriage lies with the Legislature, not with the judiciary. Today, the court has transformed its role as protector of individual rights into the role of creator of rights, and (we) respectfully dissent."

Here's another recent case to illustrate a court dispute where the law was changed to meet changing social conditions:

In *Bozman v. Bozman, 2003 WL 21915874 (Md. App. 2003)*, while plaintiff and defendant were separated prior to their divorce, defendant allegedly stalked and harassed her. She then complained to the police and had a prior protective order enforced against him. He then sued her for the tort of malicious prosecution, contending that her claims were false and was just part of divorce strategy. The trial court dismissed his suit under the doctrine of interspousal immunity, which prohibits one spouse from suing the other for an intentional tort, except in certain cases of outrageous conduct.

On appeal the decision was reversed and the court decided to change Maryland law by no longer following the doctrine. It noted that even though the stare decisis doctrine of precedent normally required a court to follow earlier judicial decisions when the same points arise in litigation, the time for a change in the law had arrived.

"The overwhelming weight of authority supports the petitioner's argument that the interspousal immunity doctrine should be abrogated. Joining the many of our sister States that have already done so, we abrogate (it), a vestige of the past, whose time has come and gone, as to all cases alleging an intentional tort.

B.   Here are two recent Constitutional Law cases that illustrate common disputes between citizens and their own governmental units concerning the enforceability of certain laws. Note how the Constitutional Law principles operate as a crucial part of the checks and balances protecting private rights:

1) In *State of Georgia v. Heretic, Inc., 588 S.E.2d 224 (Ga. 2003)*, the defendant bar was prohibited from selling alcoholic beverages on Sunday, even though the State law's Sunday ban had exceptions for stadiums and eating establishments deriving at least one-half of their gross sales from meals. Defendant didn't qualify for the exception and successfully sued to have the law declared unconstitutional as being a denial of their right to equal protection under the law.

On appeal the decision was reversed because the Court felt that the exception classification had a rational basis and was not therefore arbitrarily discriminatory. "The (law) is intended to enhance the recreational atmosphere of Sunday."

2) In *Livestock Marketing Assoc. v. U.S. Department of Agriculture, 335 F.3d 711 (8th Cir. 2003)*, the plaintiff beef growers objected to the requirements of the Beef Promotion and Research Act of 1985 that required all beef producers to contribute money to a national advertising campaign – "Beef, It's what's for dinner!" The plaintiff complained the law was unconstitutional and the trial court agreed.

On appeal the decision was affirmed. "The Beef Act violated the First Amendment free association and free speech rights of beef producers who did not wish to pay for the advertising campaign. This is compelled payment for speech with which some payers disagreed. The government's interest in protecting the welfare of the beef industry is not sufficiently substantial to justify this infringement of the First Amendment."

      C.   The inherent conflict between governmental units and private citizens over permissible uses of their property often results in litigation. Here are six recent cases involving whether private property was legally "taken" for public use under governmental powers of eminent domain that require payment of just compensation to the affected landowners. Note the inconsistent results:

1. In *SWIDA v. National City Environmental, 768 N.E.1 (Ill. 2002)*, a private raceway asked plaintiff, a municipal corporation created by the state to promote economic development, sought to condemn 149 acres of land owned by defendant on which it ran a recycling plant and landfill. Plaintiff offered defendant $1 million for the land, which would be paid by the raceway. When defendant refused, plaintiff filed this action under the announced public purpose of improving traffic flow and reducing blight. The trial court approved the taking, but the court of appeals reversed it in favor of defendant.

The State Supreme Court affirmed the appellate ruling. "The taking would not achieve a legitimate public purpose and was unconstitutional. Using the power of eminent domain for private purposes, to allow the racetrack to expand its facilities in a cost-efficient manner by avoiding the open real estate market was a misuse of the power entrusted by the public."

2. In *DABE Inc. v. City of Toledo, 393 F.3d 692 (6th Cir. 2005)*, the City had enacted an ordinance strictly limiting smoking in bars and restaurants only if they had a "separate smoking lounge" that was walled-off from the majority of customers and contained its own ventilation system.

A group of bar and restaurant owners challenged the constitutionality of the law, claiming it was an uncompensated regulatory taking that violated the 5th and 14th Amendments. The trial court ruled for the city and that decision was affirmed on appeal. The Court ruled that while the business owners might lose some business and were required to spend money to have smoking sections, they were not prohibited from running their business.

"The regulation does not deny the business owners some economically viable use of their property, so it is not a regulatory taking."

3. In *Kelo v. City of New London, Conn., 2005 WL 1459118 (U.S. 2005)*, the Court was asked to decide the constitutionality of a controversial City law that allowed exercise of eminent domain to gain title to land from parties previously unwilling to sell to private developers for a residential project. The City condemned their land and then sold it to the developers. Plaintiffs claimed this was an improper taking for "private" rather than "public" use, as required by law. The City claimed the area was sufficiently run-down to justify a program of economic rejuvenation to create jobs and increase tax revenue. The Connecticut Supreme Court approved the taking, and the U.S. Supreme Court affirmed by a split 5-4 vote. The case elicited a firestorm of negative criticism from critics as a dangerous precedent. As a result Congress proposed legislation such as the "Protection of Homes, Small Businesses and Private Property Act of 2005" to prevent the federal government from taking private property for economic development and to restrict local government's use of federal funds for any project where they are using eminent domain for private gain.

4. In *Smith v. Town of Mendon, 789 N.Y.S.2d 696 (N.Y. App. 2004)*, another apparent governmental taking was allowed. In that case, plaintiffs owned a 10-acre parcel of land, various parts of which were subject to town environmental building restrictions. When they applied for a building permit for a single-family home on the part of the property not affected by the restrictions it was granted, subject to a new conservation restriction imposing new limits on land use and allowing entry to safeguard environmentally sensitive parcels. They unsuccessfully sued, claiming the new restrictions were an eminent domain "taking" for which they were entitled to just compensation. The court said, "this does not constitute a taking because the new restriction is consistent with existing rules, there is no physical taking of the property, and the impact on the value of the property is small."

5. In *Vulcan Materials Co. v. City of Tchuacana, 369 F.3d 882 (5th Cir. 2004)*, plaintiff was licensed to engage in quarrying operations in and next to the City. Some residents objected to the noise, dust and vibrations and the City passed an ordinance prohibiting quarrying within city limits. Plaintiff sued, contending the ordinance was an inverse condemnation and unconstitutional taking without payment of compensation. The trial court held for the City, but that decision was reversed in favor of Plaintiff on appeal.

"Vulcan's property was rendered nearly useless by the regulation, so it is a compensable taking of private property. It is possible that the quarrying activity was a nuisance, but that is a separate legal issue."

6. In *Karnes City v. Kendall, 2005 WL 1025362 (Tex. App. 2005)*, the Kendalls bought a house and learned afterward that the city claimed an unrecorded sewer line easement across their property. Several times, during heavy rains, it overflowed through a manhole onto their property.

After complaining to local and state authorities, they sued claiming the placement of the sewer line without a recorded easement was an unconstitutional taking of private property for public use, or at the very least a public nuisance. The trial court ruled in their favor, but the appellate court reversed in favor of the City.

"To recover on a nuisance claim against a governmental entity based on a waiver of governmental immunity, a claimant must establish that the nuisance rises to the level of a constitutional taking. This may happen when the government 1)knows that a specific act is causing identifiable harm, or 2)knows that the specific property damage is substantially certain to result from an authorized action that is incidental to or a consequence of the government's action. The gross negligence here does not rise to the level of a taking under the constitution, and so precludes the claim against the city for public nuisance."

What would be your decision if you were the judge in these "governmental taking" disputes?

D.   Here is another case of a constitutional challenge to a local law. In *Folsom v. City of Jasper, 2005 WL 949242 Ga. 2005)*, the City had an ordinance banning the advertising of the sale of alcoholic beverages. Plaintiff owned a café that advertised a New Year's Eve party that would serve champagne. The City suspended her liquor license for 30 days and imposed one-year probation. The trial court upheld the ordinance and the appellate court reversed, ruling that the law was unconstitutional and violated of the 1st Amendment because it was "a blanket prohibition against truthful speech about a lawful product."

E.   Sometimes there are conflicts between state and federal laws that courts must resolve. The first example is the following two California cases involving "catalyst fees" – awards to parties whose lawsuits result in changes beneficial to the public. The U.S. Supreme Court abolished catalyst fee awards to a prevailing party if the dispute was resolved without a judicial order in the case of *Buckhannon Board & Care Home Inc. v. West Virginia Dep't. of Health and Human Services, 532 U.S. (2001)*. But in the following two companion California cases decided in 2004, that state's highest court affirmed by 4-3 votes that such fees are permissible in private attorney general actions so long as they are based on meritorious complaints, there was a reasonable attempt to settle, and the lawsuit was a catalyst in changing the defendant's conduct.

1. Next was a dispute concerning claims of disabled persons who sued under the federal ADA to gain access to a state courthouses in *Tennessee v. Lane, 541 U.S. 509 (2004)*, where the Court ruled 5-4 that states are not immune and the affected parties had due process rights involved in court access. ADA's Title II guarantees access for the disabled to "services, programs or activities of a public entity." But in an earlier case the Court ruled in *Board of Trustees of Univ. of Alabama v. Garrett, 531 U.S. 356 (U.S. 2001)*, that states are immune from suits under ADA Title I that bars employment discrimination against the disabled.

2. Finally, in the consolidated Texas cases of *Aetna Health Inc. v. Davila, (No.02-1845) and Cigna Health Care of Texas v. Calad, No. 03-83 (542 U.S. 200)*, the U.S. Supreme Court ruled in 2004 that patients may not sue under state tort law for insurer's refusal to pay for doctor-recommended medicines and procedures. The ruling said that the 1974 Employee Retirement Income Security Act (ERISA) completely pre-empts such lawsuits, because its purpose was to "provide a uniform regulatory regime over employee benefit plans." The claims had been brought under the Texas Health Care Liability Act, and the 5th Circuit Court of Appeals had ruled them not pre-empted by ERISA. The Court's reversal was applauded by the insurance industry that had feared having to face 50 different state liability laws.

F.   Affirmative action programs created by legislative enactments and judicial interpretation to assist disadvantaged "protected classes" of minorities in achieving educational balance were originally welcomed by the law and later criticized as being unnecessary and unfair to the disaffected majority, especially if used purely "racial tiebreakers." The key determination made by the U.S. Supreme Court in upholding the use of affirmative action programs in the cases of *Gratz v. Bollinger, 539 U.S. 244(2003), and Grutter v. Bollinger, 539 U.S. 982 (2003)*, was that they had to be narrowly tailored to achieve a compelling governmental interest. Later cases from various states have repeatedly stated that race must not be the main criterion in admissions decisions on both college and high school levels.

In a case of first impression, *Doe v. Kamehameha Schools, 416 F.3d 1025 (9th Cir 2005)*, the court ruled that a private Hawaiian school's policy of accepting only native Hawaiian students amounted to racial discrimination and violated federal law, reversing the trial judge who had ruled the policy was "a valid, race-conscious remedial affirmative action program."

The Schools argued that they received no public funding and did admit non-Hawaiian students after first offering admission to native-born students who met admission criteria. The appellate court said, "It does not follow ... that Congress may authorize a private school to exclusively restrict admission on the basis of an express racial classification."

G.   Title VII of the 1964 Civil Rights Act is recently the subject of court disputes over who or what is a female "protected class." In *Price Waterhouse v. Hopkins, 490 U.S. 228 (1989)*, the Court had ruled that a woman passed over for promotion because she did not act as feminine as her employer required was protected and could sue for discrimination. In *Smith v. City of Salem, 378 F.3d 566 (6th Cir. 2004)*, a transsexual firefighter was accorded the same protection. But in *Elsitty v. Utah Transit Authority, No. 2:04CV616 DS (Dist. Ct. Utah 2005)*, this trend was reversed by the rejection of the discrimination claims of a transsexual bus driver. So the legal question of whether transsexuals are a protected class will not be clarified until ruled upon by the U.S. Supreme Court.

In *Wheatley v. Wicomico County, Maryland, 390 F.3d 328 (4ᵗʰ Cir. 2004)*, two female emergency service department supervisors unsuccessfully sued their employer, claiming violations of Title VII and the Equal Pay Act because male supervisors were paid significantly more than they were. The court ruled that the plaintiffs didn't perform work equal to male department directors, different skills were required, and different educational levels were required.

"For example, the head of the public works department is required to have graduate degrees in civil engineering. In contrast, plaintiff's positions require no particular educational background. ... Just because titles within an organization are similar does not mean the work or its value is equal."

H.   Nowhere are judicial activism and the use of the courts to achieve social justice more evident than in the claims of Nazi Holocaust survivors to recover damages for assets looted during and after the conclusion of World War II.

1.   The Hungarian Gold Train – In 1944 Germany occupied Hungary and swiftly confiscated all property belonging to Jewish residents. A train loaded with more than two dozen boxcars of art, religious items, rare Persian rugs and valuable jewelry worth between $50 million to $120 million (current value) was taken to Austria. After the war the train was turned over to the U.S. Army to return its contents to the rightful owners. Instead, as reported for the first time in 1999 by the Presidential Advisory commission on Holocaust Assets in the U.S., the property was mishandled, no inventory taken, and was allegedly looted by senior U.S. military officers. Eventually, the U.S. auctioned off the remaining items in 1948 with proceeds to go to refugee organizations, rather than the needy Hungarian owners. A federal class action filed in Miami Federal District Court in 2004 against the U.S. was settled whereby the U.S. agreed to pay $25.5 million to the owners.

2.   The U.S. pressured European governments, businesses and banks in the early 1990's to pay Holocaust reparations victims and the families. Swiss banks had been criticized for many years after World War II for holding huge sums in Holocaust assets in their secret accounts.

In Re: *Holocaust Victims Assets Litigation, 96-4849 (E.D.N.Y. 2004)* brought these claims to the judicial arena. After many years of litigation a settlement was reached with the Swiss banks for over $1.3 billion to be distributed in a complicated formula to survivors worldwide. It allocated $800 million for lost bank deposits (a list of account holders who were probably victims of Nazi persecution was finally completed in early 2005), $200 million to survivors who were slave laborers, $200 million to those who attempted to flee to Switzerland and were mistreated, and $100 million to a looted assets subclass. The deadline for filing claims was July, 2005.

3.   Similar class action lawsuits were also filed against German and Austrian banks for alleged unlawful receipt and conversion of stolen and/or looted assets and personal property.

(In re Austrian and German Bank Litigation, 80 F.Supp.2d 164 (S.D.N.Y. 2000) A $40 million settlement was reached and approved by the court in *D'Amato v. Deutsche Bank, 236 F.3d 78 (2nd Cir. 2001).* Another similar lawsuit was filed styled *Association of Holocaust Victims v. Bank Austria Creditanstalt, 2000 U.S. Dist. LEXIS 17411 (S.D.N.Y. 2005),* seeking $1 billion in damages but was dismissed as being sham litigation and the filing attorney was sanctioned by the court.

Other banks in other countries also settled. All compensation to be distributed (a difficult task after so many years in locating rightful claimants), including the Swiss banks totals almost $51 billion of which approximately $15 billion had been distributed in the U.S. and an alleged disproportionate amount of only $444 million to former Soviet Union claimants. The New York proceedings will continue for quite some time in resolution of conflicting claims.

I.   As the working population gets older, there are disputes where claims of age discrimination are made based on alleged violation of state and federal laws. Here are five recent cases:

1. In *Palasota v. Haggar Clothing Co., 342 F.3d 569 (5th Cir. 2003),* plaintiff worked for defendant for 28 years when he was fired at age 51. He oversaw major accounts and was highly regarded for his work with customers. Defendant decided to adopt a more youthful image ("the company needs racehorses, not plowhorses") and transferred many sales functions to a group of new, young women who replaced males over age 40. Plaintiff sued for age and (reverse) gender discrimination. The trial jury ruled for plaintiff and awarded him $842,219 in back pay, but the judge overturned the verdict ruling that he had failed to prove age was a determining factor in his firing.

The appellate court reversed, holding that the jury had the evidence on which the jury based its decision was sufficient to uphold a finding of age discrimination. The court noted the governing rules of law:

"Evidence of age discrimination must be: 1) age related; 2) proximate in time to the termination; 3) made by an individual with authority over the termination; and 4) related to the employment decision."

2. In *Coryell v. Bank One Trust Co., 803 N.E.2d 781 (Ohio 2004),* plaintiff worked for defendant for 19 years until he was fired at age 49 and replaced by a man aged 42. He sued for age discrimination and the trial court dismissed, ruling that he failed to establish a prima facie case because the person who replaced him was also over age 40. The appellate court affirmed, but the state Supreme Court reversed and remanded.

"There is no greater inference of age discrimination when a 40-year-old is replaced by a 39-year-old than when a 56-year-old is replaced by a 40-year-old. The ultimate inquiry is whether a plaintiff was discharged on account of age."

"... The question in this case is whether Bank One articulated a nondiscriminatory ground for firing Coryell, so the case may proceed."

3. In *Cariglia v. Hertz Equipment Rental Corp.*, 363 F.3d 77 (1st Cir. 2004), plaintiff was hired in 1980, promoted to Boston branch manager in 1992, was commended for his work and received high annual evaluations through 1995, and was then fired for "gross misconduct" in 1996 at age 62. Plaintiff's supervisor, Heard, ordered the company auditor to dig up supporting information for the firing, and had been heard to remark that plaintiff was "over the hill." Plaintiff sued for age discrimination.

The trial judge dismissed the suit but the appellate court vacated that order and remanded for further proceedings. "Evidence that age bias existed by Heard, while it may not have been the only cause of Cariglia's dismissal, could be found by a jury to be a material factor in the dismissal. That bias could be imputed to Hertz."

4. In *General Dynamics Land Systems v. Cline, 124 S. Ct. 1236 (2004)*, the Supreme Court was presented with a dispute about the applicability of the federal Age Discrimination in Employment Act (ADEA). A collective bargaining agreement between the employer and the union eliminated the need to provide health benefits for employees when they retired, except for current workers at least 50-years old. Cline and other employees over age 40 but not yet age 50 sued, contending the agreement violated the ADEA. The trial court dismissed the suit, the appeals court reversed holding that the younger workers were protected, and then the Supreme Court reversed, holding that the younger workers were not covered by the Act.

"The purpose of the ADEA is to protect relatively old workers from discrimination that works to the advantage of relatively young workers. Discrimination against relatively young workers is outside of the Act's protection. The employer did not illegally discriminate against workers age 40-49 by eliminating the retiree health insurance benefits for workers then under age 50. The action did not target relatively old workers."

5. In *Machinchick v. PB Power, Inc.*, 398 F.3d 345 (5th Cir. 2005), plaintiff worked for defendant for 6 years during which he received excellent reviews and was promoted to vice-president. However when the company adopted a new management scheme, top managers were told to "hand-pick employees whose mindset resides in the 21st Century" and plaintiff's supervisor criticized him for failing "to adapt to a rapidly changing business environment and a new company management style." A week later plaintiff was fired, at age 63, for poor performance and replaced by a 42-year old, and then sued for age discrimination.

The trial court granted summary judgment to defendant, but the case was reversed and remanded on appeal in favor of plaintiff, allowing the case to be fully heard. It ruled that plaintiff had established a prima facie case (based on the same rules of law as stated in the *Palasota v. Haggar* case).

"At trial, the burden shifts to (defendant) to show a legitimate, nondiscriminatory reason for its employment action. Malinchick need not produce evidence of actual discriminatory intent; instead, if he can show that the reason articulated by the employer for his dismissal is a pretext for illegal behavior, then the inference of age discrimination is likely to hold. The evidence of age discrimination can be circumstantial, such as indirect references to age."

3.
THE SOURCES OF LAWS:
WHAT ARE THEY?

The cornerstone of the anticipatory thinking approach to preventive law is awareness of potential business law time bombs before transactions are negotiated and finalized.

This requires identification of the five traditional federal and state sources of law discussed in the text – court cases, statutes, administrative regulations, constitutions and bill of rights.

But once generally located, we have to zero in on our particular type of commercial involvement and have its pros and cons highlighted as to legal viability?

How can we accomplish this quickly and accurately? Before the internet revolution of the 1990's, legal research of any kind was an extremely laborious process. The only people who had even a small working knowledge of the hundreds of scholarly articles produced every year in law schools and business think tanks were either professional librarians, researchers or the authors themselves. Many of the most dangerous business law time bombs remained hidden until an unfortunate participant in a failed business deal experienced one exploding firsthand.

That is now a thing of the past because there is now no excuse to be ignorant of the law. Although they are not official sources of law from a category standpoint, the major on-line search engines and private websites nevertheless can provide instant access to almost every legal issue that might be relevant to one's pending transaction and lead to the needed source.

Here are a few more helpful internet addresses:

- *www.google.com* – aside from being the leading search engine and instant provider of every kind of information imaginable, a little-known feature is legal questions and answers that are provided by a number of providers, some on a pay-per-item basis and some free. These links cover the spectrum of possible commercial transactional issues, totaling more than 4,650,000 potential hits.

- *www.lawsource.com* – provides fast access to 12 pages of links for current court opinions at all court levels, state and federal, including historic decisions of the U.S. Supreme Court; federal and state legislative enactments; and 20 pages of assorted law reviews and periodicals from the 50 states.

- *www.startingpage.com* – **lists the best law sites, legal resources and accompanying links for self help in various areas of the law as well as sources of free legal forms and legal documents in those particular areas.**

- *www.lexisone.com* - **bills itself as the resource for small law firms. Even though you are not a lawyer, you can and should be familiar with the general area of law concerning your proposed transaction. This site can help through its topical linked index of the categories of usual business involvements, free forms, jurisdictional state-by-state links, and legal web site directory.**

- *www.swlearning.com/blaw/cases/topic_index.html* - **presents legal subject links to all major topical areas of the law that access a comprehensive list of applicable cases in chronological order starting with the most recent and working backwards in time.**

4.

TO SUE OR NOT TO SUE

We live in the most litigious country in the world but, as pointed out in the text, the movement away from suing and toward alternate ways to resolve conflict is expanding daily.

More and more contracts are drawn with clauses that name arbitration as the required method of dispute resolution rather than litigation. Business principals are seeking less combative and damaging ways to conclude their disputed transactions, so that the parties to a dispute can continue to do business in the future. The privacy of the proceedings also helps considerably to avoid "washing your dirty clothes in public," and destroying former business relationships. The participants usually can walk away from one of these alternative dispute resolution proceedings saying, "Nothing personal, it's just business," and mean it.

When combined with advantages of a faster resolution and less cost than litigation, it is no wonder the ADR trend is accelerating and its specific uses clarified.

Here is an overview courtesy of www.law.cornell.edu/topics/adr.html :

alternative dispute resolution (adr): an overview

Alternative Dispute Resolution ("ADR") refers to any means of settling disputes outside of the courtroom. ADR typically includes arbitration, mediation, early neutral evaluation, and conciliation. As burgeoning court queues, rising costs of litigation, and time delays continue to plague litigants, more states have begun experimenting with ADR programs. Some of these programs are voluntary; others are mandatory.

The two most common forms of ADR are arbitration and mediation. Arbitration is a simplified version of a trial involving no discovery and simplified rules of evidence. Either both sides agree on one arbitrator, or each side selects one arbitrator and the two arbitrators elect the third to comprise a panel. Arbitration hearings usually last only a few hours and the opinions are not public record. Arbitration has long been used in labor, construction, and securities regulation, but is now gaining popularity in other business disputes.

Title 9 of the U.S. Code establishes Federal law supporting arbitration. It is based on Congress's plenary power over interstate commerce. Where it applies its terms prevail over state law. There are, however, numerous state laws on ADR. Thirty-five states have adopted the Uniform Arbitration Act as state law. Thus, the arbitration agreement and decision of the arbiter may be enforceable under state and federal law.

In 1970, the United States joined the <u>UN Convention on the Recognition and Enforcement of Foreign Arbitral Awards</u>.

Mediation is an even less formal alternative to litigation. Mediators are individuals trained in negotiations who bring opposing parties together and attempt to work out a settlement or agreement that both parties accept or reject. Mediation is used for a wide gamut of case-types: ranging from juvenile felonies to Federal government negotiations with Native American Indian tribes.

These five recent cases also illustrate the growth of Arbitration and Mediation. Notice the different agendas of plaintiffs, who prefer to sue at law in our public judicial system with possible large jury awards, and defendants who prefer to stay out of court and privately arbitrate or mediate:

1. *Blue Cross Blue Shield of Texas v. Juneau, 114 S.W.3d 126 (Tex. App. 2003)* Arbitrators, like judges, are immune from personal liability for their judicial acts. A party to the arbitration proceedings was barred from suing the arbitrator for failing to disclose a prior relationship with the opposing party's attorney.

2. *Fisher v. GE Medical Systems, 2003 WL 21939479 (M.D. Tenn. 2003)* Mediation agreements are covered by the Federal Arbitration Act, which strongly supports the use of alternate dispute resolution procedures. Employees who sued their company claiming it violated the federal Fair Labor Standards Act because it refused to pay overtime wages could be required to have the matter resolved through mediation, as specified in their employment handbook.

3. *Pacificare Health Systems, Inc. v. Book, 123 U.S. 1531 (2003)* RICO claims are subject to arbitration. A group of physicians who made RICO claims against managed-health-care organizations for failing to reimburse them for patient services were required to arbitrate those claims.

4. *Boise Cascade Corp. v. Paper Allied-Industrial, 309 F.3d 1075 (8th Cir. 2002)* Arbitration awards that follow the terms of the party's contract will stand even if the arbitrator committed a serious error. Where a union member was fired after numerous disciplinary proceedings and the matter was referred to binding arbitration under the collective bargaining agreement – an arbitrator's decision based on "industrial justice" rather than the terms of the agreement was vacated.

5. *Parfi Holding AB v. Mirror Image Internet, 2002 WL 31277125 (Del. 2002)* Contract arbitration clauses only cover the matters mentioned in the agreement. Suit by minority shareholders who claimed their rights had been violated in the initial stock subscription agreement could be litigated in Delaware, notwithstanding a general arbitration clause that produced an adverse result for them in Sweden.

There is an old saying that, "a bird in the hand is worth two in the bush." Translated into litigation terms it often means, like the old trial lawyer's adage, "a bad settlement may be better than a good lawsuit."

This was illustrated in the case of *Yvonne Gil-de-Rebolloo v. The Miami Heat Associations, Inc., Inc., 137 F.3d 56 (1ˢᵗ Cir. 1998).* In that case, plaintiff was attending an exhibition basketball game in Puerto Rico between the Miami Heat and Atlanta Hawks when Burnie, the Heat mascot approached her and grabbed her hand as part of a planned entertainment routine during a time-out. She resisted and told him no, but he persisted "because in his experience people often were reluctant at first but later changed their minds." However he pulled her with such force that she surged forward and fell to the floor, sustaining physical and emotional injuries.

After the incident, plaintiff filed misdemeanor battery charges against the mascot for which he was convicted. She also sued at law for her damages. During the course of litigation the parties made several efforts to settle. Plaintiff's initial demand was $1 million. Defendant made offer of judgment for $80,000 which plaintiff rejected and she countered with a demand of $600,000 and a public apology. This was rejected and trial commenced.

At the first trial the jury awarded her $10,000. Afterwards, defendant made a 2ⁿᵈ offer of judgment for $70,000 which she rejected again and countered with a demand of $250,000. Then defendant made a 3ʳᵈ offer of judgment for $100,000 which plaintiff again rejected, demanding $180,000. Her appeal (*949 F. Supp. 62 (S.P.R. 1996)* was granted and a new trial ordered. It resulted in a jury verdict in her favor of $50,000, which was less than all three offers of judgment.

On appeal the jury verdict was upheld. In addition, the court, apparently fed up with plaintiff and her attorney, denied her request for attorney's fees, denied her any court costs incurred after the first offer of judgment, and further required her to pay the costs of the appeal, "Because the plaintiff's appeal was wholly without merit …"

Many employers specify Arbitration to resolve disputes as a condition of their employment agreements, and thus avoid costly and public litigation. This is now the standard dispute procedure in the securities industry as shown in *Gold v. Deutsche Aktiengesellschaft, 365 F.3d 144 (2ⁿᵈ Cir. 2004).* In that case, plaintiff's employment agreement with the bank contained the standard NASD arbitration clause. He was fired, and then sued at law in federal court for damages, claiming sexual harassment due to his gay orientation, and further claiming not to be bound by the arbitration clause because it was too broad and difficult to understand. His suit was dismissed and that decision was affirmed on appeal.

"While he claims that he did not understand the form and its reference to NASD procedures, as a competent adult with an MBA, he was capable of asking for the needed materials to understand the form."

"In the absence of fraud or other wrongful conduct by one of the contracting parties, the parties to a contract are presumed to know (its) contents and to have assented to them."

The alternate dispute resolution movement has gained even more momentum with many Internet sites that specialize in attempting to untangle Web disputes:

- cybersettle.com
- squaretrade.com
- smartsettle.com
- icourthouse.com
- webdispute.com
- internetneutral.com
- clicknsettle.com
- settleonline.com

The Federal Trade Commission receives about 6,000 consumer complaints weekly, and more than half are Internet – related. It enters all complaints into a database to be monitored for scams, which may be criminally prosecuted or referred to state agencies. "But many complaints do not involve fraud, just a misunderstanding," says their legal department, "there very well may be another side of the story … That's where ADR can provide a viable option."

5.
HIRING A LAWYER

The attorney-client relationship is a legal agreement and is governed by the principles of contract law. It is also a legal "fiduciary relationship", regarded as one involving special trust and confidence which elevates the lawyer to the highest standard of conduct in dealing with clients.

A breach of this duty of care that results in financial loss to the client is the tort of "malpractice", based on the law of negligence. The standard of care to be to be followed is based upon generally accepted standards of the legal professional, as promulgated by state and local bar associations in the form of rules of professional conduct.

A.   In addition to lawsuits by clients for alleged malpractice, attorneys are also sometimes judicially punished for improper conduct by being held in contempt of court or being required to pay fines. For example, in the case of *Stewart v. Colonial Western Agency, 105 Cal. Rptr.2d 115 (Cal. App. 2001)*, money sanctions were imposed against a defendant's attorney who improperly instructed an employee of the defendant not to answer questions at a discovery deposition. "Since the information sought at the deposition was discoverable, and the defendant's attorney prevented discovery, the imposition of sanctions against the attorney was proper."

Solo attorney Timothy C. Spayne of Norwich, Connecticut was indicted on civil charges under the federal False Claims Act for over-billing a U.S. Navy boat contractor for his legal work. He was paid over $3.3 million over a 30-month period during which he billed for legal work up to 94 hours in a single day. He agreed to pay fines of $1.24 million to settle the allegations.

B.   Sometimes attorneys make mistakes in meeting time deadlines, often because they delegate those responsibilities to others in their busy offices. *Pincay and McCarron v. Andrews, C.D.O.S. 10158 (9th Cir. 2004)*, was a case brought by a two Hall of Fame jockeys who claimed financial mismanagement by their investment advisory company. The firm of famed litigator David Boies represented the defendant. After the plaintiffs won in the trial court, Boies' calendaring clerk thought the deadline to file an appeal was 60 days instead of the usual 30 days and missed the required filing date. Boies sought court relief on grounds of "excusable neglect" due to problems of delegating duties to staff in a busy office. He won by a vote of 8 to 3, with the dissenting judges stating that the error was "inexcusable."

What would you decide if presented with this dispute?

C.   The attorney-client privilege is a foundation of hiring a lawyer. In *HLC Properties Ltd. v. MCA Records Inc. and Universal Studios Inc., 105 P.3d 560 (Cal. 2005),* the company that managed the entertainment empire of famous singer Bing Crosby (who died in 1977) sued five major recording companies alleging they owed $16 million in underpaid royalties on recording contracts dating back to 1943. The defendant's responded by subpoenaing 59 documents that HLC claimed were protected by the attorney-client privilege. The defendants successfully argued that confidentiality ceases when an estate is closed and the personal representative discharged, and that the privilege could not be held by the company.

In *Mike Price v. Time Inc., 2005 U.S. App. LEXIS 19883 (11th Cir. 2005),* a $20 million libel suit was brought by the former University of Alabama football coach regarding a Sports Illustrated magazine story in 2003 that reported he had a sexual liaison with strippers in a hotel room. He was fired shortly thereafter. He demanded in the case that the magazine identify its confidential source and it refused, consistent with a long-standing tradition of protecting sources. The trial judge ordered disclosure but the appellate court vacated that order. However it ordered the lawyer for the magazine to identify the confidential source, despite his reliance on the protection of the attorney-client privilege.

D.   The law is a multi-edged sword, and lawyers can be sanctioned when they cross the line of being an advocate for their clients and abuse the power of their position, as ruled in a case involving the creator of the popular "Lord of the Dance" Irish folk dance production. *Flatley v. Mauro, 18 Cal. Rptr.3d 472 (Cal. App.2004),* was a case where the world-famous dancer sued an Illinois lawyer for $100 million for alleged extortion.

Mauro had sued Flatley for $35 million on behalf of Robertson, an ex-stripper who claimed he raped her in Las Vegas in 2002. He denied the claim, stating they had consensual sex. Mauro spent the next few months calling Flatley's lawyers and threatening to "go public" with the rape allegations, and "ruin" Flatley. He demanded $1 million for his and his client's silence and threatened to send news releases to major media outlets. The suit against Flatley was filed by Robertson in 2003, but dropped soon after he countersued her and her attorney Mauro for civil extortion. Mauro then filed an anti-SLAPP motion claiming he had been seeking a proper settlement and was, therefore, engaged in protected activity. The motion was denied and the extortion claim allowed to proceed.

The court noted that Mauro had not just stated that his lawsuit would draw media attention due to the defendant's celebrity status. Instead he went too far by threatening direct action of his own, outside the lawsuit, to brand Flatley a rapist throughout the world.

E.   Hiring the right attorney is often the key to a successful outcome to a client's dispute. Here are some tips to a good hire, courtesy of http://nwitimes.com (The Times):

HOW TO CHOOSE AN ATTORNEY

We are a nation of laws. Chances are, sooner or later, you'll need a lawyer to help you navigate through those laws. Hiring the right attorney can make a huge difference in the outcome of your case. But there are so many lawyers, how do you select the right one? Following these simple instructions will help you make the right choice and ensure the best outcome in your legal matter.

Civil or Criminal?

If you've been arrested and charged with a crime, you'll need a criminal lawyer. Practically every other legal matter involves the civil law. Civil matters include personal injury, wrongful death, family law, business or personal disputes, wills, probate, contracts and bankruptcy. Because the vast majority of legal matters are civil not criminal, these tips focus on civil matters.

Fees: Contingent or Hourly?

Lawyers generally charge either hourly, typically between $75 and $375 per hour, a flat fee or on a contingent basis. A contingent fee is one which is paid only if you win. Contingent fees are best because they enable you to hire a top-rated lawyer, without paying any cash up-front or incurring high hourly fees. Unfortunately, contingent fees are prohibited in criminal and family law cases and some lawyers refuse to offer them, altogether.

Never hire an attorney in a personal injury or wrongful death case unless the fee is contingent. The usual fee percentage is 1/3 of a settlement or 40% if litigation is required. Remember: a contingent fee is the same whether you hire the best lawyer or the worst one, so follow the steps below to make sure you get your money's worth.

Find a Specialist

Because the laws are complicated and change every day, it's a good idea to hire an attorney whose practice is limited to one area of the law, exclusively. Remember the old adage: Jack of All Trades, Master of None! Hiring a specialist is the surest way to achieve a successful outcome in your case. But beware. Lawyers pay to be placed on referral lists. So calling the local Bar Association or dialing a toll-free number (like 1-800 LAWYERS or 1-800-INJURED) does not ensure that you will receive a specialist or even be referred to a quality attorney. You will simply be referred to whoever paid a fee to be placed on that list!

Searching the internet for a lawyer is not necessarily helpful, either. This is so because lawyers can only handle cases in the state where they are licensed or "admitted to practice." While an out-of-state attorney found over the internet may "accept" your case, he or she will ultimately refer your case to another lawyer--one you did not select-who will then end up handling your matter. You are better off conducting your search locally so that the lawyer you hire will be the one who really handles your case.

The best way to conduct your search is to check your local phone directory for lawyers who specialize. However, realize that the Bar Association limits what lawyers can say in ads. Sometimes it will be unclear whether a lawyer really specializes in one area of law or is instead soliciting cases in one area, like personal injury, but also handling other types of matters. One way to tell is to call that lawyer's office and, before describing your case, ask if they will accept a different kind of matter. For example, if you are looking for a personal injury specialist, first ask if they handle drunk driving cases. If they say yes, try another law firm.

If possible, find a lawyer whose entire law firm is devoted only to handling matters like yours, whether that is divorce, bankruptcy, personal injury or another matter. The best lawyers take only one type of case and refuse all others. And the best lawyers are selective. According to Injury Attorney Kenneth J. Allen, "our law firm only handles serious injury and death cases and we only accept about one client in ten. We are selective because it's important to believe in our clients in order to fight passionately for them and win." If you can find an entire law firm that specializes in your type of legal case, hire them!

Winning Track Record

Comparing past verdicts and results will allow you to separate the best lawyer from the others. Unfortunately, Indiana lawyers are prohibited from listing past results in their advertisements. So you must inquire. But don't simply accept what you are told. Be certain to request some proof of prior verdicts such as the court records or newspaper reports.

The percentage of winning cases and the dollar amount an attorney has won can be the single most important factor in hiring an injury or wrongful death lawyer. Why? Because all insurance companies base their settlement decisions on past verdicts. If your lawyer has a solid history of winning large verdicts at trial, the chances are the insurance company will want to avoid trial by paying you a top-dollar settlement. Equally so, if the lawyer has little or no experience winning at trial, the insurance company will likely offer little or nothing knowing that the odds are in their favor. Always hire a lawyer who is a proven winner!

Adequate Resources

Some lawyers have the best of intentions, but limited staff and resources. If you have an important case or a powerful adversary, make sure you hire a law firm –not just a single lawyer–so that you will have the resources necessary to prevail. It helps to find a lawyer with membership in a specialized organization, like the American Trial Lawyers Association, which supplies members with resources and information. Make sure the lawyer is either a sustaining member or an officer in that organization. Also, look for cum laude (with honors) law school graduates and those who have professional publications. The best lawyers have good academic backgrounds and are often selected to write or teach seminars to other lawyers.

Hiring the right attorney can make a huge difference. By following these simple steps, you will be on the right path to selecting the best attorney for you.

Here are some additional tips, courtesy of www.nfib.com (National Federation of Independent Business):

Use Good Judgment! In business, conflicts are inevitable -- but messy lawsuits don't have to be. Should you get into a dispute and need help, first try to avoid the time, money, and stress involved in filing a lawsuit by making phone calls, writing letters, or setting up meetings with the other party to find a way to resolve the problem. However, the National Federation of Independent Business and Citizens Against Lawsuit Abuse understand that sometimes you will need a lawyer, if only to find out your legal options. If you find your-self in this situation, don't panic! We've compiled the following tips to help guide you through the process of choosing the right legal counsel. After all, being a smart legal consumer can be the best weapon against lawsuit abuse.

Tip #1 -- Find the Right Lawyer

Finding a lawyer with the right credentials can be essential to a successful case. You can find legal counsel through several resources:

State Bar Associations Your local bar association can help you identify the names of people who specialize in your problem and let you know if the lawyer has been the subject of an ethical complaint or inquiry. A listing of State Bar Associations may be found at www.bestcase.com/statebar.htm.

Lawyer Referral Services You can contact a lawyer referral service, which will connect you with a lawyer who specializes in your problem for around $30. Some services will allow you to talk with a lawyer for the first half-hour at no charge. These services can be found in the yellow pages under "Attorney Referral Services," "Attorneys" or "Lawyers."

Recommendation Talk to your friends. Some of the most reliable referrals are from people you trust - fellow business owners, friends and family - who have used lawyers recently. If you already know lawyers, talk to them as well.

Advertisements Don't believe everything you see in an advertisement. If it sounds too good to be true, it probably is. Be cautious of words such as "free" and "no charge." Many reputable lawyers do not advertise, so don't assume that the size of the ad is related to the quality of the lawyer. Don't hire a lawyer who comes knocking at your door. If a lawyer solicits your business without your permission, he or she may be "ambulance chasing." And "ambulance chasing," also known as barratry, is a violation of most state bar rules. If a lawyer can't follow rules to win clients, can you expect him to follow the rules to win your case?

Tip #2 -- Choose the Right Lawyer

Even if you have an urgent legal matter, interview a few lawyers before making your final decision. It is important that you find the lawyer whom you are most comfortable working with, and that this person has the necessary skills to win your case. On your interviews: Be sure to bring the general points of your case and all the names, addresses and phone numbers of everyone associated with your case. Don't be shy about asking the lawyer questions- after all he or she will be asking you many questions in the long run.

You should feel free to ask when the lawyer last handled a matter like yours and the outcome of the case.

It is important to find out all of your legal options according to that lawyer. You should also find out how long the lawyer expects your case to take, if a less experienced lawyer will be handling your case, and the litigation fees involved. Make sure the lawyers don't overwhelm you with legal jargon. If you don't understand something, ask for clarification. A good lawyer is always willing to make sure you comprehend everything and are fully satisfied. It is important that you understand the terms of your agreement with the lawyer. Never sign anything until you have time to review it and consider other offers.

Tip #3-- Understand All the Legal Costs Before You Sign the Dotted Line

Hourly Rates If you choose to pay by the hour, you agree to pay the lawyer's bill regardless of the outcome of your case. You should also expect to pay for out-of-pocket fees associated with the case, such as postage, photocopies and long distance calls. Ask your lawyer to keep a detailed record of hours worked on the case. Make sure the contract states the lawyer's and his employees' billing rates, and your right to audit records and expenses.

Contingency Fees A contingency fee arrangement means that you do not pay the lawyer a fee unless the case is won or settled out of court. Typically, contingency fees amount to less than 33% of an award if cases are settled, and up to 50% if the case goes to court. Before you sign the contract, be sure to negotiate the fee. Most contingency fee arrangements also deduct out-of-pocket costs, such as photocopying and phone calls. Determine if the fee will be paid before or after the lawyer's expenses are deducted, and if you will be responsible for those fees if the case is lost. Be sure to get all this information in writing.

Tip #4-- Control Your Legal Costs

After hiring a lawyer: It is important that you are comfortable with how your case is executed, which includes sticking within the budget. To keep legal costs down: Don't make unnecessary phone calls to your lawyer's office. When possible, put your concerns in writing and keep a copy for yourself. This gives you a record and allows for efficient communication. Require your attorney to receive your authorization for expenses that exceed $200.00. Ask for copies of all receipts. Meet quarterly with your lawyer to assess the progress of your case compared to your budget.

F.   The taxation of contingent attorney's fees paid by a winning client has been the subject of continuing interpretation. The American Jobs Creation Act of 2004 ended the double taxation of contingent fees (winning taxpayer must declare the entire award as income including the contingency portion paid to the attorney) in several areas such as employment, whistleblower claims, and civil rights litigation. Congress had previously allowed taxation of only net awards in personal injury cases.

But in other types of commercial litigation, the contingent fee portion of settlements and awards is taxable to the client, even though the attorney pays taxes on his contingent share, due to the unanimous Court decisions in *Commissioner of Internal Revenue v. Banks and Banaitis, 125 S.Ct. 826 (2005)*. Experts forecast more costly settlements as a result of these decisions because winning plaintiffs may insist that their extra tax be tacked onto the settlement.

G.   Courts are becoming increasingly critical of the actions of litigants and their lawyers that constitute "abuse of legal process" or "malicious prosecution". They are beginning to punish the offending parties even without a separate tort claim being filed for such conduct.

Many states have statutes that give a judge discretionary power to impose sanctions against a losing party and his attorney for improperly manipulating the judicial process, including reimbursement of expenses and payment of attorney's fees. This is even being extended to the issue of "frivolous appeals."

492

While on the books for years, these laws were rarely implemented until recently, but the tide seems to be turning in favor of enforcement. *Pitts Properties v. Auburn Bank, 2005 Ga. App. LEXIS 793 (Ga. App. 2005)* assessed a $2,000 penalty against appellant and its attorney for a frivolous appeal.

While the legal profession, like any business, is deserving of criticism when it falls below expected standards of conduct, it also does many good things that escape public attention. Pro bono free legal services for the poor have been implemented by most all state bar associations. This has filled the void created by the elimination of funding for these programs by the federal government.

H.   In *Federal Trade Commission v. Assail Inc., 410 F.3d 256 (5th Cir. 2005),* a case of first impression, the court ruled that a civil attorney is bound by the same general ethics rules that require criminal defense attorneys to investigate the source of the funds they receive from clients as a retainer and/or payment of fees.

In that case the defendant company was accused of violating the Federal Trade Commission Act in a telemarketing scheme, and when the FTC filed the civil action the trial court granted a temporary injunction that froze its assets. The company hired an attorney to defend it and paid him a $210,000 retainer, allegedly not from the tainted funds. Nevertheless, as a part of the court judgment against defendant, the lawyer was ordered to return his retainer.

The appellate court affirmed the lower court judgment and said, "The circumstances of Draskovich's fee payment should have alerted him that something was awry. He knew that his client was accused of perpetrating massive telemarketing fraud, that all of his assets were frozen, and that supposedly unrelated third parties were paying his fees. These facts should have raised Draskovich's suspicions."

Legal experts agree that this case clarifies the duty of an attorney to investigate whether or not fees paid by a client are tainted, and it could apply to all manner of civil lawyers who litigate over a disputed source of funds.

6.
THE LEGAL REMEDY

A.   Punitive Damages:

In *Robinson Helicopter v. Dana, 102 P.3d 268 (Cal. 2004)*, plaintiff sued for fraud, alleging that defendant concealed that its parts that keep helicopter blades rotating through loss of power were not up to federal specifications. Plaintiff was awarded $1.5 million in compensatory damages and $6 million in punitive damages.

On appeal, that decision was reversed based on a finding that punitive damages were not permissible under the state's "economic loss rule", which prohibits tort damages in contract disputes unless someone is physically injured. None of the helicopters with faulty parts had crashed.

The California Supreme Court reversed and reinstated the trial court award, ruling that there is an exception to the economic loss rule that does not bar fraud claims if they are independent of the underlying breach.

B.   Non-Monetary Remedies:

1. The non – monetary remedy of injunctive relief has found increased usage in the business marketplace. It commonly is used by employers to protect trade secrets by preventing key employees from breaching their employment contracts or non-compete agreements by working for competitors.

The case of *Ormco Corp. v. Johns, 2003 WL 2007816 (Ala. 2003)* is typical. The employee had signed a covenant not to compete for one year after leaving the company, but ignored it when he went to work for a competing supplier of orthodontic equipment. The employer's request for injunctive relief was denied by the trial court but was granted on appeal.

"Courts will not use the extraordinary power of injunctive relief merely to allay an apprehension of a possible injury; the injury must be imminent and irreparable in a court of law. Here there is a rebuttable inference of irreparable injury because Johns is in direct contact with Ormco's customers."

Injunctions are also commonly sought to prevent perceived unfair competition in the commercial marketplace. In *Johnson & Johnson Vision Care v. 1-800 Contacts, 299 F.3d 1242 (11th Cir. 2002)*, a contact lens maker sued a competitor over its alleged false advertising that claimed that consumers preferred the competitors lenses "by a 5 to 1 ratio." The trial court issued the requested preliminary injunction for making false claims under the Lanham Act, but that decision was reversed on appeal.

"The injunction is not justified here because the statements made by 1-800 were not shown to be literally false. J&J could not disprove statements in 1-800's advertising. The matter may be litigated, but there is not sufficient evidence to justify an injunction."

2. Here's a recent non-monetary remedy case about rescission and restitution:

In *Harley-Davidson Motor Co. v. Power Sports, Inc., 319 F.3d 973 (7th Cir. 2003)*, plaintiff approved the transfer of one of its dealerships to defendant and then learned that the proposed method of operating would violate their stated dealership guidelines and was contrary to representations made during contract negotiations. Plaintiff sued for both rescissions of the transfer and money damages. The trial court ruled for defendant, finding that the lack of economic loss denied the claim.

On appeal the decision was reversed in favor of plaintiff. "Under Wisconsin law, if a party's assent to a contract is induced by (fraud), that person can either seek rescission or damages, but cannot seek both; however, a party electing rescission may recover restitution to restore it to the position it would have occupied had no contract ever been made."

C.   Duty to Mitigate Damages:
One of the long-standing fairness principles for awarding contract damages is that the non-breaching part has a duty to act reasonably and therefore lessen the final amount of damages caused by the breaching party. This doctrine is raised frequently in landlord-tenant disputes, such as *Circuit City Stores, Inc. v. Rockville Pike Joint Venture, LP, 829 A.2d 976 (Md. App. 2003)*.

In that case Rockville, as landlord, entered into a 20-year lease with Circuit City, as tenant, to occupy space in its retail shopping center. After nine years of occupancy the tenant decided to move, although it didn't tell the landlord of its plans until the following year when landlord was attempting to refinance the shopping center. Tenant hired a broker to try to find a suitable replacement tenant, as required under its lease. A music retailer was offered as a sub-lessee but was rejected because it was one-half the size of the tenant. Finally tenant closed the store and abandoned the premises. Landlord subsequently demolished the premises and erected a larger building, which was necessary to attract a replacement tenant.

Landlord sued tenant for breach of its lease, and tenant defendant claiming landlord had failed to properly mitigate damages by accepting the replacement tenant it had offered. The trial court ruled for the landlord, and after several interim appeals that resulted in a decision that the tenant had no further lease obligation after it vacated the premises and they were demolished, this court reversed again in favor of the landlord.

"We have recognized generally, that when one party breaches a contract, the other party is sustained from the breach and can charge the defaulting party only with such damages as, 'with reasonable endeavors and expense and without risk of additional loss or injury, he could not prevent.' The principle applies as well to damages resulting from a tenant's abandonment of leased premises."

D.   Contract Tort of Bad Faith:

1. In *U.S. v. Schneider, 03-1764 (2nd Cir. 2004)*, the Hyde Amendment, which allows for attorney's fees to be assessed in Federal criminal cases where "the position of the United States was vexatious, frivolous, or in bad faith", was tested in court for the first time. Defendant had been charged in 2002 with conspiracy to defraud the government and wire fraud for his alleged role in a multi-million dollar scheme. After his acquittal, defendant's demand for attorney's fees was denied, since the court felt there was no evidence of bad faith by the prosecutors.

2. In M*uirhead v.Great River Ins. Co. v. Baker, Donelson, et. al.*, an unreported 2004 Mississippi case, plaintiff was involved in an altercation at the annual sales meeting of his employer (Empire Truck Sales) and both he and his employer were sued by an injured patron who was awarded $2,900 in damages by the trial jury. Great River was the employer's insurer. Plaintiff asked it to reimburse his cost of defending the lawsuit and it hired the Baker law firm for a legal opinion. Coverage was then denied based on the opinion, and plaintiff filed a successful bad-faith lawsuit against Great River. It then fired the law firm, settled with plaintiff for more than $500,000 and the law firm was successfully sued for legal malpractice.

3. In *Cassim v. Allstate Ins. Co., 94 P.3d 513 (Cal. 2004)*, plaintiffs sued their homeowner's policy insurer-defendant for its bad-faith actions in resisting their claim for fire damages to their home. The insurer claimed that it was suspicious the plaintiff's had set the fire themselves. The trial jury found that defendant had acted in bad faith and awarded plaintiffs a combined $3.6 million in compensatory damages and $5 million in punitive damages. The judge also awarded, without explanation, additional insurer bad-faith fees including plaintiff's legal costs and related expenses as allowed by *Brandt v. Superior Court, 37 Cal.3d 813 (1985)*, in the amount of $1.2 million. The trial jury's award was affirmed on appeal, but the award of *Brandt* fees was disallowed as being unsupported by the evidence.

4. In *Calich v. Allstate Insurance Co., 2004 Ohio 1619 (Ohio App. 2004)*, an Ohio jury found that Allstate acted in bad faith when it refused to settle a claim brought by an auto crash victim against their insured. The 20-year-old victim had suffered brain injuries that permanently affected her speech and walking abilities while a passenger in a car driven by the teen-age driver plaintiff that was speeding, flipped and hit a utility pole. Allstate sat on the case for 28 days after the crash, could have settled the case for the $50,000 policy limits. The victim entered into a consent judgment with the plaintiff driver for $1 million, and plaintiff took an assignment of all the driver's claims against Allstate for its failure to settle.

The trial jury awarded $1 million in damages. But on appeal that judgment was reversed in favor of the insurer because "an adjudicated excess judgment against the insurance company must exist before a claim of bad faith arises."

In a dissenting opinion pointing out that this was a case of 1st impression in the state, it was pointed out that "traditionally, there have been two schools of thought concerning the imposition of liability upon an insurer for failing to exercise good faith which results in an excess judgment against the insured."

"An increasing majority of jurisdictions have adopted the 'judgment rule,' which advocates the reasoning that an entry of judgment in excess alone is sufficient damage to sustain a recovery from an insurer for its breach of duty to act in good faith in defending the insured's case." (Dissent - plaintiff wins.)

"A decreasing minority of jurisdictions adopt the 'payment rule,' which advocates the reasoning that, is an insured did not and cannot pay out any money in satisfaction of an excess judgment, the insured was not harmed, and, therefore, the insurer is not to be held responsible for its bad faith in defending the insured's case." (Majority – defendant wins.)

7.
WHERE TO SUE

The litigation process is a strategic battle of wits between the parties and their legal representatives that has a basic objective. One of the parties wants to win and therefore not lose. Winning or losing is usually relative since settlement is the common result at any stage of the proceeding. And the key to settlement success is answering the following question, "What can I do to induce my adversary to give in and end the dispute on my terms?"

One of the hidden strategy battlefields is after the plaintiff has decided to sue, chosen the legal remedy, and then decides to file suit in state or federal court. After the lawsuit summons is properly served on the defendant, the strategy shifts to where must the case be defended. Cases often are ended at any of these early stages as one party gains a strategic advantage and this change in perceived strength or weakness of the respective case induces the other party to settle. Here are some recent cases that highlight these jurisdictional disputes:

A.   Jurisdiction over the person:
1. In *Snowney v. Harrah's Entertainment, 11 Cal. Rptr.3d 35 (Cal. App. 2004)*, plaintiff sued defendant and other Nevada casino operators in a class action claiming unfair competition, breach of contract and false advertising. The suit was filed in California state court and defendant's motion to dismiss for lack of personal jurisdiction was granted. On appeal the case was reversed.

"The hotels and casinos purposefully directed advertising at California residents; they also conducted business with some residents by an interactive web site. They solicited and received the patronage of California residents. These activities created sufficient connections for California courts to have personal jurisdiction over the hotels and casinos."

2. In *Hollinger v. Sifers, 2003 WL 22997218 (Mo. App. 2003)*, plaintiff, a Missouri resident, who saw a TV interview with defendant, a Kansas licensed doctor, and contracted for a surgical procedure which was performed in Kansas. The surgery resulted in complications and plaintiff sued for malpractice in his home state of Missouri, serving process on defendant in Kansas under the long-arm statute. The trial court dismissed for lack of personal jurisdiction.

On appeal the decision was affirmed, based upon the facts that the non-resident defendant was providing a service and not selling a product in commerce, he didn't advertise his services in Missouri, and the tort did not occur there. "For a non-resident defendant to be subject to the long-arm jurisdiction of this state, two elements must be present:

First, the suit must arise out of one of the activities enumerated in Missouri's long-arm statute; and second, the defendant must have sufficient minimum contacts with Missouri to satisfy due process requirements."

3. In *Brown v. Thaler, 2005 WL 1459118 (Maine 2005)*, plaintiff mailed the summons and complaint to defendant by certified mail. State law allowed this direct service by mail if an "acknowledgement form" accompanied the papers and was received back by the sender within 20 days. Otherwise personal service of process was required. Plaintiff's mailing didn't contain an acknowledgement form, defendant didn't reply, plaintiff received a default judgment, it was vacated after defendant contested its entry, and plaintiff's complaint was dismissed. Plaintiff unsuccessfully appealed that ruling. "Service by mail without an acknowledgement is not proper service ... and means the trial court does not have personal jurisdiction over the defendant."

4. In *Burden v. Copco Refrigeration, 2004 WL 1058814 (Ore. App. 2004)*, plaintiff sued defendant for injuries suffered in an auto accident. Defendant claimed inadequate service of process and moved to dismiss. Oregon law allows service of process on a defendant by delivering a true copy of the summons and complaint to any person 14 years of age or older at the defendant's residence. The trial court denied the motion and upheld service of process but the appellate court reversed.

"The plaintiff only offered an unsworn statement from the process server stating that service had been completed properly. That is hearsay, not competent evidence, so the presumption is that adequate service never occurred. The matter may not proceed unless proper service can be established."

B.   Forum Non Conveniens Jurisdiction Issues:
1. In *Ex parte Kia Motors America, Inc., 2003 WL 210400313 (Ala. 2003)*, administrators of the estates of three Alabama residents who were killed in a high-speed accident in Florida sued Kia in Alabama state court for product liability. Kia's request to move the case to Florida on grounds of "forum non conveniens" was initially denied by the trial court but reversed on appeal. "The causes of action accrued in Florida and (that) almost all witnesses were in Florida. Most of the witnesses could not be subpoenaed to personally appear in Alabama court."

2. In *Esfeld v. Costa Crociere, SPA, 289 F.3d 1300 (11th Cir. 2002)*, six plaintiffs were injured in Vietnam. Four resided in Washington and two resided in California. At the time of the accident they were on a van tour cruise on a ship owned by the Italian defendant with a Miami, Florida sales office from which the trip was marketed. The trip started in Singapore and docked in Vietnam when the van accident occurred. The plaintiffs sued in Miami state court and the defendants were successful in having it removed to federal court where it was dismissed based upon forum non conveniens.

On appeal that decision was reversed. "Under the Erie doctrine, a federal court in a diversity case applies state substantive law and federal procedural law. In this case, federal procedure controls because of the diversity of the parties involved, so the suit will be heard in federal court, but Florida law will govern the substance of the dispute."

C.   Federal Court Removal Jurisdiction:
1. In *Terrebonne Homecare, Inc. v. SMA Health Plan,Inc., 271 F.3d 186 (5th Cir. 2001),* defendant had originally sued in Louisiana state court claiming unfair competition and violation of state antitrust law when it was terminated as a preferred provider. THI worded their complaint to fall within federal court federal question jurisdiction. But the case was required to be returned to state court by the appellate court. "The artful pleading doctrine does not apply, however, unless federal law completely preempts the field." In this case state antitrust laws were not completely preempted, so the federal removal was improper.

2. In *Murphy Brothers, Inc. v. Michetti Pipe Stringing, Inc., 119 S.Ct. 1322 (1999),* defendant was a Canadian corporation sued in Alabama state court by plaintiff, an Illinois corporation for breach of contract and fraud. Defendant removed the case to federal court based on diversity jurisdiction on the 30th day after service of process of the complaint, but 44 days after its counsel had received a courtesy copy of the complaint. Plaintiff claimed untimely removal under the "30-day rule" and requested a remand back to state court.

The Court clarified the removal rule by holding that, "the 30-day time period for removal under Section 1446(b) does not begin to run until actual service on the defendant." This further assumes that the complaint is "removable on its face"; meaning that it clearly shows proper jurisdictional amount and diversity of citizenship between plaintiff and defendant, or the case involves a "federal question." (Section 1446 (b) also provides: "A case may not be removed on the basis of jurisdiction conferred by Section 1332 (diversity jurisdiction) of this title more than one year after commencement of the action (filing the complaint)."

D.   Federal Court Diversity Jurisdiction:
1. In the consolidated cases of *Exxon Mobil Corp. v. Allapattah Services, 125 S.Ct. 2611 (2005) and Ortega v. Star-Kist Foods, 125 S.Ct. 314 (2004),* a group of Exxon dealers in the first case and a girl whose finger was cut on a tuna can in the second, sued in federal court under diversity jurisdiction. Their claims were unsuccessfully challenged because some of the plaintiffs could not claim injury over the then jurisdictional amount requirement of $75,000. The Court interpreted the supplemental jurisdiction of federal courts in diversity cases to mean that the smaller-claim plaintiffs should be included. "When the well-pleaded complaint contains at least one claim that satisfies the amount-in-controversy requirement," the District Court has jurisdiction over all others involved in the same incident."

2. In *Roche v. Lincoln Property Co., 373 F.3d 610(4ᵗʰ Cir. 2004)*, plaintiffs originally sued in Virginia state court claiming personal injury and property damage from toxic levels of mold in their apartment owned by defendant, a Texas-based corporation. The defendant filed a motion for removal to federal court based on "diversity of citizenship" of the parties under 28 U.S.C. Sec. 1447 that was granted by the federal court. Plaintiffs then appealed, arguing that the case should remain in state court because both parties were really citizens of Virginia. The appellate court agreed that despite defendant's Texas incorporation, it was in fact a citizen of Virginia having a "close nexus" to the state because it owned a Virginia subsidiary that was "the real and substantial party in interest."

3. In *Chadbourne & Parke v. Remote Solutions, 603037/04 (N.Y. Sup. Ct. 2005)*, an attorney's fee collection suit for $117,000 was brought by a New York law firm against a South Korean company which hired the firm through representatives and via e-mail to represent it in a patent infringement dispute pending in Delaware. Plaintiffs argued that the company's hiring and subsequent communications and e-mails provided sufficient "minimum contacts" for New York courts to exercise jurisdiction over the non-resident defendant under the state's long-arm statute. The court ruled for the defendant, based on the fact that it had not even visited New York to hire plaintiff. "The fact that lawyers located in (plaintiff's) New York office performed legal services for the Korean client ... is insufficient to find that the client transacted any business in the State of New York in relation to the claim."

E.   Class Action Federal Jurisdiction:
1. In February, 2005 President Bush signed into law "The Class Action Fairness Act" as a part of the federal and state trend toward tort reform. It aims to discourage class action lawsuits by having stricter federal judges take them away from more liberal state courts. Under the law, class action suits seeking $5 million or more would be heard in state court only if the primary defendant and more than 1/3 of the plaintiffs are from the same state. But if less than 1/3 of the plaintiffs are from the same state as the primary defendant and more than $5 million is at stake, the case would have to be heard in federal court.

F.   Choice of law – doing business – contacts test:
1. "Resolving choice-of-law issues in contract disputes where there is no choice-of-law provision means the courts consider: 1) the place of contracting; 2) the place of negotiation of the contract; 3) the place of performance; 4) the location of the subject matter of the contract, and 5) the domicile, residence, nationality, place of incorporation and place of business of the parties." *Salt Lake Tribune Publishing Co. v. Management Planning, Inc., 390 F.3d 684 (10ᵗʰ Cir. 2005)*.

2. In *Jaffe v. Pallotta Teamworks, 374 F.3d 1223 (D.C. App. 2004)*, plaintiff's daughter volunteered to participate in AIDSRide, a multiple-day bicycle ride to raise funds for AIDS charities. She signed a liability waiver in D.C. that held the organizer – defendant, a California corporation, harmless in the event of her injury or death. She began the ride in North Carolina.

Later in the day while in Virginia she felt poorly, went to a medical station for treatment where she was given intravenous fluids. But her condition worsened and she died. Plaintiff, her mother, sued in D.C. for negligence claiming that the medical station was run by untrained volunteers who over-hydrated her daughter and caused her death. The trial court granted summary judgment to defendant because of the liability waiver. On appeal, the case was reversed and remanded because the court ruled that the law of Virginia, not D.C., should be applied.

"Under D.C. choice of law rules, Virginia law, rather than D.C. law, governs the issue of the effect of the waiver signed by Jaffe. D.C. applies the *substantial interest test* for determining choice of law in tort cases: 1) where the injury occurred; 2) where the conduct that caused the injury occurred; 3) the residency of the parties; and 4) the place where the relationship is centered. Virginia has a more substantial interest in this matter than does D.C., so Virginia law will govern the case."

3. In *Schwartzenegger v. Fred Martin Motor Co.*, 374 F.3d 797 (9th Cir. 2004), defendant, an Ohio car dealer, ran a series of full-page color advertisements in an Akron, Ohio newspaper showing a photo of plaintiff as the Terminator, his famous movie role, without plaintiff's permission. Plaintiff sued in his California home state court for the tort of right of publicity based upon unauthorized use of his image. Defendant removed the case to California federal court under diversity jurisdiction and moved to dismiss for lack of personal jurisdiction. The trial court granted the motion and it was affirmed on appeal.

"Martin does not have sufficient *minimum contacts* with California arising from, or related to, its actions in distributing an ad in Ohio. The complained of acts took place in Ohio. The plaintiff bears the proof of showing that the court would have jurisdiction, which was not done. The fact that some of Martin's cars were imported through California from Japan was not sufficient to create minimum contacts for business in California. The fact that people in California could see the Martin website was also insufficient to create minimum contacts in California."

(This case is significant in its apparent limiting of the trend toward allowing court jurisdiction to be imposed anywhere the website of a goods or service vendor could be accessed on the Internet. The traditional offline "minimum contacts" test of where a party is "doing business" was applied even to an online party.)

G.   Use of Special Courts:
1. Family lawyers, especially those representing wealthy clients, are increasingly opting to go to a "private judge" rather than wait months and years for their cases to be heard clogged divorce courts. Experienced private judges can be hired for $300 to $800 per hour and can by mutual agreement resolve a case within a few days, in private non-jury proceedings that protect the reputations of the parties involved.

2. Several states are considering creating "medical malpractice courts" as part of the tort reform movement, to streamline otherwise time-consuming, costly and complex litigation. In these courts, judges with medical expertise would decide the disputes privately, with the assistance of court-appointed experts. Opponents insist that this would take away a party's constitutional right to trial by jury.

3. "Homeless court" is an experimental way for homeless persons to clear criminal misdemeanor offenses and outstanding warrants from their records so that their eligibility for government aid, driver's licenses, job training, certain housing programs and alcohol or drug rehab is not adversely affected. Homeless persons cannot participate unless referred to the court by a shelter where they have completed recovery and self-help programs.

7.

WHERE TO SUE

The litigation process is a strategic battle of wits between the parties and their legal representatives that has a basic objective. One of the parties wants to win and therefore not lose. Winning or losing is usually relative since settlement is the common result at any stage of the proceeding. And the key to settlement success is answering the following question, "What can I do to induce my adversary to give in and end the dispute on my terms?"

One of the hidden strategy battlefields is after the plaintiff has decided to sue, chosen the legal remedy, and then decides to file suit in state or federal court. After the lawsuit summons is properly served on the defendant, the strategy shifts to where must the case be defended. Cases often are ended at any of these early stages as one party gains a strategic advantage and this change in perceived strength or weakness of the respective case induces the other party to settle. Here are some recent cases that highlight these jurisdictional disputes:

A.   Jurisdiction over the person:
1. In *Snowney v. Harrah's Entertainment, 11 Cal. Rptr.3d 35 (Cal. App. 2004)*, plaintiff sued defendant and other Nevada casino operators in a class action claiming unfair competition, breach of contract and false advertising. The suit was filed in California state court and defendant's motion to dismiss for lack of personal jurisdiction was granted. On appeal the case was reversed.

"The hotels and casinos purposefully directed advertising at California residents; they also conducted business with some residents by an interactive web site. They solicited and received the patronage of California residents. These activities created sufficient connections for California courts to have personal jurisdiction over the hotels and casinos."

2. In *Hollinger v. Sifers, 2003 WL 22997218 (Mo. App. 2003)*, plaintiff, a Missouri resident, who saw a TV interview with defendant, a Kansas licensed doctor, and contracted for a surgical procedure which was performed in Kansas. The surgery resulted in complications and plaintiff sued for malpractice in his home state of Missouri, serving process on defendant in Kansas under the long-arm statute. The trial court dismissed for lack of personal jurisdiction.

On appeal the decision was affirmed, based upon the facts that the non-resident defendant was providing a service and not selling a product in commerce, he didn't advertise his services in Missouri, and the tort did not occur there. "For a non-resident defendant to be subject to the long-arm jurisdiction of this state, two elements must be present:

504

First, the suit must arise out of one of the activities enumerated in Missouri's long-arm statute; and second, the defendant must have sufficient minimum contacts with Missouri to satisfy due process requirements."

3. In *Brown v. Thaler, 2005 WL 1459118 (Maine 2005)*, plaintiff mailed the summons and complaint to defendant by certified mail. State law allowed this direct service by mail if an "acknowledgement form" accompanied the papers and was received back by the sender within 20 days. Otherwise personal service of process was required. Plaintiff's mailing didn't contain an acknowledgement form, defendant didn't reply, plaintiff received a default judgment, it was vacated after defendant contested its entry, and plaintiff's complaint was dismissed. Plaintiff unsuccessfully appealed that ruling. "Service by mail without an acknowledgement is not proper service ... and means the trial court does not have personal jurisdiction over the defendant."

5. In *Burden v. Copco Refrigeration, 2004 WL 1058814 (Ore. App. 2004)*, plaintiff sued defendant for injuries suffered in an auto accident. Defendant claimed inadequate service of process and moved to dismiss. Oregon law allows service of process on a defendant by delivering a true copy of the summons and complaint to any person 14 years of age or older at the defendant's residence. The trial court denied the motion and upheld service of process but the appellate court reversed.

"The plaintiff only offered an unsworn statement from the process server stating that service had been completed properly. That is hearsay, not competent evidence, so the presumption is that adequate service never occurred. The matter may not proceed unless proper service can be established."

B.   Forum Non Conveniens Jurisdiction Issues:

1. In *Ex parte Kia Motors America, Inc., 2003 WL 210400313 (Ala. 2003)*, administrators of the estates of three Alabama residents who were killed in a high-speed accident in Florida sued Kia in Alabama state court for product liability. Kia's request to move the case to Florida on grounds of "forum non conveniens" was initially denied by the trial court but reversed on appeal. "The causes of action accrued in Florida and (that) almost all witnesses were in Florida. Most of the witnesses could not be subpoenaed to personally appear in Alabama court."

2. In *Esfeld v. Costa Crociere, SPA, 289 F.3d 1300 (11th Cir. 2002)*, six plaintiffs were injured in Vietnam. Four resided in Washington and two resided in California. At the time of the accident they were on a van tour cruise on a ship owned by the Italian defendant with a Miami, Florida sales office from which the trip was marketed. The trip started in Singapore and docked in Vietnam when the van accident occurred. The plaintiffs sued in Miami state court and the defendants were successful in having it removed to federal court where it was dismissed based upon forum non conveniens.

On appeal that decision was reversed. "Under the Erie doctrine, a federal court in a diversity case applies state substantive law and federal procedural law. In this case, federal procedure controls because of the diversity of the parties involved, so the suit will be heard in federal court, but Florida law will govern the substance of the dispute."

C.   Federal Court Removal Jurisdiction:

1. In *Terrebonne Homecare, Inc. v. SMA Health Plan,Inc., 271 F.3d 186 (5th Cir. 2001),* defendant had originally sued in Louisiana state court claiming unfair competition and violation of state antitrust law when it was terminated as a preferred provider. THI worded their complaint to fall within federal court federal question jurisdiction. But the case was required to be returned to state court by the appellate court. "The artful pleading doctrine does not apply, however, unless federal law completely preempts the field." In this case state antitrust laws were not completely preempted, so the federal removal was improper.

2. In *Murphy Brothers, Inc. v. Michetti Pipe Stringing, Inc., 119 S.Ct. 1322 (1999),* defendant was a Canadian corporation sued in Alabama state court by plaintiff, an Illinois corporation for breach of contract and fraud. Defendant removed the case to federal court based on diversity jurisdiction on the 30th day after service of process of the complaint, but 44 days after its counsel had received a courtesy copy of the complaint. Plaintiff claimed untimely removal under the "30-day rule" and requested a remand back to state court.

The Court clarified the removal rule by holding that, "the 30-day time period for removal under Section 1446(b) does not begin to run until actual service on the defendant." This further assumes that the complaint is "removable on its face"; meaning that it clearly shows proper jurisdictional amount and diversity of citizenship between plaintiff and defendant, or the case involves a "federal question." (Section 1446 (b) also provides: "A case may not be removed on the basis of jurisdiction conferred by Section 1332 (diversity jurisdiction) of this title more than one year after commencement of the action (filing the complaint)."

D.   Federal Court Diversity Jurisdiction:

1. In the consolidated cases of *Exxon Mobil Corp. v. Allapattah Services, 125 S.Ct. 2611 (2005) and Ortega v. Star-Kist Foods, 125 S.Ct. 314 (2004),* a group of Exxon dealers in the first case and a girl whose finger was cut on a tuna can in the second, sued in federal court under diversity jurisdiction. Their claims were unsuccessfully challenged because some of the plaintiffs could not claim injury over the then jurisdictional amount requirement of $75,000. The Court interpreted the supplemental jurisdiction of federal courts in diversity cases to mean that the smaller-claim plaintiffs should be included. "When the well-pleaded complaint contains at least one claim that satisfies the amount-in-controversy requirement," the District Court has jurisdiction over all others involved in the same incident."

2. In *Roche v. Lincoln Property Co., 373 F.3d 610(4ᵗʰ Cir. 2004)*, plaintiffs originally sued in Virginia state court claiming personal injury and property damage from toxic levels of mold in their apartment owned by defendant, a Texas-based corporation. The defendant filed a motion for removal to federal court based on "diversity of citizenship" of the parties under 28 U.S.C. Sec. 1447 that was granted by the federal court. Plaintiffs then appealed, arguing that the case should remain in state court because both parties were really citizens of Virginia. The appellate court agreed that despite defendant's Texas incorporation, it was in fact a citizen of Virginia having a "close nexus" to the state because it owned a Virginia subsidiary that was "the real and substantial party in interest."

3. In *Chadbourne & Parke v. Remote Solutions, 603037/04 (N.Y. Sup. Ct. 2005)*, an attorney's fee collection suit for $117,000 was brought by a New York law firm against a South Korean company which hired the firm through representatives and via e-mail to represent it in a patent infringement dispute pending in Delaware. Plaintiffs argued that the company's hiring and subsequent communications and e-mails provided sufficient "minimum contacts" for New York courts to exercise jurisdiction over the non-resident defendant under the state's long-arm statute. The court ruled for the defendant, based on the fact that it had not even visited New York to hire plaintiff. "The fact that lawyers located in (plaintiff's) New York office performed legal services for the Korean client ... is insufficient to find that the client transacted any business in the State of New York in relation to the claim."

E.   Class Action Federal Jurisdiction:
1. In February, 2005 President Bush signed into law "The Class Action Fairness Act" as a part of the federal and state trend toward tort reform. It aims to discourage class action lawsuits by having stricter federal judges take them away from more liberal state courts. Under the law, class action suits seeking $5 million or more would be heard in state court only if the primary defendant and more than 1/3 of the plaintiffs are from the same state. But if less than 1/3 of the plaintiffs are from the same state as the primary defendant and more than $5 million is at stake, the case would have to be heard in federal court.

F.   Choice of law – doing business – contacts test:
1. "Resolving choice-of-law issues in contract disputes where there is no choice-of-law provision means the courts consider: 1) the place of contracting; 2) the place of negotiation of the contract; 3) the place of performance; 4) the location of the subject matter of the contract, and 5) the domicile, residence, nationality, place of incorporation and place of business of the parties." *Salt Lake Tribune Publishing Co. v. Management Planning, Inc., 390 F.3d 684 (10ᵗʰ Cir. 2005).*

3. In *Jaffe v. Pallotta Teamworks, 374 F.3d 1223 (D.C. App. 2004)*, plaintiff's daughter volunteered to participate in AIDSRide, a multiple-day bicycle ride to raise funds for AIDS charities. She signed a liability waiver in D.C. that held the organizer – defendant, a California corporation, harmless in the event of her injury or death. She began the ride in North Carolina.

Later in the day while in Virginia she felt poorly, went to a medical station for treatment where she was given intravenous fluids. But her condition worsened and she died. Plaintiff, her mother, sued in D.C. for negligence claiming that the medical station was run by untrained volunteers who over-hydrated her daughter and caused her death. The trial court granted summary judgment to defendant because of the liability waiver. On appeal, the case was reversed and remanded because the court ruled that the law of Virginia, not D.C., should be applied.

"Under D.C. choice of law rules, Virginia law, rather than D.C. law, governs the issue of the effect of the waiver signed by Jaffe. D.C. applies the *substantial interest test* for determining choice of law in tort cases: 1) where the injury occurred; 2) where the conduct that caused the injury occurred; 3) the residency of the parties; and 4) the place where the relationship is centered. Virginia has a more substantial interest in this matter than does D.C., so Virginia law will govern the case."

3. In *Schwartzenegger v. Fred Martin Motor Co., 374 F.3d 797 (9ᵗʰ Cir. 2004)*, defendant, an Ohio car dealer, ran a series of full-page color advertisements in an Akron, Ohio newspaper showing a photo of plaintiff as the Terminator, his famous movie role, without plaintiff's permission. Plaintiff sued in his California home state court for the tort of right of publicity based upon unauthorized use of his image. Defendant removed the case to California federal court under diversity jurisdiction and moved to dismiss for lack of personal jurisdiction. The trial court granted the motion and it was affirmed on appeal.

"Martin does not have sufficient *minimum contacts* with California arising from, or related to, its actions in distributing an ad in Ohio. The complained of acts took place in Ohio. The plaintiff bears the proof of showing that the court would have jurisdiction, which was not done. The fact that some of Martin's cars were imported through California from Japan was not sufficient to create minimum contacts for business in California. The fact that people in California could see the Martin website was also insufficient to create minimum contacts in California."

(This case is significant in its apparent limiting of the trend toward allowing court jurisdiction to be imposed anywhere the website of a goods or service vendor could be accessed on the Internet. The traditional offline "minimum contacts" test of where a party is "doing business" was applied even to an online party.)

G.   Use of Special Courts:
1. Family lawyers, especially those representing wealthy clients, are increasingly opting to go to a "private judge" rather than wait months and years for their cases to be heard clogged divorce courts. Experienced private judges can be hired for $300 to $800 per hour and can by mutual agreement resolve a case within a few days, in private non-jury proceedings that protect the reputations of the parties involved.

2. Several states are considering creating "medical malpractice courts" as part of the tort reform movement, to streamline otherwise time-consuming, costly and complex litigation. In these courts, judges with medical expertise would decide the disputes privately, with the assistance of court-appointed experts. Opponents insist that this would take away a party's constitutional right to trial by jury.

3. "Homeless court" is an experimental way for homeless persons to clear criminal misdemeanor offenses and outstanding warrants from their records so that their eligibility for government aid, driver's licenses, job training, certain housing programs and alcohol or drug rehab is not adversely affected. Homeless persons cannot participate unless referred to the court by a shelter where they have completed recovery and self-help programs.

8.
HOW TO SUE

After a dispute occurs, you check out the sources of law to see if you are "right", you choose an appropriate remedy and litigate in an appropriate jurisdictional forum – the preliminaries are over.

Now we are ready for the main event. This is the actual trial of the civil lawsuit before a judge sitting alone or with a requested jury. The steps of a typical lawsuit each carry the same give and take pendulum swing of activity back and forth between plaintiff and defendant until a final decision is reached or the dispute is resolved by settlement.

Here are five cases relating to the trial stage of the dispute:

1. In *O'Hearn v. Hillcrest Gym and Fitness Center, 2004 WL 178961 (Cal. App. 2004),* plaintiff was a professional bodybuilder who earned compensation by product endorsements and personal appearances. Defendant used a promotional brochure that contained a photo of plaintiff taken from a magazine without his consent. Plaintiff sued defendant and the marketing company that prepared the brochure for commercial appropriation and invasion of privacy. The marketing company settled for $29,500 and the court deducted this amount from the $144,000 awarded plaintiff against defendant at the trial. This was reversed on appeal.

The appellate court ruled that it was improper for a trial court to allow evidence of the amount of a settlement. "Settlement agreements are not to be a part of the trial record." If evidence of settlements is used at trial, it will discourage the parties from attempting to resolve their disputes out-of-court. Most courts will only allow a simple reference to the fact that a matter was settled, but no details or other information can be shared.

2. In *Butler v. Continental Airlines, Inc., 2003 WL 21911160 (Tex. App. 2003),* plaintiff sued defendant in Texas state court for alleged unauthorized copying and use in their computer reservation system of macros he had created. The case was dismissed for lack of subject matter jurisdiction because the court ruled it governed by the Federal Copyright Act. Plaintiff then sued in federal court but his case was dismissed. He then re-filed the same case in another and his case was dismissed with prejudice.

On appeal, the court affirmed the final dismissal. "When the case was dismissed the first time ... that decision was res judicata on the issue of whether any Texas state court had subject matter jurisdiction."

Plaintiff should have raised all his claims in the first lawsuit and is prohibited from returning later to the same court with new claims brought on the same matter.

3. In *Fama v. Yi, 2003 WL 179205 (N.J. App. 2003)*, plaintiff sued for personal injuries suffered in an auto accident when defendant ran a stop sign. After the jury ruled for defendant, plaintiff sued his own insurance company for PIP medical expenses he incurred in the accident. It was granted a summary judgment by the trial court on the issue of whether plaintiff could re-litigate the matter.

On appeal, the decision was affirmed. "Collateral estoppel applies if the issue decided in the prior action is identical to the one presented in the subsequent action, if the issue was actually litigated – that is, there was a full and fair opportunity to litigate the issue – in the prior action, if there was a final judgment on the merits ..."

4. In *Smith v. BMW North America, Inc., 308 F.3d 913 (8th Cir. 2002)*, plaintiff sued for severe neck injuries she suffered in an automobile accident, claiming a faulty air bag in her 1994 BMW increased their severity. Her expert, a forensic pathologist, testified that proper deployment of the airbag would have prevented or reduced her injuries. That testimony conflicted with some of defendant's experts and the court excluded it, resulting in plaintiff's case being dismissed for lack of evidence.

On appeal, that decision was reversed on the grounds that the trial judge had abused his discretion. "The fact that experts in other fields might also be able to form opinions regarding the cause of Smith's neck injury and would base those opinions on factors other than those used by Dr. Erickson does not disqualify Dr. Erickson from offering testimony that would be helpful to the jury."

5. In *Chewning v. Ford Motor Company, 2001 WL 589969 (S.C. App. 2001)*, plaintiff sued for injuries suffered in a rollover crash of a Ford Bronco, resulting in a jury verdict for defendant. Eight years later plaintiff uncovered documents that should have been produced by defendant at the trial showing that the same expert had been critical of the Bronco. In addition she discovered that documents showing that Ford's lawyers had paid large sums to the expert to give perjured testimony.

Plaintiff sued again, claiming the fraud by the defendant allowed her to re-file her claim. The trial court dismissed based on a state rule that "fraud at trial must be shown within one year of the trial."

The appellate court reversed in plaintiff's favor. South Carolina law maintains a distinction between intrinsic and extrinsic fraud.

"Intrinsic fraud concerns fraud presented and considered in the judgment that is being questioned that goes to the merits of the case There is a one-year time limit on such issues to be raised after the trial.

Extrinsic fraud refers to frauds such as bribery or other misleading acts which prevent the movant from presenting all of his case (and carries no time limitation)."

At the conclusion of the presentation of all evidence in a jury trial, when both plaintiff and defendant have rested their cases, the parties and the presiding judge meet in a "charging conference" for the purpose of determining the governing rules of law that will be presented by the judge to the jurors in the form of written "jury instructions" before they retire to deliberate a decision by fitting the unique facts of the applicable law. A common complaint about the standard jury instructions used is that their legalese wording is so complicated that they are hard to understand and use. The Judicial Council of California's Task Force on Jury Instructions has been working for eight years to create new 'plain English' jury instructions, and other states are considering doing the same.

9.
CREATING THE CONTRACT
A. BASIC CONTRACT CONCEPTS

The two primary fairness doctrines of our U.S. contract law are Quasi Contract and Promissory Estoppel. They present concepts that are both interesting to legal scholars and frustrating to the business community because they allow contract enforcement of non-contracts.

Try to logically explain how a party can become obligated to pay for beneficial services they never ordered that are mistakenly furnished (Quasi Contract), or how otherwise unenforceable promises made by a party can become legally binding if the other party financially relies on them (Promissory Estoppel).

But the fairness considerations that govern both concepts outweigh logic, and enable the scales of justice to maintain their balance between general legal rules and special factual fairness exceptions.

Here are six current cases in the area:

1. In *Bruce v. Weekly World News, Inc., 310 F.3d 25 (1st Cir. 2002)*, plaintiff was a commercial photographer who took a photo of President-to-be Clinton shaking hands with a secret service agent. He licensed it to a photo stock agency and it was ultimately used by the defendant in its tabloid publication, superimposing a space alien next to Clinton. This was done without permission of plaintiff. That photo was then used in other publications, on t-shirts and produced substantial income for defendant. Plaintiff was paid $1,775 in licensing fees but demanded much more and sued for copyright infringement, quasi contract and damages.

The trial court awarded him $20,142 but he appealed contending he was owed another $359,000. The appellate court ruled that the defendant had been "unjustly enriched" by its mass reproduction of the photograph. Damages would be re-calculated based upon the industry standard of plaintiff receiving a 50% share of the normal licensing fee.

2. In *Ritchie Paving, Inc. v. City of Deerfield, 61 P.3d 669 (Kan. 2003)*, plaintiff was the low bidder, at $760,505 on defendant's call for bids for a public works project. The request for bids specified that the job would go to the low bidder. Defendant did not accept its bid for unspecified reasons and plaintiff sued in promissory estoppel to recover its expenses of $6,642 in preparing the bid. The trial court dismissed plaintiff's case and it appealed.

On appeal the decision was reversed. The court ruled that the defendant did not act consistently with its own competitive bid laws, and promissory estoppel was the proper remedy for an unsuccessful responsible low bidder to recover bid preparation costs. (That doctrine is also sometimes used to require specific performance of the construction contract, or a claim of loss of profit money damages for breach of that contract.)

3. In *Wilson v. Los Angeles County Metropolitan Transportation Agency, 96 Cal. Rptr.2d 747 (Cal. 2000)*, defendant solicited bids for a governmental project. When the job was awarded to another bidder, plaintiff protested that the required Disadvantaged Business Enterprise rules had not been followed. Defendant then rejected all bids and solicited new ones. Plaintiff's low bid was rejected because of an unwritten policy regarding the structuring of DBE bids, and suit was filed again. Plaintiff was awarded $924,000 for lost profits and bid expenses.

On appeal by defendant, the court reversed the award of lost profits because they were not recoverable under state law. "Promissory estoppel is a doctrine which employs equitable principles to satisfy the requirement that consideration must be given in exchange for the promise sought to be enforced."

4. In *DeCelles v. Morgan Cleaners & Laundry, Inc., 2003 WL 21093776 (Ga. App. 2003)*, Morgan Cleaners claimed it had an oral contract to sell a dry cleaning store to DeCelles for $88,550. Payment was to be made over time by payments made to Morgan for processing cleaning that customers brought to the buyer's store, through a 7% surcharge above their normal cleaning rate. In reliance upon the verbal agreement, Morgan closed one of its stores and supported DeCelles in his new store run under the name of "Morgan Cleaners." After 15 months, DeCelles stopped sending clothing for processing but continued to use the company name. Suit was filed for breach of contract, seeking the unpaid balance of $66,290.

The trial jury ruled in favor of Morgan Cleaners and the appellate court affirmed. "Promissory estoppel means a promise which the promisor should reasonably expect to induce action of forbearance on the part of the promise or a third person and which does induce such action or forbearance. It is binding if injustice can be avoided only by enforcement of the promise."

5. In *Universal Acupuncture Pain Services, P.C. v. Quadrino & Schwartz, 370 F.2d 259 (2nd Cir. 2004)*, the defendant law firm was retained by plaintiff on a 20% contingency fee basis to seek reimbursement for medical services from an insurance company. The firm was fired midway through the case, and sued to recover its reasonable attorney's fees up to that time on the quasi-contract basis of "quantum meruit" or "unjust enrichment." The trial judge ruled against the firm, saying: "Clients who enter into a contingency fee arrangement do not expect to pay their attorneys unless they recover on their claims." The appellate court reversed and remanded the case, to determine whether the discharge was with or without cause.

"If a lawyer is discharged for cause, (even if employed on a contingent fee basis) he or she is not entitled to legal fees. If the lawyer is discharged without cause and prior to the conclusion of the case, however, he or she may recover either (1) in quantum meruit, the fair and reasonable value of the services rendered, or (2) a contingent portion of the former client's ultimate recovery, but only if both of the parties have so agreed."

6. In *Pennsylvania Employees Benefits Trust Fund v. Bayer,* a class of third-party payors who paid for advance supplies of Baycol, the anti-cholesterol drug pulled off the market in 2001 because of safety concerns, sued for damages based on breach of implied warranty and unjust enrichment. Their case was severed from involvement in the main action *In Re: Pennsylvania Baycol Third-Party Payor Litigation, No. 1874 (Pa. Comm. Pleas Ct. 2005).* The trial judge granted partial summary judgment to plaintiffs.

The class of third-party payors included insurers, self-insured employees, and health benefit plans that purchased 30 or 90 day supplies of Baycol, or reimbursed their members for Baycol supplies in the weeks before the drug was recalled by Bayer. The damages sought included a refund of the costs of the drugs the payors paid for in the 38 days before it was removed from the market, the cost of disposing of the advance drug supplies, and the costs payors incurred when their members switched to an alternative anti-cholesterol drug therapy.

Whether or not the Uniform Commercial Code (UCC) applies to a dispute is critical to any analysis of contract concepts. Many common-law rules of law are supplanted or modified by UCC exceptions if it applies. Here are two recent cases about whether the disputes are a sale of goods (UCC) or a sale of services (no UCC) and the impact of that decision on the Statute of Frauds (UCC Sec. 2-201 – a contract for the sale of goods for $500 or more):

1. In *Propulsion Technologies, Inc. (PowerTech) v. Attwood Corp., 369 F.3d 896 (5th Cir. 2004),* defendant operated a foundry and contracted to produce custom designed unfinished propeller castings to be finished by plaintiff for the boating business. The contract was mixed in its descriptions that specifically referred to the propellers as a "product" that was to be "produced." Plaintiff sued for breach of contract under common-law rules and sought $7 million in damages. Defendant contended the UCC governed the transaction, its statute of limitations applied, and the statute of frauds barred recovery due to a lack of required written terms. The trial court ruled for the plaintiff, but that decision was reversed on appeal and the court held that the UCC governed the transaction.

2. In *Fallsview Glatt Kosher Caterers v. Rosenfeld, 794 N.Y.S.2d 790 (City of N.Y. Civ. Ct. 2005,* defendant allegedly orally agreed to pay $24,000 for 15 members of his extended family to attend a 10-day Passover retreat in which the plaintiffs would provide food, entertainment and country club lodging.

Neither defendant nor the family members ever showed up and plaintiff sued for the agreed price. Defendant claimed the transaction was governed by the UCC and violated the statute of frauds writing requirements for a sale of "goods" for $500 or more. Plaintiff successfully claimed that this hybrid sales-service contract had as its "predominant purpose" a sale of "services" and was therefore not subject to the statute of frauds.

"A review of the characteristics of the program, which is the subject matter of the alleged agreement, leads the Court to conclude that the essence of the family communal experience is defined by services and not by goods."

10.
CREATING THE CONTRACT
B. IS THERE A VALID OFFER?

Whether or not there is a valid offer starts the analysis of all agreements, since by definition offer + acceptance = agreement. The lack of a valid offer ends the possibility for a legal contract to exist, even if there is a valid acceptance of the ostensible offer.

In *Audio Visual Associates, Inc. v. Sharp Electronics Corp., 210 F.3d 254 (4th Cir. 2000),* plaintiff verbally contacted defendant for the purpose of buying 1,400 calculators it intended to resell to CSR, a small business company that was going to resell them to the U.S. Navy. Sharp quoted an offer price of $62.99 each and AV quoted a price to CSR of $71 each. Two days later, Sharp informed AV it had decided to "dump" the calculators and quoted a price of $31 each. AV then faxed Sharp a purchase order to buy at the lower price. "When Audio Visual followed up with a telephone call, however, Sharp stated that the calculators were sold out and that Audio Visual's order would not be filled."

AV sued for breach of contract and other relief, and its complaint was dismissed based upon the trial court's ruling that "Audio Visual's faxed purchase order was at most an offer that was rejected by Sharp and that no contract between Sharp and Audio visual for the sale of calculators ever came into existence."

On appeal that ruling was affirmed. "Price quotations are a daily part of commerce by which products are shopped and commercial transactions initiated. Without more, they amount to an invitation to enter into negotiations, but generally they are not offers that can be accepted to form binding contracts, It would bring an end to the competitive practice of shopping products if every quotation exposed the "quoter" to an enforceable contract on whatever terms the "quotee" chose, regardless of product availability. Typically, a seller's price quotation is an invitation for an offer, and the offer usually takes the form of a purchase order, providing product choice, quantity, price, and terms of delivery."

In *Echols v. Pelullo, 377 F.3d 272 (3rd Cir. 2004),* Plaintiff, a boxer, signed an agreement with defendant promoter that paid him a $30,000 bonus and gave defendant exclusive right for four years to secure all boxing bouts. Plaintiff was to be paid on a fight-by-fight basis for four years depending on the kind of fights. If he lost a fight, his payments could be lowered. After he lost a championship bout he sued contending the agreement was unenforceable because of indefinite terms.

The trial court agreed with plaintiff, but the appellate court reversed. "The agreement was not a contract to enter into a future contract, but rather, it contained all material and essential terms required ..."

Irwin Schiff, the self-styled tax rebel who was a party to the *Newman v. Schiff* case mentioned in the text that illustrated the principle – "You are the master of your offer – apparently didn't fully learn his lesson after twice serving time in federal prison for failing to file personal income tax returns.

Upon his last release after his 1985 conviction, while he no longer personally violated the tax laws he encouraged his customers to do so. He continued to conduct seminars and sell books, tapes and CD's on three Web sites that urged others to fraudulently declare zero tax liability and not to withhold taxes from their pay.

In *U.S. v. Schiff, 269 F.Supp. 2d 1262 (Dist. NEV. 2003)*, the Tax division of the Justice Department won a temporary restraining order enjoining him and his co-workers from these unlawful activities. The federal court pointed out the nature of his scheme. "Schiff's operation is based on the premise that the 'income tax is voluntary.' ... Pursuant to the scheme, Schiff advises his customers that 'for income tax purposes, you can legally report zero income and pay no taxes regardless of how much you might have earned.' ... Schiff takes the position that the Constitution limits Congress' power to tax only "corporate profits." According to Schiff, "for tax purposes, 'income' only means corporate profit. Therefore, no individual receives anything that is reportable as 'income.' In essence we have a profits tax, not an income tax."

The court also pointed out that over the past three years IRS identified nearly 5,000 zero-income federal income tax returns filed by 3,100 customers of Schiff's organization, representing $56 million in attempted tax evasion.

Schiff's request for a stay of the injunction order was denied in *U.S. v. Schiff, 2003 U.S. Dist. LEXIS 16321 (Dist. NEV. 2003)*. It would appear that he may be going to federal prison a third time in the near future unless he complies with the court's ruling.

11.
CREATING THE CONTRACT
C. IS THERE A VALID ACCEPTANCE?

Whether or not there is a valid acceptance completes the analysis of the agreement. The lack of a valid acceptance ends the possibility for a legal contract to exist, despite the fact that there a valid offer was made.

In *Kahn Lucas Lancaster, Inc. v. Lark International, Ltd., 1997 WL 458785 (S.D. N. Y. 1997),* plaintiff sent two purchase orders to defendant, a Hong Kong buying agent subcontractor, for clothing to be manufactured abroad, and then sold to its customer Sears in the U.S. Defendant did not sign the purchase orders, but performed required duties under them including helping plaintiff select producers in the Philippines to fill the orders. When the orders were not filled properly, plaintiff sued for breach of contract. Defendant claimed no contract liability because it hadn't accepted the purchase orders as evidenced by it not signing them.

On this contract issue the court ruled that defendant was legally bound. "In this case, the purchase orders were offers to buy, which Lark accepted when it performed pursuant to the orders. The orders themselves state on their face that they can be accepted by failure to object within ten days, by delivering all or part of the goods, or by otherwise manifesting assent. Lark accepted the offer embodied in the purchase orders by ordering the goods from the manufacturers, overseeing production, complying with the other terms of the letters of credit, and arranging for the shipment of the goods.

Section 2-206(1)(a) of the Uniform Commercial Code states that: an offer to make a contract shall be construed as inviting acceptance in any manner and by any medium reasonable under the circumstances. The following subsection, Section 2-206(1)(b) states that: an order or other offer to buy goods for prompt or current shipment shall be construed as inviting acceptance either by a prompt promise to ship or by the prompt or current shipment ..."

(Since the contract was found valid and it contained an arbitration clause, the court ordered Lark to be bound by arbitration. But this issue, not the contract acceptance issue, was reversed on appeal in *186 F.3d 210* (2nd Cir. 1999).

12.
IS THE AGREEMENT LEGALLY ENFORCEABLE?

Not all valid agreements are legally enforceable as we well know. The legal definition of a contract requires, "An agreement between two or more parties that a court will enforce in the event of a breach." Therefore, the mere fact that a valid agreement has been created does not equate with there being an equally valid and enforceable "contract."

A.   The fairness doctrine of promissory estoppel (detrimental reliance) appears frequently in business law to render an otherwise invalid promise legally enforceable. It is recognized as a form of legal contract (Text chapter 9). It is an exception to the general rule that the offeror may revoke his offer at any time before acceptance (Text chapter 10). And it is recognized as an exception to the general rule requiring legally sufficient consideration, so that it may be used for enforcement of gift promises and other otherwise unenforceable agreements where there has not been a required current bargained-for exchange of legal benefit and detriment. (Text chapter 12).

In *Chrysler Corporation v. Chaplake Holdings, Ltd., 822 A.2d 1024 (Del. 2003)*, Chaplake, a U.K. company, owned Portman Lamborghini, Ltd. Between 1984 and 1987 Portman sold 30 new vehicles per year, at an average price of $250,000 each, making it the world's largest Lamborghini dealer. Chrysler bought Lamborghini in 1987 and an expansion plan was presented by its chairman Lee Iacocca to increase yearly production from 250 cars to 5,000 cars and produce a new model, the P140 with a retail price of $70,000.

Portman was told by Chrysler that in order to keep its exclusive U.K. market it had to expand its operational capacity to 400 cars by 1992. So it engaged in additional financing, hired new staff, acquired new facilities and built a new distribution center. Due to development and production problems at Lamborghini and a general economic recession, Chrysler decided to reduce its expansion plans by 2/3. Factory production delays caused Portman to become unprofitable and it went into receivership in 1992. Suit was filed against Chrysler for breach of contract, seeking money damages based upon promissory estoppel.

The trial jury awarded substantial money damages against Chrysler based upon promissory estoppel, and the appellate court affirmed.

"The prevention of injustice is the 'fundamental idea' underlying the doctrine of promissory estoppel."

"There were a series of promises made by Chrysler and its various representatives to Portman, Chaplake and their representatives ... promising that the Lamborghini line would expand ten-fold, and that Portman would retain its exclusivity deal *only* if it expanded its operational capacity.

By making these promises, Chrysler should have expected that Portman and Chaplake would be induced to expand its operations in accordance with the promised expansion of the Lamborghini line of automobiles.

Portman and Chaplake reasonably relied upon the promises made by Chrysler, and took action to their detriment."

B. The "illusory promise" issue often arises in real estate contract clauses that attempt to define the remedies of seller and buyer in the event of a default. In *Ocean Dunes of Hutchinson Island Development Corporation v. Colangelo, 463 So.2d 437 (Fla. App. 1985),* the contract buyers of a condominium unit sued for specific performance after the developer refused to close (due probably to interim price appreciation) and the seller claimed it only had to return their deposit.

Due to a material discrepancy in the seller and buyer contract default clauses, the trial court ruled for plaintiff and the appellate court affirmed that, "Because the contract provides no reasonable remedy for its breach, the equitable remedy of specific performance fashioned by the trial court was correct."

"In this contract, the seller's obligations are wholly illusory, while the buyers' are quite real. The developer can opt to sell the unit to any new buyer willing to pay a higher price than the existing contract price, or even fail to show title to be vested in the developer as required by paragraph 5 of the Agreement, with absolutely no harmful consequences; the developer must only return the buyer's *own* money. A return of one's own money hardly constitutes damages in any meaningful sense. It is especially unconscionable in this case in light of the buyer's deprivation of the use of their money for several years."

"The developer, on the other hand, in the event of a breach by the buyers, is able to choose between retaining the buyers' deposit or resorting 'to any other legal or equitable remedy to which Developer may be entitled."

13.
DEFENSES TO ENFORCEMENT OF THE CONTRACT
A. CAPACITY OF THE PARTIES

The inter-connection between the various chapter concepts of Business Law is reflected by how often the legal rules and exceptions discussed in one chapter find application in whole or part in other chapters.

In the area of minor's contracts, while the law wants to protect underage parties from the legal effects of their contracts, it also weighs this protection against the harm done to innocent adults who may suffer financial harm if their otherwise valid contracts may be legally avoided.

While the general rule allowing minor's to disaffirm their contracts is a prime example of a fairness doctrine protecting that class of contracting parties, the "necessities" exception to that rule similarly extends the same fairness principles to the adult party supplying the minor with needed goods or services.

The minor has the protection of the "voidable contracts" general rules while lacking legal capacity, and the adult has the protection of the fairness doctrine of "unjust enrichment" if the minor refuses to pay for necessities provided by the adult.

In *Yale Diagnostic Radiology v. Estate of Fountain, 838 A.2d 179 (Conn. 2003),* plaintiff furnished emergency medical services in the amount of $17,694 to the defendant minor after he was shot in the head by a playmate. It billed defendant's mother who did not pay, and then after obtaining a collection judgment against her, she filed for bankruptcy and all her debts were discharged. A tort action was filed on defendant's behalf against the boy who shot him resulting in a large settlement that was placed in the estate created on defendant's behalf. Plaintiff filed a claim in the estate for payment of its debt, but the Probate Court barred the claim on the basis that minor children could not enter into a legally binding contract.

On appeal that decision was reversed based upon the minor's contract doctrine of necessaries. "Connecticut has long recognized the common-law rule that a minor's contracts are voidable. Under this rule, a minor may, upon reaching majority, choose either to ratify or to avoid contractual obligations entered into during his minority ... The rule is further supported by a policy of protecting children from unscrupulous individuals seeking to profit from their youth and inexperience.

An exception to this rule, eponymously known as the doctrine of necessaries, is that a minor may not avoid a contract for goods or services necessary for his health and sustenance. Such contracts are binding even if entered into during minority, and a minor, upon reaching majority, may not, as a matter of law, disaffirm them.

We have not heretofore articulated the particular legal theory underlying the doctrine of necessaries. We therefore take this occasion to do so, and we conclude that the most apt theory is that of an implied in law contract, also sometimes referred to as a quasi-contract."

The court then went on to explain the contractual principles behind the necessities rule:

"Thus, when a medical service provider renders necessary medical care to an injured minor, two contracts arise: the primary contract between the provider and the minor's parents; and an implied in law contract between the provider and the minor himself. The primary contract between the provider and the parents is based on the parent's duty to pay for their children's necessary expenses, under both common law and statute. Such contracts, where not express, may be implied in fact and generally arise both from the parties' conduct (implied in fact) and their reasonable expectations. The primacy of this contract means that the provider of necessaries must make all reasonable efforts to collect from the parents before resorting to the secondary, implied in law contract with the minor."

A similar case to *Yale* was *Schmidt v. Prince George's Hospital, 784 A.2d 1112 (Md. App. 2001),* where Schmidt was a 16-year old injured in an auto accident and treated at the hospital's emergency room for a brain concussion and an open scalp wound. She was insured through her father's company, but when it sent a check to pay the hospital's bill of $1,756.24, the funds were used to buy her a car and the bill remained unpaid. After she reached age 18 and still refused to pay, the hospital sued her to collect. Both trial and appellate courts ruled for the hospital based upon the doctrine of necessaries.

"In the absence of a statute to the contrary, the prevailing modern rule is that a minor's contracts are voidable; nevertheless, it is also well established that a minor may be liable for the value of necessaries furnished to him or her.

By the common law, persons, under the age of twenty-one years, are not bound by their contracts, *except for necessaries*, nor can they do any act, to the injury of their property, which they may not avoid, when arrived at full age …Their power, thus to contract for necessaries, is for their benefit, because the procurement of these things is essential to their existence, and if they were not permitted so to bind themselves they might suffer."

14.
DEFENSES TO ENFORCEMENT OF THE CONTRACT
B. LEGALITY OF THE TRANSACTION

The primary reason for commercial business law disputes is simply that, although at the time of contracting both parties were satisfied with the transaction, something has occurred afterward to cause one of the parties to believe they made a bad deal. The search now is for a way to be released from legal responsibility.

Every contract element, as presented in the numbered chapters in the text starting with offer and acceptance and running through each succeeding chapter, guides both parties in enforcing or avoiding the agreement.

A claimed lack of legality of the transaction which may render the agreement of the parties void and unenforceable is a frequent subject of litigation as evidenced by the following current cases presented in the order in which their topics are presented in this text chapter:

A.   Usury:
1. In *State of Colorado v. The Cash Now Store, Inc., 31 P.3d 161 (Colo. 2001),* defendant provided a check cashing service to customers that included loaning them 50-60% of the face value on their assignments to it of their anticipated income tax refunds. The state's small loan regulation agency demanded an injunction to stop the practice, claiming the difference between the amount paid and tax refund received was equivalent to a high interest rate loan and violated the Uniform Consumer Credit Code. Defendant contended that the transactions were purchases of an asset receivable, not loans. The trial court ruled for defendant, but that decision was reversed on appeal in a case of first impression.

"The UCCC regulates the law governing retail installment sales, consumer credit, small loans, and usury. Among other restrictions, the UCCC limits the finance charge that a creditor may impose on consumer credit transactions. The UCCC also requires that a creditor obtain a license before making certain types of high-interest loans.

Cash Now reasons that because it does not require the taxpayer to repay the money it has advanced unless the amount of the refund received is less than the amount anticipated, its transactions do not constitute 'loans' under the UCCC. We disagree ... the definition of a loan under the UCCC does not require repayment."

B.   Non-Compete Contracts:
        1.   In *Hess v. Gebhard & Co., 2002 WL 31318803 (Pa.2002)*. Plaintiff worked for an insurance agency and his employment contract included a covenant not to compete in the area for five years should he leave.

        After 20 years, the business was sold to defendant who fired plaintiff. He was offered a job by a competitor but they withdrew that offer after defendant sent a letter stating it would sue to enforce plaintiff's non-compete. Plaintiff sued, claiming the non-compete was illegal and unenforceable. The trial court ruled against plaintiff, but that decision was reversed on appeal. This ruling was based upon the fact that the defendant had neglected to include in the non-compete an assignability clause and therefore, without plaintiff's consent, "the covenant was extinguished upon the sale of the business."

        Florida passed statute 542.335 in 1996 that requires, "In the case of an assignee or successor, the restrictive covenant expressly authorized enforcement by a party's assignee or successor." Otherwise, the result is the same as the *Hess* case, as was the case in the pre-1966 statute 542.33 where Florida law allowed corporations that acquired other companies through mergers, consolidations or other stock buyouts to enforce non-competition agreements created under prior management.

        2.   This was the case in *Corporate Express Office Products, Inc. v. Phillips, 847 So.2d 406 (Fla. 2003)*, where plaintiff sued defendant and other former employees who quit in 2000 after it took over their former companies for an injunction to enforce their prior non-compete agreements, signed in the 1980's. "The former employees raised as a defense that the noncompete agreements had been entered into with prior employers and not (plaintiff)," and were not enforceable against them without their consent. The trial court granted the injunction in favor of plaintiff, the appellate court reversed in favor of defendant, and the conflict between that ruling and one of another appellate district caused the Florida Supreme Court to accept jurisdiction. It followed the trial court's decision, based upon the pre-1996 non-competes.

        "The noncompete agreements between former employees ... and their original employers were enforceable by Corporate Express ... the rights of the merged corporation become those of the surviving corporation."

        2.   In *Boulanger v. Dunkin' Donuts, Inc., 815 N.E.2d 572 (Mass. 2004)*, plaintiff bought three franchises over a period of 5 years. Each franchise agreement stated that, regardless of how the franchise terminated, the franchisee agreed not to compete for 2 years within 5 miles of any Dunkin' Donuts shop. In 2002 plaintiff sold his franchises and asked Honey Dew Donuts about owning one of their franchises. They refused to deal with him until his non-compete expired, so plaintiff sued to have it declared unenforceable as an unfair trade practice.

The trial court ruled against the plaintiff and the appellate court affirmed, stating as follows: "A covenant not to compete is enforceable only if it is necessary to protect a legitimate business interest, reasonably limited in time and space, and consonant with the public interest."

"In case of employment, the courts look at such covenants more strictly than in cases involving a business interest, such as the sale of a business, as in this case. In such cases, there is less inequality of bargaining power than in the employment context."

3. In *Traffic Control Services v. United Rentals Northwest, 87 P.3d 1054 (Nev. 2004),* Burkhardt was employed by NES and was paid $10,000 to sign a non-competition agreement for one year after he left its employ and further promised to protect confidential information. Later, NES was sold to United Rentals but Burkhardt refused to sign a new non-compete and left to work for Traffic Control. United sued them both for violating the original non-compete. The trial court agreed that it was enforceable for one year, but the appellate court reversed.

"An employee's covenant not to compete is personal in nature and is unassignable absent the employee's express consent or an express clause permitting assignment that has been negotiated at arms-length with the employee and supported by additional and separate consideration."

C. Exculpatory Clauses:

1. In *Hyson v. White Water Mountain Resorts of Connecticut 829 A.2d 827 (Conn. 2003),* plaintiff was injured while snow tubing at defendant's resort. She had signed a standard release of liability, but it did not contain express language whereby it included "negligence" of the defendant. She claimed her injuries were caused by defendant's failure to properly groom and maintain the hill or place warning signs indicate its slippery condition, and she was unable to stop at its bottom. The trial court dismissed her suit, but the appellate court reversed in a case of first impression, where it adopted the rule that requires specific release wording:

"We conclude that the better rule is that a party cannot be released from liability for injuries resulting from its future negligence in the absence of language that expressly so provides.

The release signed in the present case illustrates the need for such a rule. A person of ordinary intelligence reasonably could believe that, by signing this release, he or she was releasing the defendant only from liability for damages caused by dangers inherent in the activity of snow tubing. A requirement of express language releasing the defendant from liability for its negligence prevents individuals from inadvertently releasing valuable legal rights. Furthermore, the requirement that parties seeking to be released from liability for their negligence expressly so indicate does not impose on them any significant cost."

Michigan and Maryland do not impose the strict language requirement on releases of liability, but requires that they "clearly indicate to the reader that by accepting its terms he is giving up the right to assert a negligence claim." *Xu v. Gay, 668 N.W.2d 166 (Mich. App. 2003),* or it "clearly and specifically indicates the intent to release the defendant from liability for personal injury caused by the defendant's negligence." *Seigneur v. National Fitness Institute, Inc., 752 A.2d 631 (Md. App. 2000).*

But if the damages sought are based upon proven gross negligence, all states will allow recovery. In *Xu,* Yan went to defendant's fitness center to use a one-week complimentary pass and before each visit signed a release of liability that said defendant would not assume responsibility, "any injuries and/or sickness incurred to me or any accompanying minor person as a result of entering the premises and/or using any of the facilities." While using a treadmill Yan fell, hit his head, and died.
His widow sued alleging both ordinary and gross negligence of defendant. The trial court granted summary judgment for defendant and the appellate court reversed on both negligence issues.

Seigneur also involved alleged fitness club injuries suffered by plaintiff as she was undergoing an initial evaluation. However the release she signed stated, "I do expressly hereby forever release and discharge NFI, Inc. from all claims, demands, injuries, damages, actions, or courses of action, and from all acts of active or passive negligence on the part of NFI, Inc., its servants, agents or employees." Summary judgment for defendant was affirmed, and would probably have been granted even with the specific "negligence" wording of the release because the language would pass the "clear and specific wording" test.

2. In *Roag v. Atkins, 111539/02 (N.Y. Sup. Ct. 2005),* a Manhattan judge dismissed a motion to dismiss a lawsuit against the estate of Dr. Robert Atkins, the now-deceased guru of low-carbohydrate diets. Rubick underwent conventional medical treatment for breast cancer, and then after hearing Dr. Atkins promote alternative treatments on the radio, made an appointment at the local Atkins Center, where she was allegedly told that a regimen of vitamins and anti-oxidants would cure her cancer. Before proceeding she was required to sign a consent form containing an exculpatory release of liability. Unfortunately it spread to her spine, she died shortly thereafter, and her estate sued for damages.

The consent form was explicit: "I cannot offer this procedure to you except upon the condition that you release my office and myself and any treating persons from any legal responsibility fir harm resulting from its use in your case. Your signature on this agreement will constitute a full and final release of any legal responsibility."

Nevertheless, the trial judge ruled the release unenforceable, on grounds that it offended public policy. "Additionally, the 'agreement' consists of several sentences in the middle of the informed consent form signed by plaintiff's decedent;

no separate heading or caption was present to alert the decedent that she was foregoing the right to bring suit."

This decision is troubling, because it expands the exculpatory release doctrine beyond analysis of whether or not the released party remains liable due to the "negligence" exception into a case fact analysis of overall unfairness. It will probably be reversed on appeal for this reason.

D.   Unconscionable Contracts:

In *Lucier v. Williams, 2004 WL 257036 (N.J. App. Div. 2004)*, plaintiffs hired defendant to perform a house inspection. Its hiring agreement limited its liability for any inspection-related matter to 50% of the inspection fee of $385. The report was issued "clean", showing no problems with the home.

After plaintiff took occupancy they noticed a roof leak and, upon investigation by a roofer, were told the roof was defective because it had no flashing and would need replacement at a cost between $8,000 to $10,000. Plaintiffs sued for breach of contract, fraud and breach of warranty. Defendant claimed liability was limited to $192.50 per the agreement.

The trial court ruled for defendant, but that decision was reversed based upon the unconscionability doctrine. "This is a classic contract of adhesion. There were no negotiations leading up to its preparation. The contract was presented to Lucier on a standardized pre-printed form, prepared by (defendant), on a take-it-or-leave-it bases, without any opportunity for him to negotiate or modify any of its terms.

15.
DEFENSES TO ENFORCEMENT OF THE CONTRACT
C. REAL CONSENT

Even if there is a party with full legal capacity appears to have consented to a legal agreement that involved a consideration exchange of benefit, its ultimate enforceability may be challenged on grounds that the consent was not voluntary and/or knowing.

The key determination is whether the claim of invalidity is legally sustainable in one of the genuine, or just based upon a re-examination of the perceived advantages / disadvantages of the pending business deal. The recent cases that follow present examples of these types of situations:

1. Undue Influence / Duress – In *Fischer v. Schefers, 656 N.W.2d 592 (Minn. App. 2003),* defendants owned a farm adjacent to elderly Lentner, who moved from it to a local nursing home in 1999. In early 2000 he offered to sell his farm to Brenny for $50,000 plus $10,000 for equipment and miscellaneous personal property. Even though Brenny thought it a fair price, the transaction was never completed.

A few months later defendants contacted Lentner about buying his farm, and after a period of time when they visited him engaged in small talk and watched him play cards, he agreed to sell the farm to them for the same price as previously offered to Brenny. They delivered the funds to him, drove him to his bank, and took him to the title company where a deed was prepared and signed conveying ownership.

Soon after the sale, plaintiff was appointed special conservator for Lentner. A court-appointed doctor evaluated him (long after the sale) and stated he, "lacked the requisite intellectual ability to sell his farm and equipment." Plaintiff sought to set aside the transaction based on undue influence, but the trial judge found that he was competent and defendants "were bona fide purchasers for value and respondents did not subject Lentner to duress."

On appeal that decision was affirme d. "there is sufficient evidence in the record to sustain the district court's finding that Lentner was competent on the date of the transaction. (The party who) drafted the transfer documents testified that Lentner ... ably responded to all of (his) questions. We further note that (the title agent's) testimony related to Lentner's competency at the actual time of the transaction and not days, weeks or months thereafter."

In order to show undue influence: the evidence must go beyond suspicion and conjecture and show, not only that the influence was in fact exerted, but that it was so dominant and controlling of the (person's) mind that, in making the (contract), he ceased to act of his own free volition and became a mere puppet of the wielder of that influence."

2. Mistake:

Mutual Mistake – In *Mattson v. Rachetto, 591 N.W.2d 814 (S.D. 1999),* after Jerry Rachetto finished law school he went to work for Jon Mattson, the husband of his sister Barbara. When Jerry later expressed a desire to build a house on plaintiff's land they deeded it to him as a gift. Later after building the house, defendants wanted to buy an adjoining tract to ensure no further development. This was acceptable to plaintiffs so long as they had an agricultural leaseback provision allowing them to cultivate hay and graze cattle for their lifetime. The two lawyers, Jerry and Jon, drafted the necessary documents which were signed in 1984.

Twelve years later the parties discovered a state law invalidating agricultural leases of more than 20 years. Plaintiffs sued to rescind the entire transaction based upon mutual mistake. Defendants claimed the requested cancellation was solely because the land had greatly appreciated in value over the years, and lawyers are presumed to know the law.

The trial court allowed rescission and the appellate court affirmed. "Although there clearly was a mistake of law neither side took advantage of the other. Both parties admitted they did not know the agricultural leaseback was illegal. Mattson and Rachetto were licensed attorneys working in the same office who negotiated the terms of the agreement in good faith which went through several drafts before becoming acceptable to all parties.

The mere fact the statute is a public record is not the controlling factor in this case. It is a statutorily recognized exception to the old axiom 'ignorance of the law is no excuse.' Freedom from negligence is not a requirement to invoke the mistake of law claim. A mutual mistake or misapprehension of the law by all parties, all supposing that they knew and understood it generally presupposes negligence as the law is a public record and citizens are charged with knowledge of its requirements."

Unilateral Mistake – In *Welkener v. Welkener, 71 S.W. 3d 364 (Tex. App. 2001),* the parties were involved in a divorce proceeding and appeared at a court hearing to "prove up" the various matters, including the agreed division of their community estate. At the hearing Mrs. W agreed she would receive $1,098.84 per month from Mr. W's retirement account, and that was the order entered by the court.

At a later hearing Mrs. W asked that the court order be modified to recite that she receive 32.7% of Mr. W's retirement account, rather than a sum certain, "so that she would be able to share in any future increase on (his) monthly benefit." She claimed, "that when the agreement was announced in open court, she described the agreement in terms of dollars and cents, but this was merely a shorthand method for describing the percentage she is entitled to receive." The court entered an order which incorporated the original dollars and cents agreement. Mrs. W then sought a new trial based on unilateral mistake, which was denied. On appeal, that decision was affirmed.

"A unilateral mistake by a party to the agreement ordinarily will not constitute grounds for relief when the mistake was not known to or induced by the other party.

Generally, to be entitled to relief, the party must show that: 1) the mistake is of so great a consequence that to enforce the contract as made would be unconscionable; 2) the mistake relates to a material feature of the contract; 3) the mistake must have been made regardless of the exercise of ordinary care; 4) the parties can be placed in status quo in the equity sense, i.e., rescission must not result in prejudice to the other party except for the loss of his bargain."

The court then analyzed the facts of the case in the context of the unilateral mistake rule and found that "the dollar amount agreed to was, at the time of trial, the equivalent to the percentage," and Mrs. W had reviewed the proposed agreement, prepared by her counsel, before appearing in court.

(See also *In re Owens Corning et. al., Debtors in Possession, 91 BR 329 (2003),* in which the contract dispute involved a drafting error by one of the parties "so huge that to enforce the contract would be unconscionable." The quoted price for plastic sheets (packed 200 to a box) used by Owens Corning as dividers to separate asphalt containers was "$172.50 per box," but because of improper input of computer information their purchase order said "$172.50 per sheet," resulting in an erroneous total price of $1,078.195 instead of $7,072.50. The contract was reformed by the court to reflect the correct price.)

3. Fraud – In *Johnson v. Davis, 480 So.2d 625 (Fla. 1985),* Florida created an important exception to the general rule that silence or failure to speak is not usually fraud. It involved a dispute between the seller and buyer of a house, where after the contract but before the closing, sellers made statements intending to reassure buyers concerning possible roof damage – "it was a minor problem that had long since been corrected," and that there were "no problems with the roof." The contract allowed the buyer to inspect the roof before closing and repair any damage at seller's expense.

Before closing there were heavy rains and the buyers discovered large roof leaks that could only be fixed by installation of a new roof at a cost of $15,000.

Buyers chose to cancel the purchase and successfully demanded full return of their deposit. "We hold that where the seller of a home knows of facts materially affecting the value of the property which are not readily observable and are not known to the buyer, the seller is under a duty to disclose them to the buyer." This language was incorporated by the Florida Legislature in statute 475.278 regulating real estate brokers, salespersons, schools and appraisers and specifying their required duties.

The "misrepresentation of a material fact" made by a defendant, "with knowledge of its falsity," that "induces the plaintiff to reasonably rely to his detriment" ordinarily refers to an affirmative statement of deceit.

Silence as fraud on the other hand involves the defendant's failure to speak when he has a legal duty to do so. The older cases, before *Johnson* in Florida and in most other states, only considered hidden problems that could affect the buyer's health or safety as the type of matters that would impose a duty to speak. Now most all states have adopted the "value test" as a recognized exception to the "silence is not fraud" rule.

The text case examples of house sales that were rescinded due to being haunted or because a murder took place were based upon alleged diminished value from disclosure of these hidden facts. But, as also pointed out in the text, our modern society places a high value on this type of notoriety.

Travel Web sites currently advertise several haunted bed-and-breakfasts that they claim are visited by ghosts regularly:

"Peacock Bed & Breakfast, a former bordello in Manitou Springs, Colorado; Captain Grant's Inn, Poquetanuck, Connecticut, where strange knocks are reported at odd hours; John Denham House, Monticello, Florida, in a town claiming several haunted homes; and Katherine's Bed and Breakfast, Asheville, North Carolina, with a ghost who sometimes likes a hug." www.bedandbreakfast.com

16.
WRITTEN FORM

Our busy commercial marketplace and litigious society demands that, for one's own protection, almost all business communications should be reduced to some type of writing. Whether that writing is a formal contract; confirming letter, fax or electronic communication; file notation; office memorandum or other form – the importance of preserving what took place in the verbal conversations that precede the making of any business agreement is essential.

The parol evidence rule penalizes one's failure to properly include all essential factual matters in the writing that follows a negotiation. It is also referred to as the "merger rule", whereby all prior oral communications between the parties are deemed incorporated in the final unambiguous writing, and may not therefore be used in evidence to change its specific terms.

In *First Data POS, Inc. v. Willis, 546 S.E.2d 781 (Ga. 2001)*, plaintiff purchased a software development company (COIN) from defendant for $2.5 million. The final written agreement stated that additional payments would be made to COIN for three years if they generated certain levels of new business, but also stated that plaintiff could "at any time without limitation and without notice ... reorganize or merge COIN out of existence or cease the sale of any of the products or services of COIN." The agreement also contained a standard merger clause providing that it, "constitutes the entire agreement between the parties ... and supercedes all prior agreements and understandings, both oral and written by and between the parties hereto with respect to the subject matter hereof."

Approximately three years after signing the purchase and sale agreement, Defendant filed suit alleging that during pre-contractual negotiations plaintiff had "misrepresented its intention to increase COIN's business after it acquired the company, and that those misrepresentations had induced appellees to enter into the Agreement and to sell COIN's stock for less than its-then-current market value."

The trial court ruled for the plaintiff – buyer based on the merger rule, but the appellate court reversed in favor of the defendant –seller, concluding that the Agreement's merger clause did not preclude their claim of fraud in the inducement. On appeal to the Georgia Supreme Court, the case was again reversed in favor of the buyer and the merger clause upheld.

"This court has held that 'the rational basis for merger clauses is that where parties enter into a final contract all prior negotiations, understandings, and agreements on the same subject are merged into the final contract, and are accordingly extinguished.'

Merger clauses exist in written contracts specifically to 'preclude any claim of deceit by prior representations.'"

Guaranty promises are often made in the course of business negotiations to give some additional assurances that may be required to close the deal. The legal rule is clear that a purely verbal guaranty promise of legally unenforceable unless reduced to proper written form. But what about situations where there are written "promises", "assurances", or "representations" made to complete a transaction? Are they only given in a representative capacity or is personal liability intended? And what about differing business practices in different countries? This is the business law time bomb in *Material Partnerships, Inc. v. Ventura, 102 S.W.3d 252 (Tex. App. 2003).*

In that case, defendant was owner and general manager of a Mexican bag manufacturer that contracted to buy production materials from plaintiff. He was multi-lingual, an experienced businessman, and had made more than 200 trips to the U.S. After plaintiff supplied over $900,000 in goods on open account and the invoice remained unpaid it requested, "written assurances in regards to the outstanding debts and obligations that you have with us," and specifically asked defendant to, "forward a personal guarantee covering all past and future obligations."

In response, defendant wrote, "I ... want to certify you that I, personally guarantee all outstandings and liabilities of Sacos Tubulares with Material Partnerships as well as future shipments." Defendant drafted the letter himself and signed it over the designation, "Jorge Lopez Ventura, General Manager."

After receiving the letter plaintiff resumed shipments of additional $200,000 value. When only one payment of $60,000 was received they stopped shipping and sued for the balance, seeking to recover from the company which became insolvent, and then the defendant on his guaranty. He claimed that he intended to sign the letter only as a corporate guaranty on the company's behalf, and not individually. He also claimed that in Mexico the concept of *aval* means a guaranty. "But for the aval to qualify as a personal *aval*, the signator must specify that he is signing in an individual capacity."

The trial court ruled that defendant was not liable in an individual capacity, but that decision was reversed on appeal in plaintiff's favor. "We conclude Lopez's September 25 letter is an unambiguous and enforceable personal guaranty of Saco's debt to MPI." The court entered judgment against defendant in the amount of $962,140 plus interest. In a concurring opinion, the court noted the practical reasoning for its decision:

"Lopez's characterization of the September 25th letter as a 'corporate guaranty' of Sacos is a *non sequitur* in this factual context. The only way there could be a corporate guaranty of the Sacos debt is if another *corporation* had guaranteed the debt. ... It simply makes no sense for Sacos to be both the account debtor and the corporate guarantor because a guarantor is one who stands for the debt of another. MPI would have no reason to request or obtain a guaranty from Sacos for Sacos's own debt. Thus, if we were to hold that the September 25th letter did not create an individual obligation for Lopez, then we would have to hold that it did not create an obligation at all.

By adding the modifier 'personally' to that verb (guarantee), Lopez took that obligation on himself. He effectively removed his hat as 'General Manager' of Sacos and individually undertook to answer for the debt of the corporation."

(Note: This case is also a good example of how a failure to use anticipatory thinking or the preventive law method could result in financial disaster.)

The hi-tech nature of the commercial marketplace is reflected in the recent case of *Lamle v. Mattel, Inc.,* 394 F.3d 1355 (Fed. Cir. 2005), in which plaintiff owned a game called "Farook" defendant was interested in distributing. The parties signed an agreement granting defendant exclusive negotiation rights for 4 months, but any distribution agreement reached would have to be in a separate written contract.

At the end of the negotiation period the parties met, defendant asked plaintiff to memorialize "the deal", and defendant sent an email letter entitled "Farook deal" repeating the key terms that had been mutually agreed at the meeting. One month later defendant sent plaintiff a fax saying it was "waiting for a draft licensing agreement," and plaintiff sent it to them one week later. Defendant then told plaintiff it was no longer interested in the deal and plaintiff sued for breach of contract.

The trial court dismissed the suit but the appellate court reversed and remanded in favor of plaintiff, ruling that an email describing the terms of an agreement can satisfy the Statute of Frauds. "Under the statute of frauds, there must be a writing that contains the material terms if the agreement. The email sent by Bucher (defendant's agent) is a valid writing and signature that satisfies California's statute of frauds. The question to b e determined at trial is if there was a binding oral agreement that was memorialized sufficiently in the email sent by Bucher."

THE BUSINESS LAW SURVIVAL GUIDE
CHAPTER CASE UPDATES

17.
RIGHTS OF THIRD PARTIES

The typical disputes in third-party rights cases involve scenarios where a non-contracting party claims enforceable rights against one of the original parties to the contract - either through an assignment of rights, a delegation of duties, or as a third-party intended beneficiary.

The four recent cases that follow are illustrative:

(1) In *Credit General Insurance Company v. Nations Bank, 299 F.3d 943 (8th Cir. 2002),* L&S contractors bought a $100,000 certificate of deposit from the bank and later assigned it to plaintiff as collateral security for performance and payment bonds on a Howard Johnson construction project. Plaintiff promptly sent the bank written notice of the assignment that stated, "Please hold this account as assigned to us until demanded or released by us." When the CD periodically matured it was rolled over by the bank into short-term CD's, but the bank's records only showed L&S as the principal/payee.

On maturity L&S withdrew the proceeds without the knowledge or consent of plaintiff. Thereafter plaintiff made written demand for payment, and after being advised by the bank that the CD had already been redeemed, it sued for wrongful payment of the proceeds. Plaintiff was granted summary judgment and upon appeal that decision was affirmed.

"In Missouri, a validly executed assignment vests the rights and interests of the assignor in the assignee, and divests the assignor of all right of control over the subject matter. An assignment of proceeds is a contract between the assignor and assignee, which upon receipt of notice requires debtor to pay the proceeds due only to the assignee. The failure of a debtor to make payment to an assignee after receiving notice of the assignment gives rise to a cause of action by the assignee for wrongful payment."

(2) In *Union Pacific Railroad Co. v. Novus International, Inc., 113 S.W.3d 418 (Tex. App. 2003),* defendant claimed the right to sue as a third – party beneficiary of a rail contract between plaintiff and Union Carbide Co. That rail contract related to the fact that defendant arranged to buy from Union Carbide an important chemical ingredient for its poultry-feed supplement, and plaintiff was contracted by Union Carbide to be the rail carrier for delivery to defendant.

Due to difficulties arising from its merger with Southern Pacific, Union Pacific's rail service was severely disrupted and it's inability to transport required quantities of product to defendant caused them to incur financial loss and additional expense by having to make other faster and more expensive shipping arrangements.

At the trial court level, defendant was found to properly be a third-party beneficiary and the case proceeded to a jury decision in its favor. On appeal that decision was reversed, since the court ruled that, at best, defendant was only an incidental beneficiary and had no enforceable legal rights.

"It is well-settled that third-party beneficiary claims succeed or fail according to the provisions of the contract upon which suit is brought ... The fact that a person might receive an incidental benefit from a contract to which he is not a party does not give that person a right of action to enforce the contract.

There exists a strong presumption against third-party-beneficiary recovery. Because the rail contract did not 'fully and clearly spell out' that Novus was an intended third-party beneficiary, Novus was instead an incidental beneficiary without standing to sue. Novus is never named in the contract and all of the obligations flow between Union Pacific and Carbide. Nowhere in the rail contract is it stated that the parties are contracting for the benefit of Carbide's *customers*."

(Note that Novus could have easily protected itself in this situation by requiring transit delay insurance in its purchase and sale agreement with Union Carbide, or inserting in that contract a form of "Force Majeure" clause providing that it would be compensated for loss of profits and/or additional expenses from shipping delays.)

3. The collapsed merger between Consolidated Edison and Northeast Utilities resulted in a class action lawsuit by disgruntled shareholders as intended third-party beneficiaries of the scheduled merger. (*Consolidated Edison v.Northeast Utilities and Rimkoskie, 332 F.Supp.2d 639 (S.D.N.Y. 2004).*

ConEd signed an agreement in October, 1999 to buy all outstanding shares of Northeast at $26.50 per share at a time when the pre-announcement market price was $18.56 per share. But in March, 2001 ConEd said it would not proceed due to alleged fraud in its inducement to do the deal, and it brought a declaratory judgment action to be relieved of its obligations. Notheast counterclaimed for the $27 million it spent on regulatory approval and $1.2 billion based on the lost premium that would have been paid to its shareholders if the merger had occurred.

Northeast shareholders were ruled to be third-party beneficiaries and it was authorized to sue on their behalf, but the legal issue was whether the shareholders having these rights were current or former. The trial judge noted this was a case of 1st impression and stated the legal issue as follows:

"Where shareholders are third-party beneficiaries of a contract between the corporate issuer and a third party, is the right to sue that third party for breach of contract automatically transferred to a *subsequent* purchaser of the stock?" The question was answered in the negative, since that would allow later purchasers of stock to, in effect, buy a lawsuit. The judge ruled that the intended third-party beneficiaries of the scheduled merger were only those shareholders who owned the stock on the day the merger broke down. But because of the far-reaching implications of the decision, the case was certified as an interlocutory appeal to the U.S. Court of Appeals.

4. In *Benton v. Vanderbilt University, 137 S.W.3d 614 (Tenn. 2004)*, plaintiff was an injured passenger in an auto collision and was treated in defendant's hospital for an amount of medical expenses of $31,500. He was insured by Blue Cross, which had a contract with the hospital that it would bill for services at a discounted rate, and not bill members for the excess between the full bill and the discounted rate of $14,800 in this case. Plaintiff, as third-party beneficiary of that contract, sued to recover that billing excess from the driver of the car and joined defendant. Defendant moved to compel arbitration based on a clause in the insurance contract.

The trial court ruled that plaintiff was not bound by the arbitration clause and could proceed at law. The appeals court reversed and their decision was affirmed. "A third party is an intended third-party beneficiary of a contract and is entitle to (bound by) its terms where 1) the parties to the contract have not agreed otherwise, 2) recognition of the third-party's right to performance is appropriate to effectuate the parties' intent, and 3) terms or circumstances indicate that performance of the promise is intended or will satisfy an obligation owed by the promise to the third party."

18.
LEGAL EXCUSES FOR NON-PERFORMANCE

Condition contracts disputes often involve the same underlying business considerations as other areas of business law – one of the parties perceives they are either selling too low or buying too high and looks for a way to be legally discharged from contract liability.

If in fact their contract is expressly conditioned on the occurrence or non-occurrence of some future event, the failure of this condition precedent to arise will release either party from any further legal obligation. The wording of the contract will reveal such a condition.

But a claim of "implied" condition, based not upon the contract itself but some outside agreements, circumstances, customs, industry standards or other extraneous matters will normally be denied. That was the result in *Powell v. Swine Graphics Enterprises, 2002 WL 180883 (Ia. App. 2002)*.

In that case, plaintiff operated a hog farm and provided nursery space for defendant, a hog producer. The parties negotiated and then agreed upon plaintiff's request to expand by constructing a new facility near a neighboring farm owned by Anderson. But when Anderson objected, defendant withdrew from the project, claiming that its "Good Neighbor" policy required permission from neighbors before construction could proceed, and since this condition did not occur it had no contract liability.

The trial jury awarded plaintiff damages of $111,069 and defendant unsuccessfully appealed, the court noting that, "Swine Graphics has no written good neighbor policy, has no definition of who constitutes a neighbor, and has no requirement that the building party secure written approval of neighbors." Thus the agreement between the parties was not conditional at all.

"Conditions precedent are those facts and events, occurring subsequent to the making of a valid contract, that must exist or occur before there is a right to immediate performance, before there is a breach of contract duty, and before the usual judicial remedies are available.

A determination that a condition precedent exists depends not on the particular form of words used, but upon the intention of the parties gathered from the language of the entire instrument. Nonperformance of a condition precedent will vitiate a contract or proposed contract."

The engagement ring cases are also decided in a majority of jurisdictions by conditional contract rules, whereby the ripening of an engagement into marriage between the parties is the condition precedent that must occur for the gift of the ring to be irrevocable. Illustrative is *Fierro v. Hoel, 465 N.W.2d 669 (Iowa App. 1990)*, where plaintiff gave defendant a diamond engagement ring worth $9,000. After the couple located a condominium unit to buy in New York City for their marriage residence, defendant refused to join in signing a mortgage on the unit since plaintiff's parents had loaned the purchase monies. Shortly thereafter plaintiff broke the engagement and requested return of the ring. Plaintiff refused and suit ensued to establish its ownership. The trial court ruled defendant could keep the ring as a completed gift, but the appellate court reversed on grounds that the gift was conditioned upon the subsequent marriage.

"We hold an engagement ring is an inherently conditional gift and therefore reverse. ... The jurisdictions which have considered cases dealing with the gift of an engagement ring uniformly hold that marriage is an implied condition of the transfer of title and that the gift does not become absolute until the marriage occurs."

"This court adopts the 'no-fault' approach ... Since the major purpose of the engagement period is to allow a couple time to test the permanency of their feelings, it would seem highly ironic to penalize the donor for taking steps to prevent a possibly unhappy marriage."

The recent case of *Lucchetti v. DiGaetano, 109231/05 (N.Y. Sup. Ct. 2005)* echoes the same sentiments and ruling. Plaintiff had given defendant a $53,000 engagement ring in July, 2003. Defendant then ended it. Plaintiff sought a restraining order to prevent him from selling it, and both parties asked for a court judgment of ownership. Both parties also agreed on the applicable law to the effect that engagement ring gifts were conditioned on marriage regarding of fault, but plaintiff claimed there was no engagement since, "he did not intend to marry her as he would not set a wedding date and had one other romantic interest during their alleged engagement."

The trial judge disagreed with plaintiff and ordered the ring returned:

"Our courts recognize that an engagement ring is a type of gift that enjoys a special status. It's deemed conditional until the marriage actually takes place. If it does not take place, then it's one of the rare times that the court will rule that the gift never was completed, even though it sits on the finger of the recipient."

Interestingly enough, the day before the trial judge issued the decision ordering return of the ring, the parties agreed to a settlement and it was voluntarily returned.

But some states have statutes, like New York, that allow reimbursement for wedding expenses even if the ceremony never occurs.

In *DeFina v. Scott, 755 N.Y.S.2d 587 (N.Y. 2003),* the parties were self-supporting professionals, plaintiff a nurse practitioner and defendant an attorney. They became engaged to be married in 2000, and defendant bought plaintiff an expensive engagement ring at Tiffany & Co. They also agreed that the plaintiff would pay the wedding-related expenses in exchange for defendant conveying her a ½ interest in his condominium unit prior to the marriage.

In early 2001 the engagement ended. Defendant demanded return of the ring and the ½ interest in his condo, while plaintiff claimed ownership of the ring and reimbursement for her $16,000 of wedding expenses. While the case was pending the ring vanished from plaintiff's apartment shortly after the events of 9/11/01 and defendant was paid for its loss by his insurance company.

The trial judge and appellate court followed New York law that "does not require a court to direct return of gifts given solely in contemplation of a marriage which did not occur." Thus, the defendant owned the ring and could retain the insurance proceeds. But, but also ruled that plaintiff's expenses were a proper item of reimbursement and awarded her a lien for that amount against the defendant's previously gifted ½ interest in the condo which she must re-convey to him.

"The court starts with application of the traditional principle of New York law holding that an engagement ring is the property of the male donor when an engagement is terminated … fault in relation to the breaking of the engagement plays no part in the determination to be made. 'In one sense the engagement period has been successful if the engagement is broken since one of the parties has wisely utilized this time so as to avoid a marriage that in all probability would fail.'

On the other hand, the statute specifically contemplates that the donee may contribute to some extent towards the gift in question and, if such a contribution is made, the donee is entitled to a lien to the extent of the contribution."

19.

SPECIAL RULES FOR SALES OF GOODS

The sheer volume of commercial transaction falling in the UCC category of "sales of goods" is staggering. We are talking about billions of dollars annually. It is not surprising therefore that disputes frequently occur and result in cases that refine the governing business law rules and exceptions. Here are two recent disputes:

1. In *Neal v. SMC Corporation, 99 S.W.3d 813 (Tex. App. 2003)*, plaintiff purchased a new motor coach for $290,000 from R&K Camping Center that was manufactured by defendant's subsidiary company, Beaver. It had a serious electrical problem that was not corrected to their satisfaction. They sued both the seller and the manufacturer for revocation of the sale, claiming joint and several liability. The trial court and the appellate court agreed that plaintiff could revoke its acceptance and recover damages only from the seller.

In this case of first impression, the issue before the court was, "whether a manufacturer is a 'seller' under section 2.608 of the UCC. (It) provides: (a) The buyer may revoke his acceptance ... if he has accepted it (1) on the reasonable assumption that its non-conformity would be cured and it has not been seasonably cured; or (2) without discovery of such non-conformity if his acceptance was reasonably induced either by the difficulty or discovery before acceptance or by the seller's assurances."

"Unlike a claim of warranty that seeks a fix for defective goods or damages, a revocation seeks to put the buyer in the same position as if he had rejected the goods at the time of delivery. Revocation cancels a contract of sale and returns the goods to the seller and the purchase price to the buyer. It places the parties in the same position as before the sale. A manufacturer, having no part in the sales transaction, would have no part in returning the parties to a status quo. The nature of a revocation claim logically requires privity of contract."

2. In *Weil v. Murray, 161 F.Supp.2d 250 (S.D.N.Y. 2001)*, plaintiff was the owner of a valuable Edgar Degas painting. Defendant was an art dealer in New York. Defendant traveled to plaintiff's home in Alabama to view their extensive art collection, examined the Degas under ultraviolet light, and expressed an interest in buying it for an undisclosed client. An agreement was made whereby the Degas would be consigned to Murray's gallery "for a private inspection in New York for a period of a week", and defendant's employee returned to New York with the painting. Murray then agreed to sell the painting to another local dealer, Peck, for $1,250,000 and then contracted to buy the painting from plaintiff for $1,000,000.

The purchase price was never paid to plaintiff, but defendant maintained possession of the painting for additional months, until plaintiff demanded its return. Plaintiff then sued for specific performance of the purchase contract, and defendant claimed that he had no liability. The federal trial court granted summary judgment for plaintiff.

"To recover on an action for the price pursuant to Section 2-709(1)(a) of the New York UCC, plaintiffs must show that 1) they had a contract; 2) the buyer failed to pay the purchase price; and 3) the buyer accepted the goods. ... The undisputed facts establish that Murray accepted the Degas. 'Goods that a buyer has in its possession necessarily are accepted or rejected by the time a reasonable opportunity for inspecting them passes.' ... There is no evidence that Murray found the painting unsatisfactory or non-conforming. ... Buyer's return of accepted goods does not deprive seller of its 2-9709 right to the price."

20.
SPECIAL RULES FOR PRODUCT LIABILITY

The commercial marketplace expands every year as more and more goods are bought and sold. With every such volume and variety increase there is a corresponding rise in disputes where buyers allege that the goods they purchased were defective in some way, resulting in legally recoverable damages.

Here are some interesting, topical and rather unusual recent cases, organized in the same manner as the text material, including situations of reality television, tobacco smoking, hot coffee spills and the three types of warranties.

A.   **Negligent Breach of Duty:**
Graves v. Warner Bros., 656 N.W.2d 195 (Mich. App. 2002) was the Jenny Jones Show murder civil action. Scott Amedure and Jonathan Schmitz appeared together for the taping of an episode of the nationally syndicated TV talk show, and Schmitz "was surprised by Amedure's revelation (on camera) that he had a secret crush on him." Defendants, producers of the show, had intentionally withheld from Schmitz the fact that "the true topic of the show was same-sex crushes." Schmitz was embarrassed and humiliated, began a drinking binge, and three days later when he found a sexually suggestive note from Amedure on his front door, he bought a shotgun, confronted Amedure and killed him. Schmitz was convicted of second-degree murder and is currently serving a 25-50 year sentence.

The personal representatives of Amedure's estate filed this wrongful death action, based on negligence, claiming that defendant "ambushed" him by not informing him in advance of the show's true purpose, and it knew or should have known that their actions would incite violence and owed a legal duty not to place him in that position. The trial jury returned a plaintiff's verdict for $29,332.686 and defendant appealed.

The appellate court reversed. "Briefly reiterated, a negligence action maybe maintained only if a legal duty exists that requires the defendant to conform to a particular standard of conduct in order to protect others against unreasonable risks of harm... criminal activity, by its deviant nature, is normally unforeseeable. Under all ordinary and normal circumstances, in the absence of any reason to expect the contrary, the actor may reasonably proceed upon the assumption that others will obey the criminal law."

"This case presents no exceptional circumstances warranting the departure from that general rule because the evidence at trial disclosed no reason to expect the contrary here.

Schmitz gave every appearance of being a normal, well-adjusted adult who consented to being surprised on the show by a secret admirer of unknown sex and identity. The evidence of record indicated that nothing in Schmitz' demeanor, or in any of his interactions with the show, put defendants on notice that he posed a risk of violence to others…While defendant's actions in creating and producing this episode of the show may re regarded by many as the epitome of bad taste and sensationalism, such actions are, under the circumstances, insufficient to impute the requisite relationship between the parties that would give rise to a legally cognizable duty."

A dissenting opinion had a contrary view, and would have upheld the jury verdict: "I believe that the issue was properly left to the jury where the evidence indicated that Jonathan Schmitz was humiliated and devastated on a show scheduled to be broadcast on national television by defendants through the revelation of a homosexual crush and lurid sexual fantasy by Scott Amedure after Schmitz told defendants that he did not want the crush to be that of another man, and where defendants nevertheless proceeded with the production of the show, using deceit, sensationalism, and outrageous behavior. I reach my conclusion taking into consideration Schmitz' personal history, which included mental illness, alcohol and drug abuse, suicide attempts, anger management problems, and sexual identity concerns."

> B.   Product Liability Negligence – Tobacco:
> 1. *Wright v. Brooke Group Limited, 652 N.W.2d 159 (Iowa 2002)* was a personal injury action filed by a smoker against the large cigarette manufacturers based on all the product liability theories of negligence, strict liability and breach of warranty. After the defendants motion to dismiss was denied, they raised various first impression questions of law regarding smoking cases, which were certified to the Iowa Supreme Court and answered.

(a) As to a claim of defective design – the "risk-utility test" set forth by Restatement 2nd of Torts section 402A is adopted, combining negligence and strict liability, rather than the "consumer expectations test" in which they are kept separate. The Court said, "Both claims rest on an identical risk-utility evaluation. Therefore, we prefer to label a claim based on a defective product design as a design defect claim without reference to strict liability or negligence."

"A plaintiff seeking to recover damages on the basis of a design defect must prove 'the foreseeable risks of harm posed by the product could have been reduced or avoided by the adoption of a reasonable alternative design by the seller or other distributor, or a predecessor in the commercial chain of distribution, and the omission of the alternative design renders the product not reasonably safe.'"

"The mere fact that a risk presented by a product design is open and obvious, or generally known, and that the product thus satisfies expectations does not prevent a finding that the design is defective."

(Note: this means the plaintiff no longer has to prove that cigarettes are "dangerously defective", which as a practical matter previously prevented recovery by plaintiffs in most cases.)

(b) As to a claim of failure to warn – "The common knowledge of consumers of the health risks associated with smoking does not necessarily preclude liability. Consumer expectations about product performance and the dangers attendant to product use affect how risks are perceived and relate to foreseeability and frequency of the risks of harm … (but) a product seller is not subject to liability for failing to warn or instruct regarding risks and risk-avoidance measures that should be obvious to, or generally known by, foreseeable product users. When a risk is obvious or generally known, the prospective addressee of a warning will or should already know of its existence."

(c) As to a claim of fraud – "In summary, a manufacturer's failure to warn or disclose material information does not give rise to a fraud claim when the relationship between a plaintiff and a defendant is solely that of a customer/buyer and manufacturer with two exceptions. Those exceptions are limited to instances where the manufacturer (1) has made misleading statements of fact intended to influence consumers, or (2) has made true statements of fact designed to influence consumers and subsequently acquires information rendering the prior statements untrue or misleading."

(d) As to a claim of breach of warranty – "When a product is manufactured as intended and is like no other products of that type, there is no breach of the implied warranty of merchantability… a warranty of merchantability is based on a purchaser's reasonable expectation that goods will be free of significant defects and will perform in the way goods of that kind should perform… We conclude therefore, that under Iowa law, a seller's warranty that goods are fit for the ordinary purposes for which such goods are used gives rise to the same obligation owed by manufacturers under tort law (design defects/ failure to warn) with respect to the avoidance of personal injury to others."

2. *Spain v. Brown & Williamson Tobacco Corp., 363 F.3d 1183 (11ᵗʰ Cir. (2004)* presented an alternative way to sue cigarette makers in tort. Plaintiff has started smoking in 1962 and died of lung cancer in 1999. Her husband sued for products liability and negligence. The trial court dismissed the tort claims since under Alabama law cigarettes were not considered unreasonably dangerous products and there were product health warnings for smokers. But the appellate court reversed, allowing the case to proceed under the law of warranty. "However, Spain's suit may proceed on the basis of breach of implied warranty of merchantability under UCC Sec. 2-214. The basis of the claim is that the cigarettes were unfit for the ordinary purpose for which they were used because they caused cancer."

C.   **Product Liability Negligence – Hot Coffee Spills:**
       1. *Liebeck v. McDonald's Restaurants, No. CV-93-02419 (N.M. Dist. 1994)*
was the landmark "hot coffee"case. What at first appeared to be a frivolous lawsuit
and baseless jury award of damages, as reported by the media, turned out upon
closer inspection to be a valid and properly sustainable legal claim. The lesson is
valuable – appearances can be deceiving - one must look at all the relevant facts of a
dispute before reaching a decision.

       This is, of course, the fundamental basis of our jury trial system where the
jury is the arbiter of the facts and applied them to the rules of law furnished by the
judge, so that their verdict can then be rendered.

       The facts of *Liebeck*, reported by the media were as follows: She was a 79-
year old retired sales clerk, riding in the passenger seat of a car driven by her
grandson, who bought a 49-cent cup of coffee served in a Styrofoam cup from a
McDonald's drive-through. After receiving the order, the grandson pulled the car
forward and stopped so she could add cream and sugar to her coffee. As she placed
the cup between her knees and attempted to remove the plastic lid from the cup, its
entire contents spilled into her lap.

       She claimed that the seller was negligent as in selling such hot coffee and
failing to warn the public of the dangers. The trial jury awarded her $160,000 in
compensatory damages and $2.9 million in punitive damages. (Later reduced by the
judge to $480,000 and the case was privately settled) Newspaper headlines after the
decision painted the picture of a runaway jury and strongly criticized the legal
system.

       The full facts included these points:
- The coffee was super-heated at 180-190 degrees per company policy. The
  sweatpants she was wearing absorbed the coffee and held it next to her skin.
  Scientists testifying agreed that any coffee spilled at hotter than 130 degrees
  could cause severe burns in three seconds.

- Plaintiff suffered third-degree burns over 6% of her body including the inner
  thighs, genital and buttocks area, and was hospitalized for eight days during
  which she received several skin grafts. She was scarred and disabled for two
  years after the incident.

- Before a suit was filed, plaintiff asked only to be reimbursed for her $11,000
  in medical bills, and defendant countered with an offer of $800. After filing
  suit but before trial, she offered through her counsel to settle for $300,000,
  and the trial judge ordered both sides into a mediated settlement conference
  where the mediator recommended that defendant settle for $225,000. It
  refused.

- Defendant admitted during trial it had known about the risk of serious burns from its coffee for more than 10 years, in which time it had received more than 700 reports of burns and scalding, and for which it had paid our more than $500,000 in claim settlements. Defendant also admitted it did not warn customers of possible dangers from hot coffee.

- Defendant's own quality assurance manager testified that the company actively enforced the super-heating requirement for its coffee, and admitted that at the temperature it was poured into Styrofoam cups it was *not fit for human consumption* because it would burn the mouth and throat. He also stated that the company still had no intention of reducing coffee temperature, since it made $1.35 million daily in its coffee sales alone.

But one day after the verdict, a local reporter tested the coffee temperature at the same store that had served plaintiff and it registered 158 degrees.

2. A more recent "hot coffee" case was *Nadel v. Burger King Corporation, 695 N.E.2d 1185 Ohio App. 1997),* where a Father was driving his children to school, stopped at defendant's drive-through ordering breakfast and two cups of coffee, passed the coffee to his wife in the passenger seat who said it was too hot to taste, and as she placed it in its carry-container on the floor it spilled on their minor son who was seated between them causing second degree burns. The usual temperature of coffee served by defendant was 175 degrees.

Plaintiffs sued for personal injury damages, including punitive damages, under theories of breach of warranty of merchantability and fitness for a particular purpose and products liability negligence for defective design (coffee too hot) and failure to warn (danger of the hot coffee). Summary judgment was granted by the trial judge on all theories, but on appeal it was reversed as to the possible products liability negligence.

"Here, the trial court granted summary judgment solely on the basis of its conclusion that (son's) injury resulting from spilled hot coffee was, as a matter of law, the result of intervening, superseding causes attributable to (father and mother). Only a reasonably unforeseeable action may constitute an intervening, superseding cause. A spilled drink at fast-food windows or shortly after pulling away from fast-food windows occurs with enough frequency that it cannot be said to be so unforeseeable that it constitutes an intervening, superseding cause as a matter of law."

"Generally, the determination of whether a design defect exists is a question of fact. Here the question is not whether the Nadels expected it to be hot, but rather *how hot* did they, or a reasonable consumer in their shoes, expect the coffee to be … the issue (on failure to warn) is not whether the coffee was hot or expected to be hot, but whether the coffee was so exceedingly hot that serving it without a warning of unforeseen danger was unreasonable."

D.   Breach of Warranty:

1. Express Warranty – In *Sheffield v. Darby, 535 S.E.2d 776 (Ga. App. 2000)*, plaintiff purchased a horse from defendants for $8,500 after watching him successfully perform at a horse show and then ride him. "The Darby's assured her that the horse has no problems and would make a good show horse for use in competition." Within three weeks plaintiff discovered the horse was lame and sued for fraud and breach of warranty. The trial court entered summary judgment for defendants and the appellate court affirmed.

"A party may not justifiably rely on and assume to be true representations consisting of mere expressions of opinion, hope, expectation, puffing, and the like; rather, the party must inquire into and examine such representations to ascertain the truth."

2. Implied Sale of Goods Warranty – In *Villette v. Sheldorado Aluminun Products, Inc., 2001 WL 881055 (N.Y.Civ. Ct. 2001)*, defendant installed an aluminum awning on the back of plaintiff's home for use as a carport. The only writing was a one-page order/bill called a "contract", but it contained no express warranties, nor were there any representations made or advertising materials or use instructions furnished by defendant. The awning collapsed on top of plaintiff's new car, and she sued to recover the $3,000 she had paid for the awning. Defendant denied liability, claiming an accumulation of snow caused the collapse. Plaintiff won the case.

"A hybrid service-sale transaction like our cause can give rise to a cause of action for breach of warranty if the sales aspect of the transaction predominates and the service aspect is merely incidental... where the services are comprised merely of installing the goods, and making them operational, the contract has been considered a sale of goods... there is nothing in this writing that suggests that the parties understood their transaction to be predominantly for services. Rather, everything suggests a sale of goods, with the incidental service of installation. Since the predominant purpose of the transaction is a sale of goods, Article 2 of the (UCC), including the implied warranty of merchantability applies to claimant's benefit."

"The claimant's case is quite simple: the ordinary purposes of an awning are to provide shade and other protection from the elements; an awning that leaks and then collapses is clearly not fit for those purposes. Sheldorado's defense is likewise simple: the claimant was putting the awning to an extraordinary purpose and misusing the product, because weather conditions were not ordinary and claimant failed to keep the awning from an accumulation of snow that it could not hold."

"(But) the foreseeability of the risk of the weight of snow operating upon a defective installation may reasonably be charged to the seller."

3. Food Warranty –

(a) In *Mitchell v. T.G.I. Friday's, 748 N.E.2d 89 (Ohio App. 2000)*, plaintiff was eating a fried clam strip when she bit into a one-fourth inch long piece of clam shell. She suffered immediate pain, was treated by a dentist, and eventually had to have the affected tooth extracted. She filed a product liability lawsuit, and the trial court granted summary judgment for defendant. On appeal, the decision was affirmed.

After the court reviewed the two legal tests of liability in food cases, the "foreign object" test and the "natural object – reasonable expectation" test, it ruled, "In the present case, it can not be disputed that the piece of clam shell which caused (the) injury was natural to the clam strip which she consumed...

(Referring to a prior Ohio case) the possible presence of a piece of oyster shell in or attached to an oyster is so well known to anyone who eats oysters that we can say as a matter of law that one who eats oysters can reasonably anticipate and guard against eating such a piece of shell ... We therefore hold as a matter of law, one who eats clams can reasonably anticipate and guard against eating such a piece of shell."

(b) In *Schafer v. JLC Food Systems, 2005 WL 984474 (Minn. 2005)*, plaintiff ate at a Perkins restaurant, ordered a pumpkin muffin, swallowed a bite, felt a sharp pain in her throat, and went to the hospital emergency room where she was treated for a cut in her throat, although the doctor was unable to see what caused it. She developed an infection that required a three-day hospital stay. Plaintiff then sued for product liability negligence and breach of food warranty. The trial court granted summary judgment to defendant, but that decision was reversed and remanded so that the matter could go to trial. In its ruling, the Court presented an excellent statement of the applicable rules of law:

"Under the foreign-natural test for assessing whether a food product is defective, if an object or substance in a food product is natural to any of the ingredients of the product, there is no liability for injuries caused but if the object or substance is foreign to any of the ingredients, the seller or manufacturer may be liable for any injury caused. The seller is liable to the extent that the injury-causing object in a food product would not be reasonably expected by any ordinary consumer."

"In such a case, a plaintiff may reach the jury, without direct proof of the specific injury-causing object, when the plaintiff establishes that 1) the injury-causing event was of a kind that would ordinarily only occur as a result of a defective condition in the food product, 2) the defendant was responsible for the condition, and 3) the event was not caused by anything other than a food product defect existing at the time of the product's sale."

E.   Lemon Law Motor Vehicle Sales Warranties:

1. In *Garcia v. Mazda Motor of America, 671 N.W.2d 317 (Wis. App. 2003)*, plaintiff bought a new Mazda Tribute automobile in 2001 and experienced continuous transmission problems requiring three attempted repairs in the next five months. She then sent a certified letter demanding a replacement of the vehicle. She continued to have transmission problems and filed suit under the Wisconsin Lemon Law statute.

The state statute required, "To receive a comparable new motor vehicle or a refund due …a consumer … shall offer to the manufacturer of the motor vehicle having the nonconformity to transfer title of that motor vehicle to that manufacturer. No later than 30 days after that offer, the manufacturer shall provide the consumer with the comparable new vehicle or refund."

Defendant successfully claimed that plaintiff failed to comply with the statute because she had not offered to transfer title to her vehicle. (Note: this is another of the many examples we see of how a party's lack of following the anticipatory thinking approach to preventive law results in a negative result.)

2.   In *Edwards v. Hyundai Motor America, 2005 WL 1017988 (Mo. App. 2005)*, plaintiffs bought a new Elantra in 2001 with a six-year or 72,000 mile bumper-to-bumper warranty. The car had numerous repetitive problems and the defects could not be cured. In 2004 plaintiffs sued for breach of express written warranty of sale and implied warranty of merchantability, but the trial court dismissed the case since the Lemon Law statute of limitations had expired.

On appeal, the case was reversed and remanded because UCC warranty rights might still protect the plaintiffs. "The Missouri Lemon Law does not supercede the UCC in all respects with regard to nonconforming new vehicles. The Lemon Law, which refers only to express warranties. Did not preclude any remedy for breach of implied warranty of merchantability or any other implied warranties. Hence, the four-year statute of limitations under the UCC, rather than the statute of limitations under the Lemon Law, applied to the claims, so the suit may proceed."

F.   Implied Warranty:

1.   In *Phillips v. Cricket Lighters, 2005 Pa. LEXIS 2125 (Pa. 2005)*, the court ruled that under Pennsylvania law the warranty of merchantability extended to a 2-year-old child who was a member of the buyer of a disposable butane lighter's household and a jury. He had ignited the lighter he found in his mother's purse, a fire started, and it burned down their apartment building in which three persons died. The victim's estates sued, claiming the lighter was defective because it could have been designed to be more child resistant, and also sought warranty protection. The prior courts hearing the case had dismissed all claims, but this Court on the breach of warranty issue ruled that different standards apply to warranty claims than claims of strict liability, and a jury should be allowed to hear the case.

The lower court said: "The Pennsylvania Commercial Code, which governs implied warranty law, expressly requires that goods be 'free from significant defects.' The code extends the coverage of implied warranties to 'any natural person who is in the family or household of his buyer or who is a guest in his home if it is reasonable to expect that such a person may use, consume or be affected by the goods."

(It should be noted however that an earlier Federal court decision from the same state, *Shouey v. Duck Head Apparel Co., 49 F.Supp.2d 413 (M.D. Pa. 1999)* came to a contrary decision in a similar dispute, holding that, "A lighter is purchased for the purpose of producing a flame suitable for lighting a cigarette. There is no indication that the Zippo lighter did anything other than produce a flame, nor is there any indication that the flame produced was not suitable (as for example, by being too large) for lighting a cigarette.")

2. In *Whitson v. Safeskin Corp., unreported (M.D.P.A. 2004)*, a federal judge threw out an implied warranty claim for latex gloves brought by a health care worker who received a latex allergy from wearing them. The court said that, "a seller cannot be liable for breach of an implied warranty merely because of a harmful effect due to an individual idiosyncrasy on the part of the buyer." There was no proof presented that the product, "did anything other than serve its ordinary purpose," that was to protect health-care workers from contracting blood-borne illnesses.

G.   Products Liability:
1. In *United States v. Mirama Enterprises, 04 C.D.O.S. 9648 (9th Cir. 2004)*, a home juicer manufacturer was ruled to be liable for not volunteering to the Consumer Product Safety Commission that it had been notified by consumers of its defective product. For the first time, such a company was ruled to have an affirmative legal responsibility to warn consumers of possible health defects.

2. In *Flax v. DaimlerChrysler, No. 02C1288 (Tenn. Cir. 2004)*, the defendant was sued for failing to warn consumers that its minivan seat backs were unsafe because of their tendency to collapse backwards in collisions. A speeding driver rear-ended plaintiff's vehicle, killing their 8-month-old son. At trial a former manager of the defendant testified that the automaker knew the seats in its minivans were unsafe, and colluded with a federal regulatory agency to cover up the information. Other experts said that defendant had known for over 20 years that the minivan seats were "deadly dangerous" and they had sealed court records of an undisclosed number of lawsuits involving failed minivan seat backs. The jury awarded plaintiff $105.5 million in damages, including $98 million in punitives.

H.   Defenses to Products Liability:
1. In *Ellis v. C.R. Bard, Inc., 2002 WL 31501163 (11th Cir. 2002)*, a medical device maker was not liable for plaintiff's brain damage due to product misuse of a morphine infusion pump provided plaintiff after knee replacement surgery.

The pump was factory set to deliver no more than 8 milligrams per hourly application, when the hospital nurse told plaintiff's daughter she could press the pump whenever she missed to prevent pain. The "Learned Intermediary Rule" provides that the maker of a prescription drug usually only has a duty to warn prescribing physicians of use dangers, not the patients themselves.

2. In *James v. Mazda Motor Corp., 2000 WL 1175026 (11ᵗʰ Cir. 2000)*, a wrongful death suit was brought by the survivors of the driver who was killed when his Mazda automobile was forced off the road and crashed. The driver was protected by the automatic shoulder belt but had not fastened his optional lap belt. Plaintiff's contentions of defective design and failure to warn consumers of the need to fasten the lap belt were dismissed because federal regulation of seat belts under the Federal Motor Vehicle Safety Act allowed the seat belt design chosen by defendant, and the federal law preempts conflicting state laws.

3. In *Maisonave v. Newark Bears, A-4144-02T3 (N.J. App. Div. 2004)*, plaintiff was injured at a baseball game when a foul ball struck him in the eye while he was buying beer at a mezzanine food stand. He sued for his injuries. The defendant asserted assumption-of-risk as a defense, but the court ruled that the duty of care to warn of dangers owed to spectators was expanded from their seating area to the concession stands.

"While watching the game, either seated or standing in an unprotected viewing area, spectators may reasonably be expected to pay attention and to look out for their own safety; but the activities and ambiance of the concession area predictable draw the attention of even the most experienced and the most wary fan from the action on the field of play. The team and the vendor have a concomitant duty to exercise reasonable care to protect them during such times of heightened vulnerability."

(Defendant had recognized the general rule in these cases that commercial stadium operators must provide protection in the most dangerous seating areas as ruled in *Schneider v. American Hockey and Ice Skating, Inc., 342 N.J. Super. 527 (App. Div. 1999)*. But it asserted this was only a limited duty of care and "many spectators choose to assume the ordinary risks of being struck by a flying ball or puck in order to obtain an unobstructed view of the playing field and that these are common and inherent risks of attending a baseball or hockey game." *Crawn v. Campo, 136 N.J. 494 (N.J. 1994)*.

I. Special Warranty Rules:
In *O'Connor v. BMW of North America, 2005 WL 1457718 (Fla. App. 2005)*, plaintiff leased a BMW from the dealer's financial subsidiary. While the car was under warranty it had problems that the dealer couldn't repair, so plaintiff sued under the Magnuson-Moss Warranty Act.

It permits, "a consumer who is damaged by the failure of a supplier, warrantor, or service contractor to comply with any obligation ... under a written warranty, implied warranty, or service contract" to sue for damages.

BMW unsuccessfully contended that plaintiff wasn't covered by the Act's warranty protection as a lessee. This case stands for the proposition that the Act does, in fact, cover lessees as well as owners.

21.
SPECIAL RULES FOR E-COMMERCE AND CYBERLAW

Internet law is evolving daily since many of the issues involved in current disputes have never before been litigated due to the newness of doing business in the cyberspace marketplace.

Recent developments are worthy of note in the following areas:

A. Domain Name Cybersquatting – While major companies that have an Internet Web site presence are vigilant in looking for name registration violations under the Anti-Cybersquatting Act, sometimes they overreact.

1. Microsoft admitted as much in a January, 2004 story highlighting their claim against a Toronto, Canada teenager named Mike Rowe whose website address was mikerowesoft.com. Microsoft originally demanded he change the name of his site, claiming copyright infringement, and offered to pay him $10 for his trouble. He refused, the story received media attention and his site received so many hits it had to shut down. Rowe demanded $10,000 to change the site's name. The matter then settled privately between the parties.

2. In *Lucas Nursery and Landscaping v. Grosse, 359 F.3d 806 (6th Cir. 2004)*, defendant hired plaintiff to do landscaping work, she was unhappy with it, complained, and then registered the domain name lucasnursery.com for the sole purpose of posting information about the poor work done and the fact she paid another company $5,400 to correct the problems. Plaintiff sued for violation of ACPA. The trial court dismissed the case and the appellate court affirmed because there was no evidence of the required legal element of "bad faith." Since plaintiff had no website, defendant's purpose was not to divert customers or to gain any profit. "The information of the site was informative and made its purpose clear.

B. Online Gambling – *In re Master Card International, 313 F.3d 257 (5th Cir. 2002)*. Thompson and Bradley incurred large online casino gambling debts. They used their credit cards to purchase gambling "chips credits", and losses were debited from and winnings credited to their accounts. Any new winnings were paid, on request, by offshore bank wire transfers.

Thompson lost $16,445 and Bradley lost $7,048 from online casino gambling debts. Rather than pay their credit card bills, they filed this novel class action against their credit card companies and the issuing banks under the RICO Act, claiming that they "created and operated a worldwide gambling enterprise that facilitates illegal gambling on the Internet through the use of credit cards..."

"The credit card companies facilitate the enterprise (they said) by authorizing the casinos to accept credit cards, by making credit available to gamblers, by encouraging the use of that credit through the placement of their logos on the websites, and by processing the 'gambling debts' resulting from the extension of credit. The banks that issued the gamblers' credit cards participate in the enterprise, they say, by collecting those 'gambling debts.'"

The trial court was unimpressed and granted defendants' motions to dismiss. On appeal that ruling was affirmed. The court noted that the Federal Wire Act, "requires that the object of the gambling be a sporting event or contest," and since that was not the case here there was no violation of federal law. "RICO, no matter how liberally construed, is not intended to provide a remedy to this class of plaintiff."

"Thompson and Bradley simply are not victims under the facts of these cases. Rather, as the district court wrote, 'they are independent actors who made a knowing and voluntary choice to engage in a course of conduct.' In engaging in this conduct, they got exactly what they bargained for –gambling chips with which they could place wagers. They cannot use RICO to avoid meeting obligations they voluntarily took on."

C.   Online Service Provider Liability - because ISP's have deep financial pockets and are an accessible defendant, lawsuits continue to be filed against for various theories of Internet liability.

1. In *CoStar Group, Inc. v. LoopNet, Inc., 373 F.3d 544 (4th Cir. 2004)*, plaintiff maintained a comprehensive real estate information database with copyrighted photos of the properties. Its database was available to customers via the Internet based upon their agreement not to post the photos on their own websites or those of third parties. Defendant is an ISP whose website allows real estate broker subscribers to post commercial real estate listings on the Internet, provided they also agree not to do so without permission of the photo copyright owners. When plaintiff noticed some of its photos on defendant's site it complained and they were removed. Plaintiff sued the ISP for copyright infringement and lost.

"The Digital Millennium Copyright Act provides a safe harbor for ISP operators if they are involved in automatic copying, storage and transmission of copyrighted materials. If an ISP contributes to infringement, the safe harbor is lost." The fact that LoopNet knew there were infringement problems and attempted to control them did not cause it to become liable.

2. In *In re: Pharmatrak, Inc., 329 F.3d 9 (1st Cir. 2003)*, cookies used by a pharmaceutical website operator to "intercept" personal information about the website users, even though they specified otherwise, was ruled to be a violation of the Electronic Communications Privacy Act (ECPA).

3. In *Hall v. EarthLink Network, Inc., 396 F.3d 500 (2nd Cir. 2005)*, plaintiff, a movie producer had an e-mail account with defendant and used it to send an announcement of a movie premiere to all his contacts. The ISP identified the mass mailing as spam and shut down his account, placing it into their "Net Abuse Report.". They later reinstated the e-mail account after they learned the mailing was legitimate. Plaintiff unsuccessfully sued alleging violation of the ECPA, claiming that defendant had illegally intercepted his e-mail. The court ruled that the Act wasn't violated because the ISP didn't intercept the e-mails, and its actions were in the ordinary course of its business.

D. Website Liability – popular websites and search engines also have deep pockets and are the focus of liability claims.

1. The popular auction website eBay is a litigation target when there are defamatory postings about vendors or bidders, and when fake goods are sold on its site. Here are two interesting cases:

In *Grace v. eBay, 16 Cal. Rptr.3d 192 (Cal. App. 2004)*, plaintiff had bought vintage magazines on eBay and posted negative criticisms about their delivery and condition of the material. The seller than posted a criticism of his own, saying plaintiff was "dishonest all the way" and should be banned from eBay. EBay has a user agreement that specifically protects it from liability for defamatory postings. When plaintiff for defamation the court ruled for defendant based on the agreement. But the ruling opened the door for plaintiff, since it also stated that eBay was not completely immunized from liability if it knew or had reason to know of the problems. (This created an exception to the absolute immunity of ISP's for defamatory postings established by the Zeran v. America Online case discussed in the text.)

In *Tiffany (NJ) Inc. v. eBay Inc., unreported (S.D.N.Y. 2004)*, plaintiff claimed direct infringement of its unique jewelry trademarks from advertising links that eBay purchased on popular Internet search engines mentioning its name. It also claimed contributory infringement due to failure to monitor the authenticity of plaintiff's items offered on the website, imposing an active duty on eBay to screen for counterfeits. (The practical result of this case was to cause eBay to post "buyer-beware" warnings for bidders on Tiffany items.)

2. Google is the most popular and widely used search engine. It entered into agreements in 2004 with Harvard, Stanford, Michigan and Oxford Universities and the New York Public Library to make large portions of their book collections searchable on the Internet. Writers and copyright holders claim this effort to digitize protected creative works is massive copyright infringement by Google. It claims it is only showing small "snippets of information" as permitted under the fir use exceptions to copyright infringement. Suit was filed in *Authors Guild v. Google, No. 05 CV 8136 (S.D.N.Y. 2005)*, and legal experts are predicting this case may revolutionize how far technology can impact the law of intellectual property rights.

22.
BUSINESS ETHICS

The numerous examples of corporate unethical conduct in covering up manufacturing and engineering problems and not ordering timely recalls of defective products have invariably led to individual and class action lawsuits producing costly adverse jury awards for compensatory and punitive damages.

This has especially impacted the automotive and pharmaceutical industries to the extent that large corporations are now acting in a more socially responsible manner in regard to their dealings with the consuming public.

The threat of adverse publicity and damaging litigation has appeared to turn the tide in favor of the companies ordering voluntary precautionary product recalls as a matter of standard operating procedure, rather than the isolated instances seen previously after they appeared to have no other reasonable alternative.

Future events will determine the true direction of this apparent positive shift in the corporate ethical behavior.

23.
TRENDS IN THE LAW

During the time this new edition of the book was being produced, for the first time in many years, two vacancies in the U.S. Supreme Court were filled with new Justices. The effect on future Court cases may be far-reaching and significant since most recent decisions have been hotly contested and decided by a vote of 5-4.

Many of the hot-button items discussed in this text chapter will be eventually heard or re-heard by the newly constituted Court in pending or new test cases. What we now consider to be landmark judicial pronouncements in many areas may be affirmed, reversed or significantly modified.

There has not been a time in recent memory that what will be "the law of the land" is so open to speculation and conjecture.